Praise for
More than One

"*More than One* stands out clearly from the quite large field of books intended for classes on World Religions. Dyron Daughrity is in his own right a distinguished scholar of religion and of religions worldwide. He is also a clear and persuasive writer who has given serious thought to making his text both usable and approachable. The result is a highly user-friendly text, which gains greatly from excellent illustrations."

> —**Philip Jenkins,** Distinguished Professor of History, Institute for Studies of Religion, Baylor University

"Dyron Daughrity is a scholar of enormous energy, skill, and thoughtfulness. The lucid prose and colorful illustrations of this book make it an enjoyable introduction to the study of world religions. It draws from Daughrity's vast experience and accomplishments as a teacher and a scholar of religion."

> —**Chandra Mallampalli,** Professor of History, Westmont College

"Dyron Daughrity is a historian and prolific author. His textbook for world religions is based on his experience in teaching the course for two decades and designed to support students in their study of the world's religious traditions. Apart from Daughrity's balanced approach, which his readers have learned to appreciate in his previous works, this book benefits from his encyclopedic knowledge of the subject. This text addresses different approaches to the study of religions and offers wide coverage of diverse religions. The content is presented in a captivating layout with rich illustrations and is enhanced by charts and dedicated sections for in-depth analysis. It will be an excellent choice for college courses."

> —**Enrico Beltramini,** Professor of Philosophy and Religious Studies, Notre Dame de Namur University, California; author of *Passage to India*

"Dyron Daughrity is an expert guide to the study of world religions—comprehensive in his understanding of the material, clear in his organization, and compassionate in his depiction. In short, this book offers readers everything they need to understand what religion is, what the religions of the world believe and practice, how they relate to the culture around them, and what they share in common. Readers will especially find helpful the text boxes highlighting technical terms, the beautiful pictures illuminating the content, and the glossary explaining names and subjects. I highly recommend this excellent book!"

> —**Derek Cooper,** Managing Director of Dodekagram and Thomas Institute, and author of *Christianity and World Religions*

"*More than One* is an excellent introductory textbook for learning the creeds, codes, ceremonies, and community of religions worldwide. Historical and current illustrations, a clear structure, and definitions of terms depict diverse religious realities and make the book accessible for teaching and studying. The insightful research questions and thick descriptions create valuable understandings for why religions remain important and meaningful and how people of different worldviews can relate to one another in peace and friendship in today's world."

> —**Susangeline Patrick,** PhD, Assistant Professor of World Christianity, Nazarene Theological Seminary, Kansas City, MO; faculty member, NAIITS, an Indigenous Learning Community

"*More than One* covers an impressive range of the world's religions. The presentation and superb illustrations really make the material come alive."

> —**George D. Chryssides,** York St John University, UK; author of many books, including *Jehovah's Witnesses* and *Heaven's Gate*

MORE THAN ONE

MORE THAN ONE

AN INTRODUCTION TO WORLD RELIGIONS

DYRON DAUGHRITY

Abilene Christian University Press

MORE THAN ONE
An Introduction to World Religions

ISBN 978-1-68426-399-8 | LCCN 2022014611

Printed in the United States of America

LIBRARY OF CONGRESS CATALOGING-IN-PUBLICATION DATA
Names: Daughrity, Dyron B., 1973- author.
Title: More than one : an introduction to world religions / Dyron Daughrity.
Description: Abilene, Texas : Abilene Christian University Press, [2022] | Includes bibliographical references and index.
Identifiers: LCCN 2022014611 (print) | LCCN 2022014612 (ebook) | ISBN 9781684263998 (print) | ISBN 9781684269204 (ebook)
Subjects: LCSH: Religions.
Classification: LCC BL80.3 .D375 2022 (print) | LCC BL80.3 (ebook) | DDC 200—dc23/eng20220616
LC record available at https://lccn.loc.gov/2022014611
LC ebook record available at https://lccn.loc.gov/2022014612

Cover design by Bruce Gore | Interior text design by Sandy Armstrong, Strong Design

For information, contact:
Abilene Christian University Press
ACU Box 29138
Abilene, Texas 79699

1-877-816-4455
www.acupressbooks.com

22 23 24 25 26 27 28 / 7 6 5 4 3 2 1

CONTENTS

TRIBUTE

With profound respect, the author of this book would like to pay tribute to the many dear friends from other faiths who have in some way contributed to the creation of this book. In particular, I have in mind those who offered guidance and support to me throughout the research process:

Buddhism:	Venerable Chodron and Thubten Damcho from Sravasti Abbey My teacher, Rev. Dr. Prof. Leslie Sumio Ryosho Kawamura (1935–2011) Rev. Dr. Sensai Joji Atone of Bukkyo University
Daoism and Confucianism:	Jenny Lien Master Dr. YF Huang
Hinduism:	Supriya, who was a great help to me when I lived in India in 2005
Islam:	Dr. Ozgur Koca Fatih Ates Atilla Kahveci
Jainism:	Dr. Ranjan Shah, MD
Judaism:	Rabbi Levi and Rabbi Sholom from the Malibu Chabad
Scientology:	Rev. Janet Weiland
Shintoism:	Rev. Kodo Tanaka Sensai Abigail Moore, my former student from Japan
Sikhism:	Mr. Gajinder Shah Singh of Nanak Sadan Sikh Temple
Zoroastrianism:	Rustum Chhor

Dear friends, thank you. It is a privilege to call you friends. I appreciate and respect you. You have helped me more than you know.

There are many other people from various faiths who have hosted me for dinners, welcomed me to their temples, and assisted my students and me as we strove to learn more about the religions of the world. We continue to learn about one another. It is a great joy to be on this journey with you.

The most important goal of studying world religions is to make friends. Indeed, the study of religion is nothing less than the commitment to making deep and lasting friendships with people. That's why I do it.

ACKNOWLEDGMENTS

First off, I would like to acknowledge my friend, Dr. Jason Fikes, Director of ACU Press. He and his team have invested countless hours into making my book an excellent, high-quality text for the study of world religions. I am grateful for the confidence Jason continually places in me as one of his authors.

I give thanks for my colleagues at Pepperdine who have supported my work for fifteen years now. The Religion and Philosophy Division continues to be a wonderful place to work, especially now that we seem to have survived the COVID-19 and Zoom storms that came our way over the last two years. We are starting to see blue skies once again. It was a difficult period, no doubt, but great hope is on the horizon.

I should acknowledge, by name, some of my friends at Pepperdine who sustain me with their support and collegiality daily: Randy Chesnutt, Ron Highfield, Nick Cumming, Jay Brewster, Jim Gash, Lee Kats, Michael Feltner, Rick Marrs, and Dan Rodriguez. These individuals have provided me with encouragement, diligently supported my scholarship, and opened up many opportunities for me over the years that I would not have had otherwise. Randy Chesnutt's retirement will leave a hole in our department, as well as in my work life. Jim Gash and Jay Brewster are doing a great job in their relatively new roles as President and Provost at Pepperdine. While they took the helm of our university during an extremely challenging moment in history, they have remained steadfast in their support of research and writing, and I am deeply grateful for their steely commitment to scholarship. My divisional dean, Dan Rodriguez—¡Órale!—consistently champions my scholarly development, and I offer my heartfelt thanks for his support. Lee Kats has developed a thriving program for internal grants at Pepperdine; I stand amazed at all he has done on behalf of our university's scholarly culture. And I have benefitted greatly from his hard work and his vision to foster a robust culture of scholarship at Pepperdine.

I have many wonderful students at Pepperdine, and so many of them become my friends during the course of their studies. I enjoy walking with them around the track after work. Many stop in to visit with me in my office. Every semester dozens of them come to my house to spend time with my family. My students are a well-spring of encouragement; they fill me with joy. I am deeply humbled at the end of each class period when several students inevitably say, "Thank you, professor!" What a privilege! My students are my friends. And I treasure those relationships. Where would I, a teacher, be without my students?

Thanks to college and departmental support, I always benefit from having research students. Two students in particular must be recognized here: Jen Gash and Tara Brandenberger. These two wonderful and brilliant women have invested enormous time and effort into the creation of this book. They researched, helped organize chapters, proofread, conducted interviews, indexed, and provided countless insights. Thank you, Jen and Tara. You have made this book so much better. I hope to return the favor to both of you by supporting your careers in whatever ways I can.

I gratefully acknowledge the unflagging, unwavering support of my wife, Sunde, and our four amazing children: Clare, Ross, Mande Mae, and Holly Joy. You all make our home so happy. I am so grateful to be a husband and a father to you. It is the greatest privilege of my life. Everything else is a distant second.

I acknowledge the foundation provided to me by my grandparents, my parents, and my brother. May Dell and Jerald Daughrity, my mom and dad, have consistently supported me with faithful, parental love for forty-nine years now. My brother, Varen, is equally faithful and is an inspiration to me. The Bible teaches that "a real friend sticks closer than a brother" (Prov. 18:24). But my brother sticks very close to me indeed, and for that I am eternally grateful.

I must acknowledge my church family, the Redondo Beach Church of Christ. It is a pleasure and privilege to serve shoulder to shoulder with such loving, open-minded, and committed Christians. For all the criticism of religion out there in cyberspace and on the airwaves, there are many, many houses of worship that get it right. And the Redondo Beach Church of Christ is one of them. What a wonderful place to call my church home, and what an inspiring group of people to call my church family. Specifically, I want to give thanks to my elders: Steve Gordon, Alan Henderson, and John Matsumoto. They are a steady force in my life, and I take great joy in our fellowship. What a privilege to serve alongside them!

And finally, as always, I humbly acknowledge Jesus Christ, my Lord, with the following words that have become a part of every book I have written:

Now unto him that is able to do exceeding abundantly above all that we ask or think, according to the power that worketh in us, Unto him be glory in the church by Christ Jesus throughout all ages, world without end. Amen. (Eph. 3:20–21 KJV)

Dyron B. Daughrity
Athens, Greece
24 May 2022

This book is dedicated to

Rabbi Levi, Rabbi Sholom, their precious families,

and all the wonderful people at the Malibu Chabad.

You have treated me, my family, and my students

with such respect and kindness.

I am deeply grateful for your friendship,

as well as your openness to people of all faiths.

It is a privilege to call you all my friends.

1 WHY STUDY RELIGION?

Photographer: Tetra Images, Alamy

The first divine liturgy at the Ukrainian Catholic Cathedral of Saint Nicholas in Chicago was celebrated on Christmas Day, January 7, 1915. Many Ukrainians have immigrated to the Americas in great waves, first between 1870–1914 and then after World War II. Russia's latest invasion of Ukraine in 2022 displaced millions more from their homeland.

Why study religion? Is religion becoming obsolete? Is religion even relevant anymore in highly advanced, technological, democratic societies?

Or why not begin another way: Why would anybody *avoid* the study of religion? Religion is at the very heart of most human societies. Isn't it obvious that religion should be studied carefully?

In the past, religions served a fundamental purpose: they brought people together. Scholars point out that the word **religion** probably comes from the Latin word *religare*, which means "to bind together." Maybe religions indeed bound societies together in medieval Western Europe, where almost everybody was Roman Catholic, or in the numerous indigenous tribes in the pre-Columbian era in the Americas. When tribal unity was crucial, people were united by religion for a sense of shared identity that would keep them together and provide a layer of social protection for the group. They shared the same god, participated in similar rituals, and remembered their history through religious festivals. These acts and beliefs bound their society together and provided profound unity; members of the tribe would even die for one another if they had to. In fact, dying for the tribe was the most courageous and laudable thing a person could do.

It was a similar phenomenon that continued throughout pre-Columbian American history as societies became larger to survive. This urgent need for social unity persisted, and different tribes often confederated into one as a means of protection. Similarly, Western Europeans confederated to the point that differing tribes joined together, leading to more complex people groups. However, one thing seemed to transcend tribal identity: religion. For example, in Western Europe, various people groups with various languages—Spanish, Portuguese, Italian, French, German—and numerous smaller groups, such as the Welsh, Swedish, and Dutch, all came together and united in the name of Roman Catholic Christianity. Religion had the unique capability to unite people groups from very different ethnic, lingual, and even cultural backgrounds. Religion seemed to prove its own etymology and meaning: to bind people together.

But that was a long time ago. Do we even need religion anymore? We are today living in complex, pluralistic societies. Many people do not really feel the need to fight to the death for anything. Perhaps we have moved more from a communal understanding of ourselves to a more **individualistic** understanding of the human person. We can compare it to the concept of **free agency** in professional sports. There was a time when athletes spent their entire career with one team. There was loyalty to the player, and the player had loyalty to his or her team and to that particular city. Today is very different. Professional athletes now play for the team that pays them the most! This is at the heart of free agency: *You pay me what I am worth, and I will move to your city and play for your team. But when another team comes along and offers me more, then I will gladly move to that city and play for them.*

Never Talk about Religion

There are two things you should never talk about: religion and politics. Like all stereotypical statements, there is some truth to this, but there is also an awful lot that is wrong with this statement. It is true that religion and politics are potentially controversial topics, but they can certainly be talked about. They are talked about every day. The primary issue is

Religion · a concept that is notoriously difficult to define; however, the English word is rooted in the Latin term *religare*, meaning "to tie or bind together"

Individualism · a common modern perspective that emphasizes the needs of an individual over the needs of the community

Free agency · a concept from sports in which a player is not bound to a particular team for his or her career; rather, he or she can temporarily commit to whatever team offers the highest payment

An Amish family riding along a country road in their open horse and buggy carriage. Lancaster County, Pennsylvania.

whether a person is able to talk about religion or politics in a way that does not intentionally offend.

If people talk about religion in ways that are naïve, they might accidentally ridicule people from other religions, or they might step on toes unnecessarily. They might speak about certain religions in a condescending way, albeit unintentionally.

Learning how to talk about religion is a central part of this book. Being educated about something helps everyone bring the temperature down. By educating ourselves on religion, we are better able to talk in productive, compassionate ways and in a manner that is less likely to cause offense to our neighbors, who often will have very different views from our own.

An academic course on religion helps students approach the topic of religion from a variety of angles that we will explore in this book. Some of the common approaches to religion are through the lenses of history, sociology, geography, demography, archaeology, or theology. It is important to be able to talk about religion in a somewhat academic way. This is not to say that religion must always be talked about academically, but it helps. If a person asks someone academic questions about his or her religion, he or she will be less likely to feel nervous about the questions. For instance, *Can you tell me about the life of the Buddha? Where was he born? What are some of his most important teachings?* These kinds of questions are devoid of judgment. They are academic and informational in nature.

Why is it important to talk about religion? The clearest reason is that, in a globalized world, we will

Amish · rooted in Jakob Ammann's (born 1644) approach to Anabaptism, a strict religious community that foregoes the usage of modern technology and rejects modern culture

Rumspringa · a season in which an Amish person is allowed to leave the community and participate in modern culture before choosing to commit to an Amish lifestyle

Baptism · an initiation ritual in Christian traditions

frequently meet people from other religions. We will share office space with Muslims, Jews, and Buddhists. We will travel to other nations and encounter Hindus, Muslims, and Daoists. We will collaborate with people from other religions. We might do business with Jains, Sikhs, or Zoroastrians. When we attend college, it is highly likely that we will meet people from faith backgrounds quite different from our own.

Religious diversity is everywhere in the twenty-first century. Very few people live in a silo where everybody has virtually the same religion. There are a few exceptions—for example, a person who lives in a small village in India, a Greek village where Greek Orthodoxy has dominated for more than one thousand five hundred years, or a town in Saudi Arabia that has been firmly Muslim since the days of the prophet Muhammad in the early 600s.

Or, perhaps, in an Amish community in Pennsylvania. Indeed, **Amish** people have to make a commitment to the Amish community after their season of **Rumspringa** ("running or jumping around"), when they are permitted to the leave the compound and experience non-Amish life on the outside. In their teen years, Amish youths are given the freedom to depart the compound for a while, to perhaps move to another state, get a job, and experience independence. This gives them a sense of their choices. They can then choose to live on the Amish compound for the rest of their lives, or they can choose to leave the compound and experience the typical life of an American, with all of its freedom. The decision they make, however, is forever. The choice is crucial for their future life. If they choose to become non-Amish, then, in a sense, they are leaving the only life they ever knew. It is fascinating that the vast majority of Amish people return to the compound after Rumspringa. Some of them live very rebellious lives during their Rumspringa years. There are tremendous sacrifices when returning to the compound: receiving **baptism,** growing a beard, living without electricity, surrendering a car, getting married, and committing to the extremely religious principles outlined by the elders and Amish community standards. This entire phenomenon was excellently displayed in the riveting 2002 documentary *Devil's Playground.*

Village India, small-town Greece, Saudi Arabia, or an Amish compound in Pennsylvania—these are a few examples of fairly stable religious conformity by virtually all members of the society. But most people in the world today, especially in the hyper-globalized Western world, will meet extreme diversity throughout their years. They will eat at the local Punjabi restaurant. They will have Jewish and Asian friends. They will know several immigrant families or families who immigrated to the United States in the last generation or two. They will probably go to church with people from various life backgrounds. Profound diversity is a common feature of living life in a globalized world—a world in which people from various geographic and cultural backgrounds have been integrated into a shared society. There is always give and take in a globalized context. People have to learn to share space, extend dignity and human rights to one another, do business with each other, intermarry, communicate effectively, work together, and raise children who share schools with each other.

US society is religiously plural in another way, however. The vast majority of Americans call themselves Christians. However, there are thousands of different kinds of Christianity in the United States. The largest denomination of Christianity is **Roman Catholicism**. Around one out of every five Americans is Catholic. There are also members of the Church of Jesus Christ of Latter-day Saints (**Mormons**)—a form of Christianity that supplements the Bible with other texts that are authoritative for them. There are thousands of different kinds of Protestants, too. Basically, Protestantism is a very diverse, broad category. In its most fundamental definition, a Protestant is someone who is not Catholic and is not Eastern Orthodox. World Christianity can be divided into three large, overarching branches: Roman Catholicism (comprising 50 percent of the world's 2.5 billion Christians), Eastern Orthodoxy (10 percent), and

Roman Catholicism · the largest Christian denomination in the world

Mormons · (formally known as the Church of Jesus Christ of Latter-day Saints) led by Joseph Smith and later Brigham Young, this form of Protestant Christianity emerged on the US frontier and is now a substantial global denomination

Protestantism (40 percent). The most diverse branch of Christianity, by far, is Protestantism, as there are thousands of denominations within that major grouping. There are Pentecostals, Anglicans, Baptists, Presbyterians, Restorationists, Methodists, Seventh-day Adventists, Messianic Jews, Jehovah's Witnesses, and many more.

So even when we talk about Christianity, we are talking about a religion that has thousands upon thousands of different groupings within it. Thus, in the United States, a person who is a Christian will likely have friends and acquaintances who approach life differently. Some people choose to keep their religious life fairly insular—for instance, in the case of a family that puts their children into a private Catholic school. But even there, it is common for Catholic schools to allow non-Catholics to attend! In the United States, it is almost impossible to live a religiously insular life. People will undoubtedly have to interact with others who follow a form of religion quite different from their own. A study of world religions is critical for providing tools and strategies to communicate more effectively and empathetically with people of other religious persuasions.

To return to my original point, it is meaningless to try to avoid the topic of religion altogether. It is ubiquitous and fundamental to the human experience. It is a much better strategy to learn *how* to talk about religion in a way that conveys understanding, respect, and competence. People will navigate the workplace much better, make friends out of acquaintances, and become much more humane if they understand where other people are coming from in their daily interactions with them.

The Golden Rule (Compassion)

While speaking what is probably the best-known speech in the history of humankind, Jesus Christ said, "Do to others whatever you would like them to do to you. This is the essence of all that is taught in the law and the prophets" (Matt 7:12).

It is no coincidence that virtually all religions and ethical systems include a version of this core teaching from Jesus. The central idea of the **Golden Rule** extends back to well before the life of Jesus. Confucianism, Daoism, Hinduism, and Buddhism all have a version of the Golden Rule, and all of them are older faiths than Christianity.

- Confucianism: "What you do not want done to yourself, do not do to others." (*The Analects* XV:24)
- Daoism: "Alike to good and bad, I must be good."[1]
- Hinduism: "When a person responds to the joys and sorrows of others as if they were his own, he has attained the highest state of spiritual union." (Bhagavad Gita, 6:32)
- Buddhism: "Hurt not others with what pains yourself."[2]

As crucial as the Golden Rule remains in Christian ethics, it is found in some form in virtually all of the world's religious traditions.

Why does the Golden Rule resonate within humans so deeply? One important reason is because it is effective. However, it is unnatural. It takes work. People want to be treated well, but they do not always want to treat others well. So the Golden Rule presents something of a dilemma. We want to be treated with respect, but we do not necessarily want to respect a person who is different, who mistreats us, or whom we dislike.

Thus, the Golden Rule requires great discipline. It is perhaps the best-known religious teaching in the world, but it is one of the most difficult to follow through on. As individuals, our natural instinct is to do what we want when we want. But the Golden Rule forces us to stop and think about our behavior, attitude, and actions in a new and even disruptive way. Instead of thinking, *How do I want to treat that person? How do I want to deal with them?* we have to think quite different thoughts: *How might that person wish to be treated by me? How might that person prefer to be dealt with by me?* It throws a curveball to us, and we have to rethink what we might say to someone. We might end up having to completely change how we were planning to deal with a situation. No longer do we allow ourselves to simply do what we want. Now

Golden Rule · a central tenet of many worldwide faiths that teaches practitioners to treat others as they would want to be treated

Statue of Saint Francis from inside the Convent of San Gabriel in the ancient city of Cholula, Mexico. In the sixteenth century, Franciscan missionaries established this convent on Mesoamerican land that had been formerly dedicated to Quetzalcóatl.

we have to do what we think someone else might want us to do in a given situation.

Living out the Golden Rule requires us to suppress our own desires and, in a sense, transcend our most basic instincts. No longer do we think first of our own ego. Now we must think first of others' egos. **Saint Francis of Assisi's** famous prayer in the 1200s is one of the great representations of Golden Rule thought processes:

> Lord, make me an instrument of your peace:
> where there is hatred, let me sow love;
> where there is injury, pardon;
> where there is doubt, faith;
> where there is despair, hope;
> where there is darkness, light;
> where there is sadness, joy.
>
> O divine Master, grant that I may not so much seek
> to be consoled as to console,
> to be understood as to understand,
> to be loved as to love.
> For it is in giving that we receive,
> it is in pardoning that we are pardoned,
> and it is in dying that we are born to eternal life.
> Amen.[3]

There is a decentering of the self that occurs here. Saint Francis was careful to turn away from his basic instincts, such as "seeking to be consoled," and replace them with non-egoistic thinking. He asked God to help him first wish to console others before asking for his own consolation. Love first before asking for love. Give first before receiving. Understand others before asking to be understood.

Saint Francis of Assisi · a famous Catholic saint from the 1200s who taught a decentering of the self to look instead to the needs of others

As Francis likely knew well, this decentered way of thinking comes with its own reward. Much of the time, when we decenter our own ego and put the needs of others first, then our own needs are met. There is something paradoxical but beautifully and mystically true in this logic. It is something we know to be true on a visceral level, but it defies our most basic instincts to get what we want before giving others what they want. From childhood, our nature is to look out for ourselves first and then look out for the needs of others. The Golden Rule flips that. And some people never learn how to think this way. That is why we have greed, egocentrism, and corruption. That is why we have prisoners, homeless encampments, and victims. That is why we have bullies, cost-prohibitive medicine, and gross income disparities. In our dealings with others, we tend to look out for ourselves first and others last. But Jesus and numerous other sages throughout history taught a radically different perspective. To many, this decentering of the ego is overwhelmingly difficult to attain.

In some religions, such as Buddhism, the concept of the Golden Rule is summarized in one word: compassion. The concept of compassion is similar to the Golden Rule. It is an authentic attempt to understand the other person. It is a softening of the heart. It is the desire to be kind over against the desire to be right. It is an attempt to walk in their shoes, understand their humanity, and allow their perspective to overshadow one's own.

Religions are often seen as being divisive, even cancerous. We read of human rights violations, often based on **religious zealotry**. We see **fundamentalisms**

Two young girls pose for a portrait in Michika, a northeastern Nigerian town formerly occupied by the extremist Islamic sect Boko Haram. The girls were attending a reconciliation meeting organized by Muslim and Christian leaders. The United Nations suggests that over the last decade, more than 350,000 have died, and another two million have been displaced from their homes in Nigeria, Cameroon, Chad, and Niger.

Photographer Danielle Villasana. Used by permission.

that are more concerned with following the letter of the law than with treating others with dignity and respect. We are sadly aware of genocides that have taken place throughout history, often with religion as a primary motive. Religion without the Golden Rule can swiftly descend into factious bickering. Religious ideology without compassion can be a cover for abuse, harassment, and even murder.

Theologian Hans Küng famously said, "There will be no peace among the nations without peace among the religions." Sadly, this seems true enough. At a time when religion should be binding people together in a context of rapid **globalization,** religion has tended to divide, escalate conflict, and erect barriers to human understanding. It is a sad commentary on religiosity when it gets to the point that religion does more tearing apart than binding together.

But religion's detrimental impact on the world is certainly no fait accompli. There are good reasons for thinking that religion can potentially bind up the wounds that it has inflicted. Religion has answers, and the world's religious traditions have survived for eons for good reasons: they provide meaning and hope, they help societies, and they provide conditions for human flourishing. But—this is key—religion can go either way. It can escalate conflict, pain, and even violence. But it can also provide solutions. It all depends on how the world's religions conform to their most basic modus operandi—the Golden Rule, compassion, a profound decentering of the ego.

The Golden Rule is famously associated with Jesus Christ, but it is important to point out that Jesus was a Jewish rabbi who was trained in the Torah. The context of Jesus's retelling of the Golden Rule is crucial—Leviticus 19. That chapter provides the larger body of thinking that was resonating in Jesus's mind and heart as he went about teaching the Golden Rule and his great teachings that echoed it. Leviticus 19 is a portion of the Torah that all rabbis knew well and still know well. Jesus was a part of this longstanding rabbinic tradition that knew this passage by heart:

When you harvest the crops of your land, do not harvest the grain along the edges of your fields, and do not pick up what the harvesters

drop. It is the same with your grape crop—do not strip every last bunch of grapes from the vines, and do not pick up the grapes that fall to the ground. Leave them for the poor and the foreigners living among you. I am the LORD your God.

Do not defraud or rob your neighbor.

Do not make your hired workers wait until the next day to receive their pay.

Do not insult the deaf or cause the blind to stumble. . . .

Do not twist justice in legal matters by favoring the poor or being partial to the rich and powerful. Always judge people fairly.

Do not spread slanderous gossip among your people.

Do not stand idly by when your neighbor's life is threatened. I am the LORD.

Do not nurse hatred in your heart for any of your relatives. Confront people directly so you will not be held guilty for their sin.

Do not seek revenge or bear a grudge against a fellow Israelite, but love your neighbor as yourself. I am the LORD.

Do not take advantage of foreigners who live among you in your land. Treat them like native-born Israelites, and love them as you love yourself. Remember that you were once foreigners living in the land of Egypt. I am the LORD your God. (Lev. 19:9–10, 13–18, 33–34)

For Jews, these verses represent the epitome of compassion, or of Golden Rule thinking. These are ideas that work against the

Globalization · the current phenomenon of increasing interconnectedness between international businesses, polities, and cultures

Public Domain

B. R. Ambedkar (1891–1956) was a socio-political reformer, remembered today for drafting the Indian constitution and challenging discrimination. Before his death, he formally converted to Buddhism in a massive public ceremony before an audience of half a million people. As many as twenty million Dalits (the untouchable class) have followed his example embracing this religion.

to your longstanding neighbors. Indeed, love them as you even love yourself!

What if all nations developed their policies with the Golden Rule in mind? What if businesses developed their salary scale alongside a copy of the Golden Rule? What if healthcare providers etched the Golden Rule in huge letters on the front of their hospitals and printed it on all of their letterhead? What if Christians put this teaching onto their foreheads, like many Jews do with the sacred teaching of the Shema?[4]

Crucially, the most important part of the Golden Rule is the living of it. Memorizing it is easy. Even putting it onto one's doorframe, as Jews do with the **mezuzah**, is easy. But living out compassion, living the Golden Rule, paying one's employees well, treating foreigners like locals, sharing one's goods with immigrants—these are not always easy to do. Doing so requires a decentering of one's own welfare and a privileging of the other. But imagine what a world would look like if people followed the teaching of Jesus and the rabbis on this central concept. It would be a drastically different world.

Incredibly, our world has not descended into chaos due to massive immigration into each other's countries. Perhaps surprisingly, many immigrants are treated well, receive health care and education, and rise up to become leaders. Perhaps counterintuitively, our world is binding together in critical ways, including trade and commerce, entertainment, sports, language, mass and social media, and air travel. Religion plays a role in all of this. Religion can indeed bring compassion and even peace rather than chaos and suspicion. The Golden Rule, like a lighthouse, provides direction for all who have entered into this massive, global interweaving of faith, culture, and individuals as we cross into each other's worlds. There is still a place for religion—a crucial place—if only it subscribes to its most fundamental tenets.

Why Be Religious?

There are many reasons why people are religious. Perhaps the most obvious one is that families tend to be religious. Even if one's parents do not actively participate in a religion, they probably did in their youth. Religion is something that revives with certain

grain of self-indulgence. *Do not harvest all of your grapes; let foreigners have some, as they need help. Pay people equitably. Do not pay your employees the smallest amount that you can possibly pay them. Do not make fun of people with disabilities. Do not slander people. Do not gossip. Support your neighbors. Help them when they are in trouble. Do not hate people; love them! Treat foreigners like native-born people. Love them like you love yourself!* All of us come from somewhere! All of us were aliens, strangers, and foreigners at some point in our history. Perhaps we ourselves had to move or migrate. Perhaps it was our ancestors who came to this country. We all have a sense of what it means to not belong. *When foreigners come into your life, treat them like they are locals. Give them the dignity you give*

Mezuzah · a parchment inscribed with Jewish scriptures and fixed to the doorpost of a home

generations and dies down in others. Nearly every-body has religious people in their families, and nearly everybody has something to say about their own religiosity. It is something that is innate.

Sociologist Abby Day has written brilliantly on the religious lives of British people.[5] In her research, she has discovered that the conventional religious/secular distinction has too many holes in it to be taken seriously. There is absolutely no sense that people are either/or. Rather, there are shades of religiosity within people. Some might say that they are spiritual but not religious. Other people might write on a survey that they have no religion when, in reality, they are quite religious. This is why it is often unwise to try to measure religion **quantitatively**, as in surveys and statistics.

Day found that many people who might characterize themselves as nonreligious or secular on paper were actually more interesting when interviewed. Thus, we can say that **qualitative** research is much more helpful when trying to determine what is going on inside a person's head. For instance, a person who claims no religious affiliation might actually believe in God. In fact, they might actually pray rather frequently. They might even talk to their deceased loved ones. Perhaps they take their dreams seriously, as messages conveyed to them from another realm. It is very possible that a **secular** person might actually believe in reincarnation or in heaven and hell. They might feel that there is a right or a wrong, a divine ethical system that originates in a power or force beyond us. Perhaps they believe that miracles are possible.

In other words, just because a person says they have no religion does not mean they have no religious qualities in their thinking. Rather, the greater likelihood is that their beliefs are extremely complex, individual, and unique. Some of them might be fairly standard religious beliefs, such as praying to the Virgin Mary or calling upon the Buddha when in a jam. Some Christians believe in **reincarnation**, while some Hindus believe Jesus to be a divine incarnation of a great god, such as Vishnu. There is hardly any way to completely understand a person's religious makeup.

Additionally, people evolve over time. Just as the cells in the human body die and get replaced by new cells, our religious ideologies are constantly changing.

One year we might have a firm belief in God, but then our life collapses and we wonder where God was during the dark times. We begin to doubt. Some people will rebound and return to their previously firm faith, but others might modify. They might open themselves up to another religion, or they might open themselves up to aspects of other religions. Perhaps they continue to go to the local Baptist church, but they begin to take seriously the teachings of Buddhism. So they enroll in a transcendental meditation class and start listening to dharma podcasts. They open themselves up, and thereby change, sometimes in subtle ways that cannot possibly be measured with an instrument as simple as a ten-question survey in which one fills in multiple-choice bubbles with a pencil.

Another reason people are religious is that sense of wonder within them. Jane Goodall, the famous primatologist who studied chimpanzees in Tanzania, believed the roots of religiosity could be found in chimps. For example, chimpanzees sometimes showed ecstatic wonder, such as when seeing a gushing waterfall. Chimps could solve communal conflicts through grooming one another after a fight. In Goodall's view, these and similar expressions of compassion and exuberance illustrate an embryonic form of religion.[6]

The tendency to question, to think of what is beyond us, and the profound curiosity that accompanies the human condition is evidence enough for thinking something else might be out there. We look up at the skies and ponder the vastness of the universe. Where did it come from? Why is there a sense of order in the stars and planets?

Which perspective requires more faith? The atheist one or the theist one? The atheistic view—to think that something appeared out of nothing and exploded, and rocks started circling rhythmically and, eventually, one of the rocks produced life, with a complexification of life occurring to the point that we have humans—seems somewhat difficult to conceive. To some people,

Quantitative · a way of studying religion that utilizes surveys and statistics

Qualitative · a way of studying religion that uses interviews and individual experiences

Secular · unaffiliated with religion

Reincarnation · the cycle of rebirth into a new body after death

all of this complexity, life, and order points to something outside of materiality. What we see around us seems like a creation—something created, rather than something that occurred by chance.

True atheism is somewhat difficult to come by. In 2014, the Pew Research Center found that only about 3 percent of Americans are **atheist**.[7] However, in 2019, when Pew interviewed (qualitative research) those who identified as atheists in a survey (quantitative research), they found that nearly 20 percent actually said that they *do* believe in a higher power. Curiously, they also found that the atheists they talked with seemed to want to reject the Bible rather than reject the possibility of a creator. They also discovered the intriguing fact that the vast majority of those who claimed atheism were young men, a fact that perhaps points to a sociological issue.[8]

Further, some scholars, such as Mary Eberstadt, have persuasively shown that when people start their own families, they become more religious, a phenomenon she humorously calls "kids driving their parents to church."[9] All this data seems to say that while young men are somewhat more likely than others to declare themselves to be atheists, they may not be completely atheistic, if by that we mean they are mere materialists. And if they do declare themselves to be atheists when they are young men, there is a decent likelihood that they will change their views once they get out on their own, get married, start a family, and have to make crucial decisions about parenthood, such as teaching their kids about ethics, morality, and how we got here.

Another important reason people tend to engage religion has to do with meaning and value. These are concepts that scientific approaches cannot definitively measure. Science has its place in the study of religion: materiality, economics of religion, architecture, chronology, and so on. Meaning and value, however, cannot easily be measured. Why does Handel's

Messiah inspire Western civilization to the degree that it does? Why do Jain nuns pull out their hair and reject their families before entering the convent? Why do Hindu widows occasionally throw themselves onto the burning pyre of their deceased husband during the funerary cremation ritual, thus committing suicide? What inspired a Japanese warrior to commit **seppuku**—the disembowelment of oneself by slitting the abdomen? These are questions that defy measurement and virtually any kind of empirical data. These examples take us into the realm of inspiration, meaning, and what one places value upon. Value and meaning vary considerably when looking within the contexts of the world's religions.

Back to our question: Why be religious? Perhaps the most obvious answer is because it helps us. Buddhism teaches people how to overcome **dukkha**, or anxiety and suffering. Hinduism helps people get off the exhausting cycle of **samsara** and achieve peace and bliss with supreme reality. Judaism teaches a community how to live well with each other and with God. Christianity teaches its members how to live a meaningful life that conforms to the principles of love. Islam teaches its followers how to submit properly to the one God. Daoism and Confucianism prioritize living a harmonious life—harmony with nature, harmony with each other, and harmony with ancestors and deities. Many people feel that they need religion to help them find meaning and value, those twin concepts that prevent us from drifting into meaninglessness, self-destructive behaviors, or complete lack of empathy with the people around us. Without meaning, without values, without self-understanding, we are pretty much left to our own resources. We need a story that frames our reality or that provides a context within which to live our lives.

The alternative is to theorize that perhaps one has no meaning and no inherent value. Perhaps we are simply stardust, results of a bunch of explosions over billions of years, and perhaps there really is no point to anything. We simply exist for no reason. There is no right, there is no wrong, there is no purpose. We spontaneously came into being as tiny cells, and we mutated to the point that we could swim, then walk, and then think complex ideas. Eventually, we started

Muslim man giving rice as a food donation for zakat.

thinking ideas so complex as to beg for answers, such as *Why did all of this happen? Why am I here? Why did time produce all that I see and result in my existence?* The completely materialistic answers seem not to satisfy. That is not to say that materialistic speculations are wrong. Nobody knows whether they are or not. But the reality is that whether we believe we have no value or have value, both options require belief. Similarly, whether we believe we are here by chance or have purpose, both options require belief. In other words, belief is difficult to avoid. Humans have to believe in something. Saying "I do not believe in anything" seems to be a form of circular reasoning that has no rational basis. In other words, it, too, is a kind of faith. It is similar to atheism. Both theists and atheists believe. They just believe in different things.

Is religion just some ethereal, mystical set of ideas, or can something definitive and materially helpful come out of it? The answer is an obviously affirmative one. Humans would likely not have developed religious systems were it not for fundamental benefits to their daily living. But practically speaking, what are the immediately tangible benefits of religiosity?

- **Psychological benefits.** People struggle to cope with life. M. Scott Peck began his famous book *The Road Less Traveled* with these words: "Life is difficult. . . . Once we truly know that life is difficult—once we truly understand and accept it—then life is no longer difficult. Because once it is accepted, the fact that life is difficult no longer matters."[10] Religions help us come to terms with the pain of life. But religions do not leave us there. They provide tools and resources designed to get us through, such as meditation to reduce anxiety and prayer to provide hope. Study after study has shown that religion can be extremely helpful in people's life satisfaction, well-being, and relationship health.[11] This is not to say that religion is always psychologically beneficial. There are times when religion can do great psychological harm to people.

- **Social benefits.** Evangelical Christian lawmakers played a critical role in the British and US abolition movements by directing people to the biblical emphasis on each person's dignity. Islam teaches **zakat**—that Muslims must give alms to the poor and otherwise needy. Native American religions bring social cohesion through rites of passage and sacred dance. Religion has time and again brought reconciliation in contexts of war and division. This is not to say that religion is an inexorable force for social good. Indeed, religion has caused many wars throughout history.

- **Physical and economic benefits.** Studies have shown that religiosity can offer tangible physical benefits, such as lessening criminal behavior and improving physical health.[12] There are many potential areas of physical and economic benefit for religious people. For example, most religious-based marriages bring God into the vows for a sacred and lifelong expectation for the marital commitment. Instant trust and rapport often occurs between coreligionists. For instance, if an American Latter-day Saint gets off a plane in Indonesia and finds another Latter-day Saint, there is an instant connection. Business agreements are more secure if religious commitment is at the foundation of that relationship. It is often said that Jains are good people to do business with since they are not allowed to be dishonest. They are obligated to be completely forthcoming in their speech, thus lessening the possibilities for dishonest gain or confusion. If one's neighbor is a committed Christian, then there is a good chance that neighbor will treat his or her neighbor well, as Jesus's most fundamental teaching is to "love your neighbor as yourself" (Matt. 19:19).

- **Inclusion and diversity.** It is common to hear people emphasize racial and ethnic diversity, but there are other forms of diversity that are less pronounced, such as age diversity and religious diversity. Religious people are not necessarily more sensitive to others, but the opportunity is there, especially in religions in which inclusion and respect for diversity are key components. Christianity, for example, is the world's most diverse faith by far. Christianity is the largest religion in Latin America, North America, Western Europe, Eastern Europe, Africa, and Oceania. Africa is the land with the most Christians, while Latin America is the place with the highest percentage of Christians. The United States is the nation with the most Christians. Armenia is the oldest Christian nation in the world. In other words, Christians should be among the most inclusive people on Earth, since they are integrally and spiritually connected to a vast array of people groups all over the world. Jesus taught to love others, period. The **apostle Paul**, a **rabbi** who emerged in the first century CE to become a great early Christian missionary and writer, emphasized repeatedly the importance of inclusion and diversity in the church—an example is his "one body, many parts" analogy in 1 Corinthians 12. Christianity is not the only religion that emphasizes the obligation to respect diversity and to be inclusive in one's daily activities, but it is a notable one.

Religion provides a slew of benefits that are obvious once a person joins.

There are sacrifices and obligations involved when one commits to a religion, however. For instance, living in a Muslim community means one needs to pray at least five times per day. Orthodox Jews have to give their **Sabbath**—the seventh day of each week—to God and to their synagogue. The young Latter-day Saints member must complete a one- to

Zakat · a 2.5% tithe collected for the poor, as required by Islam

Apostle Paul · a rabbi in the first century CE who became a great early Christian missionary and writer; he emphasized the importance of inclusion and diversity in the church

Rabbi · a religious teacher in Judaism

Sabbath · the seventh day of each week, which Jewish adherents are required to give to God and to their synagogue

Kamidana · a small shrine in a Shinto home dedicated to the ancestors and used for daily religious ritual

THEORIES OF RELIGION

Daniel Pals wrote one of the best books about how scholars have tended to study religion. The book is called *Nine Theories of Religion* and is used widely in religious studies courses that focus on method and theory in the study of religion.[14] Pals argues that there are five "leading patterns, or dominant agendas" in the study of religion: (1) humanistic, (2) psychological, (3) sociological, (4) political-economic, and (5) anthropological.[15] He breaks down this typology further into nine theories of religion pioneered by towering scholars in the larger field of religious studies, devoting a chapter to each:

- **E. B. Tylor and J. G. Frazer** were early anthropologists who studied magic, taboo, animism, and totemism.
- **Sigmund Freud**, a father of psychotherapy, speculated widely on what he saw as religion's origins being located in human illusions or wishful thinking.
- **Emile Durkheim** saw religion as a complex sociological phenomenon meant to bring coherence to the individual and his or her own specific society.
- **Karl Marx** saw religion as endemic to class struggle. His view of religion was extremely critical and tended to depict religion as something the elites of society use to keep the masses placated and docile. He famously claimed religion was "the opium of the people," meaning religion only kept people in a state of sedation so they would accept their unfavorable conditions in life.
- **Max Weber**, more than the others on this list, saw deep complexity in religion and its causes. Whereas other major theorists can be criticized for reducing religion to a singular cause, Weber's sophisticated comparison of numerous religions becomes unwieldy because of its social and historical nuance.
- **William James** was an American psychologist who focused more on religious experience than on religious institutions, as the truest form of religious life is found within human experience.
- **Mircea Eliade's** chief contribution to religious studies was his categorization of human experience into the categories of sacred and profane. The realm of the sacred—or religious—is vast and defies reductionist approaches.
- **E. E. Evans-Pritchard** was an Oxford anthropologist who believed strongly in the importance of fieldwork—actually living with the people one studies—so that the student can understand the larger worldview at work in his or her subjects.
- **Clifford Geertz**, too, was an anthropologist who believed strongly in the merits of doing actual fieldwork—befriending and living among the people one studies. Two of his important theories are **thick description** and **frames of meaning**, which emphasize the whole social context within which religious phenomena occur.

> **Thick description** · describing human social action not just with observable behaviors but also with their context, as interpreted by a member of the social community
>
> **Frames of meaning** · the conceptual framework in which a community's beliefs and behaviors are rooted and understood

The above scholars are among the most significant in the study of religion, although none of them can come close to understanding the totality of lenses by which scholars investigate religion in the twenty-first century. Some scholars attempt to study religion with a degree of scientific objectivity. Others, such as Evans-Pritchard and Geertz, realize that there is no objective place from which to study religion.

two-year mission, usually by going abroad. A Shinto will devote time to ancestors at the **kamidana** that has been set up in her home for daily religious ritual. The Buddhist will spend significant time in **meditation**, sometimes hours per day. The Daoist will visit the grave of his **ancestors** with regularity and will pledge to keep the ancestral burial sites clean and tidy.

While most adherents of religion enjoy numerous benefits by getting involved with a religion, there are expectations placed onto the individual as well. Religion is always a reciprocal process between the individual and the community. This can be looked at either positively or negatively. Sigmund Freud described this relationship in his book *Civilization and Its Discontents*.[13] He describes how being involved in a community involves both sacrifices and rewards, and it is not always immediately evident whether an individual is better off joining the community or better off being uncommitted. If the benefits outweigh the sacrifices, then perhaps one should consider joining a particular community. But if the sacrifices are so onerous that they begin to outweigh the benefits, then perhaps it is time to reconsider involvement in the association. These are subjective matters, however, and each individual person has to weigh and balance obligations with benefits.

Methodology in Studying Religion

There are countless ways to study religion. This is an important fact to bear in mind, as some people want to equate the study of the existence of gods with the study of religion. In other words, someone might say, "I do not believe in God; therefore, I am not religious." This is faulty thinking, however, because there are major

world religions, such as Buddhism, that do not believe in a supreme being. If someone rejects the concept of God, that is one thing. But if someone rejects all religions everywhere, then that is another issue entirely. The rejection of any kind of religion is a quite radical position to take because religion takes so many different forms throughout history and across the Earth. An atheist can still be religious, as in the case of many practicing Buddhists. Similarly, Jainism rejects the idea of a supreme being, or a creator god. Jainism is often described as being an **agnostic** religion, meaning that it does not take a position on whether there are gods. Some Jains may speak of a god, but when pressed, they concede to believing something closer to "trans-theism," meaning that while the gods may exist, they too are subject to samsara—being reborn as various life forms over and over again. The cycle of samsara "transcends" the gods. Even gods yearn to attain moksha, or spiritual release, from the cycle of samsara.

Put differently, the study of religion often involves understanding what people believe. There is no way to neatly isolate religion from other spheres of thinking. At times when someone says they reject religion, they are rejecting only an aspect of religion, such as belief in God, an afterlife, or the subscription to a particular system of ritual. Religion is impossible to define. Many have tried, but any definition has severe flaws and limitations. When we understand the universality and incredible diversity of religion, we realize that there is no unified theory or definition that works well. Religion transcends all attempts to clearly describe it. It defies academic categories of thought. This does not mean, however, that it cannot be studied. Certainly, it can be studied, but it cannot be studied definitively or exhaustively.

One cannot fully understand a religion as the practitioner experiences it unless one somehow climbs inside the culture and lives as if they, too, were on the "inside." Second, how can one ever truly get inside the culture and the religion if one does not fully commit to the religion with the heart, soul, and mind? Third, since our scientific instruments fail us when it comes to understanding the fullness of religion, then how can we claim to have true knowledge of a religion at

Max Müller's translation work as well as his essays on religion and philosophy greatly impacted the field of religious studies.

all? Our methods seem so inadequate. These are some of the problems and impediments in studying religion, but the alternative is to avoid them, thus depriving ourselves of the insights that religions have to offer us. And that is a far worse place to be since, obviously, religion is such a massive motivational force in the lives of many, if not most, of the world's people.

The study of religion has changed drastically since the field first started coming together as an academic discipline in the 1800s. Perhaps the most important trailblazer from that era was Max Müller (1823–1900). Müller was raised in Germany but spent the better part of his academic career at Oxford University. He became famous for his research on India, as well as his editorial oversight of the *Sacred Books of the East*, a fifty-volume set of English translations of important religious writings from Asia that were published between 1879 and 1910.

Max Müller's famous dictum was "To know one is to know none." Virtually all first-year religious studies students will encounter this phrase. Basically, it means that if one only knows their own religion, then one has no basis for comprehending larger concepts in religion.

If one only knows one approach to anything, then one is not able to comment on other approaches. Müller was a Christian, but he taught his students that, to have a better grasp of religion as a universal concept, they must be conversant in numerous religions to make comparisons and more sophisticated observations about them. By widening one's understanding, vocabulary, and worldview, the researcher is better able to make judgments about larger religious beliefs and practices. Müller's viewpoint gave rise to the field of religious studies, as many people realized the power of his observations. If one understands only one religion, then one is clearly not in a position to understand multiple religions. Only the study of multiple religions can provide that broader perspective.

Today, the study of world religions goes by several names. Some people call it **comparative religion**. Some call it **history of religions**. Some call it **religious studies**. But what is central is that the field of world religions is different than studying theology or apologetics. When people study **theology**, they are usually studying one faith—their own. They are trying to learn more about their own religion so that they can perhaps connect with God on a deeper level. Or perhaps they study in preparation for ordained ministry in a church.

People who study **apologetics** learn about other religions to refute them. They learn about Hinduism or Islam but primarily to evangelize their adherents.

When people enter into the field of religious studies, it is not primarily for evangelistic purposes. The primary purpose is to understand those religions on their own terms—to learn their vocabularies, to understand their texts and rituals, and to

Comparative religion · a term for the study of world religions that emphasizes the comparison of the various religious traditions

History of religions · a term for the study of world religions that emphasizes the historical background of religious traditions

Religious studies · a term for the study of world religions; approaches religion with an academic and critical lens

Theology · the study of the religious doctrines of a particular faith, generally to connect deeper with God or to strengthen one's belief

Apologetics · the study of one religion in order to defend it against critics and to refute competing belief systems

THE STUDY OF RELIGION

The study of religion can usually begin by focusing on the "four C's": creed, code, ceremonies, and community.

- **Creed** is the cognitive aspect of a religion. What do they believe? What do they think about this or that aspect of life? What do they think happens after death? Who is God? These are all aspects of religion that will be found in their creeds.
- **Codes** define behavior and ethics. Most religions have rules and lists of rules. The **Ten Commandments** is a good example of a religion's most important law code. How must a person conduct himself or herself in the temple? How must one treat their elders? What are the do's and don'ts that a community must abide by?
- **Ceremonies** include times of celebration, mourning, or other moments of collectivist activity, from church services to weddings to festivals. Ceremonies are sacred times when the individual or the community encounters the divine or sits in the presence of their conception of ultimate reality. There might also be practical ceremonies, such as **Brit Milah**, when a Jewish boy is circumcised on the eighth day of his life by the **mohel**.
- **Community** is the religion in its collectivist sense. A committed Christian is a member of the worldwide family of God—the church. A Muslim is a member of the global **ummah**. Some communities have an ethnic sensibility to them, such as Hindus being mainly from India and Sikhs having a shared connection to the Punjab. Jews, of course, have a shared ethnic heritage for the most part.

The four C's—creed, code, ceremonies, and community—are helpful when first trying to understand a religion. If one can get a decent grasp of the four C's, then they will be much better positioned for observing another religion or having respectful interreligious dialogue with an interlocutor.

The US Supreme Court has ruled that the display of the Ten Commandments inside a courthouse or classroom represents a violation of the establishment clause of the First Amendment. The court has subsequently ruled that outdoor religious monuments are permissible under certain circumstances. Pictured here is a monument of the Ten Commandments on the capitol grounds of the state of Texas.

become familiar with their thought processes. This is why the field of religious studies is usually distinct from the study of theology or apologetics. Of course, a person may enter into a religious studies program with the hope that they will one day be able to evangelize people. But the approach is different when taking a religious studies perspective as opposed to theological approaches.

As the study of world religions has become more popular, it has also become much easier to do. Not only are texts much more widely available, but people from other religions are widespread in the twenty-first century. It is quite common to have a Jew as a coworker. College students may encounter Muslims and Hindus in their dorm. Americans will certainly meet people from India, who may be Zoroastrian, Jain, Sikh, Hindu, Muslim, or even Christian. After all, Christianity is the third-largest religion in India, after Hinduism and Islam. One might do business with a Shinto from Japan or a Buddhist from Southeast Asia.

Thus, today, the study of world religions is something one can do quite readily from the United States. One can easily visit the local mosque or gurdwara. One will likely have friends from other faiths. Interfaith dialogue is increasingly common on college campuses, where people of various faiths share perspectives on any number of issues in the public square. Interfaith marriage is increasingly common. The various religions of the world are intermixing in profound ways, and the student of world religions can easily make

Ten Commandments · the basic moral code of Judaism

friends with people from different religions and learn about them firsthand.

Thus, the study of religion involves a level of humility and charity that is important to come to terms with. The student of world religions needs to see himself or herself as a guest in the **gurdwara**, for example. The gurdwara is the place of worship for Sikhs. When an American visits the Sikh place of worship, she can enjoy the scene, listen to the music, and even eat **langar** with the people, but she must do so with a spirit of inquiry and respect. Visitors are there to learn, not to teach. They are there to understand, not to be understood. They are there to listen. It requires a posture of humility and reverence. Shoes must be removed. Sikhs will give visitors something to cover their hair for when they enter the presence of the **Guru Granth Sahib**, the holy text of Sikhism. With a spirit of humility, there is no limit to what one can learn when one puts oneself at the mercy of another religious group that has welcomed a visitor into their sacred space. Indeed, the visitor is on holy ground—*their* holy ground. The hosts deserve kind attentiveness, respect toward their traditions, and a spirit of goodwill as visitors participate or observe.

Meaningful engagement with neighbors of other faiths can be a wonderful experience and can lead to friendships. Friendship with people from other religious traditions can be immensely satisfying. One might get invited to attend **Purim** with a Jewish family—this can be joyful and filled with humor. One might get invited to celebrate **Eid al-Fitr** with

Gurdwara · a Sikh house of worship

Langar · a free meal given to worshippers and guests following a Sikh service

Guru Granth Sahib · the holy text of Sikhism

Purim · a Jewish festival celebrating the day the Jewish people were saved from a genocide plot during the reign of the First Persian Empire

Eid al-Fitr · a Muslim celebration marking the end of the daylight fasts of the holy month of Ramadan

A Muslim woman enjoys a meal with her family after Sunset during Ramadan.

Drazen Zigic, Adobe Stock

A young girl celebrates Chinese New Year with a traditional dancing lion.

M-image, Adobe Stock

Muslim friends, and they will eat amazing meals that they have probably never tasted before. One's Daoist friends might extend an invitation to celebrate **Chinese New Year** with them. It is such an honor to be invited to these kinds of gatherings, and they can be a major learning opportunity in themselves. Do not ever pass up an opportunity to attend a **bar mitzvah**, a Greek wedding, or a **Diwali** celebration! These are opportunities for making friendships that can last a lifetime.

Another important way to understand other religions is to reckon with what they perceive to be the goal of their religion. Christians have the idea of **salvation**. In other words, they live their lives hoping that God will save them from death when they die. They hope in the final resurrection, when God will raise them up and bring them into his eternal kingdom in heaven.

Liberation, or **moksha**, is a common goal of life for Hindus, who understand life as a wheel of existence. We are reborn many times over the course of thousands of years, and eventually, we hope to achieve liberation from this continuous cycle. The goal of life, therefore, is to get off of the wheel and enjoy eternal bliss with **Brahman**.

Enlightenment is a word used often in the Buddhist context. Siddhartha Gautama—also known as the **Buddha**—is the "enlightened one," as he came to see reality as it truly is. The Buddha also achieved **nirvana**—a blowing out of all one's desires. One no longer craves or lusts. Desires keep us in the cycle of rebirth, so if we can blow out our desires, then we can potentially become fully enlightened.

Heaven is a common endpoint in the world's religions. Islam, Christianity, and even some forms of Buddhism have paradise-like places for those who die in good faith. These are places of reward where rest is offered along with peace and complete fulfillment.

One more principle that is helpful in studying world religions should be mentioned: "The scale creates the phenomenon."[16] By studying religion, we are better able to understand the context of any religious phenomenon, such as a ritual, a god, or a description of the afterlife. As Max Müller noticed, if we understand only one scale, then how can we possibly understand something that does not register on our own scale? Virtually every judgment we make comes from the scale that we find ourselves on. Is somebody a political liberal or a conservative? Well, it depends on the scale. If one lives in California, their scale is going to be different than if they live in Arkansas or Wyoming, where people tend to be more conservative politically. Does one make a good salary? It depends on the scale one has been exposed to. If one's family is from a long line of oil tycoons, their scale will be different than a person's whose family members are all public school teachers.

None of us are from static situations in life. We are all from particular backgrounds; therefore, we have a particular exposure to the various phenomena that we encounter. This concept can also be called **preunderstanding**. Before we try to understand another religion or another religious practice, then we must come to terms with the fact that we have a particular preunderstanding about it. We have a particular frame of reference that was handed to us from our parents, our society, our nation, our social status, and our previous exposure. By coming to terms with our preunderstanding, then we can keep our judgments in check, making it far more enjoyable to learn without having to make judgments about everything we are learning about a religion.

If one is from India, then India is their "scale"—meaning that is what they are used to seeing. India is their frame of reference. Therefore, reincarnation is not a shocking concept at all. However, if one has never met a person who believes in reincarnation, then it will be a very foreign concept. It will be difficult to face the idea that a good percentage of the world's population believes in reincarnation.

The scale that one is on will often determine how one hears other perspectives. If one has studied classical music, one will better understand what is happening at the opera. If one has never been exposed to classical music with any kind of sophistication, then their scale is essentially devoid of classical music, and it may sound odd, perhaps displeasing, or monotonous.

By studying the world's religious traditions, we are expanding our scale. We establish a fairly broad context for comprehending what people believe, how they think, and what motivates them. We gain a better appreciation for *why* people believe things that others might find bizarre. **Sati**, widow burning, was seen as horrible and shockingly barbaric to the British when they first encountered India. But if one is an Indian, then sati has more to do with honor, sacrifice, and extreme devotion to one's life partner.

To understand that the scale creates the phenomenon means that instead of just studying a religion, a person must first think deeply about *how* one might study a religion. Their interpretive framework and how this question is answered will create understanding. One must come to terms with the fact that not only are perceptions limited by one's own past experiences, but that those past experiences define a person's scale.

Liberation · the central goal of Hinduism

Moksha · the liberation of the soul from the cycle of rebirth in Hinduism and other Eastern traditions

Brahman · the eternal and ultimate reality in Hinduism

Enlightenment · the central goal of Buddhism

Buddha · "the enlightened one," Siddhartha Gautama

Nirvana · the extinguishment of all of one's desires

Heaven · a common endpoint for many of the world's religions; a place of paradise that can be reached through correct action on Earth

The scale creates the phenomenon · an important principle when studying religion, as people are better able to understand the context of any religious phenomenon, such as a ritual, a god, or a description of the afterlife, if they have learned other religious perspectives, or scales

Preunderstanding · our preexisting frame of reference through which we judge new information

Sati · widow burning, a controversial, now-banned, practice in India

In 2006, the Palace of Peace and Reconciliation opened in Nur-Sultan, Kazakhstan, as a venue for the triennial Congress of Leaders of World and Traditional Religions. However, the United Nations Human Rights Council has observed that Kazakhstan's mandatory registration and strict monitoring of "non-traditional" religions compromises international standards for freedom of religion and belief.

The following principles can guide the study of religion:

- **Religion is a panhuman phenomenon.** It seems to have been part of the earliest human civilizations. And for all the talk of Western people abandoning religion, the fact is that, upon further investigation, they have not abandoned spirituality. Even so-called secular people believe in things that religious studies scholars would classify as being religious. For example, Yoga, meditation, prayer, belief in afterlife, superstitions, rituals, ideas of God, morality, ethical systems, and judgments are all ideas that are deeply rooted in religiousness throughout history. For instance, it is difficult to talk about right and wrong without resorting to religious categories to one degree or another.

- When people say that one should never talk about religion or politics, what they mean is that **one should not talk about these things unless one can do so appropriately.** It is mistaken to say that one should never talk about religion or politics. However, if one is the type of person who cannot talk about religion or politics without losing one's temper, then perhaps it is time to learn *how* to talk about these topics in a compassionate, empathetic, and disciplined way.

- The Golden Rule is helpful for living life well, and **learning to respect other people is a key part of religious studies.** Putting one's neighbor's needs ahead of one's own can facilitate friendship and foster great trust. The Golden Rule—also known as compassion—can not only help us individually, but it can also lead to greater understanding among the world's peoples. If one can accomplish compassion in one's personal life, then one is well on their way toward comprehending the infinite wisdom found in the world's great religious traditions.

- There are terrific benefits that come with being religious *if one learns how to channel them correctly.* One can have less anxiety, a healthier body, powerful hope, and a decency toward other people that will impact the people around them for the better. Religion offers much to the practitioner, as well as to the curious student.

- Studying religion can be enjoyable and *can be done from a wide variety of approaches.* Whether one travels to Indonesia to study a tribe, like Clifford Geertz did, or whether one befriends a Sikh classmate at college, there are many ways to learn about other religions. This book will guide the reader toward a greater understanding of the world's religions, but a true education in world religions requires more: it requires participation. It requires a willingness to get to know other people, to eat with them and converse with them. One will be surprised by how many new friends they make along the way. Indeed, that might just be the best way to understand a worldview different from one's own—to understand it through the explanations of a friend.

2 INDIGENOUS RELIGIONS

Religion before the World Religions

One of four indigenous clans living in Northwestern Siberia, the nomadic Nenet people are known for their reindeer herding. In the 1940s, when the Soviet Union exerted influence in the region, they described their religious practices as "shamanism."

Religion has been with humans from the beginning. Wherever bones of the first humans are found, there are signs that those humans were probably religious in certain ways. The problem is what to call those early religions. Scholars have suggested various umbrella terms under which these smaller religions can be categorized. Early anthropologists often called them **primitive religions**, which is a label that has been rejected in recent times. This was a Darwinian-influenced term that held to the notion that early religions were less sophisticated. Tylor and Frazer held that primitive religions were an earlier phase of religion that they often referred to as magic. The next major phase in world history was larger, more-organized world religions. And finally, they argued, humanity would enter the age of science and would eventually have no use for magic, superstition, gods, or religious belief. Science was thus considered the apex of human achievement.

A Druid monument in North Yorkshire.

Thus, Tylor and Frazer's **three stages of human belief** were (1) **magic**, (2) **religion**, and (3) **science**. Clearly, they had a preference for science. After a long history of humans believing in magic, they believed humans entered into another long phase of religiosity. However, we have finally arrived at a fact-based worldview called science. In their minds, scientific reasoning would increasingly supplant erroneous superstitions and mythical religions. Ultimately, they reasoned, magic and religion would simply fade away due to the power and ubiquity of science. This hypothesis—that science will eventually eclipse religious belief—has survived to the present day.

Other scholars have used the term **basic religions**, which makes some sense but is still not altogether clear on its meaning. Another term, usually associated with the field of sociology, is **small-scale societies**. The only problem with this term is that it is much broader than terms dealing more directly with religion. The influential religion scholar **Huston Smith** preferred the term **primal religions**.

Some scholars have called these earlier belief systems

Primitive religions · a term used by early anthropologists for indigenous religions that has been rejected in recent times

Three stages of human belief · a theory set forth by E. B. Tylor and J. G. Frazer that states that human belief evolves through three stages, from magic to religion and finally to science

Magic · according to Tylor and Frazer, the first and most primitive form of human belief, characterized by attempts to control nature through ritual

Religion · according to Tylor and Frazer, the second stage of human belief, in which magic evolves into organized and standardized religious practice

Science · according to Tylor and Frazer, the final stage of human belief, in which people shed superstitions and myth in favor of fact-based science

Basic religions · another term for indigenous religions

Small-scale societies · a term for indigenous cultures that emphasizes a sociological approach

Huston Smith · an influential religious studies scholar

Primal religions · a term for indigenous religions used by Huston Smith

animistic religions, but that term also falls short in ways. **Animism** is a vague term based on the Latin word for "spirit," "life," or "breath." It is a word that is often used to describe the idea that spirits animate people, animals, places, trees, weather, bodies of water, and even rocks.

In this chapter, we will use the term **indigenous religions**, which preserves several important aspects of these earlier definitions, including their localized context, their often ancient character as religions, and their geographically limited scope. They rose up at a certain time and in a certain place. These religions did not spread to the far reaches of the planet; rather, they grew up in a specific context.

There is one extremely important point about indigenous religions that often goes neglected: indigenous religions are still with us. Religions are fluid. They evolve. They do not just suddenly turn on or off like a light switch. Religions supplant each other sometimes, but the new religion among a people will often absorb key aspects of the previous religion. Thus, most world religions today are actually laced with aspects of the preexisting religions.

When Christianity came to the Americas, it did not simply supplant all of the indigenous religions. Rather, indigenous peoples often had little choice but to "convert" to Christianity. However, when they accepted Jesus into their worldview, they often kept many practices, sayings, taboos, and cultural beliefs from their indigenous traditions. Even today, many indigenous peoples consider themselves Christian, but these groups eagerly practice their pre-Christian traditions such as dances, vision quests, sweat lodges, and many beliefs that have been passed down through their ancestors. Over the years, some Christians have tried to purge these pre-Christian beliefs and practices, but many of them have survived and reveal quite complex and sophisticated theologies and sociocultural practices.

The irony of this situation is that even the European Christians, who may have looked down upon these indigenous traditions, also had their own pre-Christian, ancestral beliefs. They had just all but forgotten them. For instance, the custom of having a Christmas tree in one's house is actually a tradition that dates to pre-Christian times in Europe. There is no such thing as pure Christianity. One cannot somehow step into the world of the New Testament and replicate what happened there during the life of the apostles. Everyone has a culture, and every culture that adopted Christianity over the centuries had to negotiate to what extent to allow Christian teaching to come into its own worldview. But more times than not, the preexistent religion remains in place. We just have to look around to find those pre-Christian practices.

Thunderbird House Totem Pole replica, carved in 1987 (artist Tony Hunt). Original by Kwakwaka'wakw artist Charlie James in the early 1900s.

Photographer: Ymblanter, (CC BY-SA 4.0)

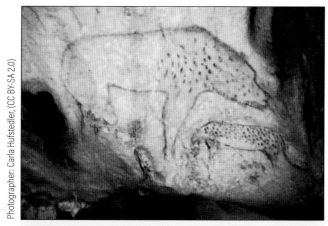

Cave painting in Chauvet Cave, France, known to be thirty-two thousand years old.

Sources of Information

Written history only goes back five thousand years or so, to Mesopotamian and Egyptian cultures. Scholars have access to **cave paintings**, **burial grounds**, **oral traditions**, and other ancient repositories of knowledge. Intelligible written language, however, is a fairly recent phenomenon in the grand sweep of human history.

An important point is that we cannot accurately reconstruct the past. Whenever we visit museums, we see paintings and depictions of what the ancient past may have looked like. This is mostly conjecture, however. History and "the past" are two different things. "The past" is what happened, but it is lost to us. History is someone's recollection. History comes from a particular viewpoint. We cannot accurately reconstruct the past because we do not have direct access to it. Therefore, we rely on historians to reconstruct their expert view of what the past may have looked like. We trust their perspective because they have the academic credentials. But the fact is that their depiction of the past may not be entirely accurate.

History is an interpretation based on a variety of motives: one's worldview, the preservation of something determined to be valuable, or an opportunity to gain power over one's surroundings. The studying of history is a valuable enterprise that can help us immensely. For example, by studying history, we can learn from our mistakes, thereby improving our prospects for the future. History also helps us acquire power that can shape our future. One of the ways we shape our future is by reconstructing our past. If we have the power to reconstruct the past, we can mold it and shape it in ways that might be helpful. The obvious dilemma is that history is always a human construct. Thus, there must always be a degree of suspicion when studying history. It is usually the victors who win

Cave paintings · the artwork of ancient peoples preserved on the walls of caves; a repository of knowledge for modern scholars

Burial grounds · sites of burial used by ancient peoples; a repository of knowledge for modern scholars

Oral traditions · stories of a people's history and myths that are passed down orally from generation to generation; a repository of knowledge for modern scholars

History · an interpretation of the past, influenced by motives and biases

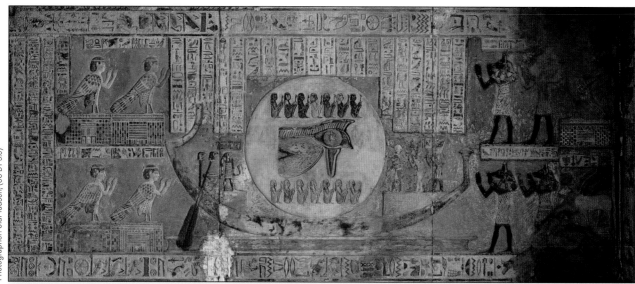

Egyptian hieroglyphs from a temple in Dendera prominently displaying the Eye of Horus in the center.

the opportunity to reconstruct the past to serve them in the future.

The writing of history has always been subject to bias. If one reads a Russian account of World War II written during the Cold War, then one will learn an entirely different story of that war than if one reads, for example, an American historian's account of it from the same era. After World War II, Russia and the United States became enemies, and they both propagandized their populations to achieve dominance on the world scene. Thus, when somebody researches World War II today, they will likely want to access both perspectives to get a more well-rounded view of what actually happened. By taking into consideration multiple sources, their history will be much more nuanced.

Another issue is **language**. Cultures use language as a way to understand. However, while language is extremely important for understanding history, it is simply not available to us in the ancient past. Many cultures had no written language, so when a culture became dominated by another culture, the history writing was done by the victorious group. Thus, language is always prone to biases and prejudices. In those cultures where written language did not even exist, we then have to rely on sources of knowledge like pottery, burial grounds, and trash heaps. To understand the ancient religions of the world, scholars have to do a lot of guesswork because there are so many gaps in their knowledge of those societies, many of which were preliterate.

Information about indigenous religions typically comes from two reservoirs of knowledge: (1) religions that are old but are still in existence today and (2) **archaeology**. Clearly, we cannot reconstruct extremely accurate depictions of indigenous religions using only these two sources. Sometimes our conjecture about these religions might simply be wrong. For example, just because we infer that a culture in 2000 BCE worshiped the Sun as the one god, it is difficult to assume they worshiped that god exactly that same way in 1000 BCE or in 3500 BCE. All religions change and evolve, and therefore, understandings of the gods evolve. Christianity in 200 CE was different from Christianity in 2000 CE, for example. Christianity has changed hands over the course of many generations, leading to a belief system that has connections to the past, but some aspects of it have been dramatically reimagined by its members. Another good example is the Roman Catholic Church. The Roman Catholic Church of the 1800s was different than the Roman Catholic Church of the 2000s. The Second Vatican Council in the 1960s altered almost every aspect of church doctrine and life. If an alien visited Earth in the 1800s, he would hardly recognize our planet in the 2000s. Everything has changed so dramatically, including many of our planet's religions. Thus, religions that are very old but are still with us today can help us to understand ancient religion but cannot offer us precision in our understanding, as religions are always in flux.

Archaeologists are extremely helpful to the study of religion, but like people in any discipline, they too have their biases and their imagination. One archaeologist might think a person buried in the fetal position shows that their culture believed in reincarnation, another archaeologist might think fetal burial had to do with entering the underworld, and another archaeologist might simply think fetal burial was a way of taking up less space in the grave, opening up room for more people to be buried there.

Nevertheless, archaeologists do a great service to the study of religion. They use physical remains to figure out the meanings behind those objects. They analyze coins, inscriptions, gravesites, building remains, various forms of art, cookware, and weaponry. They help us understand the nature of relationships between societies and their surroundings. They shed light on how people waged war, and they perhaps speculate on why. They

Language · can provide insight into ancient peoples; however, many cultures had no written language, and surviving accounts might provide deeply biased information

Archaeology · an extremely important field to the study of religion, as archaeologists can study the most ancient and preliterate religions by examining the remains of burial grounds and of surviving artifacts

Anthropology · an important field to the study of religion; anthropologists scientifically study human behavior, biology, and society from ancient to present times

Theology · an important field in the study of religion; **theologians** are concerned with the doctrinal beliefs of a particular religion

Neanderthal cave wall drawing, ocher paint.

speculate on how humans interacted with animals, and they try to figure out the diets of peoples in the past.

Literate cultures, of course, offer much more nuanced information in their texts. Scholars can interpret the past much better with texts. But let's not miss the point: without texts, scholars have to do a lot of speculating. Even with texts, scholars have to use their imagination when trying to understand older cultures. But without texts, it is difficult to understand what was happening with any degree of certitude. Archaeologists, anthropologists, and other scholars do a tremendous service to religious studies by offering up their attempts at historical reconstruction.

This all points to the need for the study of religion to be a multidisciplinary field. The archaeologists need the **anthropologists**, who need the **theologians**, who need the **linguistic scholars**, who need the **historians**. That is precisely what has happened in the field of religious studies. It is an extremely multidisciplinary field due to the complications involved in studying something as complex as religion.

Prehistoric Beginnings of Indigenous Religions

Neanderthal religion. Neanderthals were similar to humans, only a bit shorter and stockier. Neanderthal men were typically about five feet five inches, and the women were around five feet tall on average. This is not all that different from the height averages of preindustrial humans. Neanderthals went extinct around thirty-five thousand years ago, probably due to a climate event or disease. Some have hypothesized that humans may have fought with Neanderthals, contributing to their demise. Geneticists have shown that humans and Neanderthals not only coexisted but that they also interbred, which

Linguistic scholars · an important field in the study of religion; linguistic scholars can trace the migrations of and interactions between different peoples based on the evolution of their languages

Historians · experts in the field of history, providing historical context to the understanding of many other fields of study

Neanderthal religion · Neanderthals buried their dead with tools, pointing to a belief in the afterlife; an unusual number of bear bones and skulls have been found near Neanderthal sites, possibly for religious reasons

Taforalt (Cave of Pigeons) in Morocco is one of the earliest prehistoric burial sites, with evidence of occupation as early as 85000 BCE.

Photographer: Nicolas Perrault III, (CC0 1.0)

may also have led to their demise through the sharing of disease.

Some scholars have asserted that Neanderthals practiced religion to some degree. They buried their dead, often with tools and weapons, pointing to some sense of meaning attached to death. There exists good evidence gathered from over one hundred archaeological sites in Western Europe that Neanderthals had a special kinship with bears but also competed with them for resources. Archaeologists currently debate whether bears were somehow part of Neanderthal religion due to many bear bones, especially skulls, being positioned in seemingly intentional ways in Neanderthal caves.

Cro-Magnon religion. Cro-Magnon peoples, also known as **Early European modern humans**, were our near relatives. They existed from about forty thousand years ago to ten thousand years ago. They coexisted with Neanderthals, but it is much debated whether they were able to interbreed with them. Cro-Magnons may have vanquished Neanderthals, but this is conjecture. They were similar to humans, and their DNA is still with us. Like Neanderthals, they provide signs of religiosity—for example, burying their dead in an organized way, with tools and weapons. They were artistic, and they painted using reddish-colored ochre. They also painted deep inside of the caves they inhabited, causing some scholars to theorize a belief in **imitative magic**—painting a scene of hunting to bring good luck. This is a practice that was common in shamanistic societies. Cro-Magnons are famous for their Venus figurines made of stone, ivory, and bone, which have been found all across Europe and Siberia.

Neolithic religion. The word **neolithic** means "new stone age." It is an imprecise era, perhaps from around 7000 BCE to 3000 BCE. What is important about this era, however, is that new characteristics began to emerge among humans during this time. Famously, this was the era of the development of agriculture, which led to huge changes in humans. Once food became much more regulated and managed, lifestyles became much more sedentary for a certain population of society. Humans now had food reserves and were no longer forced to hunt and gather each day. People were able to settle and develop more sophisticated towns and cities.

With a more settled population, humans achieved incredible advances in property ownership and leisure. More cerebral and philosophical religions developed due to the lower burden on physical labor and transience.

This was the beginning of more organized religions for larger people groups. These early religions were more focused on fertility to ensure successful harvests, and they focused intensely on the natural elements, the planets, and the agricultural cycles. Deities became personifications of the planets and the seasons. Neolithic people's megalithic monuments were impressive—for example, **Stonehenge** in England and the **Carnac stones site** in the Brittany region of France. While there is no consensus as to what these stones mean exactly, there is almost certainly a religious dimension.

Common Features of Indigenous Religions

One of the most common terms in the study of indigenous religions is animism, meaning that spirits are within almost everything and can impact human life in important ways. Animism is a highly spiritualized understanding of one's surroundings. Virtually all religions have some animistic elements—for example, in the worship of nature or in devotion to religious sites. Trees, stones, people, rivers, mountains, the Sun and Moon, planets—almost anything can be home to spirits.

Magic is another important concept in the academic study of religion. In general, magic is the attempt to control nature through some means such as a ritual. In the minds of practitioners, rituals can lead to rain, fertility, or success in the hunt. As discussed earlier, some see magic as an earlier phase in the development of human beliefs. Some people have attached magical significance to mundane things such as a rabbit's foot, a particular bone, a special stone, heirlooms, a holy staff, or even religious texts such as the Quran or the Bible. For example, there was a time in modern Western culture when a Bible was thought to protect a person during war or to keep away unwanted spirits while sleeping.

Divination is another concept that is used in religious studies. Usually, a priest or shaman will use divination to predict the future, to discover the guilt or innocence of a person, or even to hear from a divine power by means of an **oracle**. An oracle can be virtually anything, such as a text or a person who claims to speak on behalf of a god or ancestor. Other interesting oracles that have been found useful in indigenous religions include entrails of animals, flight patterns of birds, rolling of dice, crack patterns

in shells, manipulation of plants through rubbing, or poison being administered to a person or an animal. For example, the Azande people used to feed poison to a chicken, and if the chicken died, it meant something different than if the chicken lived. Similarly, as cited Numbers 5:11–29 of the Hebrew Bible, there was a test that was to be administered to a wife suspected of infidelity. She was required to "drink the bitter water that brings on the curse" (Num. 5:24). If she was guilty, "her abdomen will swell and her womb will shrink" (Num. 5:27). These kinds of tests were usually administered by the religious leaders such as the priests, shamans, or prophets.

Taboo is another important concept in indigenous religions. The term *taboo* comes from a Polynesian context and typically means something that is prohibited or forbidden. If something is considered taboo by the group, then undesirable outcomes could happen if transgression occurs. Taboos are mechanisms by which societies keep a clear distinction between what is sacred and what is profane. While taboos are found in virtually all societies, there is extraordinary complexity around the concept. Some things are considered taboo if they are too holy—for example, approaching the main altar in a cathedral; that is why the main altars are often blocked off with a small fence. Walking over a grave is often considered taboo. Speaking directly to a king or a royal family can be taboo. Some cultures revere twins, while other cultures consider them taboo, a kind of curse. In the Hebrew Bible, touching the Ark of the Covenant could lead to immediate death.

Across the world, human diet is an area rife with taboos—for example, the eating of beef in Hinduism. Hindus revere cows as holy; thus, eating beef is considered forbidden. There

Stonehenge · an impressive religious monument in England from Neolithic times

Carnac stone site · a Neolithic religious site found in the Brittany region of France

Divination · rituals designed to predict the future, to discover the guilt or innocence of a person, or even to hear from a divine power by means of an *oracle*

Oracle · a person, text, or object that speaks on behalf of a divine power or ancestor

Taboo · something that is forbidden in a society, with the belief that undesirable outcomes will occur if the prohibition is broken

Photographer: Vyacheslav Argenberg. (CC BY-SA 4.0)

Hinduism raises the status of a cow to the level of a goddess. Vagator, India.

are many food taboos in the world's cultures. Some people even avoid any meat at all based on religious reasons. In Jainism, there is a taboo against eating root vegetables since, by pulling a vegetable out of the ground, one might expose insects who could then die. Some taboos are entirely unrelated to religiosity, such as the tendency to avoid drinking tap water in Europe. Some taboos are based on how the food will impact one's health, whereas others are seemingly disconnected from health factors. For example, Jews and Muslims do not typically consume pork, despite the fact that pork is perfectly safe to eat. Lobster is forbidden by Jews but is consumed by Christians. Taboo can even occur *within* a religion. For instance, some Buddhists eat meat, while other Buddhists are vegetarians. Similarly, alcohol is considered taboo by some Christians (and virtually all Muslims), whereas other Christians drink wine even during the Christian Eucharist. There is often no rhyme or reason; these taboos have complex histories and arose for a host of reasons that are often lost to history.

Totems are often invoked in indigenous religious traditions. Many religion scholars emphasize the importance of totemic animals in small-scale societies. Totems are typically—but not always—animals that get absorbed into a tribe's self-understanding. The totemic animal is usually considered sacred. Sometimes the people connect the totem animal to the afterlife. Some people groups actually consume the totemic animals on sacred occasions to reinforce the animal's sacredness and to provide strength to the humans eating it. More modern ideas of the totemic principle include a particular animal being attached to the larger culture's self-identity, such as the bear on the California flag or the bald eagle being a sacred symbol for citizens of the United States of America.

Sacrifice is an extremely common component of indigenous religions. Animal and plant sacrifice are found in indigenous cultures all over the world, whether the sacrifice of bulls and goats in Judaism or the frequent use of tobacco as a sacrificial object in indigenous American traditions. Occasionally, cultures will sacrifice humans, as with the famous **human sacrificial system** among the Aztecs or the god **Moloch**

Totems · animals that are absorbed into a tribe's self-understanding

Sacrifice · offering animals, plants, food, alcohol, or other desired goods to a deity in order to appease a spiritual power

Human sacrificial system · the sacrifice of human life to placate a higher power

Moloch · a god in the Hebrew Bible whose devotees practiced child sacrifice

Jesus Christ · believed to be a human sacrifice on behalf of humanity in order to expiate the sins that have been committed by his followers

(or Molech) in the Hebrew Bible, who was associated with child sacrifice. **Jesus Christ** is a kind of human sacrifice on behalf of humanity to expiate the sins that have been committed by his followers.

In some indigenous religions, rulers were buried with animals and servants, possibly with the understanding that they would serve the royal person in the afterlife. For example, **Puabi**, a woman of high status and possibly a queen, was found in the **Sumerian** city of **Ur** in a grave dated to around 2600 BCE. She was buried with dozens of servants, many of them wearing gold and silver. She was buried with animals that indicated high status, as well as with a chariot. It is unknown how the servants died—whether they were killed or voluntarily drank poison.

Many objects are still used in religions for sacrifice—for example, presenting fruit to ancestor gravesites in China or presenting alcohol to departed loved ones in Mexico during the **Día de los Muertos** (Day of the Dead) festival. Indeed, sacrifices are often made to humans in world religions, especially to the faithfully departed ancestors.

In the Hebrew Bible, there is a sense that Yahweh enjoyed the smell of cooked flesh and would thus be pleased by inhaling the smoke from the sacrifice. In Greco-Roman society, there were large-scale sacrifices of animals meant to feed substantial numbers of people in the community. The early Christians debated whether Christians could eat meat that had been sacrificed to pagan gods or to idols. The apostle Paul's conclusion in 1 Corinthians 8 was essentially that eating meat sacrificed to idols was permissible as

Puabi · a high-ranking Sumerian woman, possibly a queen, who was found buried with dozens of servants and animals, indicating human and animal sacrifice

Sumerian · the most ancient Mesopotamian civilization

Ur · an ancient city in which Puabi's burial site was discovered

Día de los Muertos · a Hispanic holiday commemorating deceased loved ones, often including the sacrifice of alcohol to their spirits

Day of the Dead Offering in Coyoacán, Mexico (2014).

Fragment of the *Epic of Gilgamesh*, dating back to the Old Babylonian Period (2003–1595 BCE). Sulaymaniyah Museum in Iraq.

Myth · an embellished cultural tale that may or may not be based on true events

Epic of Gilgamesh · an ancient Sumerian religious text that corroborates a version of the flood myth from Genesis

Rituals · vehicles of teaching and reinforcing myths to a community

Priests · religious leaders who perform rituals

Shaman · a powerful, often eccentric person who communicates with the world of the dead, provides healing, and calls upon the spirits to provide a successful hunt, fertility, or rain

Eucharist · a Catholic ritual commemorating the death and resurrection of Jesus Christ

Rites of passage · rituals denoting that a person has passed from one phase of life into the next

Arnold van Gennep · an ethnographer who posited that there are three phases to rites of passage: separation, transition, and incorporation

long as it did not cause offense to "the weak"—presumably those Christians whose faith was less mature.

Myth is a concept in religious studies that is often misunderstood. Some people might think a myth is simply a fictitious story. That is not at all what religion scholars have in mind, however. Myths may or may not be based on true events. Sometimes there is truth to myths, while other times they seem to be almost completely fictitious. The story of Noah's Ark may well be based upon an actual primeval flood, since somewhat similar flood stories exist from that same era and general geographical location. For example, the Sumerian-language *Epic of Gilgamesh* (written c. 2000 BCE), which includes a flood story, is one of the world's oldest known religious texts. Thus, while there may have been a massive flood in that vicinity, the cultures

that survived the flood interpreted the catastrophe in different ways, pulling away lessons for their own civilization and posterity.

Historical accuracy is not the most important quality of myths, however. What makes them important for religion scholars is their value to specific communities. The memory of the person or event has been preserved for important reasons. These stories provide guidance and meaning to the members of the community. The major point of analyzing myths is not to figure out if something actually occurred or not. Most of the time that is not completely verifiable. Scholars think in terms of plausibility when it comes to whether certain events in a myth may have happened or not. The crucial aspect of myths, however, is how the myths have impacted the community's formation, self-reflection, and significance. People groups define themselves by these events, stories, heroes, and places. Meaning gets

A Hindu Bengali family taking part in a Sacred Thread Ceremony. West Bengal, India.

constructed as the community reflects upon itself in light of its great collective stories.

In nonliterate societies, myths are often elevated to a kind of sacred scripture. Myths can be written, but they can also be passed down orally, in dance, in art, or in community ritual. Myths are vitally important for religious communities, and they are also vital for scholars trying to understand more about that community.

Rituals are often integrally connected to a culture's myths. Leaders, **priests**, or **shamans** will often perform certain rituals in front of a group to reinforce a myth. Rituals are a primary vehicle of teaching for both literate and nonliterate societies. Typically, rituals incorporate the important elements, heroes, gods, or characters of a particular religion. Ritual meals are common in virtually all religions, including indigenous religions. Communal meals reinforce identity and provide an opportunity for members to further solidify the bonds that keep their group intact. Ritual eating reminds members of who holds membership in the community. Guests can occasionally be invited to a ritual meal, but there is a degree of distance involved. For example, non-Catholics may attend a Roman Catholic **Eucharist**, but there is a degree of separation that gets reinforced when a non-Catholic goes forward to receive the elements. Typically, the priest will bless the individual but will withhold the bread or wine.

Rites of passage have been studied extensively by scholars such as the ethnographer **Arnold van Gennep** (1873–1957). In 1909, van Gennep proposed a famous theory of rites of passage. In his theory, there is usually a threefold phase to rites of passage: **separation, transition**, and **incorporation** (or reincorporation). First, the individual separates from his or her old status in the community. Second, the individual goes through a period of waiting or some kind of action that signifies a crossing of a boundary into the new status. Third, the person gets reincorporated into the community with a slightly altered identity or perhaps a new function or position. World religions are rife with rites of passage:

> Rites of passage are usually full of symbol and ritual, and they typically involve many community members.

Christian **baptism**, puberty rites (for example, **bar and bat mitzvah** and the **Sacred Thread Ceremony**), **confirmation**, **circumcision**, marriage, and death.

Rites of passage are usually full of symbol and ritual, and they typically involve many community members. Gods and ancestors are often invoked. They symbolize changing of status—for example, from a girl to a woman, from unborn to born, from outsider to insider, from single to married, from working to retired, from the realm of the living to the realm of the ancestors, from the death of an old way of life to the rebirth of the individual. In religious studies, the period of transition is often referred to as a **liminal** state, or liminality. The word *liminal* comes from a Latin word meaning "a threshold" and signifies somebody standing at the threshold but not yet entering a new status.

Ancestor veneration is common in indigenous religions. Religion scholars typically avoid the expression "ancestor worship," although it is commonly used by non-scholars. Worship is not exactly what is happening with ancestor veneration, as worship is usually reserved for gods or religious heroes such as founders. **Joseph Campbell** (1904–87), for example, wrote a famous study of religious and mythological heroes called

Separation · the first phase of a rite of passage in which the individual separates from his or her old status in the community

Transition · the second phase of a rite of passage in which the individual undergoes a period of waiting or takes a specific action that signifies the crossing of a boundary into a new status

Incorporation · the final phase of a rite of passage in which the individual is reincorporated into the community with a slightly altered identity or a new function or position

Baptism · a Christian rite of passage that symbolizes rebirth from an old sinful life into a new purified life

Bar and bat mitzvah · Jewish rites of passage symbolizing the passage from childhood into adulthood

Sacred Thread Ceremony · a Hindu rite of passage undergone by upper-caste boys

Confirmation · a Catholic and Lutheran rite of passage

Circumcision · a Jewish rite of passage for boys on the eighth day of their lives

Liminality · the period of transition involved in a rite of passage; taken from a Latin word meaning "a threshold"

Ancestor veneration · a common religious practice in which practitioners commemorate and sometimes sacrifice to the deceased; should not be equated with "ancestor worship"

The Hero with a Thousand Faces that profoundly influenced the young director George Lucas and his famous *Star Wars* movies. Thus, the term *ancestor veneration* is preferred since it emphasizes the idea that the hero was at one time one of us—an exemplary person within their own community who became exalted after death.

Ancestors can make appearances in the realm of the living. They can be spotted in dreams. They are not dead in the minds of the community; they are still with us, very much alive. They can help the community in various ways. On certain occasions, they can even punish, haunt, or avenge. Ancestors, therefore, must be placated through ritual appeasement. Indigenous communities often look to the ancestors for fertility of crops, successful hunts, and the safety of the tribe from outside threats. Ancestor veneration is very much alive today, even

Koku dancer celebrating the national Vodun festival in Benin (2019). The child is coated in a ceremonial mustard mixture.

Photographer: Daniel Greenberg, (CC BY-SA 4.0)

within the larger world religions. It is entirely common for Christians in Africa, for example, to invoke ancestors during important gatherings and rituals. The realm of the living must avoid disrespecting the ancestors, as it may come at a heavy cost. The dead can reenter this world in mystical ways and wreak havoc.

African Indigenous Religions

The continent of Africa consists of more than fifty nations, more than three thousand ethnic and linguistic groups, and more than a billion people. Missionaries, ethnographers, linguists, and anthropologists have studied African people groups for nearly two centuries, and they have produced a vast amount of scholarship that is being analyzed afresh by scholars today. Part of the problem with studying indigenous religions is that there is so much material for a topic like African religion. Another problem is that previous generations of scholars were often profoundly biased. This does not mean that their research is rubbish; rather, it means we must approach their research with caution.

Their research may be quite useful, but we must acknowledge that it took place in a different era, and scientific research is constantly under scrutiny and self-correction. The research scholars produce today will one day be subject to another generation of scrutiny, and their research, too, will be critiqued. It is important to discuss these matters when approaching any religion, but it is particularly important when we study religions that cannot respond to what scholars write about them. There must be a high level of sensitivity when approaching people, ideas, languages, and cultures of the past.

Many African indigenous religions were **polytheistic**. However, they often held to the notion of a **High God** who created the world and who may still be involved with creation. Lesser gods, often called spirits, are far more accessible than the great High God. Many African societies also hold to the notion of a Mother Earth figure who is closely connected to fertility.

Ancestor veneration is crucial in African indigenous religions. Ancestors are still connected to the community and are still part of virtually every sphere of life. Ancestors are often placated by sacrifice and offerings such as slaughtered animals or a liquid such

Photographer: Sharon Dawn, (CC BY-SA 4.0)

A Ugandan teenager reading the Bible during the COVID-19 pandemic (2020).

as beer or milk poured onto the ground in acknowledgment of them.

Blood sacrifice was and is common in African indigenous religions. Larger animals can be sacrificed when there is a major deity being placated or a major problem in the community that needs to be addressed.

Rites of passage are critical in African indigenous religions, and the birthing of children is crucial to the social order. Childlessness can be considered a major problem because having children essentially guarantees oneself a place in the ancestor realm. Without children, there is often a notion that a person may not be allowed into the realm of the ancestors. Circumcision is an important rite of passage in many African indigenous contexts, and this practice lives on in both African Christianity and African Islam. Female circumcision is also practiced in some African cultures and has been highly debated in modern times.

The largest religion in Africa is Christianity, as nearly half of the continent's inhabitants are Christians. Around 40 percent of Africans are Muslim. Around 10 percent are members of indigenous religions. Importantly, as discussed earlier, the indigenous religions do not stop when a person adopts Christianity or Islam. Rather, the indigenous traditions and beliefs live on in fascinating ways. This important fact is often neglected. When members of indigenous religions claim Christianity or Islam, they bring much from their previous religion. This is a common phenomenon in any form of religious conversion. It is virtually impossible to completely cut oneself off from one's past; thus, the past lives into one's present reality in complex ways.

Christianity and Judaism have deep roots in Africa, going back to Old Testament times. According to their interpretation of 1 Kings 10:1–13, Ethiopians claim that Solomon had a son with the **Queen of Sheba**, named **Makeda**, in the tenth century BCE. They claim that their rulers after that union were descendants of Solomon and Makeda. The Gospels record that Jesus lived in Egypt as a child for a time, and Christianity entered Ethiopia in the early years of the faith, shortly after Jesus died. Philip, one of the twelve apostles, evangelized a high-ranking Ethiopian who was on pilgrimage in Jerusalem, according to Acts 8. This incident would place Christianity in Ethiopia very early on, which helps to explain why King Ezana of Axum (in modern-day Ethiopia) adopted Christianity as a state religion, probably in the 330s CE.

Islam spread across northern Africa in the seventh century CE and had great success in taking root. Today, Islam is by far the largest religion in northern Africa. Christianity tends to be associated with sub-Saharan Africa, and much of that shift to Christianity took place only in the nineteenth and twentieth centuries.

Ancient Egyptian Religion

The most important ancient religion of Africa is found in Egypt, which, starting in around 3100 BCE, became one of the most sophisticated cultures in the world. Home to some of the greatest achievements in the ancient world, Egypt developed the famous pyramids of Giza around 2600

Queen of Sheba · also known as ***Makeda***, traveled from Ethiopia to visit King Solomon of Israel and Judah in the tenth century BCE; Ethiopians claim her son was fathered by Solomon

Hieroglyphics · the written language of the ancient Egyptians

Nubians · an ancient people with extensive interaction with the Egyptians

Hyksos · an ancient people who at one time conquered Egypt

Amenhotep IV · an Egyptian Pharaoh who briefly forced Egypt into monotheism by worshiping Aten exclusively

Aten · the Sun, symbolized in Egyptian hieroglyphics as a disk, often with rays of light shooting out

Akhenaten · the new name that Amenhotep IV took to emphasize his devotion to Aten

King Tutankhamun · Akhenaten's son who reinstated polytheism in Egypt and then died young; the discovery of his tomb brought worldwide attention to ancient Egypt

Osiris · the Egyptian Lord of the Dead, who was killed and dismembered by his brother Seth and reassembled by his wife Isis

Isis · Osiris's wife who brought him back to life to reign in the underworld

BCE. Weighing over two tons each, the stones were shaped into blocks and constructed as burial chambers, and they gave the pharaohs a proper royal afterlife. The Great Pyramid alone required around 2.3 million of these massive blocks. It is hard to imagine how sophisticated and ambitious these people were.

The Egyptians had a **hieroglyphic** written language that has proven extremely helpful to scholars trying to reconstruct their culture, especially their complex religious beliefs. The reason their religion was so complex was because it changed dramatically over long periods of time. When the Egyptians conquered a people or were conquered by a people, some level of assimilation occurred. As a result, the new culture's beliefs would permeate Egyptian beliefs, as is precisely what happened with the **Nubians** and the **Hyksos**.

While ancient Egypt is usually described as a polytheistic culture, there was a time in the 1300s BCE when the ancient Egyptians became monotheistic while ruled by Pharaoh **Amenhotep IV**. Amenhotep IV was a worshiper of the Sun, which he called **Aten**. Aten is symbolized in Egyptian hieroglyphics as a disk, often with rays of light shooting out. Amenhotep IV became so devoted to Aten that he renamed himself **Akhenaten**.

Akhenaten's successor was his son, who became known as **King Tutankhamun** ("King Tut"). While rising to the throne as only a boy, Tutankhamun eventually led his people back to the traditional Egyptian polytheistic religion. King Tut's tomb was famously discovered in 1922 by Egyptologist Howard Carter and brought worldwide attention to ancient Egypt, the pyramids, the Egyptian Book of the Dead, and Egyptian hieroglyphics.

Ancient Egyptians believed the natural elements—the sky, rivers, the Sun—all had great power, so they personified these elements over time. The Sun was the High God. Two other important gods were **Osiris** and **Isis**, a married couple. They had a son named **Horus** who was also important. **Amun-Ra** was another god who rose to high status due to his association with the Sun, **Ra** (also known as **Re**). He is easily identified in Egyptian art because of the Sun rays connected to his head.

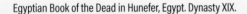

Egyptian Book of the Dead in Hunefer, Egypt. Dynasty XIX.

Full view of the pyramids in Giza, Egypt.

Max Müller believed that the personification of the elements led to religion, a process he called the **disease of language theory**. Although first applying his theories to Hinduism, Müller argued that ancient peoples tended to personify the natural elements. They used words to explain natural elements, or natural phenomena, and, over time, those words would take on a life of their own. Using **etymology**, Müller argued that the various names for gods could be traced back to a root word for a natural occurrence or a particular object. Metaphorical understanding of the natural world, over time, evolved (or "diseased") into a god. Müller's highly **philological** theory (from the field of **philology**) examines religion from the perspective of language development.

Other Egyptian gods were often depicted as half-human and half-animal creatures, all with different meanings. **Cats** are associated with Egyptian religion because they were considered to bring good luck and were highly praised in ancient Egypt, likely because of the protection they offered, including protection from poisonous snakes.

Mummification is associated with ancient Egyptian religion because ancient Egyptians believed in the notion of a resurrected body. Thus, they pioneered excellent and advanced methods for preserving the human body after death. It could take seventy days to prepare a body for mummification as they extracted the organs, dried the corpse, added salt and other preservatives, and wrapped the body tightly with linens. Then there was an **opening of the mouth ceremony,** wherein spells were made to keep the mouth of the dead open in the afterlife so it could eat, drink, and

Horus · the son of Osiris and Isis who avenged his father by killing Seth

Amun-Ra · an Egyptian god who rose to very high status because of his association with the Sun

Ra · also known as **Re**, the Egyptian Sun god

Max Müller · a religion scholar famous for his "disease of language theory"

Disease of language theory · the idea that ancient peoples used specific words to refer to the natural elements; over time, those words were personified into deities

Etymology · the study of the origin and history of words

Philology · the study of the structure and development of and relationships between languages

Cats · highly prized in ancient Egypt as protectors and good luck charms

Mummification · a complex and rather effective means of preserving the human body from decay

Opening of the mouth ceremony · ancient Egyptian spells meant to keep the mouth of the dead open in the afterlife so it could eat, drink, and breathe

breathe. The mouth was not literally opened; rather, it was a metaphorical ritual that took place before the coffin, surrogate statue, or **mummy**.

In the earlier periods of the Egyptian Empire, only royalty became mummified, as the rituals ensured the deceased pharaoh would travel across the sky with the Sun god, Ra. Gradually, the wealthier families started practicing mummification as well, and eventually, it became widespread across the society. The pharaohs were not subject to judgment since they were considered divine. However, average people had to be judged by Osiris—the Egyptian Lord of the Dead. In Egyptian mythology, Osiris had been killed by his evil brother **Seth** (or **Set**). Seth had tricked Osiris by getting him to lay down in a coffin. Seth then chopped Osiris into pieces and scattered the body parts. Isis, however, found the pieces and reassembled them with magic so she could conceive a son with her husband. Their son, Horus, resulted from their union and avenged his father's death by killing Seth. Osiris, then, descended to the underworld to become the Lord of the Dead. Mummification was closely linked to this myth, as the practice connected to Isis magically reassembling her husband Osiris's body parts so that he could come back to life. Ancient Egyptians believed that people who died went to the underworld, where Osiris was in charge. The Isis–Osiris myth was also linked to the annual rising and falling of the Nile, which constantly reinforced the story. The tears of Isis, mourning her deceased husband Osiris, caused the river to rise.

Inside the ancient Egyptian pyramids, carved into the innermost walls of the rooms where the pharaohs lay, are **Pyramid Texts**. These texts point to a divine standard called **Ma'at**, meaning truth, justice, and righteousness. Ma'at was the ultimate standard and was eventually personified as a goddess. It was often symbolized as a feather, as one's heart was weighed against a feather to determine whether it would go to paradise. Pharaohs did not have to face the laws of Ma'at, but nearly everyone else had to have their lives and conduct weighed. The righteous ones were forgiven, and their wrongdoings were wiped out. The wicked, however, would be destroyed.

Later on in Egyptian history, this judgment scenario became quite elaborate. The ancient texts dealing with this are called **the Egyptian Book of the Dead**. These texts were meant to assist the deceased person on their journey to the next world and to prepare the person for judgment.

In Egypt, if mummification occurred, the human stood a chance of immortality. Judgment was based on the objective standard of Ma'at, and there was no way to get around it, unless one was a pharaoh. Judgment was absolute as well, once and for all.

Azande Religion

One of the best-known studies of African indigenous religions was from the British anthropologist **E. E. Evans-Pritchard** (1902–73). Evans-Pritchard conducted fieldwork in the Sudan in the 1920s and 1930s, focusing intensely on the **Azande** and **Nuer** peoples. His most important publication was *Witchcraft, Oracles, and Magic among the Azande*, published in 1937. It revolutionized the field because of Evans-Pritchard's willingness to live among the people, understand their culture, learn their language, and write from a sympathetic point of view rather than caricaturing or exoticizing his subjects.

Evans-Pritchard came to realize that the Azande strongly believed in **witchcraft**. If misfortune befell a person in the tribe, then witchcraft was to blame. To gain relief from suffering, Azandes would visit a holy man in the community and consult various oracles to discover the problem for why bad things were happening. There were several oracles that could reveal various solutions or answer various questions that vexed a person.

There was a hierarchy of oracles. Some were do-it-yourself kinds, and others required more guidance and perhaps even money. One oracle was the ritual of **blowing water**. Basically, if a person was misbehaving, they would have to sit and gargle water and then blow it out into the air to cool the witchcraft inside. Another was the **rubbing board (iwa) oracle**, wherein a practitioner would rub a small board and ask questions of the oracle on behalf of the person needing an answer. If the rubbing naturally stopped or became impeded, that insinuated an answer from the oracle.

The most important oracle was **benge**—the poison oracle. It involved asking questions aloud while a holy man forcibly dropped poison down the throat of a baby chicken. The death or survival of the animal would provide an official answer. If the bird died, then the person who caused the trouble would be found out. There were many possible outcomes. Perhaps a person would confess to something, such as adultery, for example. Or perhaps the culprit would be an angry ancestor who was sending witchcraft. If the case could be resolved, there was usually compensation paid to the victim by the perpetrator. In older times, benge was actually performed on humans rather than on chickens.

These oracles were supervised and carried out by various levels of professionals and healers—a class of individuals formerly known as witch doctors, shamans, or medicine men. The ultimate authority in all of this was the tribal prince, the head of the ruling class. His supervision of the benge poison oracle was a kind of supreme court.

According to Evans-Pritchard, witchcraft offered a real explanation for the world's challenges. In more modern times, scientific thinking does not completely supplant traditional beliefs. Traditional beliefs of the Azande exist alongside the new, scientific approach to knowledge. They see no contradiction in the two ways of thinking. Science explains nature, and witchcraft explains misfortune and guilt.

There are practicalities to this witchcraft system. If one harms someone else, one will be found out. Witches are unhappy, angry, and uncooperative. Thus, if one behaves like a witch, there will arise a suspicion that they just might be one. This encourages amicability in the tribe. It is a rather sophisticated system that regulates human conduct.

The entire system of witchcraft and oracles that Evans-Pritchard observed was based on assumptions that can hardly be challenged. While living with the Azande, Evans-Pritchard even took witchcraft seriously, whereas in England it did not enter into his thinking at all. When with the Azande, he thought like an Azande, and when in England, he thought like a British person. It would be unproductive to ask an Azande to imagine a world where witchcraft was not true, since it was a longstanding system that was part of their mental framework and philosophical assumptions. Evans-Pritchard's insights were partly **epistemological** (theory of knowledge) in nature. It is hardly possible for people to think outside of the accepted mental and social categories that are deemed reasonable within their society. If someone is taught that something is true, and if that "truth" has been passed down in the society for centuries or more, then it is difficult to counter that truth. To do so would effectively put someone outside the cognitive parameters of the community, relegating him or her to perceived insanity or heretical status.

American Indigenous Religions

Various estimates suggest Native Americans arrived from the Asian continent via the Bering land bridge that connected modern Alaska with Siberia around fifteen thousand or twenty thousand years ago. Some

Oracle of blowing water · if a person was misbehaving, she or he would have to sit and gargle water and then blow it out into the air in order to cool the witchcraft inside

Rubbing board (iwa) oracle · a practitioner would rub a small board and ask questions of the oracle on behalf of the person needing an answer

Benge · the poison oracle, in which a shaman asks questions while poisoning a chicken; whether or not the chicken dies corresponds to a yes or no answer to the question being asked

Epistemology · the theory of knowledge

Native American myths, however, claim that their ancestors did not immigrate to the Americas; rather, their existence began in the Americas.

Native American peoples are extremely diverse. The United States alone officially recognizes nearly six hundred tribes. Some tribes hunted and gathered and were constantly moving, while others were more settled. Sources are limited due to the fact that North American Natives were nonliterate, as opposed to **Mesoamerican** societies that invented writing systems several hundred years before Christ.

Although North American Natives did not write, there are oral sources that have been passed down, wall paintings, pottery, and carvings that reveal information. Archaeology has proven to be controversial in researching Native American sites, as some archaeologists have produced some controversial conclusions and have been criticized for their methods of research. Many Native Americans do not want outsiders digging up their ancestors' skeletons and displaying them in museums.

The history of American indigenous peoples is typically divided into the **pre-Columbian era**—before Columbus's arrival in 1492—and the **post-Columbian era**. When the Europeans arrived, there was an almost immediate power imbalance, as Europeans had guns, stronger immune systems, and steel. Jared Diamond's famous book *Guns, Germs, and Steel* (1999) surmises that these three things led to the collapse of Native autonomy and paved the way for European expansion in the New World. Over time, Native American tribes came under European rule. Christianity was usually enforced by European colonizers, and Native American religions were absorbed into Christianity through an assimilation process.

What did Native American peoples believe before Columbus? This is a difficult question for two important reasons. First, the sources are fragmentary, and second, the sources that do exist were almost completely filtered through colonial administrators or Christian missionaries.

What can be established through oral tradition is that Native peoples seemed to be animistic—they believed spirits were all around us. They believed in animal spirits; spirits of the land; spirits of the sky and underworld; and spirits animating trees, rivers, mountains, lightning, and other natural phenomena. They believed human spirits would continue on after death.

Their theologies often included a **Great Spirit**, a High God that was deeply revered. The Great Spirit

© Juulijs, Adobe Stock

45. Eine Seite aus der Mayahandschrift der Königl. Bibliothek zu Dresden.

Detail of the Dresden Codex, one of only four extant Mayan manuscripts in the world. Held in the collections of the Saxon State and University Library, it was purchased in 1739 in Vienna as a "Mexican book." It is the oldest and best-preserved Mayan text.

Francisco Pizarro has long been a polarizing figure in Peru. This bronze statue first appeared in front of Lima Cathedral in 1935. Today, it has been relocated, without its high pedestal, to a smaller, less-visible park.

was thought to be everywhere, and all existence depended on it. There was a sense, however, that this Great Spirit was so high and powerful that the preferred approach to prayer was through lesser spirits or to ancestors for intercessory purposes, such as daily needs. The Great Spirit was essentially the owner of everything and everyone and thus was not dealt with directly.

When the Europeans arrived in the Americas, there were severe clashes of worldview. Europeans were engaged in worldwide exploration and colonial expansion and had huge ambitions and costly demands. European tools and weapons were far more advanced, leading to very one-sided battles—for example, **Francisco Pizarro** dismantling the massive Inca Empire with only 167 men in 1532. Native Americans were decimated by European diseases to which they had no immunity. Once it became clear that Europeans had superior weaponry, the momentum was unstoppable for Spain and Portugal's rise to power. French and English settlers came later but experienced a similar level of dominance in what is now known as North America.

Great Spirit · the High God in many Native American religions

Francisco Pizarro · the conquistador who defeated the Inca Empire

Sacrifice

Native Americans routinely practiced sacrifice. Tobacco was a common sacrifice and was often made when a natural resource was killed or taken—for instance, the cutting down of a tree. When an animal was killed, a sacrifice might be made because the animal gave its life so that the tribe could live. Hunting rituals were often steeped in religion and reverence and concluded with sacrifice to the gods or to the animal that was killed.

Mayan pyramid at Chichen Itza in Yucatan, Mexico.

The **Aztec Empire**, located in modern-day Mexico, was advanced in comparison with other Native American societies. Just to take one example, their sanitation systems were more advanced than in Europe. Their buildings were impressive to the Europeans. They built canals and aqueducts to equip their cities with fresh water. They had a complex system of canals that allowed for quick transportation around their capital city of Tenochtitlan.

The Spanish were amazed by these feats of ingenuity, but the human sacrificial system repulsed them. The Aztec human sacrificial system was linked to the solar calendar. According to their beliefs, sacrifice was necessary to keep the universe running properly. The Aztecs were in the middle of imperial expansion when Europeans arrived. They were constantly capturing warriors from surrounding tribes in their quest to expand their borders. They believed that by sacrificing warriors from other tribes—particularly courageous ones—they could appease the gods.

Two of the great centers of Aztec human sacrifice were at **Teotihuacan** and **Chichen Itza**. Located about an hour's drive from each other, both of these locations are home to famous **Mesoamerican pyramids**. Victims were sacrificed in front of the community as a public religious ritual. The heart of the victim was often cut out, and then the victim was typically beheaded. The headless body was then rolled down the steps of the pyramid, and the head was put on display on a **tzompantli**, or **skull rack**. The victims were either eaten by the community or fed to animals.

Taboo

In Native American societies, many taboos were erected around death, particularly the notion of ancestors. When people die, they do not disappear. They actually become part of the spirit world, which is all around. Ancestors were venerated, prayed to, and sacrificed to, and there was a great fear that ancestors might come back and cause problems for the living. This is one reason why Native Americans do not want archaeologists digging around in their burial grounds;

Aztec Empire · a powerful Mesoamerican civilization that practiced human sacrifice

Teotihuacan · one of the two great centers of Aztec human sacrifice

Chichen Itza · one of the two great centers of Aztec human sacrifice

Mesoamerican pyramids · impressive Aztec structures used in religious ceremonies

Tzompantli · also known as a **skull rack**, where the heads of human sacrifices were displayed

this may disturb the spirits and cause the community harm. Today there are organized Native efforts to persuade governments to return the bones and possessions of the dead to the ground from which they were taken.

Native Dance

Native Americans used dance as a way to contact the spirit world. Dance was used for many things, such as causing rain, appeasing the gods, contacting ancestors and other spirits, and preparing for hunts. Rhythmic drumming was associated with the dances, and elaborate costuming was usually involved. The Pueblos of the American Southwest would often dance wearing **Kachina** outfits, as Kachinas were the spirits that could provide rain, fertility, and power.

Vision Quest

Native rites of passage were often centered on the notion of the vision quest, wherein a young man during puberty would go out alone into the desert, wilderness, or forest and fast until spiritual truth was revealed to him. Some tribes expected young women to participate in a vision quest as well. Accounts of vision quests vary widely, but there was often a guardian spirit figure that appeared as a mystical animal. The young person typically had a vision or dream that was interpreted by specialists when the youth returned home.

The Shaman

Native communities generally had someone who served as a religious leader or served a prophetic role for the tribe. The word shaman has been used to describe this role, although the word itself probably comes from Siberian culture. Other words have been used to describe this role, such as **medicine man** or **witch doctor**. The shaman was a powerful, often eccentric person who communicated with the world of the dead and called upon the spirits to provide a successful hunt, fertility, or rain. The chief function of the shaman was healing. Shamans were often singled out because of some ecstatic experience they had, such as an encounter with lightning. Once called to be a shaman, they typically lived a little ways outside of the community. They were revered and feared, and they knew the correct rituals to do and plants to use to bring about desired outcomes. When someone became sick or disturbed, it was the role of the shaman to identify the problem. Shamans could also perform crude surgeries.

Shamans often used chanting, and they even had dancers who would accompany them on their house calls. Fire and smoking were frequently involved in the shaman's healing rituals. Shamans often entered into a trance state, seemingly bordering on insanity. However, this was a kind of proof that the shaman was connecting to the spirit world. Shamans were usually

Kachina · in Native American religion, spirits that could provide rain, fertility, and power

Medicine man · another term for a shaman

Witch doctor · another term for a shaman

Hopi artist Brendan Kayquoptewa paints his carved Kachina dolls at the 2017 Santa Fe Indian Market. More than nine hundred people from hundreds of tribes participate in the two-day event; visitors number about one hundred thousand.

© JannHuizenga, iStock

For more than a century, members of various tribal affiliations have faced intense sanctions for their use of the peyote cactus as a ceremonial medicine. Seeking religious protection, they formed the Native American Church, first in Oklahoma in 1918, and later elsewhere.

paid a small fee for their services. They were trusted a great deal by the community for their ability to connect with the spirit realm and bring healing to a person or reconciliation to a conflict. Shamans could also serve as conduits of **channeling**, wherein they allowed their bodies to be used by the spirits who were trying to communicate something. They could become extremely tired at the end of a **séance** due to the intensity of the experience.

Tobacco and Peyote

Smoking tobacco was common among Native Americans. Smoking a ceremonial pipe, often called a **peace pipe**, could cement treaties or relationships. Smoking regularly accompanied religious ceremony.

The ingesting of the hallucinogenic **peyote** cactus is one of the more controversial aspects of Native American religion. From the 1970s through the 1990s, there were many debates about the Native use of the substance. Peyote is a small, spineless cactus that contains the hallucinogenic agent mescaline and is thus illegal for non-Natives. Taking peyote leads to hallucinations and feelings that are often described in religious terms.

The **Native American Church** combines Christianity with Native practices, and it often incorporates the use of peyote during worship services as a sacrament. These debates have found their way all the way up to the Supreme Court of the United States. Since 1994, Native American use of peyote has been protected by the US government. While some Native Americans are repulsed by the use of peyote, many still argue that the US government must stay away from their religious practices. They cite the US Constitution as guaranteeing their ability to practice their religion freely, including the use of peyote.

The Situation Today

Native Americans have by and large converted to Christianity, although they have not completely cut ties with many of their traditional views and practices, as seen in the peyote situation.

Channeling · an important function of a shaman, who provides his or her body as a conduit for spirits who want to communicate something

Séance · communication with the dead or with spirits

Peace pipe · a ceremonial pipe shared to cement treaties or relationships in Native American culture

Peyote · a controversial hallucinogenic sometimes used in Native American religious practice

Native American Church · combines Christianity with traditional Native American religion and practice, such as incorporating peyote into worship services

There is a fascinating irony at work in the world of Native religion today: while Natives have largely adopted Christianity, many Western people have adopted Native American spirituality. This is evident in several ways, such as the New Age movement, the mystical use of **crystals** and **turquoise**, modern day **sweat lodge** ceremonies, and a newfound respect for the environment among Westerners that arose largely out of the Native American worldview.

Conclusion

Virtually any place in the world where humans have roamed is home to indigenous religions. Siberian religion has been studied extensively, as have Oceanic religions—for example, in Hawaii and greater Polynesia. Indigenous Australian religion has been studied carefully. There are also indigenous European religions such as ancient Greco-Roman religions, Old Norse religions in Scandinavia, Druid and Wiccan religions, or various local paganisms.

It should be noted that **paganism** carries no derogatory meaning in the study of religion. The word *pagan* means "rural" in Latin. Pagans were country folk who were hesitant to join the dominant religion, especially Christianity as it spread across Europe. Typically, paganism connotes a form of **polytheism** or **henotheism**—the worship of one god while believing in the reality or possibility of other gods. Some have claimed that the ancient Israelites were actually henotheists rather than strict monotheists because they repeatedly worshiped gods other than Yahweh. In support of this theory, the people turned away from God shortly after Yahweh had miraculously delivered them from their Egyptian overlords. During the period when their leader, Moses, had ascended Mount Sinai to receive the Ten Commandments, the Israelites fashioned an animal-shaped idol out of gold that they could worship. They certainly believed in their ancestral God, but they were willing to try their luck with alternative deities, given the right conditions.

There is a final point on indigenous religions that was made earlier in the chapter but must be clearly emphasized here at the end. Indigenous religions rarely just evaporate. They live on, sometimes for centuries. While these smaller religions were often demonized, slandered, and denounced as dangerously heretical, they typically became absorbed into a larger tradition. This is a common pattern that takes place in the history of religion. As a larger religion spreads and manages to gain dominance, the smaller, more localized religions, rituals, and myths find a way to graft themselves into the dominant religious infrastructure. Sometimes they go underground, but sometimes they are hiding in plain sight.

Crystals · mystically used by New Age spirituality for healing and for other properties; taken originally from Native American religion

Turquoise · a particularly significant stone in Native American religion

Sweat lodge · a Native American structure resembling a sauna; often used today for health benefits

Paganism · from the Latin word for "rural," generally denoting a polytheistic or henotheistic religion

Polytheism · the worship of many deities

Henotheism · the practice of only worshiping one god while believing in the existence or the possibility of other gods

3 HINDUISM
Like a Drop of Water into the Ocean

South Asian children covered in colored powder after celebrating Holi. This festival in March marks the end of Winter and is celebrated after the full Moon.

The goal of Hinduism is for a person's soul, or **atman**, to exit the long cycle of rebirth and drop into the ocean of supreme reality, losing all individuality. It is something that might fill a Western person with dread—the cessation of life. But in Hinduism, it is a welcome relief from the terrors and difficulties we face as creatures. Being reborn again and again is painful and exhausting. Eventually, Hindus aspire to achieve **moksha**—release—from the seemingly endless cycle of rebirth, known as **samsara**. The goal of Hinduism is to get out of the cycle and blend in with **Brahman**—the eternal and ultimate reality.

Hinduism is the first and oldest of the great Indian traditions. All of the Indian religions—Jainism, Buddhism, Sikhism—find their earliest origins in Hinduism.

There are over a billion Hindus in the world, comprising around 14 percent of the world's population, making it the third-largest religion in the world today behind Christianity and Islam.

In India, Hinduism is clearly the majority religion, with around 80 percent of Indians self-identifying as Hindu. The second-largest religion in India is **Islam**, at around 14 percent of the population. **Christianity** is third, at around 2–3 percent. **Sikhism** is fourth, at around 1–2 percent. **Buddhism** is fifth, at around 0.7 percent. **Jainism** is sixth, at around 0.4 percent.

What Unites Hindus?

Hinduism is difficult to define with any kind of precision, as there is no such thing as a single, consistent Hindu religion. Unlike many other world religions, Hinduism does not have a certain doctrine, or a central concept, that binds all of its devotees together. Rather, it is a religion united by its geography. The religion itself is extremely diverse. For instance, in Christianity, Jesus is primary. In Islam, the Quran and the prophet Muhammad unite the various factions. In Hinduism, one does not have this.

The word *Hinduism* is actually a label probably coined

Atman · the soul; the same essence as Brahman inside every living thing

Moksha · the liberation of the soul from the cycle of rebirth in Hinduism and other Eastern traditions

Samsara · the cycle of rebirth

Brahman · the eternal and ultimate reality

Islam · the second-largest religion in India, at around 14 percent of the population

Christianity · the third-largest religion in India, at around 2–3 percent of the population

Sikhism · the fourth-largest religion in India, at around 1–2 percent of the population

Buddhism · the fifth-largest religion in India, at around 0.7 percent of the population

Jainism · the sixth-largest religion in India, at around 0.4 percent of the population

Aerial view of the Indus River Valley. Karakoram, Pakistan.

A close-up shot of South Asians celebrating Holi, the Festival of Colors.

by the Persians. They understood Hindus to be the people living near the **Indus River**. In Sanskrit, the river is called the **Sindhu River**, but Persians pronounced it as "Hindu."

Thus, the word *Hinduism* does not actually refer to a religion in its most primary sense, but rather to a river and to a geographical region defined by that river: the **Indus Valley** region, today located mainly in Pakistan. The Indus Valley contains the Indus River, which stretches from Tibet to Pakistan and empties in the Arabian Sea.

The word *India* probably comes from the ancient Greeks and was used to describe the land around the Indus River. Islam gradually entered India beginning in the seventh century CE; Muslims were probably the first to use the word *Hindu* in the sense that it is used today—as a religion. For Muslims, Hindus were those people who lived near the Indus River (note the similarity in terms). As Islam started conquering and colonizing India, the meaning of the word *Hindu* came to reference those who did not become Muslim during the long era of Islamic rule there. Western European powers inherited this understanding from the Muslims, and this explains why the term *Hindu* is still in use today. Thus, *Hindu* and *India* are related terms based on geography—in this case, a river (the Indus) and its surrounding region.

Since the nineteenth century CE, many Indians have called for the name of their nation to be **Bharat**, which is a word from ancient Sanskrit texts that refers to the land we now call India. Persians and Muslims over the centuries have also used the word **Hindustan** to refer to the land of India.

Thus, the "religion" of Hinduism is a bit of an error from the get-go. Hinduism is not a religion, if by that we mean there is a tradition that unites all the members.

Three Traditional Assumptions of Most Hindus Today

Hinduism presents several assumptions that do not typically appear in the monotheistic, Abrahamic faiths of Judaism, Christianity, and Islam. These are reincarnation, karma, and caste.

Indus River · the river in India from which the Persians took the name "Hindu" for the people of this region

Sindhu River · the Sanskrit name for the Indus River

Indus Valley · the geographical region around the Indus River, which spans from Tibet to Pakistan and empties into the Arabian Sea

Bharat · another name for the nation of India, taken from ancient Sanskrit texts

Hindustan · a word used by Persians and Muslims throughout the centuries to refer to the land of India

Reincarnation. About two thousand five hundred years ago in India, the idea of the transmigration of the soul (or reincarnation) arose and became fairly widespread. It is not part of the earliest Hindu texts, known as the Vedas. The earliest Vedic texts deal largely with sacrifice to the gods. The Vedas were compiled over a long period of time, so it is difficult for scholars to pinpoint when various Vedas were written. Most scholars believe that the most recent texts in the Vedic literature are the Upanishads, compiled sometime around 500 BCE. It is in the Upanishads that we are introduced to a systematic understanding of the transmigration of souls.

Belief in reincarnation is not unique to India. Many cultures have versions of reincarnation in their history, including but not limited to ancient Greeks, Celts, Germanic peoples, some Jews, and some indigenous Americans. Some Americans today believe in reincarnation or are at least open to its possibility.

In Hinduism, being caught in the cycle of reincarnation—known as samsara—is not a good thing. It is a kind of curse that humans and animals are locked into and cannot escape without learning some truth that will liberate their soul from a long cycle of rebirth that will likely go on for thousands of lifetimes. We must escape to achieve completion and final rest.

This is all different from the typical Western ways of thinking. In Christianity and Islam, people are quite attracted to the notion of eternal life. They long for it. When this life is over, they look forward to heaven, or perhaps they dread hell. What is key, however, is that Christians and Muslims assume they get one life to live, and then they are subject to the judgment of God, and afterlife begins after one has been deemed worthy to enter heaven or not.

Hindus, however, think of humans as having had many earthly lives in the past, both as animals as well as humans. Rebirth is a necessary evil. It is an assumption. Trying to tell a Christian that people reincarnate is like telling a Hindu they only have one life on this Earth. It is difficult to reconcile these two diametrically opposed ways of thinking about life and afterlife.

In Hinduism, there is little choice. There is rebirth, and the only way out of this burdensome cycle of rebirth is to achieve the solution of moksha, or release.

The key to human existence is liberation from this wheel of existence. If one considers life as being on a merry-go-round, the ride is amusing for a few spins. But if a person were to stay on the ride for thousands of cycles, eventually they would tire and want to get off and stay off.

Karma. Karma is that which keeps us in the cycle of rebirth (samsara). Some people believe karma is an actual substance that attaches itself to our souls, weighing us down so that we cannot escape to freedom. Others argue that karma is intangible, like a principle. Still others roughly compare karma to the Western notion of sin. Whatever the case may be, karma is what keeps us from attaining freedom (moksha). Karma is like that oft-repeated saying that is found in Galatians 6:7: "A man reaps what he sows" (NIV). In Hinduism, it is a kind of cause and effect. If one accumulates too much karma, they will likely be reborn into a position inferior to their current one. A Hindu might look at a person who has a miserable life and assume that their previous life must have been rather bad, perhaps full of poor decisions. If one lived selfishly—exhibiting irresponsible behavior, hurting others, committing violence, losing one's temper, and so on—then their next life may be rather unfortunate. They will be reborn into a lesser form. It is cause and effect.

Caste. In India, the words **jati** and **varna** are often used instead of the word *caste.* They are extremely similar and often interchangeable depending on the context. Some scholars make distinctions between these two concepts, which have become enmeshed

> **Transmigration** · reincarnation
>
> **Vedas** · the earliest Hindu texts, dealing primarily with sacrifices to the gods
>
> **Upanishads** · the most recent texts in Vedic literature, dealing systematically with the transmigration of the soul
>
> **Reincarnation** · the transmigration of the soul; rebirth after death into a new form
>
> **Karma** · a sticky substance that accumulates around the soul and weighs that soul down, keeping it entrenched in samsara
>
> **Jati** · literally "birth"; somewhat synonymous with caste but implying a smaller kinship group or family
>
> **Varna** · literally, "color" or "class"; somewhat synonymous with caste; referencing a time in Indian history when the castes were each associated with colors

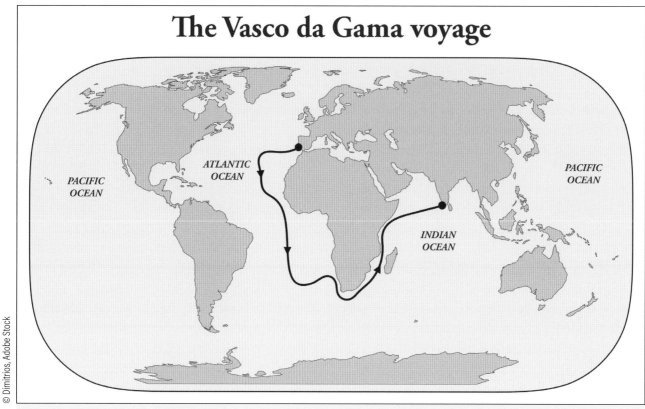

The Vasco da Gama voyage

ATLANTIC OCEAN

PACIFIC OCEAN

PACIFIC OCEAN

INDIAN OCEAN

The route of the Vasco da Gama expedition.

Caste · a Latin term that the Portuguese used to understand the complex Indian social system when Vasco da Gama first arrived to India in 1498

Caste system · a rigidly stratified socioeconomic system in which a person retains the same status as one's family throughout his or her life

Brahmins · the uppermost caste, comprising religious teachers and priests; created to be the "mouth" of existence since they are to teach the Vedas

Kshatriyas · the caste of warriors, diplomats, and rulers; created to be the "arms" of existence since they are expected to bear arms and defend

over time. Technically, the word **caste** is a Latin term that the Portuguese used to understand this complex Indian social system when Vasco da Gama first arrived in India in 1498. The term varna (meaning "color" or "class"), according to Indologist Gavin Flood, has a deep history going back to a time when castes were associated with certain colors. For example, the Brahmin priestly caste was associated with white because they were in charge of ritual purity.

The term jati (meaning "birth") implies a smaller kinship group, or a family. It refers to a person being born into a specific people group that, traditionally, had a specific job in

Indian history and society. Each person is born into a new body after they die. There is a system at play, however. One is essentially born into the caste that they deserve, according to the laws of karma. The key is that one actually deserves the life that one currently has, and how one conducts oneself in this life will shape the circumstances of his or her next life to a large extent.

Of the four major Indian-born world religions, the **caste system** is firmly upheld by Hindus and Jains. Buddhists and Sikhs, however, ignore or oppose caste distinctions in their communities.

Belonging among Hindus

Throughout Indian history, there were four major castes that arose and came to divide the population into strict groupings:

1. **Brahmins** (priests and religious teachers)
2. **Kshatriyas** (warriors, diplomats, and rulers)
3. **Vaishyas** (farmers and merchants)
4. **Shudras** (laborers)

Photographer: Domi Chung, Unsplash

Holy man (sadhu) from Kathmandu, Nepal.

Some might say that the caste system is the one unifying element in Hinduism. However, there are many today, and many throughout history, who reject and have rejected the caste system. Certainly, today the notion of caste is under fire from many progressive Hindus who think the system is unjust. Additionally, the idea of caste exists in other religions, too, so we cannot say that Hinduism is the religion of the caste system. The Hindu caste system is certainly unique, but the predominantly Hindu region is certainly not the only place in the world that has a social hierarchy.

Vegetarianism—is this what unites Hindus? No. **Vegetarianism** is common for upper-caste Hindus, particularly Brahmins—the priestly caste—but it is not widespread as a doctrine in the middle and lower classes. Over time, upper-caste Hindus became restrictive in their diets due to ideas on purity. But for most Indians, vegetarianism is more of a choice and is considered noble. Many people cannot afford meat, which is one reason why so many people are historically vegetarian in India. The widespread doctrine of **ahimsa** (nonviolence) is another reason Hindus avoid killing animals for food. But some Hindus do eat animal flesh, especially chicken and fish. Beef? Not so much.

Cows are sacred today in India; however, there was a time in ancient India when cow sacrifice in fire was common. Over time, however, cows became linked to the sustenance of the Indian people. Their manure was used for cooking fuel; it was also mixed with mud to form a protective coating (like plaster) on small houses. Obviously, dairy cows are useful to have around for milk, butter, cream, and ghee—a class of butter common in India. Cow urine is a useful and natural insecticide used commonly in Indian farming. So there are many reasons to keep cows around.

Today in India, however, whenever a cow is killed—even accidentally—there will likely be a commotion. Muslims—who traditionally eat beef—have experienced pressure in recent years to completely abandon the eating of beef in India. However, it is difficult to patrol the practice, especially in heavily Muslim areas. Some of these conflicts have even escalated to deadly levels. In recent times, Hindus have united in the name of protecting cows, and the tensions are at heights unseen in modern India.

Ahimsa, or nonviolence, is a crucial principle for many Hindus, but not for all. There have been some valiant Hindu warriors who have defended their land. Even the Bhagavad Gita discusses the necessity of violence for some, especially those in the Kshatriya caste who are expected to protect the homeland, even by violence if necessary.

Cremation is widespread in India and is sometimes seen as a kind of common denominator for Indians. But it is not always adhered to in Hinduism—for instance, in the case of holy men, who are considered pure both in body and soul. They do not need to be purified, so they do not need to be cremated. Truly holy men have achieved moksha; therefore,

Vaishyas · the caste of farmers and merchants, created to be the "thighs" of existence since they uphold society through agriculture by tending cattle, lending money, and keeping the economy running smoothly

Shudras · the caste of laborers; created to be the "feet" of existence since they serve the upper castes through their labor

Vegetarianism · a common practice among upper-caste Hindus for purity and to keep to the doctrine of ahimsa, or nonviolence

Ahimsa · nonviolence

Hinduism   65

they do not need to reincarnate. They have already vacated the body, making **cremation** rituals unnecessary. Sometimes the burial place for a Hindu holy man—also known as a **yogi**, **sadhu**, or sannyasin—becomes a holy place in itself. These holy men are typically buried in the usual Indian style—a meditation pose, with legs crossed, forearms resting on the thighs. It is also common for Hindus to bury small children—usually five or under—since they are considered to be pure and not in need of purification fires.

While all the above ideas and practices are common in Hinduism today, there is still a variety and complexity in Hinduism that must not be missed. Hinduism is best understood as a collection of beliefs and practices that can vary in countless ways, yet these ways are united by geography, and that geography is the Indian subcontinent.

A holy woman (sadhvi) in Kolkata, India.

Cremation · burning the dead instead of burial

Yogi · a Hindu holy man, also known as a sannyasin

Sadhu · a Hindu holy man, also known as a sannyasin

Twice-born · members of the Brahmin, Kshatriya, and Vaishya castes who are eligible to undergo the Sacred Thread Ceremony

Sacred Thread Ceremony · a rite of passage involving the bestowal of a sacred thread onto a boy, initiating him into the student phase of Hindu life

Upanayana · the Sanskrit word for the Sacred Thread Ceremony

Dalits · meaning "crushed" or "broken"; outcaste people who are considered untouchable to caste Hindus, comprising 20 percent of the Indian population

Harijans · "children of God"; a somewhat paternalistic term that Gandhi used to refer to the Dalits

The first three castes are considered **twice-born**, meaning they are eligible to go through the **Sacred Thread Ceremony**—a rite of passage into adulthood for upper-caste Hindu boys. The Sanskrit word for this ceremony is **Upanayana**. Shudras do not typically participate in the ceremony, nor do they wear the sacred thread. They also do not study the Vedas—the oldest and most authoritative religious texts of India.

Two important groups need to be emphasized: Dalits and Adivasis. **Dalits**, who comprise around 20 percent of Indians, are those who are deemed to be untouchable to caste Hindus. The word *Dalit* means "crushed" or "broken,"
like dal, the famous food in India made of split lentils cooked into a soup. The word *Dalit* is linked to the Sanskrit verb for "split" or "break." In other words, the Dalits feel they have been split, broken, or crushed over the course of history. Mohandas Gandhi referred to the untouchables as **Harijans**, or "children of God." Many Dalits have rejected Gandhi's term as paternalistic, suggesting that grown women and men should not be referred to as children simply because they were born to the unprivileged families of India.

Adivasi is the term used for tribal peoples in India. These are indigenous people who, like Dalits, often struggle for full participation in Indian society. Adivasis are found all across India's states and territories, and they are a strong majority in the northeastern states such as Arunachal Pradesh, Meghalaya, Mizoram, and Nagaland. These areas are considered remote in India, and the people are not traditionally connected to Hindu identity or Vedic religion. It has been estimated that around 10 percent of Indians are Adivasis.

Only the first three castes are considered twice-born, and only the twice-born are allowed to participate in the Vedic rituals. Everyone else is

Photographer: Yann Forget, (CC-BY-SA)

Adivasi girls from the Saharia tribe in Mara village, Morena district, India.

prohibited, including Shudras, Dalits, and Adivasis. The caste of a person cannot be changed except in extremely rare situations. It is linked to one's ancestry. In rare occasions throughout Indian history, castes have collectively tried to change their caste status—for example, by exiting Hinduism and joining a religion that rejects caste, such as Christianity or Buddhism. There is also the possibility that a caste can improve its social status over the course of many years or generations. Individuals, however, cannot change caste.

Where did this system come from? Why did it arise? The Vedas discuss a time when the creator god, **Brahma** (in early Vedic literature, Brahma was often known as **Prajapati**), decided to create humans. He created the people according to four varnas, or social classes, based on their duties. The Brahmins were created to be the mouth since they were to teach the Vedas. The Kshatriyas were the arms and were expected to

bear arms and defend. The Vaishyas were the thighs and were expected to uphold the society through agriculture, tending cattle, lending money, and keeping the economy running smoothly. The Shudras were the feet, and they typically served the twice-born castes through their labor and service. Shudras also included the artisan class, which in ancient Indian society meant that they often had to work with unclean items such as blood, leather, dirt, and hair.

In traditional times, caste would regulate every aspect of traditional Hindu society: what one ate, whom one marred, with whom one interacted, how one earned a living, or where one lived, for example. The entire concept is based on the notion of

Adivasis · tribal peoples in India who struggle for full participation in Indian society, comprising 10 percent of the Indian population

Brahma · the creator god; also known as **Prajapati**

Hindu water ritual being conducted in Tamil Nadu, India.

pollution. One should not cross certain lines or violate certain caste distinctions, or else one pollutes oneself, one's caste, or other people from other castes. Pollution comes through blood, death, and dirt. Thus, many Hindus, including Brahmins, choose to be vegetarians; they do not handle corpses; they do not fight; and they do not farm, sweep, or clean. High-caste people do not interact much with low-caste people other than to have them do their work. Typically, Dalits are not allowed to touch Brahmins due to cultural norms concerning pollution.

Low-caste people are needed, however, so it is not a situation of active persecution so much as it is something built into the power structures. Low-caste people struggle to gain opportunities that are wide open for high-caste people. Due to the laws of karma, many Hindus have the notion that low-caste people are low caste because of mistakes made in the past. Thus, if they follow their dharma, or their obligations in society, then they can perhaps move up the ladder in future lives.

There are thousands of subcastes in India today, but they can be traced to these major four categories and then the outcastes. Many Hindus refer to themselves as a particular subcaste rather than one of the four larger castes. Most Brahmins, however, who comprise only a small (perhaps 5 percent) portion of the Indian population, refer to themselves as Brahmins since doing so sends a powerful message in terms of duty and purity.

It should also be clarified that while modern Indian laws do not allow discrimination based on caste, it is common for Indians to have a strong sense of caste, especially when it comes to marriage and family. Today, many Indians, particularly those in the Western world or those who have attended Western institutions, express remorse or even disdain toward the caste system. Indeed, some Indians deny that caste thinking even occurs today. Regardless of these reservations, caste consciousness is real. Dalits in India continually protest against casteism. They argue that those who deny the existence of caste today are being disingenuous.

A Brief History of Hinduism

The various local religious traditions that today comprise Hinduism have very deep roots. Aspects of Hinduism go back to around 3000 BCE. This is part of the problem in understanding Hinduism; the immense variety has played out in diverse ways throughout history. In different parts of India, unique people groups worship (**puja**) different gods at different temples or many gods in one temple. There are local gods that are essentially known only by a specific community. There are the larger gods that all Hindus revere. Indeed, some scholars teach that there are tens of millions of gods in India. And while that is probably far-fetched, it is true that Hinduism is better described as an eclectic hodgepodge of religions and religious practices than as one coherent belief system.

Hinduism is alive and well in India today. It thrives. One visit to India and it becomes clear that the **secularization thesis**—the idea that people are becoming less religious over time—is completely false. In the Western world, some have proclaimed that God is dead, but in India, one might say that secularization is dead.

Hinduism is by far the majority religion in India—around 80 percent of the population. It is found in

Pollution · an underlying principle of the caste system; violating caste distinctions pollutes oneself, one's caste, or other people from other castes; also tied to blood, death, and dirt

Puja · ceremonial worship dedicated to a god

Secularization thesis · the theory that, over time, people are becoming less religious

Aryan Migration Theory · the theory that Indo-Europeans migrated from Central Asia into the Indian subcontinent

Proto-Indo-European language · a theoretical parent language of certain European and Asian languages today

other places as well, such as Nepal (80 percent), Bali (80 percent), and Mauritius (50 percent). Wherever Indian immigrants have landed, such as Malaysia, the United Kingdom, the United States, and India's neighboring nations of Bangladesh, Pakistan, and Sri Lanka, one will find Hinduism.

Hinduism is often described as a blending of various cultures that took place as a result of a large migration of people from Central Asia and Europe into the Indian subcontinent. Scholars refer to this idea as the **Aryan Migration Theory**. Based on linguistic evidence, it appears that the people of Central Asia, Persia, and both Eastern and Western Europe share many of the same words, and possibly the same ancestor language, known by nineteenth-century specialists as the **proto-Indo-European language**. English is thought to be a derivative of this ancient language. The only problem, however, is that this language is as of yet undecipherable. No one has figured out how to read its script.

Between 3300 BCE and 1300 BCE, many people lived in well-developed cities in the Indus Valley region of India, centered in modern-day Pakistan and radiating out from there. The two ancient cities of that region that have been excavated are **Mohenjo-daro** and **Harappa**, both within the borders of Pakistan today. Initially oral cultures, when the Aryan peoples of Eurasia came along, these two cities swiftly became literate societies. The Aryan peoples wrote and spoke a proto-Indo-European language that gave birth to what is today the holy language of Hinduism—Sanskrit.

The most fundamental texts of Hindus—the Vedas—are in the Sanskrit language, although they were not written down until around 1500 BCE, after a considerable fusion had taken place between the indigenous Indians and the people from the West—the Aryans, who likely came from modern-day Iran. The process of writing down the Vedas lasted for about a millennium, until around 500 BCE.

Scholars refer to the indigenous people of India as **Dravidians**. These people were quite advanced for that period of time. Their cities were organized and had populations of around fifty thousand people. They had multistory brick houses, running water, irrigation, a written language, weight and measurement systems, and a fertility-based organized religion. Estimates for the population of the entire **Indus Valley Civilization** are between one million and five million people.

According to one prominent version of the Aryan Migration Theory, the nomadic **Aryans** ("noble

Photographer: Junhi Han, © UNESCO, (CC BY-SA 3.0)

The archaeological remains of Mohenjo-daro, a thriving city of the mysterious Indus Valley civilization. The symmetry of the brickwork and the grid system of the streets suggest sophisticated urban planning measures.

Mohenjo-Daro · an ancient city in modern-day Pakistan that predates the Aryan Migration

Harappa · an ancient city in modern-day Pakistan that predates the Aryan Migration

Dravidian · the indigenous population of India, as opposed to the Aryans

Indus Valley Civilization · the ancient civilization that flourished in the Indus River Valley, boasting one to five million people

Aryans · a nomadic people who migrated from Persia into the Indian subcontinent in around 1500 BCE

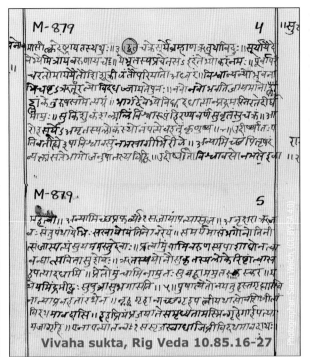

Vivaha sukta, Rig Veda 10.85.16-27

An excerpt of the Rig Veda, the earliest Hindu text.

people") came along from Persia (based in modern Iran) in around 1500 BCE. These Aryans began to interact on a significant level with the Dravidians, and, in due course, the two cultures assimilated into each other substantially, becoming one. Older interpretations of the Aryan Migration Theory are violent—the Aryans destroyed the Dravidians and pushed them into the southern regions of the subcontinent. But those theories are generally discarded today. Whether violent, peaceful, or a mix of the two, the fact is that intermixing occurred on a rampant scale. The nation of Iran is named after the Aryans. The term *Aryan* comes from the Sanskrit language and means "noble." There are many connections between ancient Persian (Iranian) religion and Vedic religion. They share many gods and concepts, and it is common for scholars to combine the two using the expression **Indo-Iranian culture**.

The Aryans also brought with them a religion of animal sacrifice. No doubt their religion merged with ideas and practices from the Dravidian religions. It is difficult for scholars to know which one influenced the other more due to limited evidence. What is known is that religion in the Indus Valley Civilization was polytheistic. Like most indigenous religions, people personified the natural elements by assigning names to them that over time came to be revered as gods. They were animistic religions, with a special focus on fertility.

Hindu Scriptures

In Hinduism, the oldest and most sacred scriptures—the Vedas—are known as **Shruti**, meaning "that which has been heard." This means that they did not originate from humans; rather, they are divine in nature. The lesser scriptures are known as Smriti, meaning "that which is remembered." **Smriti** texts are considered human in nature and therefore less authoritative in comparison to the divinely originated Vedas.

The Vedas

Originally oral traditions, four authoritative collections of Vedic literature were recorded in Sanskrit:

- **Rig Veda** ("worship knowledge")
- **Yajur Veda** ("sacrificial knowledge")
- **Sama Veda** ("chanting knowledge")
- **Atharva Veda** ("priestly knowledge")

Also, each of the four Vedas contains four major sections:

- **Samhitas** (the most ancient sections of the Vedas that include prayers, hymns, and mantras)
- **Brahmanas** (texts that direct priests how to execute their duties)
- **Aranyakas** (reflections upon rituals)
- **Upanishads** (philosophical texts that completely redefined Hinduism)

Primarily, the Vedas are collections of hymns, prayers, and stories to be used by the priests in leading worship (puja). While serving many purposes and dealing with many different themes, they are particularly concerned with fire sacrifice. **Agni**, the fire god, accepted the sacrifices. There was a highly intriguing sacrifice linked to the mysterious **soma** plant, which produced hallucinations or feelings of euphoria for those who drank it. When the **rishis**—the mystical religious leaders in the Vedic era who had visions—drank soma, they would enter an altered state of consciousness. Their euphoric mindset was deemed to be efficacious for composing great poems and chants. The rishis were seers—those who have seen the spiritual realities—and their visions are considered to be authoritative and thus comprise much of the Vedas. Eventually, the soma plant even came to be deified by the rishis, in yet another example of Max Müller's disease of language theory.

The most grandiose and enormously expensive sacrifice in the Vedic period was that of the horse. It was called the **ashvamedha** ("horse sacrifice") and was linked to the royal families. The horse would run loose for a year and was followed by the king's servants. Wherever the horse went, the king (**raja**) could claim the area as his own. When the horse returned, there was a massive sacrifice of animals, ending with the sacrifice and eating of the horse. Numerous rituals accompanied the act, and it defined the extent of a king's territorial holdings and essentially made a statement to all involved that this king was now the undisputed sovereign in the region defined by the wandering of the horse.

The Samhita collections of each of the Vedas are considered the oldest form of Hindu scripture. The Brahmana collections could be compared to the Jewish book of Leviticus—it was directed to the Levites or the priests. The Brahmanas are also famous for their scientific teachings corresponding to the Vedic era and are useful for understanding what people thought about the natural world a millennium before Christ. The Aranyaka collections are a linkage between the Brahmanas and the Upanishads. They describe how to do the intricate Vedic rituals, but they also point toward a spiritualization process that was happening in Hinduism at the time. The Upanishad collections, then took those spiritual insights from the Aranyakas and advanced a new approach to religion.

The Upanishads

Still considered authoritative in most Hindu traditions, the Upanishads, which were developed later, perhaps from 800 BCE to 300 BCE, are revered teachings that are supremely relevant to human life, reality, and worldview.

Havan Kund, a ceremonial fire pit. Sacrifice is made to the fire god Agni.

Agni · the god of fire and sacrifice

Soma · a hallucinogenic plant ingested by Vedic priests; eventually personified as a deity

Rishis · mystical religious leaders in the Vedic era who drank soma to alter their state of consciousness and have authoritative visions of the spiritual realities

Ashvamedha · a horse sacrifice in which a king would release a horse and allow it to wander for a year; wherever the horse went was considered territory of the king; at the end of the year, the horse was killed and eaten in an elaborate feast

Raja · an Indian king

The importance of the Upanishads cannot be overstated. After the Upanishads, fire sacrifice made by Brahmin priests was no longer the heart of the faith. Some people still practice animal sacrifice, even today, but over time, this practice was phased out. Few Hindus sacrifice animals today, except in more remote and provincial temple settings. In recent years, temples that still sacrifice animals have come under increasing pressure from the strongly Hindu government to eradicate the practice.

The Upanishads presented a highly spiritualized religion that critiqued the earlier forms of Vedic literature. The Upanishads were successful in their critiques, and Hinduism completely changed, much like Judaism shifted from a religion of animal sacrifice to a religion divorced from fire obligations. The other Vedic collections are today ancient texts, even for Hindus. They represent something from the distant past. The religion we see demonstrated in the Upanishads is different. It is the religion of Hinduism that we encounter today: Brahman, atman, Yoga, and transmigration of the soul.

The Upanishads teach that the supreme force in the universe is Brahman. A person's individual soul, however, is known as the atman. The secret that humans need to realize is that atman shares its essence with Brahman. Humans tend not to be able to understand all of this, however. We are blinded by our own illusion about reality, known in Hinduism as maya. It is maya—one's illusions about the nature of reality—that keeps one in the karmic system of samsara.

The Upanishads represent a shift away from actual physical sacrifices, and they emphasize mental and spiritual sacrifices. They are philosophical, as opposed to the more physically prescriptive Vedas. The Upanishads contain much speculation and philosophy, and they contain a theology very different from the Vedas. The Upanishads assume that Brahman is the underlying force behind all emanations of the divine power. Brahman is considered to be the ground of all being, the force behind all things. This is why many Hindus say that Hinduism is monotheistic—because everything goes back to this supreme reality.

The Upanishads also introduced the concepts of karma, samsara, and moksha—release from the cycle of rebirth. In the Upanishads, the central challenge is how to become aware that Brahman is atman. The person who can eventually realize this profound truth—that we are Brahman—will experience release, and their soul will join with Brahman. They are no longer in samsara. They are free. They are like a drop of water (atman) that is completely absorbed into the ocean (Brahman).

The Upanishads also developed the notion of the guru—the teacher, the master. The role of a guru is like that of a god to the student. Indeed, the guru represents a god in human form, teaching the human how to live well to achieve moksha, or release. Gurus lead the practitioner through various stages of spiritual growth. Gurus often live ascetic lives, although some gurus may have been married in the past before renouncing and moving on toward a deeper development of the spiritual life. A person who has done this is called a sannyasin, or someone who renounces all material comforts of the present life and commits themself completely to spiritual pursuits.

The greatest contribution of the Upanishads is that Hinduism became reconceptualized from a religion of sacrifice to a cerebral, spiritual religion. Our thoughts and actions affect everything and everyone, rather than the precision of our sacrifices. Good thoughts and actions have good repercussions, while bad thoughts and actions lead to bad results for us and for others. This is the concept of karma. Bad karma will cause someone to be reborn into a lower life form the next time around. One cannot reach moksha if one persists in creating karma. Thus, one tries to live a good and righteous life so one can be reborn as a Brahmin, renounce to become a sannyasin, and eventually achieve moksha. Traditional Hindus tend to believe that only Brahmin-born males can attain moksha.

Yoga · from the word yoke, meaning "to unite"; the path one takes to unite oneself to God

Maya · illusions that blind us from the nature of reality and keep us trapped in samsara

Guru · a teacher, like a god to a student, who leads a practitioner to spiritual growth

Sannyasin · someone who renounces all material comforts of the present life and commits themself completely to spiritual pursuits

Brahma Vishnu Shiva Ganesha Lakshmi

Krishna Rama Saraswati Durga Devi Parvati

Indra Agni Kartikeya Kali Hanuman

The gods of the Vedas were many and were a bit like the gods of Greece and Rome in the sense that they could be either good or bad, moral, or completely immoral. They could be frivolous, irresponsible, and petulant. They could be like the Egyptian gods in the sense that they took on different meanings, depending on context. Like animism, they were often linked to various phenomena, places, or things, such as mountains, water, or emotions. Here are a few of the more important gods of the Vedas:

- **Indra:** a creator god who defeats all chaos. He is also a warrior who fights for his people. His strengths, however, are mitigated by his struggles, as he is prone to drunkenness and hedonism.

- **Agni:** the fire god who is also the personification of sacrifice. He is often understood as the spokesman who mediated between humans and the divine realm. The sacrificial fire is thought to be his mouth.
- **Soma:** the deified plant celebrated for its hallucinogenic properties and ability to stimulate people both in body and mind. While some scholars think soma may actually be magic mushrooms, there is no consensus.
- **Varuna:** the sky god who can forgive sin and punish evildoers. He is probably the noblest of the Vedic gods in modern terms, as his virtuous life matches with most people's understandings of righteous and ethical behavior today.
- **Mitra:** the personification of an agreement or a contract. He is the god of treaties, and he is also associated with the morning. Mitra's influence has diminished over time, and his name eventually became synonymous with friendship.

There are many gods in the Vedas, but these are perhaps the most visible.

Over time, the meaning of the Vedas changed. While originally hymns of praise, they began to emphasize that careful attention must be paid to the precise prescriptions of sacrifices, like a sacrifice manual for priests. This new meaning was particularly evinced in the Brahmanas. The assumption of the Brahmanas was that if sacrifices are performed correctly, the desires of the person will be achieved. If sacrificial rituals are done sloppily or imprecisely, the desired results will fail to materialize.

Key Hindu Epics

It is nearly impossible to understand Hinduism without having a grasp of the two great epic stories of the Indian subcontinent that in many ways provide the background for the entire religion: the *Ramayana* and the *Mahabharata*. These are massive epic poems; the *Mahabharata* is about ten times as long as Homer's *Iliad* and *Odyssey* combined! The *Mahabharata* is around four times as long as the *Ramayana*. They are intricate stories that tell about the gods when they walked the Earth, as well as about Indian philosophy, history, geography, morality, and social norms. And the stories are entertaining. Hindus treasure these two epics as a kind of background scripture that unites them and provides an anchor for them through this ancestral identity. They provide a narrative about relationships, political turmoil, human behavior, and the right way to live. Perhaps the most concise way to describe them is that they are long discussions of dharma—a person's obligations in life. Obligations are sometimes difficult to navigate since there are so many competing factors in a human life. Should one be courageous and fight? Or should one be humble and patient and let things work themselves out? Should one take vengeance or forgive?

India's two great epics were composed between 400 BCE and 400 CE; however, they deal with events in Indian history from around 800 to 600 BCE. They are not categorized as Shruti (divine revelation), like the Vedas, but they are far more accessible to the common people. The stories of these two epics permeate Indian society, and hints of the stories are found everywhere, from cultural references to art to people's names. Both of them were put to the screen in India in the late 1980s, when they pulled in huge audiences over long periods of time. The televised presentation of the *Ramayana* consisted of seventy-eight episodes, while the *Mahabharata* comprised 108 episodes.

The Ramayana

The *Ramayana* (in English, "Rama's journey") is a tale about Rama, the prince of **Ayodhya**, located in modern-day **Uttar Pradesh**, the most populated state in India.[1]

There are several central characters in the *Ramayana*. Prince **Rama** is the protagonist. **Sita** is his wonderful wife. **Hanuman**, the monkey, is an extremely faithful devotee of Rama, who is also pious and powerful. **Lakshmana** and **Bharat** are loyal brothers to Rama. The antagonist of the story is **Ravana**, the demon.

Ramayana · an ancient Indian epic depicting the tale of Rama, an incarnation of Vishnu, and his wife Sita

Mahabharata · an ancient Indian epic depicting the great Kurukshetra war

Ayodhya · the kingdom in which Rama was prince in the *Ramayana*, located in modern-day Uttar Pradesh

Uttar Pradesh · the most populated state in India

Rama · the protagonist of the *Ramayana*, an incarnation of the god Vishnu

Sita · the devoted wife of Rama

Hanuman · a pious and powerful monkey god who proves to be an extremely faithful ally to Rama

Lakshmana · Rama's faithful brother

Bharat · Rama's faithful brother

Ravana · the demon antagonist of the *Ramayana* who kidnaps Sita

Kalpas · eons in Hindu cosmology, with one kalpa lasting 4.32 billion years, or one day in the life of Brahma

TIME

Hinduism teaches that our present reality has been going on for many **kalpas** (eons)—meaning billions of years. For Hindus, the length of a kalpa is 4.32 billion years, which is usually defined as a day in the life of Brahma, the creator god. There is no absolute end to the universe, however. Each kalpa has many predecessors, and many kalpas will follow our own. Over the course of billions of years, our souls (atmans) will reincarnate through innumerable life forms until we achieve release. At the end of a kalpa, everything is destroyed by fire, and the process starts over again. We are trapped in this mind-boggling circular prison of time until we manage to achieve release from it, either by ourselves or with assistance from a god or guru.

© reddees, Adobe Stock

Rama, his wife Sita, his loyal brother Lakshmana, and the Vanara, Hanuman.

Early in the story, Prince Rama fell in love with Sita and wanted to marry her. However, her adopted father, who was a king, made the stipulation that no one could marry Sita unless they could first string the great bow of Shiva. Many people had tried and failed, but when Rama came on the scene, he strung it immediately without much of a problem, until he accidentally broke it. People were impressed, and thus Rama was allowed to take Sita as his bride.

The good times did not last, unfortunately. Rama's father, King Dasharath, wanted to make Rama king, but, some years back, King Dasharath had made a vow that one of his other sons, Bharat, should be the next king. Rama decided to back down, and he exiled himself into the forest, followed by his faithful wife Sita and his loyal brother Lakshmana.

Shortly thereafter, King Dasharath died while Prince Bharat was away on holiday. When Prince Bharat returned and heard about everything that had occurred, he insisted that Rama should be the king.

Rama remained in the forest, however. Bharat was so desperate to see Rama become king that he put a pair of Rama's sandals on the throne. The people of Ayodhya all wanted Rama to become king, but he just went further and further into the forest to escape everything.

The next phase involved a demoness named Surpanakha who wanted to marry Rama. Of course, he was married to Sita, so he sent her over to his brother Lakshmana, who was single and under a vow of celibacy. The demoness Surpanakha was out of luck. She became enraged and tried to kill Sita, Rama's devoted wife. Lakshmana defended Sita and, in fact, cut off the ears and nose of the demoness Surpanakha.

The demoness Surpanakha fled to **Sri Lanka**, an island nation off the coast of South India that was ruled by her brother, a demon named Ravana. The demon king

> **Sri Lanka** · an island nation off the coast of southern India; ruled by the demon king Ravana in the *Ramayana*

Though his illustrations in *Rip Van Winkle* (1907), *Arabian Nights* (1907), and *The Fairy Book* (1913) are more famous, this 1913 color lithograph by Warwick Goble, "Rama Spurns the Demon Lover," helped popularize the story of the *Ramayana* among Westerners.

Ravana was incensed by the attack on his sister, and he vowed to take vengeance. He went on a journey to find Rama, but instead, he decided to abduct Sita. He then put Sita in his flying chariot and took her with him to Sri Lanka.

Rama then learned there was a group of **Vanara**—humanlike monkeys—that had witnessed part of the abduction. They saw the chariot flying south. Hanuman, one of the monkeys, figured out that the demon Ravana was headed toward Sri Lanka. So he assembled a monkey army to march south and build a bridge that would connect India to Sri Lanka. Rama went along, crossed the water, and

Vanara · humanlike monkeys found in the *Ramayana* as well as in Hindu religious iconography

entered Sri Lanka. He tracked down Ravana and killed him, and he rescued his wife, Sita.

But there arose a serious problem. Rama was suspicious that Sita may have defiled herself with the demon Ravana. Sita was offended by the false accusation and decided to commit suicide (sati) by throwing herself onto a funeral pyre that was burning. The fire god Agni then rose up out of the flames and carried Sita to safety, explaining to Rama that Sita had remained faithful and pure throughout her stay in Ravana's palace. Rama then accepted his wife, Sita, since she had been exonerated by Agni.

Rama then returned to Ayodhya with his wife, Sita, and he was crowned king. He ruled the kingdom with class and dignity, and it was a wonderful time for all the people. It was a time of peace and great prosperity for all—that is, until rumors began to circulate around Sita's chastity when she was with Ravana. Rama asked Sita to go through another trial by fire. She flatly refused, and Rama banished her from his kingdom.

Sita was actually pregnant with Rama's child during this exile. A hermit named Valmiki took care of Sita during this time, and she gave birth to twins: Lava and Kush. Valmiki helped Sita raise them, and he served as a kind of surrogate father, teaching them the Vedas and the arts. Valmiki was also a literate man, and he recorded the entire story he had heard from Sita; thus, he is the author of the *Ramayana*. Valmiki taught Lava and Kush to sing the *Ramayana*, although they did not know it was their own family history. The twins became so famous for their beautiful recitations of the *Ramayana* that Rama actually heard about them and summoned them to perform at his palace in Ayodhya.

When the twins arrived, it was clear that they were the children of King Rama. They looked just like him. Rama was moved, he asked Sita to come back to him, and they lived happily ever after. That is one version of the *Ramayana*, but there are other renditions of the story that are not so happy.

Another well-known ending of the *Ramayana* is that Rama decided to accept Sita back as his wife only if she could prove her chastity and purity again. Sita was deeply anguished by this and cried out so loud that the ground opened up and a goddess rescued her from this scene and descended with her into the Earth.

A scene from the *Ramayana*, the Battle of Lanka, created by influential Muslim artist Sahib Din between 1649 and 1653.

A folio from the *Mahabharata*. Kangra, India, ca. 1775–1800.

The sage Vyasa dictates the ancient Sanskrit epic, the *Mahabharata*, to Ganesh, the elephant-headed god, who acts as his scribe. Hyderabad, India.

Pandavas · a warring side of the Mahabharata, the branch of the family for which Arjuna, the hero, fights

Bhagavad Gita · a famous section of the *Mahabharata* in which the hero's chariot driver reveals himself to be Vishnu and counsels him in spiritual matters

Kauravas · a warring side of the *Mahabharata* that fights against the **Pandavas**

Kurukshetra War · the great war between the Pandavas and the Kauravas

Vyasa · the sage who composed the *Mahabharata* and is also said to have compiled and systematized the Vedas

Ganesh · the elephant-headed god who wrote the *Mahabharata* as a scribe for Vyasa; today, he is considered the remover of obstacles, and he is particularly beloved by students trying to pass exams

Rama was overcome with sadness when she was gone, and he abdicated the throne. He then descended into the waters around Ayodhya and drowned himself. Once in the water, his spirit left his body and rose up into the skies. Some versions have them reuniting in the heavens as a married couple again.

The Mahabharata

The other major Hindu epic, the *Mahabharata*, is probably even more influential in Hindu society today due to its containing the **Bhagavad Gita** story within it, the longest poem known to humankind, at around one hundred thousand verses.

The *Mahabharata* involves two branches of a family: the **Pandavas** and the **Kauravas**. They were at battle, as both of them wanted to rule. They entered into war with each other—the **Kurukshetra War**. The *Mahabharata* is said to have been composed by **Vyasa**, a sage who also compiled and systematized the Vedas.

Traditionally, Vyasa dictated the *Mahabharata*, while the elephant-headed god **Ganesh** served as his scribe and wrote the verses down.

Like the *Ramayana*, the *Mahabharata* involves family struggles, kings being exiled, and lost love. It is a complex story that involves treachery, battles for the throne, massive deaths, strategic marriages, archery competitions, and conniving dice games that resulted in horrible consequences for the losers. For example, the loser of the dice gamble would be exiled for twelve years, which would then turn into another twelve years after another loss on the dice.

The gist of the story is that tensions escalated between these two families to the point that the Kurukshetra War was inevitable. The protagonist of the story—Arjuna—was a member of the Pandavas. Arjuna led the Pandavas to a great victory. They wiped out their cousins, the Kauravas. However, the most important part of the story was the moment when

Arjuna was just about to enter into war against his cousins. He began to have doubts, and he engaged his chariot driver, Krishna—who, it turned out, was actually Lord Vishnu—in a long, philosophical dialogue. They discussed many things, and Krishna (or Lord Vishnu) explained much of what is considered to be at the very core of orthodox Hindu thought today. That section of the *Mahabharata* is known as the Bhagavad Gita.

The Bhagavad Gita (or the Song of God) is the most important and most utilized scripture in Hinduism today. It is a great story, easy to read and profound. In the story, Arjuna, a Pandava chariot warrior, was questioning before going into battle the ethics of killing. He and his driver—named Krishna—got into a long conversation about ethics and responsibility. Arjuna expressed strong misgivings about killing other people, especially relatives that he knew and loved. The chariot driver argued that since Arjuna was from the Kshatriya (warrior) caste, he must fight. However,

when he fights, Arjuna must be dispassionate. In other words, he must simply do the duty of a warrior without thinking about outcomes. His fighting must be absolutely selfless. He was not actually killing anybody, since people simply reincarnate after they die. Death is a mere changing of clothes, so fight, but stay focused on the fact that this is one's humble duty.

At a pivotal moment in the conversation, and much to Arjuna's surprise, the chariot driver revealed himself as an incarnation of the god Vishnu, and then Krishna began to teach Arjuna how he could obtain moksha. Moksha can be attained through four major ways: **Karma Yoga**, **Bhakti Yoga**, **Jnana Yoga**, and **Raja Yoga**.

The Laws of Manu

The final scripture discussed here is **Manusmriti**, better known in English as the **Laws of Manu**. Containing 2,685

Manusmriti · also known as **the Laws of Manu**, Hindu ethics codified into law

Close-up of Krishna and Arjuna statue in Kurukshetra, India.

The word Yoga is related to the word *yoke*, meaning "to unite." It usually implies one is uniting himself or herself to a god.

- *Karma Yoga: the path of action.* A person can work their way to God; however, they need to perform the duty that has been assigned to them through samsara. Deeds are measured by conformity to given obligations. A person should never do something to get certain results. For the action to be good, they have to do it simply out of a sense of duty.

- *Bhakti Yoga: the path of devotion.* This involves one expressing their deepest love for God. Complete surrender to God is the path of love. Oneness with God is the goal. Bhakti is the most important approach to Hinduism today. Rather than relying on self-discipline, most Hindus today look to their gods for grace and mercy. They develop a loving relationship with their god, showing deep devotion to one of the many deities, but usually linked to Shiva or Vishnu or one of their female consorts.

- *Jnana Yoga: the path of knowledge.* One has to learn how to renounce so that one can be released from the wheel of rebirth. The knowledge that must be realized is understanding that one's atman is actually the same thing as Brahman—the supreme reality. This realization is often referred to as **non-duality**. There is no distinction between a person and God or between two different people. We are all the same.

Vishnu in his man/lion avatar. One of the ten main incarnations, the Hindu god sits with intense concentration, apparent in the expression of his face over the ruff of mane, the taut posture, the symmetry, and the perfect proportions of his four-armed body. The Yoga band holds the crossed legs up in equilibrium. In his upper right hand, he holds the flaming discus that, when thrown, cuts through ignorance and its demonic personifications.

- *Raja Yoga: the path of discipline.* This is the path of correct breathing and posture. This path usually requires celibacy (**brahmacharya**). In Raja Yoga, one must master the mind, attaining complete stillness of thought. One unites the mind with the atman, leading to **Samadhi**, or the deepest, most tranquil phase of meditation.

The four Yogas are the bedrock of Hinduism, and virtually all Hindus draw from one or more of them in the pursuit of the good life or perhaps even of everlasting moksha.

Brahmacharya · the practice of celibacy and sexual restraint which helps a practitioner break the bonds of samsara

Samadhi · the deepest, most tranquil state of meditation

verses, they were probably first written down around the time of Christ. They evolved to become authoritative collections for regulating human conduct. According to tradition, they were articulated by Manu, an archetypal man of wisdom, but they were likely written by many people over an extended period of time.

The Laws of Manu are important because they represent a codification of Hindu ethics. The caste system gets solidified in the Laws of Manu, with the Brahmins firmly on top, almost as gods. Many accuse the Laws of Manu of being extremely patriarchal, but there are some passages that uphold the rights of women. For example, women are always to be cared for: first by her father, then her husband, and in old age, her son (9:2–4). In the Laws of Manu, this is seen as appropriate protection for women, but many in Western societies consider these laws patriarchal and oppressive.

In the Laws of Manu, we see the teaching of the **sacred cow** that is closely identified with Hinduism today. The slaying of a cow is considered a sin that requires reconciliation and penance for three months (11:109, 116), including bathing in cow urine (11:110). Cows and those from the Brahmin caste are carefully protected in the Laws of Manu (11:79–80). Cows are discussed throughout the Laws of Manu, including passages on their urine, milk, dung, and hair

(11:92–93). Cows are to be cared for (11:113) and allowed to wander into anyone's fields and eat whatever they want (11:115). This still goes on in India today, as cows wander the streets and fields without being bothered by anyone. They walk on highways as if they know they are protected.

The Laws of Manu outline four stages of life, but, as written, do not permit women to participate in the fourth stage. While the first three stages were not initially designed for women, today women do educate themselves and participate in the stages, depending upon the support of the local community. Poorer women often marry very young and thus do not

LIFE STAGES

We see the four stages of Hindu life outlined in the Laws of Manu (6:87). These stages are seen as a man's duty, or his **dharma**. They are, explicitly, only for "twice-born" males:

1. *Student phase.* A boy must study the Vedas. He is given a sacred thread or cord over his shoulder, showing he is "twice-born" (only for the upper three castes). He is "reborn" as a spiritual person. He then studies with his guru until the age of twenty-four. Brahmin boys undergo the Sacred Thread Ceremony at the age of eight. Kshatriyas undergo it at age eleven. Vaishyas undergo it at age twelve (2:36).
2. *Householder phase.* A man shall observe all the rituals and try to live out the teachings of the faith. He gets married, works, and raises children. He must entertain guests and support the faith, particularly by supporting holy men in the temples. He must have a son to whom he can give the responsibilities of the home. The son will also be responsible for leading the funeral rituals for his parents when they die.
3. *Forest-dweller phase.* When his hair turns white, a man shall leave the home to his son and go to the forest to study the scriptures and meditate (6:2, 8, 29). He is allowed to bring his wife if he wants, although he must remain chaste (6:3, 26). He must direct his full attention to spiritual matters, even sleeping at the roots of trees (6:26).
4. *Renunciation.* Those who do the optional phase of renunciation will become wandering ascetics, known in India as sannyasins. They renounce everything, including their wife. Ultimately, the idea is to unite atman with Brahman through scripture recitation and meditation. Hindus are not required to try to reach moksha in this life, but they can try if they are willing to attempt the sannyasin life, which is very difficult. The sannyasin must be "absolutely silent" and remain solitary (6:41–42). He must give up all attachments (6:81) and focus upon the bliss of moksha (6:49).

> **Dharma** · one's duty, as assigned by samsara
>
> **Sacred cow** · considered holy and linked to the sustenance of the Indian people, cows are often protected in India today

Trimurti · "three forms," the Hindu trinity of sorts, in which Brahman emanates in the three forces of creation, sustenance, and destruction, deified as Brahma, Vishnu, and Shiva

Vishnu · the god who sustains all; generally believed to have come to Earth as an avatar nine times

Avatar · an incarnation of a god on Earth

Krishna · the most popular avatar of Vishnu, from the Bhagavad Gita

Vaishnavites · devotees of Vishnu

Kalki · the tenth and final avatar of Vishnu yet to come; a messiah figure who ushers in the end of the kalpa

Lakshmi · wife of Vishnu, goddess of fertility and wealth

Hare Krishna · also known as **ISKCON**, a religious movement associated with the worship of Krishna

Hindu woman praying in the sacred Ganges River.

The Trimurti, or "three forms" of Brahman in the three principal gods of creation, sustenance, and destruction: Brahma, Vishnu, and Shiva.

study much beyond primary school. In traditional India, women are considered part of a household overseen by a man. When a couple marries, the woman usually joins the man's parents, and she lives in his home.

Developments in Hindu Theology

At around the time of Christ, there developed in Hinduism a Trinitarian theology known as the **Trimurti** (three forms). The great force of Brahman emanates in many forms, but the most important are in the acts of creation, sustenance, and destruction. These three forces have been deified in Hinduism as Brahma, Vishnu, and Shiva. The vast majority of temples in India are attached to either Shiva, Vishnu, or both.

Brahma is the most important creator god in Hinduism. In the Vedas, he was known as Prajapati. He does not receive a whole lot of attention in the scriptures. People tend not to worship him because

he is not often anthropomorphized in the scriptures. Thus, there are only a handful of Brahma temples in all of India. When he is depicted in the iconography, he usually appears with four faces and four arms, as he is linked with the four Vedas and the four directions.

Vishnu is the sustainer of all. He is typically worshiped in his **avatar** of **Krishna**—from the Bhagavad Gita. Followers of Vishnu are known as **Vaishnavites**. Vishnu is full of love and forgiveness. He sustains the universe, and he occasionally comes to Earth as an avatar when needed. Most Hindus believe he has come to Earth in nine forms: a fish, a turtle, a pig, a man/lion creature, a dwarf, and then a fierce hunter. After that he came as Rama, then Krishna, and then the Buddha. Some expect a tenth visit from Vishnu at the end of the kalpa. He will come as a messiah figure—called **Kalki**—and he will arrive on a white horse. He will punish the wicked and reward the righteous.

When in the avatar of Krishna, Vishnu is often depicted as playing a flute. His wife **Lakshmi** is popular and is the goddess of fertility and wealth. She is known for her extreme devotion to Krishna, despite the fact that many women are associated with him. Some explain that they are actually avatars of Lakshmi, however. In the United States, the **Hare Krishna** movement is associated with Vishnu and is known as **ISKCON** (International Society for Krishna Consciousness).

Shiva is the destroyer. He is often depicted meditating in the Himalayas, where he typically resides. His body is covered in ash, signifying death. He wears animal skins and sometimes a snake necklace. He often holds a trident.

Hindus who follow Shiva are known as **Shaivites**, and they sometimes paint a trident on their foreheads. Shiva is the god of death, yet he is also depicted as the four-armed **Lord of the Dance**—encircled by fire. Since death leads to rebirth in Hinduism, he is considered the god of reproduction. In Hinduism, he is often depicted by the form of the **lingam**—a smooth cylinder (typically representing a phallus) that is frequently connected to a yoni (which signifies a womb). Together, these symbols signify the creative and regenerative power of death leading to renewed life, or destruction that leads to rebirth. In Shiva temples, devotees pour milk on the Shiva lingam as an act of worship.

Shiva's female consorts are extremely important in Shaivite religion, and together, they represent the divine power of the masculine and feminine. Shiva is married to the devoted goddess **Parvati**, who is motherly and nurturing. She and

Shiva · god of destruction and reproduction, also known as the Lord of the Dance

Shaivites · devotees of Shiva

Lord of the Dance · an epithet of Shiva

Lingam · a phallic votary object symbolizing the reproductive power of the god Shiva

Yoni · a symbol of female genitalia representing reproductive power; associated with Shakti

Parvati · the wife of Shiva and mother of Ganesh

Sri Murugan Temple in Kadirampura, India. Colorful statues of Parvati holding Murugan, her six-headed baby, with Shiva, Ganesh, and Lakshmi on the side.

Photographer: Kalyan Kumar, (CC BY-SA 2.0)

Sixty-five-foot-tall statue of Shiva in Bangalore, India.

with obtaining an education and helping students to pass exams. Perhaps no other god in Hinduism today is as beloved as Ganesh, and he is featured prominently in homes and businesses as a sign of prosperity and determination.

Kali is a terrifying goddess consort of Shiva who can cause death. She is depicted with blood dripping from her tongue, she wears a garland around her neck of male skulls, and she often wears a skirt made of severed arms. **Durga** is another of Shiva's consorts. She is associated with divine wrath against oppressors, and she is depicted with weapons in her many hands. The feminine principle in Hinduism is known as **Shakti**, and it is a powerful outlet for many Hindus in their worship and devotion. Both Shiva and Vishnu temples prominently feature feminine goddesses. **Shaktism** is often associated with Tantra—one of the more esoteric forms of Hinduism.

India's Long Quest for Self-Government ("Swaraj")

For many centuries throughout its history, much of India was under the authority of other entities such as

Kali · terrifying goddess and consort of Shiva; depicted with blood, skulls, and severed limbs

Durga · consort of Shiva associated with weapons and divine wrath against oppressors

Shakti · the feminine principle, sometimes worshiped as a goddess

Shaktism · the sect of Hinduism that primarily worships Shakti

Delhi Sultanate · Islamic rule over India from 1206 to 1526

Mughal Empire · Turkish Muslim rule over India from 1526 to 1857

Babur · the first Mughal emperor

Genghis Khan · the conqueror and first great leader of the Mongol Empire

Timur · also known as **Tamerlane**, founder of the Timurid Empire

Shiva are the parents of the extremely popular Ganesh, the elephant-headed god who is the remover of obstacles and has come to be associated

The goddess Durga is depicted here with eight hands, although some say she has ten.

© Stockfoo, Adobe Stock

the Aryans, Muslims, and British. It has been a long struggle for India to achieve independence, which finally occurred in the mid-twentieth century. In India, this concept of independence is closely associated with the notion of swaraj, or "self-rule." India endured many centuries of foreign rule before independence was achieved at last after the resistance efforts of Gandhi and others.

Islam and India

Starting in the mid-seventh century CE, Islamic conquests invaded India, some with major success, especially in the northwest portion of the subcontinent, in what is today Afghanistan and Pakistan. By the 1200s, Muslims had captured considerable territory in India, and they ruled by means of a dynastic government called the **Delhi Sultanate**, which lasted from 1206 to 1526.

By the 1500s, the Muslim Turkish warriors that fought for the **Mughal Empire** overthrew the Delhi Sultanate and ruled until the British took control in 1857. **Babur** was the founder and first emperor of the Mughal Empire, which lasted from 1526 to 1857. He was deeply respected as a descendant of the great Mongolian Empire leaders **Genghis Khan** and **Timur** (or **Tamerlane**). Some of Babur's successors are legendary: **Akbar**, **Jahangir**, **Shah Jahan**, and **Aurangzeb**. The zenith of the Mughal Empire was during Aurangzeb's reign (1658–1707).

The Mughals captured the majority of the subcontinent, an amazing feat considering Muslims were in such a minority. The legacy of the Mughal Empire is manifold, but one obvious outcome is that Pakistan and Bangladesh—until 1947 part of India—remain strongly Islamic today. The Indian subcontinent has more than six hundred million Muslims today: around two hundred million each in India, **Pakistan**, and **Bangladesh**, the latter two being nearly entirely Muslim.

Due to this period of conquest, Islamic and Hindu relations are often strained. There are many important remnants of the Mughal Empire in India today,

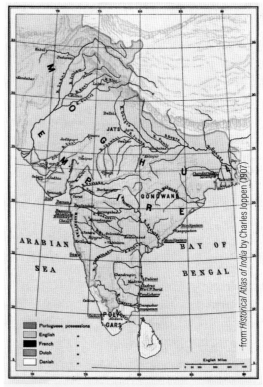

Map of India under the Mughal Empire in 1700, also showing the advent of European trading posts.

from Historical Atlas of India by Charles Joppen (1907)

Akbar · famous Mughal emperor

Jahangir · famous Mughal emperor

Shah Jahan · famous Mughal emperor; built the Taj Mahal

Aurangzeb · a famous Mughal emperor who ruled during the zenith of the empire

Pakistan · an Islamic majority nation that was created in the partition of India; contains the historic Indus River Valley

Bangladesh · an Islamic majority nation that was created in the partition of India

Taj Mahal · a mausoleum for the favorite wife of emperor Shah Jahan

Mumtaz Mahal · the favorite wife of Shah Jahan; for whom the Taj Mahal was built

particularly in the architecture, such as the **Taj Mahal**—one of the great structures of the world. Commissioned in 1632 by Mughal emperor Shah Jahan on the banks of the Yamuna River near the city of Agra, it was built as a tomb for his favorite wife, **Mumtaz Mahal**, with whom he had fourteen children. She died in childbirth, and Shah Jahan was inconsolable for a year. The Taj Mahal is a testament of his love for her and is one of the most photographed structures in the world.

Sikhism developed during the conflict of Islam and Hinduism and came to be a religion in and of itself. Some consider it a middle way between the two religions. However, while initially tolerated, the Sikhs came to be violently persecuted by the Mughals. Two of Sikhism's ten gurus were martyred by the Mughals: Guru Arjan (the fifth guru) and Guru Tegh Bahadur (the ninth guru).

European Colonialism

The Portuguese arrived in India in 1498 when Vasco da Gama anchored off the coast of Kerala. The Portuguese and the Mughals almost immediately came to blows. By 1510, the Portuguese had returned with a larger fleet and more troops, and they eventually conquered Goa under the leadership of Afonso de Albuquerque.

In around 1600, British traders set their sights on this lucrative territory, hoping to take advantage of India's major natural resources, as the Portuguese had been doing for more than a century. After establishing the East India Company, the British held a major presence in the subcontinent for over 250 years, until the queen personally took charge of the region during the high tide of European colonialism.

By the mid-1800s, the "British Raj" considered India to be the jewel of their crown, although they were often shocked by what they witnessed there. One issue that horrified them was the practice of **sati**—or widow burning. This was a custom wherein a widow would throw herself onto her husband's funeral pyre out of a deep sense of loyalty to him. The British were also outraged by the practice of **child marriage**, in which young people were betrothed at a very early age. While child marriage continues to receive scrutiny in India, **arranged marriage** is still common; it is estimated to be practiced by over 90 percent of the population. All of these issues must be looked at in context by Western readers who often do not understand the historical reasons for why various cultural practices have emerged. For example, while Westerners tend to marry relatively late in life, often after experiencing a plethora of partners, Indians marry at a comparatively young age, since dating a wide variety of people is not traditionally practiced before marital commitments. Similarly, Indian marriages rarely end in divorce. India has

one of the lowest divorce rates in the world, whereas divorce in the Western world is common—somewhere around 50 percent, depending on the nation. On a cultural level, divorce in the Western world has lost much of its former taboo. In India, however, divorce is still seen as potentially disastrous for a couple.

Recent Hindu Responses to Foreign Rule

Achieved in 1947, Indian independence was a long sequence of events with many heroes whose lives are honored in street names, institutions, and fantastic monuments. Two of the most important individuals in that sequence of events are Ram Mohan Roy and Mohandas Gandhi.

Ram Mohan Roy (1772–1833) rose up as part of the Bengali Renaissance in Calcutta (now Kolkata), which was at that time the capital city of British India. Ram Mohan Roy founded the **Brahmo Samaj**, a social reform movement that became hugely influential on several generations of Indians who worked toward self-rule. He deftly argued to his compatriots that the

Portrait of the social and religious reformer Ram Mohan Roy by an unknown Indian artist. Delhi (1820).

only way to beat the British was to learn English well and to show the British that Indians were as sophisticated and competent as the British were, in every way. He is a polarizing figure today, as some believe he went too far in trying to Anglicize Indian society. Religiously, he painted Hinduism as a monotheistic religion, and he even criticized Christianity for not being monotheistic enough (i.e., the Trinity). He became very influential among Western elites who respected him and honored him publicly in England for his work. He became attached to the **Unitarian** movement, which was popular at the time among Indologists and religious pluralists who emphasized the unity of all religions under a rather abstract notion of God.

Mohandas Gandhi (1869–1948) is probably the best-known Hindu of modern times. He is beloved in India as **Mahatma**, or Great Soul. He is also known as Bapu, or Papa, as he is often characterized as the father of Indian **swaraj** (self-rule). Gandhi studied law in Britain and became a lawyer in South Africa

Portrait of Mohandas Gandhi, famous for his role in the liberation of India from British colonialism by means of nonviolent protest.

© Elliott & Fry, public domain

for two decades. In 1915 he returned to India and eventually became the great leader of Indian independence, which was finally achieved in 1947. Gandhi was profoundly affected by Jesus Christ's Sermon on the Mount, which, combined with Indian ideas of ahimsa (nonviolence), led him to become a pacifist. Gandhi's genius was his persistence in requesting the British to leave India yet always maintaining a position of nonviolence.

Gandhiji (the ending of –ji is used to show respect to an elder in Indian society) believed in an India based on the principles of religious pluralism. Gandhi's hopes were dashed when, upon Indian independence, the nation was split into India and Pakistan along religious lines.

Gandhi's idea of a religiously pluralistic India has come under critique since around 2000 with the rise of the **Hindutva** (Hindu-ness) movement. Between Indian independence in 1947 and the early twenty-first century, the **Indian National Congress** party was the dominant political party in the nation. For many years the Indian National Congress was led by Gandhi, Jawaharlal Nehru, and their descendants. The Indian National Congress was a party that emphasized religious pluralism and tolerance. In the 1980s, however, a more nationalistic movement began gaining traction; it was known as the **Bharatiya Janata Party** (Indian People's Party, or the BJP). Over the years, the BJP continued to rise up, and in 2014, it won a landslide victory under the leadership of Narendra Modi and is today a formidable political party in India. The BJP is seen to emphasize Hindu-ness more than the pluralistic Indian National Congress did, and only time will tell which direction India will gravitate: toward more religious plurality and accommodation or toward a more Hindutva identity.

Unitarianism · emphasizes the unity of all religions under an abstract notion of God

Mohandas Gandhi · leader of the Indian independence movement

Mahatma · "Great Soul," an epithet of Gandhi

Swaraj · self-government

Hindutva · "Hindu-ness," a current Hindu nationalist movement in India

Indian National Congress · the political party that governed India from 1947 to the early twenty-first century

Bharatiya Janata Party · the formidable nationalist party in India that adheres strongly to Hindutva

HINDU LEADERS

Two other important nineteenth century Hindu leaders were **Sri Ramakrishna Paramahamsa** (1836–86) and **Swami Vivekananda** (1863–1902).

Ramakrishna was a Hindu priest from Kolkata who worshiped Kali. He came to believe that God could be worshiped in many different ways, including the worship of Allah or of Jesus Christ. According to Ramakrishna, God is one, and no matter who one might worship, one is actually worshiping the one true God who unites and transcends religions.

Ramakrishna's most famous disciple was Vivekananda, a Hindu monk who came to the United States in 1893 and spread his master's teaching at the monumental **World's Parliament of Religions**. He made a huge impression on the elites of US society, such as William James and Max Müller. US audiences had little knowledge of Hinduism, and they were ecstatic to hear this articulate and impressive sannyasin. Vivekananda stole the show and wowed the United States' educational elite, especially at a time when ideas on universalism and religious tolerance were highly fashionable.

Group photo taken on January 30, 1887. Swami Vivekananda stands third from the left with other disciples of Ramakrishna. Baranagar Math, a monastery in Kolkata, India.

Sri Ramakrishna Paramahamsa · taught that God is one, and though people may worship in different religions, they are all actually worshiping the one true God who unites and transcends religions

Swami Vivekananda · a Hindu monk who influentially spread Hinduism in the West by teaching at the World's Parliament of Religions

World's Parliament of Religions · conferences designed to facilitate a global dialogue on faith

Holi · a holiday to welcome spring and promote fertility, celebrated with lively colors; associated with Krishna and his consort, Radha

Festivals in Hinduism Today

There are many Hindu festivals and important pilgrimages that take place throughout the year in India, often based on a god such as Rama, Shiva, Krishna, or Ganesh. The great heartland of Indian celebration is the holy Ganges River, which runs from the Tibetan Himalayas to the Bay of Bengal in Bangladesh. Indians all over the subcontinent can be found celebrating at any given time. Below are only a handful of Hindu celebrations.

Holi is to welcome spring and is connected to fertility. This two-day celebration is associated with Krishna's love for his consort, Radha. It is a playful holiday wherein people throw colored powder and water all over each other. Bonfires are lit during Holi, beckoning people to gather and dance.

Diwali is probably the best-known Hindu festival in the West. This five-day celebration is known as the "festival of lights," and it indicates the victory of goodness over evil and light over dark. It occurs in October or November, and it is often connected to the goddesses Kali and Lakshmi or with Rama and Sita's return to Ayodhya after exile.

The largest gathering of humans in the world is always the Hindu pilgrimage **Kumbh Mela**. It is held every four years; however, each twelfth year, known as the **Maha Kumbh Mela**, is a massive, auspicious gathering. Tens of millions of people attend these gatherings at the important riverbank sites of **Allahabad/Prayag** (where the Ganges and Yamuna Rivers meet in Uttar Pradesh), **Haridwar** (on the Ganges River in Uttarakhand), **Nashik** (on the Godavari River in Maharashtra), and **Ujjain** (on the

Fireworks light the sky to celebrate Diwali (2012).

Shipra River in Madhya Pradesh). The pilgrimage is associated with the cleansing of sins, as at the end of the celebration the participants all enjoy a celebratory bath in the river. The pilgrimage can last up to three months. The dates for the Kumbh Mela are based on Indian astrology.

Death Rituals in Hinduism

In Hinduism, there are three possibilities for what happens after death. A person can simply be reborn, he or she can achieve moksha on rare occasions, or the person can achieve reunion with ancestors, as outlined in the Vedas. All three outcomes are widely attested in Hinduism at various times and in various schools of thought.

Death rituals are crucial for Hindus, and there are stages for how to handle the dying and the dead with proper care and reverence. Traditionally, the dying should be laid on the ground while chanted scriptures help them focus on God. After death, the body is washed, dressed, and carried from the home to the funeral pyre for cremation. The skull is cracked by the eldest surviving son to release the soul. If the heat of the fire does not crack the skull, then it is usually cracked forcibly with a long bamboo stick. Afterwards, the remains are placed into a sacred river, the most holy being the Ganges, or Mother Ganga.

A woman is not considered a widow until the skull of her husband has cracked open, as that means the soul has left. The eldest son in charge of the rituals must circumambulate the corpse alongside the priest in charge. Chants and prayers are performed to ensure the spirit of the deceased passes on its proper journey. A few groups can be buried in Hinduism,

Diwali · the Hindu Festival of Lights, celebrating the victory of goodness and light over evil and dark; connected to the goddesses Kali and Lakshmi or with Rama and Sita's return to Ayodhya after exile

Kumbh Mela · the largest gathering of humans in the world; a pilgrimage every four years to sacred rivers for the cleansing of sins

Maha Kumbh Mela · a massive, most auspicious Kumbh Mela celebrated every twelfth year

Allahabad · also known as **Prayag**, where the Ganges and the Yamuna Rivers meet in Uttar Pradesh; a pilgrimage site for Kumbh Mela

Haridwar · a pilgrimage site for Kumbh Mela on the Ganges River in Uttarakhand

Nashik · a pilgrimage site for Kumbh Mela on the Godavari River in Maharashtra

Ujjain · a pilgrimage site for Kumbh Mela on the Shipra River in Madhya Pradesh

Holi, the Hindu Festival of Colors, pictured in Barsana, India.

Kumbh Mela gathering in Nashik, India, as huge crowds bathe in the river Godavari.

such as lepers, children, and some sadhus (holy men), but the vast majority are cremated.

The fire god Agni receives the fire offering. After cremation, some bones and fragments remain, which are typically placed in the river.

Following cremation, rice balls—representing the temporary body of the deceased—are offered as gifts to funeral priests who often assist at the rituals. The rice ball represents an ancestor and is treated with reverence—often, even a small altar is set up for the rice ball. Water and sesame seeds are poured onto the rice ball for around ten days. This assures a smooth transition from the status of a ghost to the status of an ancestor.

Despite the strong notion of reincarnation, or transmigration of the soul, Hindus have a developed notion of ancestors that is alluded to frequently in the Vedas. There is also a notion of heaven for the righteous and hell for those who lived lives full of sin and irresponsibility. Hell is a spiritual place presided over by the god Yama, the god of death, who metes out justice. Hell

befalls bad people, especially people who disregard the death rituals of the Vedas. Even people in hells, heavens, and ancestor realms eventually become reborn, preferably as humans, so they can attempt moksha in their next life.

In Hinduism, as well as in several Eastern approaches to death, there is the idea that one can have a good death. A person can prepare for his or her own death by fasting and drinking holy water from a particular river. As the person nears death, the body becomes weakened, allowing the spirit to leave more easily. In Hinduism, death is a kind of voluntary offering of the body to the gods.

One should not cling to life. Death should be smooth and willing, like a sacrifice. Those who have "good" deaths are said to burn easier. In popular belief, an easy cremation is desired—almost self-igniting, with a divine glow. Bad deaths, by contrast, yield bodies that turn black like tar and resist burning. A good death, however, is a kind of final sacrifice for that particular life.

4 JAINISM
Do No Harm

© Daniel J. Rao, iStock

Lay devotees at a Jain Digambar temple. During the religious period known as Caturmas, Jain living saints, the acharyas, stop wandering because of the monsoons. These devotees are trying to entice the acharyas to have food cooked in their kitchens. It is an honor if a particular devotee's food is picked by an acharya. Ajmer, India (2011).

There are around five million Jains in the world, the vast majority of them living in India. They are not even one-half of 1 percent of India's population, making them very small in comparison with the other major religions of India: Hinduism (80 percent), Islam (14 percent), Christianity (2–3 percent), Sikhism (1–2 percent), and Buddhism (0.7 percent). Their presence, however, is ancient and important.

Jainism is known for its emphasis on **ahimsa**, or nonviolence. Perhaps a better definition for the Jain understanding of ahimsa would be "noninjury." Jains go to great lengths to avoid hurting any living things. Jainism was a major influence on Mohandas Gandhi's decision to use peaceful, non-injurious means in the struggle he led for independence from Great Britain.

A Jain woman participating in a ritual offering of rice, almonds, fruit, and money while reading from a Jain text.

A Shvetambara monk in Ahmedabad, India, holds a votive candle in his temple.

Jains are also known for their commitment to ethical living, which has led to them being highly educated, wealthy, and well-respected. In India, Jains lead in several categories, according to the Indian National Census. For example, Jains are, by far, the most literate people in Indian society today, whether male or female. They have a 94 percent literacy rate, followed by Christians, who have a literacy rate of 80 percent. Jains have fewer children than any religious group in India, which is understandable given a clear, worldwide correlation between higher rates of education and lower fertility. Jains are the likeliest of all Indians to graduate from college. The combined Jain emphases on

Ahimsa · nonviolence or noninjury toward any living thing; one of the Five Great Vows of Jainism

Top view of Shikharji Temple, one of the most visited Jain pilgrimage sites. Parasnath Hills, India.

celibacy, self-restraint, and education have the result of lowering their fertility rates.

Jain women are, by far, the least likely people to have jobs in India. They tend to remain in the home, looking after the family. Only 9 percent of Jain women attain jobs outside the home. That is far lower than the Indian average of 26 percent for female employment. In contrast, Jain men are the likeliest group in India to be employed. In India—a country where the vast majority of jobs are in farming—Jains are rarely found in that industry. This is due to their strict avoidance of harming living creatures.[1]

Jainism can be summarized in three words: do no harm. For example, many people in the world claim to be vegetarian, but Jains take it to another level. Jains do not even want to harm microscopic creatures. They eat vegetables, with the realization that vegetables, too, have

> To the outside observer, Jainism appears to be much like Hinduism. However, it was founded as a reaction movement to primarily two things: the authority of the Vedas, and the caste system—led by the Brahmin caste, whom the early Jains resented.

life in them, although they do not have nearly as much sentience as animals. Jains do not eat root vegetables such as potatoes, onions, and carrots because those plants tend to have more bacteria attached to them underneath the ground. By uprooting those plants, many insects and other living creatures will be exposed and probably die. Thus, the most responsible thing to do is live and let live. In other words, live life, but do not kill someone or something.

This is one reason that the most revered death in Jainism is the concept of **Sallekhana**, or self-starvation, also known as **holy death**. Jains do not consider this to be a form of suicide, which is usually associated with depression, hopelessness, violence, or spontaneity. Rather, Sallekhana is noble, measured, and something that only the most clear-eyed and righteous Jains participate in. It is a gradual state. First, the person stops eating, taking only milk. Eventually, the milk stops and only water is taken. As weakness sets in, the person stops drinking water. Usually around the one-month

Sallekhana · also known as **holy death**, a noble and righteous death by self-starvation, proving full victory over attachment and violence

Jina · a conqueror; one who has overcome earthly attachment and achieved moksha

Tirthankara · "ford finders"; twenty-four Jain leaders who discovered the way out of samsara and taught others to do the same; the first twenty-two are probably mythical

Parshva · the twenty-third Tirthankara and the first for whom we have historical information; an ascetic who purportedly revived Jainism when it was in decline

mark, the person meditates into death. It is a triumph for Jains, and those who die this way are true **Jinas**, or victors. True victory over one's attachments is achieved in Sallekhana. Any time humans eat any kind of food, there is the notion that something had to die. When Jains completely forego food, they make the decision to put their religious faith first and to achieve a complete renunciation of violence.

Jain Religious Communities

In Jain temples, one will often find twenty-four statues of important founders of Jainism. These men were known as **Tirthankaras**, or "ford finders." A ford is a shallow part of a river, where a person can walk across successfully without danger of drowning. The Tirthankaras were supposedly actual people who reached moksha. In other words, they "found the ford" in the river and showed people how to cross the river of reincarnation and escape the perpetual cycle of samsara. These Tirthankaras were the great leaders of Jainism.

The twenty-third Tirthankara was named **Parshva**, and the twenty-fourth Tirthankara was named **Mahavira** ("Great Hero" or "Great Man"). Parshva and Mahavira are the only Tirthankaras for whom we have any solid historical information. Even Parshva's historicity has been doubted by some, but most scholars think he probably lived between 800 BCE and 600 BCE. In the iconography, Parshva is depicted as having a cobra's hood stretched out over his head or sometimes as being a snake with many heads. He is purported to have revived Jainism at a time when it was in decline. He rejected the normal life of a householder and lived a path of **asceticism** to achieve moksha. It

Mahavira · "great hero" or "great man"; the twenty-fourth and final Tirthankara who achieved moksha through extreme asceticism and ahimsa

Asceticism · self-denial or the infliction of self-harm to rid oneself of attachment and earthly desires

Statue of Parshva, the twenty-third Tirthankara, from the Navagraha Temple. Karnataka, India (2018).

is said that he did not require **celibacy** for his followers, nor did he require the monks to go naked (or sky-clad). Having become a conqueror, a Jina, he died in the modern state of **Jharkhand**, in eastern India. The pilgrimage site of **Shikharji**, a mountainous region in Jharkhand, is one of the holiest sites for Jains, as it is said to be the place where twenty of the twenty-four Tirthankaras attained moksha.

The twenty-fourth Tirthankara was Mahavira, who lived in the 500s BCE. This period has been referred to as the **Axial Age**, a pivotal era in human history when great thinkers were creating new world religions and striving for a higher consciousness. Many of these religions had ideas that paralleled or influenced one another. Mahavira was alive at the same time as the **Buddha**, **Confucius**, **Lao Tzu**, and **Jeremiah**. Mahavira is the focal point of Jainism today, and his life will be discussed in greater detail below.

Jain nuns in meditation.

Photographer: Claude Renault, (CC BY 2.0)

Jainism is usually categorized into two groups that disagree on several key aspects of Mahavira's life and teachings. Both these monastic communities have monks and nuns: the **Shvetambaras** ("white-clad") and the **Digambaras** ("sky-clad"). While the two communities share a belief in the same five vows, they have considerable differences in how to practice the faith, particularly in the monastic/ascetic communities. They differ on the life of their founder, Mahavira, and they also differ on what should be considered scripture. Perhaps the most conspicuous differences, however, have to do with clothing and female monastics.

Shvetambara monks and nuns always wear white and are considered less strict than Digambaras, who renounce clothing. Shvetambaras do not insist on nudity for their ascetic communities. The Shvetambaras also believe that women can attain moksha in this life. They are, by far, the larger group. Nuns outnumber monks by about three to one in the Shvetambara

The Jack Daulton Collection / Photographers: Marty Kelly and Don Tuttle

Vimalanatha, the thirteenth Tirthankara, who, in Jain iconography, is shown with golden skin and whose symbol is the boar. Unknown artist, Rajasthan, India (ca. first half of the twentieth century).

Photographer: John E. Cort, MAVCOR

Shvetambar worshippers use the affixed, jeweled eyes of icons to project themselves by meditation into the presence of the living Jina. Digambars disagree with this practice, thinking that it mistakenly focuses on the external, material world. The eyes of their icons are empty and encourage inward reflection on one's own soul.[2] North Gujarat, India.

Jain Digambara monk following deliberate extraction of hair from scalp and face (kaya klesh) by hand at a temple in Ajmer, Rajasthan, India (2011).

tradition. In the Digambara tradition, monks out-number nuns by about three to one. Jainism is such a small religion that the entire monastic class is only in the thousands, perhaps around ten thousand total. Around 80 percent of the world's Jains are Shvetambar; the remaining 20 percent are Digambar.[3]

Digambaras are more conservative, and their monks do not wear clothing. The Digambaras claim that Mahavira was naked; thus, their males live naked. Living without clothes shows that one is not attached to the physical world. It is a clear sign that one has officially become unattached to all things, even clothes. Nakedness also shows no shame, which is a form of attachment to the opinions of others. This is important to Digambaras because they believe salvation only occurs when one detaches from all things. Digambaras claim that only true, male monks—unattached to everything, including clothes—will achieve moksha. Women can only hope to be reborn as men before they can try to attain moksha. Digambara nuns

do not live naked. Rather, they wear white, much like the Shvetambara nuns.

Digambara monastics carry only three items with them: (1) a **picchi**, a broom made of fallen peacock feathers to swipe away insects that might get crushed; (2) a pot of sterilized water; and (3) a religious book or manuscript.

Jain monks and nuns are usually found in smaller monastic communities consisting of only a few ascetics, rather than in larger communities, as is common in Buddhism, for example. Jain monks live difficult, austere lives. Once they commit to being a monk or nun, they

Jeremiah · a Jewish prophet; contemporary with Mahavira

Shvetambaras · "white-clad"; one of the two major branches of Jain monastics that allow clothing and believe that women can achieve moksha in this life

Digambaras · "sky-clad" (a euphemism for naked); one of the two major branches of Jain monastics that renounce clothing and believe women cannot achieve moksha in this life

Picchi · a broom made of fallen peacock feathers to swipe away insects that might get crushed

are to remain in strict solitude for most of their lives, following an extreme form of religious observation, worshiping the Tirthankaras, refraining from negative thoughts or actions, and being highly careful in their religious practices. The rigorous practices of Digambara monks are some of the most extreme in the world's religions. They must not wear clothes, bathe, or brush their teeth. They sleep on the hard ground, eat standing up, eat one meal a day, and pluck hair by hand. By rigorous observance, they hope to achieve Jina status.

After obtaining permission from their parents to become ascetics, the Jain monastic initiation ceremony involves renouncing everything and everyone. Then they complete a painful and public rite of passage called kaya klesh—having their hair plucked out of their head. They commit to a life without electricity, telephones, or any other modern conveniences. They do not eat after sunset; indeed, Digambara monastics eat only one meal per day, and that meal is extremely regulated as to what can and cannot be consumed. Fasting is common for Jain monks and nuns. They fast for various periods of time throughout the year—sometimes for up to ten days. If a Jain monk or nun breaks one of the teachings of Mahavira, he or she will likely enter into a fasting period. Jain monastics typically rise before sunrise and focus their entire lives on the teachings of their faith. They are permitted absolutely no carnal relations.

Lay Jains provide the monastics with food, and in return, the monks and nuns offer religious teaching and advice. The ascetics are deeply respected in Jainism, and confession of sins to a Jain monk or nun is a common practice. Laypeople often give of their wealth to benefit the religion—for instance, in the building and caretaking of Jain temples, some of which are quite ornate and expensive to construct. Jain laypeople also tend to imitate the monastics for short periods of time, and they are obligated to take the first three of the Five Great Vows of Jainism: nonviolence (ahimsa), truthfulness, and no stealing. The last two vows—no sex and no attachment—are for the ascetics, although laypeople abide by them for certain periods of time.

The Life of Mahavira

Mahavira was born in what we know today as the modern state of Bihar in India. According to Digambara tradition, he was born in 599 BCE and died at age seventy-two, in 527 BCE. He was the son of a wealthy raja, or ruler. They were members of the Kshatriya caste. The Shvetambaras and Digambaras differ on key aspects of Mahavira's life. Shvetambaras say that Mahavira married and had a daughter. However, the Digambaras believe women are a temptation and that Mahavira never violated the vow of chastity. Thus, Digambaras argue that he never married.

Whatever the case, Mahavira was unhappy in his youth. As a prince, he found the life of luxury to be compromising, burdensome, and lacking meaning. He wanted out, but he did not want to offend his parents. His parents died while he was in his twenties, freeing him to make his own decisions.

Thus, at the age of thirty, Mahavira became a wandering ascetic, following the teachings of Parshva, the twenty-third Tirthankara, whom his parents had also followed. Mahavira was now on the path of an ascetic, committed full-time to gaining spiritual knowledge and renouncing the world and its temptations.

Mahavira concluded that the only ways to become liberated from samsara were: (1) extreme ascetic living and (2) ahimsa (noninjury to all living things). The biographies of Mahavira tell us that he tore off his beard and hair, rid himself of all clothing, and lived naked at all times, even when it was cold. He did everything in his power to avoid stepping on insects. He even swept the road in front of his steps when he walked so as not to hurt any living thing. He would strain his water so he would not ingest any small insects. He spent twelve years punishing himself through extreme deprivation, almost dying on several occasions. He lived in silence and fasted often. He would not speak to anyone so as not to become attached to them. He would only spend one night in a place to avoid familiarity with anything.

Then, after living this way for twelve years, Mahavira conquered everything—the need for people, the need

Kaya klesh · a public rite of passage in which Jain monastics are initiated by having their hair plucked out of their head

Kevala jnana · total understanding or omniscience; achieved by a Jina who has attained moksha

Image of sitting Mahavira. Mumbai, India (2020).

for shelter, and even the need for clothes. He claimed to attain moksha—freedom from rebirths. He called himself a Jina, a Jain, a conqueror. In Jainism, the term **Kevala jnana** is often used to describe what happened when Mahavira "conquered." It is an expression that means total understanding, or omniscience. According to Jain philosophy, the original and purest state of the human soul is omniscience, but as karma is acquired, our souls take on layers of particles that weigh our souls down, keeping them locked in samsara.

After attaining Kevala jnana, Mahavira began to search for people whom he could teach. He was around forty-three years of age at that point. He traveled around India, teaching these ideas for about thirty years before achieving complete victory through fasting—Sallekhana. This

Originally, this white-marble statue of the Jain goddess Sarasvati had four arms. She is known among Jains, Hindus, and Buddhists alike as the goddess of knowledge, learning, speech, poetry, and music. Artist: Jagadeva. Gujarat, India (twelfth century).

is the holiest death for Jains—showing complete control over one's desires, even to the point of death by starvation. During those three decades of his ministry, he acquired thousands of disciples, both ascetic and lay. Some estimates are that he may have had fifty thousand ascetic followers by the time of his death, as well as possibly hundreds of thousands of lay followers.

A Challenge to Hinduism

While Mahavira rejected the Hindu scriptures, his teachings were passed orally for decades until they were eventually written down and collected, although in two different forms, according to the two different schools of Jainism—Digambara and Shvetambara. There are subsects of Jains, too, according to other important gurus and Jinas that came along throughout history.

Mahavira's thinking contrasted with Hinduism in several key ways. First of all, he rejected the Hindu notion of caste, and his disciples followed his lead in this stance. It is ironic that the Jains would, in time, begin to become caste-conscious once again, as if the caste system is simply too difficult to overcome in India. Their understanding of caste is slightly different from that of Hindus: it is based on which gurus are followed, rather than on occupations, as in Hinduism.

Jains in Austin, Texas, before an image of Mahavira (2018).

Nonetheless, most Jains have inherited a caste consciousness to one degree or another.

Mahavira also spoke against the Hindu gods and the scriptures about those gods. He said liberation could not be obtained through worshiping Hindu gods or through studying the Vedas. Only the individual could liberate himself! Mahavira did not even believe in a creator. It is ironic that later he became a divine incarnation in the minds of many of his followers. It is difficult to say with certainty whether Jains are theistic or atheistic. Many Jains believe that while there are gods and demons, they too are in the cycle of samsara; thus, they are not necessarily in a better situation than humans. Similarly, animals, microbes, and plants are also in samsara. Everyone and everything dies and is reborn.

While Jains do not venerate gods or demons, they are extremely devoted to venerating the Tirthankaras and other worthy individuals who have proven themselves victorious and omniscient due to burning off all karma. Since Mahavira is recognized as the twenty-fourth Tirthankara, his followers revere him in a way that can perhaps only be compared to the way members of theistic religions worship their deities.

As in Hinduism and Buddhism, Mahavira also believed in the notion of **karma** ("action" or "deed"), but he had a nuanced understanding of it. He argued that there were two substances in reality: (1) the soul (**jiva**), which is living, and (2) matter (**ajiva**), nonliving things. Jains think of karma as a sticky substance around the soul, like a kind of weight that keeps one down. The more accumulation of karma, the more entrenched one is in samsara—the cycle of life, death, and rebirth. The more karma one has, the lower form one will take in rebirth. The goal of life is to liberate jiva from ajiva, or to liberate the soul from the material world.

Mahavira emphasized often that religious rituals, texts, and gods were ultimately useless. Separating jiva from ajiva is only something a human can do individually. One has to become a rigid, committed, ascetic monk to get rid of all attachments and karma. One must experience prolonged hunger, thirst, pain, heat,

Karma · a sticky substance that accumulates around the soul and weighs that soul down, keeping it entrenched in samsara

Jiva · the soul; all living things

Ajiva · matter; all nonliving things

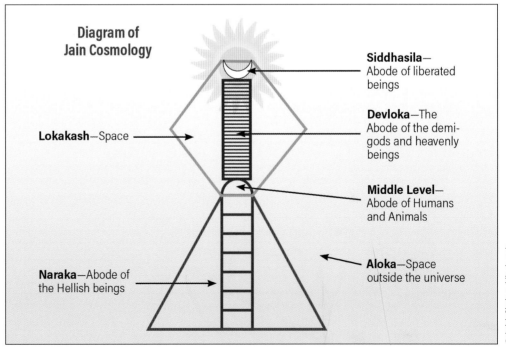

Diagram of Jain Cosmology

Lokakash—Space

Siddhasila—Abode of liberated beings

Devloka—The Abode of the demi-gods and heavenly beings

Middle Level—Abode of Humans and Animals

Aloka—Space outside the universe

Naraka—Abode of the Hellish beings

and cold. One also meditates and studies, but the more pain one puts oneself through, the more karma one will burn. By burning more karma, one will be removing the karmic buildup around one's soul, thus allowing someone to eventually be free of all attachment and defilement. Physical pain is preferable to studying scriptures or meditating if one wants to burn karma. When all accumulated karma from all of one's previous lives has been burned, then the soul can attain moksha.

Jains believe that there are many who will never be able to accomplish moksha. They will be reborn eternally. Only the few will reach liberation. It is not something that is expected. It requires dogged commitment and much pain through rigorous fasting and deprivation.

If one does reach liberation (moksha), then one will shed all physicality and will go to the top of the universe, where the liberated souls live. This realm is unique. It is a realm of no individuality. Everything is invisible and intangible. One who reaches this state is called a **siddha**, or "one who is accomplished." They are also known as Jinas ("conquerors"), as they victoriously conquered karma. This is where we get the term *Jain*, or *Jina*. The realm of the siddhas is blissful and completely identical, as all individuality ceases there. Those who make it there have been purified and thus are considered to be perfected.

The Five Great Vows of Jainism

While many people call these important teachings the five vows, some prefer to call them the five abstinences, because they are essentially sanctions on human conduct. Monks and nuns have to follow them strictly. Laypeople must observe them in various ways, but not as strictly. For example, laypeople do not have to be completely abstinent. They are allowed to marry. However, there are times when they might commit to a period of chastity within the marriage.

Nonviolence (ahimsa)—noninjury to all living things. This is the most important Jain teaching. It is first and foremost in all things. Ahimsa plays out in many ways, such as sweeping in front of one's steps; wearing a mask to avoid inhaling insects; completely avoiding meat products or anything associated with killing, such as

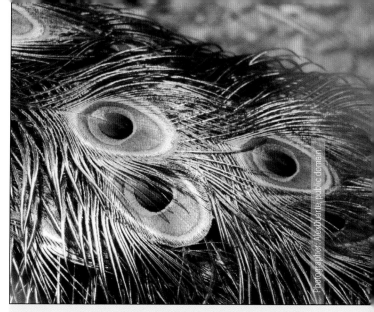

Digambara monks carry peacock feathers bound together into a broom to sweep insects away from their feet as they walk. Peacock feathers fall naturally from the bird, so no creature is harmed in their collection.

restaurants, pots, and pans that might have been used to cook meat; and straining water before drinking to avoid ingesting insects. Jains are so careful to avoid injury that they will not even kill rats during an infestation. But this teaching goes beyond the physical realm; Jains are careful to avoid causing injury during conversation, leading them to speak less than most people. They also must avoid hurtful thoughts toward people.

Truth (satya)—avoiding all falsity, lies, and everything associated with dishonesty. Typically, this leads to very little talking because Jains also recognize that all truth is relative. Jains are also inclined to see all sides of an issue rather than embrace only one perspective. In cases when telling the truth might hurt someone, Jains choose silence. Indeed, many falsehoods are rooted in a form of violence. Thus, **satya** and ahimsa are related. When people slander or lie, they are often attempting to inflict damage on another person's reputation.

Stealing (asteya)—a person must not steal anything. Other people's possessions are completely off limits. Jains have become known as trustworthy people because they must not entertain the possibility of taking something that is not theirs. Even wanting

Siddha · "one who is accomplished"; someone who has attained moksha; a Jina

Satya · truth; one of the Five Great Vows of Jainism; avoiding all falsity, lies, and everything associated with dishonesty

Plate from a Digambara Temple in South Mumbai shows Mahavira accepting alms from lay practitioners (ca. 1820).

relations outside of marriage are unthinkable for most Jains; they are particularly harmful due to the buildup of karma.

Possessiveness (Aparigraha)—attachment to possessions is forbidden in Jainism. Monks and nuns own nothing in the Digambara tradition. Shvetambars can only have a few possessions to aid their spiritual development. Jain laypeople must be careful to observe **Aparigraha**, yet in a less severe way. For example, Jain businesspeople must not charge harmful prices, as disproportionate prices are usually linked to possessiveness of something (money) that someone else has. Jains must not take something that has been dropped onto the ground; they must either return it to the owner or else leave it there. Some have argued that Aparigraha is a chief reason for Jain success. People trust Jains, so they want to do business with them. In textile, jewelry, and finance, Jain businesses prosper and often even dominate certain markets. They do everything they can to avoid greed, and people pick up on this quality of theirs, leading others to seek out Jains when it is time to make a major investment. Aparigraha also has to do with the health of an individual's soul. If people get attached to something in this life, then they will not enter moksha. Those who have anger, pride, or greed are probably attached to something in an unhealthy way. This prevents them from achieving inner freedom.

In the history of Jainism, it was understood that only the monks could follow these vows in a way that would lead to moksha. Thus, the laity were given a less rigorous set of rules, with the awareness that they would not achieve moksha in this life. It is important to note that they had to follow the first three vows: ahimsa, truthfulness at all times, and no stealing, but they were allowed to marry as long as they were committed to their spouse and only had relations in that approved context.

Jains are to practice the avoidance of greed (linked to Aparigraha), and they are to give away any of the excess. Typically, they avoid farming because of the impact that it has on insects and instead choose careers in banking, teaching, and law. Since they cannot harm any living thing, they often end up in highly skilled

what someone else has—known in the Western world as covetousness—is considered immoral. **Asteya** touches on many different areas. One must not sell imitation products. One must not receive stolen goods, so great care must be made to ensure that what one receives is genuine and given in good faith. One must not take advantage of someone during a sale—for example, when markets are in disarray. One must not use false or unclear measurements when transacting.

Chastity (brahmacharya)—this is the best way to live for Jains. It is like Western notions of chastity, but not exactly the same. Chastity is refraining from sexual activity. **Brahmacharya** has more to do with controlling one's mind and actions through asceticism. However, most Jains are not ascetics. For Jain laypeople, sexual relations are allowed but must only take place within the confines of marriage. Premarital sex is absolutely forbidden in Jainism. Sexuality is particularly prone to attract karma in the Jain religion. This even applies to sexualized thoughts. Monks and nuns must be cautious to avoid anything that might lead to sexualized thinking. Sexual

Asteya · one of the Five Great Vows of Jainism; not stealing anything, whether by theft, extortion, imitation, or unclear measurements or transactions

Brahmacharya · chastity; one of the Five Great Vows of Jainism; purity of the mind and refraining from premarital or extramarital sex

Aparigraha · non-possessiveness; one of the Five Great Vows of Jainism; strictly avoiding all attachment, possessiveness, or greed

and professionalized industries. Many lay Jains have become wealthy, making them the wealthiest religious community in India. It is ironic that although Jainism began as an ascetic movement, its members are often quite affluent today.

Laypeople are also supposed to meditate; lead simple lives; occasionally go on short-term monastic retreats, wherein they live like monks for a short period; and, of course, give alms generously to the monks.

Jains do not have a developed theology due to the suspicion of truth claims and their non-theistic roots in Mahavira's teachings. They believe the universe has no beginning or end—it is infinite. They believe in the concept of a kalpa (a rotation of time), but they do not assign a specific length of time to it. Hindus, by contrast, teach that a kalpa lasts 4.32 billion years. Jains believe everything is eternal, whether spiritual or material. They conceive of the universe and all reality in the form of a wheel, constantly turning.

Jain Scriptures

Jains call their scriptures **Agamas**, which means "that which has come down." The word *Agama* is also used in Hinduism to describe teachings that were preserved and passed down from previous times.

Throughout history, the two major groups of Jains—Digambaras and Shvetambaras—have disagreed on what precisely is considered scripture. Both sides revere the teachings of Mahavira, but they do not agree on how they have been preserved, nor do they agree on what they think Mahavira said. Thus, there is much shared material in their canonical collections, but there have always been some key differences that have led to different traditions and divergent practices.

In 1974, a large group of Jains from many different Jain sects came together to discuss the possibility of a shared scripture. They were successful in their negotiations, and since then, the vast majority of Jains in the world share a scriptural text known as the **Saman Suttam**. The text is organized into forty-four chapters that cover everything from karma, transmigration, and nonviolence to monastic vows, meditation, and Sallekhana. The scripture ends with a hymn to Mahavira:

> Right knowledge is my shelter. Right faith is my shelter. Right conduct is my shelter. Austerity and self-restraint are my shelters. Bhagavan Mahavira is my shelter. Lord Mahavira was possessed of an all-comprehensive perception, possessed of a supreme knowledge, no taker of an improper meal, possessed of patience, possessed of

Agamas · "that which has come down"; the word used for Jain scriptures

Saman Suttam · a scriptural text that is shared by each of the Jain sects; organized into forty-four chapters on everything from karma, transmigration, and nonviolence to monastic vows, meditation, and Sallekhana

An excerpt of Jain scripture.

Jains in New York City gather for Paryushana, the most important Jain festival (2012).

In this Jain celebration of Diwali, votive candles are lit before an image of Mahavira (2019).

steadiness, the supreme learned man in the world, free from all possessions, free from fear, one not going to take another birth.

That supreme wise man lived in no permanent dwelling, had crossed over the flood-of-transmigration, had a limitless vision, shown in a supreme fashion as does the sun, produced light where darkness prevailed . . .

Let victory be to the Blessed one, Mahavira, who knows as to where the mundane souls take birth, who is a teacher and a source of joy to the whole world, who is the lord and the well-wisher of the universe, who is like a grandfather to the whole world.

Let victory be to the great soul Mahavira, who is the source of all scriptural texts, who is the last among Tirthankaras, who acts as teacher to all the world.[4]

Diwali · celebrated by Jains in commemoration of Mahavira achieving moksha

Paryushana · "coming together"; an annual eight-day festival in which lay Jains live as monastics; the most important festival of Jainism

The agreements and negotiations that led to the Saman Suttam have been especially useful because the history of Jain scripture is complex. For hundreds of years, the teaching of Mahavira was preserved orally. But due to various incidents, such as famines that left important monks dead and texts forgotten, the scriptures were not easily preserved. This is also why the two major monastic schools in Jainism disagree on what precisely constitutes scripture. To ameliorate these problems, ascetics from both traditions were permitted to keep religious texts, or at least have access to them. The decisions that led to the Saman Suttam in 1974 have preserved not the entirety of the Jain canon, but the essential teachings that virtually all Jains accept. In time, the Saman Suttam may prove to have a uniting impact for the religion.

Jain Festivals and Rituals

Jains are not particularly known for their corporate worship or rituals. They do celebrate certain festivals connected to the life of Mahavira. They have periods of fasting wherein all Jains are to live as if they were a monk for short periods. They also celebrate **Diwali** with Hindus, usually in October or November. However, instead of worshiping Kali or Lakshmi, they remember the liberation and Sallekhana of Mahavira. They light lamps during this festival of lights and take pilgrimages to important Jain sites and temples as well.

By far the most important annual festival for Jains is **Paryushana**, which means "coming together." During this eight-day period, they live as if they were monks by fasting, praying, reading scripture, and meditating.

They focus on their own shortcomings, and they emphasize the Five Great Vows of Jainism throughout the festival. They ask forgiveness from anybody whom they may have offended in the previous year. Some Indian states even put an official pause on slaughtering any animals during Paryushana in observance of the central Jain idea of ahimsa.

Jains have several practices that are rather unique to them. To avoid committing any kind of harm to creatures, they live a life of great vigilance to honor the vow of ahimsa. They boil their water before drinking to allow any insects to escape during the warming of the water. They light a lamp and venerate images of the Tirthankaras, which they often keep in their homes.

Jains meditate each day in a ritual known as Samayika. The Samayika meditation lasts for forty-eight minutes and can be done one, two, or three times per day. The number forty-eight is significant because it is double the number of Tirthankaras. It involves clearing the mind, meditating on one's conduct, and detaching from anything that might lead to karmic accumulation.

When Jains perform Samayika, they recite the Namokara Mantra—the most significant mantra in the faith. Always recited in Sanskrit, this mantra is meant to destroy attachment and cultivate a deep respect for those who have conquered and have entered the realm of the siddhas. It is a prayer of humility in which the devotee vows to respect the monks, nuns, sages, and all teachers who are on the Jain path. No specific gods are mentioned, and there are no individual requests made. It is simply intended to show respect for those teachers who are leading the way toward liberation.

Photographer: Mpanchratan, (CC BY-SA 3.0)

The Jain Prateek Chihna, the official Jain symbol, adopted by all sects in 1975.

Jain funerals are unique. They always include the official Jain image, which was adopted in 1975 in commemoration of the two thousand five hundredth anniversary of Mahavira's death. The official Jain symbol is shaped as a human torso and has a swastika—an ancient symbol for Jains. Above the swastika are three dots that represent the Three Jewels of Jainism: right belief, right knowledge, and right conduct. Above the three dots is an arc with a dot inside of it that represents the realm of the siddhas—those who have conquered. The swastika itself represents the wheel of rebirth, and its four arms represent the male and female monastics, as well as the male and female laity. Below the swastika is a hand that represents openness. Inside the hand is a circle with the word *ahimsa* written in it, reminding all Jains to do no harm.

Other Jain funerary rituals are singing and scripture reading, eulogies, and the application of sandalwood powder, water, rice, and ghee. Flowers are not used since they might contain insects. A gold coin is put in the mouth of the deceased. A pearl is entered underneath the right eyelid. Forgiveness is then offered to the deceased, and the casket is closed. Cremation then occurs as soon as possible. The final rites are performed by the eldest son, as he recites the Namokara Mantra and lights the pyre with the deceased on it. Finally, milk is poured over the ashes. Whereas Hindus typically put the ashes in the nearby river, Jains put the ashes into a hole in the earth with salt applied to help break down whatever remains.

Jains believe that the soul of the deceased is reborn into a new body immediately; thus, the funerary rituals are a kind of rebirth. Wailing is uncommon at Jain funerals because of this outlook. Similarly, death anniversaries—common in other Indian traditions—are not observed in Jainism.

Samayika · a daily meditation ritual lasting forty-eight minutes (twice the number of Tirthankaras)

Namokara Mantra · the most significant mantra of Jainism; recited in Sanskrit and meant to destroy attachment and cultivate a deep respect for those who have conquered

Swastika · an ancient symbol representing the wheel of rebirth, with its four arms representing the male and female monastics, as well as the male and female laity

Three Jewels of Jainism · right belief, right knowledge, and right conduct

In 2020, more than 2,500 Japanese people traveled to India to learn from Jain teachers.

Jainism Today

Jains are often confused with Hindus, due to their many similarities. They share many practices with Hindus, such as bathing and venerating statues, meditation, and temple participation, and they assume many of the presuppositions that Hindus do, such as samsara, karma, and moksha. The differences can be subtle, but any Jain will say that the religions are not to be confused.

There are approximately 4.5 million Jains in India today. They have over forty thousand temples in India, wherein they worship the twenty-four Tirthankaras. Jains have tended to settle in the western states of Maharashtra, Rajasthan, Gujarat, Madhya Pradesh, and Karnataka.

Anekantavada · the many-sidedness of truth

JAINA · Federation of Jain Associations in North America; an ecumenical organization representing the Jains who have immigrated to North America

The Indian diaspora has meant that Jains have established themselves in other parts of the world, too, such as in East Africa, where an Indian minority has existed for generations, primarily for trade and business. There are around thirty-five thousand Jains in the United Kingdom. In Belgium, there are approximately one thousand five hundred Jains who have great influence in the diamond industry. The United States is home to roughly one hundred fifty thousand Jains, and they have erected around thirty temples there. They have formed an organization called **JAINA** (Federation of Jain Associations in North America), which has served as an ecumenical mechanism to bring together Shvetambaras and Digambaras into a united fellowship that downplays the distinctions between the two. Around ten thousand Jains have made Canada their home, primarily around Toronto.

Interestingly, thousands of Japanese people have converted to Jainism in recent years, due largely to the emphasis on ahimsa. The turbulence of the twentieth and twenty-first centuries has led many Japanese people to embrace nonviolence and peacemaking as core tenets of their identity. This has been a surprising development in the world of religion, as Jains are reluctant to propagate their faith to others because of the doctrine of **anekantavada**, or the "many-sidedness of truth." Nevertheless, many Japanese people have found the teachings of ahimsa to be uniquely attractive, and they have made journeys to India to celebrate Paryushana, to visit holy sites, and to formally convert.

For such a small and rather quiet religion, Jainism has made waves in the business world. Many important and multinational businesses have seen Jains rise to high leadership positions within them—for example, *The Times of India*, IndiGo airlines, Berkshire Hathaway, and Deutsche Bank. However, despite their success in many different professions, the defining characteristic of Jains will forever be in their deepest commitment to the concept of ahimsa, as they commit to do no harm in their daily lives.

5 BUDDHISM
Compassionate Nonattachment

Young Buddhist novices reading outside a monastery in Myanmar. Theravada Buddhists allow young men to become monks at age seven.

A famous parable in the study of Indian religions is known as the parable of the **blind men and the elephant**. We find this parable in Hinduism, Buddhism, and Jainism. The parable has been widely disbursed and is a helpful story for understanding different perspectives on the same object or phenomenon.

One of the earliest renditions of the story occurs in the *Udana*, an important Buddhist text written in the Pali language. The story was told by the Buddha to make an important point. The Buddha said there was a group of blind men who had never been around elephants. They were then introduced to the huge animal, except each one was only allowed to touch a specific part of the elephant before giving their explanation. One blind man who touched the head said the elephant felt like a large pot. Another who touched the tusk said the elephant felt like a plowshare. The one who touched the ear said it felt like a large basket. The one who touched the tail said it felt like a pestle, for crushing herbs in a bowl. The one who touched the tip of the tail said it felt like a brush. One touched the leg and said the elephant felt like a pillar. They all had extremely different ways of describing the elephant.

The men then fell into a heated argument, claiming each one was correct because they literally felt the animal, so their perspective must be accurate and all the other explanations must be badly mistaken.

The Buddha ended the upheaval by explaining that many teachers claim they have sole possession of the truth. They are ignorant of the fact that others have truly experienced a version of the truth, yet they continue to maintain that their own, limited understanding of the truth is the whole truth. The Buddha finally pointed out that each of the blind men simply quarrel out of ignorance, refusing to see the multi-sidedness of the truth. By refusing to open themselves to the experiences of the others, they deprive themselves. In short, all of the blind men were correct in their own way.

What is Buddhism? If the story of the blind men and the elephant is correct, then do we assume that all Buddhist teachers are actually right, since each of them has a slightly different explanation?

> **Blind men and the elephant ·** a parable that teaches that differing and even contradictory perspectives of the ultimate reality may actually be different ways of describing the same truth

© shoenberg3, Adobe Stock

© Steve46814, (CC BY-SA 3.0)

The Haeinsa Temple in South Korea has stored the whole of the Buddhist canon, the Tripitaka Koreana, carved onto 81,258 wooden printing blocks since 1398.

Some would claim that Buddhism is an extremely practical religion, simply a method of addressing the reality of suffering. The Buddha is often described as being a kind of physician. The diagnosis is that we all suffer. The Buddha provides the solution. To some, it is that simple. The Buddha provides the medicine to lessen our suffering. Therefore, Buddhism, in its most basic sense, is pain relief. However, as Buddhists advance in their comprehension of dukkha and its antidote, Buddhism becomes the cure.

Buddhism is misunderstood frequently in the West, since most of our exposure to it comes from the Mahayana schools of thought, which will be discussed shortly. For example, words like *karma*, *nirvana*, and

> Buddhism is misunderstood frequently in the West.

Zen are used often in the West but are completely misconstrued. Karma, for example, is often thought of as something in this life, but in Buddhism, karma impacts one's next life—one will be reborn into a life form that was determined by the karma one accumulated in the

previous life. **Nirvana** is often understood as a blissful state of existence. But many Buddhists understand nirvana as becoming extinct, or what one achieves when they extinguish all of their cravings and desires. Zen is a form of Chinese Buddhism that emphasizes one's relationship with their teacher. Phil Jackson, the legendary NBA coach, is often referred to as the "Zen master" due to his calm demeanor and his integration of Buddhist principles into coaching. However, he is not an actual Zen Buddhist master!

Origins

The Buddha's life was kept alive in oral traditions for about five hundred years until it was written down around the time of Christ. The precise dates of his life are disputed, but he lived somewhere around the 500s and 400s BCE. His followers generally agree that he died at the ripe age of eighty years old.

He was born in modern-day Nepal, in a region known today as Lumbini. His actual name was Siddhartha Gautama. He was born into the Gautama family, but the larger clan was known as the Shakyas. This is why many Buddhists refer to the Buddha as **Shakyamuni**, or the sage from the Shakya clan. His family was Kshatriya in the Indian caste system and thus were warriors and rulers.

Vishwa Shanti Stupa, a Buddhist monument in Rajgir, India.

Carving of the dream of Maya, the mother of the Buddha, in which a white elephant entered her womb as an omen of the future significance of her son. Indian Museum, Kolkata, India (100 BCE).

Buddhists believe that one night, Siddhartha's mother, named Maya, dreamed that a white elephant entered her womb through her side. The elephant had a white lotus flower in its trunk. Hindu priests were brought in to interpret this. They predicted the birth of a son who would be an important king or universal teacher.

Maya gave birth to Siddhartha while she was traveling to a nearby village to see her own parents. That site, in Nepal, is commemorated as a major pilgrimage site, with a pillar dedicated by King Ashoka (third century BCE), the most famous Buddhist ruler in history.

Gautama's mother died when he was only seven days old. He was put in the care of his aunt—Maya's sister—whom his father then married.

Siddhartha was brought up in luxury. He lacked nothing. He was the only son of his parents, and he was served by a legion of individuals at the family's three residences: one for summer, one for winter, and one for the monsoon season. He married his cousin Yasodhara when he was sixteen years old, and their son was named Rahula, which means "confined" or "unwanted." According to tradition, Siddhartha felt restricted by having a child. Eventually, however, Rahula became a Buddhist monk after training as a disciple in his father's religious community.

Siddhartha was about twenty-nine years old when he left his father's compound in what is often called "the Great Going Forth" in Buddhism. He experienced four sights that affected him tremendously, leading to his decision to leave his family and become an ascetic. These "four perceptions" were:

- Old age—an old man leaning on a staff to walk
- Sickness—a sick man in pain wallowing in his own feces
- Death—a human corpse being taken to the funeral pyre for cremation
- Monasticism—he saw an ascetic monk with a shaved head wearing a yellow robe. The monk's confidence and serenity attracted Siddhartha,

A painting from a temple in Laos depicting Siddhartha Gautama's encounter with the four perceptions.

as he lectured on compassion and nonviolence. Siddhartha immediately chose to devote himself to the life of a wandering ascetic.

The four sights profoundly impacted Siddhartha, changing the course of his life.

What is important is that Siddhartha's father, King Suddhodana, had sheltered him from all of this. Siddhartha had not seen anything like this before. So he returned to the palace and talked with his father about what he had seen and about his need to renounce and give himself to the religious life. His father argued with him in vain, and Siddhartha departed his father's kingdom, left his wife and son in the middle of the night, and determined to figure out how to escape such rampant suffering in the world. He departed with his horse as well as his charioteer, named Channa. This chapter of his life is known as "the Great Renunciation." The family was very sad that he left, but they were comforted by having Rahula around.

Siddhartha began his quest by exchanging clothes with a hunter in the woods. He pledged he would find out how to rid himself of suffering. He came to fully realize that suffering, or **dukkha**, is the central problem for humans. The word

Dukkha · suffering; dis-ease

A statue from an ascetic sect in Thailand portraying the Buddha emaciated from fasting.

dukkha is a Pali word that means several things in English: suffering, pain, anxiety, stress, misery, frustration, uneasiness, and an overall feeling of dissatisfaction. Some Buddhists define dukkha as "dis-ease."

For six years, Siddhartha struggled to figure out the solution to human suffering, or dukkha. He first went to a Hindu guru named Alara Kalama to learn meditation from him, but Siddhartha quickly mastered everything the guru could teach. Siddhartha then decided to learn from another expert named Uddaka Ramaputta, who helped his disciples dissolve their consciousness. Uddaka was so impressed with his new student that he offered to become Siddhartha's disciple! The major problem was that these Hindu gurus were unable to answer the question of why people suffer.

Siddhartha then moved on to try extreme asceticism by joining a strict religious community. This is interesting,

Bodhi tree · the tree under which the Buddha meditated until he achieved enlightenment

because Mahavira—a contemporary of the Buddha—tried extreme asceticism, and it worked well for him. Along with five other ascetics, Siddhartha tried the most amazing things: sleeping among corpses, living on a grain of rice a day, allowing filth to accumulate on his body, and putting himself through various forms of self-torture. He tried slowing down his breath to the point that he gave himself horribly painful headaches. His application of these rigorous disciplines caused his health to deteriorate until he was near death.

The traditional story is that, at this point, Siddhartha fell into a cold stream, which made him rethink everything, and he decided that he was not progressing in the quest for truth. After recovering, he realized that he had been wasting time during his six years of suffering. Nothing was gained. So he began to eat normally. He broke his intense fasting and his self-mortification. The five monks left him in disgust, assuming he had compromised. But the truth of the matter is that Siddhartha had discovered a middle path between the extremes of indulgence and asceticism.

Next, Siddhartha sat down at a tree—now known as the **Bodhi tree** (enlightenment tree)—a type of fig tree with heart-shaped leaves. That place is now one of the most famous Buddhist pilgrimage sites, located in modern-day Bodh Gaya, in Bihar, India. He sat there with his legs crossed and pledged not to move until he had figured out the antidote to suffering. At this point, a being named Mara offered three temptations:

- Mara first tempted him by telling him that everything at his home was in disarray and that his

Painting of a small Hindu temple beneath a tree in Bodh Gaya, India, by an anonymous artist (ca. 1810).

father was about to lose the kingdom. Siddhartha was unaffected.

- Mara then put three attractive women in front of Siddhartha, to tempt him. But he ignored them.
- Mara then summoned a host of demons to attack Siddhartha. Siddhartha touched the ground with the fingers on his right hand. It caused great thunder, and Mara and all of his demons became frightened and fled. Some say Mara was so impressed that, a bit later, he became a disciple of the Buddha.

Once Mara and his temptations were gone, Siddhartha meditated powerfully, in peace, thinking deeply about the nature of suffering. He went through many phases of thought and experienced numerous states of consciousness.

And then, all at once, everything was made clear to him. He instantaneously understood everything and all reality and all of existence. At the age of thirty-five, he solved the problem of suffering and how to be rid of suffering. Siddhartha was enlightened. This is why he is called the Buddha—the one who reached enlightenment. At the moment of enlightenment, he fully remembered all of his previous lives. He insisted that his followers call him Tathagata—the one who has gone into enlightenment.

Temple mural at Wat Chedi Liam, Thailand, depicting the Buddha's first sermon to his disciples.

Photographer: Kay Ess, (CC BY-SA 3.0)

Tathagata · a name for the Buddha, meaning "the one who has gone" into enlightenment

The Sangha—the Buddhist Community

For several weeks, the Buddha thought about whether he should share the message with others. He decided to tell others,

Detail of Yasodhara, the former wife of Siddhartha Gautama and the first female Buddhist monastic. Bangkok, Thailand.

Photographer: Anandajoti Bhikkhu, (CC BY 2.0)

A tenth-century illustration of Mara and his demons surrounding the Buddha. Dunhuang, China.

Image courtesy of Musée Guimet.

BUDDHIST SCRIPTURES

The Buddhist sacred scriptures belong to an open canon, which means the number of sacred texts is not fixed.

The Buddha and his earliest disciples did not write down their teachings. That came later. Like most world religions, their teachings were transmitted orally for a period of time. It was about five hundred years after the Buddha lived when his teachings were finally written down, around the time of Christ. The earliest Buddhist texts were written down in **Sri Lanka**, just off the coast of India, and they were written in the **Pali language**. Anyone who wants to study the history of Buddhist scripture must eventually find their way to the monasteries of Sri Lanka, as that is where the oldest texts are located.

The Buddhist sacred scriptures belong to an open canon, which means the number of sacred texts is not fixed. There are many writings that can be called sacred in Buddhism; thousands of texts are revered by different sects. Even texts written recently are revered in Buddhism, as long as they receive endorsement by the sangha. There are three authoritative canons in Buddhism: Pali, Chinese, and Tibetan. The two most important Buddhist textual languages are Pali and Sanskrit, as they get us back to the region where the Buddha lived. The Pali texts—the oldest Buddhist texts and therefore the sacred language for Theravada Buddhism—are the most precious, since Pali is the language of the oldest Buddhist writings.

Perhaps the most important figure in the history of Buddhist scripture and transmission is an Indian monk named **Buddhaghosa** who arrived to Sri Lanka in the fifth century CE. He collated texts, edited them, and wrote commentaries. He translated all of the texts into Pali, which is why Pali is so critical to Theravada Buddhism. Buddhaghosa can be compared to Jerome, the great Christian translator who put the Christian texts into Latin. These two distinguished scholars were contemporaries in all likelihood.

Each of the three Buddhist canons—Pali, Chinese, and Tibetan—is divided into three sections known as Tripitaka, the "three baskets." One basket contains the rules for monastics, one contains the Buddha's teachings, and one contains higher teachings intended only for monks. The Buddhist scriptures are usually in the form of **sutras**, or particular sayings or teachings of the Buddha. These sutras always begin with "Thus have I heard. At one time the Lord was staying at . . ." Usually, this kind of introduction to the Buddha's teaching comes from **Ananda**, the Buddha's attendant and one of his most important disciples. Ananda had an amazing memory. He was a first cousin to the Buddha, and he was also ordained as a monk. He was the Buddha's trusted assistant who served as a mouthpiece for the Buddha in his communications with laypeople as well as with the monastic community.

Constructed in 1859, the Kuthodaw Pagoda measures fifty-seven meters tall. There are 729 white shrines around the complex, containing marble slabs inscribed on both sides in Burmese script. Together, the 729 slabs are called "the world's largest book," each stone slab representing one of its pages.

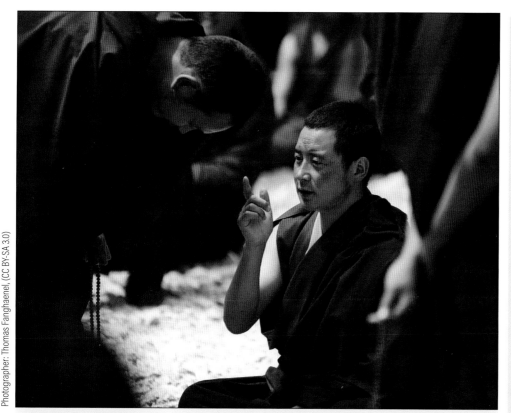

A monk gestures in a highly stylized debate at Sera Monastery in Lhasa, Tibet (2007).

Sri Lanka · the island off the coast of India where the earliest Buddhist texts were written down

Pali language · the language in which the earliest Buddhist texts were written

Buddhaghosa · an Indian monk in Sri Lanka in the fifth century CE who collated Buddhist texts, edited them, and wrote commentaries; translated the scriptures into Pali

Sutras · particular sayings or teachings of the Buddha

Ananda · the Buddha's cousin who served as a trusted assistant and a mouthpiece for the Buddha in his communications with laypeople as well as with the monastic community; advocated for women to be permitted to become monastics

The dharma · the Buddha's teachings

Sangha · the Buddhist community

knowing that some would understand but that most would not. He realized his teaching could be embraced by anyone, regardless of caste. Even low-caste people could reach enlightenment, an idea completely offensive to traditional Hindus.

The Buddha decided to find his former five companions who had deserted him. He set out to find them, and he did find them at Varanasi (formerly known as Benares), a holy city on the Ganges in India. The Buddha's teaching is known among Buddhists as **the dharma**. It was in the holy city of Benares where the Buddha preached his first sermon, the dharma, to these five monks. At first, they resisted, but then they believed him and became his disciples. His father, stepmother, and former wife all converted to his new teaching as well. Many others from all castes also joined. His pupils who achieved enlightenment were known as "arhats," or "worthy ones." The Buddha sent them out to teach others about the truth. He remained in India, but he sent out missionaries all over South Asia. His message became famous, and many people converted. Large monasteries were built during his lifetime.

The Buddha's teaching was not mastered simply by book learning. In fact, it was done orally. The Buddha realized that his discovery was profound and quite difficult to master, so it would take time for people to come to understand. The dharma is not mastered simply through lectures or written materials. It can only be mastered through a way of life. It is akin to doing an apprenticeship to acquire a life skill. Book learning only gets a person so far. Similarly, the Buddha's teaching was accompanied by learning how to conduct oneself in an ethical and holy manner. Disciples also had to learn how to master various meditative and contemplative techniques. Those who chose to join the Buddhist community—known as the **sangha**—entered into a whole new way of life. It was a complete reordering of their worldview, thought processes, and actions.

The Buddhist sangha was originally only for men. However, the Buddha's cousin Ananda—a prominent figure in early Buddhism—pleaded with him to allow women into the monastic community. The Buddha

A hand-colored woodblock print titled *Death of the Buddha*, attributed to Nishimura Shigenaga. Japan (ca. 1697–1756).

agreed and allowed an order of nuns. At that point, the sangha consisted of both males and females.

The Death of the Buddha

The Buddha had a successful mission and ministry that lasted forty-five years. Some Buddhists hold that, at the age of eighty, he died after eating spoiled pork curry, but this fact is hotly debated in the Buddhist community as many Buddhists are strict vegetarians.[1]

Nevertheless, it is clear that once the Buddha became gravely ill, he met with his disciples on one final occasion and said, "Everything decays. Work out your salvation with diligence." He then entered a deep meditative state and died, passing into **parinirvana**, or the final release from samsara. There are no more births for that person. If nirvana (enlightenment) is achieved in one's life, then parinirvana is achieved in death.

The Buddha was cremated, and his ashes became important relics. The remains were divided into eight parts and taken away to form monuments, known as **stupas** or, later, **pagodas**. Stupas tend to be large domes, whereas pagodas tend to be tower-like shrines that are often multitiered, as commonly seen in classical Chinese architecture. Virtually every Buddhist temple today has a stupa within it, where flowers and offerings are placed. Buddhists usually have a path

DHARMACHAKRA

Over time, the Buddha and his teaching came to be symbolized by a wheel known as the **dharmachakra**—the wheel of teaching. Most Buddhists will recognize this symbol immediately as the representation of Buddhism. Where one finds a dharmachakra, one will likely find a sangha.

An ornate dharmachakra atop a building in Lake Rewalsar, India (2010).

ARHAT AND BUDDHA

Some Buddhists make a distinction between an arhat and a Buddha. An arhat has achieved nirvana or enlightenment, meaning he or she has ceased from all craving, having blown out their desires. A Buddha, however, is considered to be on another level. A Buddha no longer makes mistakes in words or conduct. He or she never forgets anything; the mind is always in a state of perfect equanimity. He or she has no biases or prejudices. A Buddha will never backslide and depart from the truth he or she has learned. A Buddha is in a constant state of Samadhi—serenity, clarity, and focus. A Buddha's mind does not decline. He or she understands clearly all eighty-four thousand teachings of the Buddha.

Perhaps the greatest distinction between an arhat and a Buddha is that the arhat is focused on his or her own liberation, whereas a Buddha is focused on helping others. A Buddha has already achieved nirvana and only remains in existence due to compassion for others, trying to help them in their pursuit of enlightenment. Arhats have yet to reach that point.

around the stupa for circumambulation. Building a stupa in Buddhism comes with very good merit.

The Emergence of Distinct Buddhist Traditions

About a century after the Buddha's death, there arose a great crisis in the religion. The Buddha had appointed no successor, and the faith he stimulated was growing quickly. Disciples began to debate doctrine, practice, and issues surrounding the monastic community. One of the intense points of debate had to do with whether

King Ashoka issued numerous edicts during his reign, which were carved and displayed throughout India. Rock inscription inside a cave in Maski, India..

© WESTOCK, Adobe Stock

there was a difference between an arhat and a Buddha, as noted above, as some arhats seemed to be less than perfect in their practice. Like all successful religions that expand, there were new issues that came to the fore. New people groups joined, groups with different understandings and different cultures. People came to disagree on how to run a monastery and on what rules should be enforced.

One of the most famous converts was **King Ashoka**, who ruled almost all of the Indian subcontinent in the third century BCE. He wholeheartedly embraced Buddhism. Ashoka's contribution to Buddhism is often compared to Constantine's contribution to Christianity.

Ashoka's conquests were successful, and his empire grew until he accepted Buddhism and renounced warfare. He is purported to have become disgusted with violence after a victory when tens of thousands were killed. He built many temples and sponsored all kinds of Buddhist missions. Ashoka zealously supported

Dharmachakra · the wheel of teaching

Parinirvana · the final release from samsara; achieved at death for a person who has reached nirvana in this life

Stupas · dome-shaped shrines

Pagodas · multitiered, tower-like shrines

King Ashoka · an Indian monarch who ruled almost all of the Indian subcontinent in the third century BCE; converted to Buddhism after witnessing a violent battle, and propagated the religion throughout his kingdom

Theravadins · followers of Theravada Buddhism, or "the school of the elders"

Hinayana · also known as the small vehicle, a somewhat derogatory name for Theravada Buddhism

Mahayanists · followers of Mahayana Buddhism, or "the school of the greater vehicle"

Mahayana · also known as the **large vehicle**; a diverse set of traditions, including a belief in the divinity of the Buddha, a vast array of bodhisattvas, and sometimes even a heaven and hell; they affirm that anyone, including women and non-monastics, can be enlightened

Maitreya · a Buddha to come who will descend from heaven to Earth and revive the dharma, ruling over a new, almost Messianic age of peace and prosperity

the expansion of Buddhism during his rule. He sent out missionaries and commemorated Buddhism on stone pillars that are visible today.

After several early councils, different schools of Buddhism began to emerge. Disagreements resulted in a major division within the religion—between traditionalists and progressives. The traditionalists were called the **Theravadins**, or "the school of the elders." This oldest and most conservative form of Buddhism has been preserved for two thousand five hundred years and exists today.

The Theravada and Mahayana branches of Buddhism split at the Second Buddhist Council, which took place in around 375 BCE, about a century after Siddhartha's death. Commonly found in Sri Lanka, Myanmar, Thailand, and Cambodia, Theravada is sometimes called "Southern Buddhism" to distinguish it from the northern types of Buddhism found in Tibet, Mongolia, China, Korea, and Japan. Theravadins are sometimes classified as **Hinayana** Buddhists (meaning, in Sanskrit, "small or lesser vehicle"), but this term is somewhat derogatory. Many later traditions consider themselves superior to this ancient school of orthodoxy.

For Theravadins, nirvana is only possible for full-time, male monks. The Buddha allowed women to organize themselves into an order; however, he clearly made them a secondary movement to the men. For example, the women had to salute the males and generally be subservient to them.

Theravadins do not believe in any sort of divine Buddhas, as the **Mahayanists** do. Some Mahayanists argue there are as many Buddhas as there are sentient beings! Rather, for Theravadins, the Buddha was a great philosopher who paved the way yet was only a

Long a tool for spiritual performance, cham, the Tibetan word for dance, is performed almost exclusively by ordained monks. While the initial goal was that the audience and performers might gain access to various deities, in many cases today, performances are staged for tourists.

WORSHIP AND DISTINCTIONS OF MAHAYANISTS

Some Mahayanists worship the Buddha. They think he was much more than just a man and is more like a cosmic being. They also have a complex and vast array of bodhisattvas, or saviors. They have vivid descriptions of heaven and hell, whereas Theravadins tend not to discuss afterlife. One interesting distinction of Mahayanists is their belief in a Maitreya—a Buddha to come who will descend from heaven to Earth and revive the dharma, ruling over a new, almost Messianic age of peace and prosperity. The Maitreya is often depicted as a fat and happy Laughing Buddha, and trinkets of him are often sold at street side booths across East Asia.

Photographer: Sardaka, (CC BY-SA 4.0)

The Maitreya, pictured holding the world in his hand, outside a temple in Sydney, Australia.

Some have compared Mahayana Buddhism to Christianity. Jesus lived his life to save others, and therefore, Christians are called to live selflessly. Similarly, Mahayana Buddhists believe it is critical to seek the well-being of all people rather than myopically focus on one's own salvation. Jesus is a savior, but he is also a friend to his followers. Similarly, bodhisattvas and Buddhas are compassionate, like good friends, who seek to heal our suffering. They come to us, teaching us the path to salvation. There are many sects of Mayahana Buddhism all over the world.

man. Still, he showed us how to stop suffering, so we must follow his methods carefully.

Mahayana Buddhism includes many schools, is much more open to new interpretations, and therefore is far more diverse. The word *Mahayana* in Sanskrit means "large vehicle." Mahayana Buddhists argue that the Theravadins are too tied to the actual life of the Buddha. They argue for a "Buddha essence" in all humans—including females. Even non-monastics can become enlightened.

Madhyamika is an important form of Mahayana Buddhism founded by the Indian monk Nagarjuna in around 200 CE. Nagarjuna emphasized the middle path, claiming that a person should always take the middle position between polar opposites. He claimed dualisms were ridiculous. He believed strong claims were absurd; only a balanced middle path represents truth. He claimed that his claim of having no claim was actually not a claim.

Tantric Buddhism is considered the final development in Indian Buddhism. This esoteric form of Mahayana stems from Indian Tantric practices, which were well established even at the time of the Buddha and are rooted in the various depictions of Shiva and his female consorts. The word *Tantra* actually means "to weave." The point of Tantrism is for the devotee to obtain a mystical union with a bodhisattva, which can happen in numerous ways, including through intercourse with a partner. The "right-hand" school of Tantra maintains celibacy and views the union as symbolic. However, the "left-hand" school allows for intercourse, although it is designed to help devotees overcome desire. There are

Laughing Buddha · a fat and jolly depiction of the Maitreya, seen commonly in statuettes and imagery throughout Asia

Madhyamika · a form of Mahayana Buddhism founded by Nagarjuna around 200 CE; rejects dualisms and absolute truth claims, and focuses on always taking the balanced, middle path between extremes

Nagarjuna · an Indian monk who founded Madhyamika

Tantric Buddhism · an esoteric school of Buddhism focusing on union with a bodhisattva through Yoga and mysticism; "right-hand" tantrism practices celibacy, but "left-hand" tantrism allows for ritual intercourse

Child monks seeking alms. Don Det, Laos (2018).

A Vietnamese Buddhist nun.

many esoteric traditions in Tantric Buddhism, centered on Yoga practices. Only the more developed stages involve union, or "weaving" practices. Some schools of Tantrism teach the only way one can cure oneself of desire is through overindulgence.[2]

The Spread of Buddhism

Buddhism spread around the world in a number of ways: through diplomatic missions, missionary work, scholarship, commercial and trade routes, emigration, and, in more recent years, technology and media. The great heyday of Buddhist expansion in Asia was from 400 BCE to 800 CE. Stemming from what is today Nepal and Northeast India, Buddhism spread to Sri Lanka, Southeast Asia (Myanmar, Thailand, Malaysia, Cambodia, Vietnam, and Laos), China, Korea, and Japan, and finally, it found fertile soil in Tibet in around 800 CE. Sri Lanka is critical to the story because, over time, Hinduism enjoyed periods of revival, and, eventually, Islam came to dominate most of the subcontinent. Were it not for Sri Lanka being the Theravadin epicenter, Buddhism may have completely vanished from the Indian subcontinent.

Buddhism entered China during the Han dynasty (from approximately 200 BCE to 200 CE). The Han dynasty was powerful and dominated a huge amount of territory, ranging from Korea to central Asia and from Mongolia to Vietnam. Buddhism went through some periods of hostility and some periods of growth in China. Throughout two millennia of history, some rulers converted to Buddhism, built opulent temples, and even outlawed Daoism in their lands. Others openly smashed Buddhist temples and defrocked monks and nuns. Ironically, some of the most magnificent periods of Buddhist growth in China were followed by periods of intense persecution.

Buddhism entered Japan in the sixth century CE under the protection of Prince Shotoku, Empress Suiko, and the Soga family. They welcomed Buddhist missionaries from Korea. However, when a disease spread in Japan, some rival families blamed the foreign religion for its cause. It was too late, however, as Buddhism had already blended itself into Shintoism—Japan's traditional religion.

Over the centuries, Buddhism eventually won tremendous favor in Japan's national consciousness, as its teachings resonated with people from many walks of life. Samurai warriors, for example, found the mindfulness of Buddhism to be helpful in their training in martial arts, although their version of Buddhism shed its pacifistic reputation. Later in the twentieth century, Japanese military leaders would rely on similar training as they galvanized citizens to wage international wars against China, the United States, and the European Allies.

Japan also became a breeding ground for new sects of Buddhism. One of the most famous forms of Japanese Buddhism is called "Pure Land." It reveres a particular Buddha named **Amitabha** ("infinite light"), who was popular in India and China in the third century CE. In Japan, his name was pronounced **Amida**, and his followers believed that whoever chanted his name over and over would be reborn into the **Pure Land**—a pleasant halfway house between humanity and nirvana.

Over time, however, the Pure Land became an end in itself, and these Buddhists would say "Amida" all throughout life in hopes of reaching the Pure Land upon death. This new goal of the Buddhist faith has become one of the most important Mahayana beliefs worldwide. Japanese Pure Land Buddhists arc known as Jodoshu. Their most important teacher is Honen, who lived in Japan in around 1200 CE.

Another Japanese monk named Shinran studied under Honen but reached an entirely different conclusion. He argued that chanting was meaningless, and so was celibacy. He married a nun and had five children with her. He argued that salvation was attained merely by trusting Amida Buddha. As a result, Shinran is often thought to be "the Martin Luther of Japan." Martin Luther was a sixteenth-century German monk who also married a nun and said salvation was based on trusting Christ.

Another Japanese Buddhist movement that deserves mentioning is **Soka Gakkai**, which was founded in 1930

Amitabha · "infinite light"; a Buddha who is central to Pure Land Buddhism

Amida · the Japanese pronunciation of Amitabha; believers chant his name in the hope of being reborn in the Pure Land

Pure Land · a very pleasant halfway house between humanity and nirvana

Soka Gakkai · a Japanese Buddhist movement based on the Lotus Sutra and the teachings of Nichiren

Bentendo Hall is one of the most photographed buildings at Daigoji Temple, which was designated as a UNESCO World Heritage site in 1994. Kyoto, Japan.

Image courtesy of The British Library.

Chapter 8 of the Lotus Sutra. Commissioned by Emperor Go-Mizunoo and presented to the Toshogu Shrine in Nikko, Japan (1636).

The two central teachings of the Lotus Sutra are: (1) all Buddhist paths lead to Buddhahood, and all beings have the potential to become Buddhas; and (2) the Buddha did not pass into nirvana—rather, he is mystically present with us, teaching the dharma. He is the supreme object of faith. He actually achieved enlightenment endless eons ago, and he is the divine Buddha who is always present for us. Nichiren was persecuted and exiled for his views, but many continued to follow him over the centuries, including the members of Soka Gakkai, which is now a global organization of some twelve million people.

and has become quite large and international. Its roots go back to the thirteenth-century monk **Nichiren**, who focused on **chants** rather than meditation. He emphasized a text called the **Lotus Sutra**, which purportedly contains the final teachings of the Buddha before he passed.

Nichiren · a thirteenth-century monk who focused on chanting rather than meditation and emphasized the Lotus Sutra

Chants · repetitive rhythmic phrases uttered for spiritual purposes

Zen Buddhism

Another unique prominent school is **Zen Buddhism**. Known in China as Chan Buddhism and in Korea as Son Buddhism, it is usually associated with Japan today. Its founder was an Indian monk named Bodhidharma who traveled to China in the sixth century. These Buddhists believe in sudden insight rather than in extreme rationalism. They say they are only doing what the Buddha did—he experienced enlightenment rather suddenly once he sat under the Bodhi tree. Zen Buddhism is often associated with haiku poems and Japanese tea ceremonies. It found an audience in the Western world in the twentieth century.

Japanese Zen scholar **Daisetsu "D. T." Suzuki** (1870–1966), who spent time both in Japan and the United States, became one of Buddhism's chief interpreters for the Western world. He later joined the faculty of Columbia University in 1952 and lectured widely, stimulating great interest in Buddhism.

Tibetan Buddhism

Missionaries came to Tibet during the seventh century CE. Tibetans had an ancient indigenous religion known as Bon, which was shamanistic. The blending of Bon and Buddhism led to a unique form of Buddhism called Lamaism. Tibetan Buddhists have their own canon and their own unique system of leadership.

Tibetan Buddhism is also known as **Vajrayana** Buddhism, or **Diamond Vehicle**. The diamond ("vajra") connotes the absolutely hard truth about a person, the part that is indestructible. The word *yana* means "way" or "vehicle." It is a form of Mahayana Buddhism that contains many distinct beliefs and practices. Its popularity expanded to other Himalayan regions, such as Bhutan and Nepal. It caught on in Mongolia when its emperor converted to Buddhism in around 1300. It is so attractive because of its teaching that anyone can achieve enlightenment during their present lifetime. Prior to 1959, around 25 percent of all Tibetan males were monks. Today, the tradition of large monasteries continues, where they carry on the Buddha's lively tradition of spirited debate.

In 1951, China conquered Tibet, and under its communist regime, Buddhism has been severely persecuted. In 1959, the Tibetans attempted to declare autonomy in an uprising, but China reacted strongly by persecuting and executing tens of thousands of Tibetans. Others were imprisoned, and monasteries were looted, destroyed, or closed. The Dalai Lama escaped the crackdown in 1959, entering India when he was twenty-four years old.

At one point in its history, Tibet was ruled by a king, but over time, the **Dalai Lama** (the word *lama* means "teacher," and *dalai* means "ocean") became the absolute political and spiritual leader of the Tibetan people. The current Dalai Lama, Tibet's most famous citizen, the likeable **Tenzin Gyatso**, has denied this political authority, claiming he is only a monk. It is difficult to know if he is just trying to mislead the Chinese government or if he really has relinquished his authoritative position in Tibet.

Lotus Sutra · a text purportedly teaching the final words of the Buddha, claiming that all Buddhist paths lead to Buddhahood; that all beings have the potential to become Buddhas; and that the Buddha did not pass into nirvana but is still with us, teaching the dharma

Zen Buddhism · a Mahayana sect founded by a monk named Bodhidharma; emphasizes belief in sudden insight rather than in extreme rationalism

Daisetsu "D. T." Suzuki · a Japanese Zen Buddhist and scholar who brought acclaim to the religion in the United States; became a lecturer at Columbia University

Tibetan Buddhism · a distinct version of Mahayana Buddhism found in Tibet, Bhutan, and Nepal

Vajrayana · also known as the **Diamond Vehicle**; Tibetan Buddhist tradition that combines Mahayana with the indigenous religion of Bon

Dalai Lama · literally meaning "ocean teacher," the Dalai Lama was the political and spiritual authority in Tibet prior to its annexation by China in 1959

Tenzin Gyatso · the current Dalai Lama and Nobel Peace Prize recipient who leads Tibetan Buddhism from exile in India

Photographer: Shigeru Tamura

Photograph of the Japanese Buddhist philosopher D. T. Suzuki (1953).

Photographer: Luca Galuzzi [www.galuzzi.it], (CC BY-SA 2.5)

Tenzin Gyatso, the fourteenth and current Dalai Lama, and the head of Tibetan Buddhism. Gyatso relinquished his former political authority as the exiled ruler of Tibet, but he remains a powerful spiritual figure in the East.

BUDDHISM IN THE UNITED STATES

US interest in Buddhism has come in waves.

- Some American intellectuals, like Henry David Thoreau and Ralph Waldo Emerson, found Buddhism attractive and devoted themselves to its study.
- The mystic Helena Blavatsky's fascination with Eastern religions led her and Henry Steel Olcott to found the Theosophical Society. They traveled to Sri Lanka to learn about Buddhism, where they converted to the faith in 1880.
- The teaching of Daisetsu Suzuki, beginning with his widely known presentations at the Chicago World Parliament of Religions in 1893, sparked ongoing interest in Zen Buddhism.
- Immigration in the 1970s brought many Buddhist Vietnamese and Cambodians to the United States in the aftermath of the chaos of the Vietnamese War and the murderous regime of Pol Pot. By 1990, the Vietnamese and Cambodian population in the United States exceeded one million.
- In 1974, Robert Pirsig published his famous book, *Zen and the Art of Motorcycle Maintenance*, which became a national bestseller for decades and a cultural phenomenon. Merging Zen and Americana, he pointed toward spiritual liberation and experimentation for millions of people in a countercultural era.
- In 1997, Buddhism entered US cinema in a big way with two films focused on the Dalai Lama: *Kundun*, directed by Martin Scorsese, and *Seven Years in Tibet*, starring Brad Pitt.
- Several high-profile Hollywood actors, such as Naomi Watts, Richard Gere, Uma Thurman, Chris Evans, Orlando Bloom, and Steven Seagal, as well singer Tina Turner, have converted to Buddhism. Golfer Tiger Woods was raised as a Buddhist and has made several public comments about how his faith remains an important part of his life.
- Another important victory for US Buddhists came in 2013, when Mazie Hirono became the first Buddhist and the first Asian American female elected to the United States Senate, representing the state of Hawaii.

Theatrical poster for the motion picture *Seven Years in Tibet*.

From his home in exile in Dharamshala, India, he is the fourteenth Dalai Lama. A bestselling author, he was awarded the Nobel Peace Prize in 1989, propelling him to worldwide fame. At the very least, the Tibetan people consider him to be the embodiment of a compassionate bodhisattva. Perhaps they are beginning to accept that their traditional understanding of the Dalai Lama has been vanquished by the Chinese government.

In 2021, the Chinese government declared that it would select the next Dalai Lama upon the death of the current occupant. (Tibetan Buddhists believe each new Dalai Lama is the reincarnation of the previous Dalai Lama.) The current Dalai Lama countered that he might choose to be reborn as a woman or as a person in the United States, or perhaps he would choose not to be reborn at all. Only time will tell how this fraught situation pans out.

Tibetan Buddhism is unique in many ways. For example, the prayer wheel, ubiquitous in Tibet, is a mechanism by which Tibetan Buddhists can send out prayers simply by turning the wheel. Tibetans even leave prayer wheels out in the wind or in a stream so they are continuously turned to send out prayers of compassion for those in need.

Another distinct aspect of Tibetan Buddhism is the two schools known for their hats: the **Red Hat School** and the **Yellow Hat School**. While the Yellow Hats are associated with the Dalai Lama (the Dalai Lama is always the head of the Yellow Hat School), the Red Hats are well-known for their highly complex understanding of what happens to the recently departed.

Their famous text, the **Bardo Thodol**—or the **Tibetan Book of the Dead**—has become something of a phenomenon in Western scholarship, due largely to the famous psychologist Carl Jung, who thought it was profound. This text is an instructional manual to guide the deceased through forty-nine days of temptation and travel from one body to the next rebirth. Tibetan Buddhists study it during their earthly life so they are prepared for the journey that awaits them in death.

Six Ancient Buddhist Teachings

The Buddha did not leave a written legacy. His teachings were passed orally. When he was living, it was fairly easy to know what Buddhism entailed, since presumably one simply needed to follow his lead. But as discussed, he left no successor, so the teachings became diffuse over time. The Theravada tradition has

A Tibetan depiction of Tantrism from the late thirteenth century, with the esoteric deity Manjuvajra.

tried to keep Buddhism somewhat contained to prevent the teachings from becoming unwieldy.

Mahayana Buddhism has tended to pioneer new methods and new ideas to the point that there are innumerable schools and approaches. Some would argue that this is the genius of Mahayana Buddhism; it is like a huge buffet. One does not have to eat what everyone else eats. One can simply eat the food that satisfies. In other words, one may practice how one wants to practice, and one can believe what aspects of the larger tradition they choose to believe. One can be creative in meditation.

Some Buddhist teachers would go so far as to say that one does not even have to claim to be a Buddhist to benefit from Buddhism. One can window-shop. One can help oneself to the buffet of Buddhist teachings without taking refuge in the Buddha, the dharma, and the sangha. One can learn meditation techniques or gain inspiration from the life of the Buddha. But there is no need to go through some conversion experience and call oneself a Buddhist. In fact, the world's most famous Buddhist teacher—the Dalai Lama—has spoken out against proselytization and has claimed that religious conversion is outdated. This is quite ironic for a religion that spread like wildfire in its earliest centuries due to effective recruitment into the faith. Buddhists do, however, believe in evangelism. The key is that someone should ask to be evangelized first. One should not just proselytize without permission. Once somebody approaches a Buddhist and asks for teaching, then the Buddhist can share their beliefs.

Theosophical Society · an organization that aims to bridge the gap between Western and Eastern spirituality

Prayer wheel · a Tibetan Buddhist mechanism by which a practitioner can send out prayers simply by turning a wheel

Red Hat School · a school of Tibetan Buddhism known for its highly complex understanding of what happens to those who have recently departed

Yellow Hat School · a school of Tibetan Buddhism associated with the Dalai Lama

Bardo Thodol · also known as the **Tibetan Book of the Dead**, a Red Hat instructional manual for the recently departed, geared to guide him or her through forty-nine days of temptation and travel from one body to the next rebirth

We must not forget the Hindu context out of which the Buddha's teachings emerged. The Buddha found the teachings of Hinduism to be somehow lacking and erroneous. For example, his teaching is clearly a reaction against the caste system of India. Although he himself was upper caste, he believed caste to be of little consequence in the spiritual life. Everyone had the capacity to become enlightened, to achieve nirvana, and to exit samsara.

Fundamental to the Buddha was the assumption that we are trapped in samsara and that we therefore suffer. To stop suffering, one needs to get out of the cycle of samsara. And to get out of samsara, one needs to learn a handful of teachings, accompanied by effective and diligent practice. While the Buddha may have taught eighty-four thousand different ideas, the most important dimensions of his teachings include the following six major doctrines:

> Fundamental to the Buddha was the assumption that we are trapped in samsara and that we therefore suffer.

Denial of the existence of a creator. Many of us have traveled overseas and noticed that Buddhists seem to worship depictions of the Buddha and other important Buddhist figures. It is important to note that while Buddhists certainly venerate other beings, including gods; they believe these gods are simply beings that inhabit different regions of existence. These gods are not absolute in any sense. They, too, are trapped in samsara. According to Buddhism, we can become gods, devils, demons, and even animals, based on our karma. While Buddhists may use the term *god*, in reality, they deny the existence of a creator. All gods are subject to rebirth, just like humans and animals.

So how did the universe come into being? Buddhism teaches that the universe has been around forever. What we now see can be traced back to previous causes. There was no creation event. Some scientists argue that our current reality arose from a "big bang." They say that our universe's elements must have been tightly condensed and then, "bang," they were unleashed in a flash. However, what existed before the big bang? Obviously, there was something before that. Buddhism teaches that everything has a precedent. Therefore, there was no creation per se. Everything is connected to everything else because all things have always existed—albeit in different forms.

Much of Western cosmology depicts God creating the world, and then at the end of time there will be a judgment of all human souls, who will be consigned to either heaven or hell. Buddhism does not accept this cosmology, and neither do the other Indian religions. In Buddhism, time is cyclical. In the religions of Judaism, Christianity, and Islam, time is linear. This is a major difference between the Indian and Abrahamic religions. Further, in the Abrahamic faiths, humans are at the center of creation. In the Indian faiths, humans are not necessarily at the center. Humans are certainly in a privileged position since only humans can achieve release from samsara. But everything is cyclical. All beings, including gods and demons and animals, are trapped in samsara. There are patterns over the billions of years as individuals are constantly being reborn into different realms and various forms of awareness. Universes come into being and pass away and new ones arise and so on. This all continues forever. A trillion years is nothing; it just comes and goes.

Denial of an individual soul. Buddhists refer to this teaching as **anatman**. They deny the atman (soul), which Hindus hold to be central. The term *anatman* is usually translated as "no self." The Buddha did not believe souls exist. He thought this was sheer ignorance. In his view, everything is connected and comes and goes all the time in a massive matrix that he called **interdependent co-origination**. Some scholars refer to this as **dependent arising** or **dependent origination**. Everything that exists is completely dependent upon everything else, and everything is in constant flux. Nothing is independent but is instead interdependent—dependent on other things. Everything is changing all the time. Nothing exists independently. Therefore, there is no "I" or "me." We all are connected to our parents, out of whom we are made, and they are connected to their parents, out of whom they were made.

© bozhdb, Adobe Stock

Mandala from colored sand.

In sum, there is no independence and no permanence—only interdependence and impermanence. Why? Because there is no individual thing. There is nothing stagnant and independent; things only appear to be independent. But in reality, this is a misperception—an illusion. There is only flux, only movement. Nothing is stagnant or real; everything is in constant, interdependent flux. This is why Buddhist monks often create beautiful sand mandalas, only to destroy them shortly after completing them. Nothing is permanent; therefore, we might as well destroy the piece of art and throw it into the water, where it will eventually end up anyway.

The Four Noble Truths. First, all life forms are suffering (dukkha) and subject to decay. Not only is everything in flux, but everything is transitory and deteriorating.

Second, suffering is caused by desire. We crave and aspire. We mistakenly think certain things and certain situations will prove to be fulfilling. But it is all illusory. Nothing brings true and lasting satisfaction. When we attain things, we do not cease our suffering. Eventually, we just want more, or else we lose the thing (or person) that we thought would bring us satisfaction.

Third, the only way to stop suffering is to stop desiring. We have to stop craving or aspiring in order to stop suffering. But as long as we want something, as long as we aspire to a particular status or position, we continue to suffer.

Fourth, there is a way to stop suffering: by taking the Middle Way and the Eightfold Path. That is what Siddhartha discovered, which led to his Buddhahood.

Anatman · denial of the atman, or soul; the doctrine that there is no self

Interdependent co-origination · also known as **dependent arising** or **dependent origination**, the idea that everything is connected and comes and goes all of the time in a massive matrix in which there is no individuality and no permanence

Reclining Buddha at Wat Lokayasutharam, Ayutthaya Historical Park, Thailand. Out of respect, the statue is covered with a saffron robe.

The Middle Way. **The Middle Way** is in the middle between extreme asceticism and the worldly existence. The ascetics were too extreme in their deprivation. However, living like everybody else—always wanting more—leads only to greater desires. As we attain things, we just want more. The Buddha's solution was to learn how to take the Middle Way between the two extremes. He taught that the way to cultivate a middle path is by unlearning the things we have been taught and learning how to live the **Noble Eightfold Path**.

The Noble Eightfold Path. We must learn correct understanding (of the **Four Noble Truths**), have correct intentions, practice correct speech, have correct conduct, involve ourselves in correct occupations, cultivate correct endeavors, practice correct contemplation, and acquire correct concentration. The Noble Eightfold Path is a lifestyle. It is not linear. One does not achieve one and then move on to the next. Buddhists work on all of them throughout life as they cultivate the correct way to live. To master this path, one will become deeply transformed. It requires great discipline, but it can be done. If mastered, then nirvana is the result. The Eightfold Path is the wellspring of Buddhist ethics, morals, and behavior.

Nirvana. If one follows the Middle Way and Eightfold Path correctly, one will stop desiring (nirvana), and one will eventually achieve release from samsara. The word *nirvana* means "extinguished." One's fires of craving and desire are blown out, like a candle. Nirvana means that one has achieved compassionate nonattachment. One does not desire anything, but one does not hate anything, either. One is simply content to be

Four Noble Truths · (1) all life consists of suffering; (2) suffering is caused by desire; (3) to cease to desire is to cease to suffer; (4) to cease to desire, one must follow the Middle Way and the Noble Eightfold Path

The Middle Way · the middle ground between extreme asceticism and extreme worldliness

Noble Eightfold Path · to learn correct understanding (of the Four Noble Truths), have correct intentions, practice correct speech, have correct conduct, involve oneself in correct occupations, cultivate correct endeavors, practice correct contemplation, and acquire correct concentration; each of these are connected and cultivated over a lifetime of discipline

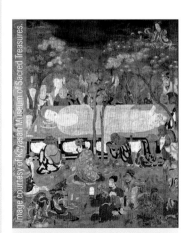

Buddha's Nirvana, dated to 1086 CE, shows the Buddha lying on his deathbed surrounded by mourners. Mount Koya, Japan.

where one is without needing to be attached to anyone or anything else.

If one has achieved nirvana, one is no longer motivated by greed, fear, or hatred. Those defilements arise because of attachment. But if one sees the truth that we are all connected and thus interdependent, then one will have compassion on everyone and will no longer allow those defilements into one's mind. This is the Buddhist awakening. One wakes up and realizes that they hold the key to their own suffering. By refusing to participate in hatred or fear or greed, one becomes free. One becomes so free that one is no longer trapped in the cycle of reincarnation. One is free now and forevermore. It is a beautiful thing to conquer attachment out of compassion for all. Not even death intimidates, because one is free. One does not even crave life anymore.

If, and only if, one achieves nirvana in this life, then one will go on to experience the ultimate nirvana. This is known in Buddhism as "parinirvana" or "maha-parinirvana." The schools of Buddhism disagree on how to describe this final nirvana. What they do agree on, however, is that it cannot be explained in extreme detail by virtue of the fact that it is beyond our comprehension, because whoever experiences it cannot come back. They have gone and will not reenter the wheel of existence, or samsara. It is final, and it is peaceful. It is bliss.

Buddhism and Mantras

Virtually all Buddhists repeat a specific mantra several times a day: "I take refuge in the Buddha, the dharma, and the sangha." These are known as the **Three Jewels of Buddhism**. Herein lies the antidote to suffering and the solution for how to escape. We are like patients who consult a doctor. We are very sick. We are suffering due to our debilitating illness. So we contact the doctor (the Buddha), who prescribes the medicine (dharma) that will heal us. However, if we do not take the medicine, then we cannot become healed. The nurses (sangha) are there to remind us to take our medicine, and they will help us in all manner of ways to ensure that we are on the correct path toward healing.

Buddhism has developed the notion of **bodhisattvas**. They are the ones who attained nirvana during their human life but chose to remain in samsara due to their profound compassion for those who suffer. Thus, they have chosen to remain in the cycle of rebirth to help people discover the truth. Bodhisattvas come in many forms: friends, strangers, and even animals. We do not typically recognize them, but they come, and they teach us. Perhaps they even cause us to become angry so we will learn how to cope. Bodhisattvas are on the path to Buddhahood and are thus unconstrained by the normal bodies that we associate with earthly existence. They can even take nonliving forms to teach us lessons.

Modern Religious Practices

Buddhists have a variety of rituals and practices. They pray often. They make offerings to Buddhas, whether in a temple or in a household shrine. In addition to reciting **mantras**, they offer a second category of chant called a **paritta**, which means "protection." It involves reciting scripture. **Hoji**, the most important service for the dead, is held on **Parinirvana Day** (February 15) and commemorates the day the Buddha's physical body expired.

Buddhists celebrate a host of festivals. Usually, the festivals are contextual and focus on a local leader or an event that occurred in their specific sect. They celebrate the birthdays of various Buddhas and bodhisattvas. Laypeople usually go to the monastery and hear teaching from the monastics. Monks and nuns celebrate the beginning and the end of the three-month retreat season, which occurs during the monsoons. Many festivals celebrate various events in the Buddha's life and can vary widely across the world.

Three Jewels of Buddhism · the Buddha, the dharma, and the sangha

Bodhisattva · those who have achieved nirvana but choose to remain in the cycle of rebirth anyway to help others discover truth

Mantras · short chants, often just a single word

Paritta · "protection"; a type of chant that involves reciting scripture to safeguard against danger

Hoji · religious services for the dead; led by priests in order to commemorate leaders, fallen soldiers, important teachers, victims of tragedies, and ancestors

Parinirvana Day · a Buddhist holiday held on February 15 to commemorate the day the Buddha's physical body expired

The community uses floating lanterns and garlands on Vesak Day as they pray and celebrate the Buddha's birthday.

The largest and most important festival for global Buddhism is called **Vesak**—named after the Indian month that roughly corresponds to the Western month of May. It commemorates the Buddha's birthday and occurs in either April or May on the full Moon of the lunar calendar. Theravada Buddhism also uses this day to celebrate the Buddha's birth, enlightenment, and death. Buddhists clean their homes and temples, put lights on trees, and bathe statues of the Buddha.

A popular practice for lay Buddhists is to live like a monk or nun for eight days. During this period, they abandon several things: sex, luxurious chairs or beds, singing, dancing, playing music, wearing perfume or jewelry or cosmetics, and snacking.

Abandoning all electronics, they pray and meditate, practice Yoga, and listen to monastic teachings.

Meditation is probably the most important aspect of Buddhist practice. There are countless ways to do it, but perhaps most importantly, meditators should be mindful of the **Five Hindrances**: lustful thoughts, malice toward a person, drowsiness, worry or depression, and doubt. Once these obstructions are overcome, the practitioner can focus on looking inside himself or herself to see the deepest nature of his or her mind.

The exercise of meditation improves with instruction, discipline, and practice. The key is to achieve calmness and to avoid "monkey mind," meaning our thoughts jump from limb to limb. We need to focus and concentrate on one thing. Calmness and serenity are called for.

The typical posture is the **lotus position**, perhaps on a mat or cushion, with a straight head and hands resting on the legs. Deep, calm breathing is key. Once calmed, the meditator must choose an object to focus the mind on, perhaps saying a mantra repeatedly. Some early-level meditators focus on something such as a flower, baseball, or kitchen pot for lengthy periods until the object is etched into their mind. The key is to **visualize** something until the subject and object dissolve into one and deeper consciousness is achieved. For advanced meditators, they can eventually stop thinking. This is called **trance meditation**.

Zen focuses very little on temples and scriptures; rather, it centers around meditation on emptiness (or nothingness). One can observe monks sitting for long periods of time, and their superiors will even strike the monks with a stick to keep them from drowsiness during their long meditation sessions known as **zazen**. It is said that Zen Buddhism punishes the body with zazen and disciplines the mind with **koans**. Koans are bizarre riddles meant to test a student's proficiency by frustrating rational analysis. Several koans have become well-known in the West: *What is the sound of one hand clapping? If a tree falls in the forest, does it make a sound? What was your face before your parents were born? If you meet the Buddha on the road, should you kill him?*

Buddhists typically have statues of the Buddha on display, although this custom did not begin until about seven hundred years after his life, in the second century CE. Typically, he is seated in the lotus position and has a dot—an **urna**—on his forehead representing the **third eye** of enlightenment. The Buddha's hand positions send messages to devotees. The "okay" sign refers to his role as teacher. The hand touching the ground symbolizes his enlightenment when he touched the ground and scared Mara and his demons. His hands formed into a circle symbolizes the dharmachakra—the wheel of dharma. The palm facing outward is a blessing. The Buddha laying down intimates his parinirvana at death.

Buddhism has various pilgrimage sites. Many are local, depending on the life of the particular teacher

Zazen · long meditation sessions in Zen Buddhism during which the superiors will strike the monks with a stick in order to keep them from drowsiness

Koans · bizarre riddles in Zen Buddhism meant to test a student's proficiency and provoke enlightenment. These statements are usually frustrating to rational analysis

Urna · a dot on the forehead representing the third eye

Third eye · the eye that represents seeing all things through an enlightened mind

Photographer: Marubatsu, public domain

Zen Buddhist monk begging for alms in Kyoto, Japan (2006).

NEUROSCIENCE

Recent neuroscience research has confirmed what many Buddhists have taught all along: there is plasticity in the brain, and meditation can mold and shape one's mental topography. Meditation has been shown to reduce chronic pain, strengthen immunity, help with depression and anxiety, and alter one's mood. Neuroscience and Buddhism agree on the fact that psychological well-being is a skill that can be taught, learned, and achieved when practiced.

The Mahabodhi Temple complex in Bodh Gaya, India, where the Buddha achieved enlightenment (2016).

Bodh Gaya · where the Buddha achieved enlightenment; the Mahabodhi Temple complex there is the most important Buddhist pilgrimage site

Kushinagar · where the Buddha died in Uttar Pradesh; the second-most important Buddhist pilgrimage site

Lumbini · where the Buddha was born; the third-most important Buddhist pilgrimage site

Sarnath · where the Buddha gave his first sermon (known as the dharma), just outside the city of Varanasi in Uttar Pradesh; the fourth-most important Buddhist pilgrimage site

being revered. Four sites in particular are visited by Buddhists globally. The first is the most important: the Mahabodhi Temple complex in the city of **Bodh Gaya**, India. Located in the state of Bihar, this is the place where the Buddha achieved enlightenment (in Pali, "bodhi"). The second is the site where the Buddha died, located in the town of **Kushinagar**, in the state of Uttar Pradesh, India. Third is the town of **Lumbini**, where Siddhartha was born. Fourth is the site of **Sarnath**, just outside of India's holy city of Varanasi, in Uttar Pradesh. It was at Sarnath where the Buddha gave his first sermon (the dharma) at the deer park.

At the center of Buddhism is the monastic community. Children can usually enter the monastery at age seven. They are placed under a teacher, have their head shaved, and adopt an ochre-colored robe. Most importantly, they must practice ahimsa. As they mature, they will need to pursue sexual abstinence and avoid any intoxicants. In their disciplined life, they will refrain from eating after midday and strictly avoid entertainment, jewelry, perfume, money, and luxurious furniture. They must be absolutely above reproach in their personal conduct, especially taking care to avoid lying and stealing. Buddhist monastics abandon normal jobs and rely on others to provide them with food. For a monastery to become established, there is the requirement of at least four fully ordained monks.

The Buddhist lay community deeply reveres its monks, and there is a reciprocity between the laity and the monastery. The laity looks after the monks and nuns, while the monastics provide teaching and guidance. Buddhist monks do not officiate weddings, as is common for clergy in the Western world. However, the Buddhist monastic presence at funerals is crucial. Monks and nuns typically visit the dying and read texts to them to help them prepare for a good death. Buddhist funeral services come from India originally and therefore are similar to Hindu death rituals. How to dispose of the dead is not prescribed in Buddhism. While cremation three days after death is commonly practiced, it is not required. In Sri Lanka and Thailand, both burial and cremation are common. In Tibet, **sky burial** is common due to a lack of trees; rather than bury or cremate, the deceased are chopped into pieces and fed to the birds.

One common question has to do with female monastics in Buddhism. There is an obvious ambivalence here. The Buddha was reluctant to ordain nuns, but eventually, with persuasion, he allowed a female order, albeit with restrictions that put them under the authority of the monks. In the medieval era, however, convents essentially died out, leading many to assume this is what the Buddha preferred anyway. There are many modern initiatives, however, to increase the number of nuns worldwide. One of Sri Lanka's three major Buddhist sects allows for nuns. In conservative Thailand and Myanmar, nuns are exceedingly rare, although the issue continues to be pressed. In Myanmar, there are legal consequences if a monk tries to ordain a nun. In Thailand, there is a class of women called mae chi who shave their heads, take vows, and wear white robes, but they are not considered to be clergy. Typically, they are poor, rural women who are in need, so they put themselves at the mercy of the monastery and devote themselves to serving the monks. Dr. Chatsumarn Kabilsingh, a former university professor, is one of a very few women who have managed to achieve ordination as a nun. She was ordained in Sri Lanka. Her work has been praised and recognized by the United Nations.

Buddhism and Death

Buddhists are often associated with the mantra: "**om mani padme hum.**" Taken literally, it means "holy, jewel, lotus flower, unity." Its meaning is something along the lines of "praise to the jewel in the lotus," but Buddhists think of it as a verbal way of connecting to their faith. Some Buddhist monks chant "**om**" over and over, as it is considered the holiest syllable. The phrase is actually a calling out to a bodhisattva, and it is supposed to infuse the caller with compassion. It is also considered to be a summary of all Buddhist teaching. Tibetan Buddhists are particularly reverent toward this mantra.

A Buddhist nun in Laos at the Boun Vat Phou Festival (2012).

Sky burial · a practice in Tibet in which the deceased is chopped into pieces and fed to the birds, instead of burial or cremation

Om mani padme hum · "praise to the jewel in the lotus"; a mantra calling out to a bodhisattva; supposed to infuse the caller with compassion

Om · the holiest syllable; often chanted in meditation

Om, the holiest syllable and most commonly chanted Buddhist mantra.

In several Asian nations, Buddhism has come to be associated with mourning and death rituals. Presumably, Buddhism has something to offer when it comes to issues related to death and afterlife. The Buddha himself talked at length about these matters. For example, on one occasion, an infant died and the mother was extremely distraught. She went to the Buddha and asked that he revive the baby. The Buddha said he would if she could bring mustard seeds from a household that had never experienced death. She quickly realized that every household had experienced death, and realizing this fact helped her to cope better. Death is everywhere. It impacts everyone. No one is exempt. We all die, and we all experience the loss of people we care about. In a way, this makes death more manageable when we realize that every single person who has ever lived has dealt with death.

Most Buddhists believe that when we die, it takes up to seven weeks—a maximum of forty-nine days—before we enter into a newly fertilized egg to be reborn. We might enter immediately, or we might have to remain in an intermediate stage for forty-nine days. This knowledge is another reason death is not to be feared. In a way, it is a fresh opportunity. With each new birth, we are still stuck in samsara, but there is a positive way of looking at it, too: we have a new opportunity to achieve nonattachment, nirvana, and, eventually, parinirvana.

Buddhists believe that people should prepare for death. They should apologize to people and reconcile if they can. They should bury the hatchet on old disagreements. They should give away their possessions and release all their concerns. It is not good when one is dying to have grudges and still feel a sense of possessiveness. Death comes much more smoothly if one can be generous, kind, compassionate, and at peace. At death, one's money and possessions will go to someone else, so it makes sense to take care of all of that while one is preparing to die.

Buddhists talk often of a good death. One does not want to be worrying about technology and medicine and treatment during death. That is why Buddhism suggests that one disconnects from technology before death. Do not clutch onto machines and medicines too much. Just die peacefully and gracefully without hanging on to the current world. Make things right with people, and freely pass on. Family members should not intervene and try every possible means to keep someone alive another hour or two. Just let them go. Dukkha comes to everyone, and it always wins. Welcome death, and see it as simply another threshold into rebirth.

If we live and die with serenity, then we improve our next reincarnation. **Karma** weighs us down in samsara and will lead us to an undesirable next life. So as we are dying, we are to get our minds ready through purification. In Buddhism, the path for purification is found in the **four opponent powers**: express remorse

Karma · that which weighs us down in samsara, leading to an undesirable next life

Four opponent powers · the path for purification: express remorse for our mistakes, emanate good thoughts toward people we have had trouble with, resolve ourselves not to repeat our mistakes, and do something positive as a remediation to offset the mistakes we have made

for our mistakes, emanate good thoughts toward people we had trouble with, resolve ourselves not to repeat our mistakes, and do something positive as a remediation to offset the mistakes we made. The four opponent powers are not just for death, however. We are to practice them often, as often as we make mistakes. But as we near death, the four powers become even more critical for us.

Buddhists believe that when we die, we will be reborn into one of six life forms: humans, gods, demigods (or titans), ghosts, dwellers in hell, or animals (including insects). The most highly desired life form is in the human realm. Those of us in the human realm have made good choices to get where we are. And if we are in the human realm, we are capable of achieving nirvana: release from suffering. Human life is precious. Only in the human existence do we have the opportunity to achieve the final goal of Buddhahood. Out of compassion, however, humans should do whatever they can to help other life forms reach the privileged human realm. For instance, some Buddhists take their dogs on walks that circumambulate Buddhist temples or stupas. These actions imprint the animals with good habits that will impact their rebirth.

Buddhism Today

Buddhism is the fourth-largest religion in the world, after Christianity, Islam, and Hinduism. Around 7 percent of the world's population is Buddhist, meaning there are currently between four hundred million and five hundred million Buddhists. That is an astounding decline from 1900, when around 32 percent of the world's population was Buddhist. Today, Buddhists have low fertility rates, which portends an even steeper decline in coming decades.

All the nations where Buddhism predominates are in Asia. China has more Buddhists, by far, than any nation in the world; around half of the world's Buddhists live there. Japan, Thailand, Vietnam, Myanmar, South Korea, Cambodia, and Sri Lanka are other Buddhist epicenters. Only around eleven million Buddhists live in India today, along with Nepal, the birthplace of the religion. In the United States, around 1 percent of the population adheres to Buddhism; that is around four million people. The vast majority of the world's Buddhists, around 87 percent, are Mahayana. Theravada accounts for around 13 percent of the world's Buddhists.

Like many faiths, Buddhism has gone global due to immigration. Seeking a better life, thousands of Chinese and Japanese people came to the western United States and Canada in the late 1800s and brought with them Confucianism, Daoism, and Buddhism. They worked hard, especially in mining, fishing, and building railroads that connected the eastern and western populations of North America. They settled in "Chinatowns" across North America, and they built temples, even in the face of persecution. By 1870, it is estimated that 10 percent of California was Chinese, which triggered the Chinese Exclusion Act of 1882 that was meant to stop Chinese laborers from immigrating to the United States. Many Chinese and Japanese people abandoned Buddhism in an effort to prove their loyalty to their newfound home. Others, however, continued to invest in Buddhism and establish places of worship, usually without monks, who rarely immigrated in those days. By the early 1900s, however, Japanese monks started immigrating to serve the US Buddhist population.

Buddhists today, particularly in the West, tend to be socially engaged. As a religion focused on compassion, Buddhists are mindful of the environment and how it is being impacted. They are active leaders in conversations about animal rights, and many have chosen vegetarianism.

Many Buddhists are also engaged in discussions around modern science. The Dalai Lama has made it clear that if science disproves something about Buddhism, then Buddhism must change. Part of the reason for this engagement with science is that Buddhism is a religion of the mind, not of the soul. Buddhists do not believe in a soul. The focus in Buddhism is on improving and correcting the mind, so science is understood to be a worthy partner.

Buddhism is active in AIDS awareness and teaches that sex is for monogamous love. **Chatsumarn Kabilsingh**, Thailand's first fully ordained Theravadin nun (in 2003),

Chatsumarn Kabilsingh · Thailand's first fully ordained Theravadin nun who advocates for abstinence outside of marriage

While women can become white-clad mae chi, with limited temple responsibilities, since 1928, the Sangha Act in Thailand has forbidden women from seeking ordination as monks. To pursue this lifestyle, one must travel overseas for training in a country that recognizes female monks and novices. Chatsumarn Kabilsingh took this approach and is assisting other Thai women in pursuing monastic orders.

teaches that Buddhist monks need to be more vocal in their stand against sex outside of marriage. She argues that the Four Noble Truths teach clearly that suffering stems from desire, so desires that lead to sex outside of marriage will likely lead to more intensive suffering.

In recent years, many Buddhists have longed for an ecumenical movement that might bring together and potentially unite these various approaches. Societies have been formed, such as the World Buddhist Sangha Council, established in 1966, to promote unity and cooperation among diverse Buddhist groups. The Young Buddhist Association (originally called YMBA—Young Men's Buddhist Association) was formed in 1974 for unity purposes. The International Association of Buddhist Studies (IABS) was established in 1976 for Buddhist students to come together in a spirit of nonsectarianism. Several Buddhist colleges have opened up in recent years to meet the needs of American Buddhists, especially in California. Dharma Realm Buddhist University (Ukiah), Institute of Buddhist Studies (Berkeley), Soka University of America (Orange County), and the University of the West (Rosemead) are some examples.

Buddhism continues to blaze trails in various places around the world. Despite its declining number of devotees, it continues to appeal. Some secular people claim that Buddhism enables them to practice meaningful rituals such as meditation without any supernatural ideas. Certain Christians have drawn on Buddhist concepts and practices to inform their Christian faith. Paul Knitter, a former Jesuit and theology professor, wrote a book explaining this phenomenon: *Without Buddha I Could Not Be a Christian*.

6 SIKHISM
Defend and Share

A family of Sikh pilgrims at the Golden Temple (Harmandir Sahib) in the Punjab region. The temple is the holiest shrine in Sikhism. Amritsar, India (2006).

When the 2002 movie *Bend It Like Beckham* was released, the movie industry was caught by surprise. How did a movie about a Sikh family in the United Kingdom surge to the top of the British box office and eventually gross over one hundred million dollars? Part of the answer to that question is that Indians are the largest ethnic minority population in the United Kingdom, and many of them were ecstatic to see a film representing their culture. The film engaged several lively topics surrounding Indians living overseas. One immediate result of the film's success was that it generated interest in Sikhism. Many people in the Western world had heard of Hinduism, Buddhism, and Islam, but they knew little about Sikhism. The movie created opportunities for educating people.

Sikhism originated in India, as did Hinduism, Buddhism, and Jainism. Its homeland is the **Punjab**, a region of South Asia that includes land in both India and Pakistan. When India and Pakistan were violently divided in 1947, the vast majority of Sikhs moved to the Indian side, to the Indian state of Punjab.

Sikhism is a much more recent religion than the other three Indian-born faiths. It began around 1500 CE, around the time the Protestant Reformation was beginning in Europe, Columbus was arriving to the Americas, and Michelangelo was sculpting David in Florence.

Today, there are about thirty million Sikhs in the world, making it the fifth-largest religion in the world, after Christianity, Islam, Hinduism, and Buddhism. As a comparison, the world's Sikh population is about twice that of the world's sixth-largest world religion: Judaism. Sikhs constitute around 0.4 percent of the world's population.

Sikhism is respected globally although often misunderstood, as it is frequently conflated with other Indian religions. The religion has taken root in the Western

Punjab · a region of South Asia that includes land in both India and Pakistan; the homeland of the Sikhs

Public domain

Photographer: Roop69, (CC BY-SA 4.0)

Map of the Punjab province of British India published in *The Imperial Gazetteer of India* in 1909. Compare with the map of the proposed state of Khalistan. The call for a separate Sikh state predates the fall of British rule in the 1940s.

SIKH DEMOGRAPHICS

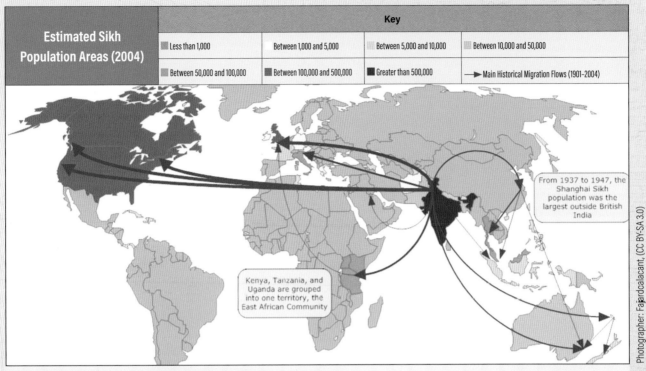

Estimated Sikh Population Areas (2004)	**Key**			
	Less than 1,000	Between 1,000 and 5,000	Between 5,000 and 10,000	Between 10,000 and 50,000
	Between 50,000 and 100,000	Between 100,000 and 500,000	Greater than 500,000	→ Main Historical Migration Flows (1901–2004)

From 1937 to 1947, the Shanghai Sikh population was the largest outside British India

Kenya, Tanzania, and Uganda are grouped into one territory, the East African Community

A map of the Sikh diaspora outside of India and across the globe.

Sikhs only comprise around 2 percent of India's population, but they are a majority in the Punjab. The majority of the world's Sikhs live in the Indian Punjab, and they hold a majority in that state. In Pakistan, it is a difficult situation for Sikhs. It is an officially Islamic state, so non-Muslims are frequent targets for persecution. The Sikhs in Pakistan are a tiny community, although some of the most important and historic Sikh gurdwaras are located in Pakistan. Caretaking these gurdwaras is the main reason a few have remained, although it is certainly a sacrifice for them to do so.

Interior of the Gurdwara Sis Ganj Sahib, one of the nine historic gurdwaras in New Delhi, India (2019).

Exterior of the Gurdwara Sis Ganj Sahib complex.

US President Bill Clinton shakes hands with Indian politician Sonia Gandhi. The future Prime Minister, Manmohan Singh, stands to her left. After this visit in March 2000, diplomatic relations between the United States and India improved dramatically.

world, and Sikh temples—known as **gurdwaras** ("door to the guru")—are becoming more common as the religion expands and gains familiarity in the diaspora. Devoted Sikh men are often recognized by their long beards, hair tucked inside a turban, and steel bracelet worn on the right wrist. Sikhs have a long history of being committed to equality, justice, and democracy, making their voices highly compatible with Western democratic societies. India, the world's largest democratic nation, was led by a Sikh man—**Dr. Manmohan Singh**—between 2004 and 2014. As prime minister of India for a decade, Dr. Singh probably did more than any Sikh in history to bring awareness to the religion.

It is difficult for religion scholars to classify Sikhism. It is often considered to be a kind of hybrid between Hinduism and Islam. Sikhs claim, however, that their religion is an entirely new revelation and is not simply a merger or blending of two faiths. One reason people tend to think of Sikhism as a combination of Hinduism and Islam is that it came about during Islam's consolidation of most of the Indian subcontinent. From the early 1500s until the mid-1800s, India was ruled mainly by Muslims in what was known as the **Mughal Empire**. It was a period of frequent tension, as the ruling Mughals were Muslim, while their subjects were largely Hindu.

This rare early nineteenth-century mural from Gurdwara Baba Atal depicts Guru Nanak. Amritsar, India.

The Beginnings of Sikhism

The founder of Sikhism was a man named Nanak, known to Sikhs as **Guru Nanak** (1469–1539). He was from a caste called Khatri, as were all ten of the later Sikh gurus. He was born into a Hindu family, in the town of Rai Bhoeki Talwandi, near Lahore; that town is today known as **Nankana Sahib** and is one of the most sacred sites in Sikhism. His elder sister, named **Bibi Nanaki**, saw the light of God in him when he was very young, and later she

Gurdwara · "door to the guru"; a Sikh temple

Dr. Manhoman Singh · a Sikh who led India from 2004 to 2014

Mughal Empire · Turkish Muslim rule over India from 1526 to 1857

Guru Nanak · the founder of Sikhism who combined certain elements of Hinduism and Islam

Nankana Sahib · the town in which Guru Nanak was born; a holy site for Sikhs today

Bibi Nanaki · Nanak's older sister and first disciple who saw the light of God in him from a young age became Nanak's first disciple. She taught him to use music as a way to connect with God.

Nanak studied both Islam and Hinduism as a boy. He was also impacted by Muslim mystics who saw compatibility between Hinduism and Islam at a time when the relationship between the two faiths was hostile. In the political sphere, Islam was expanding, and Hindus were struggling to adapt to Muslim rule.

Nanak married young, which was common at that time. His marriage was not a happy one. They did have two sons, but Nanak looked elsewhere for his successor late in his life. A common theme for world religion leaders is that their home life seems to have been less than optimal. Perhaps the extremely busy lifestyle of the father causes dysfunction on the home front.

At around the age of thirty, Nanak was working for a Muslim nobleman when he had a religious experience. He descended down to a river to bathe and emerged, uttering the words, "There is no Hindu; there is no Muslim." Nanak had perceived a way to reconcile these two religions. Nanak came to believe that God had appointed him to be the supreme guru, so he left his family to completely focus on his ministry.

Over the next thirty years, Nanak and his musically gifted partner in ministry—named Mardana—traveled all around with the message that "There is no Hindu; there is no Muslim." He dressed in a Hindu–Muslim way rather than choosing one or the other. That was rare in India at the time. He soon began to acquire followers from both Hindu and Islamic backgrounds. His followers became known as Sikhs, which is a Punjabi word for "disciples."

Nanak's divine revelation contained elements common to both Hinduism and Islam. He agreed with the Muslims that polytheism was wrong—there is only one God. He upheld the teaching of reincarnation, a quintessentially Hindu idea. But he opposed the longstanding institution of the Indian caste system and argued that asceticism—so foundational for Indian religions—was unnecessary. What eventually caused severe persecution for Sikhs was Nanak's denial of the Quran as God's final revelation.

At around the age of fifty-five, Nanak settled down in the Punjab region again. During his final fifteen years of life, he mentored a man named Angad and arranged for him to be his successor. Notably, Nanak did not choose either of his sons as successor, as he did not find them to be worthy.

Guru Nanak departed this Earth at the age of seventy, in 1539. There is an important legend about his death. Those with a Hindu background wanted to cremate him, and those with a Muslim background wanted to bury him. There arose a great quarrel about this. He told both sides to put flowers around him, and the next day, he would point out which flowers were most fresh. Whichever side had the freshest flowers would be granted the right to dispose of his body. That night, he covered himself and the flowers with a sheet. But in the morning, Nanak was not there. His body was never found. All the flowers were still there, however, and they were all fresh. Thus, even in his death, Guru Nanak proved to be a reconciler and a man of peace.

Over time, as Sikhism grew, Guru Nanak's successors attracted the attention of certain Mughal emperors, leading to a period of great violence. Many Sikhs were persecuted to the point that they began to resist and develop defensive tactics, which only antagonized the Mughal emperors. Many leading Sikhs were tortured and executed. These actions only aroused Sikh resolve. Sikhs continued to grow and thrive and defend themselves. Eventually, it became clear that Sikhism would not be destroyed.

Guru Nanak was so respected because he was perceived to be the divine light. People bowed to him, but when they bowed to him, they were bowing to the

An example of popular art that would have been sold at local bazaars and fairs, this woodcut shows Guru Nanak with Mardana (left) and Bala, one of Nanak's childhood friends and life companions. Amritsar or Lahore, India (ca. 1875).

THE TEN GURUS

According to Sikhism, God revealed his will through gurus. Nanak was the chosen instrument of God to reveal the divine will, or God's Word. After Nanak came nine more human gurus. They spread the teachings of Guru Nanak far and wide across the Indian subcontinent, shaping the religion in numerous ways.

- **Guru Nanak** (1469–1539) founded Sikhism.
- **Guru Angad** (1539–52) created a Punjabi script for the scriptures called **Gurmukhi**.
- **Guru Amar Das** (1552–74) created a Sikh clergy and geographical system, similar to the diocesan system of Christianity. Importantly, of the twenty-two top-ranked leaders he appointed, eight of them were female. Also, he preached against sati (widow burning) and purdah (seclusion of women).
- **Guru Ram Das** (1574–81) founded Amritsar, the holy city of Sikhism. He also started the tradition of appointing a blood relative as guru.
- **Guru Arjan Dev** (1581–1606) ordered the building of the Golden Temple at Amritsar—the holiest site for Sikhs. He also compiled the earliest version of the Sikh scripture, the **Adi Granth**. Under him, the guru became both the spiritual and political leader of Sikhism. He refused to convert to Islam, and he was tortured and executed on the orders of Mughal emperor Jahangir.
- **Guru Hargobind** (1606–44) became guru at age eleven, when his father died. He gave the Sikhs their warrior image, as he commissioned Sikhs to defend themselves militarily, a decision that provoked the Mughals further.
- **Guru Har Rai** (1644–61) became guru at age fourteen when his grandfather (Hargobind) died. He is notable for building up the Sikh military yet avoiding a war. This bought the Sikhs some precious time to organize themselves better.
- **Guru Har Krishan** (1661–64) became guru at age five, when his father died. He contracted smallpox and died at age seven.
- **Guru Tegh Bahadur** (1664–75) was known to be a fierce warrior, a well-traveled missionary for Sikhism, and a wonderful hymn writer. He was publicly beheaded on the orders of Emperor Aurangzeb after refusing to convert to Islam. Before his execution, he was forced to watch several of his colleagues being tortured and killed.
- **Guru Gobind Singh** (1675–1708), son of Tegh Bahadur, was the last of the human gurus. He established the Khalsa, authorized the wearing of the Five Ks, and named the Guru Granth Sahib as his successor forevermore. His four sons were all martyred by the Mughals. He led the Sikhs for thirty-three years against a fierce era of Muslim jihad.

divine light, not to the human being. Thus, all ten of the gurus, as well as the **Guru Granth Sahib**, are not venerated due to their physicality. They are venerated because of the divinity within them. In this way, the divinity that was inside Guru Nanak continues to live on in the divine light of Sikhism's scripture—the Granth Sahib.

Sikh Beliefs

Guru Nanak avoided making exclusive claims when it came to religion. He believed that he was teaching the true essence of all the religions, rather than the specificities of just one. As a result, there is some flexibility in Sikhism that is perhaps less common in most other world religions. There is an interesting story about Nanak when he was visiting the city of Mecca. He was sleeping when an attendant rudely awakened

Gurmukhi · the Punjabi script for the scriptures created by Guru Angad

Sri Guru Granth Sahib · the holy text of Sikhism as well as the eleventh and final guru; treated as a sacred person and not just a book

"Ik Onkar," or "There is one God," is the fundamental core teaching of Sikhism and its most recognizable symbol. These are the first words of the Mul Mantar, the opening verse of the Guru Granth Sahib.

him and told him that his feet were pointing toward the Ka'aba—the Islamic house of God that all Muslims must pray toward. Humbly and innocently, Nanak asked the attendant to point his feet in the direction of where God was *not*. Clearly, Nanak's point was made manifest.

First and foremost, Nanak taught that God is one. Sikhs have several names for God, probably the most important ones being **Satnam** (true name) and **Waheguru** (wondrous teacher). God is defined as being unborn and eternal, omnipotent, the creator of all, without fear or hate, and self-existent. In his doctrine of God, Nanak brilliantly merged Islam's strict understanding of monotheism with Hinduism's notion of Brahman—the supreme reality. The Sikh expression **Ik Onkar**—meaning "There is one God"—is the fundamental core of Sikhism.

In the Sikh scriptures, God is referred to as both father and mother. God is gender-neutral, and all attempts to identify God are incomplete. This is a key reason why Sikhs focus so much on gender equality. Guru Nanak argued strongly that women are of equal status to men. Besides, women cannot be inferior because they give birth to emperors and all the greatest men. Even in religious services and ceremonies, women are able to enjoy full participation and equal status.

Nanak welcomed everyone into his community, irrespective of caste, religion, creed, nationality, social class, or gender. This was countercultural at the time and scandalous to many. But Nanak held fast to there being one creator God, and therefore all human beings are brothers and sisters. This has become a pillar of Sikhism: all humans are equals and should be treated as such.

Nanak believed that humans are fundamentally good because they are fundamentally divine. Evil is simply ignorance. Guru Nanak reinterpreted the laws of karma, thus restoring a sense of dignity to humankind. This was revolutionary. Normally, Hindus understood that low-caste people received less dignity because of mistakes they had made in their past. But Guru Nanak argued against caste distinctions, choosing to focus on God's grace in spiritual

Satnam · a name for God meaning "true name"

Waheguru · a name for God meaning "wondrous teacher"

Ik Onkar · "There is one God"; a fundamental teaching of Sikhism

People crowd around a Lohri festival bonfire in 2019. Though not a religious festival, Hindus, Sikhs, Christians, and Muslims in the Punjab region and the diaspora join together to celebrate the passing of winter and the beginning of spring. At Lohri, parents and grandparents celebrate the new marriages and the birth of children that calendar year.

progress and the commonalities we all share as human beings. He also argued against asceticism and austere religious practices like fasting and celibacy. People should enjoy marriage and all the other human delights that present themselves. Instead of viewing monasticism as a virtue, Nanak considered it totally unnecessary since one can connect deeply with God while living a normal, enriched life. Sikhism

An illuminated folio from the Lahore recension of the Adi Granth (ca. seventeenth or eighteenth century).

argues that our day-to-day, material happiness is just as important as our spiritual liberation. Life is sacred because we have a divine lineage. Normal people can live a holy and sacred life.

Thus, for Nanak, the ascetic life is pointless. Elaborate rituals and monastic orders have little to do with achieving salvation. Rather, salvation depends on the goodness and grace of God's favor. The responsibility of humans is to live a good life, conduct oneself morally and ethically, and prepare one's heart for God through the **triple formula (nam dan isnan)**: praising the name (of God), giving (charity), and keeping oneself pure.

Guru Nanak became agitated at the ascetics who demanded that people renounce. Indeed, nine of the gurus were married men who had families. The only one of the ten gurus who never married was Har Krishan, because he died at the age of seven. Nanak argued that the Earth is the realm where we practice righteousness, or **Dharmsal**. We are to live out our faith in a normal human life. It makes no sense to withdraw from the world on account of one's faith. Rather, interacting with people, participating in society, and seeing the world as a place to be productive and to live out one's faith—these are the duties of a Sikh.

God can be realized by a combination of our own faith and God's grace—known in Sikhism as **Gurparshad**. This is a term that combines *guru* (teacher) and *parshad* (grace). **Parshad** is also the name of the sanctified food given at the end of a religious service in the gurdwara. It has a double meaning. It is a blessing and a gift to those gathered, but it is also a reminder that divine grace comes to those who sincerely dedicate themselves to God. God showers

Gurdwara Janam Asthan, the birthplace of Guru Nanak.

Triple formula · also known as **nam dan isnan**; prepares one's heart for God through praising his name, giving charity, and keeping oneself pure

Dharmsal · the place where we practice righteousness

Gurparshad · a combination of our own faith and God's grace; the only way to realize God

Parshad · grace; also refers to the sanctified food given at the end of a religious service in the gurdwara

people with divine grace. He assists humans on their path to know him.

> Sikhs assume the Indian religious understanding that humans are in an eternal cycle of birth and death and rebirth, or samsara.

Another related concept is **Namsimran**, which comes from *Nam* (name of God) and *Simran* (continuous remembrance). In the practice of Namsimran, Sikhs gather at the gurdwara to remember God, to meditate on God, and to recite God's holiest names: Waheguru and Satnam, often using a rosary. It should be pointed out, however, that Sikhs believe that their God is the same God that all humans have access to. God can be remembered by many names: Yahweh, Jehovah, Ram, Allah, Khuda, or Ahura Mazda.

Nanak argued that we do not know when our current universe came into being, and we do not know when it will end. Time in its largest sense is unfathomable because God, the creator, is unfathomable, limitless, and infinite. Guru Nanak emphasized this boundless and eternal nature of God; humans will never understand these matters, so it is pointless to speculate.

Sikhs assume the Indian religious understanding that humans are in an eternal cycle of birth and death and rebirth, or samsara. Guru Nanak agreed with Hinduism that humans have a soul, an atman. But for Nanak,

the soul is designed to have a longing for God. When a soul is not aligned with God, it suffers. The soul that does not love God sufficiently will exist in sorrow and remain in a state of suffering. Humans, thus, either choose to draw near to God, or they separate themselves from God.

Sikhs focus on God and believe that each human has divinity in their heart. Humans have to turn inward to find God, as the essence of God is inside of human beings. Sikhs meditate on God and listen to God's will through the guru until they become more and more in love with God. While Sikhs do have rituals, the emphasis is not on the rituals. Nor is there an emphasis on avatars and incarnations. In Sikhism, one connects directly with God without the need for intermediaries. This was one of the important reasons why Sikhism presented itself as distinct from Hinduism: it focused little on the external features that Hinduism relies heavily upon.

In some ways, Sikhism is a much simpler religion than most. Sikhs are required to abide by the **Three Pillars of Sikhism**: (1) meditate on Waheguru, (2) live honestly, and (3) share with others. As Sikhs had to defend themselves against Muslim powers, they emphasized defending themselves, as well as defending the vulnerable. Sikhism has high standards of morality.

Namsimran · a practice in which Sikhs gather at the gurdwara to remember God, to meditate on God, and to recite God's holiest names: Waheguru and Satnam, often using a rosary

Three Pillars of Sikhism · (1) meditate on Waheguru, (2) live honestly, (3) share with others

Two faithful Sikhs study the Guru Granth Sahib.

However, the strict fasting, the appeasement of deities, the various pujas directed toward various gods, the frequent holy days—these are not essential for Sikhs. Renunciation of the world has no place in Sikhism. Their priests are able to marry and have children. The ritual side of religion is rather deemphasized in Sikhism. Importantly, Sikhism shares with Islam that God should not be depicted with images, engravings, or any kind of idols.

The goal of Sikhism is to achieve union with God and liberation from samsara. Through moral progress, we improve in our new incarnations. We have all been through various animal incarnations, suffering untold miseries. Our animal incarnations were punishment for how we behaved in previous lives. Eventually, if we live without sin and with full devotion to God, then we will attain eternal peace by uniting with God. Those who fail to live in accordance with God's desires will acquire an impure mind and will enter a cycle of spiritual degeneration. They will then generate more evil and descend into a state of chaos and crisis. Eventually, if we continue to act unethically and immorally, we will be reborn as animals. With good behavior, however, we can be reborn again as humans. And if we live righteously as humans and cultivate a love for God, then we can eventually aspire to achieving release from transmigration altogether.

The Sikh word for "release from samsara" is **mukti**, which is the Punjabi pronunciation of the Sanskrit word *moksha*. When a person achieves mukti, they are liberated from the cycle of rebirth. They merge with the Supreme Soul. Sikhism assumes the Hindu teaching that there are 8.4 million forms of existence, or species, that an atman goes through prior to becoming human. Thus, human life is precious, as it presents a way toward mukti—exiting the cycle of rebirth. If humans are able to become guru-focused rather than ego- or self-focused, then they stand a chance to attain liberation. They have to detach from all of the enticements and worldly priorities that pull us downward, such as lust, anger, greed, attachment, and arrogance. Like a lotus flower that lives in the mud, Sikhs believe those who live righteously can achieve spiritual beauty, even in a sinful world.

Sikhs oppose the use of tobacco, alcohol, drugs, or any other addictive substances. Fully initiated Sikhs—known as Khalsa—have four stated prohibitions that are particularly serious and must be confessed publicly for them to be instated as Khalsa members:

- They must not have any hair cut.
- The meat they consume must have been butchered according to Sikh rules.
- They must not commit adultery.
- They must not use tobacco, alcohol, or any other intoxicants.

Perhaps most importantly, Khalsa members must wear the Five Ks, which will be discussed shortly.

Sikhs believe in four stages of the human mind. First, there is egotism—this is a life that exists in greed, selfishness, and lust. Second, there is optimism—this is when someone is aware that there is a better way forward but they remain subject to their vices. Third, there is determination—this is when a person has maneuvered himself or herself in the direction of righteousness and is truly attempting to avoid the temptations of egotism. Finally, the fourth phase is known in Sikhism as Sehaj—this is the transcendental state, enlightenment, serenity. It is heavenly bliss and is the goal of the Sikh endeavor. If a person remains in the state of the first three modes, then they cannot enter heaven. However, if one achieves Sehaj, then they have no fear, no worry, and no sadness. They are at peace and completely calm. They have no restrictions. They become absorbed into the absolute, and all desires cease. They are completely committed to following God's perfect will, both in body and in soul. Perhaps most importantly, they are no longer subject to transmigration. They are released, and therefore, they are completely free.

Interestingly, Sikhs do not believe that one has to become a Sikh to attain heavenly bliss. Anyone can achieve union with the divine, regardless of their

SIKH PRACTICES

The most well-known practices of the Sikh community are the Five Ks. It is interesting to note that these five were not obligatory for Khalsa members until the late 1800s, in the midst of a Sikh renaissance. Together, the Five Ks made for a sharper distinction between Sikhs and Hindus.

1. **Kesh:** uncut hair
2. **Kangha:** a wooden comb for the hair
3. **Kara:** an iron bracelet
4. **Kachera:** a cotton undergarment
5. **Kirpan:** an iron dagger

The Five Ks are for those Sikhs who have partaken of the **Amrit** ceremony and entered the **Khalsa**—the pure ones. Sikhs who have not taken the Amrit ceremony and/or do not abide by the Five Ks are called **Sahajdhari** ("slow adopter"), meaning they have chosen to follow the path of Sikhism but for some reason have not yet participated in the Amrit ceremony and thus are not obligated to maintain the Five Ks.

formal religious affiliation. This is one reason Sikhs do not attempt to convert others. If anyone wants to join Sikhism, they can, but Sikhs must never lure or compel another to join. Sikhism is not an exclusive faith; God can be adored by people from virtually any religion. As long as the person is virtuous and calls upon the true God, then they can achieve celestial bliss and release from samsara.

For a Sikh to fully commit to the faith and become Khalsa, they must participate in the Amrit ceremony, an initiation introduced by the tenth and last human guru, Guru Gobind Singh, in 1699. Its origin has a fascinating story. Guru Gobind Singh's father, Guru Tegh Bahadur, was the ninth guru of Sikhism, and he had been beheaded on the orders of the Mughal emperor Aurangzeb. Guru Tegh Bahadur was a warrior, and he raised his son in that same tradition. His son, Guru Gobind Singh, was also killed by the Mughals, as were Guru Gobind Singh's own four sons. This was during a long and bloody era when Mughals were persecuting the Sikhs—in fact, trying to destroy them. This is also one important reason why Gobind Singh inaugurated a new era for Sikh leadership when he declared his successor would not be a human; rather, it would be the Sikh scriptures. Indeed, he finalized and enshrined the Guru Granth Sahib as the eternal authority in Sikhism,

Amrit · the initiation ceremony to become a member of the Khalsa; involves drinking of a sweet nectar of sugar and water, which is stirred with a sword

Khalsa · "the pure ones"; the community of Sikhs who have been initiated through the Amrit ceremony and who adhere to the Five Ks and to a code of moral conduct

Sahajdhari · "slow adopter"; a Sikh who has not participated in the Amrit ceremony and does not abide by the Five Ks

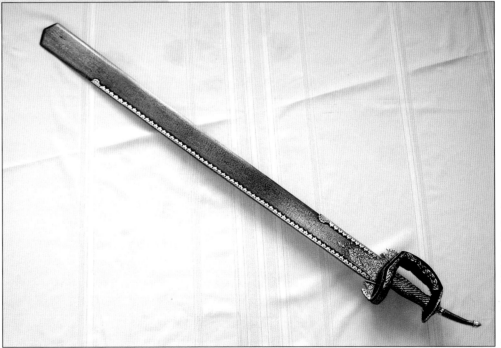

A khanda, a double-edged sword used for Sikh symbolism and ritual.

Photographer: Archit Patel, public domain

and this eliminated the possibility of yet another guru assassination.

To provide a more organized defense for his people, Guru Gobind Singh set out to establish an elite force. He called for a public gathering and spoke to the congregation from the entryway of a tent. He asked the congregation if they would like to pledge themselves to the faith by offering their head. Everyone was reluctant until, finally, one man stepped forward. Gobind Singh took him into the tent and emerged with a bloody sword. He asked for another person to offer his head, and another man stepped up. Three more men did this same thing, and each time, Gobind Singh emerged with a bloody sword. Finally, as the crowd was horrified by what was happening, Gobind Singh brought all five men out, unharmed. They emerged fully armed with weapons and dressed in excellent attire. Next, Gobind Singh kneeled before the five brave men and asked them to initiate him, their own guru, into the order of the Khalsa.

This is the origin of the Khalsa. These six men had proven themselves pure and were now members of God's army that would protect the Sikh people. This is the point where Khalsa men became known as **Singh** ("lion") and Khalsa women were called **Kaur** ("princess"). Many Sikhs today have either Singh or Kaur as part of their name.

The Amrit ceremony takes place in a gurdwara. It is administered to Sikhs who feel old enough to understand the commitment they are making. All participants must begin by bathing themselves before the service. The ceremony takes place in front of the holy text—the Guru Granth Sahib. Five already-initiated Sikhs must be there, in commemoration of the five heroes who stepped forward for Gobind Singh. There must also be a Khalsa member who leads the service. Hymns are sung, prayers are said, and the core tenets of the Sikh faith are recited and affirmed. One of the attendants must then randomly select a passage from the Guru Granth Sahib and read from it. A nectar of sugar and water is prepared and stirred with a double-edged sword, known as a **khanda**. The candidates then drink of the sweet water, all using the same bowl—demonstrating solidarity. The amrit nectar is then sprinkled on their eyes and hair five times. The remaining nectar is then shared by all present, again from the same bowl. After more prayers, readings, and affirmations, the ceremony ends with eating of the blessed, sweet-tasting food known as the parshad.

> **Singh** · "Lion"; a name taken by most Sikh men
>
> **Kaur** · "Princess"; a name taken by most Sikh women
>
> **Khanda** · a double-edged sword

If a Khalsa member falls away and, for a time, neglects the Five Ks, he or she must be assigned a penance—humiliating punishment, often manual labor—prior to going through the Amrit ceremony again. They are allowed to be readmitted, but they must pledge to do penance, with the understanding that they will henceforth be faithful.

Guru Gobind Singh is interconnected with the notion of the Five Ks, as he initiated them. The uncut hair—kesh—is how Gobind Singh lived. He did not cut his hair—not on his body, face, or head. Both Khalsa men and women must never cut any of their hair after receiving Amrit. Sikh men are easily identified due to their uncut hair—wrapped in a turban—and their uncut beard. Sikhs consider uncut hair to be the way God intended for us to be. We must not cut what God has given. God created us this way, so it is important to keep it just like the creator intended. Wearing a turban is also significant, as it shows dedication to the faith; it leads to self-respect, provides courage, and facilitates piety.

The kangha is a small wooden comb that Sikhs use to groom their hair twice per day. It is worn in the hair itself at all times and is intended to keep the hair clean and untangled.

The kara is an iron bracelet that is to be worn at all times. It means that God's hand is on the wrist of the person, providing guidance. God is with us, even holding our hand. It is also symbolic in its meaning that the Sikh is bonded, like a link in a chain, to the larger Sikh community.

The kachera is the cotton undergarment that must be tied with a knot—no elastic can be used. The symbolism is that Sikhs are always ready to battle and defend the community. Some Sikhs have even chosen to wear the kachera during baths. It is a loose-fitting

Also known as Vaisakhi, the forty-first annual Khalsa Day brought more than one hundred thousand people to the streets of Toronto. The event now includes one of the largest parades in Canada (2019).

undergarment that allows for great flexibility, enabling the soldier to engage in combat without restraint. The kachera also reminds baptized Sikhs that they should not lust. This pertains to both men and women. This garment keeps the men cool in hot weather, and it is conducive for manual labor, such as farming. While women Khalsa members wear the kachera under their clothes, they do not wear it as an outer garment as men are allowed to do.

The kirpan is the dagger that shows power, protection, and safety. Due to the threat of the Mughals, Sikhs originally were to be constantly prepared to defend themselves, violently if necessary. As was the case with all of the Five Ks, the kirpan was to be worn at all times. Today, it symbolizes that the Sikh must be prepared to stand for justice, defend the weak, and fight against evil. Sikhs are taught that if they witness a person being victimized, they are obligated to step in and help. If that means they have to fight, then the kirpan will be there to assist. Like a soldier who must be ready

for battle, Khalsa members must always be prepared. When Guru Gobind Singh started the Khalsa in 1699, there was a notion that members were part of God's army, so it made good sense that they were armed.

Sikhs have sparked legal controversy with their religious stipulation to carry a ceremonial dagger, the kirpan, at all times. This bank in Bangalore forbids all weapons, except the religious kirpans of the Sikhs.

Khalsa members have other expectations as well. Each day they must rise at dawn and meditate on Waheguru—the only God. They must marry only Sikhs. They must not worship idols. They must practice the bearing of arms and must never show their backs to the enemy during battle. They must be always willing to help the poor and offer protection to anyone who requests it. They must not observe any caste, nor should they count themselves as members of any caste. They are now and forever members of the Sikh family.

Sikhs have many celebrations and festivals, often revolving around the birthdays and martyrdoms of the ten gurus. The celebrations for the gurus are known as **Gurpurbs**, or "guru celebrations." The most important birthday celebrations commemorate Guru Nanak and Guru Gobind Singh. The two main martyrdom celebrations are for Guru Arjan and Guru Tegh Bahadur. During Gurpurbs, Sikhs have processions in which five armed Khalsa members—in commemoration of those first five—carry around the Guru Granth Sahib on a decorated palanquin.

Sikhs in the Punjab celebrate **Vaisakhi** (also pronounced "Baisakhi"), which is the first day of the month of Vaisakha and corresponds to April/May in the Gregorian calendar. Not only is this a time of **melas** (fairs) and **kirtans** (devotional singing in the gurdwara), but it is a festival that has come to specifically commemorate the birth of the Khalsa by Guru Gobind Singh.

Sikhs also celebrate **Diwali** and **Holi**, along with Hindus, but with different meanings. Whereas Hindus celebrate "the festival of lights" by remembering Lord Rama returning from exile in Sri Lanka, Sikhs remember their sixth Guru—Hargobind—being set free from prison. Emperor Jahangir released Guru Hargobind, and when he returned to the city of **Amritsar**, the Sikhs held a great party. Today, Sikhs celebrate Diwali with fireworks, and they illuminate the **Golden Temple**, also known as the **Harmandir Sahib** and the **Durbar Sahib**.

Guru Gobind Singh disapproved of the Hindu festival of Holi, where people throw colors at each other. Instead, he encouraged Sikhs to train in the martial arts and have mock battles on Holi. The Sikhs still associate the festival with martial arts, but Sikhs pronounce the festival **Hola** rather than Holi.

Sikh Scripture

Sikhs do not just view their scripture, the Sri Guru Granth Sahib ("Sir Guru Book Sir"),

Gurpurbs · "guru celebrations"; festivals commemorating the birthdays and martyrdoms of the ten human gurus

Vaisakhi · festival celebrating the birth of the Khalsa

Melas · fairs

Kirtans · devotional singing in the gurdwara

Diwali · a holiday celebrated by Sikhs in commemoration of Guru Hargobind being released from prison

Holi · a holiday in which Sikhs train in the martial arts and have mock battles

Amritsar · the holy city of Sikhism and the location of the Golden Temple

Golden Temple · also known as **Harmandir Sahib** or **Durbar Sahib**; the most important gurdwara and the most sacred site of Sikhism; a magnificent temple of white marble and gold

Hola · the Sikh pronunciation of Holi

A Sikh man reading a passage from the Guru Granth Sahib while sitting inside a gurdwara. Delhi, India (2020).

A selection of Sikh scripture from the Adi Granth.

as a book; they view it as the embodiment of the gurus. Thus, if the holy text is damaged, it is actually like someone has physically hurt their guru. There are cases in which arsonists have burned a gurdwara, and Sikhs responded by accusing the arsonists of attempted murder. Why? Because the scripture is their living guru.

The fifth guru, Arjan Dev, compiled the Sikh scriptures by editing and organizing the sacred writings of the first five gurus. He also added some Hindu and Muslim devotional writers. That text is called the **Adi Granth** ("First Book") and contains 1,430 pages. The final human guru, Gobind Singh, also added some of the writings of his father, the martyr Guru Tegh Bahadur, and he declared the text to be the final guru after his own demise. However, the new guru, the Granth Sahib, would exist in perpetuity. Sikhs are not allowed to alter the text whatsoever, not even one punctuation mark, as it comes directly from the gurus.

The Granth Sahib is written in poetic form and contains the ideals and teachings of Sikhism. It hardly mentions historical events in Sikhism. It is meant to be timeless, emphasizing love for God

Adi Granth · the first compiled collection of Sikh scripture, containing 1,430 pages of sacred teachings of the gurus as well as some Hindu and Muslim devotional writings; collected by the fifth guru, and later added to by the tenth to form the Guru Granth Sahib

Palki · a decorated seat on which the Guru Granth Sahib is prominently displayed in a gurdwara

Hukam · a daily worship practice in which the Granth is opened at random for the selection of a hymn that should be sung

A Sikh granthi sits behind the Guru Granth Sahib and waves a chaur over the sacred text.

and humankind, community service, gender equality, honesty, the importance of family, and religious tolerance. It forbids fasting and idol worship. In the gurdwara, the Granth is seated on a **Palki** (decorated seat) in a prominent location. Every day, the Granth is opened at random for the selection of a hymn that should be sung. This process is called **Hukam** (divine command).

The individuals, both male and female, who lead the worship are called **granthis** (readers) and **ragis** (musicians). During worship, a granthi sits behind the scripture and waves a **chaur** (fly whisk) over the text, a traditional practice done to honor rulers. After evening prayers, the Guru Granth Sahib is put to bed. All Sikhs are encouraged to read the complete Granth at least once in their lifetime.

Sikh State and Diaspora

Sikhs prospered and continued to expand during the eighteenth century, although Britain was gaining ground year after year in its quest to consolidate the subcontinent. From 1799 to 1849, the Sikhs established an independent state. It did not last long, however, as the British were encroaching. In the 1840s, the British military defeated the Sikhs and took much of the Punjab land as their own. From 1858 to 1947, Great Britain governed the Indian subcontinent, an era known as the British Raj. Over time, the Sikhs gained the confidence of Britain and were rewarded with favorable positions in the British Raj and British military. They were also given good positions in British territories across the world, thus beginning the Sikh diaspora to areas of the world ruled by Great Britain.

Many Sikhs were part of the Indian independence movement led by Gandhi and others. In 1947, Indian independence became a reality. However, the Sikh heartland was rent into two, with the famous **partition** of India into India and Pakistan. The Punjab area, where Sikhs are primarily located, is now partly in India and partly in Pakistan. Most Sikhs fled out of Pakistan, due to Islamic rule, and moved to

Granthis · Sikhs who lead worship services by reading from the Guru Granth Sahib and waving the chaur over the text

Ragis · musicians who lead Sikh worship services

Chaur · a fly whisk waved above the Guru Granth Sahib out of honor and respect

Partition · when the British left India, the territory was divided into three countries largely based on their religious majorities: Hindu India, Muslim Pakistan, and Muslim East Pakistan (later Bangladesh); the Sikhs' region of the Punjab was split between Pakistan and India, and Sikhism lost many of its adherents and holy sites to religious intolerance in Pakistan

Nirmala · a celibate, ascetic Sikh sect

Image courtesy of Royal Collection Trust, © Her Majesty Queen Elizabeth II 2022

Posthumous portrait of Maharaja Ranjit Singh, by Lahori artist Imam Bakhsh (active ca. 1825–45). This was the first Indian painting acquired by the young Queen Victoria in May 1843.

Image courtesy of V&A Images. Used by permission.

Collected by John Lockwood Kipling, the father of renowned English author Rudyard Kipling, this 1870s print gives a panoramic north view of the city of Lahore, Pakistan, with the first maharaja of the Sikh Empire, Ranjit Singh (1780–1839) and attendants in the foreground. Singh earned the title "Lion of the Punjab" as he consolidated control in the region.

Sikhism   153

British Sikhs continue to advocate for an independent state. In 2019, thousands cast their votes in London for a Khalistan referendum. The Indian government has strongly opposed the United Kingdom allowing these political demonstrations.

the Indian side. The Indian constitution allows much greater freedom for religions.

Many Sikhs wanted their own nation at the time of independence and partition in 1947. Hindus received their own nation in gaining India, Muslims gained Pakistan and Bangladesh, but Sikhs felt they were cheated out of a homeland. In 1983, some militaristic Sikhs captured the Golden Temple at Amritsar and declared a homeland called Khalistan. However, India's prime minister at the time, Indira Gandhi, dashed their hopes by calling in the military. The ensuing battle killed hundreds on both sides. As retaliation, the prime minister's bodyguards, who were Sikh, assassinated her in October 1984. This led to four days of violence against Sikhs. Thousands of Sikhs were killed, shops were burned, and hopes for a Khalistan were put on hold. This makes the rise of Prime Minister Manmohan Singh, a devout Sikh, all the more important in India's history, as he led India from 2004 to 2014.

Sikhs Today

There are several different denominations of Sikhs today. Some are more primitive and want to emulate the early Sikh community. Some reject the military aspect of Sikhism. There is an ascetic, celibate sect in Sikhism known as the **Nirmalas**. This ascetic sect is ironic, considering that Guru Nanak was against this concept. They wear ochre-colored robes and only own a begging bowl, just like other ascetics in India, although only a few of them go naked.

There are sects of Sikhism that emphasize going "back to the gurus." It is a common idea in religions that, at some point, certain members want to return to a previous era in the faith. There are two Sikh sects—the **Nirankaris** and the **Namdharis**—that reject the

Nirankari · a Sikh sect from the merchant class that rejects the traditional count of ten gurus, following its own guru today; known for casting the dead into rivers, rather than the customary practice of cremation

Namdhari · a vegetarian Sikh sect from the carpenter class that rejects the traditional count of ten gurus, following its own guru today; recognized by their white, homespun outfits, as well as their unique white turbans, which are tied across the forehead

SIKH CEREMONIES

Sikhs have numerous ceremonies, including:

- The **Dastar Bandi** is when a Sikh boy is taken to the gurdwara to tie on his first turban.
- The **Anand Karaj** ("act toward happiness") is the Sikh marriage ceremony. As is common in India, marriages often signify an alliance between families and are thus commonly arranged. As per tradition, remarriage is not allowed for divorcees.
- For the Sikh baby, there is a special naming ceremony called **Naam Karan**. Somebody will open the Guru Granth Sahib at random, and the first letter of the first verse on the lefthand page becomes the initial for the child's given name. Then, "Kaur" (princess) is added for girls, and "Singh" (lion) is added for boys.

traditional count of ten gurus and continue to follow their own gurus today. The Nirankaris tend to be merchants. They rose up during the era of the independent Sikh state (1799–1849). They are known for casting their dead into rivers rather than the customary practice of cremation. The Namdharis are from the carpenter caste. They are recognized by their white homespun outfits, as well as their unique white turbans, which are tied across the forehead. They are strict vegetarians. They are often called **Kukas** ("shrieking") because they shriek when they worship.

Many Sikhs came to North America—especially Canada—in the first half of the twentieth century. Like many new immigrants, they were often discriminated against with the epithet "ragheads." During this era, there were severe restrictions against Asian immigration, and it was difficult for Asians to receive citizenship in the United States. Despite racism and political opposition, the first Sikh gurdwara in the United States was established in Stockton, California, in 1912.

The Civil Rights Movement in the 1960s proved beneficial for virtually all immigrant groups. Old quotas and prohibitions against immigrants were substantially modified, allowing Sikh immigrants to come to the United States with their families to seek a better life. The early waves of Sikhs tended to be more focused on farming, so they lived in the countryside. After the 1960s, Sikh immigrants gravitated toward the United States' largest cities. California, New York, and Texas welcomed many Sikhs. Many of these post-1960s Sikhs were much more traditional than the Sikhs that were assimilated into the United States for three generations already. These newer Sikh immigrants brought Indian rules and customs, such as no shoes or chairs in the gurdwara, and they brought back traditional Indian music. They also emphasized the practice of **langar**—free vegetarian meals for all—which had faded somewhat.

Another small wave of Sikhs arrived in the 1980s, after the turbulent events of 1983 and 1984, when India's prime minister was assassinated and thousands of Sikhs were killed. These Sikhs were more politically active, and they pressed harder for a strong Khalsa identity. They talked often about **Khalistan**—an independent Sikh state—and they caused tension in the American gurdwaras.

Following the September 11, 2001, terrorist attacks, Sikhs were frequently confused with the Taliban Muslims in Afghanistan due to very similar garb and a shared commitment to turbans and beards. Sikh children were routinely criticized at school, and some Sikhs were killed

Kukas · a name for the Namdharis meaning "shrieking," since they shriek when they worship

Langar · free vegetarian meals served after every service in a gurdwara

Khalistan · a potential independent Sikh nation in Punjab

Photographer: Harisingh, (CC BY-SA 3.0)

Sikhs in the United Kingdom gather for the langar meal after their service, a free vegetarian meal prepared for all Sikh and non-Sikh guests.

Rana Singh Sodhi (left) is shown on May 3, 2011, with a photo of his late brother, Balbir, who became the first Sikh victim of a hate crime in the United States after the attacks on September 11, 2001, when he was shot and killed in front of his Mesa, Arizona, gas station on September 14, 2001.

due to the mistake. **Balbir Singh Sodhi**, a gas station owner in Mesa, Arizona, was shot and killed by a mentally unstable criminal who was angered by the attacks on the United States and mistook Sodhi for a Muslim.

In 2012, in Oak Creek, Wisconsin, a White supremacist entered a Sikh gurdwara and killed seven Sikhs as they prepared the langar meal to share with community members. Several more were injured. The shooter committed suicide on the spot.

In 2021, a nineteen-year-old shooter entered a FedEx facility in Indianapolis, Indiana, that employed a number of Sikhs. He killed eight people—four of them Sikhs—and then himself. Several others were shot but recovered.

Despite these heartbreaking events, Sikhs continue to thrive in North America. **Nikki Haley**, the daughter of Sikh immigrants from India, is perhaps the most notable American with Sikh roots. She converted to Christianity in 1997, but she still attends a gurdwara occasionally with her devout Sikh parents. Haley served as governor of South Carolina from 2011 to 2017, the first governor of the state who was not a White male. She then served as the US ambassador to the United Nations under President Trump from 2017 to 2018. Her name is often tossed around as a potential Republican candidate for the US presidency.

In 2018, Gursoch Kaur, a twenty-year-old woman from Queens, New York, became the first turbaned Sikh woman to graduate from the New York Police Academy, adding to the already two hundred or so Sikhs who work on the force, around ten of them women.

Sikhs practice cremation shortly after death. The body is washed and dressed in new clothes in preparation for burning. Ashes are gathered and placed into natural, flowing water, as is common in India (but occasionally problematic in Western nations). If the father dies, then the eldest son receives the deceased's turban, showing that the responsibility of overseeing the home has passed from father to eldest son. Prayers and scripture readings take place throughout the process.

The gurdwara is the center of Sikh life. In diaspora, Sikhs connect to the gurdwara for worship and support. In the United States, there are around three hundred gurdwaras. The epicenter for North American Sikhism, however, is probably Greater Vancouver, Canada—home to perhaps two hundred

Balbir Singh Sodhi · a gas station owner in Mesa, Arizona, who was shot and killed after September 11, 2001, by a mentally unstable criminal who mistook Sodhi for a Muslim

Nikki Haley · an American with Sikh roots who served as the governor of South Carolina and the US ambassador to the United Nations

Construction on the ninety-thousand-square-foot Sikh gurdwara in San Jose, California, began in 1984. It is now the largest gurdwara outside of India.

Volunteers prepare the langar meal for the Golden Temple in Amritsar, India—the largest free meal in the world.

The interior of the Akal Takht.

thousand Sikhs. Membership in a gurdwara is not a requirement for attending or participating. The gurdwara will always have a flag, known as a Nishan Sahib, that bears the khanda (double-edged sword). At the gurdwara, attendees can usually study Punjabi and learn how to play Sikh music. Most gurdwaras have two halls: one for worship and the other for langar.

Sikhs do not have an ordained priesthood, but granthis are typically male and must be fluent in the Gurmukhi language. Women are allowed to be granthis—in accordance with Sikhism's

The Golden Temple in Amritsar, India, at night.

egalitarianism—but female granthis are somewhat rare, particularly in India.

In the Western world, gurdwara attendance is common on Sundays. When entering the gurdwara, heads must be covered and bare feet are required. Most Sikhs will find a way to contribute **Seva** (selfless service), whether through donations, cleaning, cooking, or assisting in meditation and worship. Traditionally, men and women sit separately, as is common in India. Sweet parshad is offered at the end of services as a gift to all.

Perhaps the most notable aspect of gurdwaras for non-Sikhs is the langar meal that follows services. Instituted by Guru Amar Das (the third guru), the langar is a statement against caste. It is a basic vegetarian meal that is open to anyone and everyone. The point is to recognize that all people are on the same level and that all can eat together. This was and is revolutionary for the Indian context, with its caste consciousness. The Sikh gurdwara in Dubai entered the *Guinness World Records 2017* for feeding people from more than one hundred nations at one meal.

The ultimate authority in Sikhism is found in the **Akal Takht**, or the "Eternal Throne." The building is located in the same compound where the Golden Temple is located, in Amritsar, India. This is the location where the religion's most important discussions are had and where the most consequential decisions are made. It was founded by Guru Hargobind, the sixth Sikh guru.

The Golden Temple is the most sacred and important site in Sikhism. It has four main entrances, symbolic for welcoming people without discrimination from all four corners of the world. The temple has been damaged on several occasions, always to be rebuilt bigger and more beautiful than before. It is a white marble temple covered in resplendent gold. It is surrounded by a large pool, where Sikhs take a bath. Each day of the year, between fifty thousand and one hundred twenty thousand pilgrims take a circumambulatory walk around the compound and enjoy a vegetarian langar.

Seva · selfless service

Akal Takht · the "Eternal Throne"; the highest authority in Sikhism in Amritsar, where the religion's most important discussions are had, and where the most consequential decisions are made

Faithful Sikhs today focus on God. They meditate on him, praise him, and pray to him. They say "Waheguru" often, believing that calling upon the Lord leads to peace and will only help any given situation. Faithful Sikhs attend the gurdwara and show respect to the Guru Granth Sahib, reading from it often. They recite the **Five Banis** (meditations) each day. The **Japji Sahib** is particularly important, as it appears at the beginning of the Guru Granth Sahib. It is the first composition of Guru Nanak and is considered to be a comprehensive summation of Sikh teaching.

When Sikhs read it, they feel a connection with God and are blessed with a sensation that God will make everything work out fine. Some Sikhs emphasize the importance of physical Yoga during their meditations, and in the United States, they often welcome the public to join them in their practice.

Five Banis · daily meditations to be recited

Japji Sahib · the first composition of Guru Nanak and a comprehensive summation of Sikh teaching

7 DAOISM AND CONFUCIANISM
The Way and the Sage

Kindergarten kids in Suzhou, China, wearing Han costumes read poems during a Confucius Memorial Ceremony (2017). The event marked the 2,568th anniversary of the birthday of Confucius.

Religion in China can be mystifying for people in the Western world. Traditionally, in the West, a person was either a Christian, or a Jew, or a Muslim. But rarely will a Muslim also consider herself a Christian. However, Chinese culture allows for people to practice elements of Buddhism, Confucianism, and Daoism at the same time. There is a syncretism in China that is different from the Abrahamic faiths. Historically, Chinese religion was characterized by four phases:

1. Ancient Chinese religion: polytheism, animism and ancestor worship. Followers also offered sacrifices. This phase was very much in line with Max Müller's teachings on the origins of religion—that the natural elements became deified through language and lore.
2. The second important development was the advent of **Lao Tzu**'s teachings, as well as the philosophies of **Confucius**.
3. The third phase was Buddhism and the development of a formal Daoist religion.
4. Eventually, these movements converged, leading to varied mixtures of religion in China today.

Arguably, the twentieth century presented a fifth phase, as the philosophies of **Karl Marx** became extremely popular in China and were zealously embraced by Mao Zedong, China's leader from 1943–76. Chairman Mao's philosophies and ruminations on Marxist theory set the tone for how Chinese people engage with religion and philosophy today.

The three most important religious teachings of China—Confucianism, Daoism, and Buddhism—are complementary. Somewhere around half of the Chinese people blend these three religions together seamlessly, creating difficulties for religious demographers, especially demographers from the West. There are analogies to explain this phenomenon. For instance, some say that Chinese people are Confucian during the day, Daoist at night, and Buddhist at death. When we throw in Marxism, which only arrived relatively recently in the grand sweep of Chinese history, it gets even more complex.

Lao Tzu · also spelled Laozi, "Old Master"; the founder of Daoism and author of the *Tao Te Ching*

Confucius · "Master King"; a philosopher who emphasized the importance of ordered social relationships and wished to purify the government of corruption and incompetence

Karl Marx · a German philosopher who heavily influenced economic, social, and political thought with his theories, collectively known as Marxism

General view of the Good Wish Garden at Wong Tai Sin Temple. The Hong Kong Tourism Board approved the use of online videoconferencing applications to encourage post-COVID-19 spiritual tourism.

© winhorse, iStock

MARXISM

Another complicating factor is that **Marxism** has religious elements as well, leading to China's version of **communism**, which usually involves a commitment to atheism. Is Marxism a religion? It is difficult to say. It certainly has the typical components of a religion, particularly in China. There are texts (*Little Red Book* of **Chairman Mao Zedong**). There are parades and ritualized behaviors. There is a hierarchy. There are strong commitments to a certain moral code and ethic. There is a ruling class who oversees the group. There are even somewhat mythical stories about the movement's leaders.

Chairman Mao's *Little Red Book* on sale at Upper Lascar Row street market, Sheung Wan, Hong Kong.

Marxism · a socioeconomic philosophy that views the world through the lens of class inequalities and social conflict; religion is used as a tool of the oppressive upper class

Communism · system of government in which, in theory, all property is held in common and all work and goods are distributed according to ability and need; officially atheist or nonreligious

Little Red Book · a widely distributed Chinese communist text comprising the writings and sayings of Mao Zedong

Chairman Mao Zedong · the victor of the Chinese Civil War who redefined China along communist lines and governed the nation until 1976; heavily persecuted religion

Shang dynasty · governing kingdom of China from the 1700s to the 1100s BCE; very religious, incorporating rituals, shamanistic features, divining, animism, and human sacrifice

Shen · benevolent and helpful spirits in ancient Chinese religion

Development of Chinese Religion

The earliest Chinese dynasty of which we have any historical knowledge is the great **Shang dynasty**, which ruled from the 1700s BCE to the 1100s BCE. There were dynasties before them, but we do not know their identities. The Shang dynasty was very religious, incorporating rituals, shamanistic features, divining, and animism—the belief that spirits are all around us.

The Shang people believed in many gods and many spirits for virtually everything. They tended to divide these spirits into two categories: **Shen** and **Kuei**. The Shen were considered to be benevolent and helpful, while the Kuei were considered to be malevolent and a cause for trouble. The Shen were associated with brightness and sunshine; the Kuei were associated with darkness and gloom. People made sacrifices of vegetation and animals to placate the spirits, keeping the good spirits working on their behalf and keeping the bad spirits at bay.

Funeral human sacrifice was common in ancient China among the privileged classes. There is evidence of rulers having humans sacrificed to be buried with them, probably pointing to a belief in the afterlife. The practice was considered barbaric by some and was declared illegal on a number of occasions throughout Chinese history.

The Shang dynasty had a High God they called **Shangdi**, which means "Supreme Ruler" or "Highest Deity." This god ruled **Tian**, or heaven. Heaven was more than a place, however. It was also considered a force that was believed to be the supreme way, altogether good. Together, these two forces—Shangdi and Tian—governed the world and everything in it.

Shangdi ruled over all of the other gods, which were associated with natural elements like rivers, planets, mountains, and forests. Shangdi was not a personal god; rather, he was transcendent, and he utilized the lower categories of deities and spirits to do his work. He was the supreme ruler of a hierarchy of gods and spirits that ruled the Earth from their place in heaven (Tian). He decided the outcome of war, the success of the harvest, and everything related to the weather. Sacrifices to Shangdi determined whether or not the community would prosper. Over time, he began to be associated with being the ultimate source of reward for the good people and the ultimate source of punishment for those who do evil. Rulers were particularly accountable to him, and they had to live upright, virtuous lives for their kingdoms to function harmoniously. He showered blessings on the rulers, who were expected to govern their people with truth and righteousness.

Perhaps the most familiar concept in ancient Chinese religion is the **yin/yang**, or interdependent dualism. This is a concept that teaches the harmony and equilibrium of all things. Everything is in need of balance. Thus, everything actually needs an opposite. The **yin** is associated with human emotions, darkness, coolness, femininity, wetness, the Moon, shadows, and evil. The **yang** is associated with rational thought, brightness, warmth, masculinity, dryness, the Sun, and righteousness. These two forces are always needed, and one is not better than the other. Both are necessary and active in everything; they are dual energies that are inseparable since they represent two sides of the same thing. Rooted deeply in Chinese history, yin/yang persists as a powerful concept in Chinese religion today, particularly in Daoist thought.

One of the important ideas undergirding the philosophy of yin/yang is that people can control the world around them with **divination**. People can predict the future by analyzing plants, oracle bones, turtle shells, and many other objects. The most important and most ancient religious text in Chinese civilization is the *I Ching*, often known in the West as the *Book of Changes*. It is a Chinese diviner's manual used in all manner of ways. This text had a profound impact on subsequent developments in Chinese religion, and it is still used in Chinese civilizations today. The text operates on the assumption of **cleromancy**—that apparently random numbers and patterns

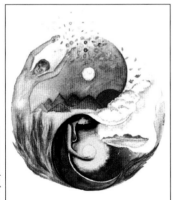

A visual illustration of what yin and yang represent. Yin is that which is emotional, dark, wet, passive, cool, feminine, yielding, nurturing, underneath; yang is all that is rational, bright, dry, powerful, warm, masculine, guiding, active, and above. Yin can represent evil, and yang can represent the good, but both polar forces are inherently and inextricably entwined and codependent.

© Nyo, public domain

can actually reveal the will of the gods. Some established forms of cleromancy are casting lots, rolling dice, flipping coins, and doing various forms of numerology. The underlying belief is that numbers can be interpreted, enabling us to understand mysteries and the future. The *I Ching* is a fundamental part of Chinese culture. It guides the reader to harmonize her or his life with the universe. The text often uses the yin/yang symbol, surrounded by sixty-four hexagrams, each comprising six lines. Specialists can offer guidance and counseling to individuals so that they can align themselves with the universe and avoid offending nature, ancestors, or spiritual beings. Some would say the interpretation of the *I Ching* has more to do with wisdom and intuition, which might be true, but a specialist is able to combine common wisdom with a sophisticated understanding of how the text is interpreted traditionally.

Shang rulers also practiced **pyromancy**—divination through analyzing a fire. It was particularly important for rulers to practice divination, as their charismatic leadership and political authority meant that they knew how to communicate effectively with the heavenly or spiritual realm, as well as with the ancestors.

Kuei · malevolent and troublesome spirits in ancient Chinese religion

Funeral human sacrifice · practiced during the Shang dynasty; sacrificing live humans to bury with the dead, probably to serve them in the afterlife

Shangdi · "Supreme Ruler" or "Highest Deity"; the transcendent High God of ancient Chinese religion

Tian · heaven; a force that was believed to be the supreme way, altogether good

Yin/yang · interdependent dualism; a concept that teaches the harmony and equilibrium of all things; since everything is in need of balance, everything needs an opposite

Yin · a force associated with emotion, darkness, coolness, femininity, wetness, the Moon, shadows, and evil

Yang · a force associated with rationality, brightness, warmth, masculinity, dryness, the Sun, and the good

Divination · prediction of the future by analyzing plants, oracle bones, turtle shells, and various other objects

I Ching · the *Book of Changes*, also written as *Yi Jing;* a diviner's manual to using cleromancy; consists of the yin/yang symbol surrounded by sixty-four hexagrams, each comprising six lines

Cleromancy · the belief that apparently random numbers and patterns can actually reveal the will of the gods

Pyromancy · divination through the analysis of a fire

DEFINING RELIGION

When looking at Chinese religion, we are forced to revisit the definition of religion. Chinese understandings of religion are quite different from Western understandings and even Indian understandings. Chinese religions have many of the same qualities of Western religions—for example, belief in the supernatural, belief in life after death, belief in gods, and morality. However, the typical Chinese way is to blend various sources rather than choosing one over the others. This points to a very different understanding of the concept of religion for most Chinese people. In China, religions do not have such exclusive authority as they do in the Western world. Rather, religions offer helpful guidance, but people are not forced to submit completely to one. There is a symbiotic relationship between people and religions that allows Chinese people to pick and choose, borrow from one or another depending on the situation, and mix and glean.

Some scholars have explained this phenomenon this way: They say that Daoism and Confucianism are not denominational religions. They do not require exclusive membership. They are like the shamanistic indigenous traditions that were common worldwide before the advent of the great world religions: Judaism, Zoroastrianism, Christianity, Hinduism, Jainism, Buddhism, and Sikhism. In other words, the ancient shamanistic, indigenous traditions allow for far more flexibility. One good Western example is found in the Native American traditions. Native Americans often converted to Christianity, but they did not abandon their rain dances, their shamanistic practices, their sweat lodges, or their mythic stories. They blended Christianity into their preexisting worldview. The Chinese religious context presents something similar.

Another complicating factor in Chinese religion is that in China today, Confucianism is not considered a religion. China currently allows for five religions: Protestantism, Catholicism, Buddhism, Daoism, and Islam. There are two noteworthy issues there. First, the Chinese government separates Protestantism and Catholicism into two

Confucian temple in Suzhou, China.

separate religions, which is something Western scholars do not do. The second issue is that Confucianism—so fundamental to a Chinese worldview—is not there. But that is strange because Confucianism has bequeathed to China the preponderance of its ethics and a good chunk of its overall worldview: marital relations, roles of males and females, roles of family members, social conduct, etiquette and ethics, love of education, veneration of elderly and ancestors, and a strong sense of respecting authority. Are these religious factors? Or are they something other than religion? It is difficult to ascertain.

If one were to argue that Confucianism is not a religion, one would point out that there is not a lot of reference to a god or gods in Confucianism. It occurs here and there with the concept of heaven, but Confucianism orients people more toward this world than another world. Confucianism does not spend much time talking about creation and afterlife either. Its focus is on relationship in this world, keeping harmony between oneself and his or her surroundings, and honoring the authorities in one's life. Confucianism certainly talks about ethics, but it does not lure a person to good behavior through divine rewards. Another reason it is difficult to call Confucianism a religion is because it does not have a revelatory text. The writings of Confucius do not pretend to be from a prophet, nor do they claim to have divine origin. The *Analects of Confucius* are simply his writings and speeches that were collected by his students.

If one were to argue that Confucianism is a religion, one would point out the temples, the ethical code, the texts that act as scripture, and the critical role that Confucius plays as an authoritative figure—like a divine sage.

Scholars have not quite answered this vexing question as to whether Confucianism is a religion, but suffice it to say, it continues to feature prominently in books about world religions, such as this one! Clearly, the consensus of scholarship is that Confucianism has enough religion in it to be carefully considered during the study of religion.

Classical Chinese religion birthed a deep-seated commitment to looking after elder family members, as well as ancestors. Chinese religion maintains that people should give the utmost respect to elders in the family, even today. There is an unequivocal deference toward elders that is unparalleled in much of the Western world. Children are expected to support their parents and grandparents, and it is common to see elderly people living with their children in Chinese culture. Proper burial, or other funerary arrangements, must be given to deceased elders. Chinese people are also expected to pay homage to their deceased relatives. There is a real sense that one's ancestors continue to exist in another form and remain with us to some degree. The ancestors reside in the spirit world but can be sought for favor, help, and advice. Even today, it would be unthinkable for a conscientious Chinese person to disregard a dead relative, as there is a potential threat of being cursed if the ancestors are ignored. Chinese often keep their ancestors alive through portable shrines or keepsakes in the home that incorporate some form of genealogy. They present small tokens of sacrifice at these home altars, and they present offerings to the headstones of their deceased ancestors.

The **Zhou dynasty** followed the Shang dynasty. It was the longest dynasty in Chinese history, lasting from around 1050 BCE to 250 BCE. During that period, the figure of Shangdi became enmeshed into a more general notion of heaven, or Tian, as the supreme force. By the time of the **Han dynasty** (200 BCE to 220 CE), the notions of Shangdi and Tian were fully conflated, both concepts completely dependent upon one another. Chinese people understood that for good luck

Analects of Confucius · the writings and speeches of Confucius, collected and preserved by his students; extremely influential to Chinese moral philosophy

Zhou dynasty · the longest dynasty in Chinese history, ruling from around 1050 to 250 BCE, during which the concepts of Shangdi and Tian started to become enmeshed

Han dynasty · governing kingdom of China from 200 BCE to 220 CE, during whose reign the concepts of Shangdi and Tian became fully conflated

Ancient Chinese religion had no fixed myth collections, largely because the stories were transmitted orally. The stories changed dramatically over time, although certain features of the stories either remained or manifested themselves repeatedly. Gods were construed in new ways. Strange animals and birds, such as dragons, were spotlighted. Both gods and goddesses were featured prominently, both evincing great powers. Over time, a divine pantheon took shape, a pantheon that highlighted the following prominent beings:

The Jade Emperor, supreme ruler of heaven (ca. sixteenth century).

Image courtesy of Museum of Fine Arts, Boston

Close-up of a small street shrine in Hong Kong.

© Stripped Pixel, Adobe Stock

- **Fuxi** (or Fu Hsi) created humanity and invented writing as well as music.
- **Shennong** is the god who invented farming and agriculture.
- Rooted in the ancient understanding of Shangdi, **the Jade Emperor** is the supreme ruler of heaven who features prominently in the Daoist pantheon later in Chinese history.
- **The Earth God**, also known as **Tudi Gong** ("land elder"), is depicted as a smiling male statue, usually only about a foot tall, frequently found in Chinese villages still today on family altars and in farmers' fields.

Anonymous eighteenth-century painting showing Mazu, dressed in red, dancing above the sea as she rescues ambassador Li Yundi on his return voyage from Korea in the early twelfth century. After this miracle, officials canonized her as a state-promoted goddess, but her popularity was not simply driven by cultural elites. Devotion spread at a grassroots level as those without power appreciated how she protected the innocent and shared their concerns.

Image courtesy of Rijksmuseum, Amsterdam

- **Mazu** is a sea goddess and is understood to be the "queen of heaven." Her story is based on Lin Moniang, a woman who lived in around 1000 CE and who saved people from danger while at sea. She is the most popular goddess in Daoism today.
- There are also many gods of protection, such as gods who are uniquely tasked with protecting certain cities. There are other gods who specialize in combating evil or fighting off pandemics. Many of these gods are rooted in actual people who lived at some point in Chinese history.

and prosperity, a person had to live in such a way that honored, or even mirrored, heaven. Rulers were particularly accountable to heaven. If they ruled well, then prosperity came to the land. If they offended the **mandate of heaven**, or the divine will, then misfortune would come—to the ruler, to those being ruled, and to the nation in general. Various signs were thought to affirm or oppose those in authority. For example, natural disasters were thought to be a mandate from heaven that a ruler was evil or unfit.

Later in Chinese history, both Lao Tzu and Confucius became revered to the point of being considered divine. In Chinese lore, the two great men met and sized each other up, but it became clear that while Confucius was more concerned with political and social stability, Lao Tzu focused on achieving internal peace within oneself. Confucius is reported to have said, "I finally met Lao Tzu, and I can only compare him to the dragon." Surely the story is fictitious, although some believe in it. Throughout Chinese history, there was tension between Daoism and Confucianism, but like yin/yang, both are absolutely critical in the development of Chinese religiosity, and, together, they have served the Chinese people well.

Later still, in around the second century CE, many Buddhas entered into the Chinese religious worldview. Chinese Buddhism tends to be Mahayana, with countless Buddhas and bodhisattvas, many of whom have been deified and are regularly venerated.

It would be remiss to neglect to point out the extent to which Mao Zedong has been deified and glorified in the collective Chinese consciousness. Famously portrayed in Tiananmen Square

Mandate of heaven · the notion that rulers were granted authority by the divine will and had to honor heaven with their actions; if tragedies occurred, then the mandate of heaven must have been revoked; if all was well, then the ruler must have the approval of heaven

Monument in front of the Mao Zedong Mausoleum on Tiananmen Square in Beijing, China.

Created during the Song dynasty (960–1279 CE), this stone carving of Laozi is one of the world's largest. Quanzhou, China.

in Beijing, Chairman Mao is like a Marxist deity who oversees the happenings in the Chinese capital, the epicenter for the Chinese Communist Party.

Daoism

In its most basic sense, Daoism is simply a philosophy from a Chinese man named Laozi (also spelled Lao Tzu). However, much later, it became a highly organized religion, with a priesthood and temples. Daoism blurs the line between a religion and the wider culture of ancient China because it has become ingrained into the culture so deeply. While Confucianism spread widely in Asia, Daoism has not expanded much beyond China and Taiwan. It is, therefore, famously difficult to comprehend; one must understand Chinese culture to fathom Daoism. The term *Daoism* did not originate in China; it came from Western Protestant missionaries who visited China in the 1830s.

Laozi (Also Spelled "Lao Tzu")

Laozi ("Old Master") is the great figure of ancient Daoism. He is credited with writing one of the greatest of all Chinese religious classics: the *Tao Te Ching* (or *Daode Jing*). His actual existence is sometimes debated by scholars. It is likely that he was a real person whose life story became embellished with time, to the point that he became deified in Chinese history. The most reliable ancient sources tell us he was the local scholar and keeper of the archives in the emperor's court in around 500 BCE, which would put him in the late Zhou dynasty. At some point in his life, he probably ventured out and became a wandering teacher, a path common among the founders of the world's great religions. (As we will see, Confucius chose a similar path.) By 300 BCE, Laozi's teachings had taken root and were widely recognized by Chinese people as a coherent religious system.

> **Tao Te Ching** · also known as **Daode Jing**, "The Book of the Way of Virtue"; a short text of eighty-one poems; the fundamental book of Daoism, teaching on the Dao and on virtuous living

Wu Wei: Nonaction

One of the most important teachings in Daoism is the principle of nonaction, or **wu wei**. It has also been translated as "nonintervention." It means one should let life take its course rather than constantly intervening and striving to change everything. To work at their best, a person should strive less, thus allowing the universe to take its course in one's life. With everything unfolding naturally, a person can live unpressured and find the best course of action. Wu wei means a person is better off if they do not micromanage their life. Even kings rule best when they establish some guidelines and then leave the people alone. The Beatles sang "Let It Be," echoing this wu wei sentiment.

Daoists are known to live quiet and simple lives: *Do not go out of your way very often. Just let go and let things play out how they will. Inaction is best. If you try to manipulate things, you will get in the way of the natural flow of reality. Live and let live. Humans do best when they cease their striving. If you try to change things, you will inevitably disrupt the flow, creating problems that should never have happened had you just left them alone.*

Daoism teaches that there should not be a distinction between work and vacation. *Life should be approached in a relaxed and amicable manner. No clenching of the fists or of the jaw; rather, allow life to happen. When it is time to work, do it in a pleasant manner. But do not make a big distinction between work and play, because that insinuates work is difficult and painstaking. Do everything naturally, and work will come rather easily.*

Similarly, inaction means nonresistance. Thus, violence is frowned upon. Violence means that one has lost control and that one is striving too hard. Do not resist an evil person or a violent person. Let them be, and they will move on to someone else. Besides, life is a great gift. Let it unfold naturally. By striving, one may find oneself disrupting one's life and getting oneself into trouble. Chapter 63 in the *Tao Te Ching* says it perfectly:

> **Wu wei** · nonaction or non-intervention; a Daoist principle encouraging us to go with the flow of life, rather than striving against the grain

After the Cultural Revolution, this Daoist temple was rebuilt. A young woman offers her prayers to the gods. Zhujiang Island, China.

© Danita Delimont, Shutterstock

Act without doing; work without effort.

Think of the small as large and the few as many.

Confront the difficult while it is still easy;

Accomplish the great task by a series of small acts.

The Master never reaches for the great; thus she achieves greatness.

When she runs into a difficulty, she stops and gives herself to it.

She does not cling to her own comfort; thus problems are no problem for her.

Foundational Writings: Tao Te Ching *and* Zhuangzi

The *Tao Te Ching* is a short text consisting of eighty-one pithy poems, usually comprising about ten to twenty lines. It has around five thousand words total. One can read it in an hour or in a lifetime. Some consider it the second-most translated text in history, after the Bible.

The *Tao Te Ching* translates into English as "Way, Virtue, Scripture"—put differently: "The Book on the Way of Virtue." It is said that about half of it deals with the Dao, and about half deals with living virtuously. It is not a typical religious text. It says nothing about afterlife. Rather, it focuses on keeping oneself in harmony with his or her surroundings. One should align with the way (**the Tao** or **the Dao**—both spellings are acceptable) of the universe. Do not try to swim upstream. Rather, remain in harmony with nature and its course. The natural course is the best course. Do not try to make something work that is not working out. The theme of the *Tao Te Ching* is that we should keep everything in perspective, because, ultimately, our individual achievements will become forgotten with time.

The *Tao Te Ching* has advice for leaders. For example, Poem 17 reads, "When the Master governs, the people are hardly aware that he exists." Even leadership should be hands-off, natural, and organic. Leadership involves tremendous trust, as Poem 17 continues, "If you don't trust the people, you make them untrustworthy." Poem 60 says, "Governing a large country is like frying a small fish; you spoil it with too much poking . . . Give evil nothing to oppose and it will disappear by itself."

The *Tao Te Ching* warns people away from indulgence. The path to serenity is to simply do one's work and then step back for a time. Do not seek approval from people. Do not "fill your bowl to the brim," because if one takes on too much, then one will disrupt the natural harmony that exists between oneself and those around them (Poem 9). Leave people alone for the most part, and focus on the task at hand. Step-by-step, one will get where they need to be, in accordance with what the Dao has assigned to them during their short life. Enjoy life, but do not take it too seriously. All one's efforts will eventually dissipate into nothingness, just as fog vanishes when the Sun comes into view.

Lao Tzu's most important student was **Zhuangzi** (also known as Chuang Tzu); they may have been contemporaries. Zhuangzi is known as the great synthesizer of Daoist thought, and the second-most important book in Daoism uses his name as its title: *Zhuangzi*. The book is fanciful and entertaining, and it features mythical animals such as dragons, huge fish, and enormous birds. It imagines numerous encounters between Laozi and Confucius, all geared to demonstrate Laozi's superiority. Confucius comes across as a pitiful character, overly concerned with political issues and what people may think about him. Political activity is seen as a hopeless endeavor that results in meaninglessness. Real change and value are found within. One must connect with the Dao on a personal and even mystical level. That is where true meaning is found. Humans should be flexible and nonjudgmental. We will be happier if we are relativists, agreeing or disagreeing in a flexible way, depending on the situation. We should accept change and not resist. This leads to greater happiness. *Zhuangzi* even encourages the reader to meditate to gain spiritual insight and personal transformation. He encourages readers to empty the mind by sitting and forgetting. We should try to attain equanimity and mental serenity. There is a definite spirituality in *Zhuangzi* that set the stage

The Tao · also written as **the Dao**, the "way"; a method of behaving as well as the supreme force of the universe, the absolute and mysterious reality of all things; formless, nameless, and impersonal; a cosmic principle instructing people to follow the natural course of the universe in life

Zhuangzi · Laozi's most important student who synthesized Daoist teaching and wrote the second most important book in Daoism, *Zhuangzi*

The Chinese character for the Dao, "the way," a method of behaving as well as the supreme force of the universe, the absolute and mysterious reality of all things.

for a full-blown Daoist religion, which developed shortly thereafter.

The Dao (Also Spelled "Tao")

The most basic concept of Daoism, and Chinese thought for that matter, is the Dao. It is commonly translated as "the way." It can also be translated as "road" or "path." Dao is essentially a method of behaving and acting or not acting. It is also an enormous concept that calls to mind the supreme force of the universe, the absolute and mysterious reality of all things. It has two components: the individual human and the universe at large. The Dao is formless and nameless. It is impersonal. We could describe it as a cosmic principle instructing people to follow the natural course of the universe in life.

A key aspect of the Dao is change. Everything is always changing. There are no exceptions. Thus, Daoists believe that everything originates in the Dao and that everything will return to the Dao. All things will return to their original state and, ultimately, everything will return to the source. This is why everything must be kept in perspective; eventually, everything returns to its source.

Sharp things will become dull again. Mountains will eventually flatten. Oceans will dry up. All life forms return to dust. Human accomplishments will be forgotten in time. Monuments and great buildings will decay and go back into the ground.

Daoists do not believe in the notion of a soul per se. Reincarnation was not initially a part of early Daoism; that came later with the advent of Buddhism into China. However, in Daoism, humans are immortal in a sense—they are part of the process of change. Humans do not have a personal soul that somehow carries on individual identity in an afterlife or in the next earthly life form. Humans are simply part of the principle of Dao, constantly changing over the long haul of eternity. The same is true with gods; they, too, must conform to the eternal cycle of change. They, too, will be forgotten and will return to the source of all things—the Dao.

While Daoists are usually reluctant to define the Dao, there are excellent clues about it in the *Tao Te Ching*. It must be clarified, however, that virtually all Daoists claim that the Dao is indefinable. By no means did Laozi invent it. He merely provided some helpful insights into the concept. Here are some descriptions of the Dao from the *Tao Te Ching*:

Daoist art is replete with scenes of tranquility in nature and a balance between dark ink and light, negative space. Pictured is a detail of Dwelling in the Fuchun Mountains by the Yuan dynasty painter Huang Guangwang (1269–1354).

Daoism and Confucianism   171

- "The Tao is like a well: used but never used up. It is like the eternal void: filled with infinite possibilities. It is hidden but always present. I don't know who gave birth to it. It is older than God" (chapter 4).
- "The Tao is called the Great Mother: empty yet inexhaustible, it gives birth to infinite worlds. It is always present within you. You can use it any way you want" (chapter 6).
- "It is serene. Empty. Solitary. Unchanging. Infinite. Eternally present. It is the mother of the universe. For lack of a better name, I call it the Tao. . . . Man follows the earth. Earth follows the universe. The universe follows the Tao. The Tao follows only itself" (chapter 25).
- "Every being in the universe is an expression of the Tao. . . . The Tao gives birth to all beings, nourishes them, maintains them . . . protects them, takes them back to itself, creating without possessing, acting without expecting, guiding without interfering. That is why love of the Tao is in the very nature of things" (chapter 51).
- "Whoever is planted in the Tao will not be rooted up. Whoever embraces the Tao will not slip away. . . . Let the Tao be present in your life and you will become genuine. Let it be present in your family and your family will flourish" (chapter 54).

Daoism emphasizes the goodness of human beings in their natural state. The wise human will become aware of the Dao and will fearlessly face it, even though it can be difficult to face. We are dust, and to dust we will return. However, there is beauty, mystery, and wisdom in this realization.

Daoism emphasizes that people should cooperate closely with nature. That is our natural state. We must be flexible, as change is always happening around us. Chapter 76 in the *Tao Te Ching* says, "Men are born soft and supple; dead they are stiff and hard. Plants are born tender and pliant; dead they are brittle and dry. Thus whoever is stiff and inflexible is a disciple of death. Whoever is soft and yielding is a disciple of life. The hard and stiff will be broken. The soft and supple will prevail." Passages such as this have convinced many that

Daoism is one of the most environmentally conscious religions due to its profound respect of nature.

One of the early ways by which the Western world came to know about Daoism was through art. Daoist art is metaphysical, gentle, and suggestive. It is mystical and can be dreamlike. It is rarely signed by an

Daoists use ephemeral materials like this silk tapestry (176 x 74 inches) to portray their rich iconography and symbolism. Shown at the top is the Queen Mother of the West riding a phoenix. She joins other immortals who have come to celebrate her birthday. Qing dynasty (1644-1912), 18th century.

> One of the early ways by which the Western world came to know about Daoism was through art. Daoist art is metaphysical, gentle, and suggestive. It is mystical and can be dreamlike.

artist, as selling art was considered to be in bad taste. Artists often abandoned public life to create their Daoist scenes of repose, bringing to mind the beauty and mysticism of nature. Sunsets, endless landscapes, trees almost deified—these are elements of Daoist art. They are meant to enmesh a person into nature and, ultimately, into the mystery of the Dao.

Daoist art often incorporates water, as water is the great strength of nature. It is fluid and cool, and it always finds the lowest and most fundamental point. There is a simplicity in Daoist art that emphasizes the beauty of nature. Sometimes humans are tiny in comparison with trees, for example, as humans are merely part of the background landscape. Daoist art tends to glorify nature through the principles of **feng shui**—a rich concept in Chinese religion that barely registers in the Western mind. Feng shui translates as "wind-water." It is a form of geomancy that purports to bring harmony with nature. For example, in feng shui, there are auspicious places to build a home or to set up one's furniture in the house. Everything around us must be placed in a particular position so as to elicit tranquility and a positive energy flow—also known as **qi** or **chi** ("air").

Feng Shui · "wind-water"; a form of geomancy that purports to bring harmony with nature, placing everything around us in a particular position so as to elicit tranquility and a positive energy flow

Qi · also spelled **chi**, "air"; the flow of cosmic energy that animates the living

Ceremonial Daoist priest robes were embroidered with various animals that have religious significance. The bottom border features blue and red dragons, unicorns, and a tortoise entwined with a snake (eighteenth century).

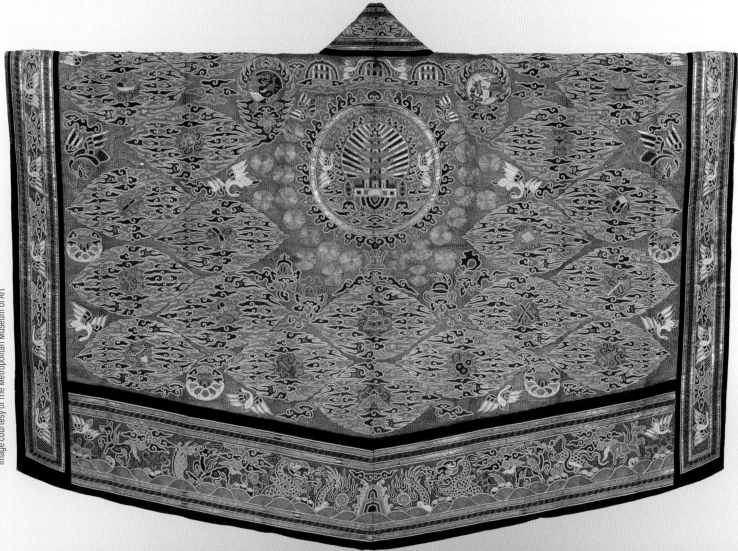

Where Do Humans Fit In?

Humans are supposed to enjoy life for as long as they can. Old age and wisdom are important for a human to achieve. Humans should remain flexible and yielding, cooperating with one another and with their surroundings to bring about harmony. We can live very long lives if we go about it naturally. The great Daoist figures either lived long lives, or else they escaped death by vanishing or ascending to the heavens and flying through the clouds like dragon spirits. Longevity is crucial in Daoism, which leads to much alchemy, meditation, conscientious eating habits, taking herbal supplements, regulating qi in the body, spending time in the freshness of nature, and having a regular routine of physical exercise.

According to Daoism, the chief problem is that people get out of sync with the universe. They become imbalanced. They deviate from the natural flow of the Dao. When people try to work against the grain of the Dao, they breed conflict. They find themselves working for no reason because, ultimately, they will fail if they do not move according to the natural flow. The Dao will always be going in one direction, so one will only cause oneself immeasurable suffering if one tries to work against this irresistible force or tries to swim upstream.

Humans are always best served by staying in harmony with the universe. When we try to conquer nature or manipulate outcomes or control our own destiny, then we attract disharmony. We need to remain simple, satisfied, and aware of our smallness in the large scheme of things. Early Daoists argued that there should not be a government, as government simply gets in the way. If everyone simply left each other alone, then the world would be a much better place. Daoism is pacific—against war. War only disturbs people, and it also extinguishes the greatest of all gifts: life. Why would one want to end life prematurely?

Man with joss sticks praying at a shrine.

Why would one want to fight for something that is doomed to decay in time? Why would one kill someone when everything is relative? Life is a wonderful gift, and Daoists typically aspire to live long, healthy lives through exercise and diet.

True Daoists do not strive to "get ahead" or achieve glory. Daoism is about humility and authenticity. Preaching one thing and doing another is absolutely shameful in Daoism. Virtuous people cultivate their own interior without worrying too much about others. Daoists are self-reliant and keep a little distance from others. They do not want to judge others, because all things are relative.

For Daoists, circumstances alter one's reactions and responses. What is right in one setting may not be the correct approach in another. Morality changes over time, circumstance, and context. There is no such thing as sin in Daoism. Rather, one's missteps will lead to consequences. If one antagonizes someone, one might receive his or her wrath. Engaging in violence is stupid, as it potentially kills. Anger receives anger in return. Similarly, when one violates the Dao, one will usually realize it immediately, as disharmony will arise. If enough people violate principles of harmony, then social disharmony will occur. Cooperate with the universe, and one will have fewer problems. Developing strict codes of conduct are counterproductive for two reasons: (1) morality inevitably changes, and (2) rigidity leads to death. It makes no sense to develop a strict moral code.

For these reasons, Daoist temples are mainly for individual purposes. Large, corporate events are uncommon. People come to the temple to make individual requests to the gods, such as help passing an exam, help with a relationship, advice for the future, or to attain a particular job. Daoists today make offerings of food and flowers at the temple altar, burn incense, or select a stick that corresponds to a section of the *I Ching* or the *Tao Te Ching*.

Temples are also meant to connect one with ancestors. Daoists tend to believe that when a person dies, the soul infuses three places: (1) heaven, (2) the grave, and (3) the **ancestral tablet**, also known as the "**spirit tablet**," which is often kept in a temple or home altar. Daoist priests assist the soul by helping it get to heaven.

They lead prayers, offer sacrifices, and burn paper effigies of things like money, cars, televisions, or even paper servants to help the deceased in the spirit realm. Feng shui is used to find a good gravesite, and the grave is meticulously maintained by the living. People who are decidedly Daoist bury their dead. Cremation is unthinkable because it destroys one's qi. Those Daoists who turn to Buddhism at death are much more likely to practice cremation.

> **Ancestral tablet** · also known as the **spirit tablet**, a tablet in which the souls of the deceased are infused upon their passing, generally kept in a temple or home altar

Ancestor veneration is crucial in Daoism. Obeying and respecting elders is perhaps the most important obligation for people in life, and in death, those same patterns of respect continue. Within one hundred days of burial, there is a memorial service commemorating the dead; it was traditionally held in the eldest son's home, but it is now generally held in a temple. An ancestral tablet containing information about the deceased is dedicated by a priest. Offerings are made routinely to the tablet, and when special family ceremonies, such as weddings, occur, the family members come and pay respect to the tablet. Some Chinese attempt to make contact with ancestors with the help of a spirit medium.

In many cases, Daoists relegate the funerary arrangements to Buddhist priests, who, of course, assume the notion of rebirth. In those cases, the soul requires forty-nine days of temptation and testing prior to being reborn in a new physical body. Daoist priests and Buddhist priests may work together, as many people identify with both religions in life; therefore, it is entirely natural for Chinese funerals to include rituals and liturgical elements from both.

Further Developments

The earlier form of Daoism taught by Laozi and Zhuangzi did not last long. Within a few centuries, it was transforming into a full-blown religion, with rituals, texts, gods, and conceptions of heaven. Buddhism's entrance into China, at around the time of Christ, made Daoism much more complex, with reincarnation and various notions of afterlife.

Daoism took a hard turn toward institutionalized religion when a man named **Zhang Daoling** (34–156 CE), also known as the Celestial Master, was purported to have been supernaturally conceived when a heavenly being put an embryonic spiritual genius into his mother's womb. He walked at birth and memorized the *Tao Te Ching* as a young lad. In adulthood, he became a mountain hermit and took a special elixir that gave him even greater power, such as exorcism and the ability to disappear and reappear. His divine calling took place in 142 CE at a site in Sichuan province called **Crane Call Mountain** (or **Heming Shan**). An avatar of Laozi—called **Lord Lao**—appeared to Zhang, substantiating his authority. Zhang was chosen to usher in a new era of peace and prosperity. He believed that the Daoist gods were calling him to abolish animal sacrifice and to turn people away from local religions. Instead, they would turn toward him—the Celestial Master.

In Daoist history, Zhang Daoling represents a new chapter. Daoism transformed from being a rather simple collection of ideas centered around following the Dao to an institutionalized religion with ordained leaders, highly structured rituals, and a commentary on the *Tao Te Ching* that was to be considered the authoritative interpretation. Once he established this new form of Daoism, Zhang Daoling appointed his son (who later appointed *his* son) as his successor, and he ascended into heaven with his wife and some of his disciples. His ascension is said to have happened at **Green City Mountain**, outside the city of Chengdu, the capital of Sichuan province. It is still a deeply revered holy site in organized Daoism.[1]

Zhang Daoling's movement grew quickly and became known as **Tianshi Dao**—the **Way of the**

Zhang Daoling · A Daoist leader six centuries after Laozi who transformed the religion from a rather simple collection of ideas centered around following the Dao to an institutionalized religion with ordained leaders, highly structured rituals, and a commentary on the *Tao Te Ching* that was to be considered the authoritative interpretation

Crane Call Mountain · also known as **Heming Shan**, the site in Sichuan province where Zhang Daoling was divinely called to usher in a new era of peace and prosperity

Lord Lao · an avatar of Laozi who purportedly appeared to and commissioned Zhang Daoling

Green City Mountain · the site outside the city of Chengdu in Sichuan province where Zhang Daoling ascended to heaven with his wife and some of his disciples

Relief of Zhang Daoling riding a tiger, and his wife. Qing dynasty or later. Baodingshan, China.

The Louguantai Temple, about 70 kilometers west of Xian, is the place where tradition says that Lao Tzu, founder of Daoism, composed the *Tao Te Ching*. Notice the statue of Lao Tzu among the trees in the back.

Celestial Masters. Colloquially, it was known as **Five Bushels of Rice** because it charged members a rice tax. Zhang's descendants became the high leaders of the movement that essentially became a theocracy—a religious government. Scholars have suggested that Tianshi Dao actually posed little threat to the Chinese imperial authority because they were so far away—in Sichuan province—and had no desire to challenge the government. The movement developed a clergy, as well as a diocesan structure with twenty-four parishes. Monasteries developed, along with hermit monks—both male and female. Monks and nuns were celibates who devoted their lives to Daoist practice and to studying and teaching the religious texts. Thousands scattered across the scenic mountains of China in pursuit of meditation and solitude. Some monks and nuns, however, established schools and developed bureaucratic administrative organizations. They developed a highly literate class, and some even worked in the service of the imperial state. Daoist monastics were rather egalitarian for their time, as the nuns were recognized as fully legitimate.

The new Daoist religion became quite regimented, developing a moral code that required members to confess and repent if they sinned. Adherents chanted religious texts, had communal feasts, celebrated births and marriages in religious ceremony, prayed to divine beings, and maintained little shrines in their homes for daily ritual. They practiced meditation and maintained dietary restrictions. The religion rose up and declined over the centuries, even to the point of being an officially recognized state religion for various periods of Chinese history. The movement spread all over China and is today an important branch of Daoism.

It is important to keep in mind that Daoism gets

> **Tianshi Dao** · also known as the **Way of the Celestial Masters** and **Five Bushels of Rice**; a theocratic movement that grew out of Zhang Daoling's teachings

interpreted in various ways, but it can be categorized into two larger approaches: (1) become an organized institution with priests and temples, or (2) maintain the spirit of Laozi—a less formal approach to Daoism that focuses on following Dao as an individual. Both of these narratives and approaches are highly popular.

While the major centers of organized Daoism are at Crane Call Mountain and Green City Mountain in Sichuan, the more independent form of Daoism regards **Lookout Tower Monastery** (also known as Louguantai)—near Xian in Shaanxi province—as ground zero for Daoism, as that is where Laozi is said to have composed the *Tao Te Ching*.

Daoism continues to develop and reform, just as it has done for two thousand years. In the 300s CE, a major school of Daoism rose up under the charismatic leadership of **Yang Xi**—a medium who claimed to be the recipient of divine revelations. This form of Daoism became famous for its scriptures, known as the **Shangqing Revelations**. These texts were influential because of their high literary quality. They focused on living a solitary life in the mountains, and they also discussed Daoist heroes who had journeyed into the celestial realms. Spiritually empowered individuals even purported to sojourn to the Moon, planets, and stars.

Another Daoist school rose up in the 400s CE—just after the breakthrough of the Shangqing Revelations. This school of thought was based on a new set of texts called the **Lingbao Scriptures**. *Lingbao* means "Divine Treasure." This school was much more communitarian in nature; liturgy for the group was a central quality. The Lingbao Scriptures borrowed freely from many sources, especially Buddhist texts. The Lingbao Scriptures represent a turning point in Daoism. Through them, Buddhism entered into the worldview of Daoism and never left. This is crucial, as this was the point at which the two religions converged, leading to the synthesis that goes on today in Chinese religion. We begin to see various Buddhas, many different hells and heavens, and a fascination with salvation. Buddhist texts were simply copied into the Lingbao Scriptures. There was no discretion used, as the two religions seamlessly became enmeshed with one another in China, as they remain to the present.

Daoism thus became a religion based largely on texts that were divine in origin, coming down from the gods to intermediaries. The canon remained open. As worthy texts came onto the scene, they were incorporated into the Daoist canon, leading to a complex collection of what is considered scripture in the Daoist faith.

There is plentiful esoteric knowledge in this era of Daoism, from the 300s CE to the 900s, when Daoism achieved its peak in China, both in terms of sophistication and influence on Chinese

Photographer: Gene Zhang, (CC-BY-2.0)

The White Cloud Temple gate in Beijing, China (2006).

TYPES OF DAOISM

The influential scholar of Daoism, Livia Kohn, has come up with a helpful typology for understanding Daoism today. She claims there are three major branches of Daoism:

1. Philosophical Daoism—this is the oldest branch. It is based on the core texts of the *Tao Te Ching* and *Zhuangzi*.
2. Religious Daoism—this is the organized religion that is associated with the Celestial Masters movement that arose around 200 CE.
3. Folk Daoism—this is the people's version of Daoism that rose up after 200 CE and is impossible to define. It is the lived religion of millions of **folk religionists** who draw freely from Daoist traditions and texts, often combining them with Buddhist and Confucian ideas as well. This third branch is as diverse as can be imagined, as there is no set way to practice folk religion. It is notable for its variety and indigeneity. It always has a localized context.

society. The **Tang dynasty** (618–907 CE) represents the zenith of Daoist power, prestige, and impact in Asia. This is not to say it lost influence. Rather, its influence has never reached the peak that it did during the Tang dynasty years. As Daoism was achieving its peak, ironically, those were the same years that Buddhism was reaching new heights in China. The Tang dynasty privileged Daoism as first, but Confucianism and Buddhism were also highly popular during that time. In fact, Buddhism had more clergy and more adherents by the Tang dynasty. But because Buddhism was a foreign religion in China, Daoism received greater national privilege. This situation illustrates the openness of the Tang dynasty; its decision to include all three religions/philosophies set the stage for the **convergence** that has continued ever since.

Not only do Daoists emphasize the importance of their huge number of texts, but they also stress the importance of living naturally; thus, they have created many mountain retreats and monasteries. One of the most famous Daoist monasteries is the White Cloud Temple in Beijing. Each Daoist school and monastery continued to create its own texts, leading to an unwieldy canonical situation. Attempts were made over the years to gather an authoritative Daoist canon. This happened under the emperors' authority in 440, 748, 1016, and 1444 CE. The Daoist canon is called **Daozang** ("Daoist canon") and consists of 5,305 volumes. Many layers of commentary and elaborations have developed around these authoritative texts as well.

Modern Practice

It is notoriously difficult to count members of the various religions in China. For Daoism, this problem is particularly acute because Daoists do not have a membership system. Devotees can practice at any temple; they do not belong to a congregation, as in Christianity. Thus, Daoists are free to go as frequently as they want to any temple that they can access. Many devotees simply practice at home, and only on occasion do they visit a temple.

Some Daoists evangelize. In China, this can be tricky, because evangelization is frowned upon by the communist government and can even land a person in jail. Proselytization can occur on temple grounds, but where it is not authorized, the penalty can be serious.

There are two Daoist seminaries operating in China today, where the clergy are trained for ministry. Daoist monks and nuns have increased rapidly in the last few decades, and according to government statistics, there are fifty thousand Daoist monastics in China. It should be kept in mind that communist government statistics on religion are thought to be suppressed.[2]

Western people started taking an interest in Daoism in the 1700s, as that is when scholars first translated the

Convergence · the phenomenon in Chinese religion where elements of Buddhism, Daoism, and Confucianism are believed and practiced in a syncretic manner

Daozang · the canon of Daoist scripture, consisting of 5,305 volumes

Folk religionists · a diverse and indefinable set of people in China who draw freely from Daoist, Buddhist, and Confucian ideas, incorporating them into their localized folk traditions; notable for their variety and indigeneity

Tao Te Ching into European languages. The first major Western scholar of Daoism was the French-Jewish scholar **Henri Maspero**. For twenty-five years, he taught Chinese history and religion at prestigious French institutions, including the Sorbonne. In 1944, his son was found to be involved in the French resistance against the Nazis, and both he and his wife were sent to Buchenwald concentration camp. He died only three weeks before the US Army liberated the camp.

Currently, Michael Saso is a leading scholar of Daoism who spent his career at the University of Hawaii. He was also one of the first Western people to become a Daoist priest. He is one of the few academicians to have been ordained in three religions: Buddhism, Daoism, and Catholicism (as a Jesuit priest).

Daoism continues to gain attention in the Western world, particularly through Chinese immigrants and through religious studies courses. Plus, there is a fairly large readership of Western texts that integrate Daoism such as the *Tao of Pooh*, the *Te of Piglet*, and the *Tao of Physics*. Some elements of Daoism have been assimilated into American culture—for instance, in martial arts and feng shui. Many people see shades of Daoism in films such as the *Star Wars* movies, *The Karate Kid*, and *Crouching Tiger, Hidden Dragon*, as well as the *Kung Fu* television series.

The first Daoist temple in the United States was built in 1852 in San Francisco. It burned down but has been rebuilt, and it stands today in the city's Chinatown. It is dedicated to the sea goddess Mazu. By the end of the nineteenth century, there were dozens of Daoist temples on the West Coast of both Canada and the United States.

Henri Maspero · the first major Western scholar of Daoism

Tao of Pooh · a book introducing Daoist thought to the West through allegory with the beloved fictional character Winnie the Pooh

Interior alchemy · esoteric religious practices intended to prolong life

Tai chi · a Chinese martial art incorporating Daoist thought

Dietetics · dieting and emphasizing nutrition for physical and spiritual health

Yangsheng · "nourishing life"; the set of practices, including alchemy, tai chi, and dietetics, which is intended to prolong one's life

Lu Dongbin · a deity and the leader of the Eight Immortals in Chinese mythology

The temple in present-day Chinatown in San Francisco.

© santirf, iStock

People practice Daoism today in many ways: Some focus on longevity, even immortality. Other devotees pray to deities and make offerings to temples and ancestors. The practice of extensive—and often esoteric—forms of **interior alchemy** (as opposed to metallic alchemy) reportedly gives adherents long lives. They meditate, practice Yoga, perform **tai chi**, focus on **dietetics**, and integrate Daoist ideas of sexual hygiene for better spiritual and physical health. This large collection of practices—geared for extending human life—is called **yangsheng** ("nourishing life").

Daoists today celebrate Chinese New Year and the summer and winter solstices, when the yang and yin energies are at their peaks, and they devote days to special deities such as the Jade Emperor, Zhang Daoling, **Lu Dongbin** (leader of the Eight Immortals, a group of legendary figures—seven men and one woman—depicted frequently in Chinese art), and, of course, Lao Tzu.

The eight figures assembled on the riverbank represent the Eight Immortals, a group of Daoist deities who originated from the legends of the Tang dynasty (618–907 CE).

The funerary rituals of Daoists center on the body of the deceased. Daoists often discuss whether someone had a good death and whether they look good after death. It is important for Daoists that the skin looks healthy at death and that the deceased looks at ease, even smiling. This all indicates a good afterlife. Daoists bury their dead after finding a good location. The entire discipline of feng shui was actually designed for good burials on peaceful and auspicious mountainsides. Only later did it enter into home and office architecture. Daoist mourners usually follow Buddhism in the forty-nine-day period of lament.

Numerous Daoist organizations have arisen in North America since the fascination with Eastern religions in the 1960s, but many of them have been criticized as **American Daoism**—in other words, not genuine. These Daoisms are usually disconnected from Chinese history and the original context of Daoism. Typically, they have almost nothing to do with China, so it is difficult for religion scholars to know how to categorize them. Nevertheless, it shows how once a

religion transcends physical borders, it can lead to surprising results.

Confucianism

Is Confucianism a religion or a philosophy? That is an oft-asked question. A case can be made either way. There are temples, but there is little emphasis on God. It does not deal with afterlife. However, it is a system intended to govern humans in their morals, politics, and dealings with one another, so in that sense, it definitely has the markings of at least a system of thought. It also appears religious in other ways, such as in the reverential approach toward ancestors and the idea of a heavenly realm.

Confucius

Confucius's life is difficult to reconstruct, as he was long dead when biographers began writing about him. In the West, his name has been pronounced

American Daoism · a critical term for forms of Daoism practiced in North America that have been separated from their original history and context

This statue of Confucius sits outside the Confucius Temple in Beijing, the second-largest Confucian temple in China.

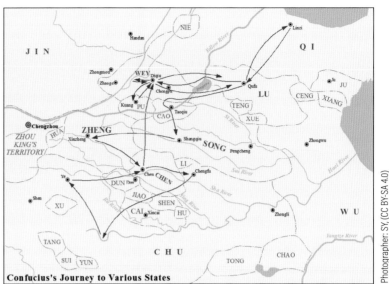

A map recounting Confucius's travels between 497 and 484 BCE.

Qufu · the city in which Confucius was born

Confucius—which means "Master King"—but he is also known as Kong Fuzi, Kongzi, Master Kong, and Kung Futzu. His actual name was Kong Qiu. The life of Confucius is told in many different ways, but over time, a scholarly consensus has emerged.

In the most important Confucian text—the *Analects*—Confucius briefly outlined his life this way (*Analects* 2:4):

At 15, I had my mind bent on learning.

At 30, I stood firm.

At 40, I had no doubts.

At 50, I knew the decrees of Heaven.

At 60, my ear was an obedient organ for the reception of the truth.

At 70, I could follow what my heart desired, without transgressing what was right.

Scholars believe Confucius was born in around 550 BCE at Mount Ni in the city of **Qufu**, which at that time was the capital of Lu state in northeast China. Birth narratives describe many auspicious signs: a unicorn, dragons, forty-nine birthmarks of a sage, celestial music, and an announcement to his mother that he would be a "king without a crown." His father was a decorated soldier, but both of his parents died while he was still young. He was a child prodigy, showing tremendous abilities. He married at age nineteen and had a son and a daughter. Some traditions say he later divorced his wife.

Confucius served in low-level governance during his day, working as a clerk and keeping accounts of the grain and produce of the community farms. He was a leader of the local civic ceremonies and thus became familiar with the rituals and beliefs of the day. For a while, he worked as a police commissioner.

In his thirties, Confucius wanted to move up in his career, but he encountered resistance at every turn. He became frustrated and decided he would turn his back on the government and teach his philosophies to anyone who would listen. He eventually assembled a group of disciples who traveled with him during a long period of itinerant teaching. Confucius was a demanding teacher. He emphasized filial piety and moral conduct, especially for society's leaders. He thought rulers should rule by example, and he pointed to the early Zhou dynasty leaders, who were heroic sage-kings of what he considered to be China's golden age.

Clearly, Confucius had misgivings about the political leaders of his day, asserting that they had wandered away from the good paths charted by their ancestors. He was an idealist. He romanticized China's past, arguing that his contemporaries needed to look to previous leaders to keep their illustrious heritage intact. This conservative perspective attracted critiques from those in power. Confucius and his students were frequently harassed by the government for their views.

In his fifties, Confucius became a chief magistrate of a town, and he began to implement his ideology into his leadership position. He was promoted up the ladder until, eventually, he became the minister of crime—one of the highest offices in the land for a commoner. Some of the lore claims that everything was safe and secure under his leadership, that crime rates dropped, and that people were honest. Once he reached those heights of his career, he realized that the other leaders were mostly corrupt. They became jealous of him and were not willing to accept his ideas, so he resigned at the age of fifty six.

At that same age of fifty-six, Confucius went back to itinerant teaching for about a decade. He gathered many disciples—some say he had three thousand people around him—who listened to his judgment that society needed to get back to the moral principles that made China great in the first place. At this stage, Confucius began to be recognized for the stable, wise thinker that he was. Some rulers sought his advice, although nobody actually implemented his teachings into the state curriculum. The reluctance of the rulers to fully endorse Confucius always frustrated him. He was dismayed by the ruling classes—having had experience in their circles—and was more sympathetic to commoners. He was offended by the behavior of government officials; they thought the government existed for them rather than the government existing for the people.

At the age of sixty-seven, Confucius moved back to his home state of Lu. He was finally able to stay in one place, giving him the time to write, reflect, and systematize his teachings. He continued with his central teaching that China needed to get back to the Dao— the old path that was followed by history's great heroes.

Confucius never saw himself as an innovator; rather, he saw himself as trying to restore the greatness of the past. Good conduct was crucial for good governance, and earthly rulers should mirror the heavenly rulers with their high standards of virtue.

After a few years of teaching and writing, Confucius died in his early seventies, believing that he had failed as a politician. In many ways, this was true. His disciples, however, deeply appreciated his cheerful and genuine approach, which may have proven to be more of an impediment in terms of a political career. While he never fully realized the lofty political ambitions he had for himself, his great legacy was that he was one of the earliest professional teachers in recorded history, which set a blueprint for what later became the teaching profession. His birthday—September 28—is one of the most important celebrations in China, as Communist Party leaders believe his teachings can counteract the social ills going on today, such as unbridled capitalism and a declining respect for authority. In many places, the celebration of Confucius's birthday lasts for ten days.

The Teachings of Confucius

In his own lifetime, Confucius's legacy was limited. However, in time, his disciples popularized his teachings. His most profound influence is in his written

First Entrance Gate to the Temple of Confucius is a steel engraving by James Tingle, based on a painting by Thomas Allom. It appeared in the book *China in a Series of Views*, Volume 2, in 1843.

© Siyuwj, public domain

The main sanctuary of the Temple of Mencius in Zoucheng, China.

legacy, the **Five Classics**, which include the *Classic of Poetry*, the *Book of Documents*, the *Book of Rites*, the *Book of Changes* (the *I Ching*), and the *Spring and Autumn Annals*. He contributed to each of them.

However, Confucius's greatest written contribution is the *Analects*. The word *analects* is actually a Greek word for "various things gathered." Confucius's *Analects* set the standard for Chinese moral philosophy, and it continues to wield a powerful influence. They were probably collected by Confucius's disciples for a few generations after his death, and they always refer to him as "the Master." Loosely organized, they contain journal entries, observations, notes, speeches, conversations, and discussions of his travels. Some scholars question whether Confucius actually wrote them, as they appear to have been assembled so haphazardly.

On a deeper level, the *Analects* advocate for social harmony and equilibrium. They emphasize humility and respect toward others, especially parents and ancestors. Respecting authority is at the heart of Confucian ethics.

> Confucius's most fundamental teaching is the notion of xiao—often translated as "filial piety."

The *Analects* are today part of the Confucian canon known as the **Four Books**. Included in the collection are the *Analects*, *Mencius*, *Great Learning*, and the *Doctrine of the Mean*.

In the history of Confucianism, Mencius is considered the second-most important teacher. He came along about a century after Confucius. He taught that humans are good and that governments should trust the people and stay out of their way as much as possible. Mencius advocated for a small government, since people generally figure out a way to coexist peacefully. He believed that the public can be trusted. Mencius was also the thinker who began to take Confucianism into a more religious direction, as he strongly emphasized the "way of heaven" as being the correct way.

Great Learning argues that political leaders must live moral lives. They should lead by example. When the leaders are morally good, then the society will follow suit. However, if the leaders are corrupt, the society will follow.

The *Doctrine of the Mean* supports a middle path in all things. People are at their best when they avoid extremes in their thoughts and conduct. Buddhism's notion of the middle path found a welcome home in China because of the trail that was blazed by this text.

Was Confucius an atheist? We do not really know. He did not deny the existence of gods, so he probably was not an atheist. He was simply more concerned with ethics and human conduct—particularly for government officials. That leads to the question of what served as his foundation for morality and ethics.

Confucius's most fundamental teaching is the notion of xiao—often translated as "filial piety." It means people should respect their parents, elders, and ancestors. They should fulfill their proper responsibilities and honor the people they are supposed to honor. Everyone has a proper place in society, and no one should resist that. Rather, people should humble themselves and respect their superiors. People should be polite and do their own specific role to maintain harmony in society. Confucius believed that China was in chaos during his days, and it was because people were not living according to xiao.

Five Classics · five works to which Confucius contributed, including the *Book of Poetry*, the *Book of Documents*, the *Book of Rites*, the *Book of Changes* (the *I Ching*), and the *Spring and Autumn Annals*

Four Books · a collection of Confucian classics including the *Analects*, *Mencius*, *Great Learning*, and the *Doctrine of the Mean*

Mencius · the second-greatest Confucian teacher, who emphasized the goodness and trustworthiness of the people, advocated for small government, and took Confucianism in a more religious direction, stressing the "way of heaven" as being the correct way

Great Learning · a Confucian text that highlights the necessity of having moral political leaders; if the leaders are corrupt, the people will be also, but if the leaders are moral, then society will be as well

Doctrine of the Mean · a Confucian text that supports a middle path in all things, avoiding extremes in thought and conduct

Xiao · "filial piety"; respecting authorities and observing one's proper place in the five fundamental relationships of parents to children, older siblings to younger siblings, husbands to wives, elders to the youths, and rulers to the ruled

At the base of xiao are five fundamental relationships that determine social harmony:

- Parents to children
- Older siblings to younger siblings
- Husbands to wives
- Elders to youths
- Rulers to those being ruled

For harmony to exist, each of the parties in these relationships must show proper respect to one another—a concept called reciprocity. The first person in each of these has more power, so the second one must readily submit. However, the one with higher social ranking must use their social power carefully and with great responsibility, protecting and looking out for the one with less privilege.

The notion of xiao has been critiqued by Western academicians as being overly patriarchal. The charge is made that Confucianism privileges men and rewards women for having sons. Education was for males only, and women were under the authority of men at every point in their lives. Women were not allowed to study the Confucian classics, widows were not permitted to marry, and foot binding became common practice, in many cases crippling women just to keep their feet small and ostensibly pretty.

Another key concept for Confucius was **ren**—being humane to people. It is a loaded term that is used often in the *Analects*. When people act with ren, they are benevolent to one another. They are good and kind. They realize that nobody functions alone in society; rather, people's lives are an interlocking web of relations with the people around them. To maintain harmony, people must practice the Confucian Golden Rule, found in two passages of the *Analects*: "Do not do to others what you would not like yourself" (12:2), and "what you do not want done to yourself, do not do to others" (15:24).

Ren · acting humanely and benevolently toward each other to maintain harmony

Li · "ritual propriety"; submitting to the subtle and overt rituals of society in order to achieve greater social harmony

Junzi · a gentleman who acts with all integrity, according to Confucian teaching

A third central concept of Confucianism—after xiao and ren—is **li**, or "ritual propriety." This means that people should submit to the subtle and overt rituals of society to achieve greater social harmony. Bow to people. Say "please" and "thank you." Allow others to go first. Give gifts to people to show appreciation. Show deference to others, making sure to dress appropriately, act respectfully, and even carry one's body in a humble way. Never talk back with defiance.

Confucius is considered the master because he modeled how people should behave toward others. He often emphasized demeanor (see *Analects* 2:8), encouraging people to show submission to one another and to be careful to have a respectful countenance. People should not talk while eating, and one should be careful about looking someone in the eye if they are a superior. Facial expressions are crucial, and one should always be aware of how others might perceive them. Even if people are irritated, they should try their best to appear pleasant.

Westerners find many of these social rules and taboos to be off-putting. The European Enlightenment emphasized personal autonomy, and in recent generations, the Western world has emphasized equality of all rather than submission to those in authority. Confucius, however, placed humility and respect atop the ladder of virtues. He thought people had abandoned proper deference in his day, which motivated him to speak strongly on concepts like xiao, ren, and li.

The *Analects* includes extensive teachings about respecting one's parents—the highest moral behavior a person can practice. It is shameful to disobey parents or to ignore them, even after their death. Confucius said, "parents, when alive, [should] be served according to propriety; that, when dead, they should be buried according to propriety; and that they should be sacrificed to according to propriety" (2:5).

A **junzi**—or a gentleman (or noble person)—should not be offended when he is not recognized by those around him. A junzi has integrity—his private and public lives correspond. He should watch his language carefully and should speak only with respect. The junzi should keep all his promises and only befriend respectful people. A junzi should not be frivolous and

The Kaohsiung Confucius Temple. Originally constructed in 1684, it is the largest Confucian temple complex in Taiwan.

should maintain a serious disposition. A junzi recognizes the accomplishments of others but does not seek accolades for himself. A junzi must be careful to avoid evil or disruptive thoughts.

The Legacy of Confucius

Earlier, Mencius was mentioned as the one given credit as the orthodox interpreter of Confucius. Like Confucius, he taught that people had the capacity to do the right thing and to live at peace. He believed, like Confucius, that humans are fundamentally good.

However, the third great figure of Confucianism is **Xunzi** (or **Hsun Tzu**), who disagreed strongly with Confucius and Mencius on one all-important issue—the nature of humanity. Born near the end of Mencius's life, Xunzi argued that humans are fundamentally evil and cannot be trusted. Without strict supervision, people lose control, and order must be imposed upon them from above. He was a Confucian, but he represented a different framework and interpretation of Confucian ideals. He thought humans are prone to err, making him a kind of Chinese Calvinist. Humans inevitably fall into bad habits and need frequent correcting. As a result of this perspective, Xunzi emphasized individual and corporate ritual in the hopes that it might bring people under control. Rituals help people to conform. People need that social pressure, or else society will explode into disharmony. Xunzi argued that without a heavy-handed government, people would completely violate the spirit of Confucius's teachings. Contradicting Mencius, it was Xunzi's belief that the government should become large and powerful, disciplining violators and bending the will of the people into submission. Perhaps it is needless to say, but Xunzi is much less popular in the West, where independence and autonomy are so prized.

Confucius's teachings profoundly shaped the Chinese people and even the cultures around them, such as in Korea and Japan. Shortly after Mencius and Xunzi, it was required that all Chinese youth had to learn Confucius's ideas and philosophies, particularly those students who would go into governance. Chinese educational systems

> **Xunzi ·** also spelled **Hsun Tzu,** the third great figure of Confucianism who disagreed strongly with Confucius and Mencius with his belief that humans are fundamentally evil and must be strictly governed in order to maintain harmony by force

officially endorsed and taught Confucius for over two millennia—from 136 BCE until the twentieth century. The Chinese civil service required all leaders in government to pass Confucian exams until this policy was abolished in 1905.

Over the centuries, Confucian temples were erected in virtually every county of China, with a school standing next door, together representing education and virtue. Confucian temples do not usually have images, as the emphasis is on his teaching rather than on the person, as is seen in Buddhism, for example. The one exception is the city of Confucius's birth, Qufu, which has become a major tourist and pilgrimage site. The city is known as "the Jerusalem of Confucianism." Confucius's descendants still control the temples and the massive cemetery there, and they proudly venerate their esteemed ancestor.

Confucian temples do not exist in North America, due to Confucius's close connection to the Chinese people and philosophical system. Confucianism might be the only religion in North America devoid of a temple. However, there are some **Confucian Centers** of learning, usually attached to universities. And, in some cases, there exists a room in the Center specifically for venerating Confucius and his chief interpreters. Many of these Centers are sponsored by the government of China, which has led to some controversy.

Like in Daoism, a metaphysical system did develop around the core principles of Confucianism, with Confucius as a supernatural being who could be sacrificed to, among other things. He became like a god in the minds of commoners. He is the great ancestor of China.

Twentieth-Century Developments

The twentieth century was an extremely turbulent one for the Chinese nation, as well as for its religions. As the society began to embrace modernity and science, it turned against traditional ways of life, especially religion. In the 1920s, Daoism underwent a crackdown that was so harsh that only two copies of the Daoist canon, the Daozang, were known to exist.

Ironically, the 1930s proved to be rather fortunate for Confucianism, as **Chiang Kai-shek**, a Christian who was religiously tolerant, initiated the **New Life Movement**. Chiang Kai-shek (also known as Jiang Jieshi) was the leader of the Republic of China from

Confucian Centers · institutions often funded by the Chinese government and attached to universities in North America that promote understanding of Chinese culture and thought

Chiang Kai-shek · the Christian leader of the Chinese Nationalist government before and during the Chinese Civil War, and leader of the Republic of China in Taiwan until 1975; founder of the New Life Movement

New Life Movement · a movement started by Chiang Kai-shek in the 1930s to bring social harmony by returning to traditional values, with an emphasis on respect and the rule of law

One-yuan 1999 banknote from China, with the image of Mao Zedong.

Photographer: Tsering Dorjee, public domain.

During the Cultural Revolution, "struggle sessions" such as this one commonly took place. They entailed a public denunciation of counterrevolutionaries, often involving acts of humiliation and torture.

Photographer: Pat B, (CC BY-SA 2.0)

This Buddhist statue, like countless other religious artifacts, was defaced during the Cultural Revolution, when religion was to be eradicated as one of the Four Olds.

Great Proletarian Cultural Revolution · a brutal purge of all traditional legacies that had survived the communist revolution in China; lasted from 1966 to Mao's death in 1976

Four Olds · old ideas, old cultures, old customs, old habits, all of which were to be violently eradicated during the Cultural Revolution

1928 until his death in 1975. In 1949, when his government was defeated by Mao and the communists, he and his party retreated to Taiwan. Before their defeat, however, Chiang Kai-shek and his government saw that traditional Confucian values strengthened the nation and gave rise to social order. The New Life Movement was designed to bring social harmony by returning to traditional values, with an emphasis on respect and the rule of law.

However, communism prevailed in China beginning in 1949 with the victory of the communists over the Nationalists in the Chinese Civil War. Communism is built on the thought of Karl Marx; thus, communism's view of religion is that it is bad for society. In Marx's words, religion is the "opiate of the people." Chairman Mao Zedong—a devout Marxist—was the leader of the Communist Party and essentially ruled China for twenty-seven years, from 1949 to his death in 1976. It was a devastating period for China's religious people. Mao explicitly referred to religion as "poison."

Communists critiqued Confucianism for passively allowing the aristocratic elites to rule over the common people. In the communist interpretation of Chinese economics, the rich enjoyed all of the benefits of society, while the lower classes suffered. The communists also critiqued the *Analects of Confucius*

for being too patriarchal and for subjugating women. The communist government was extremely critical of Confucianism. This was all part of a wider movement to rid the land of any sort of religious attachment or ideology other than that of Marxism as interpreted by Mao Zedong. All Christian missionaries were forced out in 1952. Buddhism was stamped out and humiliated—particularly in Tibet.

Mao Zedong initiated a movement called the **Great Proletarian Cultural Revolution** in 1966 that lasted until his death in 1976. It was a brutal purge of any and all religion in China. Anything associated with traditional ways of thinking was attacked. These things were known as the **Four Olds**: old ideas, old culture, old customs, and old habits. Any religious structures that had survived Mao's rule up to that point were quickly demolished or desacralized for government use. Confucius's hometown of Qufu was ransacked, and thousands of irreplaceable artifacts were destroyed. If people celebrated religious events, or if their celebrations incorporated any religious symbolism, they were singled out, publicly humiliated, and persecuted. All this had the effect of making Marxism look like a religion itself: Chairman Mao was its god, and his *Little Red Book* was its scripture. But unlike China's religious history, Maoism tolerated no competitors.

Daoism and Confucianism   189

The Temple of Confucius in Jiading now operates as a museum of the Confucian exams, required of all civil service workers from 136 BCE to 1905.

Daoism, too, was persecuted harshly during the decade of the Cultural Revolution. Nearly all temples and monasteries were shuttered, and the number of Daoists fell drastically due to government threats. Daoist leaders were either killed or sent to reeducation camps.

Mao died in 1976, and the extreme persecution lessened quickly, but certainly not completely. Still today, religion is viewed with suspicion by the communist government, which is officially atheist. Religion is allowed in China, but there are always serious restrictions. Most importantly, the government must oversee anything pertaining to religion, and fortunes can swiftly change for religious organizations.

Five religions are recognized in China: Daoism, Buddhism, Roman Catholicism, Protestantism, and Islam. Confucianism is notably absent from the list due to the Cultural Revolution's crackdown on everything tainted by Confucius. Due to Confucianism being associated with the old ways of China's past, it was used as a scapegoat for all of China's social ills. However, that situation has changed dramatically.

Confucianism has experienced a shocking resurgence in China since the death of Mao, as Chinese Communist Party leaders have begun to see an erosion of the values that Confucius taught so fervently in a society that is now, ironically, flush with cash and capital. Ancestor veneration, respect for authority, good etiquette—ideas taught by Confucius—are now emphasized by the vehemently anti-religious Chinese Communist Party. Since Confucius is seen as more of a philosopher than a religious leader, his recent rise to

President Xi Jinping · the current president of the People's Republic of China

Falun Gong · also known as **Falun Dafa**, an exercise- and meditation-based religion that was founded in the early 1990s by Li Hongzhi; brutally persecuted by the Chinese government ever since its practitioners publicly demonstrated for religious freedom in China

Li Hongzhi · the founder of Falun Gong who leads his movement from Deerpark, New York, because of the intense persecution in China

Photographer: Joffers951, (CC BY-SA 4.0)

Falun Gong involves meditation and qigong practices, such as this Falun Gong meditation in Manhattan, New York.

fame has been not only palatable but cultivated by the Chinese Communist Party (CCP). The city of Qufu is now embraced by the government as a noble pilgrimage site, and a high-speed rail line was built to haul in the masses to Qufu, increasing patriotism—all in the name of Confucius. Even a theme park now stands in Confucius's hometown as a celebration of the great sage. Hundreds of Confucian Centers have been established in China and abroad. Confucian temples are regularly visited, even by Chinese Communist Party leaders. Statues of Confucius are everywhere in China. Chinese **President Xi Jinping** quotes Confucius in his speeches and reads the *Analects* regularly. Jokes are now made that CCP stands for the Chinese Confucian Party.

Religions that fall outside of these five acceptable religions can be persecuted mercilessly, as was the case with **Falun Gong** (also known as **Falun Dafa**), an exercise- and meditation-based religion that was founded in the early 1990s by **Li Hongzhi**. It is one of thousands of **qigong** (life energy) groups that emerged in the aftermath of Mao's death. Falun Gong spread rapidly across China, but it

Qigong · "life energy"; an ancient form of traditional healing, incorporating meditation and martial arts

Chinese Communist Party · the dogmatic and formidable governing political party of China

Sinicization · to nativize into Chinese forms

Home shrines · small altars increasingly set up in Chinese homes to pay respects and burn paper money to ancestors, Daoist gods, Buddhas, and Confucius

RESURGENCE OF RELIGION IN CHINA

While China has come a long way since the era of Mao in terms of religious freedom, it is a far cry from being a religiously open society. The **Chinese Communist Party** is still reticent about religion. Despite the unpredictability of the government, religion is growing in China by all accounts. The Chinese Communist Party has called for the **Sinicization** of religion in China, meaning foreign religions are not as welcome as China-born religions.

China is now experiencing something of a religious resurgence. People have much less fear to practice their religion than in the past. Increasingly, Chinese people are setting up **home shrines**, where they pay respects and burn paper money to their ancestors, Daoist gods, various Buddhas, and Confucius.

Religious funerals are back in vogue again. Daoists and Confucians prefer burial, while those who emphasize Buddhism at death are more inclined to cremate. Today, China's dead are split: around half are buried, and around half are cremated. Cremation is more common in the big cities than in rural towns.

has been harshly suppressed since 1999, when its members publicly demonstrated for religious freedom. The persecution has been harsh and largely successful in rooting out the movement from China. The leader, Li Hongzhi, moved to the United States and established his headquarters at Dragon Springs, in Deerpark, New York.

The Falun Gong controversy has ignited questions about religious freedom in China. When the Chinese Communist Party declares a religious movement or social organization as being **xie jiao** (evil cult), the persecution begins and can become severe. The xie jiao label can be absolutely devastating for a movement and usually means it will soon disappear. Members of Falun Gong have claimed that they are not a religion; rather, they are better classified as a form of science and good health. Definitions matter, and in China, the label xie jiao has great power to marginalize.

Religion in China Today

It is notoriously difficult for scholars to try to measure religion in China today. Statistics are impossibly difficult to construct, for several reasons. Not only does the Chinese Communist Party suppress religious statistics, but the nature of religion in China itself is difficult to quantify as it is done in the Western world. As noted, much of Chinese religion is a blend of Daoism,

> It is notoriously difficult for scholars to try to measure religion in China today.

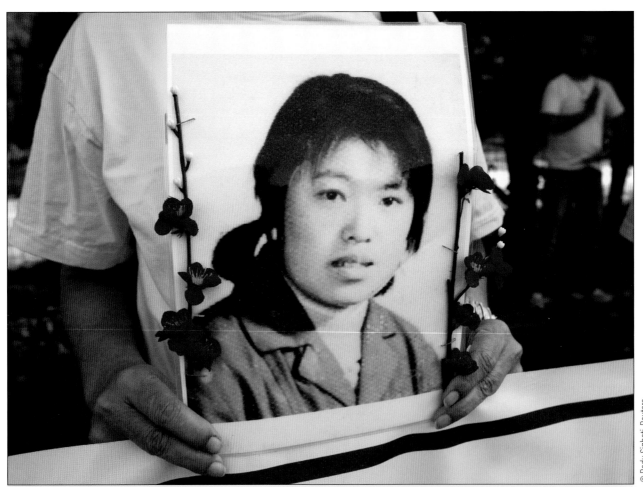

© Radu Sigheti, Reuters

During a protest against China's crackdown on Falun Gong followers in front of the Chinese embassy in Bucharest, Romania, on September 24, 2011, a Falun Gong member holds a portrait of a woman who went missing. Falun Gong was banned in China in 1999 and, according to members of the group, thousands of Chinese practitioners died in prison or due to abuse.

Confucianism, and Buddhism. There is also the influence of the one-party communist government that clearly privileges atheism, making religious people hesitant to admit their religiosity for fear of missing out on a good government job.

Some have claimed that China is simply not a very religious nation, but that conclusion is debatable to say the least. Taiwan, however, is a religious nation, showing that the difference may be political rather than truly religious. Before Mao, religion in China was prominent. The communist government demonized religion, causing a confusion around the issue of religion that persists to the present. Many demographers hold that while Chinese people may believe and practice religion, it is simply not worth it to run afoul of the authorities in some unforeseen way. Thus, they refer to themselves as irreligious by and large.

The authoritative World Religion Database counts nearly five hundred million folk religionists in China, meaning people who combine Daoism, Confucianism, and Buddhism. Surveys of Chinese religiosity tend to show that while Chinese people are reluctant to label themselves religious, they often do things that scholars associate with religious practice, most conspicuously the veneration of ancestors.

8 SHINTOISM

For Kami and Country

One of the more recognizable images of Japan, this famous torii gate off the island of Itsukushima marks the entrance from secular to sacred space.

Shinto is difficult to describe or define as a religion due to its intrinsic identification with Japanese culture in general. It is like an indigenous religion, in which there is little separation between the religion and the self-understanding of the community itself. Shinto is fundamental to the cultural identity of the Japanese nation. There is a nationalistic ethos to it, and many perceive Shintoism today as a way of life and as a vehicle for preserving Japanese traditional culture. However, it also has magical, spiritual, and ritualistic elements that would make it appear to be more of a religion. There is not a clear consensus among scholars: some see Shinto as a religion, and others see it as more of a cultural identity. In recent decades, some scholars have tried to argue that Japan has become a very **secular** nation. As we will see, however, it all depends on what we mean by the words *religious* and *secular*.

> There is not a clear consensus among scholars: some see Shinto as a religion, and others see it as more of a cultural identity.

The term *Shinto* comes from two Chinese characters: **shen** and **tao**, which translate to "the way (tao) of the spirits (shen)." The word itself was not coined until the arrival of Buddhists into Japan in the sixth century CE. This is because Shinto was not really understood by the Japanese people as their religion. It was simply the way things were, a worldview. When Buddhism entered, however, the Japanese had to give a name to their own distinct way of thinking to cope with the new Buddhist ideas coming to their shores. Thus, Shintoism became for Japanese the indigenous way of thinking, as opposed to the incoming Buddhist ideas that were entirely new to them.

Shintoism does not separate the material world from the spiritual. As with many indigenous religions, the natural elements, such as mountains, forests, waters, and heavenly spheres, become spiritualized and deified. In religious studies, this is called **animism**.

Similar to religion in China, Japanese people do not feel compelled to limit their religious affiliation to one religion. A Japanese person feels free to draw from Buddhism for one purpose and from the traditional religion of Shinto for another. These two religions have become intermixed throughout the centuries to the point that they are like a blended reality now.

Shintoism refers to both gods and spirits as **kami**. The term *kami* includes all spirits, including human, animal, plant, water, and mountain, as well as other natural objects

Secular · unaffiliated with religion

Shen · a Chinese character for "spirits," from which the word *Shinto* is derived

Tao · a Chinese character for "way," from which the word *Shinto* is derived

Animism · when the natural elements—such as mountains, forests, waters, and heavenly spheres—become spiritualized and deified

Kami · gods and all kinds of spirits, including human, animal, plant, water, mountain, as well as other natural objects and forces

Kurozumikyo · a Shinto sect centered on Amaterasu

VARIETIES OF SHINTO

Some Shintos are affiliated with mountain worship and take regular retreats. Others are neo-shamanistic. Some have been labeled as cults and are accused of being too radical. Some forms of Shinto want a return to the old ways, based mainly on the historical rituals and the ancient Shinto texts. Some, such as **Kurozumikyo**, focus on Amaterasu, the Sun goddess. Similar to Mahayana Buddhism, there are endless ways to practice Shinto. And with each new charismatic leader who rises up, there is sure to be a new school or philosophy that also comes into being.

The three most important categories of kami are: (1) distinguished ancestors, (2) great warriors, and (3) powers within nature, such as forests, animals, tsunamis, earthquakes, rocks, and rushing waters. Some examples of prominent kami are:

Tsukuyomi, the kami of the Moon.

- **Hachiman**—Japan's divine protector who is closely associated with the samurai warriors.
- **Amaterasu**—the Sun goddess and the best known of the kami; often represented by mirrors placed in Shinto shrines.
- **Izanagi** and **Izanami**—the first male and female kami. They were brother and sister, who then became husband and wife. Izanami gave birth to the Japanese islands.
- **Tenjin**—the "sky deity" kami of education and scholarship.
- **Inari**—the kami associated with fertility, agriculture, **sake** (alcoholic beverage made from rice), and prosperity.

A kitsune—a fox believed to have mythical abilities—guards the entrance to a shrine to Inari, the kami of foxes, as well as rice, sake, and fertility.

With deep reverence for nature, the kami of Shintoism often dwell in trees, rivers, or mountains. This Shinto shrine from the Saga Prefecture of Japan is built inside a 3,000-year-old camphor tree.

and forces. Historically, Shintos understood their emperor as holding a critical position within this kami worldview, as he was a link between the human realm and the realm of the kami.

Historically, the Japanese people have seen themselves as descendants of the kami, and they often refer to their religion as **kami no michi** ("way of kami"). Today, most Japanese think of Shinto as traditional spirituality in which one harmonizes herself with nature. It is natural spirituality, where the devotee listens to nature and tries to align herself with the forces of nature. There is a sense of gratitude toward nature that helps a person remain in sync with the environment.

The Way of the Kami

Shintoism revolves around the notion of kami. The kami are a diverse class of beings, including deities and spirits. Kami can also be inanimate objects such as rocks, planets, and stars. According to tradition, there are eight million kami, but in Shinto, that is not a precise number at all. It is meant to convey the limitlessness of kami all around us.

The kami are not omnipotent. They have limitations on their power and can even die and decay. They are not omnibenevolent, either. Some kami are good and helpful to people, while others are malevolent and can cause serious harm. Kami live in the same world that humans inhabit, rather than in some far-off place. There are kami for particular clans, kami that solve family problems, kami that help with fertility, and kami that guard certain geographical areas like mountains, farms, or rice paddies.

Families worshiped and relied upon the goodwill of certain kami to provide for them a good crop, particularly rice. Thus, the kami became closely associated with a family or clan, and the relationship could become quite personal, even to the point of a kami merging with a human being. This is precisely what has happened in the case of the emperor and particularly revered leaders such as holy men and military heroes. The traditional Japanese home has a **kamidana**—a shelf or altar for honoring the family's kami. The kami take up residence in homes and receive offerings of food from the family as long as the offering is made from hands that have been cleaned and ritually purified. Kami are not usually represented by iconography such as statues or paintings; they are assumed to be there based upon the traditions that have been passed down from people to people.

> **Kami no michi** · "the way of the kami"; another way of saying Shinto
>
> **Kamidana** · a shelf or altar in a home honoring the family's kami
>
> **Torii** · "bird perch"; a gateway to a Shinto shrine, reminding adherents that they are entering a sacred space

Shinto Shrines

Typically, Shinto worship is held at home or takes place quietly at one of the estimated eighty thousand shrines in Japan on any day of the week. Corporate gatherings are rare and are usually reserved for community or national events. Shinto shrines are typically rather new since they have to be torn down and rebuilt every twenty years. This prevents decay, making Shinto temples feel very fresh upon entrance.

When compared to Chinese temples, Shinto shrines are lighter, leaner, and much less ornate. One can also identify a Shinto shrine by the **torii** ("bird perch") gateway that welcomes devotees to the temple

It is common for Shinto adherents to have kamidana, or miniature shrines, on shelves in their home. Pictured is a kamidana shelf aboard the military battleship Mikasa.

The Fushimi Inari shrine in Kyoto famously has a walkway through a thousand torii gates.

The Ise Shrine is one of the most important shrines in Japan, dedicated to the Sun kami Amaterasu. Like most Shinto shrines, it is torn down and rebuilt every twenty years so that it will never be subject to decay.

Outside the honden of the controversial Yasukuni Shrine, which for over 150 years has honored all the souls who died in war for Japan—even those guilty of war crimes.

area. The torii stationed there reminds people that they are entering a place of purity.

One of the most important shrines is located in the city of Ise, in the south-central part of the country. Amaterasu is housed there at the Grand Imperial Shrine. Ise receives millions of Japanese visitors per year; they pay their respects and purchase a paper blessing at the shrine to take back to their kamidana shelves in their homes. Following World War II, national demoralization led to a decline in attendance at the shrines, but in the last couple of decades, Japan has experienced renewed interest in visitation to Shinto shrines, most notably the impressive shrines of Ise. Some of the most popular and historic shrines are on the southern side of Japan's main island, **Honshu**. Many important Buddhist temples are there, too.

One controversial Shinto shrine is the **Yasukuni Shrine** in Tokyo. For more than 150 years, it has served as a shrine commemorating those who died in the military. It honors over two million soldiers in the temple's Book of Souls. Over the years, prime ministers have attended the shrine and paid their respects, causing many people—particularly in East Asia—to bristle,

since many of the dead soldiers honored at the temple were guilty of war crimes. Hundreds of thousands of Japanese visitors come to the Yasukuni Shrine annually, stoking some of the residual tension that remains between Japan and the nations it conquered or provoked during its colonial heyday.

Shinto shrines are considered pure spaces, so no impure things, such as dead bodies, can enter. Anything that might violate norms of purity is called **tsumi**. There are two major ways people can cause impurity: (1) committing evil deeds, and (2) having contact with sickness or death.

Shinto shrines contain chozubachi so all devotees can ceremonially wash before entry. The prevalence of chozubachi demonstrates how integral purity and hygiene are to Shinto worship.

Honshu · the main island of Japan

Yasukuni Shrine · a controversial shrine honoring Japanese who have died in war, including those who are guilty of war crimes

Tsumi · anything that violates the norms of purity

Shinto worship is usually structured in four stages: purification, presentation, prayer, and participation. The first phase is for the priest to purify the setting. Next is the presentation that includes many food sacrifices and traditional music. The third phase involves the priest reading a formal prayer, either silently or by chanting. Fourth, the worshipers participate in some way, which can vary widely. Sometimes they might partake of a bit of wine on the altar, and at other times they might put a small branch onto the altar.

Cleanliness and purity are crucial concepts in Shinto, as they point to good character. Food should be fresh, and shopping is usually done daily. Homes and businesses should be tidy. One's body should be clean and well-groomed. Relationships should be open, trusting, and free of drama. Apologies are frequent and welcome. Blood and leather are polluting. One's heart should remain pure, too. Shinto teaches the goodness of human beings, but evil spirits can cause problems in a person's life, leading them to become angry, unkempt, and even physically sick. Anger and other sins will block purity from happening inside a person; thus, these evil kami must be dealt with.

When going to the shrine to pray, devotees wash their hands and mouth prior to entering. They bring a coin and drop it into a coin box for good luck. They ring a bell or strike a gong, rousing the kami's attention. Devotees then bow twice, clap their hands twice, and

Ema · a wooden plaque containing a depiction of an animal (especially a horse) on one side and blank on the other; the devotee writes a wish on the blank side and leaves it in the temple for the kami to receive

SHINTO PRIESTS

Priests in Shintoism are called **shinshokus**, which means "employee of the gods." Another word used is **kannushi**, which means "god master." They can be male or female, can marry, and can have families. Historically, the priests were male, but this has changed in the modern era. Shinshokus preside over the services at the temple, but they do not typically do Western pastoral activities such as counseling or preaching. They are supported by the offerings that come into the shrine. The largest shrines in Shintoism are usually kinship-based, meaning the positions are typically passed down from father to child, remaining in the family for many generations. Today, most priests must pass a state-prescribed course at a university to become an expert in Shintoism and in leading shrine ceremonies.

Young, unmarried women who are assistants to priests are known as **mikos**. They assist in ceremonies, clean and tidy around the facility, and help the priest in many ways. They are easy to spot, with their red skirts and white kimonos. Many mikos are daughters of the shinshokus who preside at the temple. They are trained in the **Kagura** dance, which is designed to honor the kami. The Kagura dance—accompanied by flutes and stringed instruments—is based on a myth where Amaterasu had to be lured out from a cave. The world became cold and dark without her presence, so the other gods had to cause a commotion so she would become curious and emerge from the cave.

Mikos performing the traditional Kagura dance with batons and bells.

A collection of ema at the Kamakura shrine.

bow deeply once more. At that point, worshipers either make a wish or say a prayer. Some Shintos present a wooden plaque called an **ema** that contains a depiction of an animal (especially a horse) on one side. Devotees write a wish on the backside of the ema and leave it in the temple for the kami to receive. Eventually, all of the emas are gathered together and ritually burned.

Often, after paying respects at the Shinto shrine, worshipers choose a random fortune that has been written on a small piece of paper and placed in a box. These are known as **omikuji**—forerunners of the modern-day fortune cookie, which was actually invented in the United States. Omikuji can be good or bad, so be careful before reading!

Most Shinto shrines are today organized under the Association of Shinto Shrines. However, each shrine is autonomous, self-governing, and self-supporting, and it can basically do what it wants. Shrines receive offerings and endowments from the faithful to keep the shrine active and to pay any staff that might work there.

Certain shrines become associated with certain things. For example, a shrine might have a good reputation for providing good luck in fishing. Another might be reputable for fertility. Another might recognize fallen soldiers. Another might be a peaceful place for honoring ancestors. Another might be where all the college students go to pray for good luck on their college entrance exams.

Typically, a Shinto shrine has two parts to it: a **haiden** (worship hall) and a smaller **honden** (main hall), which is in the back and is where the kami stay. Worshipers will only enter the worship hall, as they do not want to disturb the kami.

The Four Central Affirmations

There are four central affirmations in Shintoism:

- Family traditions
- Love of nature
- Purity in all things, including personal hygiene
- Honoring the kami

Omikuji · fortunes written on small pieces of paper and drawn out of a box; the forerunner of the modern-day fortune cookie

Haiden · the worship hall in a Shinto shrine, where practitioners stay so as not to disturb the kami

Honden · the main hall in a Shinto shrine; where the kami stay

お引きになられた御籤棒は元の筒にお戻し下さい。

At the Asakusa Shrine in Tokyo, Shinto practitioners draw a stick bearing a number out of a box. They then take an omikuji (fortune) from the drawer labeled with the number they drew. Unlike American fortune cookies, the omikuji can predict either good or bad fortune.

SHINTO MARRIAGES

Japanese marriages are the coming together of two families. The marriage ceremony often takes place at a Shinto shrine so the couple can be married "before the kami." Many Japanese people today prefer to be married in the Western style. Even if they have no relationship with Christianity, many Japanese today dress like Westerners for their wedding—especially the white dress for the bride—and have the ceremony in the church building.

While some shrines are major complexes, others like this Hakusan Gongen shrine in Kawagoe are small sacred spaces with a torii and a little kamidana.

Shinto ethics and morality can appear vague to Westerners since there is a level of relativity. The right thing to do might vary in certain circumstances. How a person handles a situation will have consequences for themselves, their family, their clan, or even their nation. Shintos proceed with caution, seeking to do the best that they can. In general, the great virtues are courage, loyalty, and purity (which includes personal cleanliness). These are all virtues that were exhibited in the notion of bushido, so well-illustrated in the samurai culture. Major sins in Shintoism include the murder of infants, incest, poisoning someone, and cursing with one's mouth. These sins threaten social harmony in profound ways, so they must be carefully avoided.

Shintos are concerned with the present moment and how to respond to it. How can people live appropriately right now, in this particular situation? How should a person behave in this particular circumstance? How can harmony be maintained? How can all life be protected, instead of just focusing on the protection of oneself? How can a person help all life to flourish? These are ethical questions that Shintos ask.

Shintos believe that there is life in all things, and this applies very much to food. The US food culture is

The Meoto Iwa, or the Married Couple Rocks, in the Mie Prefecture of Japan. The rope represents the bond of marital union, while the rocks represent the wedded kami Izanagi and Izanami.

The armor of a famous samurai warlord, Uesugi Kenshin.

different from the Shinto food culture. Shintos feel gratitude for their food. Life was given on our behalf so we might benefit from it. It is irresponsible to throw food in the trash or put a cigarette out on one's plate. People must respect their food. All things have divine essence within them, even plants, which, in turn, become food. Everything is alive, and by treating food with respect, people show their appreciation for the life that was given for them.

Shintoism and the Afterlife

Japanese people tend to associate afterlife with Buddhism. Some Japanese homes freely practice elements of Buddhism and even have a Buddhist altar in addition to a kamidana. The Japanese associate death with impurity. This perception comes from the *Kojiki*. Shortly after Izanami and Izanagi created the Japanese islands, Izanami died, and she descended to **Yomi**—the realm of the dead. Izanagi followed her there and saw her body decomposing with maggots all inside of her. He was horrified, and he thoroughly purified himself once he returned from the land of Yomi. This is why the Japanese do not view death favorably and therefore relegate death rituals to the Buddhist priests.

Shintos believe that life continues after death. They believe that when people die, they go down to the shadowy realm of Yomi, which is located beneath the Earth. It is not a realm of punishment, just a place where people go after death for an unspecified period of time. However, most people will become ancestral kami when they die and will get the chance to return to the land of the living. If a person does not want to return as a kami, then she or he may choose to remain in Yomi.

Most Japanese people cremate their dead. Cremation rates in Japan are the highest in the world, at around 99.8 percent. After the two-hour cremation, the relatives use chopsticks to pull out the remaining small bone fragments from the ashes. Some fragments will go into an urn that then gets buried in a graveyard, and a stone monument is erected in memoriam. Other remains are put into a family grave. Still other fragments might go to a temple or even to the site of a company where the person worked. A few days after the burial, there is a celebration of the life of the deceased person.

The *Kojiki*: Shintoism's Sacred Text

Shintoism is not a textual religion. It does not have a creed or a fixed set of doctrines. Rather, it is open-ended. Similarly, Shinto ethics and notions of morality are not static. They are flexible and relative, based upon the given situation a person finds himself in.

Nevertheless, Shinto does have some texts that influence ethics, morals, and beliefs. The most significant and historic text of Shinto is the *Kojiki*—the Record of Ancient Matters. The *Kojiki* recounts the Japanese myths that were already rooted in the culture

The creator kami, Izanagi and Izanami, ca. 1885. According to the *Kojiki*, they stirred the oceans with a spear and brought forth the Japanese islands.

Woodblock print of the Sun kami, Amaterasu Omikami, emerging from a cave—a scene from a popular myth. Artist: Utagawa Kunisada (1786–1864)

The *Kojiki* consists of three texts: the upper volume, the middle volume, and the lower volume. The style of writing is mixed: poetry, song, commentary, narration, dialogue. All the chapters are basically a genealogy. Each chapter takes either a deity or a sovereign as its title.

The first and second (or upper and middle) volumes are full of deities, such as Izanagi and Izanami. However, by the time the reader gets to the third book (lower volume), the gods do not appear much at all.

The upper volume describes the birth of the kami and recounts in some detail the era of the gods. The middle volume contains the story of the mythical first emperor of Japan—**Jimmu**. A descendant of Amaterasu, he ascended to his position in 660 BCE and founded the nation of Japan that year. He captured the region of **Yamato**, which became a strategic capital for Japan's ruling house for generations—traditionally from 250 to 710 CE. The middle volume ends with the fifteenth emperor. Much of this information is thought to be legendary by scholars.

The third (lower) volume covers events from the sixteenth to thirty-third emperors. It begins with political and social instability, which is how the middle book ended. It outlines an acrimonious succession dispute that eventually led to chaos. Subjects rebelled against the royals. Toward the end of that volume, we are introduced to Yuryaku—the first Japanese emperor of whom we have any solid historical information. He was the twenty-first emperor, and his reign lasted from around 456 to 479 CE.

Image courtesy of Tokyo Metropolitan Library

Jimmu, the mythical first emperor of Japan and descendant of Amaterasu, pictured with a longbow and a three-legged crow (ca. 1880, Tsukioka Yoshitoshi).

for many centuries prior to being written down. It was written to preserve the oral history that had been understood for generations. *Kojiki* myths are detailed, rich literature that explain the divine origins of the Japanese land, people, and emperor.

In the *Kojiki* is the important story of how the kami created the Japanese islands. They were formed by two kami named Izanagi (a male god) and his consort, Izanami. They are representative of the male and female forces in all things. The creation of the islands began one day when Izanagi and Izanami were standing together on the floating bridge of heaven. They thrust a jeweled spear into the ocean and stirred. When they pulled it out, clumps of salt dripped from the spear and hardened on the water, forming some of the Japanese lands. Izanagi and Izanami decided to live on the islands they had created. They were married, and Izanami birthed many kami, including more Japanese islands. Thus, they begat the Japanese archipelago, as well as all inhabitants of the islands.

Most importantly, Izanagi and Izanami together produced the Sun goddess, **Amaterasu**—the most important deity in Shintoism, who is linked to the imperial rulers of Japan. The Japanese imperial household is part of the divine order and is linked to certain kami.

In Japan, there are many temples dedicated to figures and events from the *Kojiki*

Jimmu · the mythical first emperor of Japan

Yamato · the strategic capital for Japan's ruling house for generations—traditionally from 250 to 710 CE

Amaterasu · the Sun goddess and most important Shinto deity, linked to the imperial rulers of Japan

Anime · a popular style of Japanese animation

Shamanesses · in early Japanese history, women who would go into trances and connect with the kami, as well as with the ancestors

Himiko · a powerful third-century queen, as well as a charismatic diviner

Empress Jingu · powerful third-century queen, as well as a charismatic diviner

myths. These temples can be huge places where national ceremonies are held. They can also be small and intimate—for example, a small shelf inside a family's home. Shinto temples and altars are ubiquitous in Japan, challenging the recent argument that Japan has become a secular, nonreligious nation.

Japan's oldest surviving written work is the *Kojiki*. It was completed in 712 CE. The oldest complete manuscript of it dates to around the fifteenth century. While accepted as sacred scripture, it is also much more. It provides ethnic and even political guidance for Japanese identity today. In the decades before World War II, the *Kojiki* contributed to nationalism and imperialism by legitimizing the distinctiveness of the Japanese people. Since Japan's profound changes in the aftermath of World War II, some of those dimensions have been dropped, but they continue to have a functionality in forming a distinct Japanese identity. Themes of the *Kojiki* can be discovered in popular film, especially **anime**. Nostalgic movies such as the Tom Cruise action drama *The Last Samurai* incorporate *Kojiki* ideas. The opening of that film is a reading from the *Kojiki*.

Japanese people today do not typically hold to a literal understanding of the *Kojiki*, but there is a sense of distinctiveness and even chosen-ness that comes from the *Kojiki*. The emperor is still a critical presence in the Japanese government. The current emperor, Naruhito, is the 126th monarch of Japan. He came to the throne in 2019. He studied at Oxford University, and he and his wife have one child, a daughter. Perhaps it goes without saying that he considers himself Shinto.

THE ROLE OF WOMEN IN SHINTO

In the earliest history of Japan, women served as mediums and **shamanesses**. They would go into trances and connect with the kami, as well as with the ancestors. Two shamanesses in the second and third centuries CE, known as **Himiko** and **Empress Jingu**, were queens as well as powerful diviners. They set a standard for charismatic female religious leaders that is seeing a small resurgence today.

Legendary Empress Jingu leading a military invasion of Korea. From an 1880 painting by Tsukioka Yoshitoshi.

Image courtesy of Waseda University Theatre Museum

However, women in Japanese religion have also been faced with strongly patriarchal norms that have proven difficult to overcome. In addition, neo-Confucianism hovers around in Japanese religion and culture, leading to the widespread notion that men are rulers of the household and that women are best in the home and are to bear sons to carry on the family legacy and name. In this understanding, women are to be loyal and subservient to their husbands. While Shintoism does have women priests today, they are somewhat rare. The shamaness role for women is not nearly as popular as the role of mikos, or assistants to priests.

When a new emperor ascends to the throne, he is required to host the leading deity, Amaterasu, as his dinner guest. No one has ever seen the meetings except the emperor himself. This ritual meal began in 712 CE and must always take place at night, as the Sun goddess Amaterasu

Emperor Naruhito, 2019.

works until evening. Since she represents brilliance and purity, the emperor must bathe and complete the "great food offering" to her. This event is held in two specially constructed log buildings at the Imperial Palace in Tokyo. During this ritual, Amaterasu gives part of her spiritual essence to the emperor, making him a living ancestor who shares deity with Amaterasu and all the kami. This is at the root of the Japanese belief that the emperor is a living deity—a half-kami, half-man figure.

The author of the *Kojiki* is purported to be **O no Yasumaro**, who compiled the history using various local sources such as oral myths and clan chronicles. It took him the better part of two years, from 711 to 712 CE. Once Yasumaro completed the *Kojiki*, he began working on the *Nihon Shoki*—the Chronicles of Japan—which were completed in 720 CE. They cover the period of the creation of the kami through Empress Jito's death in 697. She was the forty-first monarch of Japan. Yasumaro was recognized for his gifts and was made head of his clan in 716; he died in 723.

The Early History of Shintoism

Shintoism has no one founder. It is a religion that gradually came into being from the misty and inaccessible backgrounds of the Japanese people themselves. There is not even a central revered teacher or guru in Shinto. The early history of Shintoism parallels the development of other indigenous religions from all around the world. It seems to have begun as a way for people to pray for their crops, hope for their families, and remember their dead. Still today, the rhythms of Shinto are organized around the spring and fall, when

A nineteenth-century depiction of O no Yasumaro, compiler of the *Kojiki* and the *Nihon Shoki*.

Photographer: Hannah~commonswiki

rice is planted and when it is harvested. Like most indigenous religions, the gods were looked to for a good harvest.

We see consolidation of a budding Shinto religion during the reign of **Emperor Tenmu** (673–86 CE). He came up with the idea of having Japanese texts that would preserve their history. Tenmu also ordered the first Shinto shrines to be constructed at the holy site of Ise, demanding that they be rebuilt frequently, setting a precedent that continues to the present.

During the **Nara dynasty** (710–84 CE), we see more important changes, such as the imperial family claiming itself to be divine. Both Shinto and Buddhism were officially recognized during the Nara period, and the *Kojiki* was completed in 712. The Nara rulers were equally open to Buddhism and thus allowed

O no Yasumaro · the author of the *Kojiki* and the *Nihon Shoki*

Nihon Shoki · the Chronicles of Japan; a Shinto record of myth and history, covering the period of the creation of the kami through Empress Jito's death in 697

Emperor Tenmu · a Japanese emperor from the 600s CE who commissioned the writing of the *Kojiki* and established the shrine at Ise

Nara dynasty · the era during which the Japanese imperial family was proclaimed to be the divine descendants of Amaterasu and Buddhism was officially recognized in Japan, alongside Shinto

A scroll portraying Hachiman, the Shinto kami of war. His Buddhist robes illustrate the syncretism between Shinto and Buddhism for much of Japanese religious history.

The golden gate of the Ueno Tōshō-gū, a shrine honoring Tokugawa Ieyasu, founder of the Tokugawa shogunate.

Buddhist missionaries to introduce their Buddhas and bodhisattvas into the pantheon of kami that already existed, leading to a shared space for both among the Japanese people.

In time, however, Shintos began to assert their indigeneity and primacy. After all, Buddhism was a foreign faith and forever would be. Shinto was the religion of the Japanese people alone, whereas Buddhism was shared by many nations.

It was too late, however, and the two religions began to assimilate and enmesh. Buddhist temples and Shinto shrines were built right next to each other. In many cases, a Buddhist area was available in a Shinto shrine, and vice versa. The common Japanese worshiper could pray to the divinities of either religion without much discernment. Sometimes one priest would oversee both temples and would even conduct services in both. There were times when Buddhism became the more important of the two religions, while at other periods in Japanese history, an indigenous impulse would surge, clearing the way for Shintoism's rise again.

It appears that the rise of Buddhism in Japan caused Shintoism to self-reflect and to come to terms with itself as an actual religion. Prior to Buddhism, Shinto was simply the religion of the people. But with competition from Buddhism, Shinto leaders had to strategize and rethink how to distinguish the ancient Shinto faith from a form of Mahayana Buddhism that was all too happy to assimilate and melt into the population.

Christianity entered Japan in 1549 through the pioneering missionary labors of Francis Xavier, perhaps the greatest Christian missionary of all time. Within only a few decades, however, Japanese rulers began to see Christianity as a threat because of its claims of religious exclusivity. Christianity underwent severe persecution in Japan, especially during the 1630s. Shusaku Endo's famous book, *Silence*, tells this story, and it was put to film by Martin Scorsese in 2016. The suppression of Christianity was largely successful in rooting out the movement. What had originally been an extremely promising mission field turned out to be a nightmare. Both foreigners and nationals were persecuted harshly, and around forty thousand Christians were killed. Christians in Japan were forced to exist covertly.

It was largely because of the Christian religion's rapid gains that Japan began to eschew all forms of foreign religion. This led to the reasserting of Shintoism as a unique and distinctively Japanese religion. Buddhism continued to thrive, as it did not demand exclusive loyalty. During the fourteenth through the eighteenth centuries, Buddhism split into many different schools in Japan, some of which went international through mission efforts. Buddhism's creativity and willingness to assimilate protected it from a purging process like what happened with Christianity.

The years 1603–1868 are known in Japan as the **Tokugawa Shogunate** (also known as the **Edo period**). It has become romanticized in Western minds through the legacy of the samurai. The samurai were fearless Japanese warriors who were essentially bodyguards to the nobility. They were governed by a certain code of conduct known as **bushido** (warrior way), which is similar to the European notion of chivalry. The bushido code of ethics included a strong, Confucian-inspired loyalty to one's superior. This fit well in a hierarchical, feudal system. The bushido code of conduct also emphasized courage in battle—a willingness, and in some cases an eagerness, to die for a higher cause. Bushido warriors were to be men of honor—even to the point of committing suicide rather than being humiliated by an enemy or placed in a compromising situation where they might be forced to betray their superiors. If a bushido warrior had to commit suicide, he would do so using a method known in Japan as **seppuku** (belly cutting), or **hara-kiri**. It was essentially disembowelment but was often accompanied by decapitation. Even women—particularly wives of samurai—and peasants understood the notion of protecting one's honor through suicide if necessary. Sometimes, however, they would slice the arteries in the neck rather than the preferred methods used by the samurai.

Seppuku has proved perplexing to Western people, who frown upon suicide. In Japan, suicide was preferable to public humiliation or shame. These samurai ideals were also prominent during World War II, with the greatly feared **kamikaze** (divine wind) warriors who plunged their airplanes into enemy ships for a higher cause. The samurai were to be men of justice and honor, choosing to live in extreme deference to their authorities and, most importantly, to their direct superiors.

The Tokugawa period is known as an isolationist period for Japan, when nearly all foreigners, particularly Europeans, were perceived as threats. Chinese people fared better, and some Dutch merchants were permitted, but most others who tried to enter Japan during this era could be captured or killed.

Photographer: Oren Rozen, (CC BY-SA 4.0)

This memorial at the controversial Yasukuni Shrine honors the 5,843 kamikaze pilots who died in suicide attacks against the Allied forces in World War II. The plaque to the left lists their names in their memory.

Tokugawa Shogunate · also known as the **Edo period**, the period between 1603 and 1867 in Japanese history; an age often romanticized as the days of the samurai and of strict codes of honor

Bushido · a code of conduct for samurai similar to medieval notions of chivalry

Seppuku · also known as **hara-kiri**; ritual self-disembowelment required by honor in certain circumstances

Kamikaze · "divine wind"; warriors during World War II who plunged their airplanes into enemy ships

A self-portrait (ca. 1773) of Motoori Norinaga, an early nationalist who promoted a return to Shinto and to the pure Japanese way before it was influenced by Chinese philosophies.

IMPERIAL SHINTO

State-sponsored Shinto—or **Koshitsu**—is no more. Chiefly associated with the supreme role of the emperor, it was abolished in the national reforms that took place in the aftermath of World War II. **Jinja** Shintoism is the largest form of Shintoism and is the traditional kind that has been practiced throughout Japanese history. Most of Japan's eighty thousand shrines are Jinja and are overseen by the Jinja Honcho—the Association of Shinto Shrines. **Minzoku** is folk Shinto and is practiced predominantly in the countryside villages to celebrate the harvest and rites of passage within the local community. It was never formally associated with the national government, and it incorporates much from Buddhism and Daoism. **Kyoha** ("sect") is independent Shintoism. It is often called sectarian, as their members tend to practice in houses or lecture halls rather than in shrines. Underneath the umbrella of Kyoha Shinto are thirteen independent sects—most of them emerging in the nineteenth century—that are recognized by the Japanese government. **Tenrikyo** Shinto, or "Religion of Heavenly Wisdom," was begun by Nakayama Miki, a poor farmer's wife who received revelations for fifty years. She claimed that the one true God of the universe was speaking to her. Her followers call her Oyasama, which means "honored parent." Today there are around two million Tenrikyo members practicing in seventeen thousand centers in Japan. They also operate many mission centers worldwide.

Japan's **Meiji Constitution** of 1889 adopted a British-style approach to religion and state, and it lasted until 1947. In Confucian and top-down form, it elevated the role of the emperor and adopted Shinto as the official religion. Other religions were allowed to exist in principle, but this era was known for its explicitly pro-Shinto policies. Shinto became state-supported, and all citizens were to pay respect to the nation's Shinto past. The state took control of the shrines and began to support the priests. The shrines were to be dedicated to gods that were popular in a specific region.

The mother goddess of Japan, Amaterasu, was revered above all others in the entire pantheon. Worshipers had to face Tokyo during their prayers, as the emperor—who was divine—lived there. Criticism of Shintoism or the emperor was declared to be a crime. It was thoroughly Confucian in character, as this top-down approach was not to be criticized; everyone was to respect the nobility without question. There were, however, several movements within Shinto that resisted conformity to the government and remained disconnected from the state.

This painting, Conference on Drafting a Constitution by Goseda Hōryū (1926), memorializes the creation of the Meiji Constitution. Note the Western-style clothing and other Western influences in the image.

© Goseda Hōryū II, public domain

Koshitsu · state-sponsored Shinto, associated with the supremacy of the emperor; abolished in the national reforms after World War II

Jinja · the largest form of Shinto and the traditional kind that has been practiced throughout Japanese history

Minzoku · folk Shinto, practiced predominantly in the countryside villages to celebrate the harvest and rites of passage within the local community

Kyoha · independent, sectarian forms of Shinto

Tenrikyo · "Religion of Heavenly Wisdom"; founded by a poor farmer's wife, Nakayama Miki, in the 1830s when she began receiving revelations from the one true God; claims two million adherents today

Meiji Constitution · a strictly hierarchical and British-style constitution adopted in 1889 and followed until the end of World War II; elevated the emperor and established Shinto as the official religion of Japan

One of the most memorable figures of the Edo period was **Motoori Norinaga** (1730–1801). He was a scholar and physician who wanted to turn away from Buddhism and Confucianism and turn back to Japan, as well as to the Shinto classics. He wrote commentaries on the *Kojiki*, and he emphasized Japan's own history and culture, as opposed to allowing Chinese influence to be so strong in the nation. Norinaga's work had a major influence in bringing out the national pride in the Japanese people.

Japan was forced to open itself up to the Western world when Commodore Matthew Perry and a small fleet of US Navy ships arrived in 1853 and rather suddenly created trading relations between Japan and the United States, setting the stage for Western influence in the previously introverted Japanese nation.

© Sekai Gahō, public domain

The Hitler Youth organization, sponsored by the Nazi party, visits the extremely controversial (and still operable) Yasukuni Shrine in 1938, led by Shinto kannushi.

Shintoism after World War II

World War II was a crucial turning point in the history of Japan and, therefore, in Shintoism. After Japanese surrender in 1945, the US government occupied the nation. This was a humiliating era, as Japan had been a major colonial power in the years before and during the war. They had invaded, annexed, and/or colonized many nations and territories, including Taiwan, Korea, South Sakhalin Island (today in Russia), Northern Mariana Islands, Caroline Islands, Marshall Islands, Guam, Hong Kong, Manchuria, parts of Northeast India, other parts of China, the Philippines, Indonesia, Malaysia, Singapore, Myanmar, and Thailand.

Japan attacked the Hawaiian Islands during the bombing of Pearl Harbor on December 7, 1941, resulting in the United States' more deliberate entrance into World War II and Japan's humiliating defeat after the atomic bombs were dropped. The first atom bomb fell on the Japanese city of Hiroshima on August 6, 1945, and three days later, another atom bomb was dropped on the city of Nagasaki. At least one hundred twenty thousand civilians were killed instantly. On August 9, the Soviet Union declared war on Japan in an effort to roll back geographical gains made by the Japanese Empire. On

Motoori Norinaga · a scholar of the Edo period who promoted a return to the traditional Japanese way, emphasizing Shinto over Buddhism and Confucianism

September 2, Japan formally surrendered to the Allied forces. The Allies occupied Japan from 1945 to 1952.

The US government, notably General Douglas MacArthur, abolished state support of Shintoism in 1946. MacArthur became the de facto ruler of Japan during the occupation. The US government was instrumental in pressuring the Japanese government to remove Shinto religion from the schools, divorce the religion from the state, and force the emperor of Japan to renounce his divinity.

The result of these actions was that Shintoism was disestablished, and freedom of religion was the law of the land. The new Japanese constitution prohibited discrimination against any religion. The indoctrination of Shinto ethics into the citizens of Japan was forbidden. Freedom of religion (including Shinto) was announced, with the stipulation that no religion would be funded by the government. As in the United States, religious institutions would have to be funded by the citizenry. There was to be no compulsion in religion whatsoever. People were free to forsake religion. All of these rather sudden changes sent shock waves throughout Japan. Japan's emperor had been humiliated. It was clear that he was not in command. Many Shintos were disoriented and found themselves questioning how the emperor was still connected to Amaterasu, if at all.

Shintoism, Festivals, and Life Events

Shintos celebrate all manner of life events—for example, the **anzan kigan** ceremony is a prayer at the shrine for a pregnant woman to have a safe delivery of her child. The ceremony is associated with dogs, since dogs are viewed as having easy pregnancies and births. The expecting family can purchase a sash at the shrine that is meant to protect the baby while in the womb. After birth, the family returns to the shrine for another blessing.

A three-year-old boy attends the shrine for his first Shichi-Go-San festival.

Two women clad in kimono attend the Kitano Tenmangu Shrine in springtime to pray.

Another important Shinto rite of passage is **Shichi-Go-San** (the "7-5-3" celebration) for boys aged three and five and girls aged three and seven. The festival is held annually on or around November 15 and is said to have originally been a celebration of the survival of the child from infancy. In previous times, it was common for children to die as infants and toddlers.

Shinto festivals, known as **matsuris**, take place throughout the year in the larger shrines that have resident priests. The small shrines without full-time priests have services only two or three times per year. It is common for families to commission a priest and a shrine for a particular occasion. The spring and fall festivals are the most important matsuris.

Shintos celebrate the **New Year** by purifying their shrines and homes to prepare for the coming of the ancestors and kami. It is important to rid oneself of the defilements and impurities that may have built up during the year. The kamidana is prepared in anticipation of a blessing from the rice kami who will sustain the family throughout the year.

On March 3, Shintos celebrate the **Doll Festival**, wherein the girls of the home set up an elaborate doll display. In modern times, it has become quite expensive to purchase the dolls, but in previous times, the dolls were made of paper and then

Anzan kigan · a prayer ceremony at a shrine for a pregnant woman to have a safe delivery of her child

Shichi-Go-San · the "7-5-3 festival"; held annually for boys aged three and five and girls aged three and seven, on or around November 15; said to have originally been a celebration of the survival of the child from infancy

Matsuri · Shinto festival

New Year · a Shinto holiday celebrated by purifying the home and ridding oneself of any impurity; kamidanas are prepared in anticipation of a blessing from the rice kami, who will sustain the family throughout the year

Doll Festival · a celebration on March 3 during which the girls of a household set up an elaborate doll display

thrown into the river as a visual for the impurities leaving the village. Today, the Doll Festival is purely for fun and relaxation with family.

There is also a **Boys' Day** on May 5, when boys set up warrior action figures in their homes in celebration of their growth in strength and stature. In older times, the setting up of warriors was meant to drive away evil spirits.

March 23 is the spring equinox in Japan and is associated with Buddhism and the ancestors. People often return to their ancestral homes and make offerings at the gravesites of their ancestors. There is a **flower festival** on April 8 that is associated with the mountain kami who descended to the rice fields. People celebrate the flower festival by having picnics in the hills and picking wildflowers. April 8 is also the day when most of the Buddhists of the world—including Japanese Buddhists—celebrate the **birth of the Buddha**. The main ritual involves pouring tea over a statue of a baby Buddha.

Another purification festival takes place on June 30—halfway through the year—when people take a doll and rub it against themselves to symbolize their own impurity being transferred to the doll. They put the doll into the Shinto shrine, and the priests dispose of it. It is also a day of purification of the shrines, as well as the homes.

Inside and near Shinto shrines, one can often find **origami** ("paper folding")—paper creations made from folding that can be quite impressive. The most famous kind of origami is probably a crane, but virtually anything can be depicted. Initially used as wedding decorations, origami were later made as attachments to gifts. Now they are considered a form of artwork or craft.

The Future of Shintoism and Japan

Is Japan today a secular society? That is a question that can be answered in many different ways. Clearly, many draw freely from Shintoism, Buddhism, and Confucianism. Thus, those who might identify as Shintos may also accept Buddhist notions of reincarnation or may even perform Indian religious rituals such as Yoga and other meditations.

Many Japanese people keep a kamidana in their home that contains small figurines that represent gods or ancestors; important family heirlooms are kept there as well. Incense is burned. Fruits and drink are placed on a shelf as an offering. Many families preserve a list of ancestors' names, often going back many generations. Maintaining this connection to the kami and the ancestors is critical to Shinto self-understanding.

More Shinto-specific beliefs vary according to sect. Many Shintos believe that all humans are the offspring of beings in the divine world. There was a time when

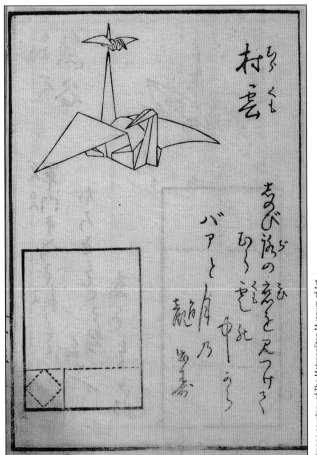

Origami paper-folding instructions from a woodblock-print book published in 1797. Attributed to Shimokōbe Shūsui.

Shintos applied this to the Japanese people only, but in modern understanding, there is the idea that people all come from the same divine source. The universe has many kami, and people should remember, respect, and celebrate them. People should enjoy life and be sincere. People should give back to society and uphold the teachings of the ancestors about the kami and about common identity.

One way to assess whether a society is religious is by observing what happens when there is a crisis. On March 11, 2011, a massive earthquake hit Japan and caused a deadly tsunami that killed nearly twenty thousand people, while more than two thousand five hundred went missing. Both Shinto and Buddhist priests stepped up to the occasion. People prayed to the kami to remove their anger or to help the nation rebuild its infrastructure. It is estimated that over $360 billion in damage occurred. Shinto purification rituals were common in the aftermath. Survivors gathered at shrines and temples to pay respects. Whether Japan is secular or religious, when the 2011 crisis occurred, there was a definite turn toward faith.

> Calculating religiosity, as one might do in the natural sciences, is terribly difficult when it comes to religion. People may be religious in one way while not in another.

Most Japanese consider themselves affiliated somehow with Shintoism as well as Buddhism, although many social scientists include Japan as a part of the secularization thesis—that it is a country that has little active participation with religion other than at ceremonial times. Calculating religiosity, as one might do in the natural sciences, is terribly difficult when it comes to religion. People may be religious in one way while not in another. Some people are religious during one season of life while not so religious in another. Some people become more religious with age or when starting a family. Many people practice religious rituals without believing everything about the religion they are participating in, so it is difficult to measure religiosity with any kind of certainty.

A Shinto man bows reverently in prayer.

As with Chinese religions, it is impossible to count members of Japanese religions. Less than 5 percent of Japanese people exclusively identify with Shintoism. However, more than 80 percent of Japanese people register their newborn babies at Shinto shrines, causing some sources to estimate that 80 percent of Japanese are Shinto. Similar to the old Roman Catholic parish system, Shinto shrines usually count all people living within the shrine's geographic district as members, regardless of their religious status. Also, most Japanese visit Shinto shrines for the New Year celebration, which seems to indicate at least some loyalty to the religion. It is just that Shintoism is not dogmatic at all, which makes it difficult to determine whether one is a member or not.

Some might say that Shintoism is a religion whose days are numbered. Shintos do not practice evangelism, the national birth rate in Japan is among the lowest in the world, and there seems to be a growing secularization pattern happening in the country. However, there are other reports saying that Shinto practices are coming back, such as kamidanas in homes. People still register their infants in the shrines, and respect for Shintoism remains high. Thus, perhaps we could say that as long as there are Japanese people, the spirit of the kami will still be present.

On a humorous note, many Japanese consider themselves to be born the Shinto way, married the Christian (Western) way, and buried the Buddhist way. This funny quip is often right on the money!

9 ZOROASTRIANISM
Good Thoughts, Good Words, Good Deeds

An Iraqi Kurd, who recently converted from Islam to Zoroastrianism, holds a pendant representing Zoroaster, in Dohuk, Iraq (2020).

Zoroastrianism is a very old faith. We do not even know how old it is. It is a small faith today, with less than two hundred thousand adherents. However, it is taught in world religions courses because it represents a shift in world religion. Scholars agree that Zoroastrianism influenced all three of the Abrahamic faiths: Judaism, Christianity, and Islam. The extent of that influence is a topic of hot debate.

Zoroastrians often refer to their faith as "the good religion" since they understand their God to be good and because they strive to do good deeds. According to Zoroastrianism, humans have free will, and they should always try to choose the good in their conduct and decisions. The most famous Zoroastrian mantra is: **"Good thoughts, good words, good deeds."**

The symbol of Zoroastrianism is the **faravahar**—a bearded man with eagle's wings. One of his hands is open to God—known as **Ahura Mazda** in the Zoroastrian faith. The other hand holds a large ring, representing faithfulness to the religion. The wings have three layers, representing "good thoughts,

good words, good deeds." Below the man is a three-layered tail, representing "bad thoughts, bad words, bad deeds." There are two streamers going in opposite directions below the man. The symbol of the faravahar is an attempt to show that all humans must make choices for good or for bad. We have no way of avoiding this. Good decisions will propel us upward to God. If we make poor decisions, however, we must face those consequences. Zoroastrianism has been defined from within as "the brotherhood and the sisterhood of those who do good."[1]

Origins and Development

Zoroastrianism is probably better pronounced **Zarathustrianism** after its founder, Zarathustra, which is his name in the **Avestan** language. The word *Zoroaster* is the Greek pronunciation, which was handed down to the Romans and therefore stuck with the Western languages. Zoroastrians refer to

Good thoughts, good words, good deeds · the most famous Zoroastrian mantra

Faravahar · the symbol of Zoroastrianism; a bearded man with eagle's wings

Ahura Mazda · a dualistic interpretation of God in which God has two sides—an evil side known as Angra Mainyu and a good side known as Spenta Mainyu; the two sides are in a cosmic struggle against each other

Zarathustrianism · another word for Zoroastrianism, after the Avestan pronunciation of Zoroaster's name, Zarathustra

Avestan · an old Iranian language similar to Vedic Sanskrit; the language of the Zoroastrian scriptures

An intricately carved faravahar atop the Fire Temple of Yazd.

Mazdayasna · "Worship of the Lord (Mazda)"; the name Zoroastrians use to refer to their religion

Sacred Thread Ceremony · a rite of passage in ancient Persia for male children signifying their new status as young men with new responsibilities

Superman · also known as the **overman**; Nietzsche's theory that humankind can evolve beyond categories of moral good and evil to realize our full potential

A temple in Naqsh-e Rostam, Iran, from the Achaemenid period, known as the Ka'bah of Zoroaster.

their religion as **Mazdayasna**—meaning "worship of the Lord (Mazda)."

Zoroaster's precise years are debated. Some say he may have lived as recently as the 500s BCE. Other scholars, particularly linguists, argue that he probably lived around 1200 BCE. Some say he may have lived as early as 1700 BCE. Were he to have lived before 1000 BCE, this would make him one of the first of the great prophets in world religion.

Zoroaster was probably born into a warrior tribe with a connection to the royal bloodline in Persia. According to Zoroastrianism, at around the age of fifteen, he went through a **Sacred Thread Ceremony** that was passed on to early Hinduism and is still practiced to the present day. The Sacred Thread Ceremony is the rite of passage of a male child into a young adult man with responsibilities. It was at that time that Zoroaster became a priest in the Persian religion. According to tradition, he had three wives and fathered six children.

At the age of twenty, Zoroaster went traveling, looking for truth and studying with various teachers. After about a decade, when he was thirty years old, he had an experience that changed him. He came to a river, where he was confronted by a shining angel who had several beings with him. The angel told him the secret

of monotheism: that Ahura Mazda is the only true God. The angel told Zoroaster that he was to become the chief prophet of God. Various angels continued to

Scenes from the life of Zoroaster, centered on his revelation of Ahura Mazda as the one God.

appear to him and reveal more about his mission. He began to preach without success. For a decade, no one listened to him. His people condemned and rejected his teachings. Eventually, he was successful in converting his cousin to his beliefs.

Zoroaster had little success until one of those important moments in history. He and his cousin traveled northeast and appeared before the ruling prince of Bactria in modern-day Tajikistan, Uzbekistan, and northern Afghanistan. The prince, named Vishtaspa, did not immediately convert. However, after a tumultuous quarrel during which Zoroaster had to debate the local priests and was even thrown into prison, the prince eventually converted to Zoroaster's teachings. Some sources say it was because Zoroaster healed the prince's favorite horse. Whatever the case, it is clear that Vishtaspa and his wife, Hutaosa, became believers and declared Zoroastrianism the religion of their kingdom. They also became patrons of Zoroaster as he traveled to spread the religion of Ahura Mazda across Central Asia.

Zoroastrianism spread rapidly, particularly among the Aryan people. The religion seems to have spread chiefly through holy war. During one battle, Zoroaster was killed while in the temple worshiping before a sacred fire. He was in his seventies when he died.

God is dead · Nietzsche's theory that humankind has evolved past its need for primitive dependence on false superstitions, and with the advent of modern science, we have put "God" to death

Will to power · according to Nietzsche, this is the driving force in humans

Eternal return · Nietzsche's theory that all reality, and all events, come and go and repeat themselves in an eternal cycle of reality forever and ever

NIETZSCHE

Many Western people were introduced to Zoroaster through the writings of Friedrich Nietzsche, who authored the book *Thus Spoke Zarathustra* in the 1880s. The book was intentionally provocative. Nietzsche considered it to be his masterpiece, the greatest gift ever given to humanity. He finished writing the book shortly before he went insane in the late 1880s. A core concept in the book is that morality should be rejected in favor of the **superman**—or the **overman**—who has grown beyond categories of good and evil. It contains his famous **God is dead** hypothesis, his **will to power** idea, and his belief in the cyclical nature of reality—known as the **eternal return** conception of the universe.

Nietzsche argued that all reality, and all events, would come and go and repeat themselves in an eternal cycle of reality forever and ever. He carefully provoked his readers, choosing Zarathustra as the main character in the book and intentionally mocking Christianity as a refuge for the weak. Only the strong can become supermen, according to Nietzsche, and people who do not execute their power will shrink back and become religious.

Image from *Nietzsche's Werke*, vol. 6 (1907)

Friedrich Nietzsche, author of *Thus Spoke Zarathustra*, which took its name from the founder of Zoroastrianism. His book is often the first or only introduction Westerners have to Zoroastrianism.

Unfortunately, Nietzsche's book has nothing to say about Zoroaster at all, leading to a mischaracterization that has confused people ever since. Zoroastrianism emphasizes morality—good thoughts, good words, good deeds—so it is ironic that a book about rejecting morality has become conflated with Nietzsche's book that interjected Zoroaster into the title. The only reason scholars even bring up Nietzsche when discussing Zoroastrianism is to help people understand that there is no connection between them. But because Nietzsche's work is standard reading at colleges and universities, it is a mistake that must be addressed.

FIRE TEMPLES

Zoroastrians are often associated with fire due to the incessant fires that burn in their houses of worship, known as **fire temples**. In India, the fire temples are usually called **agiaries**. They have a priesthood that looks after the sacred fires and preserves them from all contaminants, including their own breath, which is why they wear masks when attending the fire. In India, this tradition is still intact, but in Iran, the faith has been so suppressed over the years that many have abandoned the old purification rituals. Instead, they emphasize their high standards of ethics and morality—good thoughts, good words, good deeds. There are few practicing priests in Iran. The intensely detailed rituals so characteristic of Zoroastrianism are seldom practiced anymore.

Throughout the history of Zoroastrianism, the fire temples were at the very center of the religion. Men and women had to wear head coverings when they entered, and a fire burned perpetually. It was tended by a priest who wore a face covering and had metal tools that hung on the wall. There was an outer area for laypeople to watch the fire from many feet away, while the inner room was exclusively for priests. The fire was usually in an urn that sat on the floor. The inner room consisted of two domes that had vents for the smoke to escape. Usually, the walls of the inner room were made of tile and marble, with no light except the fire—this was the holiest, most sacred place for Zoroastrians. This is where Ahura Mazda was encountered. Non-Zoroastrians were forbidden from seeing the fire, so they had to remain outside.

The Zoroastrian eternal flame, burning in a fire temple in Yazd, Iran.

Sacrifices to Ahura Mazda included haoma, bread, and milk. Laypeople would bring wood to the priests to fuel the perpetual fire, and they would also present incense and spices to go into the fire.

In more recent years, Iranian Zoroastrians have started allowing guests to come into the fire temples, but the Indian context tends to be far more conservative and, thus, there are posts that read "Parsis only" on the outside of the temples. In conservative India, women who have married outside the faith have been ostracized, and their children are not allowed into the fire temples (agiaries).

Fire temples today typically have several rooms, as well as a source of fresh water for performing purification rituals. They have a special kitchen for the preparation of ritually clean food. There is usually a meeting hall for festivals, celebrations, and other such gatherings. The fire room is constructed in such a way that the smoke is vented out, but outside rain does not threaten the flame. Fires are tended carefully, and it is considered a catastrophe for a fire to become extinguished. The tending priests wear masks to prevent saliva or breath from contaminating the fire. On special occasions, haoma is still incorporated into the fire ceremonies. Today, the haoma is a mixture of water, ephedra, pomegranate, and goat's milk.

Zoroastrians have various levels of special fire ceremonies, with a host of different accompanying liturgies. There are three levels of fires. By far the most common is the **Appointed Place Fire**, which is consecrated by two priests during a two-hour ceremony. The second level is the **Fire of Fires**. It requires eight priests over a period of three weeks. The highest level is the **Fire of Victory**. It requires thirty-two priests and takes nearly a year to consecrate. It brings together sixteen different flames, each from a different source. Only eight of these fires exist in the world today.

Fire temple · a Zoroastrian temple named for its sacred, eternally burning fires

Agiaries · the term used in India for fire temples

Appointed Place Fire · the least sacred and the most common of the three kinds of special fires; consecrated by two priests over a two-hour ceremony

Fire of Fires · the second-most sacred kind of fire in Zoroastrianism; consecrated by eight priests over a period of three weeks

Fire of Victory · the most sacred fire in Zoroastrianism, requiring thirty-two priests to consecrate the fire over the course of a year, bringing together sixteen different types of flame; only eight Fires of Victory exist in the world

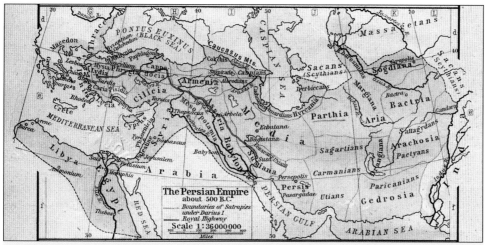

A map of the Achaemenid Empire at its height from William R. Shepherd's *Historical Atlas* (1923).

The Persian Empire and Zoroastrianism

Zoroastrianism became the religion of the **First Persian Empire**, also known as the **Achaemenid Empire**. At one time, this empire was huge; it controlled most of the entire Middle East for two centuries in the sixth to fourth centuries BCE, or from about 550 BCE to around 330 BCE, when it was conquered by **Alexander the Great**. It was the largest empire in world history up to that time. Its area stretched from the Balkans in Eastern Europe to the Indus Valley—roughly the border region of India and Pakistan.

The Persian Empire and some of its kings are mentioned in the Christian Bible in many of the Old Testament books, including 2 Chronicles, Ezra, Nehemiah, Esther, Isaiah, Ezekiel, and Daniel. **Cyrus the Great**, the founder of the First Persian Empire, is considered to be a hero of sorts to the Jews, even today, due to his liberating the Jews from Babylonian captivity after he defeated the Babylonians in 539 BCE. Cyrus is even called the Lord's anointed one by the prophet Isaiah (Isa. 45:1).

First Persian Empire · also known as the **Achaemenid Empire**, an empire that controlled most of the entire Middle East in the sixth to fourth centuries BCE; the largest empire in history up to that time; Zoroastrianism was its official religion

Alexander the Great · the Greek conqueror who brought down the Achaemenid Empire

Cyrus the Great · the founder of the First Persian Empire, considered to be a hero of sorts to the Jews, even today, due to his liberating the Jews from Babylonian captivity

The tomb of Cyrus the Great, founder of the First Persian Empire (539–330 BCE), located in the ancient Persian city of Pasargadae (present-day Iran).

Ṭāq-e Bostān, near present-day Kermanshah, Iran, is known for its Persian rock carvings from the Sassanid Empire (third to seventh century CE).

King Darius is another important Persian king who recurs in the Bible. He credited Ahura Mazda with bringing him to the throne. He was the third king of the Persian Empire, and he is mentioned in the biblical books of Haggai, Zechariah, Ezra, and Nehemiah. He elevated the status of the Magi, and he made Zoroastrianism the religion of his empire. Another of the Persian kings in the Hebrew Bible who followed Ahura Mazda is **Xerxes the Great**. He may have even married **Esther**, a story that is recounted in the biblical book of her name.

It is clear that the Persians had a significant influence on Judaism due to their extensive interactions with one another. The question that cannot be answered in any precise way is: How much influence? While the New Testament does not address the Persian Empire or Zoroastrianism explicitly, it is possible that the **Wise Men**, or **Magi**, from the Gospel of Matthew were Zoroastrian priests who took great interest in astrology. These Wise Men likely came from Parthian Iran, which lasted from 247 BCE to 224 CE. The Parthian Empire tended to equate Iranian and Greek deities due to the cultural gains made by Alexander the Great when he conquered Persia in 330 BCE. For example, Ahura Mazda was often identified with Zeus, and Angra Mainyu was the equivalent of Hades.

The empire that succeeded the Parthians was the **Sassanid Empire** (also known as the Sasanian Empire), which lasted from 224 CE to 651 CE. It was much larger than the Parthian Empire. It practiced a form of Zoroastrianism that was quite different from its predecessors, and it changed the religion in key

King Darius · an important Persian king and follower of Ahura Mazda who recurs in the Bible

Xerxes the Great · a Persian king who appears in the Bible in the book of Esther

Esther · an ancient Jewish woman who purportedly married Xerxes the Great and wielded her influence as queen to save the Jewish people

Wise Men · also known as **Magi**, Zoroastrian priests and astrologers who appear in the New Testament

ways that are still in existence. The Sassanids actually demoted Ahura Mazda to the second-most important god, behind **Zurvan**, the creator god. Their theological argument was that if God consisted of twins—a key idea in Zoroastrianism—then there must be a father god who created the twins. It was the Sassanids who introduced a priestly hierarchy, the tending of the sacred flame, the priestly practice of wearing a mask while attending the flame, and the notion of exposing the dead so that they do not pollute the Earth. All of these innovations are still with Zoroastrianism, showing the power of the Sassanid influence. The Sassanids were conquered by the Arabs in the seventh century CE, leading to the long decline of Zoroastrianism.

The Arabs adopted the religion of Islam and quickly conquered much of the Middle East, North Africa, Southern Europe, and the Byzantine Empire. When they conquered Persia, they initially considered the Zoroastrians to be monotheists. This was a critical decision, as according to Islam, non-Muslim monotheists have the right to exist as long as they live in servitude under the concept of **dhimmitude**. They have to pay higher taxes, and they do not enjoy the same privileges as do those who submit to Islam. However, after about a century, the Arabs removed the protections for Zoroastrians. That led to serious persecution, as well as a mass exodus from the Zoroastrian faith. Zoroastrianism in the former Persian empires has been on a steady decline ever since.

Charles Posten was buried in this pyramid outside of Florence, Arizona, in 1907. There are no other hills in a ten-mile radius.

Photographer: Scott Surgent. Used by permission.

The Zoroastrian Diaspora

As Zoroastrianism has spread, it has interacted with various religions across time. The religion of **Manichaeism**, in the third century CE, was founded by a prophet named **Mani** who borrowed heavily from Zoroastrianism, especially its dualistic teachings. Christianity's most famous theologian, Augustine (354–430 CE), was a Manichaean for a period of time, and he wrote about Manichaeism extensively. In ninth-century China, the Tang dynasty adopted Daoism and persecuted other religions in the empire, including Christianity and Zoroastrianism.

Over the centuries, **Iranis**, Zoroastrians living in Iran, have moved away from the homeland because of unbearable persecution. In India, they are known as **Parsis**, due to their homeland being in Persia. Elsewhere in the Muslim world, they are known as **Majoos** (or **Majus**)—named after the Magi. There exists today a small Zoroastrian diaspora in various places across the world. Zoroastrians first arrived in North America in the 1860s and formed their first religious congregation in 1929 in New York City. In 1973, the Zoroastrian community in New York created an organization called ZAGNY—the Zoroastrian Association of Greater New York.

Interestingly, the first fire temple in the United States was built in 1878 in the town of Florence, Arizona, by Charles Poston, the "father of Arizona," as he convinced President

Sassanid Empire · also known as the Sasanian Empire, the empire that ruled Persia from 224 to 651 CE; demoted Ahura Mazda to the second-most important god behind Zurvan; introduced a priestly hierarchy, the tending of the sacred flame, the priestly practice of wearing a mask while attending the flame, and the notion of exposing the dead so that they do not pollute the Earth

Zurvan · the creator god in Sassanid mythology who fathered Ahura Mazda

Dhimmitude · a legal provision for non-Muslim monotheists living in Muslim territory who are allowed to continue practicing their religion so long as they pay higher taxes and do not enjoy the same privileges as do those who submit to Islam

Manichaeism · a religion founded in the third century CE that borrowed heavily from Zoroastrianism

Mani · the prophet who founded Manichaeism

Iranis · Zoroastrians who are still in Iran

Parsis · Zoroastrians who moved to India

Majoos · also spelled **Majus**; the Muslim term for Zoroastrians

Lincoln to make Arizona a territory of the United States. Poston became an Arizona delegate to Congress. When his wife and daughter died, he set out on a trip to Asia and became fascinated with the Parsi community in India. When he returned to the United States, he built a pyramidal temple with a fire in it in commemoration of his adopted Zoroastrian faith, although the fire died out after a few months. He was later buried at that place, which is today called Poston's Butte, although initially he named it Parsee Hill.

One of the first Americans to learn about Zoroastrianism was Benjamin Franklin. After reading a bit from the Avesta, he made the remark, "I have cast my eye over the religious part; it seems to contain a nice morality, mix'd with abundance of prayers, ceremonies, and observations."[2]

Zoroastrian Scriptures

The Zoroastrian scriptures are known as the **Avesta**. The language of this text, Avestan, is an early Iranian language that shares much with the Indo-European family of languages. Old Avestan is quite similar to Vedic Sanskrit.

The Avesta text takes its name from the language Avestan. Only when the Zoroastrian scriptures are in Avestan are they properly considered authoritative—a phenomenon similar in Islam. The Quran is only considered sacred scripture when it is untranslated, in the Arabic language. This Avesta contains various forms and styles of writing such as prayers, liturgies (known as the **Gathas**), hymns, and ritual texts. There are other scriptures that contain more philosophical material and myths. Some of the texts were supposedly written by Zoroaster himself. Scholars tend to date the Avesta to whatever they believe to have been Zoroaster's years; thus, there is a wide range for the possible origins of the text: from around 1300 BCE to 550 BCE. The Gathas have not been available in Western languages for all that long; they were first translated into English in 1860.

There are five sections that make up the Avesta:

- The **Yasna** is the collection of recitations for priests during the liturgy. At the heart of the Yasna are the Gathas—hymns that Zoroaster is thought to have written. These texts are closely associated with the life of Zoroaster, and they deal with a broad array of themes such as origins, ethics, the dual nature of God, the last things, and the critically important concept of **Asha**, or "truth and righteousness." In the Zoroastrian worldview, virtually everything can be categorized as Asha or **Druj**—"falsehood and deception." Asha and Druj are a core reason why Zoroastrianism is considered a dualistic faith.

- The *Visperad* is a collection of liturgical texts used for festivals, such as the Zoroastrian New Year. It is only used in conjunction with the Yasna.

- The *Vendidad*, or "Against the Demons," is a text that explains how believers are to avoid getting caught by evil spirits. This text is fascinating, as it includes conversations between Ahura Mazda and Zoroaster. Included are a creation myth, a flood myth, as well as sections on personal hygiene, atonement for sins, and instructions on how to care for and dispose of the dead. It also deals with social aspects such as marriage, wealth, charity, and what to do when a contract is violated.

- The *Yashts* are a collection of twenty-one hymns that extol Zoroaster and the virtues he represented, such as wisdom, truth, and justice. This

A copy of the Avestan text of the Yasna (1250 CE).

Like many other world religions, Zoroastrianism began as an oral religion. Its liturgical texts and teachings were not written down until centuries after their original composition. This Sogdian (a medieval Iranian language) fragment dates from around the ninth century CE and was discovered in Central China by British archaeologist Aurel Stein in 1907.

text also discusses angels that should be venerated, as the angels are associated with particular virtues.

- The *Khordeh* is the final section of the Avesta and is often called the **Little Avesta**. It contains sections of the Avesta that are useful to laypeople. It outlines prayers that should occur five times a day. It discusses what believers should pray before certain daily tasks and how to pray before meals. Some have compared the *Khordeh* to the *Book of Common Prayer* used by Anglicans.

There are also some other texts that are respected in Zoroastrianism, such as the *Bundahishn* ("Primal Creation") and the *Denkard* ("Acts of Religion"), but they are not considered scripture. They are worthy texts that many Zoroastrians study and revere, but they are not given canonical status. This is largely because they were written down much later, at around 700 CE to 1000 CE. Also, they were written in the much later language of **Pahlavi**, or **Middle Persian**. Pahlavi is a kind of link between Old Persian (similar to Avestan) and Modern Persian (Farsi). **Farsi** is a language used commonly in Iran, Afghanistan, and Tajikistan.

The Yasna tells a long, detailed story about Ahura Mazda—The Wise Lord— who made a plan for creation and recruited some guardian spirits called **fravashis** to help guide humans toward living good, ethical lives. Ahura Mazda has two sides— an evil side and a good side. The evil side is called **Angra Mainyu**, and the good side is called **Spenta Mainyu**. The good side, Spenta Mainyu, then overpowered Angra Mainyu, attacking him so hard that Angra Mainyu was dazed and powerless for three thousand years. During that three-thousand-year period, Spenta Mainyu created the physical world.

The Yasna explains that the period from creation to the final triumph of good over evil lasts for twelve thousand years. Zoroastrians believe the universe to be cyclical. History more or less repeats itself. There is always good and bad in the world until the end of the twelve-thousand-year period, when good triumphs over evil. But then it all starts over again.

Yashts · a collection of twenty-one hymns that extol Zoroaster and the virtues he represented, such as wisdom, truth, and justice

Khordeh · also known as the **Little Avesta**, the final section of the Avesta, containing instructions for laypeople

Bundahishn · "Primal Creation"; a text respected in Zoroastrianism but not considered scripture

Denkard · "Acts of Religion"; a text respected in Zoroastrianism but not considered scripture

Pahlavi · also known as **Middle Persian**, the language in which the *Bundahishn* and the *Denkard* are written; a link between Old Persian (Avestan) and Modern Persian (Farsi)

Farsi · a modern language used commonly in Iran, Afghanistan, and Tajikistan

Fravashis · guardian spirits who help guide humans toward good, ethical lives

Angra Mainyu · the bad side of Ahura Mazda and a force of chaos who wars with Spenta Mainyu and will ultimately be vanquished

Spenta Mainyu · the good side of Ahura Mazda, a force of order and benevolence, who wars against Angra Mainyu and will ultimately be victorious

Discovered in 1922, this shrine from the second century CE in the ancient city of Capua (northern Italy) shows Mithra slaying a sacred bull.

© DinoPh, Adobe Stock

Image courtesy of Yale Art Museum

The Romans conquered the city of Dura-Europos (in modern-day Syria) in 165 CE and converted a house into a Mithraeum which remained in use for more than seventy years. Pictured is an anonymous person, likely a portrait of a leading member of the community.

In a fascinating turn of history that still confounds historians, the god Mithra also surfaced much later in the Roman Empire, in the first to fourth centuries CE. Scholars are not altogether clear how this happened. What we do know from the evidence is that one of the Roman **mystery religions** centered on the god Mithra. It was a secret society religion that was mainly practiced by the soldiers in the Imperial Roman Army, as well as by some of the nobility in the Roman Empire. Initiation for this secret religion involved the killing of a sacred bull. They organized themselves into a complex ranking system that would have fit well into the culture of the military. Evidence of this secret **Mithraism** was found even at the edges of the Roman Empire, in England, where it was clearly practiced by upper-ranking officers. The religion declined sharply, however, and it was quickly extinct in the late fourth century as Christianity was being hailed as the religion of the Roman Empire. Further, Constantine, known to be a great warrior, converted to Christianity in the fourth century, paving the way for Roman soldiers to become Christians.

Pre-Zoroastrian Persians

The First Persian Empire had connections to India. The migrants who wandered from Iran to the Indus Valley region called themselves **Aryans**, or the **noble ones**. As discussed in the chapter on Hinduism, scholars are divided over whether the Aryans came in peace or came to conquer. The Aryans took their religion to the nation we call India today, inaugurating the great Vedic age in India. This process of two cultures mixing led to the earliest form of what we now understand to be the religion of Hinduism.

The Avesta provides some scattered information on the **pre-Zoroastrian Persians**. First, they were animists. They believed in the sacredness of nature. They were polytheistic—almost everything was associated with a god. Many of their gods and goddesses were carried over into Hinduism. Their evil gods they called **devas**, often spelled **daevas**. Devas cause chaos in the world, and they are to be avoided. The Zoroastrian text known as the *Vendidad* advises the faithful on how to avoid or combat these evil deities.

Among all of the gods of the pre-Zoroastrian Persians, the greatest one was **Mithra**; he was associated with cattle, covenants, truth, and obedience. Mithra's named morphed to Mitra when he was absorbed into the classical Indian Vedic literature. His roles changed over time in the Vedas. Often associated with the sky god **Varuna**, he was the god of covenants and was often linked to the Sun.

There are other clear lines of connection between the pre-Zoroastrian Persians and the Hindus. In the early Vedic form of Hinduism, there was a famous drink called **soma** that was considered hallucinogenic and sacred. Similarly, in pre-Zoroastrian religion, that same sacred plant-based drink existed, except in the Avestan language, it is called **haoma**.

Despite the many gods, spirits, and deities in pre-Zoroastrian Persia, there was one important divine reality that was frequently emphasized—Ahura Mazda—The Wise Lord. This concept is somewhat similar to Hinduism's notion of **Brahman**. The pre-Zoroastrian Persians believed that while people worship many gods, there was one underlying supreme force that was beyond human comprehension. That being they called Ahura Mazda.

Some scholars suggest that Zoroaster may have been the first monotheist. He clearly devoted himself to Ahura Mazda and tried to discredit the other gods that were prominent. If Zoroaster did try to pioneer a form of monotheism, then we know he was not successful immediately, as many other gods remained popular. Mithra, in particular, continued to be prominent. He came to be associated with the ultimate **Judgment Day** scene a little later in Zoroastrianism. He made the final decisions about everyone's afterlife. Zoroaster was probably not advocating the more adamant kind of monotheism that emerged in Judaism and later in Islam.

Another clear connection between the Vedic Hindus and the pre-Zoroastrian Persians was that both of them practiced a complex system of animal sacrifice, with all manner of rituals, accompanying prayers, and incantations.

Importantly, the pre-Zoroastrian Persians believed in prophets. They called the prophets **Saoshyants**, or "those who bring benefit to the community." Thus, when Zoroaster came preaching a new message to his people, they were somewhat open to the idea, as they believed Saoshyants could come to Earth occasionally and restore the original purity of their religion, which had become corrupt.

Mystery religions · secret cults that flourished in Greco-Roman times

Mithraism · a Roman mystery religion practiced by imperial soldiers that focused on the ancient Persian god Mithra; initiation ceremonies involved killing a sacred bull

Aryans · "noble ones"; Indo-Iranians in pre-Zoroastrian Persia

Pre-Zoroastrian Persians · polytheistic animists who believed in the sacredness of nature

Devas · also spelled **daevas**; evil gods of pre-Zoroastrian Persian religion who cause chaos and are to be avoided

Mithra · the greatest of the pre-Zoroastrian Persian gods; associated with cattle, covenants, truth, and obedience

Varuna · the Vedic sky god

Soma · sacred hallucinogenic drink in Vedic India

Haoma · the Avestan name for soma

Brahman · in Hinduism, the eternal and ultimate reality; has a similar transcendence to pre-Zoroastrian Persia's Ahura Mazda

Judgment Day · after death, Mithra weighs a person's good and bad deeds to determine whether the person will go to the Zoroastrian heaven or hell

Saoshyants · "those who bring benefit to the community"; prophets who come to Earth occasionally to restore the original purity of religion, which has become corrupt

Faravahar relief, the winged Sun symbol of Zoroastrianism, in Persepolis portraying a bearded man with eagle's wings holding his hand out to Ahura Mazda.

This is a supremely important concept shared by the Abrahamic faiths as well. For example, in Islam, Muhammad characterized himself as the great, and last, purifier of religion. He viewed his role as a purifier of a previous pristine form of revealed religion that had become corrupted. Zoroaster was many centuries prior to Muhammad, but he was a part of a longstanding tradition in the Middle East. Zoroaster claimed to be a Saoshyant—one benefitting the community by purifying the religion of the people. The pre-Zoroastrian Persians knew of this idea and likely opened themselves up to the teaching of Zoroaster because of it.

Ahura Mazda

The most important teaching of Zoroaster was that he believed Ahura Mazda to be the creator of the world and the most important, if not the only existing, God. If he taught that there was no other god in existence,

then he would be revolutionary indeed. However, it is difficult to definitively prove that he was actually arguing for a staunch form of monotheism. The scholarly community has the same problems with Abraham and Moses. Were they monotheists? Or were they henotheists?

We do know this: Zoroaster had in mind Ahura Mazda as his chief God. The Persians would have been familiar with Ahura Mazda, as they had worshiped him as the distant and extremely powerful High God, although people did not typically communicate with this god. Ahura Mazda was considered a power beyond humans and therefore impossible to connect with on a personal level.

The word *Ahura* means "Lord," and *Mazda* means "wisdom." Thus, Ahura Mazda is generally translated "The Wise Lord." Many other names are used for this deity in the Zoroastrian scriptures, but Ahura Mazda is the most common. Ahura Mazda has thirty

yazatas, or divine entities (like angels), that serve him. The thirty yazatas correspond to the days of month in the Zoroastrian calendar. The greatest of the benevolent powers is Spenta Mainyu—the Holy Spirit. Another important one is Mithra, who is conceived of as a valiant soldier. There is also Asha—truth and righteousness.

Zoroaster taught that God had revealed itself throughout history through six powers. Three of them were male, and three were female. Scholars think these deities were similar to great angels, but Zoroastrians think more in terms of great forces consisting of both the cosmic male and female principles. In other words, God is a balance of male and female. The names for these "powers" used in Zoroastrianism are actually descriptions of God. Thus, the six powers are six concepts: knowledge, love, service, piety, perfection, and immortality. These six qualities, combined with the male and female principles, constitute God's nature.

During the days of the Sassanid Empire (224–651 CE), the Persian people spoke the language of Pahlavi—also known as Middle Persian. In Pahlavi, the name for

A tenth-century depiction of Ahriman being slain.

Photographer: Wellcome Images, (CC BY 4.0)

God (Ahura Mazda) was actually pronounced **Ohrmazd** (say Ahura Mazda very quickly, and this is the result). The name for the devil—Angra Mainyu—during the Sassanid period was **Ahriman** (again, possibly a truncated pronunciation).

Zoroastrians claim to follow a monotheistic religion. They believe in Ahura Mazda, who is a righteous, eternal, and omnipotent God. However, Ahura Mazda has two sides to its nature. The good side is Spenta Mainyu— the "Holy Spirit" within. Angra Mainyu is the bad, destructive side of God. This is somewhat similar to the Hindu notion of God, in which there are the positive powers of Brahma and Vishnu (creator/sustainer) and the negative powers of Shiva (the destroyer). It is a core belief of both Hinduism and Zoroastrianism that God has twin spirits within, which manifest in opposing ways.

Dualism—Good versus Evil in Zoroastrianism

Zoroastrianism is the quintessential example of a **dualistic** religion, meaning there are two opposing forces dueling it out throughout history. In the study of world religions, Zoroaster is often credited with being the great developer of the notion of a cosmic force of evil that is working against the cosmic force of good. These two powers are constantly fighting for the hearts of men and women.

Zoroaster seemed to have conceived of God as being like the Chinese notion of yin and yang—God emanates both good (Spenta Mainyu) and bad (Angra Mainyu). They coexist. In Christianity, everything was good at one time, and God allowed one of his angels to become bad; thus, evil began. In Zoroastrianism, evil was there from the very beginning. The Avesta speaks of these forces as being twins. Zoroastrianism holds that there are many angels and demons that work

> **Yazatas ·** thirty divine entities who serve Ahura Mazda like angels
>
> **Ohrmazd ·** a truncated pronunciation of Ahura Mazda that came into use during the Sassanid Empire
>
> **Ahriman ·** a truncated pronunciation of Angra Mainyu that came into use during the Sassanid Empire
>
> **Dualism ·** the concept that there are two opposing forces constantly dueling with one another throughout history

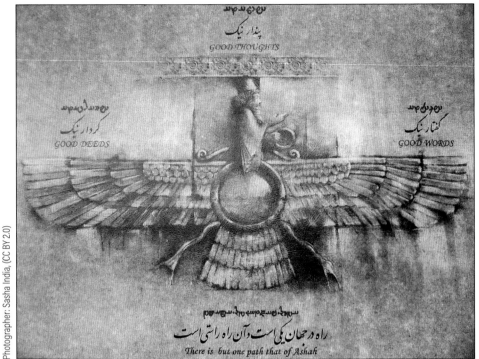

The mantra of Zoroastrianism—good thoughts, good words, good deeds—written around a faravahar.

Intertestamental literature · Jewish literature written during the four-hundred-year period between the Old and New Testaments; reveals a strong belief in Satan and angelic beings

while humans were born pure, they would eventually have to choose whether to be good or evil. By participating in either good or evil deeds, humans would essentially choose sides with their life decisions. Each human being had to make a decision for good or for evil. Zoroastrians believe strongly in the notion of free will. Humans must make a decision using their capacity to reason.

Zoroaster taught other forms of dualism. For example, he taught that reality is divided into two realms: spirit and matter. Another of Zoroaster's dualisms, mentioned earlier, is Asha (truth and, therefore, order) versus Druj (lies and, therefore, chaos). True thoughts lead to order in one's life, but a life built on deceit leads to individual chaos.

All reality is a grand war between Spenta Mainyu and Angra Mainyu. These are the two primal spirits that are at war, and the victor will bring either order or chaos to the world. The yazatas fight on behalf of the good, while the daevas afflict the world with evil and discord.

> Zoroaster taught that humans were the battlefield for the two forces of God. Humans had free will and could align with either side.

on behalf of Ahura Mazda and also Angra Mainyu.

Many scholars hold that Abrahamic faiths were influenced by Zoroastrian ideas about good and evil angelic beings. Some scholars believe Judaism had no distinct figure of Satan until after being influenced by the Persian Empire right before the Second Temple period. This was when Cyrus the Great and his Persians defeated the Babylonians in 539 BCE and liberated the Jews from Babylonian captivity.

Old Testament literature has only a few, somewhat obscure references to Satan, but the Jewish **intertestamental** (between the end of the Old Testament and the beginning of the New) **literature** has many. Indeed, the New Testament reveals a strong belief in the existence of Satan. Thus, there is a development of the notion of Satan throughout the Bible that very well may have been impacted by the Persian period, as well as the interaction of Jews with Zoroastrians.

Zoroaster taught that humans were the battlefield for the two forces of God. Humans had free will and could align with either side. He taught that

Death and Afterlife in Zoroastrianism

Zoroastrians believe that humans will eventually be judged in the afterlife. They do not believe in reincarnation. Zoroaster taught that all humans would have their deeds carefully weighed by Mithra. Perhaps more than anything else, Zoroastrianism is a religion in which salvation is affected by one's deeds. If one chooses a life of evil, one will be condemned. If one chooses a life of good, one will be rewarded.

Zoroaster taught that when people die, their soul stays with them for three days. They are then introduced to their Daena, which is the representation of their decisions during life. If the person lived well—according to the principles of Asha—then the Daena appears as a young, attractive woman. If the person lived a sinful existence—according to the principles of Druj—then the Daena appears as an old and terribly unattractive woman. The soul is usually aware of whether it chose the good or the bad during human existence.

On the fourth day, the individual's soul must be judged and sentenced. Mithra is the presiding judge and determines whether the bad deeds or the good deeds are heaviest. It is often a close measurement, and the person who has even the slightest amount in favor of good will go to a paradise realm. On the way to paradise, souls have to cross the **Chinvat Bridge**, which is guarded by a couple of intimidating **four-eyed dogs**. It is easy to cross if the person lived well. If the person lived immorally, then the bridge appears narrow, and it is impossible to cross, as demons will emerge and pull the soul into the abyss of hell below.

If the soul passes the judgment, then they are allowed to the other side, which is a paradise. It has good music, fragrant smells, and beautiful light. If they fail the judgment, then they fall down into the hellish depths below. Hell is called **druj-demana**, or the **House of Lies**, and it is an absolutely awful place. There are horrific smells, it is dark and crowded, and the food is rancid.

Paradise or hell is temporary in Zoroastrianism, however. Souls are only kept there until the day of resurrection. There is a massive, cosmic resurrection at the end of time. All human beings will eventually be purified, even if they chose to live a depraved human life while on Earth.

This grand finale will be signaled by the appearance of a Saoshyant born of a virgin. His mother became pregnant when she entered a freshwater lake that had miraculously preserved the seed of the prophet Zoroaster for centuries. Thus, this Saoshyant is the son of a virgin and the great prophet. However, this Saoshyant is also the representation of Ahura Mazda. He will supervise the resurrection and miraculously

bring together the scattered particles of all people who have ever died, from the ends of the Earth. He will bring together all people who have ever lived. This massive resurrection will take around fifty years to complete.

All people will rise up out of the Earth or out of the oceans, and they will be easily distinguishable as having come from a state of salvation or condemnation, from paradise or hell. They will be given their bodies back, and they will be returned to either heaven

Detail from a Zoroastrian manuscript, showing demons torturing a person who failed to cross the Chinvat Bridge. Collected by Samuel Guise, a surgeon working for the East India Company. Copyist: Peshotan Jiv Hirji Homji in 1789.

Image courtesy of the John Rylands Library, University of Manchester, (CC BY-SA 4.0)

Daena · the representation of one's life decisions after death; a righteous person's daena will be young and attractive, but an evil person's daena will appear old and ugly

Chinvat Bridge · the bridge souls cross at judgment after death; the righteous walk safely across to paradise, but the wicked are pulled down into the abyss below by demons

Four-eyed dogs · intimidating creatures who guard the Chinvat Bridge

Druj-demana · also known as the **House of Lies**, the Zoroastrian hell; an awful, albeit temporary, place of torment for the wicked

ANIMALS IN ZOROASTRIANISM

Zoroastrians have notions of good and bad animals. The good animals are associated with Spenta Mainyu and include horses, oxen, and dogs. If a person kills a dog, then they must do many different forms of penance, including the killing of cats. This brought conflict with Muslims, who much prefer cats over unclean dogs. The Zoroastrian list of bad animals—associated with Angra Mainyu—includes flies, ants, snakes, toads, and, predictably, cats.

Though now abandoned, this Tower of Silence, located fifteen kilometers southeast of Yazd, Iran, remains a vibrant tourist destination. Since the 1970s, Iran has outlawed the use of dakhmas.

or hell one last time—for three more days. They will experience either excruciating punishment or exhilarating comfort.

Finally, however, all will be purified. The skies will open up, and there will be all kinds of cosmic chaos. All humans will be purified by passing through rivers of fiery metal. In the end, all will be saved. All will gather together to give praise to Ahura Mazda. All will live forever in the transformed world. People will be reunited with their families, and life will continue, beautifully, forever. People will not grow old, and all misery will be vanquished.

There is one last chapter, however. There will be a final battle between good and evil. It will last for three thousand years. Ahura Mazda must defeat Angra Mainyu (or Ahriman) one last time, bind him, and throw him into hell forever. Only good will then remain, as the source of evil will finally be abolished.

Zoroastrians have a strong belief that humans should not pollute the elements: earth, wind, fire, water. Thus, there is a problem in the area of

> **Dakhma** · also known as the **Tower of Silence**; the structure on which a deceased body is placed to be eaten by the vultures so that its flesh will not pollute the Earth

The stairway leading up to the Tower of Silence in Yazd, Iran.

disposal of the dead. How does one handle a corpse if it is polluting? The solution in ancient times was that Zoroastrians would feed their dead to the birds.

The corpse is washed and dressed in white for the funerary rituals, which involve a sacred fire. In ancient times, a "four-eyed dog" (a spot above each eye) was brought near to the corpse to scare away evil spirits. Next, the clothes are removed, and the corpse is placed onto a raised, circular structure known as a **dakhma**, or **Tower of Silence**. Then the body becomes food for

PURITY

Zoroastrians have always had a powerful concern for purity. Thus, members must keep themselves pure. There are all manner of rituals for cleansing oneself after using the restroom, sneezing, receiving a haircut, or even using a toothpick. The most powerful symbol of purity is the extreme care taken when it comes to disposal of the dead. Zoroastrianism is adamant that the Earth must not be violated by a corpse, and they take great pains to avoid compromising on this important virtue of the faith.

---

expectant vultures, who strategically live nearby. It takes about an hour for the vultures to complete the task. The bones are then dried out in the Sun, and they are swept into a large stone box in the central part of the Tower of Silence. On the all-important fourth day of the funerary rituals, the soul appears before Ahura Mazda, is judged, and will be sent to either paradise or hell until the physical resurrection.

It is not required that birds eat the flesh, as occasionally other animals, such as wild dogs, feast on the corpses as well. Vultures are commonly associated with this ritual, however. Some members of the Zoroastrian community still practice the laying out of the dead in the Tower of Silence.

In the Western world, Zoroastrians are not permitted to leave their dead to wild animals, so they do one of two things: either cremate the body with an electrically generated flame (thus, not a true flame, so they do not contaminate it), or they buy a completely sealed casket that is lined in a secure way so that the Earth is not desecrated by the decaying corpse.

Zoroastrians have struggled to figure out a consensus on how to dispose of their dead. The exposure of the dead to vultures is rarely practiced in Iran today. In India, it still goes on, but less and less by the year. The vulture population has become very small today, especially in the urban sprawl of Mumbai, where most of the Parsis live. The vultures often cannot consume the flesh completely, and the body remains in a state of decay for much longer than in old times. Additionally,

the vultures are dying from the medicines given to people in their final stages of life. When the vultures eat the human flesh, they absorb these drugs. These problems have caused many Parsis to opt either for cremation or burial. The more traditional of the Parsis have opposed these practices, arguing that they pollute the Earth, which is forbidden in Zoroastrianism. There are current programs geared to grow the vulture population so the Parsi community can return to the disposal methods of their ancestors. However, many Zoroastrians, even in India, foresee a time when the exposure of the dead to animals will eventually fade away completely.

Perhaps the most famous Zoroastrian of modern times was Freddie Mercury (1946–91), the lead singer of the internationally celebrated band Queen. He was not faithful to his religion in most of his adulthood, but he did request a Zoroastrian funeral. When he

Farrokh Busara, as he was named at birth by his Persian-descended Parsi parents. Freddie Mercury (1946–91) became the most well-known Zoroastrian in the West.

A restored fire temple near Khinalig village, Azerbaijan.

died, he was cremated, and it stirred a debate in the Zoroastrian community about whether cremation should be acceptable.

Zoroastrian Religion Today

Today, there are between one hundred thousand and two hundred thousand Zoroastrians in the world. Over half of them live in India, concentrated mostly in Mumbai. Around twenty-five thousand live in Iran. Approximately fifteen thousand live in the Kurdistan Region of northern Iraq. North America is home to around twenty thousand Zoroastrians. Worldwide, it is a community that is shrinking fast. At one point in time, at the height of the faith, there were probably around forty million Zoroastrians, making it one of the great religions in history, especially considering the world's population during the golden age of the Persian empires.

In Iran, Zoroastrians are marginalized and sometimes persecuted due to their non-Muslim status in an officially Islamic nation. However, members of the Baha'i faith fare even worse in Iran. Sometimes, Baha'is even register themselves as Zoroastrians to avoid unwanted scrutiny.

Zoroastrians are typically understood as being deeply ethical people, probably due to the notion that they are judged by their deeds. In India, they tend to be an educated group and are known as being good businesspeople because of their high standards of integrity.

In Iran, it is a distinctly different story, as they have experienced serious persecution and harassment. After Islamic conquest, they were pushed into remote regions of the deserts. They were often perceived as being backward due to their marginalized status. They persevere, however, hanging on to their ancient traditions, despite rampant persecution. Some Iranian Zoroastrians have migrated into Tehran in search of a better life, and a few have even succeeded in business there.

Modern Rituals

Zoroastrians have many rituals today. For example, they still practice an ancient Sacred Thread Ceremony, called **Navjote** in India. In Iran, it is called **Sedreh Pushi**. It is the Zoroastrian initiation ceremony. Once the initiates have sufficiently learned about Zoroastrian history and practice, they offer a prayer of repentance and a declaration of faith. They are given a **sedreh**—a sacred undershirt. They are also given a **kushti**—a sacred belt with seventy-two strands worn around the waist. All Zoroastrians should wear both the sedreh and the kushti during their entire lives after the Sacred Thread Ceremony; they only remove them while bathing. The seventy-two threads of the sacred belt correspond to the seventy-two chapters of the Yasna, which is the holiest section of the Avesta. These garments are worn to remind the believer to fight against evil. The last part of the Navjote, or Sedreh Pushi, is a statement of faith and a blessing from the priest.

Zoroastrians have many religious rituals that they practice privately inside their homes. They pray five times a day in accordance with the positioning of the Sun. In total, a faithful Zoroastrian spends about an hour in prayer per day. It is said that this teaching was issued by Zoroaster himself. The daily prayers often include untying and tying the kushti strands while reciting scriptural texts. Prayers also require a short ritual purification that involves washing the face, forearms, hands, and feet with clean water. While these ritual **ablutions** take only a few minutes to complete,

Navjote · the term in India for the Zoroastrian Sacred Thread Ceremony

Sedreh Pushi · the term in Iran for the Zoroastrian Sacred Thread Ceremony

Sedreh · a sacred undershirt

Kushti · a sacred belt with seventy-two strands worn around the waist

there are longer ablutions. For instance, the **nahn**—a sacred bath ceremony—requires washing the entire body, and it is required of Zoroastrians just before their wedding.

The Zoroastrian calendar is complex and elaborate, and there are many disagreements among devotees themselves about the calendar's intricacies. Days are named after various deities and angels. They have many feast days, along with seven annual holy days that are obligatory for Zoroastrians. The most popular holy day is **Nowruz**, the Zoroastrian New Year, and it is associated with the **Amesha Spenta** (seven good deities that emanate from Ahura Mazda), as well as with fire.

There is no such thing as congregational worship in Zoroastrianism. Members simply pray individually to Ahura Mazda. The daily practice of a layperson includes good thoughts, good words, and good deeds. Zoroastrian teaching emphasizes the gift of life; therefore, kindness toward all—including animals—is expected. One interesting custom that illustrates this priority is that at mealtime, dogs eat prior to the people. Zoroastrians do not fast from food or drink.

> There is no such thing as congregational worship in Zoroastrianism. Members simply pray individually to Ahura Mazda. The daily practice of a layperson includes good thoughts, good words, and good deeds.

Celebration of the Sadeh festival in Iran, a tradition dating back to Achaemenid times. Sadeh is celebrated fifty days before Nowruz.

© Farzac j, public domain

MARRIAGE AND FAMILY

Zoroastrians are expected to marry and have children. Celibacy is a sin in Zoroastrianism, as it is avoiding one's duty to procreate and expand on what Ahura Mazda has given.

Priests are an important part of the Zoroastrian faith, but they undertake ceremonies for the benefit of the community, presiding at events inside and outside the fire temple. Training for the priesthood involves memorizing texts from an early age, as priests begin training when they are children. The more traditional and therefore rigorous training is in India, where Zoroastrianism still functions much as it always has. The Irani community is far less traditional, and priests typically have secular careers to avoid poverty. It is expected that priests will marry and raise children. Traditionally, priests were to marry women from priestly families, but this has started to change, especially in Iran.

In Iran, due to a serious shortage of priests and a loosening of tradition, the Zoroastrian community has started to ordain women. In India, there have been vehement debates about whether converts to Zoroastrianism can become priests, as there is a strong preference for the priesthood to be passed down through families.

Priests are important to have around because religious ceremonies and festivals can hardly occur without them. In addition, a major part of Zoroastrianism is confessing one's sins to a priest—a ritual known as **patet** (or "confession"). After the patet, the devotee is to verbally commit to the priest that they will avoid that sin in the future. In Zoroastrianism, priests do not

Ablutions · ritually purifying one's face, forearms, hands, and feet with clean water before prayer

Nahn · a sacred bath ceremony that requires washing the entire body just before one's wedding

Nowruz · the Zoroastrian New Year and most popular holy day; associated with the Amesha Spenta and with fire

Amesha Spenta · seven good deities that emanate from Ahura Mazda

Patet · ritual confession to a Zoroastrian priest

The fire temple in Yazd, Iran. Of the nine fire temples in the world that burn Fires of Victory, the holiest Zoroastrian flame, this temple is the only one in Iran, the historic homeland of Zoroastrianism. The other eight are in India.

preach or teach much. Their most important duty is to tend to the sacred fire, offering prayers and sacrifice to it. Other duties include memorizing and chanting—without any instrumental music—the scriptures and prayers when the community gathers.

Women and Zoroastrianism

Traditionally, Zoroastrianism was quite patriarchal. The first role of a woman was to be a faithful and obedient wife to her husband. Her second role was to be a good mother. This is all changing somewhat due to modernization, and women in Iran can now become priests—a move geared to stave off the religion's extinction. In India, women are not allowed to become priests. Menstruation has always had an unusually high level of pollution attached to it in Zoroastrianism, and during menses, women had to stay fifteen steps away from men, fire, water, and religious utensils. In traditional times, a woman was only considered clean from menses after she had been washed with bull's urine—a traditional disinfectant.

Much of this is changing, however, especially in Iran. For example, an important discussion around scriptural interpretation has arisen in Zoroastrianism, a discussion that affects the roles of women. The Gathas—the most important texts due to them being from Zoroaster himself—address men and women together. This has led some to argue that while Zoroaster was egalitarian, the religion mistakenly became extremely patriarchal without scriptural sanction. Women have always worn the sedreh and kushti—again, indicating an egalitarianism that goes back to Zoroaster. Women have equal rights to the temple, unless, of course, they are menstruating, so some Zoroastrians are searching the scriptures to determine if perhaps the patriarchy was not intrinsic to the faith. Perhaps it rose up later and is mainly a cultural issue.

Importance of Studying Zoroastrianism Today

There are important reasons for studying this tiny faith. It seems to have had an influence on the Abrahamic faiths of Judaism, Christianity, and Islam. The figure of Satan may have been a Zoroastrian idea that was incorporated into Judaism. Also, Judaism did not have a highly developed notion of afterlife until its encounter with Persia. The Day of Judgment in Christianity and Islam may have incorporated ideas from Zoroastrianism, since there is scant attention paid to these ideas prior to the Second Temple period when the Jews were freed from Babylonian captivity by the Persians.

If some key Abrahamic faith teachings find their origins in Zoroastrianism, then it is not far off the mark to say that the majority of people in the world today—meaning Christians and Muslims—have been in some measure affected by the teachings of this ancient prophet Zoroaster.

There are serious differences between Zoroastrianism and the Abrahamic faiths, however. One of the most important is that Ahura Mazda seems to have both a good nature and an evil nature: Spenta Mainyu and Angra Mainyu. In other words, God created evil because evil is part of God.

In the Abrahamic faiths, however, God did not create evil. Rather, an angel led a rebellion that caused evil in the divine realm. Thus, when humans were created, that separate power—call it Satan—already existed and was able to integrate evil into the human realm as well. Abrahamic faiths cannot accept the idea that God contains evil and is therefore the origin of all evil.

The Zoroastrian community is divided today, mainly along the lines of Iranis and Parsis. The Iranis are marginalized, often live in poverty, and have shown a strong willingness to reconceive the faith along modern lines—due largely to survival. In India, the Parsis are faring much better and tend to be of a higher socioeconomic class. Parsis were privileged during the days of the British Raj in the nineteenth and twentieth centuries. The British found the caste system repulsive and incomprehensible, so they tended to recruit Parsis for respectable positions in the Raj. The Parsis benefitted greatly from this situation and therefore have more social power today. This enables them to stick to their old traditions, support their priests, and finance the expenditures of the religion—most importantly the agiaries (fire temples).

The Iranis and Parsis differ in other areas as well—for example, in the wearing of the sedreh and kushti. Parsis wear the undershirt and belt all the time, untying and tying them several times throughout the day according to ancient tradition. The Iranis, however, only wear their sacred undergarments when attending the fire temple. This situation has caused deep tensions. For example, some Iranis who immigrate to India are often disallowed from entering the temples over this issue. There are other issues that are pulling at the seams of this ancient faith, such as burial customs, intermarriage, and issues around ethnicity and Zoroastrian membership.

The world's Zoroastrian population is tiny and in decline. In Iran, Zoroastrians are harshly treated and are subject to discrimination and persecution. Their situation became worse in 1979 when the secular shah government was overthrown and Ayatollah Khomeini's Islamic regime came to power. The Indian

ZARATHUSHTRIAN ASSEMBLY

A group in California known as the Zarathushtrian Assembly was organized in 1990 to advocate for a much more modern interpretation of the faith. It has been controversial, as the organization advocates many nontraditional stances. For example, it allows people from outside the traditional ethnicities to convert to the faith—a move that has caused a firestorm of criticism. The Assembly also permits Zoroastrians to marry non-Zoroastrians. For centuries, Zoroastrians have been prohibited from marrying outside the faith. In India, Parsis tend to be very traditional and vehemently oppose this practice.

Parsis fare much better, but even there, the future of the faith is tenuous.

Worldwide numbers of Zoroastrians are shrinking. They have low birthrates, and until recently, they have not allowed people to convert into their religion. Traditionally, to be a Zoroastrian, both parents must be Zoroastrian, although that concept is being fiercely debated. Ethnicity has been so embedded into the Zoroastrian culture that some refer to their religion as "the faith of kindred marriage." Many Zoroastrians predict that either their theory of conversion must change, or else they will become extinct in the not-too-distant future.

Two of the most important Zoroastrian locations in the world today are in Yazd, Iran, and Mumbai, India, for different reasons. Yazd, in the center of Iran, is the historical epicenter of the faith. It has a beautiful, well-maintained fire temple that has been burning a sacred fire for over a millennium. Yazd's old city is a UNESCO World Heritage Site. Mumbai is the modern-day epicenter of the faith, as that is where over half of the world's Zoroastrians currently live and where the old traditions of this ancient faith are still practiced on a day-to-day basis.

10 JUDAISM
Hear, O Israel

To remember the murder of six million Jews, each year students from all over the world meet for the March of the Living. Held near the former German concentration camp at Auschwitz in Poland, an important aspect of the program is the participation of Holocaust survivors who share their memories of wartime experiences.

YomHaShoah / © wjarek, iStock

Over half of the world's population is connected to Judaism since it is an ancestor faith to both Christianity and Islam. Without Judaism, those two faiths would not exist, as they are built upon the foundation of Judaism.

Judaism comes in many shapes and sizes. There is not one Judaism. It has expanded over the centuries to mean many things for those who adhere to it. There are Jews who live according to a strict interpretation of the Torah; there are those who have extremely flexible interpretations of the Torah. There are secular Jews—those who are Jewish in ethnicity but scarcely follow the tenets of the faith. There are Jews who select which aspects of the faith they want to follow—an approach found in virtually all religions. Even in the nation of Israel one can find a whole variety of different kinds of Judaism, with various levels of commitment.

As with many religions of the world, the moment one tries to define it, one's definition runs into problems. Similar to the concept of religion itself, pinning down Judaism proves to be elusive. However, there can be no denying that Judaism exists. It is a religion with deep roots. It has impacted humanity powerfully for four millennia. Even today, the nation of Israel is the **axis mundi**—the center of the world—for many Jews, Christians, and Muslims. Some have opined that if there is a third world war, it will surely involve the nation of Israel.

Judaism's stories resonate deeply within humankind. A huge percentage of the world's population is familiar with the story of Judaism—a rather small kingdom that occupied a tiny part of the world nearly

> **Axis mundi** · the "center of the world"; commonly seen as Jerusalem in Israel for Jews, Christians, and Muslims

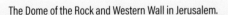

The Dome of the Rock and Western Wall in Jerusalem.

© AnastasiiaUsoltceva, Adobe Stock

Genesis. cap: 12. v. 1. 2. etc.

דברה

Linquenda tellus & domus

An engraving by Czech-born artist Wenceslaus Hollar (1607–77), titled *God Calls to Abraham*. Note that God's Hebrew words to Abraham are translated into Latin.

Abraham · the patriarch of the Jewish people

Israel · the "promised land" that God had vowed to give to the descendants of Abraham to constitute a holy nation dedicated to and protected by their creator

Canaan · an ancient name for the land of Palestine

Palestine · the geographical region encompassing the modern-day states of Palestine and Israel

Israelites · the descendants of Abraham's grandson Jacob, whose name was changed to Israel after a dramatic encounter with God

three millennia ago. Its legacy, however, has proven to be enormous when it comes to religion, politics, ethics, and global affairs.

In the book of Genesis, God promised **Abraham**, at a ripe old age, that he and his also-elderly wife Sarah would have a son and that their descendants would be plentiful. Armed with this information, Abraham took his wife Sarah, his concubine Hagar, and his flocks, and he headed for the place that God would show him, which

ended up being the land of **Israel**, also known from early times as **Canaan**, or **Palestine**.

Abraham submitted to God and did what God said, and God blessed him with a son named Isaac. Isaac had a son named Jacob. Jacob's name was changed by God to Israel, and this is where we get the name **Israelites**.

Repeatedly in the Hebrew scriptures, the Israelites are known as God's firstborn. By no means does this mean that God dislikes the other nations. Rather, Israel was the first to enter into a covenant with this particular god, and God would always remember them as the firstborn. Being the firstborn comes with expectations, responsibilities, and hopes. Some firstborn children may resent having the responsibilities of being the first child. Nevertheless, there is always a special connection between parents and the firstborn child. The firstborn child has certain rights but also many responsibilities, such as taking a leadership role among the rest of the children.

The Hebrew Bible is known as the **Tanakh**—an acronym made from the Hebrew initials of each of its three components: Torah, Nevi'im, and Ketuvim. The **Torah** is understood to be the central and most fundamental **teaching**, or the **law**. The **Nevi'im** are the **prophets**. Third, there are the **Ketuvim**, also known as the **writings**.

The **Torah** is the cornerstone upon which Judaism is built. It is often referred to as the **Pentateuch** (meaning "five books"), or the **Five Books of Moses**, as legend claims Moses wrote it. The Torah comprises Genesis (the book of beginnings), Exodus (the book of redemption), Leviticus (the instructions of the priests), Numbers (the book of the censuses), and Deuteronomy (the repetition of the Torah). These are the first five books of the Hebrew Bible, as well as the Christian Bible.

At the most fundamental level, the Torah reveals how existence began, what we are called to do, and who is in charge. The obvious answer to that last question is God—the central character of the Hebrew Bible. God is described concisely in the Torah, in Exodus 34:6–7 (NIV):

> The LORD, the LORD, the compassionate and gracious God, slow to anger, abounding in love and faithfulness, maintaining love to thousands, and forgiving wickedness, rebellion and sin. Yet he does not leave the guilty unpunished; he punishes the children and their children for the sin of the parents to the third and fourth generation.

Two important aspects stand out in that definition: love and justice. God loves, but God also disciplines those whom he loves. These two themes are reinforced throughout the Hebrew Bible in myriad ways.

Tanakh · the Hebrew Bible; an acronym formed from the initials of each of its three component parts: Torah, Nevi'im, and Ketuvim

Torah · "teaching" or "law"; the first section of the Tanakh, which contains the fundamental instructions of God to his people, as well as the story of Israel's origins and early history

Nevi'im · "prophets"; the second section of the Tanakh, which continues the story of Israel from the Torah and contains the writings of the prophets, who warned Israel to repent of its sins and follow God, or else the nation would face divine retribution

Ketuvim · "writings"; the final section of the Tanakh, which contains books of poetry, wisdom literature, stories with female protagonists, and the story of Jerusalem's restoration after its defeat and exile

Pentateuch · also known as the **Five Books of Moses**; the five books purportedly written by Moses that comprise the Torah: Genesis, Exodus, Leviticus, Numbers, and Deuteronomy

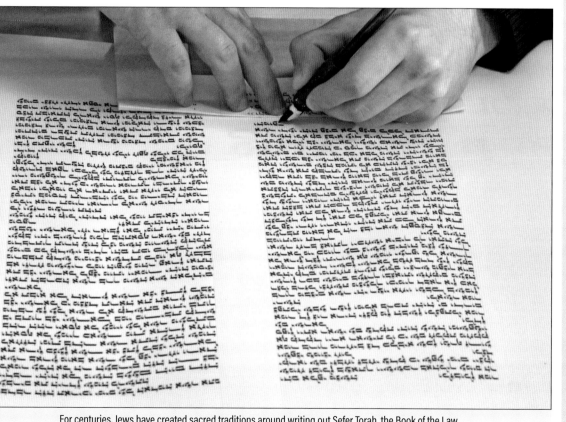

For centuries, Jews have created sacred traditions around writing out Sefer Torah, the Book of the Law.

God has many names in the Hebrew Bible and in Jewish liturgy, and those names get translated into different configurations when integrated into different languages. For instance, God told Moses in Exodus 6:3, "I appeared to Abraham, to Isaac, and to Jacob as El-Shaddai—'God Almighty,' but I did not reveal my name, Yahweh, to them." Other words used to refer to God in the Hebrew Bible are: El (God), Elohim (God), El Shaddai (God Almighty), El Olam (Everlasting God), Adonai (My Lords), Elyon (God Most High), Hashem (the Name), and Shalom (Peace).

For non-Jews, one familiar name for God derived from the Hebrew Bible is **Jehovah**, which is actually a Latinized pronunciation of God's proper name: **YHWH**. These four letters, often pronounced by non-Jews as **Yahveh** or **Yahweh**, are known as the **Tetragrammaton** (four-letter name). In Hebrew, these four letters are pronounced "Yod-Hay-Vav-Hay." This holy name is actually never vocalized in Hebrew—it is too sacred and too powerful to be uttered. Reading the four-letter name aloud, Jews will say "Adonai," "Elohim," or "Hashem." Jewish mystics tend to think that the Tetragrammaton has unusual power attached to it. The Tetragrammaton is frequently shortened to Yah, Yahu, or Yeho—for instance, when used in combination with other names or phrases: Yehoshua (Joshua, meaning "the Lord is my salvation"), Eliyahu (Elijah, meaning "my God is the Lord"), and **Hallelujah** ("praise the Lord").

Many observant Jews do not write the vernacular equivalent of the sacred names, preferring, for example, "G-d"

or "L-rd." While the English names for God are not technically Hebrew terms, many Jews choose to err on the side of caution due to the important law in the Ten Commandments that they should not use the Lord's name in vain.

Judaism does not prohibit writing the name of God per se, but it does prohibit erasing or defacing a name of God. Consequently, observant Jews avoid writing any name of God casually because of the risk that it might later be defaced or destroyed, even by accident. The commandment not to erase or deface the name of God is derived from Deuteronomy 12:3. This prohibition applies only to names that are written in some permanent form. Recent rabbinical decisions have held that typing on a computer is not a permanent form, thus it is not a violation to type God's name into a computer and then backspace over it, or cut and paste it, or copy and delete files that include God's name. However, once the document is printed, it becomes permanent and is more easily defaced or destroyed. Jewish websites commonly address this. The safest course of action is to avoid altogether saying or typing one of the holy names for God.

> Judaism does not prohibit writing the name of God per se, but it does prohibit erasing or defacing a name of God.

Alongside the names and nature of God, the most central teachings in the Torah are the **Shema** (which means "hear") and the **Decalogue** (Ten Commandments). The Shema is found in Deuteronomy 6:4–5 (NIV): "Hear, O Israel: The LORD our God, the LORD is one. Love the LORD your God with all your heart and with all your soul and with all your strength."

The Ten Commandments are located in Exodus 20 and Deuteronomy 5. The first four have to do with human relationships with God: worship no other gods, keep no idols, honor God's name, and remember to uphold the **Sabbath**. The ensuing six commandments have to do with human-to-human relationships: obey parents, do not murder, do not commit adultery, do not commit theft, do not say falsehoods against a

Jehovah · a Latinized pronunciation of God's name; derived from the Hebrew characters YHWH

YHWH · the highly sacred name of God; too holy to be uttered aloud and often left unwritten out of respect

Yahweh · a common non-Jewish pronunciation of the Tetragrammaton; also pronounced **Yahveh**

Tetragrammaton · "four-letter name"; a term for the four-character name of God, YHWH

Hallelujah · an exclamation meaning "praise the Lord," with the last syllable "jah" (yah) derived from a shortened version of Yahweh

Shema · "hear"; taken from the first words of Deuteronomy 6:4-5; one of the most central teachings of the Torah

Decalogue · the Ten Commandments

Sabbath · also known as Shabbat, meaning "cease"; the seventh day of each week that is set aside for rest and for remembrance of God

MEZUZAH

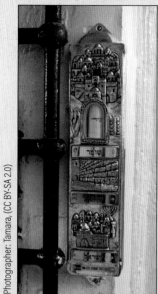

Jewish homes usually have a mezuzah affixed to their doorpost. The mezuzah is a case containing a parchment with the Shema written on it. It is a statement of allegiance to God, and it is an act of obedience to the command in Deuteronomy 6:9 that Jews put God's words on their doorposts.

This mezuzah is attached to the doorpost of King David's tomb in Jerusalem, a site popularly (though not historically) believed to be the burial place of the great Hebrew monarch.

Photographer: Tamara, (CC BY-SA 2.0)

neighbor, and do not covet (strongly desire) something that belongs to someone else.

The Torah holds a special place in the hearts and minds of Jews. Indeed, it holds a special place in the **synagogue** as well. For a synagogue to be a synagogue, it is required that there is a copy of the Torah scrolls. Without Torah scrolls, there is no synagogue. The Torah is like a family album. It is a collection of stories of a family in a land that still exists. When Jews read the Torah, they feel they are reading about their grandparents and great-grandparents. Only Jews tend to feel this sensation, as they consider themselves to be part of the family descending from the heroes in these powerful stories that have survived the test of time like few others.

The Nevi'im, or the "prophets," essentially constitutes the continuation of the history given in the Torah. Moses dies at the end of Deuteronomy, and then in the first book of the Nevi'im—Joshua—the Jews launch a series of conquests to take the land promised to them by God. The books of the Nevi'im are: Joshua, Judges, Samuel, and Kings, followed by the major prophets (Isaiah, Jeremiah, Ezekiel) and the minor prophets (Hosea, Joel, Amos, Obadiah, Jonah,

Micah, Nahum, Habakkuk, Zephaniah, Haggai, Zechariah, Malachi).

The Nevi'im goes on to discuss the rise and fall of Israel's kingdom, which was eventually split into two and later conquered by the **Assyrians** (who conquered the Northern Kingdom) and the **Babylonians** (who conquered the Southern Kingdom). The thesis of the Nevi'im is that because of the Israelites' failure to honor God and obey his commands, they essentially forfeited their role in the **covenant**, which went back to Abraham, and God ultimately allowed their defeat.

The Ketuvim, or "writings," includes books of poetry, wisdom literature (teachings on virtue), and stories with female protagonists. These books include Psalms, Proverbs, Job, Song of Songs, Ruth, Lamentations, Ecclesiastes, and Esther. The Ketuvim also contains the story of the rebuilding of Jerusalem after its destruction by the Babylonians in the books of Ezra and Nehemiah. Also included is the fascinating story of Daniel, as well as the Chronicles—a summary of the history of Israel up to the point at which the Persians defeated the Babylonians and allowed the Jews to rebuild their temple and their capital in Jerusalem.

The Broad Story of the Hebrew Bible

There is a reason that the Hebrew Bible is one of the most read books of all time: it reads quite well. It is certainly tragic in places, yet it is filled with hope. These people rose from obscurity, from Abraham and Sarah. They grew into a community, eventually becoming a powerful kingdom. Under King Solomon—King David's son—they built a massive temple compound in Jerusalem during the 900s BCE. The remnants of that temple are among the most revered religious sites in the world today.

Synagogue · "assembly"; a place of Jewish gathering and worship that requires the presence of the Torah scrolls and a minyan

Assyrians · an ancient Near Eastern people group who conquered the Northern Kingdom of Israel

Babylonians · an ancient Near Eastern people group who conquered the Southern Kingdom of Judah

Covenant · a central theme of the Hebrew Bible; God makes covenant agreements that bind the Israelites to him for obedience, sacrifice, protection, and love

Some have summarized the central content of the Tanakh in this way: God makes a covenant in the Torah, it is broken by Israel in the Nevi'im, and restored by God in the Ketuvim. God establishes covenants with his people all throughout Jewish history: "I will claim you as my own people, and I will be your God" (Exodus 6:7, for example). God also establishes ritualistic covenants between himself and the Israelites, such as male **circumcision**. Perhaps the most important item marking God's covenant with Israel was the **Ark of the Covenant**. Inside that ark were three items:

- A jar of manna—this was food from God that sustained the Israelites in the wilderness.
- Aaron's staff—Moses's brother Aaron had a miraculous walking stick.
- The Ten Commandments—tablets of stone containing the most crucial Jewish teachings.

The Ark of the Covenant has been imagined and reimagined by artists for centuries.

God's covenant with Israel included other phenomena, such as clouds that would serve as guidance, fires to light up their nights, miraculously provided food, and water given to them even in the barren desert. The Jewish people had to observe many rituals to maintain this covenant with God, such as male circumcision, animal sacrifice, and exclusive loyalty to God. Over time, the nation of Israel created a semipermanent structure (the **Tabernacle**) to house the Ark of the Covenant. This building, with the Ark of the Covenant inside it, was interpreted as a primary symbol of God's presence. The same was true for Solomon's Temple, which was constructed a few generations later.

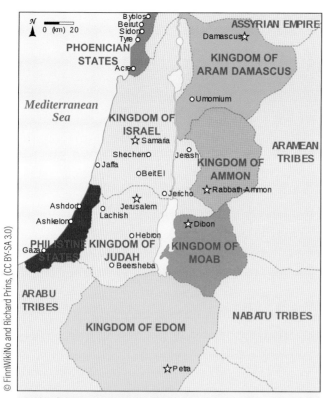

Regional map in the ninth century BCE.

The strength of the Israelite Empire was short-lived, as the northern part of it (known as Israel) was conquered by the Assyrian Empire in the 720s BCE. In the early 600s BCE, the Babylonians defeated the Assyrians, who had previously conquered northern Israel. The southern Jewish empire (known as Judah) fell in 586 BCE when the Babylonians destroyed the city of Jerusalem, along with its beloved temple. Babylon used the Israelites as their slaves. When Israel was defeated by Babylon in 586 BCE, it was the second time in history that the Jewish people had been enslaved. The Jews had been slaves to the Egyptians way back in the days of Moses, in the 1200s BCE. Moses led them to freedom from Egyptian bondage in the epic story recounted in the book of Exodus. That famous moment is probably

Circumcision · a ritual required by the covenant for all Jewish males on the eighth day of their life

Ark of the Covenant · a sacred container that held the tablets on which the Ten Commandments were written, Aaron's staff, and manna—all symbols of the covenant

Tabernacle · a tent used as a sanctuary for the Ark of the Covenant

Model of the Second Temple in ancient Jerusalem.

the most important story in the history of Judaism.

Second Temple Judaism

It was a miraculous moment for the Jews in 539 BCE, when Babylon was defeated by the Persian Empire. The victorious Persian king, named **Cyrus**, unexpectedly liberated the Jews, allowing them to rebuild their beloved city of Jerusalem, reconstruct their temple, and restore their culture that had been suppressed by Babylon. This return to Jerusalem and to the homeland is understood to be the beginning of **Second Temple Judaism**.

The story of the Hebrew Bible pretty much ends there, with a message of hope for the future after terrible trauma and threats to their culture's survival. There is little known about Judaism for a couple hundred years after that. It is often called the **Persian period** and lasted from 539 BCE to 333 BCE, when Alexander the Great introduced Greek/Hellenistic culture to the region. Scholars believe much of the Hebrew Bible was written during the Persian period, as the Jews were intent on reconstructing and reviving their culture and faith. It is commonly thought that, during the Persian period, the Jews appropriated a number

First written between 150–100 BCE, the Letter of Aristeas contains one of the oldest narrations of the creation of the Septuagint. This copy, held at the Vatican Library, is from the eleventh century.

of Zoroastrian ideas, particularly regarding Satan, Judgment Day, the afterlife, resurrection, and more expansive teachings about angels.

Something else was going on in the Levant and Southern Europe during the three centuries prior to Jesus that would affect Judaism a great deal: the process of **Hellenization**—a sociocultural change begun by Alexander the Great that was intended to implement Greek language and culture across all their territories. Greek rule lasted until 31 BCE, when the Roman **Caesar Augustus** defeated **Cleopatra** and took the Greek city of Alexandria, now in modern-day Egypt. A strong Hellenistic influence persisted for centuries, giving rise to a **Greco-Roman** (Greek and Roman) culture and empire.

Alexander the Great (356–323 BCE) conquered a huge swath of biblical territory: Persia, Asia Minor (modern-day Turkey), Egypt, Greece, and lands all the way to India. In the wake of his conquests, what emerged was a Panhellenic culture in place of the many separate cultures and languages of the time. This new situation of a large, shared culture would set the stage for later Roman conquest, chiefly by integrating a common language: Greek. In response to Panhellenism, Jews translated their holy texts into Greek and gave them the name **Septuagint**, which means "seventy," based on a legend that the translation of the Hebrew Bible into Greek was carried out by seventy Jewish scholars. In the first and second centuries CE, Jewish rabbis made decisions about which books should be included into the Jewish canon, and by 200 CE, the Jewish canon was effectively closed.

In the 160s BCE, there was a Jewish rebellion known as the **Maccabean Revolt** against encroaching Hellenistic influence. One of the successor states to Alexander the Great's legacy was called the Seleucid Empire, and through it, Greek influence expanded and was cemented in the entire region, including Judea. Some Jews were comfortable with the Hellenization process taking place, but others, led by Judas Maccabeus, strongly resented the Greek influence, as it threatened to overwhelm Jewish religion, culture, and language. The Maccabees had great success in their revolt and actually reclaimed the city of Jerusalem and rededicated the temple. This is what is celebrated annually in the festival of **Hanukkah**. The Jews enjoyed a century of relative independence until the capture of Jerusalem by the Romans in 63 BCE. Judea became a client kingdom to the Romans at that point, although not without Jewish resistance.

The Jewish rabbis seem to be identified with a school of teachers known as **Pharisees**, a group that acquired a negative reputation by the early Christians. In the Gospels, Jesus often found himself being critiqued by Pharisees, and they quarreled often. One thing is unmistakable, however; the Pharisees scrupulously followed the traditions of their ancestors. They spent much of their lives debating copious issues related to religious law and tradition. What they did was no

After the destruction of Jerusalem, the Romans produced a series of Judea Capta coins. Obverse: Emperor Vespasian; reverse: humbled Judeans under a symbol of victory.

During his short revolt, Simon bar Kokhba ran a centralized administration and overstruck coins, often defacing existing Roman currency with his own design. Silver coin showing the temple and a grain offering (obverse and reverse). 134–35 CE.

ESCAPE FROM 70 CE

One of the great stories of this period involves **Rabbi Yohanan ben Zakkai**, who escaped the 70 CE **siege of Jerusalem** in a coffin and established a new center for Judaism at the town of **Yavne**. Today, Jews identify Rabbi Zakkai as the instigator of Rabbinic Judaism and as the pivotal person who changed the loyalty of the Jews from animal sacrifice to a religion centered on text and prayer.

---

small feat: they transformed the Jewish religious system to be one in which animal sacrifice was no longer necessary. Rather, ritual purity, prayer, devotion, and knowledge of the texts—these were the crucial ideas that kept the Jewish community in covenant with God.

Life after the Temple

In 70 CE, the Jerusalem temple was again destroyed, but this time by the Romans, because of a Jewish revolt that had begun in 66 CE. It was catastrophic. The Jewish sacrificial system could not continue, as the temple was utterly destroyed. Jews who escaped with their lives were forced out of the immediate area or compelled into slavery. This resulted in a major **Jewish diaspora**.

The Jewish people made one final charge for independence in the 130s CE. It succeeded for three years under a leader by the name of **Bar Kokhba**. However, Bar

Pharisees · a group of religious teachers who scrupulously practiced tradition and law; transformed Judaism from a religion of animal sacrifice to one focused on ritual purity, prayer, devotion, and knowledge of the texts

Jewish diaspora · the mass dispersal of the Jewish people following the failed revolts against Rome

Bar Kokhba · a revolutionary in the 130s CE who led the last great Jewish rebellion against Rome

Rabbi Yohanan ben Zakkai · the pivotal person who changed the loyalty of the Jews from animal sacrifice to a religion centered on text and prayer; escaped the 70 CE siege of Jerusalem in a coffin and founded a new center for Judaism in Yavne

Siege of Jerusalem · a Roman offensive against the Jewish revolt that culminated in the destruction of the Second Temple and the sacking of Jerusalem

Yavne · the new center for Judaism after the fall of Jerusalem in 70 CE

Dead Sea Scroll

Essenes · a Jewish movement in the first century CE that isolated itself from the rest of the contemporary culture to maintain its religious authenticity

Dead Sea Scrolls · ancient Jewish religious literature remarkably preserved and discovered in caves near Qumran; containing scrolls from as early as the fifth century BCE

Sadducees · a group of political elites who tended to control political offices as well as the Jewish temple; rejected the veracity of the Oral Torah and resurrection

Zealots · a discontented political group that opposed Roman domination through the use of violence

Sicarii · a sub-group of the Zealots who carried small daggers concealed in their cloaks to stab Roman sympathizers at public gatherings

Samaritans · a people group with religious beliefs similar to Judaism, with the exception that the holiest site was Mount Gerazim rather than Zion in Jerusalem

While the Pharisees likely birthed the rabbinic movement, there were other Jewish movements that were active during the first century CE as well. For instance, the **Essenes** were Jews who isolated themselves, most famously around the Dead Sea region, where they produced the now celebrated **Dead Sea Scrolls**—the most ancient manuscripts of the Hebrew scriptures. They were extremely concerned about maintaining their autonomy and therefore inhabited this harsh and remote part of Judea.

Another Jewish group was the **Sadducees**, a group of political elites who tended to control political offices as well as the Jewish temple. They rejected the Oral Torah, and therefore, they died out alongside the rise of the rabbis. Early Christian writers noted that the Sadducees rejected the concept of resurrection.

The **Zealots** were a discontented political group that was militant in nature and eager to fight against Rome. One of its subgroups—the **Sicarii**—carried small daggers around with them, concealed in their cloaks. They would often blend into a crowd at public gatherings and stab Roman sympathizers. They were thought to be based in Galilee.

A final group was the **Samaritans**. They were ethnically related to Jews, but they used an altered version of the Torah as their text, written in the Samaritan language. Their holiest site was on Mount Gerizim, in the West Bank, rather than the Temple Mount in Jerusalem. This difference led to deep suspicion between Jews and Samaritans. The Samaritans nearly went extinct in the 1800s but have rebounded to the point that there are now around 840 of them living in Israel and the West Bank.

The hills at Qumran where the Dead Sea Scrolls were discovered in Israel.

Kokhba's revolt ended in disaster, and the Jews were severely defeated. Some have referred to it as a genocide, although the Jews put up a powerful defense that took a heavy toll on the Romans. Romans became severe and punishing in their dealings with Jews. The consequent brutality caused the vast majority of Jews to live in diaspora, far away from their homeland, from 136 CE (the end of Bar Kokhba's rebellion) until the late 1800s, when Jews started moving back to the **Holy Land** in hopes of reestablishing a Jewish state.

How was Judaism to survive without access to Jerusalem? How could Judaism exist without its temple that was erected on the land promised by God? How could the Israelites continue on their path of being God's chosen people if they lost Israel—the chosen place for their existence?

This is where the rabbis began to provide answers. Through amazing creativity, they were able to transfer allegiance from a system of animal sacrifice at the temple to the teaching of the Holy Scriptures. They would switch from ritual blood sacrifice to faithful and diligent study of God's will. This ingenious move enabled them to keep their faith alive amid the destruction of their homeland.

It was in this context that Torah began to take on two meanings: (1) the written Torah, but also (2) the interpretive tradition around the Torah, preserved by the rabbis and guarded by the rabbis. Rabbinic tradition is crucial for the Jewish faith. Both tradition *and* text comprise Torah. To present times, Jews study the written Torah as well as the **Oral Torah**. Both of them are crucial for Jews. The Oral Torah has now been written down into a collection of texts, but for centuries, these texts were passed down orally from generation to generation.

Rabbis are crucial to Judaism because they are the people trained to interpret the Torah, and their interpretations are crucial for the faith. They tell the Jewish people how the text is to play out in real life. This entire system of interpreting the Torah, both in the past as well as today, is known as **Rabbinic Judaism**.

Holy Land · the former land owned by ancient Israel to which the Jews longed to return and reestablish as a Jewish state

Oral Torah · the authoritative interpretive tradition around the Torah; recorded and preserved by the rabbis

Rabbinic Judaism · the prevailing Jewish practice since the fall of Jerusalem; centered on the Torah as interpreted by the traditions of the rabbis

Though the Talmud indicates that he lived in the larger city of Sepphoris, the traditional tomb of Rabbi Judah ha-Nasi is located in the Galilean village of Bet She'arim.

Khirbet Susiya, south of Hebron in Israel, had a notable Jewish community between the fourth and seventh centuries CE. Synagogue courtyard, looking southeast.

Photographer: Steve Werlin. Used by permission.

View of the interior of the main hall of the synagogue, showing the central mosaic carpet, benches in the background, and bema to the right.

Photographer: Steve Werlin. Used by permission.

The earliest document that records the rabbinic tradition is known to us as the **Mishnah** (the "Repeated Tradition" or "Repetition") and dates to around CE 200. Supposedly, it was compiled by **Rabbi Judah ha-Nasi** (135–217 CE), also known as **Judah the Prince**, a highly esteemed rabbi who served as Rome's contact person for Palestinian Jews.

After Judah ha-Nasi compiled and edited the Mishnah, Jews wrote major compilations of commentary and teachings about its contents. These commentaries on the Mishnah are called the **Gemara**. The **Talmud** is a combination of the Mishnah and the Gemara. There are many collections, but two are most important: the **Jerusalem Talmud** (also known as the **Palestinian Talmud**) and the **Babylonian Talmud**. The former was developed in Israel in the area of Galilee and was compiled in around 350 CE. The latter was compiled in around 500 CE in the modern-day region of Iraq but was not completed until around 700 CE.

The crucial role of the rabbis up to the completion of the Talmud was that they interpreted what the Torah was saying to them. Important decisions were made that live on in Judaism today. For instance, according to rabbinic counting, the Torah has 613 teachings, or **mitzvoth**. Jews cannot observe every single one of them today, as some are heavily agrarian in nature. However, the vast majority of them can be obeyed. Rabbis help Jews identify the obligations they should fulfill, and they provide instruction on how exactly they are to be fulfilled in a given context.

Medieval Judaism

Islam rose up in the 600s CE and became a major empire. Under Islam, Jews were usually given peace in return for higher tax rates (called **jizya**) and certain limitations in social privileges. Overall, however, medieval Jews may have fared better in Islamic lands than in Christian ones.

Traditionally, Muslims considered Jews and Christians to be People of the Book, or monotheists who did not understand the fullness of truth because, ostensibly, their scriptures had become corrupted over time. Thus, Christians and Jews were allowed to exist in Islamic lands, with hopes that they would eventually accept the Quran. **Al-Andalus** (Moorish Spain and Portugal), for example, was a rather peaceful place for Jews (711 CE to 1492 CE).

Jews could potentially thrive in Al-Andalus. The most important figure during that centuries-long era

JEWISH KOSHER LAWS

Jews separated themselves culturally—for instance, by maintaining biblical food laws. Jewish **kosher** ("fit") laws have been highly important for maintaining Jewish distinctiveness. Under normal kosher laws, only certain animals may be consumed (Leviticus 11 and Deuteronomy 14), and those animals must be killed according to prescribed methods. Dairy and meat may not be cooked or eaten together. Consuming blood is forbidden.

Bronze statue of Maimonides in Córdoba, Spain.

was **Maimonides**, known also as Moses ben Maimon, or Rambam. Maimonides lived in the 1100s and became famous as a Jewish intellectual in the Islamic world. He was known to be one of the greatest physicians of his time, even serving as Saladin's personal physician. Saladin was an Egyptian sultan who famously defeated the Christian crusaders to win back Palestine for Islam. Maimonides wrote many important Jewish texts, including an authoritative fourteen-volume commentary on the Talmud (the **Mishneh Torah**), as well as his *Guide for the Perplexed*, an attempt to reconcile **Aristotelianism** with Judaism. Maimonides believed strongly in the interdependence of science and religion; he argued that they both work together harmoniously and ultimately come from God.

Judaism took many different forms under Christian and Islamic rule. Its existence was always closely connected to and dependent on the ruling power. Jews never quite knew whether they were going to be punished, tolerated, or even courted by political entities. It all depended upon the whims of the people who governed them, which could switch dramatically.

In the late Renaissance era, as Christianity was on the rise after centuries under Islamic rule, Judaism struggled. This was part of a larger movement to assert Christianity as the state religion again. For example, by the late fifteenth century, Christianity had reconquered (**Reconquista**) the Iberian Peninsula, and in the aftermath, many Jews and Muslims were harshly punished. Islam had ruled the region for nearly eight centuries, and Christians were eager to take full control and eliminate any threats to a new Christendom. The year 1492 was an important year. Not only was this when Columbus famously set sail, but it is also the year Spain exhorted Jews and Muslims to convert to Christianity or leave the region. Many Jews became or were forced to become **conversos**, or converts. However, some merely claimed to convert, but in private, they continued practicing Judaism. If they were ever found out, they could be tortured and killed under the laws of the **Spanish Inquisition**, established in 1478.

Kosher · Jewish dietary laws restricting what animals may be consumed and how those animals must be killed and prepared

Maimonides · a famous Jewish intellectual and physician who wrote commentaries on the Talmud as well as a book reconciling science and religion

Mishneh Torah · Maimonides's authoritative fourteen-volume commentary on the Talmud

Guide for the Perplexed · Maimonides's written attempt to reconcile Judaism with Aristotelianism

Aristotelianism · the philosophical tradition of Aristotle; characterized by deductive logic and the analytical, inductive study of nature and natural law

Reconquista · Christian Spain's crusade to reconquer the Iberian Peninsula from the Moors

Conversos · "converts" to Christianity during Spanish persecution of non-Christians

Spanish Inquisition · a religious court that tried and punished non-Christians utilizing methods of torture and execution

Passover seder plate with traditional food.

According to rabbinic teaching, God created the world in 3761 BCE, which is essentially Year 1 for Jews. Shabbat sets the tone for each week, as it comes closer into view each passing day. And while Shabbat is at the core of Jewish communal identity, there are several significant annual holy days and ritual celebrations that emphasize various aspects of being Jewish.

Passover (Pesach) is a commemoration of Israel's escape from Egyptian bondage, and it is the most celebrated holiday in Judaism. For one week, Jews eat thin, unleavened flatbread called **matzah**, a reminder of the "bread of affliction" (Deut. 16:3 NIV) that their ancestors ate when hurrying out of Egypt.[1] On the first night of **Passover**, Jews eat an elaborate meal—called a seder—in the home, and the youngest child asks numerous questions while the leader provides answers, all based on the Exodus story. Jews keep an empty place at the **seder** table for the prophet Elijah, who will one day return to announce the coming of the Messiah.

Shavuot (Feast of Weeks) is celebrated fifty days after the first night of Pesach. Originally a wheat harvest holiday, it commemorates the covenant established between God and Israel on Mount Sinai. Orthodox Jews often stay awake from the evening meal until dawn, studying the Torah and reading the biblical book of Ruth, as she was an ancestor to David and is said to have been born and died on **Shavuot**. They also work through the 613 commandments in the Torah and eat mainly dairy foods.

Sukkot (Feast of Tabernacles) commemorates the years of wandering in the desert after escaping from Egypt. This celebration lasts for a week and is best known for the construction of a small, thatch-covered hut called a sukkah (also called a booth or tabernacle). Meals are eaten inside this hut during this festival. Some even sleep in the hut, which is a reflection on Leviticus 23:42–43, which describes the Israelites living in **sukkot** (plural of sukkah) in the wilderness for forty years after escaping Egypt.

Rosh Hashanah is the Jewish New Year that is celebrated in September or October on the Gregorian calendar. Considered an anniversary of the creation of Adam and Eve, **Rosh Hashanah** is also a time of repentance. The **shofar** (ram's horn) is blown, and apples dipped in honey are consumed.

Yom Kippur is the holiest of Jewish holidays; even secular Jews attend synagogue on **Yom Kippur**. It is the **Day of Atonement**, when the people of Israel receive forgiveness of their sins and are closest to God. Jews fast for the day and attend synagogue for prayers. Jews seek

A Yemenite man blowing the shofar, a ram's horn used in the Jewish New Year celebration (1947).

Matzah · "bread of affliction"; unleavened flatbread eaten during the Passover in remembrance of the unleavened bread the Israelites ate in a hurry when they left Egypt

Passover · a weeklong Jewish festival celebrating the Jews' deliverance from bondage in Egypt

Seder · an elaborate meal eaten on the first night of Passover

Shavuot · the Feast of Weeks, celebrated fifty days after Passover and commemorating the covenant God made with the Jews at Mount Sinai

Sukkot · the Feast of Tabernacles, celebrated by constructing temporary huts in which Jews will eat and sometimes sleep for a week, remembering the temporary dwellings of their ancestors when they lived in the desert for forty years

Rosh Hashanah · Jewish New Year; the anniversary of the creation of Adam and Eve and a time of repentance for sins

forgiveness from God and extend forgiveness to others. It is also a day for giving to charity.

Hanukkah is a minor holiday in Judaism but has taken on more significance since it occurs in late November or December, making it a kind of Jewish parallel to Christmas. It celebrates a Jewish fighter—**Judas Maccabeus** (Judas the Hammer)—who fought the Seleucids (Syrian Greeks) in the 160s BCE and rededicated the temple after it had been desecrated by Zeus worshipers. The Jews rededicated the temple using one small container of oil that, miraculously, lasted for eight days. Using a nine-branch menorah (rather than the typical seven-branch), Jews light a candle each day for eight days. The central candle is a helper candle and is used to light the others.

A Hanukkah celebration in front of Brandenburg Gate in Berlin, with the signature nine-pointed menorah.

Purim is the celebration of Esther's Jewish pride and the self-assertion of the Jews in the face of persecution. In the biblical book of Esther, Jews were to be destroyed at the behest of a Persian official named Haman, but Esther saved them and eventually became the queen of Persia. **Purim** are "lots," a form of dice. The lots were cast to determine when to destroy the Jews, but Esther saved them by working some political magic (along with her beauty), and she watched her nemesis, Haman, hang on the gallows. Purim is full of feasting, celebration, and a public reading of the book of Esther. Jews often dress up in costumes and masks and eat pastries known as "Haman's ears."

Bar mitzvah ("son of commandment"). A Jewish boy is considered a man at age thirteen; thus, on his **bar mitzvah**, he shows his maturity by reading from the Torah publicly and giving a short sermon. After the ceremony, he is officially part of the minyan—the requirement of ten men for a synagogue to be valid. The **bat mitzvah** is for girls but is mainly practiced by Reform Jews. There are disagreements in Judaism about whether women can publicly read the Torah in the presence of men.

Two boys wearing tallits gather at a bar mitzvah, a rite of passage for thirteen-year-old Jewish males. After their bar mitzvah, Jewish boys officially become a part of the minyan at their synagogue.

There are other Jewish holidays as well, such as **Yom HaShoah** (Holocaust Remembrance Day), Israel's Independence Day, and Jerusalem Reunification Day.

Shofar · a ram's horn blown during Rosh Hashanah

Yom Kippur · also known as the **Day of Atonement**, the holiest of Jewish holidays, during which Jews fast, pray, and seek forgiveness from God and from others

Judas Maccabeus · "Judas the Hammer"; the Jewish revolutionary who led his people to victory in their rebellion against the Seleucid Empire

Menorah · a lampstand, typically with seven branches, modeled after the one of pure gold that Moses made for the tabernacle of the Lord in the desert and later used in the temple

Purim · the celebration of Esther's Jewish pride and the self-assertion of the Jews in the face of persecution; full of feasting, celebration, and a public reading of the book of Esther

Bar mitzvah · a rite of passage for Jewish males when they turn thirteen and are officially considered adult men in the synagogue; they demonstrate their maturity by publicly reading from the Torah and giving a short sermon

Bat mitzvah · a rite of passage for Jewish girls when they turn thirteen; practiced mainly by Reform Jews

Yom HaShoah · Holocaust Remembrance Day

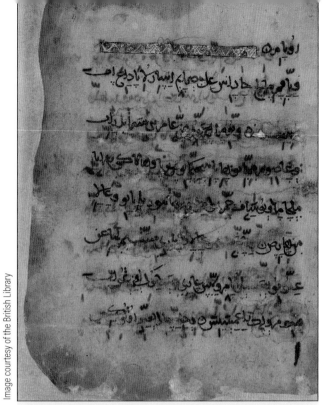

Founded in the eighth century CE in Babylonia, the Karaites used an Arabic script to transcribe the Hebrew Bible, adding in vowels with red ink. This tenth-century Karaite manuscript of the book of Exodus remains an important source of our knowledge of pronunciation traditions of Hebrew.

There were several different forms of Judaism that proliferated in the medieval era. One large and influential group was the **Karaites**, known as the anti-traditionalists. The Karaites rejected rabbinic claims to authority and distrusted human commentary on scripture. To them, the Oral Torah was a human construct. Some Karaite Jews still exist today in both the United States and Israel.

Medieval Judaism also saw the birth and flourishing of the **Kabbalah** movement in southern France in the late twelfth century. It spread rapidly to Spain, Islamic North Africa, and the Middle East. Kabbalah took the Jewish world by storm. Eventually, a leader in the Kabbalah, **Isaac Luria** (1534–72), rose up in the Galilee region of Israel. Later, his teachings became known as Lurianic Kabbalah and greatly impacted the **Hasidic** movement of the eighteenth century.

The primary text of Kabbalists is the **Zohar**—the Book of Splendor. It is a mystical commentary on the Torah. Over time, the Zohar became authoritative to

Under the leadership of Isaac Luria, the small Galilean town of Safed became the intellectual center of Jewish mysticism. Pictured is old-town Safed, which approximates the small residential quarters in which Jews likely lived in the sixteenth century.

Built at the end of the sixteenth century, the Sarajevo Synagogue served as a place of worship until the outbreak of war in the Balkans dramatically affected the Jewish community. After a series of renovations in 2000, the building became the Jewish Museum of Bosnia and Herzegovina.

Kabbalists. Eventually, most of them believed that without the Zohar, the Torah could not be interpreted correctly. The Kabbalists were mystics, and their understanding of God was highly complex and esoteric. To them, God was infinite, unknowable, beyond form, beyond gender, beyond all concepts of any kind. God became known to them as **Ein Sof**—the infinite.

Kabbalists attempt to mystically unite themselves to God. They claim a hidden tradition of scriptural interpretation, known only to a few. By figuring out the secret meaning of the written Torah, they develop a love relationship with it. They are known for their unique methods of interpretation through numerology and configurations of letters in the Hebrew Bible. They are also known for some rather unorthodox teachings, such as denying evil and even an openness to the reality of reincarnation.

In medieval times, the Jews of Northern Europe developed a distinct culture known as **Ashkenazic**. Ashkenaz was a descendant of Noah mentioned briefly in the Bible (Jer. 51:27–28) and, over time, his name came to be associated with Northern Europe, especially German and Slavic regions. (Scholars do not know why Northern European Jews came to associate themselves with Ashkenaz.) The culture reached a zenith in the 1500s and 1600s. Most North American Jews and probably half of all Israeli Jews are of Ashkenazic descent. It is estimated that between 65 to 75 percent of the world's Jews are Ashkenazic. Ashkenazi Jews speak **Yiddish**—German and Hebrew mixed, with some additional Slavic influence.

Another form of medieval Judaism is **Sephardic**—Jews who lived in Spain and Portugal between the eighth and fifteenth centuries, along with their descendants. While the Iberian Peninsula was under Islamic rule, this group thrived. They were dismissed en masse following the Christian expulsions of the 1490s, during the Reconquista. The word *Sephardi* comes from a vague biblical passage, this one in Obadiah 1:20, that may refer to Spain. Muslim Spain, or

Karaites · an anti-traditionalist Jewish sect that arose in the Middle Ages; rejected rabbinical authority, the Oral Torah, and human commentaries on scripture

Kabbalah · a movement of Jewish mysticism that claimed to discover the hidden meaning of the Torah

Isaac Luria · a Kabbalist leader in Galilee whose teachings became known as the Lurianic Kabbalah

Hasidic · a Jewish anti-intellectual movement that emphasizes personal piety and expressing ecstatic, emotional love for God

Zohar · the Book of Splendor; a mystical commentary on the Torah authoritative to the Kabbalists

Ein Sof · "the infinite"; the Kabbalist understanding of God as unknowable, beyond form, beyond gender, and beyond all concepts of any kind

Ashkenazic · the culture that emerged from the Jewish communities living in Northern Europe

Yiddish · the language of the Ashkenazi Jews; a mixture of German and Hebrew with some Slavic influence

Sephardic · the culture that emerged from the Jewish communities living in Moorish Spain and Portugal

Old Canton Synagogue in the Jewish Ghetto of Venice. The second-oldest Venetian synagogue (1532).

Moorish Spain, shared much with the culture of North Africa. Sephardic Jews succeeded at the highest levels, as they were physicians, statesmen, and philosophers. After being expelled from Spain, Sephardic Jews spread to other areas such as North Africa, the Netherlands, the Balkans, and the Middle East. Today, Sephardic Jews live mainly in Israel, France, and the United States, although there are smaller populations in the tens of thousands in Argentina, Spain, Brazil, Italy, Turkey, and Canada. Sephardi Jews speak **Ladino**, a language based on Old Spanish that incorporates many religious terms from Hebrew.

The Protestant Reformation, which began in 1517, represented a transition from medieval to modern. Most medieval and Reformation-era Europeans were anti-**Semitic**. The Catholic Inquisition laws were oppressive toward Jews. Martin Luther became intensely anti-Semitic later in life. As Protestants and Catholics entered centuries of war in the aftermath of the Protestant Reformation, Jews were often caught in the crossfire and could quickly become scapegoats. The idea of the **Jewish ghetto** may have originated in Rome in the 1500s, and it caught on rapidly across Europe. The Jewish ghetto in Rome was under the authority of the papacy until the fall of the Papal States in 1870. The Jewish ghetto could be a demeaning place for Jews, as they were typically sequestered away from the Christian population. This led to crushing poverty and rampant discrimination. Opportunities to leave the ghetto were limited. Jews were often required to wear yellow to clearly identify themselves. This and other demeaning practices set the stage for centuries of escalating anti-Semitism that culminated in the **Shoah**, also known as the **Holocaust**.

Modern Judaism

There are three important individuals who stand out in modern Judaism, all for different reasons. But they help to explain the varieties of narratives pertaining to Jews in the modern era.

Ladino · the language of the Sephardi Jews, based on Old Spanish with the incorporation of Hebrew religious terms

Semitic · one of the oldest known language groups, with some texts over five thousand years old; connected to the family of Afro-Asiatic languages and centered in the Levant

Jewish ghetto · the practice of sequestering Jewish people into specific districts, leading to crushing poverty and discrimination; originated in Rome in the sixteenth century and spread throughout Europe

Shoah · "calamity," "catastrophe," or "destruction"; the Hebrew word for the Holocaust

Holocaust · "completely burned"; the name given to the systematic mass extermination of six million Jewish people by Nazi Germany

© Olga Popova, Shutterstock

This 1979 stamp printed in Germany shows Jewish philosopher Moses Mendelssohn.

Sabbatai Zevi (1626–76)

Sabbatai Zevi was a Sephardic, Kabbalist rabbi in the 1600s who claimed to be the long-awaited Jewish Messiah promised in the Hebrew Bible. His messianic movement spread rapidly, as many Jews believed his claims, hoping he would lead them out of their crushing poverty across Europe. However, he was arrested at Constantinople and given the choice of whether to convert to Islam and live or to retain his messianic claims and die; he converted to Islam. Many Jews had actually believed he was the long-awaited Messiah, and around three hundred families followed him into Islam.

Moses Mendelssohn (1729–86)

Moses Mendelssohn was a German Jew in the 1700s who represented an embracing of European culture. Mendelssohn urged his Jewish compatriots to modernize and integrate into European society, a task he fully accomplished himself. Rising up from a poor background, he stunningly succeeded in this anti-Semitic milieu, becoming an admired Jewish intellectual and achieving fame as a scholar of religion and philosophy. He urged Jews to blend into society, to compete as equals, to speak the German language, and to get out of their insular ghettos. Two of his grandchildren—Fanny and Felix—became renowned music composers.

Israel ben Eliezer (1700–60)

Israel ben Eliezer was born a Polish Jew in the 1700s and represented the opposite of Moses Mendelssohn. As a mystical healer of profound piety, he took on the title of **Baal Shem Tov**, or "Master of the Good Name." Colloquially, he was known as the Besht—an acronym for Baal Shem Tov. He opposed intellectualism, a trend that was captivating most Europeans of the day and that was starting to attract more academically inclined Jews as well. He advocated a pious, heartfelt faith that had little to do with intellect and much more to do with worshiping God. Israel ben Eliezer is considered the founder of the Hasidic ("pious ones") movement, which rose to the point that, in much of Eastern Europe, there were actually more Hasidic synagogues than rabbinic ones. He was a master of the Kabbalist approach to Judaism. Many rabbis opposed his anti-intellectual stance, but thousands of lay Jews were powerfully attracted to this movement toward personal piety. The Besht taught people to pray frequently, sing to God throughout the day, and express love to God in ecstatic, overtly emotional ways.

Sabbatai Zevi · a Sephardic, Kabbalist rabbi in the 1600s who claimed to be the long-awaited Jewish Messiah but then converted to Islam under threat of death, convincing several hundred Jewish families to do the same

Moses Mendelssohn · a German Jew in the 1700s who encouraged the Jewish community to assimilate into European culture

Israel ben Eliezer · the founder of the Hasidic ("pious ones") movement

Baal Shem Tov · "Master of the Good Name"; the title adopted by Israel ben Eliezer

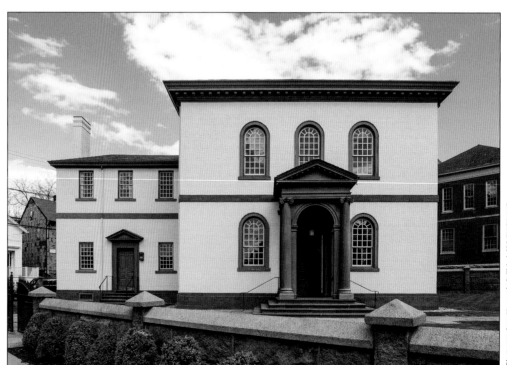

The Touro Synagogue in Newport, Rhode Island (2017).

Photographer: Kenneth C. Zirkel, (CC BY-SA 4.0)

In the late 1700s, amid the proliferation of various forms of Judaism, Europe was showing signs of religious tolerance toward Jews. The French Revolution of 1789 represented a watershed moment for Jews in Europe, as the French government began to remove longstanding laws against Jews, such as poll taxes and limitations of Jewish rights of residence and movement. Somewhat surprisingly, Napoleon emerged as a champion of Jewish rights, offering them full **emancipation** and even full citizenship throughout the French Empire. He even declared Judaism an official religion, alongside Roman Catholicism, Lutheranism, and Calvinism. Napoleon's decisions had a huge impact on Judaism across Europe, and there seemed to be hope that the longstanding anti-Semitism on the European continent would soon come to an end.

Also in the late 1700s, the new nation of the United States of America wrote into its Constitution, via the Bill of Rights, that religious discrimination was illegal. Many Jews came to the United States precisely for this reason—to reside in a nation that formally recognized them as full citizens regardless of their religious beliefs. The first Jewish congregation in the United States was formed in 1654, while the **Touro Synagogue** in Newport, Rhode Island, claims to be the oldest synagogue in the United States still in existence. Jews have risen to great heights in the US government. There have been eight Jewish Supreme Court justices, including Ruth Bader Ginsburg, Stephen Breyer, and Elena Kagan. Jewish representation in the US Congress nearly always exceeds the percentage of Jews in the general population.

Reform Judaism

The origins of Reform Judaism go back to Napoleon's emancipation decrees. Jews were suddenly able to move about and take residence outside of their traditional ghettos. They were able to dress like people dressed in wider society. In many cases, they had access to public schools.

The first Reform temple opened in Seesen, Germany, in 1810, under the leadership of a layman, Israel Jacobson. Their liturgy was in German rather than Hebrew, they used an organ for music, and references to a coming Messiah were jettisoned from the liturgy. This new form of Judaism was intentionally progressive and was based on four pillars:

- Judaism must continue to evolve—it is not stagnant.
- The Talmud is an ancient text and does not apply today.
- There is no Messiah.
- There is no homeland. Jews are citizens only of the land of their birth.

Reform Judaism introduced many changes. Worship was modernized along Protestant Christian lines, with organs and the introduction of choirs. The term **Jewish temple** replaced the traditional term *synagogue*. Kosher food laws were much less stringent, if observed at all. Head coverings became completely optional. The Sabbath did not require a cessation of work. Men and women could sit together during worship.

Another important leader of the Reform movement was the German **Rabbi Abraham Geiger** (1810–74), who oversaw Reform Judaism's expansion across Europe. In the 1820s, Reform Judaism made its way

Emancipation · the liberation of the Jewish people from oppressive and discriminatory policies in medieval and early modern Europe

Touro Synagogue · The United States' oldest synagogue still in existence; located in Newport, Rhode Island

Reform Judaism · a progressive branch of Judaism that promotes the evolution of the religion and the rejection of outdated ideas such as Talmudic authority, a coming Messiah, and a return to the Jewish holy land

Jewish temple · the Reform term for a synagogue

Rabbi Abraham Geiger · the most important leader of Reform Judaism; oversaw its expansion throughout Europe

In 1938, the Nazi regime destroyed the Jacobstempel in Seesen, Germany, but with the assistance of photos, drawings, and 3D technology, the former synagogue has been digitally reconstructed.

into the United States, and the first Reform congregation was established in 1841, in Charleston, South Carolina. Reform Judaism flourished in the United States under the leadership of **Rabbi Isaac Mayer Wise** (1819–1900), who was based in Cincinnati. **Hebrew Union College**, the first permanent Jewish institution of higher learning in the New World, was established in Cincinnati in 1875, under the leadership of Rabbi Wise.

Back in Europe, several anti-Jewish **pogroms** broke out in Russia, causing many Jews to leave. In some cases, Jewish freedoms were rolled back after they went into effect, leaving many Jews confused about whether Europe was, in fact, changing from its anti-Semitic ways. This led many Jews to consider where they could possibly establish an independent nation that was not subject to the vagaries that came with European hegemony over them.

The Birth of Modern Zionism

The father of Zionism was **Theodor Herzl** (1860–1904), a journalist who argued that Jews would always be subject to persecution unless they obtained land of their own. Being subject to other powers while living in diaspora nearly always meant being subject to persecution. The only way to avoid being subject to

WOMEN IN JUDAISM

The topic of women in Judaism is highly researched today. Women are vital to the faith in several key ways. For example, Jewish identity is **matrilineal**—it passes through the mother. Deborah was a leader over Israel. Two books of the Bible—Ruth and Esther—have female protagonists. However, there are elements of the Torah that have been interpreted as overly patriarchal, such as menstruation causing ritual impurity. More progressive forms of Judaism have lifted all limitations on women, even to the point of having an egalitarian rabbinate.

another power was to have sovereignty and political independence. Herzl and others began searching for land. Naturally, the land of Palestine was at the top of the list, as this was the homeland for Jews, the land of their ancestors. But there were other regions that were considered as well, such as Uganda, Argentina, and the Jewish Autonomous Oblast in Russia, which did, in fact, come into being in 1934.

In the late 1800s and early 1900s, many Jews, led by Herzl, began to organize and raise funds with the

Image courtesy of Museum of Rishon LeZion

Esther Shapira (1881–1966) immigrated during the First Aliyah and became a kindergarten teacher in Rishon LeZion, south of Tel Aviv. Scholars have observed that her work helped reintroduce spoken Hebrew into many Jewish households (image ca. 1898).

Rabbi Isaac Mayer Wise · an important leader of Reform Judaism in the United States; based out of Cincinnati

Hebrew Union College · the first permanent Jewish institution of higher learning in the New World; established in Cincinnati in 1875 under the leadership of Rabbi Isaac Mayer Wise

Pogroms · organized massacres of Jewish people

Theodor Herzl · the father of Zionism who argued that Jews would always be subject to persecution unless they obtained land of their own

Matrilineal · Jewish identity is passed through the mother

intention of purchasing land in and relocating to Palestine. This movement of people toward Palestine became known as **Zionism**, named after a hill in Jerusalem called Mount Zion. For Jews, **Zion** is a word used as shorthand for both Jerusalem as well as the nation of Israel.

In the 1880s and 1890s, the first wave of agricultural immigrants from Russia arrived in Palestine, in a movement known as the **First Aliyah**. Many farming settlements were established, where Russian Jews applied their modern techniques, rapidly developing the region. The Second Aliyah (1904–14) was mainly from Russia and Poland and occurred in the aftermath of terrible uprisings and pogroms against Jews in Eastern Europe. They, too, got to work buying land and building agricultural settlements. The Third Aliyah (1919–23) included many Russian Zionist socialists, as the Bolshevik Revolution had captured the imaginations of many Russian Jews at the time. Further Aliyah waves came in the 1920s and 1930s, increasingly from Germany, and they included many professionals who brought much needed capital and financial resources into Palestine. German Jews began to realize that Hitler's rise was not in their best interests; thus, immigration rates to Palestine expanded dramatically.

The Ottoman Empire had controlled Palestine for centuries; however, after World War I (1914–18), the British took control of the region. This encouraged more and more immigrants to the area. Many Arabs, both Muslim and Christian, resented the influx and argued to the British that there should be limitations to the number of immigrants admitted. The British conceded and began enforcing quotas. The limitations placed on Jews trying to escape Germany coincided with Hitler's policies in the 1930s. Many Jews could have escaped the Shoah but were legally unable to leave Germany due to the quotas placed on them.

The Shoah

Beginning in 1933, Hitler's dictatorship was rife with anti-Semitic policies. Jews were relegated to second-class status and robbed of virtually all civil rights, including their citizenship. They were forbidden from marrying non-Jews. Hitler argued many rogue theories, such as the superiority of the Aryan race. Jews were eventually declared enemies of the state. Many Jews tried to flee, but the British policy was being emulated in many places, including the United States and Canada, where quotas were put in place. At the same time, Hitler charged Jews an oppressive emigration tax and restricted their ability to withdraw their savings from German banks.

Hitler reintroduced many old medieval strategies for marginalizing Jews, such as the **yellow badge policy** and the ghettos. Increasingly, Hitler described Jews as a problem for Germany, and he fomented propaganda that described Jews as vermin. At first, Hitler "solved" **the Jewish problem** (or **Jewish question**) by establishing more than a thousand **concentration camps** between 1933 and 1945. However, concentration camps quickly evolved into death camps with gas chambers for more efficient mass execution.

Child survivors of Auschwitz liberated by the Red Army in 1945.

Image courtesy of Wiener Holocaust Library

In the Ukrainian city of Lviv, a pogrom broke out against the Jewish population in July 1941. Here, a woman, stripped and beaten, flees assault from a uniformed boy with a stick, as well as another adolescent.

Introduced in 1941, the **Final Solution** was the last stage of Hitler's strategy. Many Jews were worked to death, many starved, many died due to unsanitary conditions, and many were executed upon arrival to the camps. Millions of bodies were mass-cremated. In the end, six million Jews were murdered—a third of their global population. It was an organized genocide of unspeakable proportions. The word assigned to this event is *Holocaust*, which means "completely burned." Jews typically use the Hebrew word *Shoah*, which is translated as "calamity," "catastrophe," or "destruction."

How did something this atrocious and barbaric happen in the twentieth century? There are many answers, but four stand out:

- ***Anti-Semitism,*** a centuries-long history of anti-Jewish racism that persists even today.
- ***A fabricated document known as the Protocols of the Elders of Zion,*** which emerged in Russia in 1903 and was translated into many languages. It was circulated widely in Europe, and it claimed that Jews wanted to take over the world. Many people believed it to be genuine, even though it was proven to be a hoax in the 1920s.
- ***The industrialization of mass murder through modern technology.***
- ***Global acquiescence.*** Most of the world's population did not know about the extent of the horrors while they were occurring, though many political leaders were aware of details. When the German nation realized what was happening, many remained quiet out of fear for their lives. Plus, they had been highly indoctrinated by the Nazi government to despise Jews.

The Nazis were finally defeated in 1945. However, what was to be done with the surviving Jews? Many were displaced, fearful, distrustful, and saw hope in Israel. However, most Palestinians strongly opposed a Jewish state.

In 1947, the United Nations (formed in 1945) voted to partition Palestine into a Jewish and an Arab state. The British withdrew in 1948, and Israel declared its statehood. Israel was immediately attacked by Arab soldiers from several nearby nations, beginning the **1948 Arab–Israeli War**. Further major attacks occurred in 1967 (**Six-Day War**) and 1973 (**Yom Kippur War**). Smaller attacks and battles occur routinely, as tensions between Israel and the Arab world continue to simmer. Israel is seen by many Arabs as a foreign occupying power, while Israelis tend to view the situation entirely differently; they see Israel as their homeland from which they were forcibly expelled centuries ago. This is why immigrating to Israel is tantamount to coming home for Jews.

Judaism Today

Very few religions have survived such crushing defeats as the Jews have, from the sackings of Jerusalem, the destruction of the temple, the expulsions out of Israel, centuries of anti-Semitism, a

Final Solution • Hitler's answer to the Jewish Problem; a complete genocide of the Jewish people

Protocols of the Elders of Zion • a fabricated document that emerged in Russia in 1903 and circulated throughout Europe in a number of languages; claimed that the Jews schemed to take over the world

1948 Arab-Israeli War • a war launched by a coalition of Islamic Arab powers against the newly formed state of Israel in protest of the new nation's intrusion into Palestine

Six-Day War • a brief war between Israel and its Arab neighbors in 1967

Yom Kippur War • a war between Israel and the surrounding powers in 1973

CHAI AND STAR OF DAVID

The Star of David is a generally recognized symbol of Jewish identity and Judaism.

Photographer: Alex Proimos, (CC BY 2.0)

The term **chai** (pronounced "kai") is a Jewish affirmation of life. The word means "living" or "to life." The chai symbol is often worn as a necklace by Jews. Other important symbols in Judaism are the **Star of David** and the flag of Israel (which contains the Star of David).

Chai · "living" or "to life"

Star of David · a hexagram that symbolizes Jewish identity

Shalom · peace

Minyan · ten Jewish males over the age of thirteen; the quorum required for a synagogue

Dome of the Rock · an Islamic shrine built on the Temple Mount in Jerusalem in commemoration of Muhammad's Night Journey

Al-Aqsa Mosque · a mosque built on the Temple Mount in Jerusalem; the third-holiest site in Islam

Cantors · Jews tasked with leading a congregation's music and prayer during worship

far-flung constituency living in diaspora, and the Holocaust. However, the Jewish faith has not only managed to survive, but it has thrived.

Living in diaspora for centuries, Jews have gathered every Sabbath (Shabbat), observing it as a day of rest and worship. This rhythm of Jewish religious life mirrors the order of creation with the setting and rising of the Sun. As noted in the book of Genesis, each day began with darkness, an evening followed by a morning. After six creative days, God rested and blessed the seventh day, making it holy. Thus, Jewish people commemorate God's resting after his acts of creation.

No work is allowed on the Sabbath, and worship is leisurely on that day. The day is welcomed shortly before sunset, God's creative act. The candles must already have been lit. When the stars show in the sky on Saturday evening, Shabbat is over. To end Shabbat, Jews light a candle, bless wine and sweet spices, and praise God in prayer.

For ultra-Orthodox Jews—the most observant—there are many restrictions that come with Shabbat: they cannot write or erase, they cannot turn on or off lights, and the precooked food is kept on low heat for the entire period of rest. The only activities allowed are prayer, eating, Torah study, strolling, and sleeping. Even children must slow down and relax. The entire

Many Jews customarily eat challah bread on Shabbat.

© Rafael Ben-Ari, Adobe Stock

period is supposed to be a foretaste of the wholeness and **shalom** (peace) that will be restored to the world when God makes all things perfect.

Today, Jews continue to gather together in synagogues. The word *synagogue* simply means "assembly." It has also come to mean a worship building. There are two things required for a synagogue to be official: a copy of the Torah, and a **minyan**—ten adult Jewish males over the age of thirteen. Some have characterized the synagogue system as being like a temporary replacement of the Jerusalem Temple until it is rebuilt. This is a controversial idea, as a rebuilding of the Jerusalem Temple would interfere with two Islamic structures on the present grounds: the **Dome of the Rock** and the **Al-Aqsa Mosque**.

Rabbis have kept the Jewish community together for two millennia. In the synagogue, rabbis are accompanied by **cantors**—those tasked with leading the congregation's music and prayer during worship. **Brit Milah** (male circumcision) is kept alive in Judaism through the **mohels** who are trained in performing this critically important rite of passage for Jewish boys on the eighth day of their life. Jews are expected to commit to **tzedakah**—giving to charity—as an obligation commanded by God.

Many Jews today choose to dress like people dress in the larger society around them, although more Orthodox Jews can be recognized by certain articles of clothing such as the **tallit** (fringed prayer shawl), the **tefillin** (or phylactery)—leather boxes containing Torah readings worn on the head and arm, and the **kippah** (or yarmulke)—a brimless cap worn on the crown of the head.

In the United States, Jews are often divided into one of three different groupings: Orthodox, Conservative, or Reform. These are not watertight classifications. In general, the most observant Jews are called **Orthodox**. They are biblical and Talmudic.

Brit Milah · the ritual of male circumcision

Mohel · the person who performs the circumcision

Tzedakah · giving to charity, an obligation commanded by God

Tallit · fringed prayer shawl worn by Orthodox Jews

Tefillin · also known as the phylactery; leather boxes containing Torah readings worn on the head and arm

Kippah · also known as a yarmulke; a brimless cap worn on the crown of the head

Orthodox Judaism · the most observant branch of Judaism, which affirms Talmudic authority, Kosher laws, Sabbath observance, the separation of men and women in worship, head coverings, and the use of Hebrew as the language of worship

Mourner's Kaddish · after a death, a prayer recited each day by the children of the deceased for a year after their passing

Shiva · after a death, a seven-day period in which the family of the deceased stays at home to receive visitors

DEATH AND AFTERLIFE

Jewish practices concerning death are that the deceased should be buried that very day in a simple coffin and according to a simple funeral. The children of the deceased should recite the **Mourner's Kaddish** prayer for a year after the loss. The family stays at home for a week to receive visitors in a practice known as **shiva** (seven). Traditional Judaism discourages cremation, as it is seen as defiling to the human body, particularly in the aftermath of the Shoah. Many Jews long to be buried in Israel.

Jewish belief in afterlife is quite open to interpretation. There is a general idea that there will be a purgative period after death and a coming resurrection in a messianic age that will be like a renewed Garden of Eden. Beyond that, interpretations vary a great deal. Elijah is a forerunner of resurrection, as he never tasted death. Orthodox Jews believe in a post-resurrection messianic age, centered on the land of Israel. Very few people will escape an afterlife punishment, but eternal punishment—hell—is rejected in Judaism. The reasoning is that God would not torture his children eternally. Extremely evil people will simply become annihilated.

Related to notions of purity, Judaism rejects a dualistic understanding of the body and soul. Rather, the body and soul are both vital for personhood, and both can be made holy again. This idea is important for understanding bodily resurrection in Judaism, a profound affirmation of humanity's physicality.

THE WESTERN WALL

Photographer: Ori Lubin, (CC BY-SA 4.0)

A Hasidic Jew in prayer at the Western Wall, the most sacred place in Judaism.

The **Western Wall** of the Second Jerusalem Temple is the most sacred place in Judaism. It is a place of prayer and hope for a restored Israel. Twice a year, the written prayers of people from all over the world are gathered from the Wall and solemnly buried on the nearby Mount of Olives.

Western Wall · the most sacred place in Judaism; a place of prayer and hope for restoration

Haredim · a term for Orthodox Jews in Israel meaning "tremblers," and usually translated as "ultra-Orthodox"

Yeshiva · a Jewish school devoted to the study of the Torah and the Talmud

Sally Jane Priesand · ordained in 1972 in Cincinnati; the first female rabbi of Reform Judaism

Regina Jonas · a German woman ordained as a rabbi in 1935, though her case was hotly debated at the time

Conservative Judaism · also known as **Masorti**; a middle ground between Orthodox and Reform Judaism

Kosher laws, Sabbath observance, and the separation of men and women in the synagogue are normative. They worship in the Hebrew language and cover their heads during worship. In Israel, they are known as the **Haredim** ("tremblers"), which is usually translated into English as ultra-Orthodox. They separate themselves in closed neighborhoods and wear distinctive clothing. They typically have very high fertility rates, and many of their men devote themselves full-time to Torah study in the yeshiva—a traditional Jewish school for the study of religious texts.

Reform Jews are the most progressive of practicing Jews.

They are modern in their interpretation of the faith, even emphasizing the equality of all religions. Men and women sit together and do not usually cover their heads. They use the local language and do not normally observe kosher laws. Reform women have been ordained as rabbis since 1972, when **Sally Jane Priesand** was ordained in Cincinnati. It should be pointed out that a German woman, **Regina Jonas**, was ordained in 1935, but her case was hotly debated among Jews at the time. She was killed in the Shoah.[2]

Conservative Judaism, also known as **Masorti** ("traditional"), is considered to be a kind of middle ground between Orthodox and Reform. It emerged in the nineteenth century and formally launched in 1887 at the Jewish Theological Seminary in New York City. Conservative Jews follow kosher dietary laws, pray daily, and observe Shabbat and the Jewish holidays. However, they are often more progressive on social issues, such as those involving gender and sexuality.

There are also many **secular Jews** who are Jewish only in ethnicity. They might put up menorahs and nominally celebrate high holidays, but they live largely secular lives. In Israel, they are called **Hiloni** ("secular").

There are many small Jewish communities scattered around the world, although many of them are moving to Israel due to Israel's pro-Zionist policy for those who are ethnically Jewish and have some evidence to prove it.

Messianic Jews are Jews who believe in Jesus Christ as the long-awaited Messiah. Most Jews consider them to be Jewish in ethnicity but Christian in religion. Messianic Jews often observe Jewish rituals faithfully, with the caveat that Jesus is the fulfillment of their faith. They often worship in Hebrew in their synagogues and celebrate the Jewish holy days.

> Judaism is a small faith. It accounts for only around 0.2 percent of the global population. However, its teachings and texts have become widespread due to the global success of its offspring religions: Christianity and Islam.

While Judaism is both a religion and an ethnicity, it is possible to convert to it. It requires a full year of study, a commitment to join the Jewish community, interviews by a court of rabbis, a covenant of circumcision for males, and immersion in water—in a **mikvah**. The convert is then given a Jewish name.

Judaism is a small faith. It accounts for only around 0.2 percent of the global population. However, its teachings and texts have become widespread due to the global success of its offspring religions: Christianity and Islam. Thus, it is a little surprising that Jews have been badly mistreated by these two religions throughout history. While medieval Christianity was often a hostile context for Jews, the creation of a Jewish state in 1948 led to widespread opposition in the Islamic world. In the decades since the founding of Israel, the vast majority of Jews have emigrated out of Islamic lands due to tensions and now reside mainly in Israel or in the United States.

There are approximately fifteen million Jews today, with around 40 percent living in the United States and over 40 percent living in Israel. The rest of the world's Jews are scattered in many countries, such as France, Canada, Russia, and the United Kingdom. There are over thirty nations in the world with at least ten thousand Jewish citizens. Around 1.5 million Jews live in New York City alone, the highest urban concentration in the world. Over 2 percent of the US population identifies as Jewish.

In 1950, Israeli legislators passed the **Law of Return**, which grants to any Jew worldwide the right to immigrate to Israel. Around 45 percent of them lead secular lives, but they are certainly not anti-religious. Over half of Israeli Jews practice their faith to some degree, with nearly a quarter of the population describing themselves as Orthodox or ultra-Orthodox (Haredi).[3]

A Jewish synagogue known as Temple Emanu-El in New York.

Secular Jews · Jews in ethnicity but not in religious practice

Hiloni · "secular"; the term for secular Jews in Israel

Messianic Jews · Jews who believe that Jesus Christ was the long-awaited Jewish Messiah but who often still practice traditional Jewish rituals

Mikvah · a bath for ritual immersion to attain purity

Law of Return · legislation allowing any Jew worldwide the right to immigrate to Israel

11 CHRISTIANITY
Unto the Ends of the Earth

A devout follower prays as Pope Francis leads a mass in Kampala, Uganda (2015). On his five-day apostolic journey, the pope visited Kenya, Uganda, and the Central African Republic.

The world's population is around eight billion people, and Christianity claims around 33 percent of that population, or 2.64 billion. For over a century now, Christianity has been the religion of about one-third of the human race. It is a religion that is growing worldwide, both in sheer numbers and as the percentage of the global population. If current trends continue, by 2050, Christianity will have increased its percentage of the global population to 35 percent.[1]

> Christianity is the only religion to be found in all nations of the world and on every continent. It is the most widespread religion in human history, and it is the only religion that fully meets the criteria of being a "world" religion, if by that we mean it exists in every nation of the world.

The United States has more Christians than any nation in the world. While around 80 percent of its citizens self-identify as Christians, only about two-thirds of them report being members of a congregation. Rounding out the top five, the other nations with the most Christians are Brazil, Mexico, Russia, and China.

Jewish Heritage

Jesus was a Jew, and he was called rabbi ("my master") by many. He was an itinerant preacher, which was common at that time. He was a healer, and he attracted crowds due to his reputation as such. Very quickly, he acquired a faithful group of disciples, and he was killed after a mere few years of ministry, yet stories began to emerge that he was resurrected. His followers believed that his life, death, and resurrection held the key not only to understanding Judaism, but for understanding God's entire plan for humankind.

Christianity emerged as a Jewish sect. Its worldview was similar to the worldview of Judaism. However, Christians quickly began to see themselves as unique, as something available to the whole world. Jews tended not to think this way. Due to this outward thinking,

At left, Jesus touches and heals a blind man. At right, Jesus brings Lazarus back to life, accompanied by St. John and the sisters of Lazarus, Mary and Martha. Fresco transferred to canvas from the hermitage in San Baudelio de Berlanga, near Soria, Spain (early twelfth century).

Image courtesy of the Metropolitan Museum of Art.

Christianity grew extremely fast, and within three hundred years, it was the most important religion in the Roman Empire. The **apostle Paul**—the author of much of the New Testament—argued persuasively that Gentiles were as welcome as Jews were to the inchoate faith of Christianity. Paul traveled far and wide to argue this crucial point. The destruction of the Jewish temple in 70 CE contributed to the Jewish–Christian divide, as some followers of Jesus made it clear that they were not Jewish rebels; rather, they were merely followers of the Messiah who happened to have been Jewish.

The fall of the Jewish temple was the culmination of a four-year war known as the **Great Jewish Revolt**, which ended in catastrophe for the Jews. This Jewish–Roman war caused some Christians to want to distance themselves from Jewish revolutionaries who used violence in their struggle for independence from Rome. As a result, the early church transitioned into a largely **Gentile** population. But initially, the early church consisted almost entirely of Jews who believed that Jesus was the Messiah.

New Testament Scriptures and Early Christianity

Early on, the Christian scriptures were the Jewish scriptures. Christians simply tried to explain Jesus as Messiah, according to the Jewish scriptures. In fact, very little of the **New Testament** was written with the awareness that it would become canonical scripture. The New Testament documents are, essentially, letters and stories about Jesus and his earlier disciples. Written in the first century CE, the New Testament is quite different from the Old Testament because, clearly, Jesus Christ is its central figure. Christians continue to use the Hebrew Bible, which they often refer to as the Old Testament. The word *testament* means "covenant." Thus, most Christians believe that when Jesus came, a new kind of covenant was established between God and humankind. The new covenant anchored Jesus as the focus of all human history. Put differently, the Old Testament was fulfilled by the coming of Jesus.

Early Christians were an expectant people. They expected Jesus to come back at any moment to resurrect his deceased followers and join them with his living disciples in heaven. However, the second coming did not occur, thus indicating the need for a set of teachings enshrined in text.

The Christian New Testament consists of twenty-seven books loosely grouped into the following

P66, a late second- or early third-century papyrus codex containing the Gospel of John in Greek.

Image courtesy of Martin Bodmer at Université de Genève in Geneva, Switzerland

Seventeenth-century oil painting by Valentin de Boulogne titled, "Saint Paul Writing His Epistles." Much of the Christian New Testament comprises letters attributed to Paul, an integral apostle of the early Christian church.

categories: **Gospels** (good news of Jesus), **Acts of the Apostles** (early church history dealing with the apostles—the earliest followers of Jesus), **Epistles** (apostolic letters), and the book of **Revelation** (also known as the apocalypse).

The four texts that are central to Christianity are the Gospels. These crucial documents are essentially biographies of Jesus's birth, ministry, death, and resurrection. They include his sermons, miracles, parables (short stories intended to teach a spiritual lesson), and conversations with the people around him. The Gospel accounts of Matthew, Mark, Luke, and John recall a similar story, albeit from the vantage point of four different authors. The death and resurrection of Jesus, discussed near the end of each Gospel, must be considered the most crucial component of all four. Without a resurrection, the life of Jesus becomes merely a great life. With a resurrection, the life of Jesus suddenly becomes much more than a human story about a gifted rabbi.

However, the letters of Paul are also critical, because they interpret how a life devoted to Jesus should be lived. They unpack the implications of the resurrection on the life of the individual believer, and they set the rules and standards for how Christians should function until the second coming of Christ. Paul was a controversial figure in his own lifetime, and in twenty-first-century Christianity, his writings are often hotly debated. Although he was uniquely chosen by Jesus to establish the Christian church among the Gentiles, some have questioned his authority since he was not among the original disciples. Still others, however, especially in modern times, have raised significant concerns about whether Paul promoted patriarchy and possessed an overly strict understanding of human sexuality. However one interprets Paul, one thing cannot be denied: the early church believed his writings were inspired by God and should guide the Christian community into the future.

Many Christians also revere a set of texts known as the **Apocrypha**. Christians differ on what texts should be included in the Apocrypha, but they are essentially second-tier books that are useful for instruction but not to be placed into the same sphere of authority as the sixty-six-book canon of the Old and New Testaments.

The Christian scriptures accepted as standard today are the result of a fierce ideological battle between different groups of Christians who struggled to represent mainstream Christianity: the Marcionites, various groups of **Gnostics**, the Montanists, and several others. It was the **Orthodox** ("correct opinion") Christians who won out, however, giving birth to a religious movement that grew to become a major world faith.

Christian Calendar

The **Lord's Day**, or the first day of the week, is the liturgical centerpiece for most Christians, although there are a few Christian denominations that have maintained the Jewish Sabbath—Saturday—as the primary day for corporate worship. **Easter** is the celebration of Christ's resurrection. **Christmas**, the feast of Christ's

Epistles · formal letters written by the apostles that contain theological insight and instruction

Revelation · a heavily symbolic apocalyptic text; the last book in the Christian Bible

Apocrypha · a set of religious texts that Christians generally consider to be useful but that do not carry the same authority as canonical literature

Gnostics · a heretical strand of early Christian thought obsessed with esoteric secret knowledge

Orthodox · "correct opinion"; the set of Christian beliefs that were accepted as truth, with all competing views declared to be heresy

Lord's Day · Sunday, the first day of the week and the day on which Jesus rose from the dead; typically the day used for corporate worship services

Easter · the celebration of Christ's resurrection

Christmas · the feast of Christ's birth, celebrated on December 25 for Catholics and Protestants and on January 7 for Orthodox Christians

DIVISIONS IN CHRISTIANITY

Gregorian calendar · the mainstream calendar used by most of the world today; adopted in the sixteenth century by Pope Gregory XIII to fix a minor flaw in the old Julian calendar

Julian calendar · the calendar used from the time of Julius Caesar until the adoption of the Gregorian calendar in 1582; still used in the liturgical calendar of Eastern Orthodoxy

Epiphany · the feast celebrating the revelation of Jesus as God incarnate to the Wise Men from the East

Protestantism · the third branch of Christianity, which was born out of Martin Luther's protests against the excesses and corruptions of the Roman Catholic Church

Wise Men · according to the Gospel of Matthew, Wise Men from the East came to worship and present gifts to Jesus shortly after his birth; possibly Zoroastrian Magi

Passion Week · the week before Easter and the holiest segment of the Christian calendar

Palm Sunday · the celebration of the day Jesus rode into Jerusalem and was embraced with joyous singing and the waving of palm branches

Maundy Thursday · the day commemorating the Last Supper and Jesus's washing of his disciples' feet

Good Friday · the day on which Jesus was crucified; remembered solemnly in the Christian faith

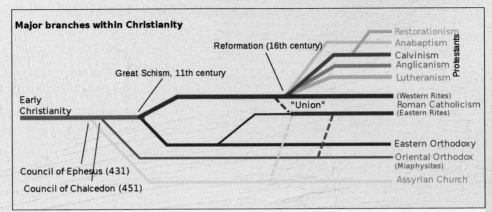

A diagram of the main schisms among Christian branches, from the Council of Ephesus to the Reformation era.

Designed by Hogweard, public domain

Christianity consisted of two large bodies—Eastern and Western—until a German monk by the name of Martin Luther came along. He changed Christianity forever in 1517, with the publication of his 95 *Theses*, or complaints against the Roman Catholic Church. With that act of protest, **Protestantism** began, and by the twenty-first century, it had claimed an ever-increasing share of Christianity—around 40 percent worldwide.

birth, is fixed at December 25 for Catholics and Protestants using the **Gregorian calendar**, but it occurs on January 7 for Orthodox Christians, as they continue to observe the old **Julian calendar**. The feast of **Epiphany** (revealing) celebrates the revelation of Jesus as God incarnate to the **Wise Men** from the East. **Pentecost** is observed on the fiftieth day from Easter Sunday to mark the birth of the church, with the descent of the Holy Spirit onto the early Christians, as recounted in Acts 2. **Passion Week** is the week before Easter and is the holiest segment of the Christian calendar. It includes the special days of **Palm Sunday, Maundy Thursday,** and **Good Friday.**

The forty-day period before Easter is known as **Lent** and is a period of self-denial, repentance, and fasting. It begins with **Ash Wednesday**, when Christians burn the palm leaves from the previous Palm Sunday and use the ashes to mark observers' foreheads with a cross. All Hallows' Eve—**Halloween**—is the day before All Hallows' Day (**All Saints' Day**) on November 1. **Advent** is the month of December prior to Christmas. In churches that observe the traditional Christian liturgy, different colors decorate the church building during each of the above seasons, and the sermons and liturgy are all guided by the historic readings that correspond to the Christian calendar. The **lectionary** is a three-year cycle of readings that attempts to expose Christians to much of the Bible's contents while emphasizing the important holy days.

In the Western world, the Christian holy days have largely been secularized. Easter is a day for children to celebrate rabbits and receive eggs and candy. Christmas is now dominated by the figure of Santa Claus who brings gifts to everybody. Halloween is a day when kids dress up and knock on doors to receive candy from neighbors. Increasingly, the religious atmosphere of Sundays is dissipating, as sports and activities now encroach on the once-sacred day of worship and resting with family. Pentecost is almost unobserved in the wider culture. The traditions of self-denial surrounding Christian holidays in the West—fasting, abstinence, remorse, repentance—are virtually unobserved. In the **Global South** and in the Eastern Orthodox realms of influence, however, most of these traditions are kept alive, especially in Ethiopia, which carefully maintains ancient Christian practices.

Central Christian Beliefs

Christian **cosmology** holds that God created the world out of nothing and continues to sustain it. The origin story in the book of Genesis is accepted by Christians as essentially true. God created the world, the animals and plants, and all that is. Whether one accepts evolution or other scientific theories such as the big bang is beside the point, as Christians all over the world have different takes on how literally to read Genesis. Whatever else happened to bring our reality into existence, it was God's doing. God created the laws that our natural world abides by, and it is God who will destroy and/or redeem the world.

Humans were created in the likeness of God. All humans have the image of God within them. Humans will eventually be judged by God and will either go

to heaven, hell, or an intermediary place of purgation, which typically culminates in entrance into heaven.

Like Jews, Christians are considered monotheists, although their version of **monotheism** is more nuanced. The Christian scriptures testify to a God who revealed himself fully in the form of a human (Jesus Christ), but that God still remained in heaven. However, God and Jesus (God on Earth) are undivided and unified.

Christians believe Jesus was the long-awaited Jewish messiah. Therefore, Jesus's teaching must be considered directly from God since Jesus and God were and are one and the same.

However, many of the early Christians debated this new kind of monotheism, as they had to uphold conflicting ideas: (1) that their God was still the God of the Jews but that (2) their God also had to be the same thing as Jesus. This conflict led to major controversies about the nature of Jesus Christ. How can he be the true God yet truly a man at the same time?

One early thinker named **Marcion** (85–160 CE) concluded that there must be two different gods because the Jewish God was radically different from Jesus. Marcion's group had many followers and for a time threatened to outnumber the mainstream

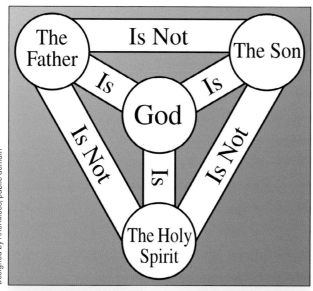

Christians have a nuanced understanding of monotheism. This Western, somewhat popular shield diagram from the twelfth century explains a commonly held version of the Trinity.

Lent · a forty-day period of self-denial, repentance, and fasting that begins on Ash Wednesday and leads to Easter

Ash Wednesday · the beginning of Lent, when Christians burn the palm leaves from the previous Palm Sunday and use the ashes to mark observers' foreheads with a cross

Halloween · All Hallows' Eve; the night before All Saints' Day on November 1

All Saints' Day · the Christian holiday that commemorates all of the saints, both known and unknown

Advent · the month of December, leading up to Christmas

Lectionary · a three-year cycle of readings that attempts to expose Christians to much of the Bible's contents while emphasizing the important holy days

Global South · a geographical term referring to Latin America, Asia, Africa, and Oceania

Cosmology · the study of the origin of the universe; in Christianity, believed to be creation by God, which is sustained by and through him

Monotheism · the belief that there is only one God; nuanced in Christianity to include three distinct persons of God in one unified deity

Marcion · a second-century heretic who believed that the God of the Old Testament was irreconcilably different from the person of Jesus

church. However, a class of Christian teachers known today as the **church fathers** condemned Marcion as a heretic—a person with religiously unacceptable views.

Early Christians began to understand God chiefly as a father. This was not an entirely new way of understanding God, but it represented a new interpretation of Christian monotheism nonetheless. The typical Jewish names for God did not emphasize God as a father, but Jesus repeatedly addressed God as his father, often in warm and familial terms, such as in the use of the word **abba**.

In addition to conceiving God as Father and God as the Son of God—Jesus Christ—there is a third idea that Christians incorporate into their unique understanding of monotheism: the **Holy Spirit**. Jesus taught that when he ascended to heaven after his

> In addition to conceiving God as Father and God as the Son of God—Jesus Christ—there is a third idea that Christians incorporate into their unique understanding of monotheism: the Holy Spirit.

resurrection, he would send God's Holy Spirit to live inside of the people who believed in him to help them. There is a famous Christian scene in the New Testament book of Acts where the Holy Spirit comes upon the followers of Jesus, enabling them to perform signs and wonders. The event happened on **Pentecost Sunday** and is commemorated each year in the Christian liturgical calendar. It is also a critically important event for those who use that scene as a badge of identification, calling themselves **Pentecostal Christians**.

The form of monotheism that was ultimately declared Orthodox in the Christian tradition looked something like this: God is one but has three distinct entities: Father, Son, and Holy Spirit. This is the Trinity—the unity of three. They are all equal and are fully divine. The **Council of Nicaea** in 325 CE used

Church fathers · an influential class of early church leaders who established much of the Orthodox tradition and doctrine

Abba · "Father"; a familial term that Jesus used to refer to God; Christians tend to see God in this same loving, fatherly role

Holy Spirit · the third person of the Trinity whom Jesus told his followers he would send to guide them after his ascension into heaven

Pentecost Sunday · the Christian holiday commemorating the descent of the Holy Spirit onto the apostles in Jerusalem on Pentecost after Jesus's ascension

Pentecostalism · the largest form of Protestantism in the world, which is spreading quickly; emphasizes miraculous gifts of the Holy Spirit such as healing, prophecy, and speaking in angelic tongues

Council of Nicaea · an ecumenical Christian council of church leaders in 325 CE who articulated the doctrine of the Trinity

Nicene Creed · the statement of belief created at the Council of Nicaea and still used as the basis for Christian doctrine to the present day

Tradition states that Bishop Nicholas of Myra attended the Council of Nicaea, pictured above. This fresco was fully restored in 2018 and appears in Saint Nicholas Church in Antalya Province, Turkey. It served as a house of worship for Orthodox Christians between the fifth and twelfth centuries.

Greek philosophy and terminology to spell out this novel concept. The participants in that conference created the Nicene Creed that is still used as the basis of Christian doctrine to the present day.

In Christianity, the authority of Jesus Christ was pivotal. In the Gospels (Matt. 28:18), Jesus claimed he had absolute authority granted to him by God. Jesus eventually passed authority on to his apostles, and the authority of the apostles was strong in earliest Christianity. For centuries, the Christian faith managed to keep a tradition of authority alive, called **episcopal succession** or **apostolic succession**. The apostles ordained bishops who ordained bishops who ordained bishops throughout two millennia of Christian history. In this view, the authority of bishops, still today, comes from this long line of succession that goes all the way back to Jesus. One core responsibility of bishops is that they ordain and appoint priests. Priests are the ones who oversee the local church, usually called a parish.

The Protestant Reformation disrupted this notion of episcopal succession. Protestant leaders argued that this understanding of a chain of authority going back to Jesus is unnecessary and unbiblical. Using the Bible as their sole source of authority, many Protestant churches do not even attempt to trace succession back to the apostles. Most of them claim that each person—using the Bible—should be his or her own authority in matters of faith, without interference from others. They reason that if the Holy Spirit lives within each person, then, strictly speaking, no intermediaries are required. Each person is accountable exclusively to God.

The Early Church and Society

Clearly, Christianity was a persecuted minority faith from its origins. Jesus was executed, as were most of the apostles. The writings of the New Testament reveal extensive persecution of the apostle Paul and his companions. This pattern continued for two centuries. Christians were critiqued publicly, in scholarship, and by the government. While some claims of Christian persecution have been exaggerated, it would be ridiculous to claim, as some have, that the persecution of Christianity was mythic—meaning it scarcely happened. The truth is that while it may have been sporadic and geographically contained, actual Christians

died because of it. It is regrettable and disingenuous that some scholars have tried to downplay the persecution and murder of Christians in the first two centuries of the religion. It happened. Repeatedly, it happened. And while the persecution may have been exaggerated by some during those first two centuries CE, it was likely because they were frightened and were being slandered by many. After all, their friends and family had been killed because of their allegiance to Christ.

In 250 CE, the Roman emperor Decius launched a religious and political persecution that caused the deaths of many believers, including **Pope Fabian** himself. Other sporadic persecutions followed, most notably under the reign of **Emperor Diocletian** (284–305 CE), who rescinded the civil, legal, and religious rights of Christians, culminating in a bloodbath of thousands and migrations by others to less hostile lands. However, according to the church father **Tertullian**, "the blood of the martyrs was the seed of the church." People stood up for Christ, they suffered and died for Christ, and they fled for Christ—leading to unintended evangelism that spurred new rounds of Christian conversion.

Christianity gained a massive and unexpected victory in 313 CE with the **Edict of Milan**, propounded by co-emperors Constantine and Licinius. But the real force behind it was **Emperor Constantine**, a Christian convert who later had Licinius killed. This edict offered official toleration and legality to Christians

Episcopal succession · also known as **apostolic succession**; the unbroken chain of ordination passed down from the apostles to the first bishops and all the way to bishops today

Pope Fabian · a third-century Bishop of Rome who was martyred under the reign of Emperor Decius

Emperor Diocletian · the supreme ruler of the Roman Empire from 284 to 305 CE; rescinded the civil, legal, and religious rights of Christians, instigating a period of intense persecution

Tertullian · late second- to early third-century Latin church father and apologist from North Africa

Edict of Milan · a landmark decree by Emperors Constantine and Licinius in 313 CE that extended official legality and toleration to Christians

Emperor Constantine · the fourth-century Roman emperor who legalized and favored Christianity, thus sparking a significant increase in conversion; revered in the Eastern Orthodox tradition as "Equal to the Apostles"

in the Roman Empire. In a stunning reversal of imperial policy, Christians went from being despised and persecuted to enjoying great imperial favor. In 300 CE, Christianity was the religion of around 10.5 percent of the Roman Empire. When Constantine died in 337, Christianity was the religion of over half of the Roman Empire.[2] The emperor Constantine was surely one of the most successful Christian influencers of all time, and he is honored in Eastern Orthodoxy as the Equal to the Apostles.

Early Christianity was an urban faith. It grew mainly in the cities. This is why the word **pagan** was assigned to non-Christians early on. The Latin word *pagan* meant "country person." Thus, the head bishops of five strategic cities in the Roman Empire came to be especially respected and authoritative. This "rule of five" came to be known as the **pentarchy**:

- Jerusalem: the holy city, where Christianity began.
- Antioch: Paul's mission base. It was also the city where Christ's followers were first called "Christians."
- Alexandria: the second city of the empire, named after Alexander the Great.
- Rome: the ancient capital of the empire.
- Constantinople: later, it became the new capital of the Roman Empire, so designated by Emperor Constantine.

The bishops of these cities were given the title of first among equals, meaning they were bishops of special importance among all the hundreds of bishops in the Christian world. However, a battle for supremacy among the bishops of these cities quickly ensued.

Saint Leo the Great, who served as Pope from 440 to 461 CE and famously defended the church from heretical assaults against orthodoxy. History remembers him for reasoning with Attila the Hun and dissuading him from pillaging the Italian peninsula.

It was the Roman bishop, Pope Leo I, or **Leo the Great**, who insisted on supremacy among the five **patriarchs** in around 450. He based his authority on a saying Jesus had made to Peter, "Upon this rock [*petros*] I will build my church" (Matt. 16:18). Peter, traditionally, was thought to be the leader of the church at Rome, and after Leo the Great, popes often linked their authority to Peter. Orthodox Christians concluded that authority in all church matters was in the collective voice of the Christian bishops, most conspicuously at the church councils. Still today, the Orthodox Christians believe that Christian doctrine was propounded at the **Seven Ecumenical Councils**, held between 325 and 787 CE.

In actuality, Christianity had been drifting into regional halves early on: a Latin West and a Greek East. The Roman Empire became known as the Western church, or the Roman Catholic Church. The Eastern Orthodox Church was based in the city of **Constantinople**, the capital of the **Byzantine Empire**.

Many historians point to 476 CE as a reasonable origin for medieval Christianity, as that was the year when the last Roman emperor, Romulus, was deposed, although he was only eleven years old at the time. Thus, Christianity is often organized in this way:

- Antiquity (early church): 33 CE (Christ's death) to 476
- Medieval: 476 to 1517 (Martin Luther's protests)
- Modern: 1517 to today

Some want to argue for a "postmodern" era, but the concept has failed to attract consensus globally.

Christian Society in the Patristic and Medieval Periods

Medieval Christianity lasted a millennium or so, and it impacted Christianity in ways that are still with us. Some have tried to dismiss this long period of time as the **Dark Ages**, but that is an outdated perspective. The discoveries, advances, and ingenuity of this era are impressive. One only has to look at medieval cathedrals to realize these engineers, craftsmen, and architects were anything but dimwits. Breathtaking cathedrals were built all across Christendom during this period, defying facile claims that medieval people were somehow inferior to those before and after. That condescending and erroneous perspective on the medieval era is finally being put to rest.

Some of the important developments in the medieval Christian era are the following:

Monasticism **began in Egypt in the 200s CE with** *Saint Anthony the Great;* the tradition produced a wealth of scholars, including the master linguist **Jerome**, who translated the Bible into Latin in around 400 CE.

An icon of Saint Anthony the Great, the father of Christian monasticism, above the entrance of the church of Saint Spyridon in the Pagrati area of central Athens.

Seven Ecumenical Councils · great assemblies of church leaders between 325 and 787 that propounded official Christian doctrine before the Orthodox and Catholic churches split; considered the primary authority in Eastern Orthodoxy today

Constantinople · the center of Eastern Orthodoxy and the capital of the Byzantine Empire

Byzantine Empire · the eastern half of the Roman Empire that survived the fall of Rome and persisted until the fifteenth century, when it fell to the Ottoman Turks

Dark Ages · an outdated and ignorant historical term for the medieval era

Monasticism · an institution of self-denial and of careful study of God, which flourished in early and medieval Christianity and prompted a great tradition of monastic scholars

Saint Anthony the Great · the father of Christian monasticism; an ascetic in Egypt in the 200s CE

Jerome · a fourth-century linguist and scholar who translated the Bible into Latin

Christianity   277

During the medieval era, *Christians established many orphanages, hospitals, and institutes of higher education*, all geared to improve the lives of those around them. Monasteries and convents doubled as orphanages. Those injured or exhausted during travel were nurtured, fed, and cared for at pilgrimage stops. Beginning in the eleventh century, monastic institutions in Bologna, Oxford, Salamanca, Paris, and Cambridge rose up to offer training in the emerging arts and sciences.

The writings of patristic church father Augustine (d. 430 CE) remained the touchstone for medieval Christianity and profoundly shaped the Western theological tradition, both Catholic and Protestant. Augustine is often credited with defining key—though not universally agreed upon—Christian doctrines such as original sin, predestination, and just war theory (or justified war).

The defeat of Islam at the Battle of Tours *in 732 CE* was a crucial moment in the medieval era. In that battle, Charles Martel led his troops to thwart the invading Muslims who had already taken the Iberian Peninsula (Spain and Portugal) and southern France. They had

Constructed by order of Emperor Charlemagne, who was buried there in 814 CE, the Palatine Chapel at Aachen Cathedral is one of the oldest in Europe.

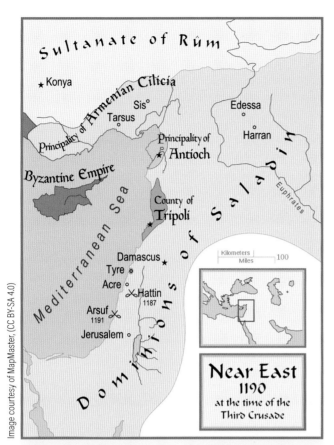

The First Crusade established a series of crusader states throughout the Levant, which fell to the Muslim armies under Saladin. This map depicts the surviving crusader states and the dominions of Saladin at the time of the Third Crusade in 1190.

The Crusades *were a series of attempts by Christians to take back the Holy Land from Islam between 1095 and 1204.* While there were some short-term successes with the Crusades, the end result came when Saladin defeated the Christians in 1187 and reasserted Muslim dominance. Unfortunately, Roman Catholic armies unexpectedly sacked the Christian city of Constantinople in 1204, leading to a lasting and insurmountable division within the worldwide Christian community.

Thomas Aquinas (1200s CE) was the greatest Christian theologian of the High Middle Ages (eleventh to thirteenth centuries). A Dominican friar, Aquinas carefully studied the ancient Greek philosophers—most notably Aristotle—alongside Christian theology. Considered the high point of **Scholasticism**, his school of thought is today known as **Thomism**. His book *Summa Theologica* is considered one of the greatest works of Roman Catholic theology to the present day.

Between 1309 and 1376, a scandal rocked the Roman Catholic Church. *Today, that scandal is known as the* *Avignon Papacy,* also known as the **Babylonian Captivity of the Church** or the **Western Schism**. During that period, the Roman pope moved his headquarters to Avignon, France, which outraged those

Pilgrimages · religious trips undertaken to relics and to important Christian sites, often to seek healing or the absolution of sins

Great Schism · the severe rift between the Eastern Orthodox and Roman Catholic churches, which broke apart in 1054 and have remained divided ever since

The Crusades · a series of Christian invasions into the Muslim-controlled Holy Land between 1095 and 1204

Thomas Aquinas · the greatest theologian of the High Middle Ages who reconciled Aristotelianism with Christian theology

Scholasticism · a philosophical school that combined Aristotelian logic with Christian dogma

Thomism · the school of thought that arose from the teachings of Thomas Aquinas

Summa Theologica · the principal scholastic text of Thomas Aquinas; considered to be one of the greatest works of Roman Catholic theology to the present day

Avignon Papacy · also known as the **Babylonian Captivity of the Church** and the **Western Schism**; a scandal in the Roman Catholic Church from 1309 to 1376, when the papacy was moved to Avignon, France, and there were briefly multiple, simultaneous popes

their sights on consolidating Europe. This battle may have been the most pivotal moment for the future of Western Europe's religious affiliations. Had the battle gone to the Muslim armies, Christendom in Western Europe would have likely ended.

Pilgrimage **sites rose up all across Eastern and Western Europe**, attracting Christians to pay their respects to important relic collections (objects of religious significance—often a saint's bones) to receive absolution for their sins.

The *Great Schism of Christianity occurred in 1054*, resulting in the development of Eastern (Orthodox) and Western (Roman Catholic) forms of Christian faith. The Great Schism was theological in nature but evinced a sociopolitical rift in the formerly unified Roman Empire. From then on, there was a definite distinction between a Greek (Byzantine) East and a Latin West. Attempts at reconciliation continue to the present.

who thought the papacy should forever remain in Rome. The nadir of the episode was when three different bishops claimed the title of pope! The debacle was finally resolved at the Council of Constance in the early 1400s, when the papacy was moved back to Rome.

During the medieval era, critical thinking increased dramatically as universities spread across Europe, giving birth to a powerful network of institutions that focused largely on theology, but also on secular matters. The groundwork was laid for a university system in which academicians and intellectuals gathered to exchange knowledge. Latin became the lingua franca of the universities, so Europeans from virtually any region could participate in the life of the mind as long as they learned Latin. Professorships were established, huge gains were made in the arts and sciences, and the spreading of knowledge accelerated dramatically.

Authority, Leadership, and Conflict among Christians

Christians established levels of authority early on. By the end of the first century CE, **bishops** were considered the successors to the apostles, who were the successors of Jesus, who was the ultimate representation of God on Earth. To the present day, most Christians are still led by a roster of bishops that guide the church in doctrine, liturgy, and practice. Bishops typically have charge of a region, called a **diocese**. Underneath the authority of bishops are **priests**—those who lead in local congregations. The Orthodox and Roman

The people of the Czech Republic remember Jan Hus (1372–1415), a key predecessor to the Protestant reformers, as a martyr who opposed ecclesiastical control. Pictured is the Jan Hus Memorial in the old town square in Prague.

MEDIEVAL CATHOLIC THEOLOGY

Theology was considered the **queen of the sciences** in the medieval Christian universities, as it explained how humans could escape condemnation and achieve salvation with God in heaven. In the medieval era, salvation was linked to behavior. To sin was to jeopardize one's salvation; thus, a lengthy list of rules and taboos developed, and the list was preached as unassailable truth for centuries. For example, Wednesday and Friday were always for fasting, and a bath could not even be taken on those days. It was forbidden to work or have intimate relations on Sundays. And the lists went on. Sins were split into two categories: **mortal sins** (kept one out of heaven if not confessed) and **venial sins** (lesser sins).

There developed a special list of **seven deadly sins**: pride, greed, wrath, envy, lust, gluttony, and sloth (laziness). All sins had to be confessed to a priest, and as the representative of Christ, he held the power of forgiveness. Christians were expected to confess their sins and repent, usually by doing acts of **penance** prescribed by the priest during **confession**.

During the medieval era, the idea of **purgatory** developed in the West. It was described as a flaming place of torment, sometimes thought to exist beneath the Earth's crust. The concept became quite elaborate in the High Middle Ages, although it probably did not achieve widespread consensus among Roman Catholic leaders until the thirteenth century. The doctrine taught that when a person died, they would go on an arduous journey to purge their sins, beginning from the place their deeds had put them. If someone lived with several sins, they had a lot of work to do in the hereafter. If they led a pretty good life, they did not have to do so much to purge themselves.

Only the holiest individuals—typically saints and monastics—could enter heaven directly. Those who were unfortunate enough to go to **hell** were thought to go to the Earth's core, reserved for the unbaptized, the heretics, and the unrepentant. Their afterlife punishment would be in perpetuity, without any system for working a way out of it. The lesson was clear: even if a person sinned wantonly, they must stay in good faith with the church. The church was God's authority on Earth, and without its help, one's afterlife would be very bleak.

© Bibliothèque Nationale, Paris. Used by permission.

In the ninth century, Byzantine scribes compiled Parisinus 923, a large collection of biblical and patristic quotations. This manuscript is notable for its lavish use of gold and miniature church father illustrations in the margins.

Queen of the sciences · theology, according to medieval Christian universities, as it can explain how humans can escape condemnation and achieve salvation

Mortal sins · serious and deliberate sins that keep transgressors out of heaven if left unconfessed

Venial sins · lesser sins

Seven deadly sins · pride, greed, wrath, envy, lust, gluttony, and laziness

Penance · acts meant to punish and restore a sinner to a correct posture of righteousness

Confession · the admission of one's sins to a priest to receive grace and reconciliation with God

Purgatory · a middle ground between heaven and hell in which a soul purges itself of all lingering sins and impurities to prepare for the perfect divine presence of God in heaven

Hell · a place of endless torment that serves as punishment for the unbaptized, the heretics, and the unrepentant

Catholic churches, as well as many Protestants, continue to use the old system of bishops and priests.

That model of leadership—of bishops and priests—was undisturbed until the Protestant Reformation in the 1500s. Protestants often went in creative directions when it came to clergy and church authority. From about 400 to 1500 CE, Christianity's hierarchy kept the scriptures firmly in the hands of church elites. In the late medieval period, this long-established tradition began to be challenged. John Wycliffe (1300s England), Martin Luther (1500s Germany), and William Tyndale (1500s England) subverted that tradition with their translating of the New Testament into local languages rather than relying on the Latin translation of the original Greek scriptures. By putting the Bible into the languages of the common people, a revolution in Christian history was unleashed. While these pioneering biblical translators were a turning point, they could not have been nearly as effective as they were without the invention of the printing press by Johannes Gutenberg (1400–68), which opened the floodgates to literacy and biblical access.

Perhaps one unintended consequence of the Reformation is that it made religious authority a private matter. Reformers taught people that they should read the Bible for themselves, but, naturally, that led to a massive proliferation of ways to interpret the Bible. People began to form their own judgment on religious matters. This led to a great proliferation of Protestant sects—something that continues today with each new denomination. There are always people who will have different ideas from their group; thus, they branch out and form newer denominations. What results is constant innovation within the faith, as well as a common rejection of religious authority. The Reformation unleashed religious innovation, but it also fragmented Christianity, like broken glass, into an irretrievably broken body of different ideologies.

In Northern Europe, the heart of the Reformation, the Roman Catholic clergy quickly lost their exclusive handle on scripture and the notion of authority, and much of Christianity began to change. When people read the Bible for themselves, in their own language, they critiqued the institutional church, and, in many cases, they rebelled against the clergy.

Sola scriptura (scripture alone) was the cry of the Protestant reformers. The leaders of the Reformation took a suspicious view toward the clergy and especially the pope. Luther condemned the distinction between clergy and laity. He argued that clergymen

---

John Wycliffe · a fourteenth-century reformer who translated the Bible into English

Martin Luther · the architect of the Protestant Reformation and the author of the *95 Theses*, which indicted the Roman Catholic Church on all of its historical abuses of power

William Tyndale · a sixteenth-century reformer who translated the Bible into English

Johannes Gutenberg · the inventor of the printing press

Pastor · the most common Protestant term for a minister

Sola scriptura · "scripture alone"; a central tenet of Protestantism in which scripture, not the clergy, is authoritative for Christians

John Calvin · the father of Reformed Christianity who taught a fivefold teaching known by its acronym of TULIP

Reformed Christianity · a sect of Protestantism begun by John Calvin and centered on a strong belief in predestination

Geneva · the home of Reformed Christianity; greatly influenced by John Calvin

---

PROTESTANT LEADERSHIP

Protestants today are extremely innovative in the area of church leadership. Some Protestant churches have essentially mirrored US corporate culture in their leadership, with CFOs, CEOs, presidents of church boards, executive pastors, flowcharts, and mission statements. Some churches prefer simplicity: there is a pastor and perhaps an assistant. Some churches prefer to borrow strictly biblical terminology, such as overseers, deacons, and evangelists. Some Protestants call their clergy ministers, some call them preachers, but most today prefer the term **pastor**. Most pastors are paid a salary, as their church work occupies a good portion of their time. Some are paid handsomely in high-income churches, whereas others eke out a living in places where individuals live hand-to-mouth.

were only necessary to preach the Word. They were not to be considered magical in any way, especially in their administering the sacraments (holy rituals), which under the Roman Catholic system had become their greatest power. People knew that if a priest refused them the sacraments, then their soul would be in danger. This made the clergymen extremely powerful in the medieval era. Martin Luther, John Calvin, and the other Protestants sought to overturn this way of thinking about clergy. Many leaders of the Reformation, including Martin Luther and Ulrich Zwingli, went so far as to identify the pope as the Antichrist.

John Calvin, the father of **Reformed Christianity**, lived in the Swiss city of **Geneva** in the sixteenth century. It had a population of around ten thousand people, and before the Reformation, the city was home to four hundred clergymen—one cleric for every twenty-five people! After the Reformation, the city had only ten clerics. Clergy privileges were removed, and Protestant clergy became just ordinary citizens. They had to pay taxes and could be prosecuted in civil court,

The International Monument to the Reformation, also known as the Reformation Wall (inaugurated 1909), was built to commemorate the 400th anniversary of John Calvin's birth and the 350th anniversary of the University of Geneva's establishment.

unlike the Catholic model, where priests were generally immune from prosecution. Strangely, however, Geneva became probably the strictest, most puritanical city in all of Europe, even with only a few clergymen. The city passed laws forbidding the wearing of shoes thought to be sexy. Foul language was policed. Even giving one's child a secular name—rather than a biblical name—could result in jail time. John Calvin became like a Genevan pope, and he even exercised his ability to condemn and kill heretics. Although his own writings contain far more nuance, many modern believers summarize Calvinist Christian doctrine using a simplified fivefold acronym—**TULIP**:

- Total depravity: people are completely evil.
- Unconditional election: God elects some for salvation, and others he does not.
- Limited atonement: Jesus died only for the elect, not for everyone else.
- Irresistible grace: if God elects a person, they cannot resist him.
- Perseverance of the saints: once saved, always saved.

This is the form of Christianity that inspired the Puritans who immigrated to America on the Mayflower in 1620.

It was the **Anabaptists** (re-baptizers) who began to argue that church and state should be separated. People should only volunteer to be a part of the church, and Christian doctrine should not be policed by civil authorities. The Anabaptists were ahead of their time, and their ideas eventually led to the option of secularization. In their minds, people should have a choice of whether or not to be religious. Anabaptists were labeled **radicals**, and they were often persecuted and even killed for their ideas. One of their great legacies is their teaching that babies should not be baptized; rather, only people who can properly profess faith in Christ should be baptized. This raised the age of baptism significantly from infancy to usually the teenage years, or even later.

The Roman Catholic Church realized that it was losing numbers rapidly. Most of Northern Europe became Protestant, for example. In 1545, the Roman Church summoned its bishops to the **Council of Trent** in an attempt to curb the hemorrhaging of church members. This council set in motion the **Counter-Reformation**. At this council, the Roman Church basically dug in its heels, reaffirmed the supremacy of the Latin version of the Bible (known as the **Vulgate**), reaffirmed the exclusive right to biblical interpretation to Catholic clergy, and condemned the Protestant movements altogether.

Alongside the rise of the Protestant movement, we also witness the rise of a strategically important order of Catholic missionaries who would change the world: the **Jesuits**, formally known as the **Society of Jesus**, founded by Ignatius Loyola in 1534. The Jesuits traveled widely across land and sea to bring Asia, Africa, and Latin America into the fold of the Roman Catholic Church, and they had huge successes. Entire regions of the world became Catholic due to their valiant efforts. Many of the nations that are Catholic today were strongly impacted by the herculean work and travels of the Jesuits.

It is interesting that in the vast number of cases, the nations and regions of the world that became or remained Catholic during the sixteenth century are still Catholic, and the nations that became Protestant in the sixteenth century are still mainly Protestant nations. The Orthodox nations of the world, mainly in Eastern Europe, took little interest in the

TULIP · the five main doctrines of Reformed Christianity: total depravity, unconditional election, limited atonement, irresistible grace, and the perseverance of the saints

Anabaptists · a radical subgroup of the Reformation that denounced infant baptism, teaching instead that only those who could profess their own faith in Christ should be baptized

Radicals · Anabaptists, who were often persecuted or even killed for their beliefs

Council of Trent · a Roman Catholic council held in 1545 in response to the Reformation; the council condemned Protestantism, upheld Latin as the language of scripture and liturgy, and confirmed exclusive religious authority to the Catholic hierarchy of religious offices

Counter-Reformation · a firm reassertion of Catholicism in the face of the Protestant Reformation

Vulgate · Jerome's Latin translation of the Bible

Jesuits · formally known as the **Society of Jesus**; a Catholic missionary society founded by Ignatius Loyola in 1534 that took Catholicism to Asia, Latin America, and Africa

Image courtesy of Hessisches Landesmuseum Darmstadt.

Diptych showing Martin Luther and his wife, Katharina von Bora. Artist: Lucas Cranach (1529).

The Reformation gave birth to new Christian denominations, new translations of the Bible, and new theologies, and, by doing so, it provoked the Catholic Church to attack. Protestant–Catholic wars raged across the European continent and abroad for centuries. The Reformation made dramatic changes within the church culture—for example, it challenged the idea of monasticism. Reformers argued that clergy should be married, as in their view, **celibacy** was not at all commanded in the Bible. Jesus was celibate, but the Bible actually encouraged marriage in many places, including for religious leaders. Besides, the Catholic mandate that urged priests to remain celibate was only authorized in around 1000 CE. The Eastern Orthodox churches never required celibacy of priests, and many, such as Luther, argued that forced celibacy often led to secret sexual promiscuity. Thus, Luther married, and he urged Protestant pastors to marry, too. With the rise of the Protestant Reformation, the convents and monasteries virtually emptied, and the monks and nuns tended to marry each other.

> **Celibacy** · unnecessary, according to the reformers, who supported clerical marriage

Image courtesy of Lyndon Baines Johnson Library and Museum.
Photographer: Yoichi Okamoto, public domain

Anglicans · also known as the Church of England, or in the United States, the Episcopal Church; a Protestant denomination that came into being when King Henry VIII split with Rome after the pope denied him an annulment

King Henry VIII · the king of England in the sixteenth century who cut ties with Rome over a marital conflict

Martin Luther King, Jr. · an African American Baptist preacher renowned for his civil rights advocacy

Liturgy · from the Greek word for "public service"; consists of prayer, ritual, and public worship

Martin Luther King Jr., a devout Baptist preacher who advocated powerfully in the Civil Rights Movement, meeting with President Lyndon B. Johnson on March 18, 1966.

Reformation or the Counter-Reformation, and they have remained Orthodox.

The **Anglicans** (**Church of England**, or **Episcopal Church** in America) arose due to a marital and political conflict. In 1525, **King Henry VIII** wanted an annulment from his wife, Catherine of Aragon, but the pope declined. Like most of the European monarchs of this period, Henry believed himself to be a God-ordained king. He firmly believed that Rome was overstepping its authority as it interfered with the English crown. Consequently, Henry appointed his own archbishop (Thomas Cranmer) and remarried another woman without the approval of the pope. This all set the stage for a political break between the Church of England and the Roman Catholic Church. King Henry VIII resented the pope's refusal to grant the annulment, and he cut England's ties with Rome, declaring himself the supreme head of the church on English soil.

Christianity and Civil Rights

Christianity's core doctrines have persisted up to the present, and they have given birth to numerous movements and institutions worldwide. History has judged some of them as good and some of them as regrettable. For instance, the abolition of slavery emerged from British Evangelicals in the early nineteenth century. Some of the great civil rights movements throughout history—such as the Magna Carta in the early thirteenth century—were profoundly impacted by Christianity. In the United States, Christians were at the vanguard of both women's rights and universal civil rights throughout the nineteenth and twentieth centuries. The notable African American Baptist pastor, **Martin Luther King Jr.**, captivated a nation when he argued powerfully that, "I have a dream that my four little children will one day live in a nation where they will not be judged by the color of their skin but by the content of their character."

However, Christians have also found themselves enmeshed with movements of repression, such as the various Catholic Inquisitions, murderous wars, and participation in the wretched institution of slavery throughout history. These were striking developments, as Jesus clearly taught to "turn to them the other cheek" (Matt. 5:39 NIV), to "love your enemies" (Matt. 5:44), and to "set the oppressed free" (Luke 4:18 NIV).

Christian Worship and Rituals

Since the earliest Christian times, disciples of Jesus were to gather frequently to remember Jesus and worship him together. For Christians, prayer, ritual, and public worship are known as **liturgy**, a Greek word that means "public service." Bible reading, recitation of creeds, prayer, Eucharist, and singing or chanting are all important parts of the liturgy.

Prayer is the most fundamental way that Christians communicate with God on a personal level, although there are many different ways to pray. Many Catholic and Orthodox Christians pray through saints. Protestants typically pray directly to God. Roman Catholics often pray to Mary, the mother of God, known to many as the **theotokos** ("God-bearer").

Early Christians also fasted regularly as a way to honor Christ. Jesus fasted for forty days before launching his ministry. **Fasting** is encouraged in the Bible, although Western Christians have largely abandoned the practice. Orthodox Christians—especially in the Ethiopian, Coptic, Armenian, and Syrian traditions—continue to fast regularly. Fasting on Fridays, the day of Christ's passion, remained an observance for Roman Catholics until the mid-twentieth century, when the practice started to decline alongside Western **secularization**.

A central practice of Christian worship is the initiation of new believers in the sacrament of **baptism**. Jesus was baptized by his cousin John the Baptist,

beginning a practice that continued into the apostolic era. Baptism is a universal practice in Christianity. Most Christians are baptized as infants, although those Christians in the Anabaptist traditions baptize people whenever they can make their own profession of faith in Christ. Baptism with water is often linked to God's forgiveness and salvation. Jews practiced ritual cleansing in water, but the Christian practice of baptism supplanted Jewish circumcision as the fundamental mark of entering a covenantal relationship with God.

Jesus Christ celebrated the Jewish Passover with his disciples, but he stipulated it should be commemorated in remembrance of him. For Christians, the bread and the wine now represent the body and blood of Christ. This meal came to be known as the **Eucharist**, a Greek word that means "giving thanks."

Roman Catholics believe that once the bread and wine are transformed into Christ's body and blood, they do not revert back, thus Catholics hold the consecrated bread and wine in high regard, considering it actually the body and blood of Jesus. Priests may eat all the bread and drink all the wine, even rubbing their hands over the wine so that Christ's body and blood are not desecrated. Or else they will put the remainder into a tabernacle—a locked box for holding unused bread and wine that has already been consecrated. Catholic priests often refer to the body and blood as the **host**, which comes from the Latin word *hostia*, meaning "sacrifice."

The elements involved in the sacrament of Eucharist, or Communion, include bread and a chalice of wine. According to the Christian tradition, the night before Jesus was crucified, he gave his disciples bread and wine, representing his body and blood, and he told them to continue the ritual in memory of him.

© zolnierek, Adobe Stock

Theotokos · literally "God-bearer" or "mother of God"; a term Catholic and Orthodox Christians use to refer to Mary; generally not used in Protestant circles

Fasting · abstaining from food and/or drink as a religious observance; encouraged by the Bible and regularly practiced by Orthodox and sometimes Catholic Christians

Secularization · the decline of religiosity that has been witnessed in Western Europe and, to a lesser extent, North America

Baptism · an initiation ritual in the Christian faith that is associated with cleansing, renewal, and salvation; the fundamental mark of entering a covenantal relationship with God

Eucharist · "giving thanks"; partaking in the bread and wine of Passover; associated with the sacrifice of Jesus's body and blood as a remembrance of him

Host · a term for the bread and wine of the Eucharist, which, once consecrated, becomes the literal body and blood of Christ in the Catholic tradition

Divine Liturgies · the Orthodox term for the Eucharist

Mass · the Catholic term for the Eucharist

Communion · also known as the **Lord's Supper**, the Protestant term for the Eucharist

A cappella · "in the style of the chapel"; singing without the accompaniment of musical instruments; the typical Orthodox manner of worship

Iconostasis · a prominent screen near the altar in an Orthodox church that separates the clergy from the laity

Icons · images of the holy saints from the history of Christianity

Sacraments · sacred rites that confer God's grace onto the participant

Eastern Orthodox Christians generally call their eucharistic celebrations **Divine Liturgies**, while Catholics call them **Mass**. The word *Mass* comes from the old Latin phrase at the end of a service: "*Ite, missa est*," or "Go, it is the dismissal." Protestant Christians often refer to the Eucharist as **Communion** or the **Lord's Supper**.

During medieval times, Masses became common for a variety of purposes, such as to heal illness, to help with fertility, to ensure a good harvest, and to honor those who had departed this life.

The Eastern Orthodox churches have worship services that are similar to Catholics, but they differ in key ways. While both Catholics and Protestants typically use musical instruments in worship, Eastern Orthodox Christians tend to worship **a cappella**—"in the chapel style"—the style of the church. Additionally, Orthodox churches have a prominent screen near the altar that separates the clergy from the laity. This screen is called an **iconostasis** and has three doors that are opened throughout the worship service. The iconostasis is covered in many **icons**—images of holy saints from the history of Christianity.

The Protestant leader Martin Luther contested many of the core teachings of the Roman Catholic Church. He reduced the list of sacraments from seven to two: baptism and Eucharist. He argued that confession to a priest was not needed, since forgiveness came from God alone. He argued that monasticism was completely useless, as all are equal before God. Luther taught that virginity and celibacy were no longer great virtues, as God is equally pleased by marriage, and celibacy often leads to sexual vice. Importantly, Luther argued against the existence of purgatory, saying that it was unbiblical.

Protestant worship services today, especially in the Western world, have tended to conform to cultural norms. It is common to attend Protestant and Independent services with a rock-and-roll band, complete with electric guitars and drum sets. Many Protestant pastors dress like everybody else, with no costume that reveals his or her status as a cleric. Protestant services are often relaxed and spontaneous. Jokes are often told from the pulpit, coffee is served at

SACRAMENTS

Roman Catholic and Orthodox Christians believe in and practice seven **sacraments**:

- **Baptism**
- **Confirmation** (anointing with oil)—Catholics administer it at the age of reason, while Orthodox administer it at the time of baptism.
- **Eucharist**
- **Penance**—confession to a priest
- **Holy orders**—ordination of the clergy
- **Marriage**—after the tenth century, most Catholic priests were not allowed to marry; Orthodox priests can marry before ordination.
- **Extreme unction** (last rites)—anointing of the sick with oil, often when gravely ill

A contemporary worship team at Harvest Community Church in Goshen, Indiana (2016).

View to the north and east walls of the Great Mausoleum, Forest Lawn Memorial Park, Glendale, California (2013).

the entrance, and preachers lace their sermons with cultural references, such as movie scenes and Internet memes on a giant screen up front.

Christianity and Funerary Rites

Christian funerary practices can vary a great deal, due to the three main traditions—Orthodox, Catholic, Protestant—as well as the wide variety of cultural contexts within which Christians find themselves. Throughout history, Christians have buried their dead, since the belief in a bodily resurrection has been assumed. Only heretics and witches were burned, and that was a punishment by denying them the opportunity to resurrect. However, cremation has become an option for many Christians in the Western world due largely to environmental concerns. Some Christians argue that burial in the twenty-first century includes embalming chemicals and an industrialized system that pollutes the Earth. Others have argued that,

theologically, God is entirely capable of collecting scattered bits of dust and resurrecting the person regardless of the state of their remains. Most Christians outside of the Western world—which means the vast majority of the world's Christians—hold to the traditional practice of burial after death. Orthodox Christians forbid the practice of cremation. Cremation was forbidden in the Roman Catholic Church until 1963. In Canada and the United Kingdom, the vast majority of people use cremation today. In the United States, cremation has slightly exceeded burial since 2016, but each state is different. More secular states tend to cremate, while more Christianized states, especially in the South, tend to prefer burial.

Many Christians offer a **wake** for their departed loved ones. This is often done at

> **Wake** · a funerary tradition held in the home of the bereaved shortly before the funeral, in which friends and relatives visit to comfort those mourning the deceased

Christianity   289

home, where friends and relatives can visit and comfort the bereaved. Christians do not have a prescribed amount of time that should pass between death and burial, although a few days is relatively common.

Funeral services can vary a great deal, especially in the Protestant and Independent services. Focus is usually placed upon eulogizing the dead, allowing family and close friends to publicly comment, and focusing on scriptures having to do with the resurrection as a source of hope. Catholics and Orthodox Christians usually celebrate the Eucharist at funerals.

Funerals are typically followed by a trip to the cemetery, where the coffin is lowered into the ground and a handful of dirt is often thrown onto the casket. After a brief graveside service, a meal for all mourners is usually held at the church hall. While most Christians do not have a formal period of mourning, in the Orthodox churches it is common for the spouse of the deceased to wear black clothing for forty days.

Christian Material Culture

The transplanting of Christianity to the Global South—Asia, Africa, Latin America and the Caribbean, and Oceania—during the age of discovery caused various forms of Christianity to spring up all over the world, making Christianity the most widespread religion in world history. There are many examples globally that highlight this important point. It is common to find American forms of Christianity in India, and, vice versa, Indian Christians faithfully practicing in America. The largest two Roman Catholic nations in the world are Brazil and Mexico. Africa has vastly more Anglicans than North America, the United Kingdom, and Australia combined. And it is interesting to see how cultures assimilate the old rituals planted onto their shores by Western missionaries. For example, actual crucifixions take place in the Philippines each year, although not unto death. In New Mexico, upturned bathtubs decorated with the Virgin Mary stand in people's front yards. Religious syncretism occurs in many

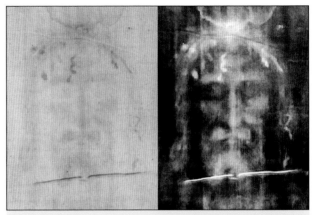

The Shroud of Turin, a relic believed by the Catholic Church to be the burial cloth of Jesus of Nazareth. Digital processing on the right tries to recreate what his face might have looked like from the imprint on the shroud. However, radiocarbon dating on the shroud has shown its origin to be in the High Middle Ages, not at the time of Christ.

> All of this intermixing of global cultures has led to a fascinating material culture in Christianity that connects the Christian world.

transplanted Christian immigrant communities, such as with the case of Vodou in Haiti.

All of this intermixing of global cultures has led to a fascinating material culture in Christianity that connects the Christian world. Local traditions become global traditions. Once-local pilgrimages, for example, have opened up a kind of Christian pilgrimage that is common today. For example, the **Shroud of Turin**, a relic said to be the burial garment of Jesus, has become a major religious tourist destination in northern Italy whenever the pope decides to put it on display. **Our Lady of Guadalupe** in Mexico City is the most visited Christian pilgrimage site in the world, with around twenty million visitors per year. Christians have always longed to see the Holy City of Jerusalem, and with the modern-day convenience of cheap travel, it has become common for Christians worldwide to take trips to the city where Jesus died and was resurrected. Pilgrims visit the Holy Sepulcher, the Garden Tomb, and the Mount of Olives. In a short drive, one can see the Jordan River, the Sea of Galilee, Bethlehem, and many other sites in Israel associated with Jesus Christ.

Martyr veneration is a powerful attraction to Christian pilgrims both today and over the last two

Shroud of Turin · purportedly the burial cloth of Jesus

Our Lady of Guadalupe · the most visited Christian pilgrimage site in the world, with around twenty million visitors per year

millennia. Relics of Christian martyrs have been prized throughout history, although many of them are of dubious provenance. Nevertheless, the assumed remains of saints and other important objects have attracted Christian pilgrims for centuries. To be in the presence of a deceased martyr was to be in the presence of the holy. Relics were often the source of controversy, as Christians jostled for possession of them, as they are thought to contain real power. Relics were seen as a nexus between the physical and spiritual realms. Since the soul of the martyr was thought to be in heaven, the body had special significance, as it was still on Earth.

People believed, then and now, that relics could heal, and many stories and examples circulated, lending credence to their authenticity. In former times, many Christians believed relics were the most trustworthy form of healing available to them in an era of crude and often ineffective medicines.

When Christianity became legal in the fourth century, the adoration of relics burgeoned, and churches were built over them. Many of these structures are known as **basilicas** ("royal place"). The most prized relics were bodies of the apostles, great early Christians, and martyrs. All manner of relics rose up, many associated with the life of Jesus—for example, the **True Cross**, the **Holy Grail** (chalice), and the burial shroud of Christ.

Christian architecture did not really exist until the fourth century, when Christianity was declared legal. Both Christian art and architecture blossomed dramatically when Constantine embraced the faith. Some of the earliest Christian art can still be viewed in the **catacombs** outside of Rome, a labyrinth of underground corridors where Christians buried their dead. Romans considered cemeteries to be sacred property; thus, Christians enjoyed relative safety in the catacombs. In the catacombs, Christians met, worshiped, mourned their dead, and created art on the walls. The dead were placed onto niches carved into the walls. The catacomb paintings are still some of the most important sources for early Christianity.

When Christianity became legal in 313 CE, church buildings were erected around two rituals: the Eucharist and the veneration of relics. Christians gathered and encountered the mystical presence of Christ as well as the physical presence of the holy saints. During the 300s, Christianity grew dramatically at the expense of paganism, and many pagan temples were converted into churches.

These buildings usually contained a **narthex** (entrance), leading to a long, open assembly space called a **nave**, as well as a **sanctuary** that contained the altar or eucharistic table. The altar, situated beneath

© Ch.Andrew, public domain

Fourth-century church father John Chrysostom explains the power of relics, the human fragments that the church preserved: "[they] repulse the onslaughts, not only of those enemies which can be seen and heard, but also the attacks of the invisible demons ... This they do with ease too, just as a vigorous man will turn back and frustrate the playful advances of children."[3]

Basilica · "royal place"; a special class of church building in Catholicism, many of which were built over the burial place of a saint and/ or martyr

True Cross · the alleged remains of the cross on which Jesus was crucified

Holy Grail · the cup used by Jesus at the Last Supper

Catacombs · a labyrinth of underground corridors outside of Rome where Christians buried their dead

Narthex · the entrance of a cathedral

Nave · the open assembly space within a cathedral

Sanctuary · the room of a cathedral or church building that contains the altar or Eucharistic table

Apse · the domed roof directly over the altar in a cathedral

Crypt · a room underneath a church building used for burial

Hagia Sophia · a magnificent sixth-century church building in Constantinople, which was eventually converted to a mosque after the Ottoman conquest of the Byzantine Empire

St. Peter's Basilica · a famous church building in Vatican City; purportedly built over the burial site of Peter, the apostle of Jesus

Romanesque · a dark and solemn style of church architecture with rounded arches and small windows

Cruciform · in the shape of a cross

Gothic · a late medieval style of church architecture characterized by enormous, pointed arches and stained glass windows

The Hagia Sophia, built by Emperor Justinian in the sixth century CE. Legend says that upon completion of his masterpiece, Justinian said, "O Solomon, I have outdone thee." When the Hagia Sophia was taken over by the Ottomans, the minarets were added to Justinian's design.

The cloisters of Gloucester Cathedral in the United Kingdom, intricately designed in the Gothic style.

the ceiling's **apse**, was the holiest place, as that is where Christ became present in the Eucharist. Altars were often situated directly over a special relic or a saint's tomb. During medieval times, wealthy families erected side chapels and altars in the church building, and they were often buried in a separate wing or downstairs in a **crypt**. People of lower social class were typically buried in consecrated ground adjacent to the church.

The heyday of the Byzantine Empire may have been the most important era for elaborate church construction. For example, the **Hagia Sophia** (built in the sixth century) in Constantinople dwarfed all other churches until the construction of **St. Peter's Basilica** (built in the sixteenth and seventeenth centuries) in Rome. The Muslim Turks captured the Hagia Sophia in 1453 and converted it into a mosque, but visitors today are typically astounded at how something so breathtakingly immense could have been constructed in the 500s.

Church architecture in the Western Latin world was characterized by the **Romanesque** style: rounded arches and small windows. They tended to be dark and solemn. They were also **cruciform**—built in the shape of a cross. The **Gothic** style caught on in the twelfth century and extended outward from northern France. By the fifteenth century, it was the dominant style. It was well-suited for enormous structures featuring pointed arches, large windows, and lots of glass.

The stained glass creations in these churches are still marvelous to observe.

It is confounding how rather poor and technologically limited communities in the medieval ages could build such massive, opulent structures. With great care and great pride, they devoted themselves to massive engineering feats, constructing their beloved masterpieces, sometimes taking well over a century to complete. These structures were built to overwhelm the senses—colorful vestments, sparkling gold and silver vessels, dazzling marble, fine wood structures, shimmering textiles, and ornate candelabras, complete with sweet incense wafting through the air.

Powerful bells called the faithful to worship and tolled for the dead. Bell towers dominated the skyline of Christian cities and villages. Choirs developed to aid the music of the liturgy. In the 800s, pipe organs were introduced in Western European churches and eventually became common. In the Eastern Orthodox churches, chanting without instruments remained the norm.

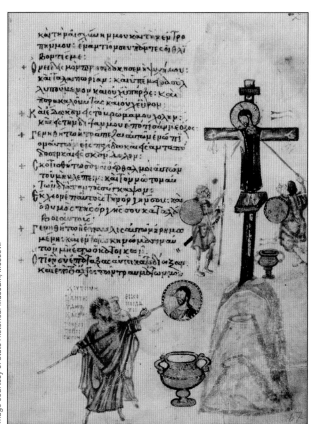

This anti-iconoclastic image from the Chludov Psalter parallels the soldiers that pierced the side of Jesus with an iconoclast that whitewashes an icon (mid-ninth century).

Image courtesy of State Historical Museum, Moscow.

In the 700s and 800s, Eastern Orthodox Christians struggled over the issue of whether icons should be permitted in the churches. A movement called **iconoclasm**, which means "image smashing," arose. Important pieces of art were destroyed during these turbulent centuries. Many people died trying to save holy icons. Several Byzantine emperors despised icon veneration and instigated persecutions against the **iconodules**. In 843, it was finally decided that icons could be venerated, a decision celebrated in the Orthodox Church each year on the first Sunday of Lent, which is called **Orthodox Sunday** or **Triumph of Orthodoxy**.

The Protestant Reformation rose up alongside the rising popularity of the printing press. Gutenberg invented his press around 1440, opening the floodgates for book printing. Literacy rose immediately. The power of the book was amazing in how knowledge and ideas could be transported almost immediately, not unlike the invention of the Internet in modern times. Early on, the Roman Catholic Church used the printing press to mass-produce indulgences—the paper certificates that fueled the birth of the Protestant Reformation. Luther was outraged that the Catholic Church had the audacity to sell certificates offering people forgiveness of their sins. Once the Catholic Church realized that the printing press unleashed anti-Catholic teaching with unprecedented efficiency, it became unsettled, and it produced the infamous **Index of Forbidden Books**. Of course, Luther was enemy number one, and faithful Catholics were advised to avoid reading his books.

The Bible was translated into vernacular languages as a result of the Reformation. Protestant opinion was that it was the right of every person to be able to read God's Word. However, the price of the

Iconoclasm · "image smashing"; a movement that arose in the 700s and 800s to end the veneration of icons

Iconodule · a person who supported the veneration of icons

Orthodox Sunday · also known as the **Triumph of Orthodoxy**; an annual Orthodox celebration held on the first Sunday of Lent to celebrate the final decision in 843 CE in favor of the veneration of icons

Index of Forbidden Books · a list published by the Roman Catholic Church of all the heretical books that Catholics were forbidden from reading; begun during the Protestant Reformation and abolished at the Second Vatican Council in the 1960s

Catacomb of Domitilla in 1974. Second-century Christians buried their dead in catacombs, honoring them with wall frescoes.

Ichthus · the Greek word for fish and an acronym used by the ancient church to represent Christianity, hence the fish symbol still used today by Christian adherents

Crucifix · an image of the cross that bears the body of Jesus

Perpetual virginity · the Catholic and Orthodox belief that Mary remained a virgin until her death

Virginal conception of Jesus · the Christian doctrine that Jesus was conceived while Mary was still a virgin

initial runs of Bibles was extremely expensive, and only the wealthy could obtain them. Eventually, however, the proliferation of published Bibles drove down production costs, and Protestants began keeping Bibles in their homes for private reading and even for protection from evil—a mentality that continues today.

Christian symbols have evolved over the centuries. The earliest depictions of Christianity, in the catacombs, were of Jonah and the whale, Noah's Ark, and the Great Shepherd carrying a lamb on his shoulders. A fish symbol rose up early on, due to the acronym for the Greek word for fish: **ichthus**. The acronym stood for: "Jesus-Christ-God's-Son-Savior." It is a symbol that has survived the test of time and is still used today. The cross did not catch on until the 300s, as it was a symbol of a brutal death in the Roman world. However, once adopted, it became the most powerful symbol for Christianity. Catholics tend to use the **crucifix**, which includes Jesus on the cross. Protestants tend to use the empty cross, representing the resurrection. The Greeks tend to use a cross of four extensions of equal length. Catholic and Orthodox Christians both depict the cross with their fingers over their chests during worship, as well as during private prayer.

Women in Christianity

The Virgin Mary has been adored by Christians since the second century CE. Catholic and Orthodox

Christians call her the theotokos—the mother of God. Protestants rarely uphold Mary in this way, although they do respect her as a godly woman. Protestants believe Mary had other children with Joseph after Jesus was born. Orthodox and Catholic Christians believe Mary was celibate to the end of her life and thus believe in her **perpetual virginity**. Mary's authority in the Orthodox and Catholic churches has steadily increased over the centuries. In recent times, some liberal Protestant churches have abandoned the doctrine of the **virginal conception of Jesus**. It should be kept in mind that the Catholic doctrine of the **Immaculate Conception** actually refers to Mary herself being conceived, within the womb of her mother Anna, without the stain of original sin.

The New Testament makes it clear that many women followed Jesus during his earthly ministry. Much debate has circled around two names in Paul's epistle to the Romans (chapter 16). One is **Phoebe**, who is called a **deaconess**, and the other is **Junia**, who is referred to as an apostle. The word *deaconess* could simply mean "servant," but some churches have included women in the diaconate. More perplexing is the issue of what Paul meant when he referred to Junia as an apostle. While there is much debate within the scholarship about whether Junia was, in fact, a woman, it would be fascinating if this woman was counted among the apostles of the Lord in the mind of Paul. It is clear that Paul had a more expansive view of the term *apostle*, as he considered himself one, although he never actually met Jesus. This expanded meaning of the word *apostle* might shed light on Paul's controversial inclusion of Junia as an apostle.

While the early church had patriarchal tendencies compatible with the Greco-Roman culture around it, there were also allowances made to women that were rare for that time. Thus, on one hand, Paul wrote that women must be silent and must not teach or speak in Christian assemblies (1 Cor. 14:34). However, on the other hand, Paul was prone to single out women in more egalitarian ways, such as when he referred to the wife–husband team of Priscilla and Aquila as his coworkers in ministry (Rom. 16:3).

The medieval church produced several notable Christian women who are still today held in high regard:

- **Hildegard of Bingen** was a twelfth-century Benedictine **abbess** in Germany; she was respected for her musical compositions as well as for her mystical visions.
- **Julian of Norwich** was a fourteenth-century mystic whose book *Revelations of Divine Love* might be the first book written by a woman in the English language.
- **Margery Kempe** was a fourteenth- to fifteenth-century mystic who wrote the earliest autobiography in the English language. Her work discusses her fascinating pilgrimages to the Holy Land, Italy, the Netherlands, Poland, Germany, and the famous **Santiago de Compostela** church in Spain. Margery was greatly inspired by Julian of Norwich, whom she had met and spent time with.
- **Bridget of Sweden** was a fourteenth-century mystic who founded the Bridgettine order of nuns and monks. Like Margery Kempe, she also took pilgrimages to the Santiago de Compostela, to the Holy Land, and to Rome, where she died.

In the modern era, ordained women preachers got their start in the seventeenth century with the **Quaker** movement—known formally as the **Society of Friends**. The Quakers taught equality of women and men in ministry,

Immaculate Conception · the Catholic doctrine that Mary was conceived in the womb of her mother Anna without the stain of original sin

Phoebe · a female leader in the early church; called a deaconess by Paul

Deaconess · an office of leadership in the church

Junia · a female leader in the early church; called an apostle by Paul

Abbess · the head of an abbey of nuns

Santiago de Compostela · a revered church and pilgrimage site in Spain at the burial place of James, the son of Zebedee and apostle of Jesus

Quakers · also known as the **Society of Friends**; a pacifistic and egalitarian sect of Christianity that began ordaining women preachers as early as the seventeenth century

Sojourner Truth · an American slave who escaped in 1826 and became a famous abolitionist and preacher

Jarena Lee · an eighteenth- and nineteenth-century African American preacher in the African Methodist Episcopal Church who fought against slavery and gender inequality; possibly the first African American woman to write an autobiography

African Methodist Episcopal Church · the first Black denomination in North America; founded in 1816 by Richard Allen

Church of Christ, Scientist · a Christian denomination focused on miraculous healing; founded by Mary Baker Eddy in Boston in 1879

Aimee Semple McPherson · a Pentecostal preacher from Canada who founded the Foursquare Church denomination and Angelus Temple in Los Angeles

Foursquare Church · a Pentecostal denomination founded by Aimee Semple McPherson that today boasts nine million members

Angelus Temple · one of the most successful megachurches; founded by Aimee Semple McPherson in 1923

Methodist · a mainline denomination with roots in the teachings of John Wesley

Presbyterian · a mainline denomination with roots in the Church of Scotland, which was influenced heavily by John Calvin's Reformed theology

and they produced many women preachers. They made a lasting impact on the notion of ordained female ministers, and they were way ahead of their time.

Sojourner Truth was an American slave who escaped in 1826 and became a famous abolitionist. She was also a highly regarded preacher, captivating audiences by her six feet of height as well as her vocal, physical, and psychological strength.

Jarena Lee was an eighteenth- to nineteenth-century African American preacher in the **African Methodist Episcopal Church**. She fought against slavery as well as against longstanding gender norms. She is thought to be the first African American woman to write an autobiography.

In the late nineteenth century, women started founding denominations. Mary Baker Eddy established the **Church of Christ, Scientist**, in Boston in 1879. **Aimee Semple McPherson**, a famous Pentecostal preacher from Canada, established the **Foursquare Church** denomination in Los Angeles in 1923. Perhaps the best-known preacher in her day, she built up **Angelus Temple** to become one of the most successful megachurches in the world at that time (1920s–1940s). She evangelized by radio and brought

Pentecostalism to the masses. Her denomination now claims a global membership of around nine million members.

Both the **Methodist** and **Presbyterian** denominations started ordaining women as pastors in 1956. The Black church traditions, however, made allowances for female preachers earlier on, due largely to matriarchal patterns of leadership common in Africa. For example, many African American churches have a tradition of **mother boards**, which consist of prominent church women who hold significant power in the congregation.

While some **Baptist** denominations allow for women to serve as ordained pastors, the largest one—the Southern Baptist Convention—has consistently taught that only men can be ordained as teaching pastors over the entire mixed assembly. **Rick Warren**, the famous American pastor of the largest Southern Baptist congregation, ordained three women in 2021, igniting major controversy in the denomination.

The ancient Christian traditions—Roman Catholic and Orthodox churches—have never ordained

Sojourner Truth, an escaped slave and powerful abolitionist and feminist, known for her famous "Ain't I a Woman?" speech.

Photo of Mother Teresa taken in Washington, D.C. (1986).

women as priests, although women are highly involved in other areas of church life, such as church administration, educational institutions, and ecclesial charities.

Mary Daly (1928–2010) was a prominent Catholic theologian who, while serving as a professor at the Jesuit-run Boston College, became an outspoken feminist and LGBTQ advocate. She famously argued, "If God is male, then the male is God." She exhorted women to leave Christianity and organize themselves into a distinct sisterhood. Her work has helped to inspire feminist movements such as womanist theology (Black feminist) and mujerista theology (Latina feminist).

Perhaps the most famous woman Christian leader of the twentieth century was Mother Teresa (1910–97), a Roman Catholic nun who founded the Missionaries of Charity order while serving the poor and sick in the streets of Kolkata, India. She grew to international fame and won the Nobel Peace Prize in 1979, inspiring millions around the world for putting her Christian faith into action.

Christianity Today

Christianity today can be split into three major categories: Roman Catholic (50 percent of the global Christian population), Protestant and Independent (40 percent), and Eastern Orthodox (10 percent). The Roman Catholic Church is led by the pope, who still resides within an independent enclave in Rome, in a small city-state known as Vatican City. Orthodox churches are organized mainly along national lines, so each nation tends to have its own autonomous framework of authority; however, there is a shared posture of respect among Eastern Orthodox Christians that their spiritual leader—the "first among equals"—is the Patriarch of Constantinople. There are somewhere around forty thousand Protestant denominations in the world, each having a different structure of authority, so it is virtually impossible to point to a consistent Protestant authoritative framework. There are thousands of them.

The Roman Catholic Church, by far the largest Christian denomination in the world, went through massive changes in the 1960s at the Second Vatican Council. Some major decisions were made at that

Mother boards · an African American church tradition in which a board of prominent women holds significant power in the congregation

Baptist · an Evangelical denomination born out of the Anabaptist movement of the Reformation

Rick Warren · a famous US pastor of the largest Southern Baptist congregation; ignited controversy in 2021 when he ordained three women

Mary Daly · a prominent Catholic theologian who, while serving as a professor at the Jesuit-run Boston College, became an outspoken feminist and LGBTQ advocate; exhorted women to leave Christianity and organize themselves into a distinct sisterhood

Womanist theology · an approach to faith that emphasizes and centers the experiences of Black women

Mujerista theology · an approach to faith that emphasizes and centers the experiences of Latina women

Mother Teresa · a Roman Catholic nun who founded the Missionaries of Charity order while serving the poor and sick in the streets of Kolkata, India; received the Nobel Peace Prize in 1979

Missionaries of Charity · a Catholic missionary society founded by Mother Teresa that serves those in the greatest depths of poverty

Patriarch of Constantinople · the spiritual leader of the Eastern Orthodox Churches; the "first among equals"

In addition to her journalism and activism, Dorothy Day (1897–1980) purchased an eighty-seven-acre plot in 1964 to create a farm and hospitality house. The community survived until 1978.

Image courtesy of Bob Fitch photography archive, © Stanford University Libraries. Used by permission.

Second Vatican Council · a council in the 1960s that implemented sweeping reforms to the Roman Catholic Church, including the recognition of Protestant and Orthodox Christians as true Christians, using the vernacular language for Mass, abolishing the Index of Forbidden Books, disassociating Jews from the death of Jesus, and promoting interfaith dialogue

Filioque · a word meaning "and the Son"; added to the Nicene Creed by the Catholic Church without the approval of the Orthodox churches or of an ecumenical council; a major source of division between the Catholic and Orthodox branches of Christianity

conference that changed the nature of the Roman Catholic Church:

- Non-Roman Catholic Christians were recognized as being true Christians.
- Vernacular languages replaced Latin in the Mass.
- The Index of Forbidden Books was abolished.
- The priest now faced the people rather than facing the altar, which meant more involvement for the laity.
- Jews were disassociated from the death of Jesus.
- Interreligious dialogue was encouraged.

The Roman Catholic Church claims well over a billion people—the largest religious organization in human history. It thrives today as a robust religious movement that continues to see steady growth.

The Eastern Orthodox churches thrive today as well, in the aftermath of the Soviet Union, which was brutal for Christians. By far the largest Orthodox nation is Russia, where about half of the Eastern Orthodox Christians live. Other important Orthodox nations are Ukraine, Romania, Greece, Serbia, Bulgaria, and Georgia. There are four major disagreements between Catholic and Orthodox churches:

- ***The Nicene Creed.*** At the Council of Toledo, held in Spain in 447, the Roman Church added the word **filioque** ("and the son") to the creed. The original creed states that the Holy Spirit proceeds from the Father. Catholics added the filioque without approval from other churches, leading them into doctrinal error, according to Orthodox Christians.
- ***Authority***. The Orthodox churches do not believe the Bishop of Rome is the supreme authority in Christendom. They believe in a more collective approach to authority—the collective voice of the bishops.
- ***Immaculate Conception***. This doctrine, devised by the Roman Church and approved only in 1854, has never been accepted by Orthodox Christians.

- *Liturgy.* Since the Orthodox–Catholic split in 1054, many differences in liturgy have arisen over the centuries.

While there is an ongoing Orthodox and Catholic dialogue, the reconciliation efforts between Eastern Orthodox and Oriental Orthodox are the most promising in Christianity today.

The **Oriental Orthodox churches** are similar to the Eastern Orthodox, although they have key points of doctrinal difference that have kept them apart since the **Council of Chalcedon** in 451 CE. These two ecclesial families are today working hard to heal their historic divisions. The Oriental Orthodox churches are found in Egypt (the Coptic Church), Armenia, India, Ethiopia, Eritrea, and Syria.

Clearly, the Protestant churches struggle with what to do about the further proliferation of divisions. A twentieth-century Protestant-led initiative is the **ecumenical movement**, a desire among Protestant Christians to unite with other Christians.

There is irony here, as Protestants are prone to divide. Nevertheless, the movement continues, mainly through the work of the **World Council of Churches (WCC)**, based in Geneva, Switzerland. The WCC comprises Protestant and Orthodox churches, while Roman Catholics may participate as observers but not as voting members.

One major form of Christianity that has grown in recent years and has garnered much media attention in the United States is Evangelicalism. Scholar David Bebbington

Oriental Orthodox Churches · a group of churches that split from Orthodoxy at the Council of Chalcedon in 451; found today in Egypt, Armenia, India, Ethiopia, Eritrea, and Syria

Council of Chalcedon · an ecumenical council in 451 that affirmed the hypostatic union that Jesus was simultaneously 100 percent man and 100 percent God

Ecumenical movement · a twentieth-century Protestant movement striving for Christian unity across denominational lines

World Council of Churches (WCC) · a vehicle of ecumenism, based in Geneva, Switzerland, through which differing Christian denominations can come together in unity for the common good of the faith

Every seven years or so, the World Council of Churches gathers. In 2013, about five thousand Christians representing three hundred churches and one hundred countries met for the tenth assembly in Busan, South Korea.

While there are thousands of Protestant denominations, the vast majority of them fit under the umbrella of one of these six movements:

- **Lutheranism**—begun by Martin Luther.
- Reformed (Presbyterianism)—begun largely by John Calvin.
- Anabaptism (Mennonites, the Restoration Movement, Brethren, Baptists)—associated with **Thomas Müntzer** and the Radical Reformation.
- Anglicanism (Church of England)—begun by King Henry VIII.
- Methodism—begun by John Wesley in England.
- Pentecostalism—an offshoot of Wesleyan Christianity that has grown to become the largest form of Protestantism in the world. Roughly a quarter of the world's Christians are Pentecostal, and that number is rising at a staggering pace. Pentecostal Christianity is often thought to be the future of Christianity due to its ability to connect with the poor and marginalized in society. It emphasizes the gifts of the Holy Spirit, healing, and miracles. Many Africans, Latin Americans, and Asians joined Pentecostal movements in recent decades. In 1980, roughly 8 percent of the world's Christians were Pentecostal, but in 2020, this number had risen to around 25 percent.

Lutheran · a Protestant denomination begun by the reforms of Martin Luther

Thomas Müntzer · a Protestant reformer associated with the Anabaptists and the Radical Reformation

Evangelical Quadrilateral · according to David Bebbington, the four primary elements of Evangelicalism are activism, biblicism, conversionism, and crucicentrism

George Whitefield · a British clergyman and a close friend of John Wesley; traveled seven times to the American colonies to preach the gospel, setting into motion the First Great Awakening

First Great Awakening · a widespread religious revival in eighteenth-century North America and Britain

famously outlined four primary elements found in Evangelicalism, known to scholars as the **Evangelical Quadrilateral**:

- Conversionism—typically a "born again" experience wherein people see themselves as dying to an old (sinful) way of life and being born into a new (Christian) identity.
- Biblicism—a belief in the divine inspiration of the Bible.
- Cruicentrism—the cross is at the center of Christianity, as Jesus's sacrifice was an atoning death for those who trust in him.
- Activism—an urge to evangelize people and bring them into the Christian faith.

These qualities emerged during the mid-1700s when **George Whitefield**, a British clergyman and a close friend of John Wesley, traveled seven times to the American colonies to preach the gospel, setting into motion the **First Great Awakening**. His preaching was extraordinary, due largely to his background in theater. He mesmerized American audiences for decades and profoundly shaped American Christianity.

Another significant form of Christianity that is present in world Christianity today is often described as **fundamentalism**. While impossible to define with any precision, there are aspects of fundamentalism that arise repeatedly, such as an emphasis on biblical inerrancy and a suspicion of modern biblical criticism. There is also an emphasis on a doctrine known as the **rapture**, when Christians will meet Christ in the air during his return to Earth and will be with him during a tribulation period. During the tribulation, satanic forces—led by the **Antichrist**—will wreak havoc on the Earth for a period of time, often thought to be a thousand years. Some fundamentalists are leery about getting too close to those who do not share their beliefs, as they want to remain uncorrupted from worldly influences.

On the opposite end of the spectrum from fundamentalism is **liberal Protestantism**, which used to be called **mainline Protestantism** before their numbers of followers collapsed so markedly. Liberal Protestants in the United States tend to emphasize universal salvation and hold to an ecumenical outlook. Many of them are religious pluralists—meaning many religions are true. They tend to be in favor of the ordination of females as well as gay and lesbian clergy. Virtually all mainline Protestant groups have declined dramatically since the 1960s, which was their numerical high point.

Christianity in the United States has a fascinating history. The United States was one of the first examples of a separation model, in which religion was separate from state influence. This is different from how most nations understood the relationship between religion and politics over the centuries. Quickly, the United States became a place where people could come and practice their religion freely without interference from the government. Indeed, the government was legally prohibited from persecuting anyone on the basis of religion. For this reason, the United States is at the epicenter of world Christianity today. No other nation in the world has more Christians within its borders than the United States. However, while the United States remains fairly religious, statisticians are starting to notice declines there, too, although certainly not as rapidly as what happened in Western Europe during the last half of the twentieth century.

The Roman Catholic Church is by far the largest

Fundamentalism · an Evangelical movement to recommit to the "fundamental" aspects of the Christian faith in the face of modern criticism and reform

Rapture · an apocalyptic theory that Christians will be swept up into the sky to meet Jesus upon his return and will remain safe with him while satanic forces wreak havoc on the Earth

Antichrist · an apocalyptic figure that some believe will arise in the end times and lead many astray

Liberal Protestantism · also known as **mainline Protestantism**; a collection of Protestant churches that embraces modern scholarly criticism of the Bible, feminism, LGBTQ activism, and pluralism

An American Methodist layman, John R. Mott (1865–1955) won a Nobel Peace Prize in 1946 and is remembered for leading many ecumenical and missionary efforts that were designed to bring about political, racial, social, and religious cooperation.

An outstanding progressive theologian and social thinker, Reinhold Niebuhr (1892–1971) may be best known for his widely-adapted "serenity prayer." In its earliest version, the prayer asked "for courage to change what must be altered, serenity to accept what cannot be helped, and insight to know the one from the other."

Photograph of William Seymour of the Azusa Street Revival, the birthplace of the modern Pentecostal movement.

Church of Christ, Disciples of Christ, and Christian churches—collectively known as the **Restoration Movement**—originated in the United States during a revival known as the **Second Great Awakening** in the early 1800s. As mentioned earlier, the most important religious product coming from the United States is the Pentecostal movement, which began in 1906 in Los Angeles at a gathering called the **Azusa Street Revival**. Led by a partially blind African American preacher whose parents were enslaved, **William Seymour** launched a global movement that is now the most significant form of Protestantism on the face of the Earth. Some projections are that global Pentecostalism will surpass Roman Catholicism by the end of the present century.

Restoration Movement · a group of Protestant denominations whose goal is to restore the original practices and beliefs of the early church; includes the Church of Christ, Disciples of Christ, and Christian Churches

Second Great Awakening · a nineteenth-century religious revival in North America that culminated in many social reform movements, as well as the Restoration Movement

Azusa Street Revival · a revival in Los Angeles in 1906 that is often seen as the birth of modern Pentecostalism

William Seymour · the African American preacher who led the Azusa Street Revival

Christian denomination in the United States, with around seventy million members, or around 22 percent of the nation's population. The largest Protestant denomination is the Southern Baptist Convention, with around fourteen million members.

Many Christian denominations, such as the Church of Jesus Christ of Latter-day Saints, were actually founded in the United States. The Church of Jesus Christ of Latter-day Saints has nearly seven million members in the United States and nearly seventeen million worldwide. The

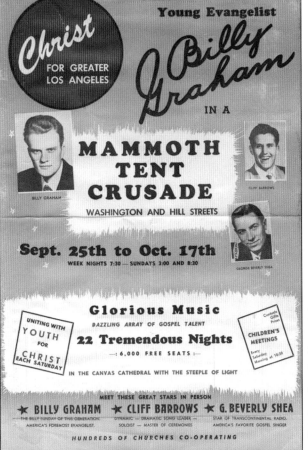

A 1949 crusade in Los Angeles catapulted a young Billy Graham into an international spotlight. The meeting space, a temporary "canvas cathedral," seated about six thousand to seven thousand people. Over fifty-seven days, more than three hundred fifty thousand people attended. Around three thousand people made decisions to follow Christ.

Christians in Laos face constant pressure and persecution from the Buddhist majority (67 percent) in the country. Protestants make up about 2 percent of the total population; 0.7 percent are Catholic.

During the twentieth century, Christianity became a faith based mainly in the southern hemisphere, or the Global South. Christianity is today largely a Latin American and African religion, as the Western world—primarily Western Europe—continues to move away from Christianity. Africa already has more Christians than Muslims, a fact that would have been considered totally impossible in 1900. Certain pockets of Asia are largely Christian; South Korea and the Philippines are examples. There are many Christians in China, perhaps as high as 8 percent of the country, although scholars do not really know. Latin America is thoroughly Christian, as it is the heart of the Roman Catholic Church.

Global South Christianity has grown rapidly largely because of higher-than-average fertility rates, especially in Africa, where fertility rates continue to outpace the rest of the world by far. Christianity in the Global South also tends to be far more conservative than Christianity in the United States and Western Europe. Demographers now note that liberal Protestantism tends to decline over time for a number of reasons: lower fertility rates; higher education rates, which are linked to lower fertility; and theology that tends not to promote evangelism. In liberal Protestantism, there is a pluralistic emphasis that tends to shy away from religious conversion, as it is often associated with colonial or imperial approaches to other cultures.

A fifty-six-foot-tall statue of Christ the Redeemer at Hundred Islands National Park, Pangasinan, Philippines.

12 ISLAM
As-Salamu Alaykum

Women praying at a mosque during Ramadan. Historically, attitudes about women's mosque attendance have varied widely. In some countries, women are not permitted to enter a mosque.

©Rawpixel.com, Adobe Stock

T he standard greeting said millions of times a day across the Muslim world is "**As-salamu alaykum**," which means "Peace be upon you." The appropriate response to this greeting is "Wa-alaykumu s-salam," or "And peace be upon you also." The **Quran** (10:10) actually commands Muslims to greet each other with a blessing of peace.

Islam is the second-largest religion in the world. There are nearly two billion Muslims in the world, around 24 percent of the global population. Some religious demographers suggest that Islam will surpass Christianity as the world's largest religion by the end of the century. This forecast is possible because Islam grows at a rate faster than most religions due to its slightly higher fertility rate. One interesting fact that

A woman from Malaysia appearing in a Muslim fashion show.

Photographer: Firdaus Latif (CC BY-SA 2.0)

Islam is the second-largest religion in the world. There are nearly two billion Muslims in the world, around 24 percent of the global population.

shows Islam's popularity is that **Muhammad**, the final prophet in Islam, is the most common first name in the world.

Islam is a fairly young religion compared to most of the other major world religions. It began in the 600s CE in what is Saudi Arabia today. Its rise to prominence occurred relatively quickly, as shortly after Muhammad died, his followers fanned out far and wide to spread the message of Islam. It grew to dominate the Middle East rather quickly, in about a century. The global Muslim community is called the **ummah**.

There are around twenty-seven nations (among the nearly two hundred nations of the world) that have formally adopted Islam as the state religion. Around fifty of the world's nations have an Islamic majority.[1] There are some nations that have a significant Muslim minority population, such as in India, where over two hundred million Muslims reside. The Indian subcontinent, now divided into India, Pakistan, and Bangladesh, is home to around one-third of the world's Muslim population. Indonesia is the nation with the most Muslims in the world, at well over two hundred million. Pakistan and India are not far behind, followed by Bangladesh, which has more than 150 million Muslims. Four African nations are in the world's top ten Muslim populations: Nigeria, Egypt, Algeria, and Sudan. Most people associate Islam with the Arab world, but

As-salamu alaykum · the standard greeting in the Muslim world, meaning "Peace be upon you"

Quran · "the recitation"; the words of the angel Gabriel to Muhammad that related God's final revelation to humankind

Muhammad · the founder of Islam; the last and greatest Messenger of God

Ummah · the global Muslim community

Muslim men bowing, kneeling, and praying inside of a mosque in Constantine, Algeria.

only about 20 percent of the world's Muslims reside in Arab countries.[2] Many parts of the world have an almost entirely Muslim population, with over 98 percent adhering to Islam, in places such as Mauritania, Western Sahara, Somalia, Tunisia, Afghanistan, Algeria, Iran, Yemen, Morocco, Niger, and others.

Basic Beliefs

Islam is strongly connected to Judaism and Christianity, although it developed in a unique trajectory, as we will see. Islam is an uncompromisingly monotheistic faith. It rebels against the Christian doctrine of the Trinity, preferring to declare that God is one—without qualification. In Islam, the oneness of God is called **Tawhid**. While *Tawhid* is not a word found in the Quran, it is known to Muslims as the most prized doctrine.[3]

Tawhid · the Islamic doctrine of the indivisible oneness of God

Jihad · "to struggle"; a doctrine that can signify the inner battle against temptation as well as the physical struggle against enemies of the faith

Allah · the Arabic word for God

The word *Islam* has a dual meaning: "submit" and "peace." Thus, Muslims are those who submit to the will of God and, in doing so, achieve personal and social peace. Muslims do not separate peace and justice. Thus, peace as understood in Islam has the connotation of justice having been done to achieve peace. Muslims promote the idea that the achievement of peace requires a struggle, or **jihad**.

Arabic for Allah, or God. Muslims are known for refraining from depicting God in artwork, as he is too great and inexpressible.

In Arabic, the word *God* is pronounced "**Allah**." Islam holds that while God revealed himself to past prophets, the final revelation was to Muhammad. Muslims declare two ideas above all others: (1) that God is one and (2) that Muhammad's interpretation of God is the final one and therefore the most authoritative. Muhammad is not worshiped. He is respected in the highest of terms, but he is not worshiped. He is seen as the model human and occupies a tender place in every Muslim's heart.

Muslims believe strongly that one's destiny is in God's hands. Islam has a strong notion of God's sovereignty. God will decide one's fate in the afterlife. The believer's duty is to live for God, submit to him, and struggle on behalf of Islam. Hopefully, God willing, the believer will be granted entrance into paradise at the final day. Evildoers suffer badly in Islam. They might scheme against other humans and win for a time, but ultimately, they will lose. God will surround evildoers and punish them harshly, but he will richly reward those who live righteously and believe in God. Islam believes strongly in the justice of God. Evildoers and schemers will not be able to escape the judgment of God, and they will suffer harsh punishments in the afterlife. Muslims have no reticence when describing the reality of hell. It is real, and there is no escape from it for those consigned by God to live there in the afterlife. In Islam, hell is called Jahannam and is derived directly from the biblical word *Gehenna*—the preferred term used by Jesus for hell.

Muslims believe that God created the world to reveal himself in nature. The idea here is that by observing the Earth, the order in the universe, and all of the intricately connected forms of life, one will eventually come to perceive that there is a God who created the world. The Quran affirms the Genesis story of God creating the world in six days (7:54), although scholars debate whether this means six literal twenty-four-hour periods.

Pre-Islamic Religion in Arabia

Populations in the Middle East, particularly in Arabia, practiced several religious traditions prior to Muhammad. Many tribes were polytheistic, while others were Christians of the Eastern varieties—Syrian, Nestorian, Byzantine, and Oriental Orthodox. Eastern Christianity was strong in the nearby patriarchate cities of Jerusalem, Antioch, and Alexandria. Damascus and Caesarea were strongly Christian and were also nearby. Judaism was present due to forced expulsions from Israel in 70 CE and the 130s CE. Zoroastrianism, the religion of the Persians, had a significant presence. Perhaps more than religion, Arabs in the time before Muhammad were more concerned with their tribal loyalties. While they may not have had a highly developed theological tradition, they did have a strong sense of loyalty to their kin that expressed itself in a willingness to fight and even die for the clan's survival.

Muhammad was fairly tolerant of other monotheists. The people he condemned harshly were polytheists, who had a supreme God whom they called Allah, as well as several other deities that were often considered to be descendants of Allah. Theirs was a statue-based faith, which he rejected as idolatrous. There was also animal sacrifice going on at the time. These polytheistic religions also had several other classes of beings such as angels, fairies, and demons. They were animistic, believing spirits occupied the natural elements, such as trees, rocks, and rivers.

The Meccans were particularly fond of a dark-colored stone—known in Islam as the Black Stone—that may have been a meteor. That stone now sits on the eastern corner of Islam's most sacred building: the Kaaba ("the Cube"). This is the holiest site in Islam and is the location of the world's most important mosque: the Masjid al-Haram, also known as the Grand Mosque. Muslims believe the Black Stone fell from heaven during the lives of Adam and Eve and helped them to know where to build an altar to God. That altar was rebuilt and enlarged many times throughout history, most famously by the prophet Abraham and his son, Ishmael. Eventually, it was constructed as a cube, and it now serves as Islam's geographical and spiritual epicenter. Muslims are strongly encouraged to visit the Kaaba at least once in their lifetime, and while there,

Jahannam · the Islamic hell, a place of extreme and eternal torment

Black Stone · a revered rock, possibly from a meteor, currently situated in the eastern corner of the Kaaba; believed to have fallen from heaven in the days of Adam and Eve

Kaaba · Islam's most sacred building and holiest site to which Muslims travel on pilgrimage and toward which Muslims pray five times daily

Masjid al-Haram · also known as the **Grand Mosque**; the mosque in Mecca in which the Kaaba is located

Panoramic view of the entire Masjid al-Haram mosque, Saudi Arabia (2018).

they should try to kiss the Black Stone if they manage to get close enough to it. This experience is a powerful one for Muslims, as they unite themselves to Islam's past, present, and future.

Muhammad

Muhammad lived from 570 CE to 632 CE. He was born into the **Quraysh** tribe. His father died before he was born, and his mother died when he was only six years old. His paternal uncle, a chief of the Quraysh, raised him. Muhammad never received formal education and was thus illiterate.

In his youth, Muhammad found work with a merchant caravan. He eventually married a wealthy widow named **Khadija** who was a businesswoman and head of a caravan. Muhammad married her when he was twenty-five years old and she was forty. Muhammad remained faithful and monogamous to her until she died. They were married for twenty-five years, and she bore him two sons and four daughters. Both sons died very young. Only one girl outlived Muhammad; it was his youngest daughter, named **Fatimah**. She is important in the history of Islam and revered for her true righteousness. She was loved deeply by her father.

Because Khadija was wealthy, Muhammad did not have to work. He devoted himself to praying and meditating in the hills around **Mecca**. One day, he was in a cave on Mount Hira when he was visited by the angel Gabriel during the Arabic month of Ramadan. He was given a command to "recite." Then Gabriel spoke, with the expectation that Muhammad would memorize the recitations. This was to be the first of many such encounters. These visits were purported by Muhammad to be the basis of God's final revelation to humankind, which Muhammad dictated to others so that they could be written down and preserved. These recitations are the basis of the Quran, which means "the recitation." Muhammad did not like these revelatory experiences, as they were accompanied by sweating and a ringing in his ears, causing him physical and mental anguish. He was depressed for three

Quraysh · the tribe into which Muhammad was born

Khadija · Muhammad's first wife; a wealthy widow and business owner who was fifteen years older than Muhammad

Fatimah · the youngest and beloved daughter of Muhammad; revered for her true righteousness

Mecca · Islam's holiest city, home to the Grand Mosque and the Kaaba

years after receiving the first revelation, and the revelations did not resume until he had recovered from his distressed state of mind.

The angelic visits from Gabriel began in 610 CE and continued for around twenty-two years, until his death in 632. They all occurred in the Arabian cities of Mecca and Medina.

One significant event in Muhammad's life is known as the **Night Journey**, which took place in 621. During that night, Muhammad flew on a winged horse from Mecca to Jerusalem. When he arrived at Jerusalem's Temple Mount, he ascended into heaven and visited with many of the prophets from Judaism and Christianity. He led them all in prayer. Once he came back to Earth, he mounted the winged horse again and flew back to Mecca. While the Quran mentions a night journey from one mosque to a far-off mosque (17:1), the details of the Night Journey arose over the centuries through various traditions. Muslims erected the **Dome of the Rock** at the site in 692 CE, where it can be seen from all over Jerusalem. The dome is erected over a rock that is believed to be where God created Adam, where Abraham nearly sacrificed his son (Ishmael in the Islamic tradition), and where God's presence on Earth is strongest and clearest. Jews continue to face the site for many of their prayers, as it is the location of their most revered place on Earth: Solomon's Temple. Muslims hold that Muhammad ascended to heaven from the rock located within the structure. The Dome of the Rock is considered crucial for understanding early Islam, as it was erected only about six decades after the death of Muhammad, and it displays many Muslim teachings that are inscribed into it.

Muhammad began to teach that there was only one God in existence and that all other gods were false. He taught about the final judgment and resurrection

Night Journey · Muhammad's sole miracle, during which he was taken by night from Mecca to Jerusalem on a winged horse, ascended to heaven to pray with the Judeo-Christian prophets, and then returned

Dome of the Rock · a shrine erected by Muslims in 692 CE over the rock believed to be the site where God created Adam and where Abraham nearly sacrificed his son

Image courtesy of the Metropolitan Museum of Art

The prophet Muhammad's celestial Night Journey. He is shown mounted on the Buraq, a steed with the face of a human, accompanied by angels. Nineteenth-century folio from Iran.

Photographer: Paolo Massa, (CC BY-SA 2.0)

The Dome of the Rock in Jerusalem, built on the Temple Mount in 692 CE on the rock believed to be the site of the near-sacrifice of Ishmael.

Hijra · the event of 622 CE when Muhammad and his followers migrated from Mecca to Yathrib to evade persecution

Yathrib · later renamed Medina; a city 250 miles north of Mecca that invited Muhammad to become its leader and from which Muhammad eventually conquered Mecca

Medina · originally Yathrib; the city that welcomed Muhammad and first fully embraced Islam

Qibla · the direction Muslims face during prayer; originally to Jerusalem but changed to Mecca during Muhammad's tenure in Medina

and gave vivid descriptions of heaven and hell. He urged people to be chaste, to pray often, to give to the poor, and to avoid the love of money. He also claimed he was the final prophet; thus, his message was superior to the previous ones. Muhammad did not see himself as a miracle worker, like Jesus Christ. Rather, he simply saw himself as the one chosen by God to reveal the final words of God to humans.

Muhammad's preaching soon became controversial, especially since he was opposed to the selling and worshiping of idols. The problem was that idols were a big business in that time and, therefore, threatened the livelihood of many. But one by one, people began to believe Muhammad's claims, beginning with his wife, Khadija, honored as the first Muslim. She died when Muhammad was about fifty years old. He then married several other women after her death.

The year 622 CE marks the year of the **Hijra**— "the migration." This was the year Muhammad and many of his followers moved from Mecca to **Yathrib**, which later changed its name to **Medina**. Muhammad was now fifty-two years old, and he had been invited to serve as leader of the city. His stature had grown in Mecca considerably, and he had acquired a large, though rivaled, following. In Mecca, there were threats on his life, his group was persecuted, and he had to be vigilant due to tribal jealousies. Thus, moving to Yathrib made sense, as Muhammad was very popular there. By the time Muhammad and his supporters migrated, most of the residents of Yathrib had already accepted Islam. However, there were other reasons they recruited Muhammad to come—for example, they desperately needed a respected diplomat to adjudicate their clan conflicts.

Muhammad was joyfully welcomed to Yathrib as the unquestioned leader of the city. Immediately, he had a small mosque built, as well as houses for all of those who immigrated with him. He issued a charter that spelled out the rights and responsibilities of all citizens of the city. The charter focused on religious freedom for those who committed themselves to protecting Yathrib. In earliest Islam, Muslims faced Jerusalem for their prayers, but in Yathrib, Muhammad changed the **qibla**—the direction for prayer—to Mecca after tensions with Jews arose. The call to prayer would

The prophet Muhammad asked his friend and wealthy trader Abu Bakr to emancipate Bilal, an enslaved Ethiopian who had recently converted to the message of Islam. Bilal is pictured here issuing a call to prayer from a rooftop. Folio from the *Hamla-i-Haidari*, which contains stories of the life of Muhammad (ca. 1820).

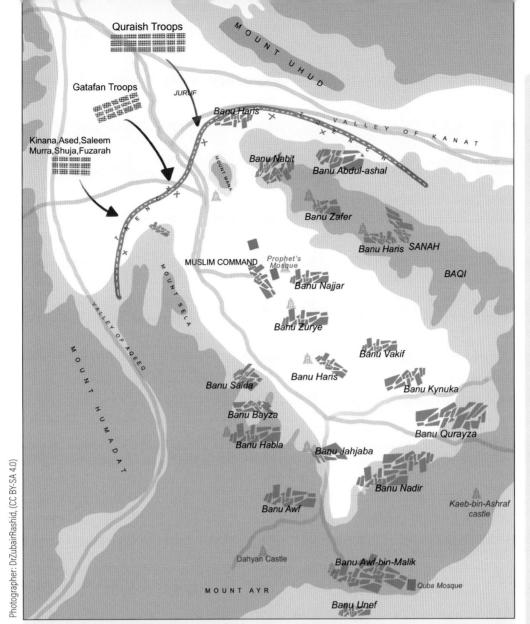

Surrounded by mountains, the residents of Medina withstood a siege by building a trench.

Bilal · a young Black slave in Medina who became the first muezzin

Zakat · a mandatory alms-giving, generally 2.5 percent of one's income, used to support widows and the poor

People of the Book · a term in the Quran for Jews and Christians that references their shared religious heritage with Islam; sometimes mentioned favorably and other times considered unbelievers to live in a state of subjection

Dhimmi · also known as **dhimmitude**; the institution of second-class status to People of the Book under Muslim rule

Battle of the Trench · a famous military engagement in 627 CE during which Muhammad led his small force to victory against a great confederate army of opposing Jews and Arabs; a major turning point in Islamic history

be done exclusively by the pristine human voice. The first person to call the Yathrib Muslims to prayer was a young Black slave named **Bilal**. Muhammad also ruled that the city should fast during the daylight hours during the month of Ramadan. He instituted the **zakat**—the giving of alms for the poor—during this time as well.[4] Islam was institutionalizing.

Muhammad realized there would be tensions with people from other religious backgrounds, and while he had little toleration for polytheists, he was more ambivalent about Jews and Christians, referred to in the Quran as **People of the Book**. These are the people who received earlier revelations from God through the biblical prophets. The Quran mentions this category of people more than fifty times. In some passages, the

Quran mentions People of the Book favorably, but in others, they are considered to be unbelievers and must live in a state of subjection (2:105, 59:2, 98:1, 5:57, 9:29), a concept known in Islam as **dhimmi** or **dhimmitude**.

Shortly after Muhammad consolidated power in Medina, he began to wage war against the city of Mecca, located 250 miles south of Medina. He and his followers also began to fight various Jewish tribes in Yathrib and the surrounding regions over issues related to land, resources (oases), trade, political loyalty, and military alliances. Tensions reached a height at the famous **Battle of the Trench** (627 CE), where three thousand Muslims defeated a confederate army of ten thousand Arabs and Jews at Medina. Afterwards, Muslim armies besieged the Banu Qurayza Jewish population and executed the men whom they considered traitors, while the women and children were taken as captives, many of them being sold into slavery later. The Battle of the Trench dramatically strengthened the resolve of the Muslim community and represents a turning point in the history of Islam.

The following year, in 628 CE, the **Battle of Khaybar** occurred, in which Muslims led by Muhammad defeated Jews in the oasis town of Khaybar. After the battle, a Jewish woman named **Zaynab bint Al-Harith** cooked a lamb shoulder for Muhammad after seasoning it with poison. Muhammad noticed it tasted bad and confronted her. She admitted to it, but Muhammad chose to spare her life. However, some of Muhammad's companions had already eaten and died. Muhammad claimed that the assassination attempt actually caused him physical pain for the rest of his life. About a year after the assassination attempt, Zaynab was captured by relatives of Muhammad's deceased companions, and she was put to death for her deed.

In the aftermath of the Battle of Khaybar, defeated Jews were required to give half of all their produce to the Muslims. This move set a precedent in Islamic history, known today as the **jizya**. The jizya is an annual tax that dhimmi people must pay if they refuse to convert to Islam. It allows them a regulated measure of freedom under Islamic rule, subject to payment. This battle, the assassination attempt, and the solution of an annual jizya is believed to have caused lasting tensions between the Muslim and Jewish communities in the region that radiated out from there.

By 629 CE, Muhammad and his warriors were unstoppable, and they made their way to do what Muhammad had long aspired to—conquer the city of Mecca and consolidate the entire Arabian Peninsula under the banner of Islam. Muhammad became known as a great military strategist, which enhanced the attraction of his religion. In the context of Arabia, great military leaders received immense respect.

When Muhammad conquered Mecca, he immediately purged the Kaaba of all statues, idols, and sacred objects, with one exception—the Black Stone. Muhammad kissed the stone, beginning a ritual that all Muslims emulate while on pilgrimage in Mecca. If they cannot manage to get close enough to kiss

Battle of Khaybar · a battle in 628 CE during which Muhammad and his forces defeated a Jewish community at the oasis town of Khaybar; after the battle, a Jewish woman attempted to take Muhammad's life

Zaynab bint Al-Harith · a Jewish woman who served Muhammad a lamb shoulder seasoned with poison in an assassination attempt; Muhammad survived and showed her mercy, but some of his companions perished, and their families sought justice by taking Zaynab's life

Jizya · an annual tax that dhimmi people must pay if they refuse to convert to Islam

Allahu akbar · "Allah is greater"; a repeated phrase during the five daily prayers

Hajj · a pilgrimage to the Kaaba taken during the last month of the Islamic calendar

The door of the Kaaba at Al-Haram in Mecca, Saudi Arabia (2019).

Photographer: as-artmedia, Adobe Stock

Photographer: Cri Piatelli, (CC BY-SA 4.0)

Air-conditioned tents set up in Mina City, located two miles from Mecca, to house pilgrims on Hajj.

Farewell Sermon · Muhammad's speech in the last year of his life, 632 CE, in which he addressed equality for all men, advocated for good treatment of women (unless they act indecently), and outlined inheritance law

Aisha · Muhammad's third and youngest wife, said to be his favorite

Abu Bakr · Muhammad's close friend and the father of Aisha; chosen to be the first caliph

Ali · Muhammad's son-in-law and cousin, whom some Muslims believed to be the rightful successor to Muhammad; eventually became the fourth caliph

the stone, then they should at least point to it. Some Muslims argue that on Judgment Day, the Black Stone will appear with eyes and a tongue and will testify to those who kissed it with true devotion in their hearts.

After conquering Mecca, Muhammad became the most powerful leader of the Arabian people. Most Meccans converted to Islam during his final years of life as his influence grew. He sent missionaries out to spread Islam. He engaged in several key battles, and he required those he defeated to either convert to Islam or pay the jizya tax. Muhammad married a total of thirteen women, eleven of them in the final decade of his life, as he continued to have great militaristic success.

In 632 CE, the year of his death, Muhammad completed a pilgrimage to Mecca, which set the precedent for the concept of **Hajj**—one of the Five Pillars of Islam. He preached his famous **Farewell Sermon** that addressed the equality of all men, and he advocated for good treatment of women, unless they acted indecently. He also outlined his views of how inheritance law should work.

In 632, at the age of sixty-two, Muhammad died in the arms of **Aisha**—his third and youngest wife, said to be his favorite. Upon his death, there was a major fracture in the ummah regarding who should lead the Islamic community. Some thought it should be **Abu Bakr**, Muhammad's close friend and the father of Aisha, while others believed Muhammad's son-in-law (and cousin), **Ali**, should be the successor. Abu Bakr was chosen to become the first

CALL TO PRAYER

The call to prayer usually follows this format:

- **Allahu akbar**, or Allah is greater (four times).
- I testify there is no god but Allah (two times).
- I testify that Muhammad is the Messenger of Allah (two times).
- Hasten to the prayer (two times).
- Hasten to salvation (two times).
- Allah is greater (two times).
- There is no god but Allah (one time).

There are slight variations of the prayers within different schools of Islam.

caliph (successor). The party of Ali, however, believed strongly that Muhammad had appointed Ali as successor; they became known as the **Shi'as**, or "the party." The party that supported Abu Bakr as caliph was known as the **Sunni**, or "lawful." This was the beginning of the Sunni/Shi'a divide in Islam that continues to haunt global Islam today.

The Five Pillars

These **Five Pillars** are the most important practical obligations to which faithful Muslims must adhere:

1. *Shahada* (testimony of faith). "There is no God but God, and Muhammad is the Messenger of God." This is whispered by a father into the ear of a newborn baby, and it is also whispered into the ear of a dying person. This is how a person converts to Islam; they merely say the **Shahada**, with sincerity and preferably with witnesses.

2. *Salah* (prayer). Five times throughout the day, faithful Muslims devote themselves to prayer. An **adhan**—call to prayer—is issued by the **muezzin**, who traditionally stands atop the minaret (although it is done on loudspeakers in modern times).

   Muslims must engage in washing prior to praying. The washing process is called **wudu**, and it consists of washing the face, arms, head, and feet. Women and men are separated for prayer due to possible temptation (24:30–31). In Middle Eastern countries, women normally do not enter the mosque, as Muhammad urged women to pray at home instead.[5]

   Reciting the Quran is crucial for **salah**. During each of the five obligatory prayers, the al-Fatiha (the opening surah of the Quran) is recited, as well as other passages according to one's own choosing.

3. *Zakat* (almsgiving). This is an amount of money given to charity, mandatory for all Muslims who have enough to give. It can range in amount but is often around 2.5 percent. Many Muslim nations simply withhold the zakat as a tax, as the money is used to help the poor and needy.

4. *Sawm* (fasting). Muslims are required to fast, or **sawm**, during the holy month of Ramadan—when the Quran was first revealed to Muhammad. They are obligated to fast all day, but they can function normally before sunrise or after sunset. They fast from all eating, drinking, smoking, and sex during the daylight hours of Ramadan. Daylight and dark are defined as being able to determine the difference between a white or black thread. The sick, those traveling, new mothers, soldiers on active duty, and small children are exempt. Muslims end each day of Ramadan with a large and wholesome meal—called an **iftar**—that is often taken with friends and family. Those who complete the fast properly will be rewarded with absolution of their sins.

5. *Hajj* (pilgrimage). Pilgrimage to the Kaaba went on even before Muhammad's time. Muslims revere the structure, and whoever can afford to go must do so at least once in their lives. The special pilgrimage must be done during the year's twelfth and final month, known as **Dhu al-Hijjah**. Islam allows pilgrimages to Mecca at any time of the year. These pilgrimages are known as **umrah**, but they are not nearly as important as the Hajj, which has specific dates in accordance with the Muslim calendar. During the Hajj, Muslims from all lands travel to Mecca to complete several rituals. It is said that the gates to hell are closed during the Hajj; thus, if one dies on a Hajj, one is guaranteed entrance to paradise. During Hajj, Muslims have to walk a great distance to the Kaaba and must wear simple garments, usually white (but not required to be any color). Non-Muslims are prohibited from entering the city of Mecca. Non-Muslims can visit Medina, but they must not get anywhere near the Prophet's Mosque, built by Muhammad.

Muslims visit Medina as they perform Hajj.

During Hajj, Muslims complete several noteworthy rituals that are often ancient, some even going back to the time of Abraham:

- Walk quickly seven times between the hills of Safa and Marwah.
- Drink from the well of Zamzam, which has connections to Ishmael—the father of all Arabs.
- Make seven circumambulations around the Kaaba.
- Kiss (or point toward) the Black Stone.
- Sacrifice an animal to remember Abraham's near-sacrifice of Ishmael.
- Visit Medina, where Muhammad is buried.
- Throw stones at pillars representing the devil.

Those who complete the Hajj typically shave or trim their heads (men) or trim their hair (women). Those who successfully complete the requirements are given the label **Haji**.

Additional Beliefs of Muslims

Muslims, like Jews, insist there is no division in God. They are monotheists and deny the existence of any other gods. Some theorize that Islam spread so rapidly partly because Christians were so divided about the notion of the Trinity.

Muslims believe **there are ninety-nine names for God in the Quran.** God is merciful and compassionate but also perfectly just, and he will not make any mistakes about who goes to heaven or hell.

Muslims believe **there are three spiritual classes of beings:**

- **Jinn** (also known as **djinn** or **genie**), which are made of fire and air and can either serve humans faithfully or pester them with misfortune. Some jinn are good, and some are bad.

Sunni · the largest sect of Islam, representing 85 percent of the ummah, that believes the caliph need not be a direct descendant of Muhammad; they also reject the innate authority of an imam in favor of elevating the Quran and the Hadith as the ultimate sources of authority

Shahada · a testimony of faith; the public confession that "there is no God but God, and Muhammad is the Messenger of God"

Adhan · the call to prayer issued by the muezzin at set times throughout the day

Muezzin · the man who issues the adhan from atop a minaret

Wudu · the washing process in which Muslims engage prior to praying

Salah · ritualized prayers practiced five times per day

Sawm · required fasting during the daylight hours of the holy month of Ramadan

Iftar · the large and wholesome meal taken after dark by a Muslim family during Ramadan

Dhu al-Hijjah · the twelfth and final month of the Islamic calendar, during which practitioners take the Hajj

Umrah · pilgrimages not taken during the month of Dhu al-Hijjah

Haji · a person who has successfully completed the Hajj

Jinn · also known as **djinn** or **genie**; spiritual beings made of fire and air who can either serve humans faithfully or pester them with misfortune

- **Shayatin** are devils or demons that were created from the fires of hell and are grotesque in appearance. They tempt humans by whispering into their hearts. Their leader is **Iblis**—the Satan figure of Islam who is the father of the Shayatin. Iblis is the tempter of humans, much like in the Judeo-Christian traditions.
- **Angels** were created from light and are the servants of God. Led by the four archangels, Gabriel, Michael, **Azrael** (angel of death), and **Israfil** (who will blow a trumpet to signal the Judgment Day), the angels interact with humans. They protect Muslims from the attacks of demons. Angels are also associated with judgment in Islam, as they record the deeds of humankind, both evil and good.

Muslims, like most Christians, believe **there will be a Judgment Day**. They believe that souls sleep until the Resurrection Day—a day ushered in by the archangel Israfil's trumpet blasts. People will be judged according to their own book of deeds that God will reveal to them. Everyone will be consigned to either heaven or hell. Heaven is a place of abundance, where all desires will be met. It is described as a paradise garden (**al-Janna**) in Islam, and it appears eighty times in the Quran. There will be mansions, flowing rivers, expensive carpets, and all manner of delicious meats and fruits. People will wear gold, pearls, and fine silks. They will also be married to beautiful spouses (2:25) and enjoy their children who also ended up in paradise. The greatest part of being in heaven is that those who enter will experience God's approval. One irony is that

An eighteenth-century depiction of Israfil, the archangel who will blow a trumpet to signal the arrival of Judgment Day.

while alcohol is forbidden to Muslims on Earth, in heaven, they will be able to drink wine without becoming intoxicated.

Jahannam is **the concept of hell in Islam.** It is a place of excruciating pain and punishment, based on the evils one committed in the flesh. Punishments will be both physical and mental, and most Muslims believe it will last eternally. There are various levels of hell, depending upon how wicked the person behaved on Earth. Reminiscent of Dante's descriptions, those who enter hell will experience all manner of suffering and torture, from boiling water poured on them to hooks into their bodies, dragging them. People will plead for forgiveness, but to no avail.

Shayatin · devils or demons that were created from the fires of hell and are grotesque in appearance; they tempt humans by whispering into their hearts

Iblis · the Satan figure of Islam who is the father of the Shayatin and the tempter of humans

Angels · spiritual beings who were created from light and are the servants of God

Azrael · one of the four archangels; the angel of death

Israfil · one of the four archangels who will blow a trumpet to signal Judgment Day

al-Janna · heaven; a paradise garden where all desires will be met

Shariah · literally "the path leading to water"; a legal code derived from the laws of God

Muslims believe that *humans should live according to God's laws while on Earth;* thus, there is a notion of **Shariah**—the path leading to water—that has been developed over time. Shariah law is rooted in the Quran and in the **Sunnah**—the traditions and practices of Muhammad—and can be quite complicated, depending upon various schools of jurisprudence. Muslims do not agree on how Shariah law should work. Some are more adamant that the early ummah's example should be followed, whereas many modern Muslims have essentially replaced Shariah law with European and American approaches to social and even personal conduct. For instance, some Muslims have no problem shaking hands with non-Muslims. However, traditional Shi'a Muslims believe that if they shake hands with a non-Muslim, then they will be obligated to do ritual purification. There are also concerns about male–female interaction in Shariah law. Many Muslims believe that touching a non-family member of the opposite sex—even shaking of hands—is forbidden. Some Muslims hold that women may not even be seen by nonfamily members of the opposite sex unless they are covered partially or fully.

The Quran

The holy text of Islam is the Quran, which means "recitation." Muslims believe there is a heavenly prototype, written on a preserved tablet (85:22), which is in heaven with God (13:39). It was revealed to Muhammad through the angel Gabriel. The ninety-sixth chapter of the Quran is generally thought to be the first revelation from Gabriel to Muhammad:

> *Read! In the name of your Lord who created. He created man from a clot. Read! Your Lord is the Most Bountiful One, who taught by the pen, who taught man what he did not know. But man is rebellious when he thinks he is self-sufficient.*[6]

Muhammad's secretary, named **Zayd bin Thabit**, wrote down the recitations because Muhammad was illiterate; he could neither read nor write (7:157). Islam teaches that Muhammad's illiteracy shows the veracity of the revelation that came down through him. The Quran claims that Muhammad is the **Seal**

of the **Prophets** (33:40)—meaning there will never be another divine revelation after Muhammad, nor will there ever be another earthly prophet until Judgment Day.

The Quran is organized according to the length of chapters, which are known as **surahs** (in Arabic, the plural of surah is suwar). There are 114 chapters. The longest ones are early, with the exception of the first one, the **al-Fatiha**, or "the Opening," and the shorter ones appear later in the text. The Quran is roughly the same size as the Christian New Testament. Each surah has a title and begins with these words: "In the Name of Allah, the Most Gracious, the Most Merciful." The only

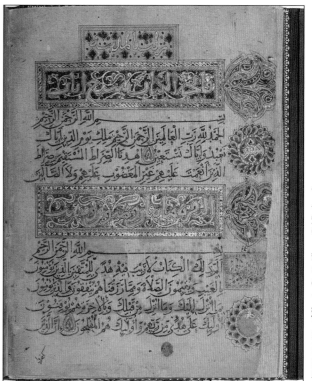

Headings for the first two chapters of the Quran, the al-Fatiha and the al-Baqara. Calligraphed by Ibn al-Bawwab (d. 1022 CE).

Image courtesy of Chester Beatty Library. Public domain.

Named the "Pink Quran" because of its use of expensive parchment from one of the earliest paper mills in Spain, this ornate thirteenth-century manuscript uses gold disks as verse numbers. The blue outlined teardrop is a prostration mark to guide the reader when to kneel.

This is one of the big differences regarding scripture and religion—in Islam, people must learn Arabic so they can understand God. Typically, Muslims require converts to learn at least some Arabic.

The Quran's sacrosanct presence in Islam is reinforced through calligraphy—the preferred art form for Muslims. Quranic calligraphy is seen commonly on Islamic art and architecture, as well as in Islamic homes. Muslims also revere memorizing the Quran. A person who memorizes the complete Quran is known as a **hafiz**, or a guardian of the Quran. The Islamic world supports many television shows and competitions geared to helping people reach the status of hafiz. In some cases, large cash prizes are given to the champions who recite the entire Quran excellently. Muslims from all over the world compete in these competitions, which are often held in Egypt and Saudi Arabia.

There is a general misconception that Muslims may not have art depicting humans or animals because of the tendency of humans to fall into idolatry. This idea is not quite accurate. It is true that Muslims today tend not to depict humans or animals on their architecture, preferring instead calligraphy or geometric designs. But there are plenty of examples of Muslims depicting Muhammad and other prophets in art, both throughout history and even still today. A cursory glance at Muslim children's books shows ample depictions of humans, prophets, and animals. The issue is that Muslims are not supposed to depict God in their art, as God is too great. In Islam, God is inexpressible.

The Quran is held in high esteem in Islam, to the point that the very book itself is treated with reverence. Muslims never put the Quran on the floor. They wash their hands before handling it. They kiss it and put it on their heads for a blessing. Some even complete a full religious ablution before reading it: washing hands, arms, mouth, nostrils, head, and feet—with running water—before taking it up and reading it.

Muslims have a theological concept called **I'jaz**, or **inimitability**, which applies to the Quran. This means that there is nothing else as beautiful as the Quran. It surpasses all in terms of reliability and truth. It is incomparable because it is miraculous. It is so self-evidently superior to anything else on Earth that it proves the prophetic authority of Muhammad. How could a

exception is surah 9 (al-Tawbah, "the Repentance"), which does not begin with the **Bismillah** ("In the name of Allah").

Bismillah · the invocation, "In the Name of Allah, the Most Gracious, the Most Merciful," which opens every surah in the Quran except surah 9

Hafiz · "guardian of the Quran"; someone who memorizes the Quran in its entirety

I'jaz · also known as **inimitability**; the belief that the Quran miraculously surpasses all in its reliability and truth and that nothing else on Earth can match it

Muslims believe their scripture is not simply inspired text. Rather, the words of the Quran are the very words of God. Muslims believe the Quran is God's final words to humans before Judgment Day. Muslims believe that while God can easily speak all human languages, his preferred language is Arabic. Thus, Muslims view translations with suspicion. The Quran is not truly the Quran when it becomes translated into another language.

QURANIC DISPUTES

The compilation of the Quran began when Muhammad died and Abu Bakr, the first caliph, began to rule the ummah. However, many others claimed to be prophets and thus turned away from Abu Bakr. In response, Abu Bakr launched a series of wars—the Ridda Wars (Apostasy Wars) to kill these self-proclaimed prophets and to bring their followers back into the ummah. The problem was that many Muslims died during the Ridda Wars, and as a result, many of the people who knew the recitations of Muhammad died in battle. Abu Bakr decided to consult Zayd—Muhammad's scribe—and ask him to assist in compiling a written Quran before it would become impossible to do so. He wanted to preserve the text while some of those who knew Muhammad were still living. Thus, Abu Bakr, Zayd, and Umar (the second caliph) gathered the scattered sources into one text. They identified important pieces of Quranic text from stones, palm leaf stalks, parchments (skins), and camel bones, as well as various oral traditions. Eventually, they put together what they believed to be a complete text of the Quran.

However, the third caliph, Uthman, did something controversial. He gathered up all the previous texts and versions of Qurans, created a new version (authorized by himself), and had all other available texts burned. Whether they were small manuscripts or completed versions, he had them destroyed. He then proclaimed that his authorized version should be distributed to the Muslim community, which was, by that point, scattered in many places. By doing this celebrated act, he became the protector of the Quran, supposedly in its truest and purest form.

There is one more important piece to this story, however. Shi'ites doubt key aspects of the Sunni version of the story of how the Quran came into being. Rather, they believe that Muhammad supervised the compilation of the Quran with the assistance of Ali, who became the fourth caliph. The problem is that Abu Bakr rejected Ali's copy of the Quran, which was more chronological in nature. In addition, Ali's Quran probably contained additional material. Even the possibility that some of the Quran may have been lost is an idea highly offensive to the Sunni community. Shi'ites profoundly regret the fact that Ali's version is now lost to history. These events are crucial and are at the very core the Sunni/Shi'a conflict.[7]

> **Ridda Wars** · also known as the **Apostasy Wars**; a series of wars launched by Abu Bakr against self-proclaimed prophets who arose after Muhammad's death
>
> **Uthman** · the third caliph and husband of two of Muhammad's daughters who conquered more Persian territory, part of Afghanistan, and part of Armenia; one of the oldest caliphs in history

© Bridgeman Images

Nineteenth-century engraving of the first four successors to the prophet Muhammad that, according to Sunni tradition, "rightly guided" the community: Abu Bakr (r. 632–34), Umar ibn al-Khattab (r. 634–44), Uthman ibn Affan (r. 644–56), and Ali ibn Abi Talib (r. 656–61).

man have invented something so perfect? According to Muslims, the Quran exceeds anything else on Earth and therefore must be divine in origin.

The Quran is believed to grant a level of safety and security to Muslims, which is why Quranic verses are often placed on jewelry and clothes. Verses adorn mosques and appear on walls. Quranic passages are worn on pendants and emblazoned on soldiers' apparel.

The Quran is divine in origin and comes directly from the mouth of God, and it therefore brings peace and security to a Muslim's mind and heart.

Muslims look to the Quran for authoritative advice on how to live—everything from how children should treat their parents to matters pertaining to the environment are directly or indirectly addressed. The core of the Quran, however, is how to submit to God to avoid hell and eventually end up in paradise. Judgment plays a critical role in the Quran.

The Quran gives careful attention to various prophets throughout history to advise people on how to live righteously. According to Islam, God sent one hundred twenty four thousand prophets to humankind over the years, the first being Adam and the last being Muhammad. However, the most important prophets, such as Moses, Jesus, and Muhammad, are of a unique class and are also known as **Messengers** because their words have been preserved in written text.

There are some prophets in the Quran who do not appear in the Old or New Testaments, such as Hud, Saleh, and Shu'ayb. However, the vast majority of the prophets mentioned, such as Adam, Enoch, Noah, Abraham, Ishmael, Joseph, Moses, Elijah, David, Jonah, John the Baptist, and Jesus, are familiar to both Jews and Muslims. The stories are often a little different than the biblical versions, however. For example, in

Circumcision · required in Islam for all boys, though the age of circumcision varies from culture to culture

Messengers · a unique class of the most important prophets that God has sent to Earth, such as Moses, Jesus, and Muhammad, whose words have been preserved in a written text

CHILDREN

Islam has regional and cultural rites surrounding children. One interesting practice is when a baby is seven days old, its head is shaved, and the parents give the equivalent of the weight of the hair in currency to the poor. The father will also whisper the Shahada into the baby's ear, as well as the adhan—the call to prayer. This is also the time for the baby's name to be assigned, which, in the case of many boys, is Muhammad—widely believed to be the most popular name in the world. **Circumcision** is required for all boys in Islam, although the age can differ from culture to culture. People in some cultures circumcise babies, whereas others circumcise a boy upon puberty as a sign he has become a man. Female circumcision is a common practice in parts of the Islamic world, but there are disagreements about whether it is a cultural or religious practice.

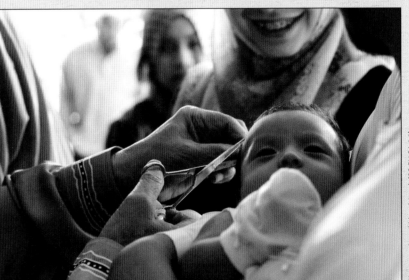

Babies receive their first haircut during aqiqah, an Islamic tradition on welcoming the birth of a child. Seremban, Malaysia (2014).

Photographer: Ikhlasul Amal, (CC BY-SA 2.0)

In the Quran, the prophet Elijah (Elias) rebukes God's people for idolatry (37:124–28). In later tradition, he rescues Prince Nur ad-Dahr from drowning in a river. Sixteenth-century illustration from the Hamzanama.

Mary with Jesus (Isa). Sixteenth-century Persian manuscript.

Islam, Abraham nearly sacrificed his son Ishmael, not Isaac. **Ishmael** (in Islam pronounced **Ismail**) receives a lot of attention in Islam, as he and his father built the Kaaba together, and Muhammad is considered to be a direct descendant of Ishmael.

Jesus—known as **Isa** in the Quran—enjoys a high status in Islam. One of his most important roles is that he announced the coming of Muhammad. In Islam, Jesus is like John the Baptist in Christianity in that he announced the coming of another (see John 14:16–17, 14:26, 15:26, and 16:7). Christians would identify the "Advocate" with the Holy Spirit, whereas Muslims argue this figure prophesied by Jesus is actually Muhammad. Otherwise, much of what the New Testament teaches about Jesus is accepted as true in the Quran: he was born of a virgin (3:42–55), he performed miracles, he is the only prophet in the Quran who is said to be strengthened by the Holy Spirit (2:87, 253), he was sent to the Israelites, he is the only person described as the Word of God in the Quran (4:171),

and there will be a second coming of Jesus that will result in universal peace and justice. Where Islam deviates, however, is in Jesus's divinity. In Islam, Jesus is only a Messenger, not part of God's nature (5:72–75). Indeed, Islam condemns the person who deifies Jesus. According to the Quran, the person who believes in the Trinity is destined for a painful afterlife in hell.

Crucially, Muslims do not believe in the crucifixion or resurrection of Jesus. They believe the apostles mistakenly thought Jesus was crucified, when in reality he was taken up into heaven, like Elijah in the Old Testament (3:55, 4:156–59, 5:117). While Muslims do not believe Jesus was resurrected, the Quran does have a passage (19:33) in which Jesus predicts his resurrection. This passage is often interpreted as being

Ishmael · pronounced **Ismail**; the son of Abraham and father of the Arab people, believed to be the direct ancestor of Muhammad; built the Kaaba with his father

Isa · the Quranic name for Jesus, believed to be a prophet who announced the coming of Muhammad

Mosques · also known as **masjids**, "places of prostration"; Islamic houses of worship

Imam · respected men who are chosen by the congregation to lead due to their competence in the Quran and their righteous lifestyle; in Shi'a Islam, revered as infallible examples of God's will for man's life

Isma · the Shi'ite doctrine of the incorruptibility of the imams, that they are morally infallible holy men who must be obeyed and respected

Madrasa · a school for studying the Quran

Mihrab · a niche in the wall indicating the direction of Mecca, the city toward which Muslims are obligated to pray

Nikah · Islamic marriage; a legal contract meant to protect women in case of widowhood or abandonment

Muslim men studying the Quran in Umayyad Mosque in Damascus, Syria.

in a future time, after Jesus's second coming. Muslims do not see a need for the crucifixion or resurrection since they do not believe in the doctrine of original sin. They believe that humans will be judged according to their own conduct, and nobody will be able to save those who have condemned themselves through a sinful life.

Worship at the Mosque

Muslims can pray anywhere and do not depend upon a building for saying their prayers. Houses of worship in Islam are called **mosques** or **masjids**; however, anywhere can be a "place of prostration," which is actually the meaning of the word *mosque*. In some nations, Muslims pray right on the street or anywhere else when the call to prayer is made.

The special day for Muslims gathering at the mosque is on Friday at noon. It is not a day of rest. This is simply the day when Muslims are obligated to attend the mosque, pray, and hear a sermon by an **imam** or another Muslim leader well-versed in the Quran. In Sunni Islam, imams are not necessarily clergymen. They are usually respected men who are chosen by the congregation to lead due to their competence in the Quran and their righteous lifestyle. Sometimes they are salaried, but not usually. They do carry out many of the tasks that clergy from other religions might assume, such as teaching, visitation, counseling, and administration of the religious organization.

Imams in Shi'a Islam are understood quite differently. They are thought to be chosen by God and are considered to be holy men who are perfect examples of living the Islamic life. This concept is called **Isma**, or incorruptible. They are morally infallible and therefore must be followed and obeyed. This is a debated topic in Islam.

Mosques often have a library for reading about the faith. They also may have a school nearby for studying the Quran, known as a **madrasa**. Common to every mosque is a **mihrab**—a niche in the wall indicating the direction of prayer toward Mecca. Mosques also typically have a minaret on the grounds, a tower used for calling Muslims to prayer. Common to mosques is also a place to wash before prayers, full of fresh and running water.

Women in Islam

Muslims believe that Islam significantly improved the status of women, especially when compared to women

BIRTH CONTROL, ABORTION, AND CELIBACY

Birth control and abortion are controversial topics in Islam. Some Muslims strongly oppose any form of birth control and any abortion. Other schools are more flexible—for example, allowing coitus interruptus—only if agreed upon by both husband and wife. Some schools, such as the Hanafi school, allow abortion up to four months of pregnancy. Most Muslims would frown upon abortion except in rare cases, and certainly anything after four months would be considered infanticide. Islamic scholarship tends to support in vitro fertilization when necessary, and it strongly opposes surrogate motherhood on the grounds that it is sinful and could cause a host of unforeseen problems for the families involved.

In Islam, celibacy is discouraged. Marriage is expected rather early to avoid sexual temptations. Any kind of sex outside of marriage is haram, or forbidden (4:25, 5:5, 17:32, 25:68). Islamic marriage is called **nikah**. It is a legal contract intended to protect the woman in case the man dies or abandons her. Marriage must be mutually consented to by both the male and the female. The couple should meet before marriage and decide on their compatibility together. Marriage requires at least two witnesses. The bridegroom must give a dowry to the woman, which can be in cash or some other form of wealth; again, this is protection for the wife in case of widowhood or singleness. A Muslim man may have four wives as long as he can take care of them equally, and the women must be monotheists. It should be pointed out the Quran clearly states that while all of a man's wives should be treated equally, practically speaking, this is impossible (4:129).

in pre-Islamic Arabia. They claim that Muhammad stopped female infanticide, which was common. Muslims claim Muhammad also helped women in terms of divorce, giving them more leverage and benefits, since under his teachings they were allowed to keep a sum of money given to them by the husband's family when they were married (4:4). He also introduced the idea that widows were to be supported for a year using funds from their husband's estate (2:240). After a year, they became free to marry. This was partly to ensure the paternity of a child, should the widow choose to remarry.

Islam holds that a woman may have only one husband, and that husband must be Muslim. Typically, an Islamic man may have up to four wives, and they should be monotheists (4:3). The wives must be provided for and treated equally. Muhammad allowed himself twelve wives after Khadija died. Some wealthy Islamic men marry numerous wives, claiming precedence from the life of Muhammad. Polygyny was common in the context of early Islam, as Islamic expansion meant many men were killed during war, leaving thousands of widows and orphans behind.

The situation of women in Islam is not monolithic. Some Islamic nations

A young Muslim woman in the Thar Desert near Jaisalmer, India (2009).

have practices that are similar to Western nations on issues related to women. For example, many Islamic nations, such as Pakistan, Bangladesh, Turkey, Indonesia, Kyrgyzstan, Kosovo, Tunisia, and others, have had female heads of state. Some Islamic countries allow women essentially the same professional opportunities as men.

Some Islamic societies are relatively patriarchal in comparison with Western societies. For instance, many Islamic societies tend to be segregated along gender lines. The most conservative types of Islam—for example, in Saudi Arabia—have many restrictions on women; they must completely cover themselves, and they must be accompanied by a related male when in public. In recent years, even the government of Saudi Arabia has loosened up in several areas of public life, such as allowing women the right to drive cars since 2018, as long as the husband consents.

While the Quran is not extremely specific about head coverings, most Islamic women nevertheless choose to cover their heads with a garment known as a **hijab**. This word, which when translated means "barrier," does not appear in the Quran, but it is interpreted to mean that women must be modest in all things. A few passages of the Quran speak about women covering themselves (24:31, 33:59). These passages have been interpreted in various ways: hijab (a bit of hair can

be seen), chador (all hair covered while face is seen), niqab (only eyes can be seen), and burqa (completely veiled). When women are in the home or exclusively with other women, they do not have to cover themselves. As Muslims immigrate to non-Muslim parts of the world, issues related to hijabs have become controversial. For example, in 2011, France imposed a ban on full-face veils in public places, citing security and cultural concerns.

Because of the fact that many passages in the Quran are directed at both men and women—for example, both women and men will be judged, and both righteous men and women will inherit paradise—it is often argued that Islam is egalitarian in key ways. All Muslims, regardless of gender, must pray, give alms, and obey God and Muhammad.

Some feminists have vocalized their opposition to unnecessarily conservative forms of Islam, arguing that Muhammad actually improved the situation of women in his day. Others, however, cite passages in the Quran, such as 4:34, that point toward patriarchy: "Men are in charge of women, because Allah hath made the one of them to excel the other, and because they spend of their property." As many Muslims interact routinely with Westerners, there are pressures on traditionalist forms of Islam to consider Western gender norms. Some traditional forms of Islam, however, argue that the Western world is not the appropriate model to follow since the majority do not adhere to Islam.

In Europe, there has been a trend toward prohibiting women from wearing face-covering veils, especially burqas or niqabs (pictured left). Most bans on religious dress have not targeted hijabs or chadors (pictured right), since neither obscure a woman's face.

© oes, Adobe Stock

© Jasmin Merdan, Adobe Stock

Meat market in Brixton, London (2008).

Restrictions in Islam

Jews have the notion of kosher. Muslims have the notions of **halal** (permitted) and **haram** (forbidden). Muslims may not eat pork, and they must slaughter animals in the name of Allah, meaning their meat should normally be slaughtered by a fellow Muslim. They must not eat carnivorous animals, including birds, and they should not drink blood or consume alcoholic beverages. Dogs are considered unclean in Islam, while cats and birds are fine as pets. Muslims may not gamble, nor can they charge interest when loaning to people, although the Muslim world has come up with creative ways to still turn a profit in industries such as banking. For instance, if a person in the Muslim world has little money yet wants to purchase a home, he or she needs the help of a bank. Thus, the bank will buy the house, raise the price of it, and then sell it back to the customer. The customer then must make payments. Some Muslims argue that this system typically saves the consumer a lot of money in comparison with the Western model, which is based on compound interest.

Jihad

The word jihad means "to struggle" and can mean to conduct warfare against unbelievers or to fight an inner battle against evil and temptation. It is often referred to as the **sixth pillar** of Islam. Sometimes Muslims differentiate the greater jihad (fighting against temptation) from the lesser jihad (warfare). Some Muslims argue that Islam should proactively fight against unbelievers, while some Muslims argue that this is not necessary

FUNERALS

When a Muslim dies, the deceased should have his or her mouth closed, eyes closed, and body covered with a clean sheet. A prayer of forgiveness is offered on behalf of the deceased, and the person should be buried as soon as possible. Autopsies and cremation are generally forbidden, as Muhammad is reported as saying in a hadith that the breaking of the bones of a dead person is like breaking the bones of a living person. Embalming is forbidden unless under extreme circumstances in which a person must be moved from one place to another. The deceased's body must not be viewed by anyone outside the family. The body is washed three times by family, and a deceased woman's hair is braided. The body is shrouded in three white sheets, and ropes are used to secure the sheets onto the body. The body is taken to a mosque for prayers. After prayers, the body is taken to the cemetery for burial. The mourning period lasts for forty days.

anymore. Muslims are divided on what jihad actually means and upon whom jihad should be declared. The European colonial era is a source of resentment in Islam, and thus, there can be found an anti-colonial, anti-Western dimension in some forms of Islam today. However, there is also a constituency of world Islam that appreciates many aspects of Western culture and even its politics.

Islam had a period of rapid expansion shortly after Muhammad died, specifically from 632 to 732 CE. The rise of Islam coincided with the fall of the Byzantine Empire (Eastern Roman Empire), as well as the fall of the Persian Empire, known in the 600s CE as the Sassanid Empire. The Islamic conquests were most successful during the one hundred years following Muhammad's death in 632. The Arabs conquered many territories, including Palestine, Syria, Persia,

> **Halal** · that which is permitted for Muslims
>
> **Haram** · that which is forbidden for Muslims
>
> **Sixth pillar** · a term sometimes used to refer to jihad to emphasize its importance in Islam

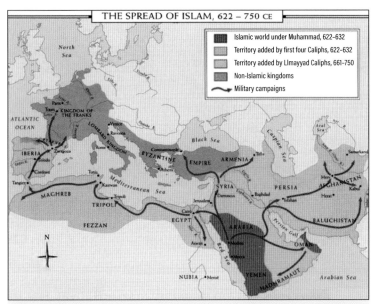

THE SPREAD OF ISLAM, 622 – 750 CE

- Islamic world under Muhammad, 622-632
- Territory added by first four Caliphs, 622-632
- Territory added by LImayyad Caliphs, 661-750
- Non-Islamic kingdoms
- Military campaigns

Islam spread in three distinct waves: under Muhammad, during the first four caliphs, and during the Umayyad Caliphate.

Christianity had become a cerebral faith at a time when Islam was offering tangible practices. Islam declared that there was only one God, that God had no children, and that if a person obeyed the Five Pillars, then he or she could inherit salvation. It was a far simpler approach to religion than the complex theological debates that had embroiled Christianity at the time.

Islam was on the verge of overtaking Europe when, in 732, at the famous Battle of Tours, **Charles Martel** ("the Hammer") defeated the invading Islamic forces and drove them back. Islam conquered Sicily in the 800s and launched attacks on Italy from there for about two hundred years. Arab armies finally conquered the hugely important city of Constantinople (New Rome—the heart of the Byzantine Empire) in 1453 and made it the de facto capital of the entire Muslim world.

Charles Martel · the French general at the Battle of Tours in 732 who halted the Muslim advance into Europe, decisively solidifying the religious history of the continent as we know it

Egypt and North Africa, Spain and southern France, much of India, Central Asia, and even parts of China. How did a relatively small number of warriors accomplish so great a feat? They believed it was God's guidance, which inspired the movement. In addition, Christianity was having serious internal problems at the time, particularly regarding the Trinity and the nature of God.

Today, the Islamic world is vast. Pakistan and Bangladesh—part of India until 1947—are almost completely Muslim. India has the third-largest Muslim population in the world, after Indonesia and Pakistan. The Middle East is strongly Muslim; the only exception is the nation of Israel. Indonesia and Malaysia became Islamic majority countries in the 1400s due to missions. Today, Islam is growing rapidly compared to most other religions due to generally higher fertility

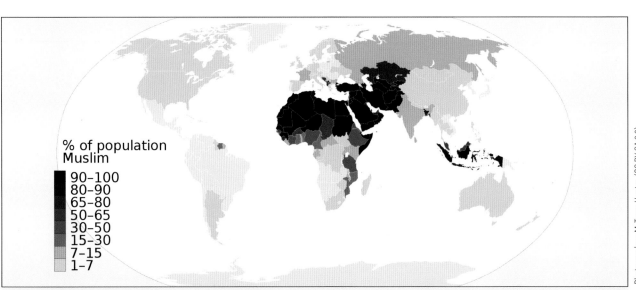

% of population Muslim

- 90–100
- 80–90
- 65–80
- 50–65
- 30–50
- 15–30
- 7–15
- 1–7

A map showing what percentage of each country is Muslim, according to Pew Research.

LUNAR CRESCENT

The Muslim symbol—the lunar crescent and star—began in the Ottoman Empire and is about five hundred years old. Several Muslim nations have adopted that symbol for their national flag, such as Algeria, Azerbaijan, Malaysia, Pakistan, and Turkey. The lunar crescent and star can be found on many mosques, too, and in some ways, it has become the universal symbol of Islam.

rates, as well as the fact that Muslim couples start having children at a relatively early age.

Islamic Leadership

After Muhammad died, there was a major crisis in leadership that has remained problematic ever since. The successor (caliph) to Muhammad was debated, and two men rose to the fore: Abu Bakr and Ali. While the Quran was the authority in Islam, earthly matters had to be decided by someone. Thus, the office of the caliphate (or khalifa) came about. The first four caliphs were the most important and are called Rashidun— the Rightly Guided Caliphs. Their names, dates of rule, and descriptions are as follows:

- **Abu Bakr** (632–34) was Muhammad's senior-most companion. His daughter, Aisha, became Muhammad's third wife when she was very young. He died of fever only two years into his caliphate.
- **Umar**, sometimes called **Omar** (634–44), also had a daughter who married Muhammad. He was an extremely successful warrior, conquering the Sassanid (Persian) Empire, as well as about two-thirds of the Byzantine (Eastern Christian) Empire. He was killed by a Persian assassin.
- **Uthman** (644–56) was married to two of Muhammad's daughters at different times. He conquered more Persian territory, part of Afghanistan, and part of Armenia. Ruling in his late sixties and seventies, he was one of the oldest caliphs in history. His last years in office were marred by accusations of nepotism, and

he was assassinated by a Muslim sect known as the Kharijites who claimed that the caliphate should be awarded to a person based on character rather than kinship or tribal politicking. In their view, the caliph should be decided only by Allah.

- **Ali** (656–61) was married to Muhammad's daughter Fatimah, along with many other wives and concubines. Shi'ite Muslims see Ali as the rightful successor to Muhammad, as well as a supremely righteous man, immune to corruption. Ali, too, was assassinated by a Kharijite.

In a short time, Islam became well-established and reigned supreme in the region under dynasties known as the Umayyads (661–750), who ruled from Damascus, Syria, and later, the Abbasids (750–1258), who ruled from Baghdad, Iraq. The Abbasids in particular became highly sophisticated in art, architecture, math, medicine, and philosophy. The Mongols, however, viciously sacked Baghdad in 1258, abruptly ending the Golden Age of Islam. Later, other Islamic empires rose up, such as the Mamluk Sultanate in Egypt (1258–1517) and the Ottoman Empire (1299–1922), which had their own caliphates within them.

Caliphate · also known as the **khalifa**; the Muslim government that rules as the successor to Muhammad until Judgment Day

Rashidun · also known as the **Rightly Guided Caliphs**; the first four Muslim caliphs: Abu Bakr, Umar, Uthman, and Ali

Umar · also known as **Omar**; the second caliph and father of one of Muhammad's wives; an extremely successful warrior who conquered the Sassanid (Persian) Empire, as well as two-thirds of the Byzantine (Eastern Christian) Empire, before falling to a Persian assassin

Kharijites · an Islamic sect that arose during the crises of leadership after Muhammad's death; responsible for assassinating both Uthman and Ali

Umayyads · an Islamic dynasty that ruled from Damascus, Syria, from 661 to 750

Abbasids · an Islamic dynasty that ruled from Baghdad, Iraq, from 750–1258; their reign is known as the Golden Age of Islam

Golden Age of Islam · an era during the Abbasid empire characterized by highly sophisticated art, architecture, math, medicine, and philosophy

Dar al-Islam · the "house of Islam"; refers to countries in the world where Muslims can freely practice their religion, generally implying Muslim control of law

Atatürk High Institute of Culture, public domain

The founding father of the Republic of Turkey, Atatürk served as its first president from 1923 until he died in 1938.

Hadith · the words, actions, and viewpoints of Muhammad, as preserved by those who knew him

Hasan · Muhammad's grandson who would have become caliph after the death of Ali but abdicated to prevent a Muslim civil war, allowing Mu'awiya to become the fifth caliph

Mu'awiya · the fifth caliph who established the Umayyad Caliphate

Husayn · Hasan's younger brother and grandson of Muhammad who was murdered by Mu'awiya's son Yazid to eliminate his competing claim to the office of caliph

The Islamic caliphate was ended in 1924 in Turkey by its secular-minded leader, Mustafa Kemal Atatürk. Some tried to revive it, but to no avail. To the present day, many Muslims long for a renaissance of the caliphate, as opposed to the Western division of nation-states. These Muslims prefer the Islamic notion of a **Dar al-Islam** (house of Islam), with a renewed caliphate at its center.

Conflict in Islam

Islam split during the early days into two parties: Sunni and Shi'a. The Sunnis are by far larger, boasting over 85 percent of all Muslims. Their name comes from the word Sunnah, which refers to the life and behavior of the prophet Muhammad. Sunnis have two sources of authority: the Quran and the **hadith**—the words, actions, and viewpoints of Muhammad. The hadith are explanations of how Muhammad made decisions and how he lived. Importantly, Sunnis reject the idea of a clergy.

Shi'ites, however, believe Muhammad appointed his son-in-law Ali as his successor. When Ali was murdered, his son **Hasan** was expected to take over after him, but Hasan abdicated to avoid a Muslim civil war. This allowed **Mu'awiya** to become the fifth caliph and establish the Umayyad Caliphate. However, Hasan and his younger brother **Husayn** were blood grandsons to Muhammad, and they therefore posed a threat to Mu'awiya's claim to the caliphate. Mu'awiya had no blood connection to Muhammad. He was one of Muhammad's scribes, and he eventually rose up through the ranks to become governor of Syria.

When Mu'awiya died, his son Yazid became the sixth caliph. However, Yazid was fearful that Husayn might claim to be caliph. Thus, Yazid had Husayn murdered in 680 CE at Karbala, in modern-day Iraq. This incident proved cataclysmic to Islam. Shi'ites commemorate this day as **Ashura** each year. It is always a tense day in the Islamic world. It is the day that Husayn—the grandson of the prophet Muhammad—and his family were unjustly martyred.

Shi'ites continue to see the leadership of Islam as related to the bloodline of Muhammad. They believe the descendants of Ali should be the leaders of the faith. The word *Shi'a* means "party" or "sect."

Classical Numistic Group, (CC BY-SA 2.5)

Before he founded the Umayyad dynasty, Mu'awiya proved himself an exceptional administrator in Damascus, Syria. Through taxes and coins, like the one pictured above, he shaped an economy and solidified his reign.

SHI'ITES

Shi'ites have several unique features that differentiate them from Sunnis:

- A slightly different Shahada—in the Shi'ite Shahada, there is an added a phrase that Ali is the rightful successor.
- A different understanding of the role of an imam—Shi'ites believe that there were twelve divinely appointed imams after Muhammad. In Shi'ism, imams are considered to be clergy, highly revered, infallible, and divinely appointed by God. There are three major forms of Shi'ites: Twelvers (by far the largest), Fivers, ("Zaydiyah"), and Ismaili. They hold to different views on how many imams came after Husayn, but all of them believe in a highly organized clergy that is authoritative—for example, the Grand Ayatollah in Iran.
- The figure of Mahdi, or a messiah figure, who will come and rule Earth for a period of time and bring an era of great justice shortly before the Judgment Day—they believe the Mahdi is actually the twelfth imam (Hujjat Allah ibn al-Hasan [ruled from 869–74 CE]), who has been in celestial hiding since 874. The Mahdi will one day appear with Jesus (Isa, the Messiah) to fight against the Antichrist.
- Reverence for Husayn, the opponent of Mu'awiya and the rightful heir to the caliphate—Husayn is celebrated as a righteous martyr who, along with his family, was unjustly killed by the armies of Yazid, Mu'awiya's son. Obviously, Sunnis do not share this belief since they view Husayn's claim to the caliphate as being illegitimate.
- A different interpretation of the Quran, and in some cases, a belief that Sunnis altered the text—importantly, they believe the Quran was tampered with by Sunnis, which explains why Ali is not mentioned as the successor to Muhammad in the surviving text of the Quran.

Ashura · the day on which Shi'ites commemorate the martyr of Husayn

Twelvers · the largest subsect of Shi'a Islam; named after their belief on how many imams came after Husayn

Grand Ayatollah · an authoritative and highly organized clerical and political office in Shi'a Islam

Mahdi · a Messiah figure in Shi'a Islam who will come and rule Earth for a period of time, ushering in an era of great justice prior to Judgment Day

Sufism · a school of Islamic mysticism that rejects luxury and legalism in favor of following a path of loving and ecstatic unity with God

Tariqas · "paths"; communities or schools that form around influential Sufi teachers

Fakirs · Arabic converts to Sufism

Dervishes · Persian converts to Sufism

There are a few majority Shi'a nations: Iran (90 percent), Azerbaijan (85 percent), Iraq (65 percent), and Bahrain (52 percent). There are Shi'a communities all over the world, and in some cases, they are sizeable. Lebanon, for example, has an equal number of Sunnis and Shi'ites. It is estimated that over a third of the entire population of the Middle East is Shi'a.

Mystical Islam

Islam tends not to encourage monasticism or celibacy; therefore, monks and nuns are exceedingly rare. However, a mystical movement in Islam does exist—it is known as Sufism. The word *Sufi* comes from the garment they wore, which was made of undyed wool (suf), signifying their forsaking luxury to unite with Allah on a spiritual and emotional level.

From early on, Sufis have had a difficult relationship with mainstream Muslims and have endured many waves of persecution. Originally, Sufism was a reaction against legalism and extreme puritanism in Islam. Sufis also reacted against the vast wealth of the Umayyad Caliphate, which was conquering many civilizations and vastly expanding the Muslim empire.

Sufis organize themselves around influential Sufi teachers, similar to the notion of a guru. Communities or schools, known as **tariqas** (paths), form around these leaders, and converts become known as **fakirs** (Arabic) or **dervishes** (Persian). Some Sufis do extravagant actions to demonstrate their unity with and devotion to God, much

Whirling dervishes at the Hodjapasha Culture Center in Turkey (2014). The Sufis meditate while spinning in place, sometimes for hours at a time.

Photographer: Kemal Kubbe, (CC BY-SA 4.0)

like other forms of mysticism. The famous **whirling dervishes** meditate while spinning in place for long periods of time, even hours. Known for their eccentricity, they have been accused of heretical beliefs—for example, arguing that all religions have the potential to lead their followers to the ultimate truth found in God.

Sufism has an illustrious history. It began under Hasan al-Basri, who was brought up by Umm Salama, one of Muhammad's wives. The first famous Sufi was Rabia al-Basri (717–801 CE), a freed slave who lived a life of poverty in the desert after she found freedom. Many proposed to her for marriage, but she rejected them, preferring to write poetry and teach others about her mystical approach to God.

Sufis try to destroy their own ego so that they only exist in God. They often deny materialism, and they live a life of profound focus on communing with God. Many of them renounce the world and reach a state of ecstasy, bliss, and unity with God.

The two most famous Sufis in history are **Ibn Arabi** (1165–1240) from Andalusia and **Rumi** (1207–73) from Persia/Turkey. Both of them have had a profound influence on Islam, especially through their poetry, and they are beloved in other religions as well.

Modern Islam

After the sacking of Baghdad and the dissolution of the Abbasid Caliphate in 1258, Islam continued its expansion, yet into new places. By no means did the sacking of Baghdad terminate Islamic growth. Rather, Islam expanded more intentionally into India and Southeast Asia. Islam had great success in Indonesia between the twelfth and sixteenth centuries. India became home to the great Mughal Empire between the sixteenth and the nineteenth centuries. The expansion of Islam in north and central Africa was profound from the fourteenth to the eighteenth century. North Africa is today one of the great heartlands of Islam, with approximately one-third of the world's Muslims living there.

While the Christian **Reconquista** of the Iberian Peninsula was seen as an aberration rather than a general trend, it soon became clear that the Christian world had become increasingly powerful. In around 1500 CE, Europe was on the rise to world military dominance, primarily through the trailblazing work of its circumnavigators, who dominated the seas and encountered far-off civilizations, bringing many of them into the Christian fold. The Muslim world was obviously surprised by the great advances made by Christians.

The European colonial era was particularly humiliating for Muslims, as virtually all of their lands became dominated by Christian empires. It was a rude awakening for Muslim empires to realize that the tables had turned and that they were no longer in charge of their own destiny.

Adding insult to injury, in 1919, at the **Paris Peace Conference**, the victors of World War I—Britain, France, Italy, and the United States—split up the entire world into various nation-states. The Muslim world was shocked to see that their fortunes had changed so dramatically. Western powers delineated the borders for Muslim countries, with little consideration of Muslim input. This process is something many Muslim nations were not comfortable with, preferring instead a unified Muslim Dar al-Islam.

The **Wahhabi** religious movement in Saudi Arabia dates to 1744 and was a reaction to the rise of the Western powers. Founded by Muhammad ibn Abd al-Wahhab, the movement argued for a decidedly conservative and puritanical form of Islam that opposed industrialization and widespread social change. Many Muslims were inspired by this resounding "no" to Western influence and culture and "yes" to the form of Islam authorized by Muhammad and the early ummah. The leading family in the Wahhabi movement was the House of Saud. After striving for a century and a half, they finally gained full control of Arabia in 1932, naming

Paris Peace Conference · the 1919 conference at the end of World War I in which the victors—Britain, France, Italy, and the United States—split up the world into various nation-states, generally without the consent of the peoples and regions involved

Wahhabi · a conservative, reactionary school of Islam that began in 1744 to oppose Western imperialism and revive Muslim culture; primarily found in Saudi Arabia today

Photograph of the Big Four at the Paris Peace Conference after World War I on May 27, 1919. From left to right: British Prime Minister David Lloyd George, Italian Premier Vittorio Orlando, French Premier Georges Clemenceau, and President of the United States Woodrow Wilson.

it after themselves. Their political rise coincided with the rise of the oil industry, which quickly made Saudi Arabia one of the wealthiest lands in the world. Due to this partnership between Saudi Arabia's wealth and Wahhabism, this more conservative form of Islam has spread all over the globe and has exerted tremendous influence over the last century. Muslim missions and global influence were empowered dramatically by oil revenues in the Middle East.

The rather sudden oil wealth propelled the Middle Eastern nations to a clear resurgence throughout the latter half of the twentieth century. Virtually all of the Western powers became utterly reliant on Middle Eastern oil. Islam's fortunes changed once again. While the Muslim nations were a mere afterthought at the Paris Peace Conference of 1919, just a few decades later, Islamic voices had become full participants at the global table of influence, a situation that remains to the present day.

Islam's influence has continued to increase in the West through immigration. In addition, Islamic nations are growing far more rapidly than Western nations due to high fertility rates. Islamic missions to the West are as robust as ever. Due to these developments, some statisticians estimate that by the end of the twenty-first century, Islam will have overtaken Christianity as the largest religion in the world.

Today, as with many other religions, Islam is navigating how to thrive in a modern, globalized context. Some Muslim nations have responded by choosing a more conservative path. For instance, in 1979, the Shi'ite nation of Iran overthrew the secular **shah** government and proclaimed the Islamic scholar Ayatollah Khomeini as its leader. He championed an Islamic revival and publicly condemned the Western world as the **Great Satan**. Upon seizing power, he famously authorized the fifty-two US diplomats who were trapped in Iran to be arrested and held hostage for over a year, a move that drastically changed the United States' previously congenial relationship with much of the Islamic world. Iran and the United States have remained in a state of suspicion toward one another

Shah · the secular government in Iran that was overthrown in 1979, with Islamic scholar Ayatollah Khomeini elevated to leadership in its place

Great Satan · the term Ayatollah Khomeini used to describe and condemn the West

Al-Qaeda · the extremist terrorist organization responsible for the attacks on September 11, 2001

Osama bin Laden · the mastermind of the September 11, 2001, attacks; killed by US Navy Seals in 2011

Taliban · a fundamentalist Islamic group in Afghanistan that eventually solidified control over the country in 2021

Islamic State · a fundamentalist Islamic group in the Levant known for its use of violence and terrorism

Levant · the geographical region comprising Syria, Lebanon, Jordan, Israel, Palestine, and parts of Iraq and Turkey.

Muslim women wearing hijabs with a stars-and-stripes pattern.

ever since, and relations between the two nations are practically nonexistent.

Wahhabi interpretations of Islam, combined with anti-colonial resentment of the West, have led to widespread tensions between certain parts of the Islamic world and much of the Western world. Tensions reached new heights on September 11, 2001, when Muslim terrorists, primarily from Saudi Arabia, carried out a plan to fly passenger airplanes into the World Trade Center towers, as well as the Pentagon. Another plane crashed into a field in Pennsylvania but was almost certainly headed toward the US Capitol Building in Washington, D.C.

Many Westerners had little knowledge of Islam up until that time, and on September 11, 2001, they were suddenly exposed to a form of Islam they found reprehensible and incomprehensible. That form of Islam was personified by a terrorist organization called **al-Qaeda** ("the foundation"). The events of that fateful day redefined political realities in the modern world, as many Western nations—led by the United States—declared war on Iraq and Afghanistan in an attempt to achieve justice. The mastermind of the attacks—**Osama bin Laden**—evaded capture for a decade, but he was finally discovered to be living on a compound in Pakistan. He was killed by US Navy Seals in 2011, bringing a sense of resolution to those who had lost loved ones on September 11.

Wahhabi interpretations of Islam have impacted many other fundamentalist groups throughout the Islamic world, such as the **Taliban** in Afghanistan and the **Islamic State** in the **Levant**—that is, Syria, Lebanon, Jordan, Israel, Palestine, and parts of Iraq and Turkey. The Islamic State is often known as ISIS in the West, but in the Muslim world, it is usually called **Daesh** ("to crush"). In many cases, the various fundamentalist groups do not associate with each other. For instance, ISIS and the Taliban are enemies who disagree on a host of matters.

It is quite clear that Islam has not been represented well in the Western media, especially since the 1979 Islamic Revolution and the events of September 11, 2001. However, many Muslims work hard to heal divisions, extend hospitality to non-Muslims, and bring

Mother Mosque of America in Cedar Rapids, Iowa. Many documents and photographs were lost in a historic flood in 2008. The Cedar River crested at thirty-one feet, filling the mosque's basement with ten feet of water.

peace to their societies. Less visible in the media are reconciliation efforts by Muslims worldwide—for instance, work in interreligious dialogue, the 1981 **Universal Islamic Declaration of Human Rights**, and tremendous social progress being made in numerous Muslim nations today.

Islam has been present in North America since early on. Many Muslim slaves from West Africa arrived during the eighteenth and nineteenth centuries. Some estimates are

Daesh · the term most commonly used in the Middle East to reference ISIS, derived as an acronym for its Arabic name, "Al-Dawla al-Islamiya al-Iraq al-Sham" ("the Islamic State of Iraq and the Levant"); coincidentally, "daesh" is also related to the Arabic word for "bullies," accounting for its popularity among those victimized by ISIS

Universal Islamic Declaration of Human Rights · a 1981 statement of the human rights protected by the Quran and Islamic doctrine

Malcolm X before a press conference in 1964.

that around 20 percent of the slaves brought from Africa in those two centuries were Muslim. The period between the two world wars saw many Muslims migrate to the United States due to political oppression or upheaval in their home countries. The oldest surviving mosque in the United States dates to 1934 and is in Cedar Rapids, Iowa. It is known as the **Mother Mosque of America**. When the United States' immigration laws were tightened to favor skilled immigrants in the 1960s, many Muslims immigrated to attend graduate schools or to work in specialized fields. Notably, many highly skilled South Asian Muslims from India and Pakistan have arrived since then, often working in science, technology, and medicine.

Many of the mosques in the United States' largest cities are organized along ethnic or racial lines, much like churches in the United States. Thus, some mosques cater mainly to Turkish people, others attract mainly Arabs, and some are frequented predominantly by Asian Muslims. However, these developments are only practical in nature, as there is a shared cultural background. One of the great points of genius of Islam is that it refuses to restrict itself to one race of people. Like Christianity, this crucial element of Islam has caused it to be embraced by peoples and nations all over the world.

One Islamic movement in the United States has received widespread attention over the years: the Black Muslim movement, also known as the **Nation of Islam**. Founded in 1930, it came into its own under the leadership of Elijah Muhammad, who led the organization from 1934 until 1975. The movement has been described as striving to equip African Americans with a sense of pride, purpose, and strength. It critiqued White oppression and reached out to African Americans. The movement has been severely critiqued by mainstream Islam due to Elijah Muhammad's claims that he—not Muhammad—was the last prophet. It has a separatist, segregationist bent to it, which goes against the racial inclusion clearly taught in mainstream Islam. The Nation of Islam also does not typically follow the Five Pillars.

The most recognizable member of the Nation of Islam is probably Malcolm X (1925–65). Formerly known as Malcolm Little, he used an X to reject what he called his slave name. **Malcolm X** was drawn into the movement while serving time in prison. He was drawn to its strong sense of Black exclusionism and denunciation of White supremacy. Malcolm X became Elijah Muhammad's right-hand man and the movement's most effective recruiter. He was revered for his powerful charisma and ability to recruit others, including notable figures such as Cassius Clay, who, upon conversion, changed his name to **Muhammad Ali**. He openly opposed Martin Luther King Jr. for his racial reconciliation efforts.

Malcolm X began to meet mainstream Muslims and soon concluded that the Nation of Islam was unorthodox. He spent increasing time with Sunni Muslims and even took a pilgrimage to Mecca, which deeply impacted him, especially on the issue of race because the Hajj included Muslims from all over the world. The Nation of Islam leadership was incensed that their most prolific member had defected, and it soon became apparent that Malcolm X would have to pay the ultimate price for his departure from the movement. On February 19, 1965, while preparing to give a lecture in New York City, he was ambushed and fatally shot in public.

When Elijah Muhammad died in 1975, his son, Wallace D. Muhammad, took over as leader of the Nation of Islam, but he swiftly disbanded the organization. Instead, he started an organization that was closer to orthodox Islam, the American Muslim Mission, which later was renamed the American Society of Muslims. Meanwhile, **Louis Farrakhan**, another Nation of Islam member, essentially took over the roles and responsibilities that Malcolm X had previously

Mother Mosque of America · the oldest surviving mosque in the United States, founded in 1934 in Cedar Rapids, Iowa

Nation of Islam · the Black Muslim movement popularized by Elijah Muhammad and Malcom X that condemned White oppression and encouraged a sense of pride, purpose, and strength among African Americans

Malcom X · Elijah Muhammad's right-hand man and fervent recruiter for the Nation of Islam; tried to steer the movement more toward orthodox Islam and was assassinated for his efforts

Muhammad Ali · a famous American boxer and convert to the Nation of Islam

Louis Farrakhan · a Nation of Islam member who recreated the movement, along with its original vision and beliefs

held. Farrakhan, however, grew disenchanted with the new direction of the movement, and he decided to defect and restart the Nation of Islam according to how it was originally envisioned. Louis Farrakhan's movement reached its zenith in 1995 with its **Million Man March** in Washington, D.C., which united many African American groups into the largest Black protest in US history.

Islam Today

Islam uses a lunar calendar that differs slightly from the Gregorian, or solar, calendar used in most of the world. The lunar calendar contains only 354 days a year. Further, the Islamic calendar begins its counting of years with the Hijra (immigration) in 622 CE, or, in Islamic terms, AH (Anno Hijra) 1. Thus, the prophet Muhammad died not in 632 CE but in AH 10—that is, ten years after the immigration to Medina.

Perhaps the most important time of the year in the Muslim calendar is the month of Ramadan, or the ninth month of the Muslim lunar calendar. It is a month of fasting when food or drink cannot be taken during daylight hours. Each evening, after the Sun goes down, Muslims enjoy an iftar meal, often with friends and family and sometimes even with non-Muslim guests. Muslims celebrate the end of the Ramadan fast with **Eid al-Fitr**, often simply called Eid or "the lesser Eid." (The word *eid* means "feast.") It is a festival that lasts for three days and includes feasting and gift exchanging. As more Muslims immigrate to the United States, Eid al-Fitr is becoming celebrated at the White House and even included on school

A family breaking their Ramadan fast together.

© Odua Images, Adobe Stock

holiday calendars. Dearborn, Michigan—the first US city with a Muslim majority city council—now recognizes Eid al-Fitr and Eid al-Adha as public holidays. **Eid al-Adha** is the "Festival of the Sacrifice" that celebrates Abraham's near sacrifice of Ishmael. During that feast, animals are sacrificed, and a third of the meat is consumed by the family, while the rest is given to the poor. Eid al-Adha is known as the "greater Eid" since it lasts for four days, compared to Eid al-Fitr, which only lasts for three days.

Many Muslims enjoy New Year festivities, as well as a celebration of the birth of Muhammad. More conservative Muslims, however, such as Wahhabis, reject these two practices as modern innovations. They claim that Muhammad did not celebrate either of these, so neither should Muslims.

Eid al-Adha · the "Festival of the Sacrifice," which commemorates Abraham's near-sacrifice of Ishmael

13 ALTERNATIVE RELIGION AND IRRELIGION
Religion Remixed

A young girl in prayer. Some believe religion will die out in the coming decades and centuries, but current evidence suggests religion remains strong.

There have always been voices who opposed religion, whether a specific religion or the concept of religion in general. For example, Christian history is replete with heretics, critics, and doubters. Since the 1700s—the so-called Enlightenment—there have been voices of dissent against religion in general, particularly in the Western world.

In the eighteenth century, some philosophers tried to make a distinction between religion and reason, as if religion were unreasonable. Thus, during the French Revolution, they erected Temples of Reason, killed Catholic priests in a bloody purge, and put the Roman Catholic Church underneath the power of the state. This touched off movements in the Western world that continue to the present day. And while not all of these movements away from or against religion have their origins in the French Revolution and Enlightenment, many of them certainly do. In the wake of the intellectual shocks of the eighteenth century have come a general distrust of religion, a tendency to disavow absolute truth, and a focus upon the natural as opposed to the supernatural. In short, the Enlightenment gave rise to a concept discussed often in religious studies today: secularization—the decline of religious authority and religious influence in various spheres of social life.

In the nineteenth century, a Danish philosopher named Søren Kierkegaard was an important forerunner to a philosophy now called existentialism, which emphasizes our current existence, as opposed to some nebulous future existence in heaven or in a future life. Existentialism prioritizes the will over reason. It deals with the practical rather than the theoretical. Its realm of concern is the personal, as opposed to the collective. It minimizes the concept of objectivity because it asserts that there is no such thing. Every subject

Image courtesy of St. Olaf College. Used by permission.

The two primary English translators for Søren Kierkegaard's work are Howard V. and Edna H. Hong. The Hong Kierkegaard Library at St. Olaf College in Northfield, Minnesota, is an internationally recognized repository and is named in their honor.

Secularization · the decline of religious authority and religious influence in various spheres of social life

Søren Kierkegaard · a nineteenth-century Danish philosopher known for his existentialism

Existentialism · a philosophy which emphasizes our current existence as opposed to some nebulous future existence in heaven or in a future life, prioritizing the will over reason, the practical over the theoretical, and the personal over the collective; important for its rejection of the possibility of objectivity

can only think and see according to one's existential location. Thus, objective conclusions are by nature inconclusive because all we can possibly do is observe and analyze according to our subjective location. One person, or even a group of people, cannot evaluate whether something is true or accurate according to all perspectives. Existentialism dislocates discussions of objective truth and puts the focus upon the subjective.

If we combine the Enlightenment's ideas on reason with the French Revolution's sudden shift to secularization and mix it well with existentialism, we arrive at a point many have referred to as **postmodernism**. While the term itself is hotly debated and highly debatable, some of the fundamental concepts are not. For instance, there has been an undoubted shift in Western intellectual circles in the last few generations. Objective truth is often seen as unattainable today. The focus, instead, is placed on cultural narratives, personal experience, and subjective truth. In other words, one person's truth is not necessarily another person's truth. The discussion centers on the concept of truth. Is there such a thing as objective truth, or are there only subjective perspectives on truth?

This line of thinking undergirds intellectual and philosophical discourse today, and it has profoundly impacted the study of religion. Are people's truths simply cultural constructs? The result has been an erosion of confidence in truth. People seem more open than ever to hearing and weighing other perspectives on truth. One ethnic group may understand truth differently than another. One gender may think differently than another gender. Is there such thing as a gender? Can even the concept of gender become a culturally conditioned idea? What about class—do upper classes actually think differently about reality than subjugated classes?

Obviously, power comes into play here. Many philosophers argue that we are exercising power whenever we

Postmodernism · the current historical and philosophical movement, which draws heavily from existentialism in its belief that all truth is relative

Secularization theory · the theory that the world is becoming more secularized and less religious

Sacralization · a theory countering the secularization thesis, which posits instead that the world's civilizations are growing more religious

> Currently, one of the center-stage debates in religious studies has to do with secularization's impact on culture at large. Are people becoming less religious over time?

assert that our truth is more valuable or "truer" than another person's truth. When one party is able to cancel another party's truth, does that simply mean that truth is always conditioned and defined by the victor's understanding and perspective? Put simply, is truth merely the result of power? One wins, and one gets to define truth. Those who lose power will have less of a voice in determining reality, truth, and meaning. The concept of will to power is at the forefront of larger meta-discussions of religion, philosophy, and even reality today. Kierkegaard's existential ideas seem to be dominant for now. But if history shows us anything, it is that all ideologies lose power eventually, given enough time.

Currently, one of the center-stage debates in religious studies has to do with secularization's impact on culture at large. Are people becoming less religious over time? Some argue that this is happening, while others are not so sure. An entire field of knowledge, **secularization theory**, has risen up—it debates why society is turning away from religion to embrace a more scientific, less supernatural worldview. The jury is still out, however, because others argue for **sacralization**—that the world's civilizations are becoming more religious. China and the former Soviet Union claimed to have effectively purged religion from their societies in the twentieth century. However, we now realize that notion was naïve and flatly mistaken. Most of the religious people in those nations simply remained silent to avoid persecution.

Now that religion is legal in Russia and China once again, there is a flourishing of religiosity in these societies. While neither Russia nor China are completely open societies, they have seemingly made the decision to stop punishing people just for embracing religion. One caveat must be emphasized: religion in both of these societies is not completely free from persecution. If one happens to be religious in a way that runs afoul of the government, then that person could certainly become punished on account of practicing an unapproved religion. Many smaller religions continue to deal with persecution in Russia and China.

Sacralization is the concept of religion becoming personalized and individuated within a person. Whereas secularization is a concept about society at large, sacralization pertains more to the individual. Sacralization is what is happening when people say, "I am spiritual but not religious." They are longing for some sense of the divine or metaphysical, but the current menu of religious options does not appeal to them. They realize a certain value in religion, so they branch out and explore alternative forms of religiosity that might not be institutionalized. Usually, this quest is described as spirituality due to the strong social connotations that arise with the term *religion*.

"Spiritual but not religious" people often stray from established orthodoxy and concoct new constructs such as God being a personalized spirit that can help them rather than God being the God of the Christian Bible. These people often experiment and incorporate ideas from different religions. They might choose to believe in angels but not in hell. They might choose to believe in a spirit but not the God of the Bible. They might choose reincarnation while also believing in the teachings of Jesus. They might meditate instead of pray. These individuals are notoriously difficult to document in scholarly discourse because they evade categories. Sometimes, they are known as the "nones"—meaning that on surveys they describe their religion as "none." However, the fact is that they are often quite religious, but "none" of the formal religions on offer fully appeal to them.

Some sociologists, such as Abby Day, have interviewed hundreds of these "no religion" people, only to find out that they tend to do religious things, such as believe in the presence of ancestors, pray to God, and frequently tap into spiritual practices characteristic of established religions. They tend not to sign up with a church or a synagogue and commit to it. They believe in free agency. They take their spirituality with them and adapt it to their everyday needs to provide an individuated experience for themselves. In these cases, their spiritual growth is a core part of their personal growth. They are certainly not what we might call secular people, although the surveys tend to be unable to untangle this fact. Thus, they are labeled as "secular," whereas in reality they are quite the opposite. They are spiritual believers in a sacred realm, and they seek a worldview with spiritual answers. This is why they are often considered to be part of a sacralization process happening in the world today, especially in the Western world. People often leave a religion only to become independently spiritual.

NRMs = New Religious Movements

The study of **New Religious Movements** (NRMs) is a burgeoning field presently. New religious movements are born each day—however, a minority of them achieve a level of popularity or influence that merits academic study. Some of these new religious movements gain enough numbers to the point that they require notice from the scholarly community. Others may be small in number but somehow attain a level of influence that demands attention. Some NRM scholars limit their focus of study to approximately the last two hundred years or so, which includes the first wave of NRMs: **Mormons**, **Jehovah's Witnesses**, **Christian Science**, and the **Seventh-day Adventists**. Others limit their focus to the last fifty years or so in an attempt to stay focused on the "new" aspect of NRMs. Today, there are thousands of distinct NRMs all around the world, with tens of millions of followers. It is a marvelously complex subfield in the study of religion.

New Religious Movements (NRMs) · alternative religious traditions which have arisen in recent times and have not yet achieved the longevity and the global adherence of world religions

Mormons · known formally as the **Church of Jesus Christ of Latter-Day Saints**, an NRM based on Christianity and on a new testament which God revealed to Joseph Smith in nineteenth-century North America

Jehovah's Witnesses · a Christian-based millenarian NRM founded by C. T. Russell known for its rejection of the Trinity and its emphasis on eschatology

Christian Science · an NRM founded by Mary Baker Eddy around the idea of prayer-induced healing and a rejection of secular medical care

Seventh-day Adventists · an NRM founded by Ellen Gould White which observes a Sabbath on the seventh day of the week and prepares for the imminent return of Jesus Christ

A Jehovah's Witness member distributing religious literature on Ban Jelacic square in Zagreb, Croatia (2010). Jehovah's Witnesses has a worldwide membership of over 8.5 million.

Members of NRMs sometimes resist the label that has been given to them since they see themselves connected to a long history and tradition. For instance, they might see themselves as the latest manifestation of a long-established religion. They have good reason for this reticence, since before the expression NRM was used, most scholars simply referred to these groups as **cults**. The term *cult*, however, has fallen into disuse among many religious studies scholars since it is clearly pejorative. It was a term that effectively put these groups on the bad list and sometimes caused them to experience repression, even violent repression. Thus, while the term *cult* has evolved to the acronym NRM, there are still some within them who are suspicious of all labels that imply that their group is too recent to be welcomed to the table of the world's major religions.

Cults · a pejorative classification for NRMs which has fallen into disuse

Some of the common features of NRMs are that they are usually founded by a charismatic leader who may have had supernatural powers or at least superb insights into God and the human condition. Due to their leader's obvious gifts, the movement rose up quickly around the leader's personality, and the leader drew many people to himself or herself. Not all NRMs last long. In fact, most of them die out quickly, as soon as something major goes wrong in the community or when the leader dies. However, other NRMs exist long enough to establish a plan for succession. No organization can succeed for long without a plan for how

Some of the common features of NRMs are that they are usually founded by a charismatic leader who may have had supernatural powers or at least superb insights into God and the human condition.

to keep the community together once the charismatic leader is out of the picture. If the community can last for generations, even centuries, it eventually becomes accepted as a religion.

NRMs usually succeed by keeping their members tightly connected and by placing extremely high expectations on them. If the group cannot manage to hold on to the children of the first generation, then they are doomed as a movement of any kind of longevity. One of the major ways NRMs maintain their numbers is by putting heavy responsibilities and expectations upon their members. Simply connecting oneself to an NRM requires courage, as outsiders will scoff at them. However, if the leaders can manage this potential problem and keep the members engaged enough to stay, then roots will eventually grow pretty deep, as will conviction and commitment. Again, a new leader can wipe out all gains, but in some cases, the second-generation leader is quite competent and manages the leadership changes effectively. That

effective passing of the baton, however, is somewhat rare.

Another aspect of NRMs is that they are generally new manifestations, or reinterpretations, of older traditions. If the older traditions seem to lack vitality, the NRMs often do a good job of updating, revising, or reimagining the older, more established religion. Mormons, formally known as the Church of Jesus Christ of Latter-day Saints, argue that God revealed himself through another testament that was unearthed in North America. Other traditions claim that a new prophet has come with a new word for the faithful. Clearly, this threatens to put the NRM at odds with the larger tradition, but many continue to follow it, usually because of the power and charisma of the community's leader. His or her teaching is more persuasive than that of other leaders in the mainline traditions. Other times, members become so socially or physically connected to the NRM that there is no easy way out. They are now part of a new social group, and it would be difficult to

Photographer: Entheta, (CC BY 2.5)

Beyond church congregations, Mormons also have temples for special religious ceremonies and practices. The Salt Lake Temple is the largest of 170 dedicated Latter-day Saints temples internationally.

Image courtesy of Community of Christ Archive, Independence Missouri

A painting of Joseph Smith, enigmatic founder of the widely prosperous Church of Jesus Christ of Latter-day Saints. Today, the Mormon church is one of the fastest-growing religious movements in the world.

extract oneself from that kind of belonging into which one has invested so heavily.

One notable feature of NRMs is that, historically, they often had women leaders at a time when female religious leaders were rare, as in the cases of **Ellen Gould White** (Seventh-day Adventists), **Mary Baker Eddy** (Christian Science), **Ann Lee** (**Shakers**), the **Fox sisters** (**Spiritualism**), and **Helena Blavatsky** (**Theosophical Society**), among others. In the case of the Mormons, women's roles were countercultural in the sense that many of the early leaders of the Mormon Church were polygamists. For example, Brigham Young, a successor to founder Joseph Smith, married a total of fifty-five women and fathered dozens of children.

Societies are often suspicious of NRMs because some of them have been linked to violence, such as Jim Jones's Peoples Temple (Guyana), David Koresh's Branch Davidians (Waco, Texas), the Order of the Solar Temple (France, Switzerland, Canada), Heaven's Gate (California), Movement for the Restoration of the Ten Commandments of God (Uganda), Lord's Resistance Army (Uganda), and Aleph (Japan). While NRMs have occasionally deviated into doomsday movements with loss of life, it is difficult to ascertain whether NRMs are any more or less deadly than other religions, philosophies, or ideologies.

Crystal healing is a hallmark of modern spirituality. First sparking widespread interest in the 1970s, today young people can often be seen purchasing crystals for their mystical properties.

© Elena Ray, Adobe Stock

Many Christian NRMs are millenarian in theology, meaning they believe that Jesus Christ will come back to Earth and establish a one-thousand-year reign of peace. Both the Jehovah's Witness and the Seventh-day Adventist movements have roots in millenarianism. The Branch Davidian movement was a unique manifestation of Seventh-day Adventism that over time became independent. Led by David Koresh, the movement came under scrutiny by the US government for stockpiling weapons and claims of child abuse within the church. A standoff with the government ensued and ended badly. Substantial gunfire was exchanged, and buildings went up in flames. Dozens of Branch Davidians were killed, including many children, along with four government officers.

In the 1970s, there was much interest in NRMs having to do with **Native American spirituality**. Crystal healing, the channeling of deceased people's spirits, and veneration of the Earth came into vogue within mainstream US society. Many have connected the increased attention toward nature in the 1970s as a clear precursor to the climate change movement so popular in the twenty-first century. The particulars of Native American spirituality—sweat lodges, ghost dances, Kachina dolls—are probably not as popular today as they were in the 1970s and 1980s. They have not disappeared entirely, however.

The discussion of NRMs is not at all specific to the Western context. Many prominent NRMs have arisen outside the West—for instance, in Asia. The **Taiping Heavenly Kingdom** movement rose up in China in the 1850s and became an empire that threatened to conquer the entire Chinese nation. The movement was led by a charismatic leader named **Hong Xiuquan** (1814–64), who claimed to be the younger brother of Jesus Christ. He blended Christianity with Chinese folk religion, and his movement expanded rapidly until it was suppressed by the government in 1865, at a

> Another family of NRMs that scholars have identified are science-based, or science fiction, depending upon one's perspective.

cost of tens of millions of lives. Oddly, the Chinese government today honors the Taiping Rebellion as an early form of communism. While Western Christians saw the movement as heterodox, there was a mixed reaction, as many Chinese were introduced to Christian teachings during the rebellion. Hong Xiuquan welcomed Western missionaries with open arms, which may have damaged Chinese understandings of Christianity in the long run.

Another family of NRMs that scholars have identified are science-based, or science fiction, depending upon one's perspective. Several religions have arisen over the last few decades that focus on unidentified flying objects (UFOs). Often, the premise of these religions is that there are gods who communicate with Earthlings through UFOs and aliens. The gods often choose certain humans to communicate with, and those humans assume the role of a prophet, speaking to the people on behalf of a god.

The first known UFO religion—the **Aetherius Society**—was founded by George King in the 1950s. He taught that there were extraterrestrial intelligences that he referred to as Cosmic Masters. Humans should rely on these Masters to solve their earthly problems

Fox sisters · Leah, Margaretta and Catherine Fox; three sisters who created the NRM known as Spiritualism by purportedly channelling spirits of the dead

Spiritualism · an NRM started by the Fox sisters which uses seances and mediums to commune with spirits

Helena Blavatsky · a founder of the Theosophical Society

Theosophical Society · a Western interpretation of Hinduism that birthed a variety of NRMs that brought together religious ideas from both the East and the West

Native American Spirituality · practices such as crystal healing, the channelling of deceased people's spirits, and veneration of the Earth; drawn from the religious traditions of Indigenous Peoples

Taiping Heavenly Kingdom · a nineteenth-century NRM which arose under the leadership of Hong Xiuquan, establishing a theocratic rebel state in China for over fifteen years before it was put down by the Chinese government

Hong Xiuquan · the self-proclaimed brother of Jesus Christ, who founded his own rebel theocracy in southern China with heterodox theology

Aetherius Society · the first known UFO religion, founded by George King in the 1950s around the belief in extraterrestrial intelligences called Cosmic Masters, who can help humans with their earthly concerns

ASIAN NRMs

The following is a list of other more recent Asian NRMs that have enjoyed great popularity:

- **Sokka Gakai** (founded in 1930) is a Japanese NRM based on the teachings of the thirteenth-century monk Nichiren, along with a reverence for an important Buddhist text known as the Lotus Sutra.

- **Falun Gong** (also known as Falun Dafa) was established by leader Li Hongzhi in the 1990s in China. It is today based in Dragon Springs, New York, with millions of followers, mainly in China despite severe government opposition.

- **The Unification Church** was founded in 1954 in South Korea by Sun Myung Moon. Borrowing several themes from Christianity, Reverend Moon claimed he would establish the kingdom of God on the Earth.

- Helen Blavatsky's Theosophical Society was a Western interpretation of Hinduism that birthed a variety of NRMs that brought together religious ideas from both the East and the West.

- The **Vedanta Society** was established in New York in 1894 by Swami Vivekananda—one of the first Indian gurus to unleash the power of Indian religion on US audiences. His message was that all religions share a similar message, but the Vedanta—or the Upanishads—are the supreme articulation of divine truth.

- The **Self-Realization Fellowship** was started in Los Angeles, California, in 1920 and brought the practice of Yoga to North Americans. Paramahansa Yogananda, the movement's charismatic leader, spoke in scientific terms, which appealed to educated Americans in particular. When George Harrison of The Beatles became an avid proponent of Yogananda's writings, it opened the floodgates for thousands of young Beatles fans to take notice of the movement.

- **Transcendental Meditation** became popular in the 1960s and 1970s due to the charismatic teaching of Maharishi Mahesh Yogi. However, it was clearly his winning of the Beatles that propelled this religious movement to international fame. Perhaps the most famous rock band of all time, the Beatles dove into the transcendental meditation movement and exposed generations of Westerners to Hindu approaches to spirituality.

- One of the most successful Indian-based NRMs is **ISKCON**—the International Society for Krishna Consciousness. Also known as the Hare Krishna movement, it was founded in 1966, as many Beatles fans were following their celebrity idols into Eastern forms of spirituality. It was founded by Swami Prabhupada, who famously translated the Bhagavad Gita into English, to great acclaim. George Harrison and Swami Prabhupada became friends, and Harrison wrote his megahit "My Sweet Lord" as a love song to the Hindu god Krishna.

Vedanta Society · an NRM established in New York in 1894 by Swami Vivekananda with the message that all religions are essentially the same, but the Vedanta—or, the Upanishads—are the supreme articulation of divine truth

Self-Realization Fellowship · an NRM started by Paramahansa Yogananda in Los Angeles, California, in 1920, which brought the practice of Yoga to North Americans

Transcendental Meditation · an NRM led by Maharishi Mahesh Yogi which became popular in the 1960s and 70s due to the endorsement of the Beatles

ISKCON · the International Society for Krishna Consciousness (ISKCON), a Hindu-based NRM also known as the Hare Krishna movement; founded by Swami Prabhupada, who famously translated the Bhagavad Gita into English

Raëlian Movement · the most well-known UFO religion, founded in the 1970s in France by Claude Vorilhon, who later took the name Raël; the movement believes that humans were created by a superior extraterrestrial species known as the Elohim, who have sent 40 Elohim-human hybrids to earth as the great prophets of the world religions

Church of Scientology · a controversial NRM founded by science fiction writer L. Ron Hubbard around the psychological self-help book *Dianetics*

Claude Vorilhon, the founder of Raëlism, was banned from entry into South Korea by the government, sparking protests from Korean Raëlians around the country.

because the Masters were sophisticated enough to help. Members of the Aetherius Society tend to be from Southern California, the United Kingdom, and New Zealand.

The **Raëlian Movement** is the most well-known UFO religion. Founded in the 1970s in France by Claude Vorilhon—known later as Raël—this movement claims an extraterrestrial species known as Elohim created humans. Raëlians do not believe in gods; rather, they believe the Elohim are a sophisticated species that have created forty hybrids (human/Elohim) that were the great prophets of humanity's history—people like Abraham, Moses, Buddha, Jesus, and Muhammad. Raëlians want world peace—therefore, they pursue the goal of building a landing pad for the Elohim to come to Earth.

Based initially in France and now in Quebec, Raëlians are proponents of human cloning as a hope for eternal life. Reliant on much of the religious infrastructure found in the Christian Bible, the group critiques Christianity for fundamentally misinterpreting the Bible.

Raël has emphasized the fluidity of gender, and he has argued that women are actually closer to the superior Elohim, which has given the religion a strong feminist bent. Some scholars have pointed to the hedonistic nature of the religion, as Raël urges members to experiment with their sexuality as a way of unifying with the universe. Raël himself is heterosexual and has been married multiple times.

Raised by a Jewish father and an atheist mother, Raël ran away from home as a young teenager and became a street musician in Paris, eventually rising to have some success on the national charts. He then became a French journalist, writing about the national car racing scene. Eventually, he, too, became a professional race car driver. In 1973, in his mid-twenties, Raël had an extraterrestrial encounter with a being called Yahweh and began writing books about how the encounter changed him. This being gave him a message that he was to take to humanity.

By far one of the most controversial and famous NRMs is the **Church of Scientology**. Founded by science fiction writer L. Ron Hubbard in the 1950s,

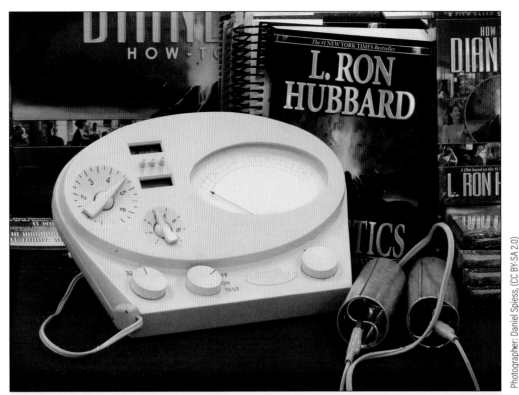

An E-meter and copies of *Dianetics*, both central to Scientology.

Engrams · in Scientology, memories that cause psychological trouble because of the negativity attached to them

E-meter · a machine in Scientology which measures one's electric currents

Clear · the status in Scientology when one is free of engrams

Rastafarianism · an NRM from Jamaica linked to the "back to Africa" movement; believes that the Ethiopian Emperor Haile Selassie was the Second Coming of Christ, ushering in a new Zion for members of the African diaspora who return to Ethiopia

the church began as a psychological self-help movement based around Hubbard's 1950 book *Dianetics: The Modern Science of Mental Health*. That book sold millions of copies and gave birth to the religion of Scientology.

The core teachings of Scientology are that people have memories—known as **engrams**—that can cause major psychological trouble due to the negativity attached to them. Hubbard developed a system of auditing in which an auditor, a Scientology therapist, uses a machine called an **E-meter** to measure a person's electric currents. The auditor helps the patient to work out these engrams so that they do not continue to distract the person and pull him or her away from enjoying their life. Once a person's mind has been freed of engrams, they are considered to be **clear**.

One of the reasons that Scientology has attracted so much attention as well as scrutiny is that many celebrities, such as Tom Cruise and John Travolta, have joined its ranks. Part of its controversial nature is that it has been critiqued trenchantly by professionals in the psychology and psychiatric industries for years. Famously, the church opposes psychological medicine,

which has put it at odds with many. The church has struggled in many countries to attain the status of a formal religion, which would exempt it from having to pay certain taxes. Many nations continue to decry it as being a cult.

Rastafarianism is an NRM that originated in Jamaica in the 1930s but focuses on events in Ethiopia. The religion is organized around the charismatic Ethiopian emperor **Haile Selassie** (1892–1975).

The imperial standard of Haile Selassie I, the Ethiopian emperor believed to be the Rastafari messiah. Christian elements include the "Lion of Judah" and the cross emblem.

Rastafarians argue that Emperor Selassie was the second coming of Jesus Christ, and he would lead all those in the African diaspora to return to resettle in Ethiopia, a new Zion. Rastafarians wear their hair long, usually in dreadlocks, and they frequently smoke cannabis as a sacrament. The movement was linked with a "back to Africa" movement that was strong during the mid-twentieth century. Ethiopia was the one African nation that was never colonized; therefore, it earned a reputation for being fiercely independent.[1] The most famous Rastafarian in history was Bob Marley (1945–81), one of the great figures in the history of reggae music. While the movement has been declining since the deaths of Selassie and Marley, there are still estimated to be close to a million followers.

Some NRMs focus on nature, such as Wicca, **Druidry**, and Neo-Paganism. **Wicca** is a witchcraft religion founded in England in the 1950s in the aftermath of a book called *Witchcraft Today* (1954), which was written by an amateur anthropologist named Gerald Gardner (1884–1964). Wicca draws upon key ideas in the ecology movement, as well as feminism. Made up predominantly of women, the religion focuses on goddesses. Two deities in particular that are favored among Wiccans are the Horned God and the Mother Goddess, both of whom are associated with fertility.

There are estimated to be around a million people in the United States who associate with witchcraft and paganism, which would mean they outnumber Jehovah's Witnesses in the United States. Witchcraft is on the rise in the Western world, partly due to its alliances with feminism and LGBTQ communities. It has also had great success in media, with hit shows impacting curiosity in the movement, such as *Harry Potter*, *Buffy the Vampire Slayer*, *Sabrina the Teenage Witch*, and *Charmed*.

Haile Selassie · an Ethiopian emperor believed by Rastafarians to be the second incarnation of Jesus Christ

Druidry · a modern NRM of harmony and connection to the natural world, based loosely on the religion of the historical Druids

Wicca · a witchcraft NRM that combines a reverence for ecology and feminism

Nature and witchcraft religions have grown more popular in recent decades as an outlet of feminist and ecologist religious expression.

© Andrey Kiselev, Adobe Stock

The **Baha'i Faith** is an NRM that branched off from Islam. Its origins are found in Persia (Iran) in the first half of the nineteenth century with two men: the **Bab** (the Gate) and **Baha'u'llah** (the Glory of God). The Bab was executed for treason and blasphemy. His followers, coming from Shi'a Islam, held that he was a Mahdi, a kind of hidden imam that would come in the last days. A few years later, one of the Bab's followers claimed he had been prophesied by the Bab. In other words, the Bab was a precursor, and a great prophet would come. That man, named Mirza Husayn Ali, took on the name Baha'u'llah and taught a radically inclusive message about the world's faiths. In his view, all the religions are valid, and all have a unified message. Baha'u'llah claimed that all prophets were necessary during their time, and the ultimate goal of all religions is harmony and peace for all people and all nations. While monotheistic, most Muslims found the prophetic claims to be offensive, as Islam holds that Muhammad is the Seal of the Prophets. The movement grew steadily, however, and is today one of the fastest growing religions in the world, with a global membership of around 8.5 million. Baha'is have experienced severe persecution in Iran and in Egypt, due to them being considered apostates from Islam.

Drugs and Religion

Numerous scholars have devoted themselves to the study of religion's interaction with drugs and **entheogenic plants** such as mescaline, peyote, LSD, and so-called magic mushrooms. Medicinal plants and herbs have been associated with religion for millennia, as in the case of soma's use within Hinduism and haoma's use within Zoroastrianism. Various plants have a long history of being associated with producing various states of consciousness and hallucination. Wine, beer, and other alcoholic drinks have long served as medicinally valuable remedies. Cannabis is smoked regularly by Rastafarians. The Native American Church continues to take peyote as a sacrament, a tradition that likely goes back centuries.

Whether these drugs and plants induce altered states of consciousness is not in doubt. They certainly do alter the mind. Adherents to many religions have taken entheogenic plants because of this altered state that can be induced. The primary questions for religion scholars concern the religious significance of these altered states and what value they serve for the individual or community.

It is clear that religious views have been enhanced, altered, or otherwise impacted due to the use of entheogenic plants and intoxicants. Scholars show that the effects of hallucinogenic drugs are explained in religious terms by approximately one-third of the general population. However, around three-fourths of religious participants in these studies explain their hallucinogenic experiences in religious terms. If a religious setting is provided for religious subjects to take

Abdul-Baha (1844–1921), the eldest son of Baha'u'llah, a central figure of the Baha'i Faith. He faced imprisonment and exile but managed to grow the Baha'i Faith through preaching and teaching the principles he learned from his father.

Young adults gather at a hookah lounge. The high of certain drugs is often compared to a religious experience.

hallucinogens, then around nine-tenths of study participants report having a religious experience.[2]

Scholars are divided on these studies. Some claim that the drugs simply impacted the brain in such a way that people used religious categories to explain unique experiences. Others, however, see a clear connection between religiosity and the effects of the drugs. In other words, can a religious "trip" truly be considered religious if it is merely a chemical impact on the mind? Isn't that an artificial experience as opposed to something real? Or perhaps the drug unlocks a part of the mind that is not typically accessed in normal day-to-day life, and the chemical opens up doors of creativity and mystical understanding.

Karen Armstrong, the famous writer on world religions, noted that when she was a nun in a convent, she had euphoric religious experiences that were often accompanied by emotional outbursts and even anguish. However, when she was diagnosed as having epilepsy, the medicine she was prescribed did two things: it stopped her painful episodes, but it also muted her religious experience dramatically. With treatment, she stopped having the episodes that she had previously interpreted as being religious.[3]

Atheism · the conviction that there are no gods nor anything supernatural or metaphysical

Scholars seem united in their conclusion that while substances can induce religious experiences, they are less likely to produce religious lives. Certainly, drugs are used to improve the mental state of patients, but is it ethical to improve the religious awareness of people through drugs? Religiosity is often associated with positive outcomes in people. Thus, is it ethical to prescribe drugs that help people become more religious, furnishing them with the positive impacts that religion provides?

Atheism and Agnosticism

Atheists uphold the idea that there are no gods in existence; therefore, religions are likely based on mistaken convictions. Pure **atheism** is rare. Throughout history, people who take a position that there are no gods are a

Staunch New Atheists Richard Dawkins and Ariane Sherine posing in front of the Atheist Bus Campaign, an effort to combat Christian evangelism in Western Europe.

small minority. There is a variety of reasons for atheism remaining so small. Some of it obviously has to do with the fact that, in many societies, atheists are demonized and persecuted. Other reasons have to do with sociological contexts. People are less likely to believe in no gods when their parents and virtually everyone else around them believe in divine beings. Even when atheists are given the freedom to take that position, it seems that the propensity for religiosity is powerful in humans. For some, atheism serves as a kind of phase that people move in and out of depending on their life circumstances. People may rebel against a religion they think offers insufficient answers to life's challenges, is a source of injury or harm, or otherwise let them down. Of all of the surveys of religious beliefs in the United States, true atheists—those who believe that there are no divine beings in existence—have never registered above 5 percent of the population, although the world atheist population is up to 7 percent.

In recent years, scholars have written about **New Atheism**—a school of thought that attacks religious belief, usually through books and in academic venues. The New Atheists, such as Christopher Hitchens, Sam Harris, Richard Dawkins, and Daniel Dennett, argue that religion is simply superstition and is therefore irrational. They are not tolerant of religious views, believing that religion is so provably false that it

should not be tolerated. It should be demonstrated for what it is: irrational. Dawkins has gone so far as to condemn those who train their children in religion as being unethical. Through indoctrination, he argues, parents are denying their children the freedom to question and to arrive at rational conclusions on their own. These atheists associate religion with undesirable social ills such as racism, violence, bigotry, tribalism, ignorance, and intolerance. However, what these New Atheists have not fully engaged, at least not yet, is how irreligion—such as Maoist China and Stalinist Russia—failed to do any better in these unsavory categories. Violence and intolerance in the name of atheism knew no bounds in the twentieth century. Obviously, not all atheists are so militant.

Agnosticism is a softer worldview that tends to refrain from taking a stance. The word *agnosticism* means "no knowledge." There are two major forms of agnosticism. First, there is the stance that one does not know because they have not thought much about the topic or have not explored the topic thoroughly. Perhaps they are searching but have not found enough evidence to support belief in a god. The second major form of agnosticism is more adamant. This is the view that there is no way for anyone to ever know, whether one way or the other. In other words, until one can prove that there is or there is not a god, then one must adhere to an

Catholicos Karekin II, the supreme head of the Armenian Apostolic Church, is a leader in the World Council of Churches and has participated in a number of ecumenical meetings with Pope Francis.

agnostic position. Intellectually, we must remain agnostic since the proof, either way, comes up short.

The Future of Religion

> The vast majority of humankind's religions have come and gone. Hieroglyphs, ancient texts, and oral stories show us that, while religions play a major role in civilizations, eventually, the vast majority of them will become replaced, or else they will become absorbed into another culture that comes along.

Religions also wax and wane during their existence. They usually rise up with great zeal and excitement and then go through an institutionalization process whereby the religion finds its way into the society's institutions. And if religions are not careful, they can ossify, eventually to the point of becoming irrelevant to the community members. If the religious ideas are not powerful enough to last, then something else will surely come along that will capture the imagination, and in time, the religion will recede and eventually evaporate.

Not all religions are destined to die, but most of them have proven how difficult it can be to survive the test of time. Christianity and Islam now claim over half of the world's population. This statistic alone shows just how competitive a religion must be to enter the marketplace. When Hinduism is added, we are getting close to three-fourths of the world's population. There just is not a lot of room for other major religions, which is why the fourth-largest religion in the world—Buddhism—is only about 6 percent of the world's population.

In some ways, competing religions are like capitalism but on a massive scale. The truly successful religions of the world will outlast any company, but the vast majority of religions—think of some of the NRMs—will be here for perhaps a few generations, maybe a few centuries, and then peter out. Only the most innovative and resilient religions will survive the long test of time.

Hinduism, for example, has survived largely because of its deep connection to the South Asian soil and its people over the millennia. Buddhism at one point posed a serious challenge, Islam came along and dominated the subcontinent for centuries, and then Christianity entered alongside colonialism. But Hinduism remained firm, against the odds. Today, Buddhism is hardly present in India. Islam is a force to contend with—at around 14 percent of the Indian population. Christianity, Sikhism, and Jainism account for less than 5 percent of the total population. But Hinduism remains firmly on top in India, with around 80 percent of the nation's population, probably due to its ability to cast itself as the ancient and authentic religion of India.

People today have to fight hard to keep their religion from slipping into irrelevance, or worse. Many Christian civilizations over time have had to fight wars to keep their religion. The Armenians have dealt with invasion after invasion for centuries. Really, Armenia should be a Muslim nation today, after so many thwarted invasions into the land. However, its religion remains firm, the religion of Orthodox Christianity. It has stood the test of time, against all odds, probably more than any nation on the Earth today. How does a little nation like Armenia defend itself against such behemoth forces over the years, such as the Persians, Zoroastrians, various Muslim empires, and the Soviet Union with its strongly atheistic principles? Yet, somehow, Armenia's Christian religion survived.

Some religions have to compromise and therefore blend. This can be a smart decision or a devastating one for the future of the religion. If the religion compromises too much, then it melts into another society and loses all distinctiveness. However, if the religion is inflexible, it can lose connection to its people. Religions inevitably wax and wane, occasionally bend, and occasionally hold firm to traditional values, but one thing is clear: religions are living things. They must adapt and move. They must migrate and fight. They must resist and reinvent. Religions that survive long-term do these things. Perhaps more than anything else, they have to maintain a hold on the hearts and minds of new generations. Religious growth occurs in three major ways: war, proselytization, and fertility rates. If religions fail at all three of these, then they eventually dissipate. If they cannot expand through territorial gains, if they do not proselytize, and if new babies are not born into the religion, then the future is grim.

The world is changing rapidly. Ever since World War II, these changes have been accelerating, and one could argue that the acceleration has been exponential since the inventions of the Internet and the cellphone. These two inventions have changed the game. People are now connected as never before. People can become millionaires without leaving their bedrooms. People can broadcast their views to almost the entire world. People can maintain connections with thousands of different people in ways unheard of a century ago. And these changes mean that religions will have to adapt to compete. If they transition well into the Internet era, then they have a chance at survival.

Political and economic power can prove tremendously helpful for religions, much like the Constantinian effect—when the emperor smiles on a religion, that religion is likely going to fare pretty well. When the Arab militaries embraced Islam, then the expansion of the Arabs also expanded the religion of Islam. When a nation like the United States of America tends to support Christianity, then that religion has a good chance of remaining relevant and strong. However, when a nation turns against a religion, as we saw with the religions of China in the twentieth century, then it could go either way. Some religions have been destroyed. There is a reason that Spain was Christian for so long, then Muslim for seven centuries, and then Christian again. There was a titanic struggle on the Iberian Peninsula. There is a reason that the Middle East—formerly almost entirely Christian—is Muslim today. There are reasons why Zoroastrianism has declined so precipitously throughout the centuries, despite at one time being the favored religion of the great Persian Empire. There is a reason why Egyptian gods are relegated to the realm of mythology today—those ancient Egyptian religions were displaced by other religions that were able to capture hearts and minds more effectively. Plus, those Egyptian religions belonged to people who were defeated in wars, and their religions died with them. It can be brutal. Like Darwinism, religions must not only survive, but they have to evolve if they plan to stick around when competitors come along.

Another approach to survival, however, is what we see in fundamentalist religions. Some religions see their future as better linked to their past. Islam, Hinduism, Judaism, and Christianity all have robust fundamentalist movements currently in the world. The

Hasidic Jews at the Western Wall in Jerusalem, with a copy of the Torah. The Hasidic movement pushes its followers to be more religious and more Orthodox, combatting the trend away from religion.

Hasidic movement in Judaism is a revivalist movement that has been characterized as "ultra-Orthodox." Instead of adapting to today's society, it opts to remember a time in the past and honor it. Similarly, many Christians choose to go "back to the Bible" with their theology instead of trying to integrate every new social issue that comes along. They prefer to return to a previous era—perhaps the era of the New Testament or the era of the church fathers. Muslims, clearly, are in the midst of a global "back to the ummah" movement that originated in Saudi Arabia but expanded to Egypt and later to Iran and has captivated the greater part of global Islam. Hindus, too, are reviving a form of fundamentalist understanding about their faith that has completely defeated the once-secular government coalition (Indian National Congress) and replaced it with an overtly Hindu government: the Bharatiya Janata Party. The notion of "returning" to a previous era in a religious tradition can be powerful and effective. Thus, adaptation and progress can move in different directions, even backwards, much of the time.

Some have wondered if perhaps atheism will ultimately win. Based on the fact that atheism's heyday was in the late 1700s, this seems unlikely. The propensity for religion is strong within people. What seems more likely is that religion will change. As globalization—Internet, air travel, communications, immigration, global corporations, English language—connect the world's population, there is bound to be some mutual discovery and mutual enhancement that will take place among the world's religions. Many Christians have already started practicing Yoga. Many Hindus argue that they are actually monotheists. Many Muslims emphasize the sensibility of love. Many Zen Buddhists have entered the capitalistic frenzy that now defines our world. These are examples of religious adaptation.

Perhaps more than anything else, migration and English as the world's lingua franca will make everybody more available to everybody else. Foreigners will become more easily integrated into new societies. For example, in the United States, immigrants from other lands already exhibit the ability to speak English exceedingly well—they have eaten at KFC and McDonald's all of their lives, and they watch the same Netflix shows as the Americans that they now join. As Thomas Friedman put it, the world is now flat. What he means by that phrase is that we all have the ability to understand each other; like no other time in history before, we have access to each other.

All these factors will likely serve to the advantage of religiosity rather than atheism or complete secularization. Religion will continue to have a role. Religions will perhaps be strengthened and challenged by one another as they encounter each other more frequently. Perhaps the competition will increase, but that will only help religions, just as it does the price and quality of hamburgers.

Religion Remixed

So what if all these various religions converge during the age of globalization? What if people start practicing a little bit of Yoga with their Bible studies? That is already being done. What if upcoming generations that declare themselves nonreligious actually are religious, just in unfamiliar ways? Perhaps they long for meaning, for spirituality, for angels and perhaps demons, but do not have formal categories for understanding their religious experiences. Indeed, that seems to be what is happening.

> The religiously remixed are often young, but increasingly, older people are moving in this direction as well—they want religion on their terms.

Studies continue to show that the "religious nones" are pretty religious. They pray and meditate and do Yoga. They read the Bhagavad Gita and the book of Genesis, sometimes in the same sitting. Sometimes they listen to "om" chants as they study, and they read inspirational quotations from the Dalai Lama and other well-known faith leaders. They travel across the Himalayas in search of meaning, all the while staying connected to their churches back home through streaming. Their phone notifications are as likely to come from Jordan Peterson—a kind of religious guru for nonreligious men—as from Ariana Grande's

A young woman thoughtfully engaged in prayer.

Instagram account. We are connected. We are hearing voices from all directions. And this has impacted our religiosity—by mixing it up. Many of us are becoming **religiously remixed**.[4]

The religiously remixed are often young, but increasingly, older people are moving in this direction as well—they want religion on their terms. They buy religious products and books on the Internet. They attend various cultural and religious festivals and gatherings without hesitance. They have friends from various religious traditions, and they learn from them. Crucially, much of their religious content and consumption comes for free on the Internet. Again, this is crucial. People today are using their phones like a "back-pocket" God—they find answers to questions, ideas on philosophy, and sermon snippets simply from doing a quick Google search on their phones (or DuckDuckGo if they want more privacy).[5]

Some studies show that retirees spend as much time connected to the Internet as young people. But it is the religiously remixed, regardless of age, who are allowing technology to shape their religious preferences and practices in profound ways. If anybody had any hesitation about consuming religion on a device, the COVID-19 pandemic all but destroyed that hesitancy, as almost everybody had to go virtual, and now everybody knows how to do it.

Perhaps Protestant Christianity is most prepared for the shifts happening in religion today due to technology and globalization. After all, Protestantism has always been the religion of the book. Protestants were born into a way of thinking that emerged from the minds of Johannes Gutenberg and Martin Luther—get

> **Religiously Remixed** · a categorization for people who draw on various traditions from multiple religions for their own personal spirituality

Modern fan communities or fandoms have a zeal often similar to religious commitment and exhibit a like-minded community analogous to that of a congregation. Souvenirs from the Wizarding World of Harry Potter experience in Madrid, Spain (2017).

the Bible into the hands of the people. People need to read. People need access. Society is better if we can all view something and shape it with our distinctive minds and unique perceptions.

Ultimately, this process is at the root of democracy. The more minds the better. But groupthink has pros and cons. On one hand, the crowd can be right, as has been proven through studies of gameshows. However, the crowd is often dead wrong, as in the case of the French revolutionaries who wanted to shoot all the Catholic priests in the streets, or such as the crowds in the Salem witch trials, who whipped themselves into a frenzy and caused the deaths of innocent people. This negative side of groupthink happens quite regularly in a connected, virtual world. It can be victimizing and terrorizing, just as in Salem.

Debate, Fandom, and Friendship

Another well-known problem with Protestant Christianity is that it constantly feeds schism. Think about it. There is one Catholic Church. The various national Orthodox churches are rather united on doctrine and praxis. But Protestantism? It is all over the place. Unificationism and Methodism are both considered successor faiths to Protestantism. There are Pentecostals, Pietists, and Presbyterians. There are now approaching fifty thousand Protestant denominations in the world. They continue to split and fracture. Why? It is because Protestants protest. That is just what they do. They were born in protest, and that remains the most significant badge of a Protestant. They protest each other's claims.

Fandom on the Internet has mixed us all together in strange ways. We might share similar interests:

Justin Bieber, deep-sea fishing, 1980s toys, to name a few. And perhaps that is a good thing. We never would have found each other otherwise. We all get mixed together in fascinating ways in the twenty-first century thanks to the remarkably sophisticated algorithms that unite and divide us.

Harry Potter, for instance, has united people on principles that seem rather religious. There is, of course, more in this literature than witches, spells, giants, and young love. J. K. Rowling's story connects with transcendent themes and has allowed a generation of readers to understand not only good and evil but the nature of deep and loyal friendships. Could it be that the religion portrayed in *Harry Potter* will have an impact on the shape of Christianity or the other well-known religions? Time will tell.

One thing that is becoming clear about millennials and Gen Z-ers is that they are less likely to get involved in traditional religious institutions. This conclusion started emerging with the Gen X-ers in the 1990s and 2000s and has continued. People under age fifty tend not to commit to social organizations such as Boy Scouts, Rotary clubs, or swim teams, as in past generations. People are not as eager to commit long-term to groups. We are more fluid in virtually everything. And as the boomers, who tend to have deep commitments to groups, pass away, that trend will probably accelerate. These trends are hitting religion hard. Religious institutions valiantly served the boomers and the Greatest Generation, but the one thing that never changes is change. Change always remains. Nothing else does.

Is religion going the way of the dinosaur? This does not seem likely. People still pray, trust their scriptures, believe in the afterlife, see the value in spiritual connection, and worship a divine presence. Even the religious "nones" have been shown to be fairly religious people, if by that we mean that they believe in spiritual practices and possibilities. Very few people absolutely reject religion and spirituality—studies have demonstrated this for more than two hundred years. Again, true atheism is rare. For many who claim to be atheists, it is a temporary phase.

Americans might be attending religious services less frequently these days, which is certainly sensible in a post-COVID world. But we will certainly keep searching for meaning. We will continue to find value in our communities. We will keep reading ancient texts of wisdom. We will keep looking for our purpose in this often confusing and at times cruel world. We will keep searching for ways to celebrate rituals—corporate prayer, worship, and confession of sin. We can hardly function without celebrating life events with others. But perhaps we are reconceiving religion. Perhaps we are entering a new era in which globalization is impacting how and what we believe by exposing us to new ideas. As our world shrinks, maybe our religions mix.

Even religious leaders in the great traditions are becoming "remixed" in key ways. For example, the Dalai Lama—the great leader of the Buddhist world—has said that religious conversion is outdated. Another religious leader in India, Amma, has shared similar sentiments. Amma's real name is Mata Amritanandamayi, but she is famously referred to as the "hugging saint." She sits in her ashram in Kerala, India, hugging devotees and other visitors for hours on end. She has become one of the leading religious celebrities in our world today for her compassionate kindness and the sympathetic looks she gives to

Mata Amritanandamayi, better known as Amma or the "hugging saint," is an Indian guru beloved for her compassion and goodwill toward all, as well as for her practice of giving hugs.

each person who collapses into her arms. Known to many as the divine mother, she has said, "It matters not whether one believes in Krishna or Christ, Mother Kali or Mother Mary; a formless God or even a flame, a mountain or an ideal."[6] Amma's warmth, kindness, and compassion inspires people. She has an appeal that transcends disparate religions. She has a beautiful and unique way of uniting people. This is one major kind of religiosity that people of all ages seem to respond to these days. Amma represents our better angels.

Amma is showing that other religions can offer resources from which we can all benefit. Another example is Yoga, which has found its way into eager Christian churches. Yoga is today a multibillion-dollar industry that, in some cases, has completely separated itself from any kind of religious context. That is what is so ironic about the religion remixed concept—even explicitly religious practices like Yoga become integrated into other religions or even get stripped of religion altogether. One never knows which direction a religious idea might eventually go.

The Khrist Bhakta movement in India has given Jesus Christ a platform that few Western missionaries could ever attain, largely because it is an indigenous movement toward Christ that is devoid of any kind of Western ideology.[7] Khrist Bhakta is a quintessential example of the religious mixing happening between East and West in a globalizing postcolonial age.

More and more, people in the United States are taking world religions classes, making friends with members of other faiths, and participating in inter-religious dialogue. It is difficult to attend a religiously monolithic university today, even if attending a so-called Christian university. Inevitably, one will find Jews, Hindus, Muslims, and Buddhists there. Certainly, one will find agnostics, nones, and the religiously remixed at a Christian university, as the United States' universities—religious or not—are globally respected.

Author, educator, and interfaith leader Eboo Patel founded Interfaith Youth Core (now known as Interfaith America) on the idea that religion should be a bridge of cooperation rather than a barrier of division.

Well-to-do families from all over the world consider it a privilege to send their children to the United States for school.

As a result, individuals are gaining exposure to other religions like never before. The temple down the road sparks curiosity. The Muslim family who invites a Christian family to an iftar is doing its best to be loving and hospitable. Christians are responding in kind—inviting members of other religions to a Christmas pageant, for example. The religious mixing going on has led to a new era of camaraderie and even a rising religious consciousness. Our world is becoming more religiously complex and probably not less religious.

> What if there is something rather than nothing? What if there is a transcendent reality? What if our thoughts and actions actually have spiritually meaningful consequences? In other words, what if it all means something?

Religion is the place where those questions get their due. The world's religions can be used for better or for worse. They provide hope and meaning, fight despair, and bring people together like nothing else can. But they can also stimulate tribalism and shame. There are aspects and consequences that derive from religion that we could certainly do without.

It is wonderful to see religious leaders from various traditions think collectively about what they can do to help address the world's conflicts and what they can do to put balm on humanity's wounds. As Hans Küng often noted, "There is no peace among the nations without there being peace among the religions."

People are starting to understand that members of other religions are potential friends. Certainly, friends have their own convictions. But friendship is a beautiful thing, perhaps especially when it involves people who think differently from each other. Like former Supreme Court justices Ruth Bader Ginsburg and Antonin Scalia—they were the closest of friends, despite their extremely different take on virtually every hot-button issue imaginable. He was a conservative Catholic; she was a secular Jew. But before their deaths in 2016 and 2020, they impressed the world by their exceedingly close friendship—to the very end. Being members of different faiths does not preclude close friendships—not at all.

GLOSSARY

CHAPTER ONE

Agnostic · a person who is uncommitted to a stance on whether or not a god or gods exist

Amish · rooted in Jakob Ammann's (born 1644) approach to Anabaptism, a strict religious community that foregoes the usage of modern technology and rejects modern culture

Ancestors · the spirits of deceased family members, often believed to be accessible through prayer and sacrifice

Apologetics · the study of one religion in order to defend it against critics and to refute competing belief systems

Apostle Paul · a rabbi in the first century CE who became a great early Christian missionary and writer; he emphasized the importance of inclusion and diversity in the church

Atheist · a person who rejects the possibility of a god

Baptism · an initiation ritual in Christian traditions

Bar mitzvah · a Jewish rite of passage undertaken by a boy on his thirteenth birthday

Brahman · the eternal and ultimate reality in Hinduism

Brit Milah · when a Jewish boy is circumcised on his eighth day

Buddha · "the enlightened one," Siddhartha Gautama

Ceremony · the sacred times in a religion when the individual or the community encounters the divine or sits in the presence of their conception of ultimate reality; varies from church services to weddings to festivals

Chinese New Year · a celebration of the New Year according to the lunar calendar

Civilization and Its Discontents · a book by Sigmund Freud, which posited that a person chooses to submit to certain obligations and sacrifices to gain the rewards of being involved in a particular community or society

Clifford Geertz · an anthropologist who believed strongly in the merits of doing actual fieldwork—befriending and living among the people one studies; contributed the important theories of "thick description" and "frames of meaning"

Code · the aspect of a religion that defines behavior and ethics

Community · the collectivist sense of a religion

Comparative religion · a term for the study of world religions that emphasizes the comparison of the various religious traditions

Creed · shared statements of faith used in confessional communities to promote unity among believers and create doctrinal borders

Diwali · the festival of lights in India

Dukkha · the Buddhist doctrine of suffering, anxiety, and dis-ease

E. B. Tylor · an early anthropologist who studied magic, taboo, animism, and totemism; believed that the beliefs of a civilization evolve from primitive magic to organized religion and eventually to modern science

E. E. Evans-Pritchard · an Oxford anthropologist who believed strongly in the importance of fieldwork—actually living with the people one studies—so that the student can understand the larger worldview at work in his or her subjects

Eid al-Fitr · a Muslim celebration marking the end of the daylight fasts of the holy month of Ramadan

Emile Durkheim · saw religion as a complex sociological phenomenon meant to bring coherence to the individual and his or her own specific society

Enlightenment · the central goal of Buddhism

Frames of meaning · the conceptual framework in which a community's beliefs and behaviors are rooted and understood

Free agency · a concept from sports in which a player is not bound to a particular team for his or her career; rather, he or she can temporarily commit to whatever team offers the highest payment

Fundamentalism · extreme commitment to the traditional aspects of a religion, often to the point of emphasizing obedience to the letter of the law over human decency and respect

Globalization · the current phenomenon of increasing interconnectedness between international businesses, polities, and cultures

Golden Rule · a central tenet of many worldwide faiths that teaches practitioners to treat others as they would want to be treated

Gurdwara · a Sikh house of worship

Guru Granth Sahib · the holy text of Sikhism

Heaven · a common endpoint for many of the world's religions; a place of paradise that can be reached through correct action on Earth

History of religions · a term for the study of world religions that emphasizes the historical background of religious traditions

Individualism · a common modern perspective that emphasizes the needs of an individual over the needs of the community

J. G. Frazer · an early anthropologist who studied magic, taboo, animism, and totemism; believed that the beliefs of a civilization evolve from primitive magic to organized religion and eventually to modern science

Kamidana · a small shrine in a Shinto home dedicated to the ancestors and used for daily religious ritual

Karl Marx · saw religion as endemic to class struggle and as used by the elites to keep the masses docile; famous for claiming that religion is the "opium of the people"

Langar · a free meal given to worshippers and guests following a Sikh service

Liberation · the central goal of Hinduism

Max Weber · saw deep complexity in religion and its causes; compared numerous religions with great social and historical nuance

Meditation · a practice of regulated breathing and mental focus employed by many world religions

Messiah · a famous and inspiring oratorio by George Frideric Handel

Mezuzah · a parchment inscribed with Jewish scriptures and fixed to the doorpost of a home

Mircea Eliade · categorized all human experience into the categories of sacred and profane

Mohel · the officiate who performs the circumcision

Moksha · the liberation of the soul from the cycle of rebirth in Hinduism and other Eastern traditions

Mormons · (formally known as the Church of Jesus Christ of Latter-day Saints) led by Joseph Smith and later Brigham Young, this form of Protestant Christianity emerged on the US frontier and is now a substantial global denomination

Nirvana · the extinguishment of all of one's desires

Preunderstanding · our preexisting frame of reference through which we judge new information

Purim · a Jewish festival celebrating the day the Jewish people were saved from a genocide plot during the reign of the First Persian Empire

Qualitative · a way of studying religion that uses interviews and individual experiences

Quantitative · a way of studying religion that utilizes surveys and statistics

Rabbi · a religious teacher in Judaism

Reincarnation · the cycle of rebirth into a new body after death

Religion · a concept that is notoriously difficult to define; however, the English word is rooted in the Latin term *religare*, meaning "to tie or bind together"

Religious studies · a term for the study of world religions; approaches religion with an academic and critical lens

Religious zealotry · extremist forms of religion that sometimes result in violence or human rights violations

Roman Catholicism · the largest Christian denomination in the world

Rumspringa · a season in which an Amish person is allowed to leave the community and participate in modern culture before choosing to commit to an Amish lifestyle

Sabbath · the seventh day of each week, which Jewish adherents are required to give to God and to their synagogue

Saint Francis of Assisi · a famous Catholic saint from the 1200s who taught a decentering of the self to look instead to the needs of others

Salvation · the central goal of the Christian religion

Samsara · the cycle of rebirth

Sati · widow burning, a controversial, now banned practice in India

The scale creates the phenomenon · an important principle when studying religion, as people are better able to understand the context of any religious phenomenon, such as a ritual, a god, or a description of the afterlife, if they have learned other religious perspectives, or scales

Secular · unaffiliated with religion

Seppuku · honorable suicide by self-disembowelment in Japanese history

Sigmund Freud · the father of psychotherapy who speculated that religion's origins are in human illusions or wishful thinking

Ten Commandments · the basic moral code of Judaism

Theology · the study of the religious doctrines of a particular faith, generally to connect deeper with God or to strengthen one's belief

Thick description · describing human social action not just with observable behaviors but also with their context, as interpreted by a member of the social community

Ummah · the global community of Muslims

William James · an American psychologist who focused on religious experience rather than religious institutions, believing that within human experience is found the truest form of religious life

Zakat · a 2.5% tithe collected for the poor, as required by Islam

CHAPTER TWO

Akhenaten · the new name that Amenhotep IV took to emphasize his devotion to Aten

Amenhotep IV · an Egyptian Pharaoh who briefly forced Egypt into monotheism by worshiping Aten exclusively

Amun-Ra · an Egyptian god who rose to very high status because of his association with the Sun

Ancestor veneration · a common religious practice in which practitioners commemorate and sometimes sacrifice to the deceased; should not be equated with "ancestor worship"

Animism · the belief that spirits animate people, animals, places, trees, weather, bodies of water, and even rocks and everyday objects

Animistic religions · a term for indigenous religions that emphasizes their common connection to animism

Anthropology · an important field to the study of religion; anthropologists scientifically study human behavior, biology, and society from ancient to present times

Archaeology · an extremely important field to the study of religion, as archaeologists can study the most ancient and preliterate religions by examining the remains of burial grounds and of surviving artifacts

Arnold van Gennep · an ethnographer who posited that there are three phases to rites of passage: separation, transition, and incorporation

Aten · the Sun, symbolized in Egyptian hieroglyphics as a disk, often with rays of light shooting out

Azande · an ethnic group of North Central Africa

Aztec Empire · a powerful Mesoamerican civilization that practiced human sacrifice

Baptism · a Christian rite of passage that symbolizes rebirth from an old sinful life into a new purified life

Bar and bat mitzvah · Jewish rites of passage symbolizing the passage from childhood into adulthood

Basic religions · another term for indigenous religions

Benge · the poison oracle, in which a shaman asks questions while poisoning a chicken; whether or not the chicken dies corresponds to a yes or no answer to the question being asked

Burial grounds · sites of burial used by ancient peoples; a repository of knowledge for modern scholars

Carnac stone site · a Neolithic religious site found in the Brittany region of France

Cats · highly prized in ancient Egypt as protectors and good luck charms

Cave paintings · the artwork of ancient peoples preserved on the walls of caves; a repository of knowledge for modern scholars

Channeling · an important function of a shaman, who provides his or her body as a conduit for spirits who want to communicate something

Chichen Itza · one of the two great centers of Aztec human sacrifice

Circumcision · a Jewish rite of passage for boys on the eighth day of their lives

Confirmation · a Catholic and Lutheran rite of passage

Cro-Magnon religion · Cro-Magnons, also known as **Early European Modern Humans**, buried their dead with tools for the afterlife, and they painted hunting scenes with ochre, probably a form of imitative magic

Crystals · mystically used by New Age spirituality for healing and for other properties; taken originally from Native American religion

Día de los Muertos · a Hispanic holiday commemorating deceased loved ones, often including the sacrifice of alcohol to their spirits

Disease of language theory · the idea that ancient peoples used specific words to refer to the natural elements; over time, those words were personified into deities

Divination · rituals designed to predict the future, to discover the guilt or innocence of a person, or even to hear from a divine power by means of an *oracle*

E. E. Evans-Pritchard · a British anthropologist who studied the Azande and Nuer peoples; wrote *Witchcraft, Oracles, and Magic among the Azande*

The Egyptian Book of the Dead · elaborate texts dealing with the afterlife

Epic of Gilgamesh · an ancient Sumerian religious text that corroborates a version of the flood myth from Genesis

Epistemology · the theory of knowledge

Etymology · the study of the origin and history of words

Eucharist · a Catholic ritual commemorating the death and resurrection of Jesus Christ

Francisco Pizarro · the conquistador who defeated the Inca Empire

Great Spirit · the High God in many Native American religions

Henotheism · the practice of only worshiping one god while believing in the existence or the possibility of other gods

The Hero with a Thousand Faces · a comparative study of myths found in religions throughout the world

Hieroglyphics · the written language of the ancient Egyptians

High God · found in many polytheistic religions, especially in African cultures; the High God created the world but is now distant and somewhat inaccessible, so various lesser gods or spirits are worshiped instead

Historians · experts in the field of history, providing historical context to the understanding of many other fields of study

History · an interpretation of the past, influenced by motives and biases

Horus · the son of Osiris and Isis who avenged his father by killing Seth

Human sacrificial system · the sacrifice of human life to placate a higher power

Huston Smith · an influential religious studies scholar

Hyksos · an ancient people who at one time conquered Egypt

Imitative magic · imitating something that one wishes to happen, such as painting a successful hunt in order to bring good luck to a hunt

Incorporation · the final phase of a rite of passage in which the individual is reincorporated into the community with a slightly altered identity or a new function or position

Indigenous religions · a term for basic religions that emphasizes their localized context, their often ancient character, and their geographically limited scope

Isis · Osiris's wife who brought him back to life to reign in the underworld

Jesus Christ · believed to be a human sacrifice on behalf of humanity in order to expiate the sins that have been committed by his followers

Joseph Campbell · wrote a famous study of religious and mythological heroes called *The Hero with a Thousand Faces*

Kachina · in Native American religion, spirits that could provide rain, fertility, and power

King Tutankhamun · Akhenaten's son who reinstated polytheism in Egypt and then died young; the discovery of his tomb brought worldwide attention to ancient Egypt

Language · can provide insight into ancient peoples; however, many cultures had no written language, and surviving accounts might provide deeply biased information

Liminality · the period of transition involved in a rite of passage; taken from a Latin word meaning "a threshold"

Linguistic scholars · an important field in the study of religion; linguistic scholars can trace the migrations of and interactions between different peoples based on the evolution of their languages

Ma'at · truth, justice, and righteousness in ancient Egyptian religion; the ultimate standard; later personified as a goddess

Magic · according to Tylor and Frazer, the first and most primitive form of human belief, characterized by attempts to control nature through ritual

Max Müller · a religion scholar famous for his "disease of language theory"

Medicine man · another term for a shaman

Mesoamerica · a historical and cultural region spanning from southern Mexico to northern Costa Rica

Mesoamerican pyramids · impressive Aztec structures used in religious ceremonies

Moloch · a god in the Hebrew Bible whose devotees practiced child sacrifice

Mummification · a complex and rather effective means of preserving the human body from decay

Mummy · the body of one who has undergone mummification

Myth · an embellished cultural tale that may or may not be based on true events

Native American Church · combines Christianity with traditional Native American religion and practice, such as incorporating peyote into worship services

Neanderthal religion · Neanderthals buried their dead with tools, pointing to a belief in the afterlife; an unusual number of bear bones and skulls have been found near Neanderthal sites, possibly for religious reasons

Neolithic religion · religion from the New Stone Age among a more settled population; centered on fertility, agriculture, and personified natural elements

Nubians · an ancient people with extensive interaction with the Egyptians

Nuer · a Nilotic ethnic group found in Ethiopia and South Sudan

Opening of the mouth ceremony · ancient Egyptian spells meant to keep the mouth of the dead open in the afterlife so it could eat, drink, and breathe

Oracle · a person, text, or object that speaks on behalf of a divine power or ancestor

Oracle of blowing water · if a person was misbehaving, she or he would have to sit and gargle water and then blow it out into the air in order to cool the witchcraft inside

Oral traditions · stories of a people's history and myths that are passed down orally from generation to generation; a repository of knowledge for modern scholars

Osiris · the Egyptian Lord of the Dead, who was killed and dismembered by his brother Seth and reassembled by his wife Isis

Paganism · from the Latin word for "rural," generally denoting a polytheistic or henotheistic religion

Peace pipe · a ceremonial pipe shared to cement treaties or relationships in Native American culture

Peyote · a controversial hallucinogenic sometimes used in Native American religious practice

Philology · the study of the structure and development of and relationships between languages

Polytheism · the worship of many deities

Post-Columbian era · the era of history in the Americas after the arrival of the Europeans

Pre-Columbian era · the era of history in the Americas prior to 1492

Priests · religious leaders who perform rituals

Primal religions · a term for indigenous religions used by Huston Smith

Primitive religions · a term used by early anthropologists for indigenous religions that has been rejected in recent times

Puabi · a high-ranking Sumerian woman, possibly a queen, who was found buried with dozens of servants and animals, indicating human and animal sacrifice

Pyramid Texts · sources on ancient Egypt that were carved onto the interior walls of pyramids

Pyramids of Giza · ancient wonders built to house the tombs of Pharaohs in around 2600 BCE

Queen of Sheba · also known as **Makeda**, traveled from Ethiopia to visit King Solomon of Israel and Judah in the tenth century BCE; Ethiopians claim her son was fathered by Solomon

Ra · also known as **Re**, the Egyptian Sun god

Religion · according to Tylor and Frazer, the second stage of human belief, in which magic evolves into organized and standardized religious practice

Rites of passage · rituals denoting that a person has passed from one phase of life into the next

Rituals · vehicles of teaching and reinforcing myths to a community

Rubbing board (iwa) oracle · a practitioner would rub a small board and ask questions of the oracle on behalf of the person needing an answer

Sacred Thread Ceremony · a Hindu rite of passage undergone by upper-caste boys

Sacrifice · offering animals, plants, food, alcohol, or other desired goods to a deity in order to appease a spiritual power

Science · according to Tylor and Frazer, the final stage of human belief, in which people shed superstitions and myth in favor of fact-based science

Séance · communication with the dead or with spirits

Separation · the first phase of a rite of passage in which the individual separates from his or her old status in the community

Seth · also spelled **Set**, the Egyptian god of chaos who killed his brother Osiris

Shaman · a powerful, often eccentric person who communicates with the world of the dead, provides healing, and calls upon the spirits to provide a successful hunt, fertility, or rain

Small-scale societies · a term for indigenous cultures that emphasizes a sociological approach

Stonehenge · an impressive religious monument in England from Neolithic times

Sumerian · the most ancient Mesopotamian civilization

Sweat lodge · a Native American structure resembling a sauna; often used today for health benefits

Taboo · something that is forbidden in a society, with the belief that undesirable outcomes will occur if the prohibition is broken

Teotihuacan · one of the two great centers of Aztec human sacrifice

Theology · an important field in the study of religion; theologians are concerned with the doctrinal beliefs of a particular religion

Three stages of human belief · a theory set forth by E. B. Tylor and J. G. Frazer that states that human belief evolves through three stages, from magic to religion and finally to science

Totems · animals that are absorbed into a tribe's self-understanding

Transition · the second phase of a rite of passage in which the individual undergoes a period of waiting or takes a specific action that signifies the crossing of a boundary into a new status

Turquoise · a particularly significant stone in Native American religion

Tzompantli · also known as a **skull rack**, where the heads of human sacrifices were displayed

Ur · an ancient city in which Puabi's burial site was discovered

Witch doctor · another term for a shaman

Witchcraft · a strong belief in magic, especially as the cause of whatever misfortune might befall a community

Witchcraft, Oracles, and Magic among the Azande **(1937)** · revolutionized the field of anthropology since its author lived among his subjects, understood their culture, learned their language, and wrote from a sympathetic point of view rather than caricaturing or exoticizing

CHAPTER THREE

Adivasis · tribal peoples in India who struggle for full participation in Indian society, comprising 10 percent of the Indian population

Afonso de Albuquerque · conquered Goa for the Portuguese in 1510

Agni · the god of fire and sacrifice

Ahimsa · nonviolence

Akbar · famous Mughal emperor

Allahabad · also known as **Prayag**, where the Ganges and the Yamuna Rivers meet in Uttar Pradesh; a pilgrimage site for Kumbh Mela

Aranyakas · a major section of the Vedas that reflects upon rituals; a link between the Bhramanas' ritual and the Upanishads' spiritual philosophy

Arranged marriage · a common Indian practice in which parents choose suitable spouses for their children; practiced by 90 percent of the Indian population

Aryan Migration Theory · the theory that Indo-Europeans migrated from Central Asia into the Indian subcontinent

Aryans · a nomadic people who migrated from Persia into the Indian subcontinent in around 1500 BCE

Ashvamedha · a horse sacrifice in which a king would release a horse and allow it to wander for a year; wherever the horse went was considered territory of the king; at the end of the year, the horse was killed and eaten in an elaborate feast

Atharva Veda · "priestly knowledge"; one of the four authoritative collections of Vedic literature

Atman · the soul; the same essence as Brahman inside every living thing

Aurangzeb · a famous Mughal emperor who ruled during the zenith of the empire

Avatar · an incarnation of a god on Earth

Ayodhya · the kingdom in which Rama was prince in the *Ramayana*, located in modern-day Uttar Pradesh

Babri Masjid · a mosque built over Rama's birthplace that was demolished by Hindu nationalists in 1992

Babur · the first Mughal emperor

Bangladesh · an Islamic majority nation that was created in the partition of India

Bhagavad Gita · a famous section of the *Mahabharata* in which the hero's chariot driver reveals himself to be Vishnu and counsels him in spiritual matters

Bhakti Yoga · the path of devotion

Bharat · another name for the nation of India, taken from ancient Sanskrit texts; also Rama's faithful brother

Bharatiya Janata Party · the formidable nationalist party in India that adheres strongly to Hindutva

Brahma · the creator god; also known as **Prajapati**

Brahmacharya · celibacy

Brahman · the eternal and ultimate reality

Brahmanas · a major section of the Vedas that directs priests how to execute their duties

Brahmins · the uppermost caste, comprising religious teachers and priests; created to be the "mouth" of existence since they are to teach the Vedas

Brahmo Samaj · a social reform movement influencing Indians who worked towards self-rule

Buddhism · the fifth-largest religion in India, at around 0.7 percent of the population

Caste · a Latin term that the Portuguese used to understand the complex Indian social system when Vasco da Gama first arrived to India in 1498

Caste system · a rigidly stratified socioeconomic system in which a person retains the same status as one's family throughout his or her life

Child marriage · an ancient Indian custom in which young people were betrothed at an early age

Christianity · the third-largest religion in India, at around 2–3 percent of the population

Cremation · burning the dead instead of burial

Dalits · meaning "crushed" or "broken"; outcaste people who are considered untouchable to caste Hindus, comprising 20 percent of the Indian population

Delhi Sultanate · Islamic rule over India from 1206 to 1526

Dharma · one's duty, as assigned by samsara

Diwali · the Festival of Lights, celebrating the victory of goodness and light over evil and dark; connected to the goddesses Kali and Lakshmi, or with Rama and Sita's return to Ayodhya after exile

Dravidian · the indigenous population of India, as opposed to the Aryans

Durga · consort of Shiva associated with weapons and divine wrath against oppressors

Forest-dweller phase · the third phase of Hindu life for a twice-born male, in which he leaves his house to dwell in the forest and meditate in self-denial and chastity

Ganesh · the elephant-headed god who wrote the *Mahabharata* as a scribe for Vyasa; today, he is considered the remover of obstacles, and he is particularly beloved by students trying to pass exams

Genghis Khan · the conqueror and first great leader of the Mongol Empire

Guru · a teacher, like a god to a student, who leads a practitioner to spiritual growth

Hanuman · a pious and powerful monkey god who proves to be an extremely faithful ally to Rama

Harappa · an ancient city in modern-day Pakistan that predates the Aryan Migration

Hare Krishna · also known as **ISKCON**, a religious movement associated with the worship of Krishna

Haridwar · a pilgrimage site for Kumbh Mela on the Ganges River in Uttarakhand

Harijans · "children of God"; a somewhat paternalistic term that Gandhi used to refer to the Dalits

Hindustan · a word used by Persians and Muslims throughout the centuries to refer to the land of India

Hindutva · "Hindu-ness," a current Hindu nationalist movement in India

Holi · a holiday to welcome spring and promote fertility, celebrated with lively colors; associated with Krishna and his consort, Radha

Householder phase · the second phase of Hindu life for a twice-born male during which he observes Hindu rituals, marries and runs a household, and supports the temples and holy men

Indian National Congress · the political party that governed India from 1947 to the early twenty-first century

Indo-Iranian culture · a term used for the many shared concepts and gods of the ancient Persian and Indian peoples

Indra · a strong but hedonistic creator god who defeats all chaos and fights for his people

Indus River · the river in India from which the Persians took the name "Hindu" for the people of this region

Indus Valley · the geographical region around the Indus River, which spans from Tibet to Pakistan and empties into the Arabian Sea

Indus Valley Civilization · the ancient civilization that flourished in the Indus River Valley, boasting one to five million people

Islam · the second-largest religion in India, at around 14 percent of the population

Jahangir · famous Mughal emperor

Jainism · the sixth-largest religion in India, at around 0.4 percent of the population

Jati · literally "birth"; somewhat synonymous with caste but implying a smaller kinship group or family

Jnana Yoga · the path of knowledge

Kali · terrifying goddess and consort of Shiva; depicted with blood, skulls, and severed limbs

Kalki · the tenth and final avatar of Vishnu yet to come; a messiah figure who ushers in the end of the kalpa

Kalpas · eons in Hindu cosmology, with one kalpa lasting 4.32 billion years, or one day in the life of Brahma

Karma · that which keeps us in the cycle of rebirth

Karma Yoga · the path of action

Kauravas · a warring side of the *Mahabharata* that fights against the Pandavas

Krishna · the most popular avatar of Vishnu, from the Bhagavad Gita

Kshatriyas · the caste of warriors, diplomats, and rulers; created to be the "arms" of existence since they are expected to bear arms and defend

Kumbh Mela · the largest gathering of humans in the world; a pilgrimage every four years to sacred rivers for the cleansing of sins

Kurukshetra War · the great war between the Pandavas and the Kauravas

Lakshmana · Rama's faithful brother

Lakshmi · wife of Vishnu, goddess of fertility and wealth

Lingam · a phallic votary object symbolizing the reproductive power of the god Shiva

Lord of the Dance · an epithet of Shiva

Maha Kumbh Mela · a massive, most auspicious Kumbh Mela celebrated every twelfth year

Mahabharata · an ancient Indian epic depicting the great Kurukshetra war

Mahatma · "Great Soul," an epithet of Gandhi

Manusmriti · also known as **the Laws of Manu**, Hindu ethics codified into law

Maya · illusions that blind us from the nature of reality and keep us trapped in samsara

Mitra · the personification of an agreement or a contract, later associated with the morning

Mohandas Gandhi · leader of the Indian independence movement

Mohenjo-Daro · an ancient city in modern-day Pakistan that predates the Aryan Migration

Moksha · liberation of the soul from the cycle of samsara

Mughal Empire · Turkish Muslim rule over India from 1526 to 1857

Mumtaz Mahal · the favorite wife of Shah Jahan; for whom the Taj Mahal was built

Nashik · a pilgrimage site for Kumbh Mela on the Godavari River in Maharashtra

Non-duality · the realization that there is no distinction between one's atman and Brahman, no difference between one and God or one and another person

Pakistan · an Islamic majority nation that was created in the partition of India; contains the historic Indus River Valley

Pandavas · a warring side of the *Mahabharata*, the branch of the family for which Arjuna, the hero, fights

Parvati · the wife of Shiva and mother of Ganesh

Pollution · an underlying principle of the caste system; violating caste distinctions pollutes oneself, one's caste, or other people from other castes; also tied to blood, death, and dirt

Proto-Indo-European language · a theoretical parent language of certain European and Asian languages today

Puja · ceremonial worship dedicated to a god

Raja · an Indian king

Raja Yoga · the path of discipline

Ram Mohan Roy · founder of the Brahmo Samaj movement; taught Indians to learn English and British customs in order to eventually achieve independence by proving their competency to the British colonialists; controversial for these accommodationist policies

Rama · the protagonist of the *Ramayana*, an incarnation of the god Vishnu

Ramayana · an ancient Indian epic depicting the tale of Rama, an incarnation of Vishnu, and his wife Sita

Ravana · the demon antagonist of the *Ramayana* who kidnaps Sita

Reincarnation · the transmigration of the soul; rebirth after death into a new form

Renunciation · the optional final phase of Hindu life for a twice-born male, in which he gives up all attachments in favor of asceticism to try and attain moksha in this life

Rig Veda · "worship knowledge"; one of the four authoritative collections of Vedic literature

Rishis · mystical religious leaders in the Vedic era who drank soma to alter their state of consciousness and have authoritative visions of the spiritual realities

Sacred cow · considered holy and linked to the sustenance of the Indian people, cows are often protected in India today

Sacred Thread Ceremony · a rite of passage involving the bestowal of a sacred thread onto a boy, initiating him into the student phase of Hindu life

Sadhu · a Hindu holy man, also known as a **sannyasin**

Sama Veda · "chanting knowledge"; one of the four authoritative collections of Vedic literature

Samadhi · the deepest, most tranquil state of meditation

Samhitas · a major section of the Vedas comprising prayers, hymns, and mantras; the oldest form of Hindu scripture

Samsara · the cycle of rebirth

Sannyasin · someone who renounces all material comforts of the present life and commits themself completely to spiritual pursuits

Sati · the practice of widows self-immolating on their husband's funeral pyre

Secularization thesis · the theory that, over time, people are becoming less religious

Shah Jahan · famous Mughal emperor; built the Taj Mahal

Shaivites · devotees of Shiva

Shakti · the feminine principle, sometimes worshiped as a goddess

Shaktism · the sect of Hinduism that primarily worships Shakti

Shiva · god of destruction and reproduction, also known as the Lord of the Dance

Shruti · "that which has been heard"; divinely originated, sacred scriptures

Shudras · the caste of laborers; created to be the "feet" of existence since they serve the upper castes through their labor

Sikhism · the fourth-largest religion in India, at around 1–2 percent of the population

Sindhu River · the Sanskrit name for the Indus River

Sita · the devoted wife of Rama

Smriti · "that which is remembered"; less authoritative scriptures of human origin

Soma · a hallucinogenic plant ingested by Vedic priests; eventually personified as a deity

Sri Lanka · an island nation off the coast of southern India; ruled by the demon king Ravana in the *Ramayana*

Sri Ramakrishna Paramahamsa · taught that God is one, and though people may worship in different religions, they are all actually worshiping the one true God who unites and transcends religions

Student phase · the first phase of Hindu life for a twice-born male, in which he studies the Vedas

Swami Vivekananda · a Hindu monk who influentially spread Hinduism in the West by teaching at the World's Parliament of Religions

Swaraj · self-government

Taj Mahal · a mausoleum for the favorite wife of emperor Shah Jahan

Timur · also known as Tamerlane, founder of the Timurid Empire

Transmigration · reincarnation

Trimurti · "three forms," the Hindu trinity of sorts, in which Brahman emanates in the three forces of creation, sustenance, and destruction, deified as Brahma, Vishnu, and Shiva

Twice-born · members of the Brahmin, Kshatriya, and Vaishya castes who are eligible to undergo the Sacred Thread Ceremony

Ujjain · a pilgrimage site for Kumbh Mela on the Shipra River in Madhya Pradesh

Unitarianism · emphasizes the unity of all religions under an abstract notion of God

Upanayana · the Sanskrit word for the Sacred Thread Ceremony

Upanishads · the most recent texts in Vedic literature, dealing systematically with the transmigration of the soul

Uttar Pradesh · the most populated state in India

Vaishnavites · devotees of Vishnu

Vaishyas · the caste of farmers and merchants, created to be the "thighs" of existence since they uphold society through agriculture by tending cattle, lending money, and keeping the economy running smoothly

Vanara · humanlike monkeys found in the *Ramayana* as well as in Hindu religious iconography

Varna · literally, "color" or "class"; somewhat synonymous with caste; referencing a time in Indian history when the castes were each associated with colors

Varuna · the god of the sky who can forgive sin and punish evil

Vasco da Gama · Portuguese explorer who sailed to India in 1498

Vedas · the earliest Hindu texts, dealing primarily with sacrifices to the gods

Vegetarianism · a common practice among upper-caste Hindus for purity and to keep to the doctrine of ahimsa, or nonviolence

Vishnu · the god who sustains all; generally believed to have come to Earth as an avatar nine times

Vyasa · the sage who composed the *Mahabharata* and is also said to have compiled and systematized the Vedas

World's Parliament of Religions · conferences designed to facilitate a global dialogue on faith

Yajur Veda · "sacrificial knowledge"; one of the four authoritative collections of Vedic literature

Yoga · from the word *yoke*, meaning "to unite"; the path one takes to unite oneself to God

Yogi · a Hindu holy man, also known as a sannyasin

Yoni · a symbol of female genitalia representing reproductive power; associated with Shakti

CHAPTER FOUR

Agamas · "that which has come down"; the word used for Jain scriptures

Ahimsa · nonviolence or noninjury toward any living thing; one of the Five Great Vows of Jainism

Ajiva · matter; all nonliving things

Anekantavada · the many-sidedness of truth

Aparigraha · non-possessiveness; one of the Five Great Vows of Jainism; strictly avoiding all attachment, possessiveness, or greed

Asceticism · self-denial or the infliction of self-harm to rid oneself of attachment and earthly desires

Asteya · one of the Five Great Vows of Jainism; not stealing anything, whether by theft, extortion, imitation, or unclear measurements or transactions

Axial Age · a pivotal era in human history when great thinkers were creating new world religions and striving for a higher consciousness

Brahmacharya · chastity; one of the Five Great Vows of Jainism; purity of the mind and refraining from premarital or extramarital sex

Buddha · a religious leader on the Indian subcontinent; contemporary with Mahavira

Celibacy · not required by Parshva for his followers, but required outside of marriage

Confucius · a philosophical and religious leader in China; contemporary with Mahavira

Digambaras · **"sky-clad"** (a euphemism for naked); one of the two major branches of Jain monastics that renounce clothing and believe women cannot achieve moksha in this life

Diwali · celebrated by Jains in commemoration of Mahavira achieving moksha

JAINA · Federation of Jain Associations in North America; an ecumenical organization representing the Jains who have immigrated to North America

Jeremiah · a Jewish prophet; contemporary with Mahavira

Jharkhand · the modern Indian state in which Parshva perished

Jina · a conqueror; one who has overcome earthly attachment and achieved moksha

Jiva · the soul; all living things

Karma · a sticky substance that accumulates around the soul and weighs that soul down, keeping it entrenched in samsara

Kaya klesh · a public rite of passage in which Jain monastics are initiated by having their hair plucked out of their head

Kevala jnana · total understanding or omniscience; achieved by a Jina who has attained moksha

Lao Tzu · a religious leader in China; contemporary with Mahavira

Mahavira · "great hero" or "great man"; the twenty-fourth and final Tirthankara who achieved moksha through extreme asceticism and ahimsa

Namokara Mantra · the most significant mantra of Jainism; recited in Sanskrit and meant to destroy attachment and cultivate a deep respect for those who have conquered

Parshva · the twenty-third Tirthankara and the first for whom we have historical information; an ascetic who purportedly revived Jainism when it was in decline

Paryushana · "coming together"; an annual eight-day festival in which lay Jains live as monastics; the most important festival of Jainism

Picchi · a broom made of fallen peacock feathers to swipe away insects that might get crushed

Sallekhana · also known as **holy death**, a noble and righteous death by self-starvation, proving full victory over attachment and violence

Saman Suttam · a scriptural text that is shared by each of the Jain sects; organized into forty-four chapters on everything from karma, transmigration, and nonviolence to monastic vows, meditation, and Sallekhana

Samayika · a daily meditation ritual lasting forty-eight minutes (twice the number of Tirthankaras)

Satya · truth; one of the Five Great Vows of Jainism; avoiding all falsity, lies, and everything associated with dishonesty

Shikharji · one of the holiest pilgrimage sites for Jains; the place in Jharkhand where twenty of the twenty-four Tirthankaras are said to have achieved moksha

Shvetambaras · "white-clad"; one of the two major branches of Jain monastics that allow clothing and believe that women can achieve moksha in this life

Siddha · "one who is accomplished"; someone who has attained moksha; a Jina

Swastika · an ancient symbol representing the wheel of rebirth, with its four arms representing the male and female monastics, as well as the male and female laity

Three Jewels of Jainism · right belief, right knowledge, and right conduct

Tirthankara · "ford finders"; twenty-four Jain leaders who discovered the way out of samsara and taught others to do the same; the first twenty-two are probably mythical

CHAPTER FIVE

Amida · the Japanese pronunciation of Amitabha; believers chant his name in the hope of being reborn in the Pure Land

Amitabha · "infinite light"; a Buddha who is central to Pure Land Buddhism

Ananda · the Buddha's cousin who served as a trusted assistant and a mouthpiece for the Buddha in his communications with laypeople as well as with the monastic community; advocated for women to be permitted to become monastics

Anatman · denial of the atman, or soul; the doctrine that there is no self

Bardo Thodol · also known as the **Tibetan Book of the Dead**, a Red Hat instructional manual for the recently departed, geared to guide him or her through forty-nine days of temptation and travel from one body to the next rebirth.

Blind men and the elephant · a parable that teaches that differing and even contradictory perspectives of the ultimate reality may actually be different ways of describing the same truth

Bodh Gaya · where the Buddha achieved enlightenment; the Mahabodhi Temple complex there is the most important Buddhist pilgrimage site

Bodhi tree · the tree under which the Buddha meditated until he achieved enlightenment

Bodhisattva · those who have achieved nirvana but choose to remain in the cycle of rebirth anyway to help others discover truth

Bon · the shamanistic indigenous religion of Tibet

Buddhaghosa · an Indian monk in Sri Lanka in the fifth century CE who collated Buddhist texts, edited them, and wrote commentaries; translated the scriptures into Pali

Chants · repetitive rhythmic phrases uttered for spiritual purposes

Chatsumarn Kabilsingh · Thailand's first fully ordained Theravadin nun who advocates for abstinence outside of marriage

Daisetsu "D. T." Suzuki · a Japanese Zen Buddhist and scholar who brought acclaim to the religion in the United States; became a lecturer at Columbia University

Dalai Lama · a bodhisattva who leads Tibetan Buddhism from exile in India

The dharma · the Buddha's teachings

Dharmachakra · the wheel of teaching

Dukkha · suffering; dis-ease

Five Hindrances · lustful thoughts, malice towards a person, drowsiness, worry or depression, and doubt

Four Noble Truths · (1) all life consists of suffering; (2) suffering is caused by desire; (3) to cease to desire is to cease to suffer; (4) to cease to desire, one must follow the Middle Way and the Noble Eightfold Path

Four opponent powers · the path for purification: express remorse for our mistakes, emanate good thoughts toward people we have had trouble with, resolve ourselves not to repeat our mistakes, and do something positive as a remediation to offset the mistakes we have made

Hinayana · also known as the **small vehicle**, a somewhat derogatory name for Theravada Buddhism

Hoji · religious services for the dead; led by priests in order to commemorate leaders, fallen soldiers, important teachers, victims of tragedies, and ancestors

Interdependent co-origination · also known as **dependent arising** or **dependent origination**, the idea that everything is connected and comes and goes all of the time in a massive matrix in which there is no individuality and no permanence

Karma · that which weighs us down in samsara, leading to an undesirable next life

King Ashoka · an Indian monarch who ruled almost all of the Indian subcontinent in the third century BCE; converted to Buddhism after witnessing a violent battle, and propagated the religion throughout his kingdom

Koans · bizarre riddles in Zen Buddhism meant to test a student's proficiency and provoke enlightenment. These statements are usually frustrating to rational analysis

Kundun · a film about the Dalai Lama, directed by Martin Scorsese

Kushinagar · where the Buddha died in Uttar Pradesh; the second-most important Buddhist pilgrimage site

Lamaism · the blending of Bon and Mahayana Buddhism

Laughing Buddha · a fat and jolly depiction of the Maitreya, seen commonly in statuettes and imagery throughout Asia

Lotus position · the typical meditation posture, with legs crossed, a straightened spine, and hands resting on the legs

Lotus Sutra · a text purportedly teaching the final words of the Buddha, claiming that all Buddhist paths lead to Buddhahood; that all beings have the potential to become Buddhas; and that the Buddha did not pass into nirvana but is still with us, teaching the dharma

Lumbini · where the Buddha was born; the third-most important Buddhist pilgrimage site

Madhyamika · a form of Mahayana Buddhism founded by Nagarjuna around 200 CE; rejects dualisms and absolute truth claims, and focuses on always taking the balanced, middle path between extremes

Mahayana · also known as the **large vehicle**; a diverse set of traditions, including a belief in the divinity of the Buddha, a vast array of bodhisattvas, and sometimes even a heaven and hell; they affirm that anyone, including women and non-monastics, can be enlightened

Mahayanists · followers of Mahayana Buddhism, or "the school of the greater vehicle"

Maitreya · a Buddha to come who will descend from heaven to Earth and revive the dharma, ruling over a new, almost Messianic age of peace and prosperity

Mantras · short chants, often just a single word

The Middle Way · the middle ground between extreme asceticism and extreme worldliness

Nagarjuna · an Indian monk who founded Madhyamika

Nichiren · a thirteenth-century monk who focused on chanting rather than meditation and emphasized the Lotus Sutra

Nirvana · an extinguishment of all craving and desire, achieving compassionate nonattachment

Noble Eightfold Path · to learn correct understanding (of the Four Noble Truths), have correct intentions, practice correct speech, have correct conduct, involve oneself in correct occupations, cultivate correct endeavors, practice correct contemplation, and acquire correct concentration; each of these are connected and cultivated over a lifetime of discipline

Om · the holiest syllable; often chanted in meditation

Om mani padme hum · "praise to the jewel in the lotus"; a mantra calling out to a bodhisattva; supposed to infuse the caller with compassion

Pagodas · multitiered, tower-like shrines

Pali language · the language in which the earliest Buddhist texts were written

Parinirvana · the final release from samsara; achieved at death for a person who has reached nirvana in this life

Parinirvana Day · a Buddhist holiday held on February 15 to commemorate the day the Buddha's physical body expired

Paritta · "protection"; a type of chant that involves reciting scripture to safeguard against danger

Prayer wheel · a Tibetan Buddhist mechanism by which a practitioner can send out prayers simply by turning a wheel

Pure Land · a very pleasant halfway house between humanity and nirvana

Red Hat School · a school of Tibetan Buddhism known for its highly complex understanding of what happens to those who have recently departed

Sangha · the Buddhist community

Sarnath · where the Buddha gave his first sermon (known as the dharma), just outside the city of Varanasi in Uttar Pradesh; the fourth-most important Buddhist pilgrimage site

Seven Years in Tibet · a film focusing on the Dalai Lama, starring Brad Pitt

Shakyamuni · a name for the Buddha meaning "sage of the Shakya clan"

Sky burial · a practice in Tibet in which the deceased is chopped into pieces and fed to the birds, instead of burial or cremation

Soka Gakkai · a Japanese Buddhist movement based on the Lotus Sutra and the teachings of Nichiren

Sri Lanka · the island off the coast of India where the earliest Buddhist texts were written down

Stupas · dome-shaped shrines

Sutras · particular sayings or teachings of the Buddha

Tantric Buddhism · an esoteric school of Buddhism focusing on union with a bodhisattva through Yoga and mysticism; "right-hand" tantrism practices celibacy, but "left-hand" tantrism allows for ritual intercourse

Tathagata · a name for the Buddha, meaning "the one who has gone" into enlightenment

Tenzin Gyatso · the current Dalai Lama

Theosophical Society · an organization that aims to bridge the gap between Western and Eastern spirituality

Theravada · a school of Buddhism that views the Buddha as a great philosopher but only a man; they deny more mystical aspects of Buddhism and believe only men can be enlightened

Theravadins · followers of Theravada Buddhism, or "the school of the elders"

Third eye · the eye that represents seeing all things through an enlightened mind

Three Jewels of Buddhism · the Buddha, the dharma, and the sangha

Tibetan Buddhism · a distinct version of Mahayana Buddhism found in Tibet, Bhutan, and Nepal

Trance meditation · an advanced state of meditation in which all thoughts cease

Urna · a dot on the forehead representing the third eye

Vajrayana · also known as the **Diamond Vehicle**; Tibetan Buddhist tradition that combines Mahayana with the indigenous religion of Bon

Vesak · the largest and most important festival for global Buddhism, commemorating the Buddha's birthday

Visualization · a meditation technique in which a practitioner pictures something until subject and object dissolve into one and deeper consciousness is achieved

Yellow Hat School · a school of Tibetan Buddhism associated with the Dalai Lama

Zazen · long meditation sessions in Zen Buddhism during which the superiors will strike the monks with a stick in order to keep them from drowsiness

Zen and the Art of Motorcycle Maintenance · a national bestseller and cultural phenomenon, this book merged Zen Buddhism with Americana, pointing towards spiritual liberation and experimentation for millions of people in a countercultural era

Zen Buddhism · a Mahayana sect founded by a monk named Bodhidharma; emphasizes belief in sudden insight rather than in extreme rationalism

Adi Granth · the first compiled collection of Sikh scripture, containing 1,430 pages of sacred teachings of the gurus as well as some Hindu and Muslim devotional writings; collected by the fifth guru, and later added to by the tenth to form the Guru Granth Sahib

Akal Takht · the "Eternal Throne"; the highest authority in Sikhism in Amritsar, where the religion's most important discussions are had, and where the most consequential decisions are made

Amrit · the initiation ceremony to become a member of the Khalsa; involves drinking of a sweet nectar of sugar and water, which is stirred with a sword

Amritsar · the holy city of Sikhism and the location of the Golden Temple

Anand Karaj · "act toward happiness"; a Sikh marriage ceremony

Balbir Singh Sodhi · a gas station owner in Mesa, Arizona, who was shot and killed after September 11, 2001, by a mentally unstable criminal who mistook Sodhi for a Muslim

Bibi Nanaki · Nanak's older sister and first disciple who saw the light of God in him from a young age

Chaur · a fly whisk waved above the Guru Granth Sahib out of honor and respect

Dastar Bandi · a ceremony in which a Sikh boy is taken to the gurdwara to tie on his first turban

Dharmsal · the place where we practice righteousness

Diwali · a holiday celebrated by Sikhs in commemoration of Guru Har Gobind being released from prison

Dr. Manhoman Singh · a Sikh who led India from 2004 to 2014

Five Banis · daily meditations to be recited

Golden Temple · also known as **Harmandir Sahib** or **Durbar Sahib**; the most important gurdwara and the most sacred site of Sikhism; a magnificent temple of white marble and gold

Granthis · Sikhs who lead worship services by reading from the Guru Granth Sahib and waving the chaur over the text

Gurdwara · "door to the guru"; a Sikh temple

Gurmukhi · the Punjabi script for the scriptures created by Guru Angad

Gurparshad · a combination of our own faith and God's grace; the only way to realize God

Gurpurbs · "guru celebrations"; festivals commemorating the birthdays and martyrdoms of the ten human gurus

Guru Amar Das · the third guru, who created a Sikh clergy and geographical system, similar to the diocesan system of Christianity, and preached against sati and purdah

Guru Angad · the second guru, who created a Punjabi script for the scriptures

Guru Arjan Dev · the fifth guru, who ordered the building of the Golden Temple and compiled the Adi Granth; martyred by the Mughal emperor

Guru Gobind Singh · the tenth and last human guru, who founded the Khalsa and declared the Granth Sahib to be his successor

Guru Har Krishan · the eighth and youngest guru, who succeeded his father at age five and died of smallpox at age seven

Guru Har Rai · the seventh guru, notable for building up the Sikh military yet avoiding a war

Guru Hargobind · the sixth guru, who gave the Sikhs their warrior image, commissioning Sikhs to defend themselves militarily

Guru Nanak · the founder of Sikhism who combined certain elements of Hinduism and Islam

Guru Ram Das · the fourth guru, who founded Amritsar

Guru Tegh Bahadur · the ninth guru, a fierce warrior, a well-traveled missionary for Sikhism, and a wonderful hymn writer; martyred by the Mughal emperor

Hola · the Sikh pronunciation of Holi

Holi · a holiday in which Sikhs train in the martial arts and have mock battles

Hukam · a daily worship practice in which the Granth is opened at random for the selection of a hymn that should be sung

Ik Onkar · "There is one God"; a fundamental teaching of Sikhism

Japji Sahib · the first composition of Guru Nanak and a comprehensive summation of Sikh teaching

Kachera · a cotton undergarment

Kangha · a wooden comb

Kara · an iron bracelet

Kaur · "Princess"; a name taken by most Sikh women

Kesh · uncut hair

Khalistan · a potential independent Sikh nation in Punjab

Khalsa · "the pure ones"; the community of Sikhs who have been initiated through the Amrit ceremony and who adhere to the Five Ks and to a code of moral conduct

Khanda · a double-edged sword

Kirpan · an iron dagger representing power, protection, and safety

Kirtans · devotional singing in the gurdwara

Kukas · a name for the Namdharis meaning "shrieking," since they shriek when they worship

Langar · free vegetarian meals served after every service in a gurdwara

Melas · fairs

Mughal Empire · Turkish Muslim rule over India from 1526 to 1857

Mukti · release from samsara; the Punjabi pronunciation of moksha

Naam Karan · a baby-naming ceremony in which someone will open the Guru Granth Sahib at random and the first letter of the first verse on the left hand page becomes the initial for the child's given name

Namdhari · a vegetarian Sikh sect from the carpenter class that rejects the traditional count of ten gurus, following its own guru today; recognized by their white, homespun outfits, as well as their unique white turbans, which are tied across the forehead

Namsimran · a practice in which Sikhs gather at the gurdwara to remember God, to meditate on God, and to recite God's holiest names: Waheguru and Satnam, often using a rosary

Nankana Sahib · the town in which Guru Nanak was born; a holy site for Sikhs today

Nikki Haley · an American with Sikh roots who served as the governor of South Carolina and the US ambassador to the United Nations

Nirankari · a Sikh sect from the merchant class that rejects the traditional count of ten gurus, following its own guru today; known for casting the dead into rivers, rather than the customary practice of cremation

Nirmala · a celibate, ascetic Sikh sect

Palki · a decorated seat on which the Guru Granth Sahib is prominently displayed in a gurdwara

Parshad · grace; also refers to the sanctified food given at the end of a religious service in the gurdwara

Partition · when the British left India, the territory was divided into three countries largely based on their religious majorities: Hindu India, Muslim Pakistan, and Muslim East Pakistan (later Bangladesh); the Sikhs' region of the Punjab was split between Pakistan and India, and Sikhism lost many of its adherents and holy sites to religious intolerance in Pakistan

Punjab · a region of South Asia that includes land in both India and Pakistan; the homeland of the Sikhs

Ragis · musicians who lead Sikh worship services

Sahajdhari · "slow adopter"; a Sikh who has not participated in the Amrit ceremony and does not abide by the Five Ks

Satnam · a name for God meaning "true name"

Sehaj · the fourth and final stage of the human mind; a transcendental state of enlightenment and bliss; the goal of Sikhism

Seva · selfless service

Singh · "Lion"; a name taken by most Sikh men

Sri Guru Granth Sahib · the holy text of Sikhism as well as the eleventh and final guru; treated as a sacred person and not just a book

Three Pillars of Sikhism · (1) meditate on Waheguru; (2) live honestly; (3) share with others

Triple formula · also known as **nam dan isnan**; prepares one's heart for God through praising his name, giving charity, and keeping oneself pure

Vaisakhi · festival celebrating the birth of the Khalsa

Waheguru · a name for God meaning "wondrous teacher"

CHAPTER SEVEN

American Daoism · a critical term for forms of Daoism practiced in North America that have been separated from their original history and context

Analects of Confucius · the writings and speeches of Confucius, collected and preserved by his students; extremely influential to Chinese moral philosophy

Ancestral tablet · also known as the **spirit tablet**, a tablet in which the souls of the deceased are infused upon their passing, generally kept in a temple or home altar

Chairman Mao Zedong · the victor of the Chinese Civil War who redefined China along communist lines and governed the nation until 1976

Chiang Kai-shek · the Christian leader of the Chinese Nationalist government before and during the Chinese Civil War, and leader of the Republic of China in Taiwan until 1975; founder of the New Life Movement

Chinese Communist Party · the dogmatic and formidable governing political party of China

Cleromancy · the belief that apparently random numbers and patterns can actually reveal the will of the gods

Communism · system of government in which, in theory, all property is held in common and all work and goods are distributed according to ability and need; officially atheist or nonreligious

Confucian Centers · institutions often funded by the Chinese government and attached to universities in North America that promote understanding of Chinese culture and thought

Confucius · "Master King"; a philosopher who emphasized the importance of ordered social relationships and wished to purify the government of corruption and incompetence

Convergence · the phenomenon in Chinese religion where elements of Buddhism, Daoism, and Confucianism are believed and practiced in a syncretic manner

Crane Call Mountain · also known as **Heming Shan**, the site in Sichuan province where Zhang Daoling was divinely called to usher in a new era of peace and prosperity

Daozang · the canon of Daoist scripture, consisting of 5,305 volumes

Dietetics · dieting and emphasizing nutrition for physical and spiritual health

Divination · prediction of the future by analyzing plants, oracle bones, turtle shells, and various other objects

Doctrine of the Mean · a Confucian text that supports a middle path in all things, avoiding extremes in thought and conduct

The Earth God · also known as **Tudi Gong**, "land elder"; a smiling male statue, usually only about a foot tall, frequently found in Chinese villages still today on family altars and in farmers' fields

Falun Gong · also known as **Falun Dafa**, an exercise- and meditation-based religion that was founded in the early 1990s by Li Hongzhi; brutally persecuted by the Chinese government ever since its practitioners publicly demonstrated for religious freedom in China

Feng shui · "wind-water"; a form of geomancy that purports to bring harmony with nature, placing everything around us in a particular position so as to elicit tranquility and a positive energy flow

Five Classics · five works to which Confucius contributed, including the *Book of Poetry*, the *Book of Documents*, the *Book of Rites*, the *Book of Changes* (the *I Ching*), and the *Spring and Autumn Annals*

Folk religionists · a diverse and indefinable set of people in China who draw freely from Daoist, Buddhist, and Confucian ideas, incorporating them into their localized folk traditions; notable for their variety and indigeneity

Four Books · a collection of Confucian classics including the *Analects*, *Mencius*, *Great Learning*, and the *Doctrine of the Mean*

Four Olds · old ideas, old cultures, old customs, old habits, all of which were to be violently eradicated during the Cultural Revolution

Funeral human sacrifice · practiced during the Shang dynasty; sacrificing live humans to bury with the dead, probably to serve them in the afterlife

Fuxi · the Chinese deity who created humanity and invented writing as well as music

Great Learning · a Confucian text that highlights the necessity of having moral political leaders; if the leaders are corrupt, the people will be also, but if the leaders are moral, then society will be as well

Great Proletarian Cultural Revolution · a brutal purge of all traditional legacies that had survived the communist revolution in China; lasted from 1966 to Mao's death in 1976

Green City Mountain · the site outside the city of Chengdu in Sichuan province where Zhang Daoling ascended to heaven with his wife and some of his disciples

Han dynasty · governing kingdom of China from 200 BCE to 220 CE, during whose reign the concepts of Shangdi and Tian became fully conflated

Henri Maspero · the first major Western scholar of Daoism

Home shrines · small altars increasingly set up in Chinese homes to pay respects and burn paper money to ancestors, Daoist gods, Buddhas, and Confucius

I Ching · the *Book of Changes*, also written as *Yi Jing*; a diviner's manual to using cleromancy; consists of the yin/yang symbol surrounded by sixty-four hexagrams, each comprising six lines

Interior alchemy · esoteric religious practices intended to prolong life

The Jade Emperor · evolved from the concept of Shangdi, the supreme ruler of heaven who features prominently in the Daoist pantheon

Junzi · a gentleman who acts with all integrity, according to Confucian teaching

Karl Marx · a German philosopher who heavily influenced economic, social, and political thought with his theories, collectively known as Marxism

Kuei · malevolent and troublesome spirits in ancient Chinese religion

Lao Tzu · also spelled **Laozi**, "Old Master"; the founder of Daoism and author of the *Tao Te Ching*

Li · "ritual propriety"; submitting to the subtle and overt rituals of society in order to achieve greater social harmony

Li Hongzhi · the founder of Falun Gong who leads his movement from Deerpark, New York, because of the intense persecution in China

Lingbao Scriptures · "Divine Treasure" scriptures; texts from a communitarian school of Daoism that incorporated Buddhist thought, including Buddhas, many different hells and heavens, and a fascination with salvation

Little Red Book · a widely distributed Chinese communist text comprising the writings and sayings of Mao Zedong

Lookout Tower Monastery · a monastery built near Xian in Shaanxi where Laozi is said to have composed the *Tao Te Ching*

Lord Lao · an avatar of Laozi who purportedly appeared to and commissioned Zhang Daoling

Lu Dongbin · a deity and the leader of the Eight Immortals in Chinese mythology

Mandate of heaven · the notion that rulers were granted authority by the divine will and had to honor heaven with their actions; if tragedies occurred, then the mandate of heaven must have been revoked; if all was well, then the ruler must have the approval of heaven

Marxism · a socioeconomic philosophy that views the world through the lens of class inequalities and social conflict; religion is used as a tool of the oppressive upper class

Mazu · a sea goddess understood to be the "queen of heaven," based on a real woman, Lin Moniang from 1000 CE who saved people from danger at sea; the most popular goddess of Daoism

Mencius · the second-greatest Confucian teacher, who emphasized the goodness and trustworthiness of the people, advocated for small government, and took Confucianism in a more religious direction, stressing the "way of heaven" as being the correct way

New Life Movement · a movement started by Chiang Kai-shek in the 1930s to bring social harmony by returning to traditional values, with an emphasis on respect and the rule of law

President Xi Jinping · the current president of the People's Republic of China

Pyromancy · divination through the analysis of a fire

Qi · also spelled **chi**, "air"; the flow of cosmic energy that animates the living

Qigong · "life energy"; an ancient form of traditional healing, incorporating meditation and martial arts

Qufu · the city in which Confucius was born

Ren · acting humanely and benevolently toward each other to maintain harmony

Shang dynasty · governing kingdom of China from the 1700s to the 1100s BCE; very religious, incorporating rituals, shamanistic features, divining, animism, and human sacrifice

Shangdi · "Supreme Ruler" or "Highest Deity"; the transcendent High God of ancient Chinese religion

Shangqing Revelations · influential scriptures written by Yang Xi focused on living a solitary life in the mountains and discussing Daoist heroes who had journeyed into the celestial realms

Shen · benevolent and helpful spirits in ancient Chinese religion

Shennong · the god who invented farming and agriculture

Sinicization · to nativize into Chinese forms

Tai chi · a Chinese martial art incorporating Daoist thought

Tang dynasty · the governing kingdom of China from 618 to 907 CE during which Daoism reached its zenith of power, prestige, and impact in Asia

The Tao · also written as **the Dao**, the "way"; a method of behaving as well as the supreme force of the universe, the absolute and mysterious reality of all things; formless, nameless, and impersonal; a cosmic principle instructing people to follow the natural course of the universe in life

Tao of Pooh · a book introducing Daoist thought to the West through allegory with the beloved fictional character Winnie the Pooh

Tao Te Ching · also known as *Daode Jing*, "The Book of the Way of Virtue"; a short text of eighty-one poems; the fundamental book of Daoism, teaching on the Dao and on virtuous living

Tian · heaven; a force that was believed to be the supreme way, altogether good

Tianshi Dao · also known as the **Way of the Celestial Masters** and **Five Bushels of Rice**; a theocratic movement that grew out of Zhang Daoling's teachings

Wu wei · nonaction or nonintervention; a Daoist principle encouraging us to go with the flow of life, rather than striving against the grain

Xiao · "filial piety"; respecting authorities and observing one's proper place in the five fundamental relationships of parents to children, older siblings to younger siblings, husbands to wives, elders to the youths, and rulers to the ruled

Xie jiao · the designation of "evil cult," which the Chinese government labels certain religions; adherents to xie jiao can be marginalized or persecuted

Xunzi · also spelled **Hsun Tzu**, the third great figure of Confucianism who disagreed strongly with Confucius and Mencius with his belief that humans are fundamentally evil and must be strictly governed in order to maintain harmony by force

Yang · a force associated with rationality, brightness, warmth, masculinity, dryness, the Sun, and the good

Yang Xi · a medium who claimed to be the recipient of divine revelations and formed his own school of Daoism

Yangsheng · "nourishing life"; the set of practices, including alchemy, tai chi, and dietetics, which is intended to prolong one's life

Yin · a force associated with emotion, darkness, coolness, femininity, wetness, the Moon, shadows, and evil

Yin/yang · interdependent dualism; a concept that teaches the harmony and equilibrium of all things; since everything is in need of balance, everything needs an opposite

Zhang Daoling · A Daoist leader six centuries after Laozi who transformed the religion from a rather simple collection of

ideas centered around following the Dao to an institutionalized religion with ordained leaders, highly structured rituals, and a commentary on the *Tao Te Ching* that was to be considered the authoritative interpretation

Zhou dynasty · the longest dynasty in Chinese history, ruling from around 1050 to 250 BCE, during which the concepts of Shangdi and Tian started to become enmeshed

Zhuangzi · Laozi's most important student who synthesized Daoist teaching and wrote the second most important book in Daoism, *Zhuangzi*

CHAPTER EIGHT

Amaterasu · the Sun goddess and most important Shinto deity, linked to the imperial rulers of Japan

Anime · a popular style of Japanese animation

Animism · when the natural elements—such as mountains, forests, waters, and heavenly spheres—become spiritualized and deified

Anzan kigan · a prayer ceremony at a shrine for a pregnant woman to have a safe delivery of her child

Birth of the Buddha · celebrated on April 8 in Japan; practitioners pour tea over a statue of the Buddha when he was a baby

Boys' Day · a celebration on May 5 during which boys set up warrior action figures in the home in celebration of their growth in strength and stature; originally meant to drive away evil spirits

Bushido · a code of conduct for samurai similar to medieval notions of chivalry

Doll Festival · a celebration on March 3 during which the girls of a household set up an elaborate doll display

Ema · a wooden plaque containing a depiction of an animal (especially a horse) on one side and blank on the other; the devotee writes a wish on the blank side and leaves it in the temple for the kami to receive

Emperor Tenmu · a Japanese emperor from the 600s CE who commissioned the writing of the *Kojiki* and established the shrine at Ise

Empress Jingu · powerful third-century queen, as well as a charismatic diviner

Flower festival · a celebration in which people have picnics in the hills and pick wildflowers in commemoration of the mountain kami descending to the rice fields

Hachiman · Japan's divine protector who is closely associated with the samurai warriors

Haiden · the worship hall in a Shinto shrine, where practitioners stay so as not to disturb the kami

Himiko · a powerful third-century queen, as well as a charismatic diviner

Honden · the main hall in a Shinto shrine; where the kami stay

Honshu · the main island of Japan

Inari · the kami associated with fertility, agriculture, sake, and prosperity

Izanagi · the first male kami, who created the Japanese islands

Izanami · the first female kami, who created the Japanese islands with Izanagi, her brother and consort; gave birth to Amaterasu

Jimmu · the mythical first emperor of Japan

Jinja · the largest form of Shinto and the traditional kind that has been practiced throughout Japanese history

Kagura · a dance, accompanied by flutes and stringed instruments, designed to honor the kami

Kami · gods and all kinds of spirits, including human, animal, plant, water, mountain, as well as other natural objects and forces

Kami no michi · "the way of the kami"; another way of saying *Shinto*

Kamidana · a shelf or altar in a home honoring the family's kami

Kamikaze · "divine wind"; warriors during World War II who plunged their airplanes into enemy ships

Kannushi · "god master"; a term for Shinto priests

Kojiki · the "Record of Ancient Matters"; the most significant book of Shinto myths, demonstrating the divine origins of the Japanese land, people, and emperor

Koshitsu · state-sponsored Shinto, associated with the supremacy of the emperor; abolished in the national reforms after World War II

Kurozumikyo · a Shinto sect centered on Amaterasu

Kyoha · independent, sectarian forms of Shinto

Matsuri · Shinto festival

Meiji Constitution · a strictly hierarchical and British-style constitution adopted in 1889 and followed until the end of World War II; elevated the emperor and established Shinto as the official religion of Japan

Mikos · young, unmarried women who are assistants to priests

Minzoku · folk Shinto, practiced predominantly in the country-side villages to celebrate the harvest and rites of passage within the local community

Motoori Norinaga · a scholar of the Edo period who pro-moted a return to the traditional Japanese way, emphasizing Shinto over Buddhism and Confucianism

Nara dynasty · the era during which the Japanese impe-rial family was proclaimed to be the divine descendants of Amaterasu and Buddhism was officially recognized in Japan, alongside Shinto

New Year · a Shinto holiday celebrated by purifying the home and ridding oneself of any impurity; kamidanas are prepared in anticipation of a blessing from the rice kami, who will sustain the family throughout the year

Nihon Shoki · the Chronicles of Japan; a Shinto record of myth and history, covering the period of the creation of the kami through Empress Jito's death in 697

O no Yasumaro · the author of the *Kojiki* and the *Nihon Shoki*

Omikuji · fortunes written on small pieces of paper and drawn out of a box; the forerunner of the modern-day fortune cookie

Origami · paper creations made from folding

Sake · an alcoholic beverage made from rice

Secular · unaffiliated with religion

Seppuku · also known as **hara-kiri**; ritual self-disembowel-ment required by honor in certain circumstances

Shamanesses · in early Japanese history, women who would go into trances and connect with the kami, as well as with the ancestors

Shen · a Chinese character for "spirits," from which the word *Shinto* is derived

Shichi-Go-San · the "7-5-3 festival"; held annually for boys aged three and five and girls aged three and seven, on or around November 15; said to have originally been a celebration of the survival of the child from infancy

Shinshokus · "employees of the gods"; a term for Shinto priests

Tao · a Chinese character for "way," from which the word *Shinto* is derived

Tenjin · the "sky deity" kami of education and scholarship

Tenrikyo · "Religion of Heavenly Wisdom"; founded by a poor farmer's wife, Nakayama Miki, in the 1830s when she began receiving revelations from the one true God; claims two million adherents today

Tokugawa Shogunate · also known as the **Edo period**, the period between 1603 and 1867 in Japanese history; an age often romanticized as the days of the samurai and of strict codes of honor

Torii · "bird perch"; a gateway to a Shinto shrine, reminding adherents that they are entering a sacred space

Tsumi · anything that violates the norms of purity

Yamato · the strategic capital for Japan's ruling house for gen-erations—traditionally from 250 to 710 CE

Yasukuni Shrine · a controversial shrine honoring Japa-nese who have died in war, including those who are guilty of war crimes

Yomi · the realm of the dead

CHAPTER NINE

Ablutions · ritually purifying one's face, forearms, hands, and feet with clean water before prayer

Agiaries · the term used in India for fire temples

Ahriman · a truncated pronunciation of Angra Mainyu that came into use during the Sassanid Empire

Ahura Mazda · a dualistic interpretation of God in which God has two sides—an evil side known as Angra Mainyu and a good side known as Spenta Mainyu; the two sides are in a cosmic struggle against each other

Alexander the Great · the Greek conqueror who brought down the Achaemenid Empire

Amesha Spenta · seven good deities that emanate from Ahura Mazda

Angra Mainyu · the bad side of Ahura Mazda and a force of chaos who wars with Spenta Mainyu and will ultimately be vanquished

Appointed Place Fire · the least sacred and the most common of the three kinds of special fires; consecrated by two priests over a two-hour ceremony

Aryans · "**noble ones**"; Indo-Iranians in pre-Zoroastrian Persia

Asha · truth and righteousness

Avesta · the Zoroastrian scriptures, named after the language in which they are written

Avestan · an old Iranian language similar to Vedic Sanskrit; the language of the Zoroastrian scriptures

Brahman · in Hinduism, the eternal and ultimate reality; has a similar transcendence to pre-Zoroastrian Persia's Ahura Mazda

Bundahishn · "Primal Creation"; a text respected in Zoroastrianism but not considered scripture

Chinvat Bridge · the bridge souls cross at judgment after death; the righteous walk safely across to paradise, but the wicked are pulled down into the abyss below by demons

Cyrus the Great · the founder of the First Persian Empire, considered to be a hero of sorts to the Jews, even today, due to his liberating the Jews from Babylonian captivity

Daena · the representation of one's life decisions after death; a righteous person's daena will be young and attractive, but an evil person's daena will appear old and ugly

Dakhma · also known as the **Tower of Silence**; the structure on which a deceased body is placed to be eaten by the vultures so that its flesh will not pollute the Earth

Denkard · "Acts of Religion"; a text respected in Zoroastrianism but not considered scripture

Devas · also spelled **daevas**; evil gods of pre-Zoroastrian Persian religion who cause chaos and are to be avoided

Dhimmitude · a legal provision for non-Muslim monotheists living in Muslim territory who are allowed to continue practicing their religion so long as they pay higher taxes and do not enjoy the same privileges as do those who submit to Islam

Druj · falsehood and deception

Druj-demana · also known as the **House of Lies**, the Zoroastrian hell; an awful, albeit temporary, place of torment for the wicked

Dualism · the concept that there are two opposing forces constantly dueling with one another throughout history

Esther · an ancient Jewish woman who purportedly married Xerxes the Great and wielded her influence as queen to save the Jewish people

Eternal return · Nietzsche's theory that all reality, and all events, come and go and repeat themselves in an eternal cycle of reality forever and ever

Faravahar · the symbol of Zoroastrianism; a bearded man with eagle's wings

Farsi · a modern language used commonly in Iran, Afghanistan, and Tajikistan

Fire of Fires · the second-most sacred kind of fire in Zoroastrianism; consecrated by eight priests over a period of three weeks

Fire of Victory · the most sacred fire in Zoroastrianism, requiring thirty-two priests to consecrate the fire over the course of a year, bringing together sixteen different types of flame; only eight Fires of Victory exist in the world

Fire temple · a Zoroastrian temple named for its sacred, eternally burning fires

First Persian Empire · also known as the **Achaemenid Empire**, an empire that controlled most of the entire Middle East in the sixth to fourth centuries BCE; the largest empire in history up to that time; Zoroastrianism was its official religion

Four-eyed dogs · intimidating creatures who guard the Chinvat Bridge

Fravashis · guardian spirits who help guide humans toward good, ethical lives

Gathas · Zoroastrian liturgies found in the Avesta

God is dead · Nietzsche's theory that humankind has evolved past its need for primitive dependence on false superstitions, and with the advent of modern science, we have put "God" to death

Good thoughts, good words, good deeds · the most famous Zoroastrian mantra

Haoma · the Avestan name for soma

Intertestamental literature · Jewish literature written during the four-hundred-year period between the Old and New Testaments; reveals a strong belief in Satan and angelic beings

Iranis · Zoroastrians who are still in Iran

Judgment Day · after death, Mithra weighs a person's good and bad deeds to determine whether the person will go to the Zoroastrian heaven or hell

Khordeh · also known as the **Little Avesta**, the final section of the Avesta, containing instructions for laypeople

King Darius · an important Persian king and follower of Ahura Mazda who recurs in the Bible

Kushti · a sacred belt with seventy-two strands worn around the waist

Majoos · also spelled **Majus**; the Muslim term for Zoroastrians

Mani · the prophet who founded Manichaeism

Manichaeism · a religion founded in the third century CE that borrowed heavily from Zoroastrianism

Mazdayasna · "Worship of the Lord (Mazda)"; the name Zoroastrians use to refer to their religion

Mithra · the greatest of the pre-Zoroastrian Persian gods; associated with cattle, covenants, truth, and obedience

Mithraism · a Roman mystery religion practiced by imperial soldiers that focused on the ancient Persian god Mithra; initiation ceremonies involved killing a sacred bull

Mystery religions · secret cults that flourished in Greco-Roman times

Nahn · a sacred bath ceremony that requires washing the entire body just before one's wedding

Navjote · the term in India for the Zoroastrian Sacred Thread Ceremony

Nowruz · the Zoroastrian New Year and most popular holy day; associated with the Amesha Spenta and with fire

Ohrmazd · a truncated pronunciation of Ahura Mazda that came into use during the Sassanid Empire

Pahlavi · also known as **Middle Persian**, the language in which the *Bundahishn* and the *Denkard* are written; a link between Old Persian (Avestan) and Modern Persian (Farsi)

Parsis · Zoroastrians who moved to India

Patet · ritual confession to a Zoroastrian priest

Pre-Zoroastrian Persians · polytheistic animists who believed in the sacredness of nature

Sacred Thread Ceremony · a rite of passage in ancient Persia for male children signifying their new status as young men with new responsibilities

Saoshyants · "those who bring benefit to the community"; prophets who come to Earth occasionally to restore the original purity of religion, which has become corrupt

Sassanid Empire · also known as the **Sasanian Empire**, the empire that ruled Persia from 224 to 651 CE; demoted Ahura Mazda to the second-most important god behind Zurvan; introduced a priestly hierarchy, the tending of the sacred flame, the priestly practice of wearing a mask while attending the flame, and the notion of exposing the dead so that they do not pollute the Earth

Sedreh · a sacred undershirt

Sedreh Pushi · the term in Iran for the Zoroastrian Sacred Thread Ceremony

Soma · sacred hallucinogenic drink in Vedic India

Spenta Mainyu · the good side of Ahura Mazda, a force of order and benevolence, who wars against Angra Mainyu and will ultimately be victorious

Superman · also known as the **overman**; Nietzsche's theory that humankind can evolve beyond categories of moral good and evil to realize our full potential

Varuna · the Vedic sky god

Vendidad · "Against the Demons"; a text that explains how believers are to avoid getting caught by evil spirits

Visperad · a collection of liturgical texts used for festivals, such as the Zoroastrian New Year; used in conjunction with the Yasna

Will to power · according to Nietzsche, this is the driving force in humans

Wise Men · also known as **Magi**, Zoroastrian priests and astrologers who appear in the New Testament

Xerxes the Great · a Persian king who appears in the Bible in the book of Esther

Yashts · a collection of twenty-one hymns that extol Zoroaster and the virtues he represented, such as wisdom, truth, and justice

Yasna · the collection of recitations for priests during the liturgy

Yazatas · thirty divine entities who serve Ahura Mazda like angels

Zarathushtrian Assembly · an organization started in California in 1990 to advocate for a modern interpretation of the faith, including letting Zoroastrians marry non-Zoroastrians

Zarathustrianism · another word for Zoroastrianism, after the Avestan pronunciation of Zoroaster's name, Zarathustra

Zurvan · the creator god in Sassanid mythology who fathered Ahura Mazda

CHAPTER TEN

1948 Arab–Israeli War · a war launched by a coalition of Islamic Arab powers against the newly formed state of Israel in protest of the new nation's intrusion into Palestine

Abraham · the patriarch of the Jewish people

Al-Andalus · Moorish Spain and Portugal, which peacefully tolerated the Jewish minority during its reign from 711 to 1492 CE

Al-Aqsa Mosque · a mosque built on the Temple Mount in Jerusalem; the third-holiest site in Islam

Aristotelianism · the philosophical tradition of Aristotle; characterized by deductive logic and the analytical, inductive study of nature and natural law

Ark of the Covenant · a sacred container that held the tablets on which the Ten Commandments were written, Aaron's staff, and manna—all symbols of the covenant

Ashkenazic · the culture that emerged from the Jewish communities living in Northern Europe

Assyrians · an ancient Near Eastern people group who conquered the Northern Kingdom of Israel

Axis mundi · the "center of the world"; commonly seen as Jerusalem in Israel for Jews, Christians, and Muslims

Baal Shem Tov · "Master of the Good Name"; the title adopted by Israel ben Eliezer

Babylonian Talmud · one of the most important collections of rabbinic tradition; compiled in around 500 CE in the modern-day region of Iraq, but not completed until around 700 CE

Babylonians · an ancient Near Eastern people group who conquered the Southern Kingdom of Judah

Bar Kokhba · a revolutionary in the 130s CE who led the last great Jewish rebellion against Rome

Bar mitzvah · a rite of passage for Jewish males when they turn thirteen and are officially considered adult men in the synagogue; they demonstrate their maturity by publicly reading from the Torah and giving a short sermon

Bat mitzvah · a rite of passage for Jewish girls when they turn thirteen; practiced mainly by Reform Jews

Brit Milah · the ritual of male circumcision

Caesar Augustus · the first Roman emperor, who conquered the Hellenized world

Canaan · an ancient name for the land of Palestine

Cantors · Jews tasked with leading a congregation's music and prayer during worship

Chai · "living" or "to life"

Circumcision · a ritual required by the covenant for all Jewish males on the eighth day of their life

Cleopatra · the last Ptolemaic ruler of Egypt; lost Alexandria to Caesar Augustus in 31 BCE before taking her own life

Concentration camps · abhorrent labor camps established throughout Nazi territory designed to work the Jews to death

Conservative Judaism · also known as **Masorti**; a middle ground between Orthodox and Reform Judaism

Conversos · "converts" to Christianity during Spanish persecution of non-Christians

Covenant · a central theme of the Hebrew Bible; God makes covenant agreements that bind the Israelites to him for obedience, sacrifice, protection, and love

Cyrus · the beloved Persian monarch who liberated the Jewish people from Babylonian oppression and allowed them to rebuild their temple and the holy city of Jerusalem

Dead Sea Scrolls · ancient Jewish religious literature remarkably preserved and discovered in caves near Qumran; containing scrolls from as early as the fifth century BCE

Decalogue · the Ten Commandments

Dome of the Rock · an Islamic shrine built on the Temple Mount in Jerusalem in commemoration of Muhammad's Night Journey

Ein Sof · "the infinite"; the Kabbalist understanding of God as unknowable, beyond form, beyond gender, and beyond all concepts of any kind

Emancipation · the liberation of the Jewish people from oppressive and discriminatory policies in medieval and early modern Europe

Essenes · a Jewish movement in the first century CE that isolated itself from the rest of the contemporary culture to maintain its religious authenticity

Final Solution · Hitler's answer to the Jewish Problem; a complete genocide of the Jewish people

First Aliyah · a wave of Jewish agricultural immigrants from Russia into Palestine in the 1880s and 1890s

Gemara · commentaries on the Mishnah

Greco-Roman · the combined Greek and Roman influence on Mediterranean culture and history

Guide for the Perplexed · Maimonides's written attempt to reconcile Judaism with Aristotelianism

Hallelujah · an exclamation meaning "praise the Lord," with the last syllable "jah" (yah) derived from a shortened version of Yahweh

Hanukkah · a Jewish holiday commemorating the miraculous rededication of the temple after retaking it from the profanities of the Seleucids

Haredim · a term for Orthodox Jews in Israel meaning "tremblers," and usually translated as "ultra-Orthodox"

Hasidic · a Jewish anti-intellectual movement that emphasizes personal piety and expressing ecstatic, emotional love for God

Hebrew Union College · the first permanent Jewish institution of higher learning in the New World; established in Cincinnati in 1875 under the leadership of Rabbi Isaac Mayer Wise

Hellenization · a sociocultural change begun by Alexander the Great that was intended to implement Greek language and culture across all Greek territories

Hiloni · "secular"; the term for secular Jews in Israel

Holocaust · "completely burned"; the name given to the systematic mass extermination of six million Jewish people by Nazi Germany

Holy Land · the former land owned by ancient Israel to which the Jews longed to return and reestablish as a Jewish state

Isaac Luria · a Kabbalist leader in Galilee whose teachings became known as the Lurianic Kabbalah

Israel · the "promised land" that God had vowed to give to the descendants of Abraham to constitute a holy nation dedicated to and protected by their creator

Israel ben Eliezer · the founder of the Hasidic ("pious ones") movement

Israelites · the descendants of Abraham's grandson Jacob, whose name was changed to Israel after a dramatic encounter with God

Jehovah · a Latinized pronunciation of God's name; derived from the Hebrew characters YHWH

Jerusalem Talmud · also known as the **Palestinian Talmud**; one of the most important collections of rabbinic tradition, which was developed in Galilee and was compiled in around 350 CE

Jewish diaspora · the mass dispersal of the Jewish people following the failed revolts against Rome

Jewish ghetto · the practice of sequestering Jewish people into specific districts, leading to crushing poverty and discrimination; originated in Rome in the sixteenth century and spread throughout Europe

The Jewish problem · also known as **the Jewish question**; the question over policy pertaining to the Jewish minority in Europe

Jewish temple · the Reform term for a synagogue

Jizya · higher tax rates for non-Muslim monotheists living in Muslim-controlled areas

Judas Maccabeus · "Judas the Hammer"; the Jewish revolutionary who led his people to victory in their rebellion against the Seleucid Empire

Kabbalah · a movement of Jewish mysticism that claimed to discover the hidden meaning of the Torah

Karaites · an anti-traditionalist Jewish sect that arose in the Middle Ages; rejected rabbinical authority, the Oral Torah, and human commentaries on scripture

Ketuvim · "writings"; the final section of the Tanakh, which contains books of poetry, wisdom literature, stories with female protagonists, and the story of Jerusalem's restoration after its defeat and exile

Kippah · also known as a yarmulke; a brimless cap worn on the crown of the head

Kosher · Jewish dietary laws restricting what animals may be consumed and how those animals must be killed and prepared

Ladino · the language of the Sephardi Jews, based on Old Spanish with the incorporation of Hebrew religious terms

Law of Return · legislation allowing any Jew worldwide the right to immigrate to Israel

Levant · a geographical region along the Eastern Mediterranean, stretching from Syria in the north to Jordan in the south

Maccabean Revolt · a successful rebellion against the Seleucid Empire led by Judas Maccabeus; led to a century of Jewish independence

Maimonides · a famous Jewish intellectual and physician who wrote commentaries on the Talmud as well as a book reconciling science and religion

Matrilineal · Jewish identity is passed through the mother

Matzah · "bread of affliction"; unleavened flatbread eaten during the Passover in remembrance of the unleavened bread the Israelites ate in a hurry when they left Egypt

Menorah · a lampstand, typically with seven branches, modeled after the one of pure gold that Moses made for the tabernacle of the Lord in the desert and later used in the temple

Messianic Jews · Jews who believe that Jesus Christ was the long-awaited Jewish Messiah but who often still practice traditional Jewish rituals

Mezuzah · a case affixed to a doorpost containing parchment with the Shema written on it; a statement of allegiance to God and an act of obedience to the command in Deuteronomy 6:9 that Jews put God's words on their doorposts

Mikvah · a bath for ritual immersion to attain purity

Minyan · ten Jewish males over the age of thirteen; the quorum required for a synagogue

Mishnah · "Repeated Tradition" or "Repetition"; the earliest recorded rabbinic commentary on the Torah from around 200 CE

Mishneh Torah · Maimonides's authoritative fourteen-volume commentary on the Talmud

Mitzvoth · commandments given by God in the Torah; according to tradition, there are 613

Mohel · the person who performs the circumcision

Moses Mendelssohn · a German Jew in the 1700s who encouraged the Jewish community to assimilate into European culture

Mourner's Kaddish · after a death, a prayer recited each day by the children of the deceased for a year after their passing

Nevi'im · "**prophets**"; the second section of the Tanakh, which continues the story of Israel from the Torah and contains the writings of the prophets, who warned Israel to repent of its sins and follow God, or else the nation would face divine retribution

Oral Torah · the authoritative interpretive tradition around the Torah; recorded and preserved by the rabbis

Orthodox Judaism · the most observant branch of Judaism, which affirms Talmudic authority, Kosher laws, Sabbath observance, the separation of men and women in worship, head coverings, and the use of Hebrew as the language of worship

Palestine · the geographical region encompassing the modern-day states of Palestine and Israel

Passover · a weeklong Jewish festival celebrating the Jews' deliverance from bondage in Egypt

Pentateuch · also known as the **Five Books of Moses**; the five books purportedly written by Moses that comprise the Torah: Genesis, Exodus, Leviticus, Numbers, and Deuteronomy

Persian period · the era of Persian domination of the ancient Near East, from 539 to 333 BCE

Pharisees · a group of religious teachers who scrupulously practiced tradition and law; transformed Judaism from a religion of animal sacrifice to one focused on ritual purity, prayer, devotion, and knowledge of the texts

Pogroms · organized massacres of Jewish people

Protocols of the Elders of Zion · a fabricated document that emerged in Russia in 1903 and circulated throughout Europe in a number of languages; claimed that the Jews schemed to take over the world

Purim · the celebration of Esther's Jewish pride and the self-assertion of the Jews in the face of persecution; full of feasting, celebration, and a public reading of the book of Esther

Rabbi Abraham Geiger · the most important leader of Reform Judaism; oversaw its expansion throughout Europe

Rabbi Isaac Mayer Wise · an important leader of Reform Judaism in the United States; based out of Cincinnati

Rabbi Judah ha-Nasi · also known as **Judah the Prince**; a highly esteemed rabbi who served as Rome's contact person for Palestinian Jews and who compiled the Mishnah

Rabbi Yohanan ben Zakkai · the pivotal person who changed the loyalty of the Jews from animal sacrifice to a religion centered on text and prayer; escaped the 70 CE siege of Jerusalem in a coffin and founded a new center for Judaism in Yavne

Rabbinic Judaism · the prevailing Jewish practice since the fall of Jerusalem; centered on the Torah as interpreted by the traditions of the rabbis

Reconquista · Christian Spain's crusade to reconquer the Iberian Peninsula from the Moors

Reform Judaism · a progressive branch of Judaism that promotes the evolution of the religion and the rejection of outdated ideas such as Talmudic authority, a coming Messiah, and a return to the Jewish holy land

Regina Jonas · a German woman ordained as a rabbi in 1935, though her case was hotly debated at the time

Rosh Hashanah · Jewish New Year; the anniversary of the creation of Adam and Eve and a time of repentance for sins

Sabbatai Zevi · a Sephardic, Kabbalist rabbi in the 1600s who claimed to be the long-awaited Jewish Messiah but then converted to Islam under threat of death, convincing several hundred Jewish families to do the same

Sabbath · also known as **Shabbat**, meaning "cease"; the seventh day of each week that is set aside for rest and for remembrance of God

Sadducees · a group of political elites who tended to control political offices as well as the Jewish temple; rejected the veracity of the Oral Torah and resurrection

Sally Jane Priesand · ordained in 1972 in Cincinnati; the first female rabbi of Reform Judaism

Samaritans · a people group with religious beliefs similar to Judaism, with the exception that the holiest site was Mount Gerazim rather than Zion in Jerusalem

Second Temple Judaism · the term for Jewish religion and culture during the time period from the reconstruction of the temple under Persian rule to the destruction of that temple by the Romans in 70 CE

Secular Jews · Jews in ethnicity but not in religious practice

Seder · an elaborate meal eaten on the first night of Passover

Semitic · one of the oldest known language groups, with some texts over five thousand years old; connected to the family of Afro-Asiatic languages and centered in the Levant

Sephardic · the culture that emerged from the Jewish communities living in Moorish Spain and Portugal

Septuagint · "seventy"; the Greek translation of the Jewish scriptures; purportedly written by seventy scholars

Shalom · peace

Shavuot · the Feast of Weeks, celebrated fifty days after Passover and commemorating the covenant God made with the Jews at Mount Sinai

Shema · "hear"; taken from the first words of Deuteronomy 6:4–5; one of the most central teachings of the Torah

Shiva · after a death, a seven-day period in which the family of the deceased stays at home to receive visitors

Shoah · "calamity," "catastrophe," or "destruction"; the Hebrew word for the Holocaust

Shofar · a ram's horn blown during Rosh Hashanah

Sicarii · a sub-group of the Zealots who carried small daggers concealed in their cloaks to stab Roman sympathizers at public gatherings

Siege of Jerusalem · a Roman offensive against the Jewish revolt that culminated in the destruction of the Second Temple and the sacking of Jerusalem

Six-Day War · a brief war between Israel and its Arab neighbors in 1967

Spanish Inquisition · a religious court that tried and punished non-Christians utilizing methods of torture and execution

Star of David · a hexagram that symbolizes Jewish identity

Sukkot · the Feast of Tabernacles, celebrated by constructing temporary huts in which Jews will eat and sometimes sleep for a week, remembering the temporary dwellings of their ancestors when they lived in the desert for forty years

Synagogue · "assembly"; a place of Jewish gathering and worship that requires the presence of the Torah scrolls and a minyan

Tabernacle · a tent used as a sanctuary for the Ark of the Covenant

Tallit · fringed prayer shawl worn by Orthodox Jews

Talmud · a combination of the Mishnah and the Gemara

Tanakh · the Hebrew Bible; an acronym formed from the initials of each of its three component parts: Torah, Nevi'im, and Ketuvim

Tefillin · also known as the phylactery; leather boxes containing Torah readings worn on the head and arm

Tetragrammaton · "four-letter name"; a term for the four-character name of God, YHWH

Theodor Herzl · the father of Zionism who argued that Jews would always be subject to persecution unless they obtained land of their own

Torah · "**teaching**" or "**law**"; the first section of the Tanakh, which contains the fundamental instructions of God to his people, as well as the story of Israel's origins and early history

Touro Synagogue · The United States' oldest synagogue still in existence; located in Newport, Rhode Island

Tzedakah · giving to charity, an obligation commanded by God

Western Wall · the most sacred place in Judaism; a place of prayer and hope for restoration

Yahweh · a common non-Jewish pronunciation of the Tetragrammaton; also pronounced **Yahveh**

Yavne · the new center for Judaism after the fall of Jerusalem in 70 CE

Yellow badge policy · discriminatory laws that required all Jews to wear yellow badges for quick identification of their ethnicity

Yeshiva · a Jewish school devoted to the study of the Torah and the Talmud

YHWH · the highly sacred name of God; too holy to be uttered aloud and often left unwritten out of respect

Yiddish · the language of the Ashkenazi Jews; a mixture of German and Hebrew with some Slavic influence

Yom HaShoah · Holocaust Remembrance Day

Yom Kippur · also known as the **Day of Atonement**, the holiest of Jewish holidays, during which Jews fast, pray, and seek forgiveness from God and from others

Yom Kippur War · a war between Israel and the surrounding powers in 1973

Zealots · a discontented political group that opposed Roman domination through the use of violence

Zion · in reference to Mount Zion, a word used as shorthand for both Jerusalem as well as the nation of Israel

Zionism · a movement for Jews to repatriate to Palestine and establish an independent nation

Zohar · the Book of Splendor; a mystical commentary on the Torah authoritative to the Kabbalists

CHAPTER ELEVEN

A cappella · "in the style of the chapel"; singing without the accompaniment of musical instruments; the typical Orthodox manner of worship

Abba · "Father"; a familial term that Jesus used to refer to God; Christians tend to see God in this same loving, fatherly role

Abbess · the head of an abbey of nuns

Acts of the Apostles · a book of the New Testament that relates the history of the early Christian church

Advent · the month of December, leading up to Christmas

African Methodist Episcopal Church · the first Black denomination in North America; founded in 1816 by Richard Allen

Aimee Semple McPherson · a Pentecostal preacher from Canada who founded the Foursquare Church denomination and Angelus Temple in Los Angeles

All Saints' Day · the Christian holiday that commemorates all of the saints, both known and unknown

Anabaptists · a radical subgroup of the Reformation that denounced infant baptism, teaching instead that only those who could profess their own faith in Christ should be baptized

Angelus Temple · one of the most successful megachurches; founded by Aimee Semple McPherson in 1923

Anglicans · also known as the **Church of England**, or in the United States, the **Episcopal Church**; a Protestant denomination that came into being when King Henry VIII split with Rome after the pope denied him an annulment

Antichrist · an apocalyptic figure that some believe will arise in the end times and lead many astray

Apocrypha · a set of religious texts that Christians generally consider to be useful but that do not carry the same authority as canonical literature

Apostle Paul · the author of much of the New Testament; advocated for the inclusion of Gentiles as well as Jews in Christianity

Apse · the domed roof directly over the altar in a cathedral

Ash Wednesday · the beginning of Lent, when Christians burn the palm leaves from the previous Palm Sunday and use the ashes to mark observers' foreheads with a cross

Augustine · a famed theologian significant to all three branches of Christianity; articulated such Christian theories as original sin, predestination, and just war

Avignon Papacy · also known as the **Babylonian Captivity of the Church** and the **Western Schism**; a scandal in the Roman Catholic Church from 1309 to 1376, when the papacy was moved to Avignon, France, and there were briefly multiple, simultaneous popes

Azusa Street Revival · a revival in Los Angeles in 1906 that is often seen as the birth of modern Pentecostalism

Baptism · an initiation ritual in the Christian faith that is associated with cleansing, renewal, and salvation; the fundamental mark of entering a covenantal relationship with God

Baptist · an Evangelical denomination born out of the Anabaptist movement of the Reformation

Basilica · "royal place"; a special class of church building in Catholicism, many of which were built over the burial place of a saint and/or martyr

Battle of Tours · a pivotal moment in Western history in 732 CE when Charles Martel defeated the advancing Muslim armies, securing Christian supremacy in Europe

Bishops · the successors of the apostles as the authorities of the church

Bridget of Sweden · a fourteenth-century mystic who founded the Bridgettine order of nuns and monks

Byzantine Empire · the eastern half of the Roman Empire that survived the fall of Rome and persisted until the fifteenth century, when it fell to the Ottoman Turks

Catacombs · a labyrinth of underground corridors outside of Rome where Christians buried their dead

Celibacy · unnecessary, according to the reformers, who supported clerical marriage

Charles Martel · the French military leader who halted the Muslim incursion into Europe

Christmas · the feast of Christ's birth, celebrated on December 25 for Catholics and Protestants and on January 7 for Orthodox Christians

Church fathers · an influential class of early church leaders who established much of the Orthodox tradition and doctrine

Church of Christ, Scientist · a Christian denomination focused on miraculous healing; founded by Mary Baker Eddy in Boston in 1879

Communion · also known as **the Lord's Supper**, the Protestant term for the Eucharist

Confession · the admission of one's sins to a priest to receive grace and reconciliation with God

Confirmation · a sacrament in which the covenant between God and a person, entered into at baptism, is affirmed and sealed with the anointing of oil in the presence of the church

Constantinople · the center of Eastern Orthodoxy and the capital of the Byzantine Empire

Cosmology · the study of the origin of the universe; in Christianity, believed to be creation by God, which is sustained by and through him

Council of Chalcedon · an ecumenical council in 451 that affirmed the hypostatic union that Jesus was simultaneously 100 percent man and 100 percent God

Council of Nicaea · an ecumenical Christian council of church leaders in 325 CE who articulated the doctrine of the Trinity

Council of Trent · a Roman Catholic council held in 1545 in response to the Reformation; the council condemned Protestantism, upheld Latin as the language of scripture and liturgy, and confirmed exclusive religious authority to the Catholic hierarchy of religious offices

Counter-Reformation · a firm reassertion of Catholicism in the face of the Protestant Reformation

Crucifix · an image of the cross that bears the body of Jesus

Cruciform · in the shape of a cross

The Crusades · a series of Christian invasions into the Muslim-controlled Holy Land between 1095 and 1204

Crypt · a room underneath a church building used for burial

Dark Ages · an outdated and ignorant historical term for the medieval era

Deaconess · an office of leadership in the church

Diocese · the region overseen by a particular bishop

Divine Liturgies · the Orthodox term for the Eucharist

Easter · the celebration of Christ's resurrection

Ecumenical movement · a twentieth-century Protestant movement striving for Christian unity across denominational lines

Edict of Milan · a landmark decree by Emperors Constantine and Licinius in 313 CE that extended official legality and toleration to Christians

Emperor Constantine · the fourth-century Roman emperor who legalized and favored Christianity, thus sparking a significant increase in conversion; revered in the Eastern Orthodox tradition as "Equal to the Apostles"

Emperor Diocletian · the supreme ruler of the Roman Empire from 284 to 305 CE; rescinded the civil, legal, and religious rights of Christians, instigating a period of intense persecution

Epiphany · the feast celebrating the revelation of Jesus as God incarnate to the Wise Men from the East

Episcopal succession · also known as **apostolic succession**; the unbroken chain of ordination passed down from the apostles to the first bishops and all the way to bishops today

Epistles · formal letters written by the apostles that contain theological insight and instruction

Eucharist · "giving thanks"; partaking in the bread and wine of Passover; associated with the sacrifice of Jesus's body and blood as a remembrance of him

Evangelical Quadrilateral · according to David Bebbington, the four primary elements of evangelicalism are activism, biblicism, conversionism, and crucicentrism

Extreme unction · a sacrament in which the gravely ill are anointed with oil

Fasting · abstaining from food and/or drink as a religious observance; encouraged by the Bible and regularly practiced by Orthodox and sometimes Catholic Christians

Filioque · a word meaning "and the Son"; added to the Nicene Creed by the Catholic Church without the approval of the Orthodox churches or of an ecumenical council; a major source of division between the Catholic and Orthodox branches of Christianity

First Great Awakening · a widespread religious revival in eighteenth-century North America and Britain

Foursquare Church · a Pentecostal denomination founded by Aimee Semple McPherson that today boasts nine million members

Fundamentalism · an Evangelical movement to recommit to the "fundamental" aspects of the Christian faith in the face of modern criticism and reform

Geneva · the home of Reformed Christianity; greatly influenced by John Calvin

Gentile · non-Jewish

George Whitefield · a British clergyman and a close friend of John Wesley; traveled seven times to the American colonies to preach the gospel, setting into motion the First Great Awakening

Global South · a geographical term referring to Latin America, Asia, Africa, and Oceania

Gnostics · a heretical strand of early Christian thought obsessed with esoteric secret knowledge

Good Friday · the day on which Jesus was crucified; remembered solemnly in the Christian faith

Gospels · literally "good news"; narrative accounts of the life of Jesus of Nazareth

Gothic · a late medieval style of church architecture characterized by enormous, pointed arches and stained glass windows

Great Jewish Revolt · a first-century rebellion against Rome that culminated in the destruction of the temple and furthered the burgeoning division between Jews and Christians

Great Schism · the severe rift between the Eastern Orthodox and Roman Catholic churches, which broke apart in 1054 and have remained divided ever since

Gregorian calendar · the mainstream calendar used by most of the world today; adopted in the sixteenth century by Pope Gregory XIII to fix a minor flaw in the old Julian calendar

Hagia Sophia · a magnificent sixth-century church building in Constantinople, which was eventually converted to a mosque after the Ottoman conquest of the Byzantine Empire

Halloween · All Hallows' Eve; the night before All Saints' Day on November 1

Hell · a place of endless torment that serves as punishment for the unbaptized, the heretics, and the unrepentant

Hildegard of Bingen · a twelfth-century Benedictine abbess in Germany; respected for her musical compositions as well as her mystical visions

Holy Grail · the cup used by Jesus at the Last Supper

Holy orders · a sacrament; the ordination of the clergy

Holy Spirit · the third person of the Trinity whom Jesus told his followers he would send to guide them after his ascension into heaven

Host · a term for the bread and wine of the Eucharist, which, once consecrated, becomes the literal body and blood of Christ in the Catholic tradition

Ichthus · the Greek word for fish and an acronym used by the ancient church to represent Christianity, hence the fish symbol still used today by Christian adherents

Iconoclasm · "image smashing"; a movement that arose in the 700s and 800s to end the veneration of icons

Iconodule · a person who supported the veneration of icons

Iconostasis · a prominent screen near the altar in an Orthodox church that separates the clergy from the laity

Icons · images of the holy saints from the history of Christianity

Immaculate Conception · the Catholic doctrine that Mary was conceived in the womb of her mother Anna without the stain of original sin

Index of Forbidden Books · a list published by the Roman Catholic Church of all the heretical books that Catholics were forbidden from reading; begun during the Protestant Reformation and abolished at the Second Vatican Council in the 1960s

Jarena Lee · an eighteenth- and nineteenth-century African American preacher in the African Methodist Episcopal Church who fought against slavery and gender inequality; possibly the first African American woman to write an autobiography

Jerome · a fourth-century linguist and scholar who translated the Bible into Latin

Jesuits · formally known as the **Society of Jesus**; a Catholic missionary society founded by Ignatius Loyola in 1534 that took Catholicism to Asia, Latin America, and Africa

Johannes Gutenberg · the inventor of the printing press

John Calvin · the father of Reformed Christianity who taught a fivefold teaching known by its acronym of TULIP

John Wycliffe · a fourteenth-century reformer who translated the Bible into English

Julian calendar · the calendar used from the time of Julius Caesar until the adoption of the Gregorian calendar in 1582; still used in the liturgical calendar of Eastern Orthodoxy

Julian of Norwich · a fourteenth-century mystic whose book *Revelations of Divine Love* might be the first book written by a woman in the English language

Junia · a female leader in the early church; called an apostle by Paul

Just war theory · the theory that, in certain circumstances, resorting to violence or war for a good cause is morally justifiable or even advisable

King Henry VIII · the king of England in the sixteenth century who cut ties with Rome over a marital conflict

Lectionary · a three-year cycle of readings that attempts to expose Christians to much of the Bible's contents while emphasizing the important holy days

Lent · a forty-day period of self-denial, repentance, and fasting that begins on Ash Wednesday and leads to Easter

Leo the Great · the first Bishop of Rome to assert supremacy over the other patriarchs in around 450 CE, based on Rome's link to Peter, to whom Jesus gave the "keys of the kingdom of heaven" in Matthew 16:19

Liberal Protestantism · also known as **mainline Protestantism**; a collection of Protestant churches that embraces modern scholarly criticism of the Bible, feminism, LGBTQ activism, and pluralism

Liturgy · from the Greek word for "public service"; consists of prayer, ritual, and public worship

Lord's Day · Sunday, the first day of the week and the day on which Jesus rose from the dead; typically the day used for corporate worship services

Lutheran · a Protestant denomination begun by the reforms of Martin Luther

Marcion · a second-century heretic who believed that the God of the Old Testament was irreconcilably different from the person of Jesus

Margery Kempe · a fourteenth- to fifteenth-century mystic who wrote what is considered to be the earliest autobiography in English

Marriage · a sacrament in the Catholic and Orthodox traditions

Martin Luther · the architect of the Protestant Reformation and the author of the *95 Theses*, which indicted the Roman Catholic Church on all of its historical abuses of power

Martin Luther King Jr. · an African American Baptist preacher renowned for his civil rights advocacy

Mary Daly · a prominent Catholic theologian who, while serving as a professor at the Jesuit-run Boston College, became an outspoken feminist and LGBTQ advocate; exhorted women to leave Christianity and organize themselves into a distinct sisterhood

Mass · the Catholic term for the Eucharist

Maundy Thursday · the day commemorating the Last Supper and Jesus's washing of his disciples' feet

Methodist · a mainline denomination with roots in the teachings of John Wesley

Missionaries of Charity · a Catholic missionary society founded by Mother Teresa that serves those in the greatest depths of poverty

Monasticism · an institution of self-denial and of careful study of God, which flourished in early and medieval Christianity and prompted a great tradition of monastic scholars

Monotheism · the belief that there is only one God; nuanced in Christianity to include three distinct persons of God in one unified deity

Mortal sins · serious and deliberate sins that keep transgressors out of heaven if left unconfessed

Mother boards · an African American church tradition in which a board of prominent women holds significant power in the congregation

Mother Teresa · a Roman Catholic nun who founded the Missionaries of Charity order while serving the poor and sick in the streets of Kolkata, India; received the Nobel Peace Prize in 1979

Mujerista theology · an approach to faith that emphasizes and centers the experiences of Latina women

Narthex · the entrance of a cathedral

Nave · the open assembly space within a cathedral

New Testament · a collection of letters and historical witnesses to the life of Jesus that comprises sacred scripture to

Christians alongside the Old Testament, which contains the same literature as the Hebrew Bible

Nicene Creed · the statement of belief created at the Council of Nicaea and still used as the basis for Christian doctrine to the present day

Oriental Orthodox Churches · a group of churches that split from Orthodoxy at the Council of Chalcedon in 451; found today in Egypt, Armenia, India, Ethiopia, Eritrea, and Syria

Original sin · the doctrine that humans are born with the inherited guilt of sin going all the way back to the first man, Adam, and are likewise inclined toward sin rather than holiness

Orphanages, hospitals, and institutes of higher education · impactful Christian contributions to society at large during the medieval era

Orthodox · "correct opinion"; the set of Christian beliefs that were accepted as truth, with all competing views declared to be heresy

Orthodox Sunday · also known as the **Triumph of Orthodoxy**; an annual Orthodox celebration held on the first Sunday of Lent to celebrate the final decision in 843 CE in favor of the veneration of icons

Our Lady of Guadalupe · the most visited Christian pilgrimage site in the world, with around twenty million visitors per year

Pagan · originally a word referring to someone from the countryside; after Christianity gained ascendency in the Roman cities, the word took on a connotation of meaning non-Christian

Palm Sunday · the celebration of the day Jesus rode into Jerusalem and was embraced with joyous singing and the waving of palm branches

Passion Week · the week before Easter and the holiest segment of the Christian calendar

Pastor · the most common Protestant term for a minister

Patriarch of Constantinople · the spiritual leader of the Eastern Orthodox Churches; the "first among equals"

Patriarchs · archbishops of the five churches of the pentarchy

Penance · acts meant to punish and restore a sinner to a correct posture of righteousness

Pentarchy · the primacy of five strategic bishoprics in the early church: Jerusalem, Antioch, Alexandria, Rome, and Constantinople

Pentecost Sunday · the Christian holiday commemorating the descent of the Holy Spirit onto the apostles in Jerusalem on Pentecost after Jesus's ascension

Pentecostalism · the largest form of Protestantism in the world, which is spreading quickly; emphasizes miraculous gifts of the Holy Spirit such as healing, prophecy, and speaking in angelic tongues

Perpetual virginity · the Catholic and Orthodox belief that Mary remained a virgin until her death

Phoebe · a female leader in the early church; called a deaconess by Paul

Pilgrimages · religious trips undertaken to relics and to important Christian sites, often to seek healing or the absolution of sins

Pope Fabian · a third-century Bishop of Rome who was martyred under the reign of Emperor Decius

Predestination · the doctrine that God has chosen whom he will save, meaning that each human awaits a predetermined fate of either salvation or damnation, which was decided long before he or she was born

Presbyterian · a mainline denomination with roots in the Church of Scotland, which was influenced heavily by John Calvin's Reformed theology

Priests · religious leaders under the authority of the bishops and in charge of individual congregations or parishes

Protestantism · the third branch of Christianity, which was born out of Martin Luther's protests against the excesses and corruptions of the Roman Catholic Church

Purgatory · a middle ground between heaven and hell in which a soul purges itself of all lingering sins and impurities to prepare for the perfect divine presence of God in heaven

Quakers · also known as the **Society of Friends**; a pacifistic and egalitarian sect of Christianity that began ordaining women preachers as early as the seventeenth century

Queen of the sciences · theology, according to medieval Christian universities, as it can explain how humans can escape condemnation and achieve salvation

Radicals · Anabaptists, who were often persecuted or even killed for their beliefs

Rapture · an apocalyptic theory that Christians will be swept up into the sky to meet Jesus upon his return and will remain safe with him while satanic forces wreak havoc on the Earth

Reformed Christianity · a sect of Protestantism begun by John Calvin and centered on a strong belief in predestination

Restoration Movement · a group of Protestant denominations whose goal is to restore the original practices and beliefs of the early church; includes the Church of Christ, Disciples of Christ, and Christian Churches

Revelation · a heavily symbolic apocalyptic text; the last book in the Christian Bible

Rick Warren · a famous US pastor of the largest Southern Baptist congregation; ignited controversy in 2021 when he ordained three women

Romanesque · a dark and solemn style of church architecture with rounded arches and small windows

Sacraments · sacred rites that confer God's grace onto the participant

Saint Anthony the Great · the father of Christian monasticism; an ascetic in Egypt in the 200s CE

Sanctuary · the room of a cathedral or church building that contains the altar or Eucharistic table

Santiago de Compostela · a revered church and pilgrimage site in Spain at the burial place of James, the son of Zebedee and apostle of Jesus

Scholasticism · a philosophical school that combined Aristotelian logic with Christian dogma

Second Great Awakening · a nineteenth-century religious revival in North America that culminated in many social reform movements, as well as the Restoration Movement

Second Vatican Council · a council in the 1960s that implemented sweeping reforms to the Roman Catholic Church, including the recognition of Protestant and Orthodox Christians as true Christians, using the vernacular language for Mass, abolishing the Index of Forbidden Books, disassociating Jews from the death of Jesus, and promoting interfaith dialogue

Secularization · the decline of religiosity that has been witnessed in Western Europe and, to a lesser extent, North America

Seven deadly sins · pride, greed, wrath, envy, lust, gluttony, and laziness

Seven Ecumenical Councils · great assemblies of church leaders between 325 and 787 that propounded official Christian doctrine before the Orthodox and Catholic churches split; considered the primary authority in Eastern Orthodoxy today

Shroud of Turin · purportedly the burial cloth of Jesus

Sojourner Truth · an American slave who escaped in 1826 and became a famous abolitionist and preacher

Sola scriptura · "scripture alone"; a central tenet of Protestantism in which scripture, not the clergy, is authoritative for Christians

St. Peter's Basilica · a famous church building in Vatican City; purportedly built over the burial site of Peter, the apostle of Jesus

Summa Theologica · the principal scholastic text of Thomas Aquinas; considered to be one of the greatest works of Roman Catholic theology to the present day

Tertullian · late second- to early third-century Latin church father and apologist from North Africa

Theotokos · literally "God-bearer" or "mother of God"; a term Catholic and Orthodox Christians use to refer to Mary; generally not used in Protestant circles

Thomas Aquinas · the greatest theologian of the High Middle Ages who reconciled Aristotelianism with Christian theology

Thomas Müntzer · a Protestant reformer associated with the Anabaptists and the Radical Reformation

Thomism · the school of thought that arose from the teachings of Thomas Aquinas

True Cross · the alleged remains of the cross on which Jesus was crucified

TULIP · the five main doctrines of Reformed Christianity: total depravity, unconditional election, limited atonement, irresistible grace, and the perseverance of the saints

Venial sins · lesser sins

Virginal conception of Jesus · the Christian doctrine that Jesus was conceived while Mary was still a virgin

Vulgate · Jerome's Latin translation of the Bible

Wake · a funerary tradition held in the home of the bereaved shortly before the funeral, in which friends and relatives visit to comfort those mourning the deceased

William Seymour · the African American preacher who led the Azusa Street Revival

William Tyndale · a sixteenth-century reformer who translated the Bible into English

Wise Men · according to the Gospel of Matthew, Wise Men from the East came to worship and present gifts to Jesus shortly after his birth; possibly Zoroastrian Magi

Womanist theology · an approach to faith that emphasizes and centers the experiences of Black women

World Council of Churches (WCC) · a vehicle of ecumenism, based in Geneva, Switzerland, through which differing Christian denominations can come together in unity for the common good of the faith

CHAPTER TWELVE

Abbasids · an Islamic dynasty that ruled from Baghdad, Iraq, from 750–1258; their reign is known as the Golden Age of Islam

Abu Bakr · Muhammad's close friend and the father of Aisha; chosen to be the first caliph

Adhan · the call to prayer issued by the muezzin at set times throughout the day

Aisha · Muhammad's third and youngest wife, said to be his favorite

Al-Fatiha · the first surah, "the Opening"; recited during each of the five daily prayers

Al-Janna · heaven; a paradise garden where all desires will be met

Al-Qaeda · the extremist terrorist organization responsible for the attacks on September 11, 2001

Ali · Muhammad's son-in-law and cousin, whom some Muslims believed to be the rightful successor to Muhammad; eventually became the fourth caliph

Allah · the Arabic word for God

Allahu akbar · "Allah is greater"; a repeated phrase during the five daily prayers

Angels · spiritual beings who were created from light and are the servants of God

As-salamu alaykum · the standard greeting in the Muslim world, meaning "Peace be upon you"

Ashura · the day on which Shi'ites commemorate the martyr of Husayn

Azrael · one of the four archangels; the angel of death

Battle of Khaybar · a battle in 628 CE during which Muhammad and his forces defeated a Jewish community at the oasis town of Khaybar; after the battle, a Jewish woman attempted to take Muhammad's life

Battle of the Trench · a famous military engagement in 627 CE during which Muhammad led his small force to victory against a great confederate army of opposing Jews and Arabs; a major turning point in Islamic history

Bilal · a young Black slave in Medina who became the first muezzin

Bismillah · the invocation, "In the Name of Allah, the Most Gracious, the Most Merciful," which opens every surah in the Quran except surah 9

Black Stone · a revered rock, possibly from a meteor, currently situated in the eastern corner of the Kaaba; believed to have fallen from heaven in the days of Adam and Eve

Caliph · the successor to Muhammad who rules the ummah under the authority of the Quran

Caliphate · also known as the **khalifa**; the Muslim government that rules as the successor to Muhammad until Judgment Day

Charles Martel · the French general at the Battle of Tours in 732 who halted the Muslim advance into Europe, decisively solidifying the religious history of the continent as we know it

Circumcision · required in Islam for all boys, though the age of circumcision varies from culture to culture

Daesh · the term most commonly used in the Middle East to reference ISIS, derived as an acronym for its Arabic name, "Al-Dawla al-Islamiya al-Iraq al-Sham" ("the Islamic State of Iraq and the Levant"); coincidentally, "daesh" is also related to the Arabic word for "bullies," accounting for its popularity among those victimized by ISIS

Dar al-Islam · the "house of Islam"; refers to countries in the world where Muslims can freely practice their religion, generally implying Muslim control of law

Dervishes · Persian converts to Sufism

Dhimmi · also known as **dhimmitude**; the institution of second-class status to People of the Book under Muslim rule

Dhu al-Hijjah · the twelfth and final month of the Islamic calendar, during which practitioners take the Hajj

Dome of the Rock · a shrine erected by Muslims in 692 CE over the rock believed to be the site where God created Adam and where Abraham nearly sacrificed his son

Eid al-Adha · the "Festival of the Sacrifice," which commemorates Abraham's near-sacrifice of Ishmael

Eid al-Fitr · a three-day festival of feasting and gifts that commemorates the end of Ramadan

Fakirs · Arabic converts to Sufism

Farewell Sermon · Muhammad's speech in the last year of his life, 632 CE, in which he addressed equality for all men, advocated for good treatment of women (unless they act indecently), and outlined inheritance law

Fatimah · the youngest and beloved daughter of Muhammad; revered for her true righteousness

Five Pillars · the five most important practical obligations to which faithful Muslims must adhere

Golden Age of Islam · an era during the Abbasid empire characterized by highly sophisticated art, architecture, math, medicine, and philosophy

Grand Ayatollah · an authoritative and highly organized clerical and political office in Shi'a Islam

Great Satan · the term Ayatollah Khomeini used to describe and condemn the West

Hadith · the words, actions, and viewpoints of Muhammad, as preserved by those who knew him

Hafiz · "guardian of the Quran"; someone who memorizes the Quran in its entirety

Haji · a person who has successfully completed the Hajj

Hajj · a pilgrimage to the Kaaba taken during the last month of the Islamic calendar

Halal · that which is permitted for Muslims

Haram · that which is forbidden for Muslims

Hasan · Muhammad's grandson who would have become caliph after the death of Ali but abdicated to prevent a Muslim civil war, allowing Mu'awiya to become the fifth caliph

Hijab · a term referring both to a female head covering and to the general concept of modesty

Hijra · the event of 622 CE when Muhammad and his followers migrated from Mecca to Yathrib to evade persecution

Husayn · Hasan's younger brother and grandson of Muhammad who was murdered by Mu'awiya's son Yazid to eliminate his competing claim to the office of caliph

I'jaz · also known as **inimitability**; the belief that the Quran miraculously surpasses all in its reliability and truth and that nothing else on Earth can match it

Iblis · the Satan figure of Islam who is the father of the Shayatin and the tempter of humans

Ibn Arabi · a famous Andalusian Sufi who lived from 1165 to 1240; influenced Islam through his writing and poetry

Iftar · the large and wholesome meal taken after dark by a Muslim family during Ramadan

Imam · respected men who are chosen by the congregation to lead due to their competence in the Quran and their righteous lifestyle; in Shi'a Islam, revered as infallible examples of God's will for man's life

Isa · the Quranic name for Jesus, believed to be a prophet who announced the coming of Muhammad

Ishmael · pronounced **Ismail**; the son of Abraham and father of the Arab people, believed to be the direct ancestor of Muhammad; built the Kaaba with his father

Islamic State · a fundamentalist Islamic group in the Levant known for its use of violence and terrorism

Isma · the Shi'ite doctrine of the incorruptibility of the imams, that they are morally infallible holy men who must be obeyed and respected

Israfil · one of the four archangels who will blow a trumpet to signal Judgment Day

Jahannam · the Islamic hell, a place of extreme and eternal torment

Jihad · "to struggle"; a doctrine that can signify the inner battle against temptation as well as the physical struggle against enemies of the faith

Jinn · also known as **djinn** or **genie**; spiritual beings made of fire and air who can either serve humans faithfully or pester them with misfortune

Jizya · an annual tax that dhimmi people must pay if they refuse to convert to Islam

Kaaba · Islam's most sacred building and holiest site to which Muslims travel on pilgrimage and toward which Muslims pray five times daily

Khadija · Muhammad's first wife; a wealthy widow and business owner who was fifteen years older than Muhammad

Kharijites · an Islamic sect that arose during the crises of leadership after Muhammad's death; responsible for assassinating both Uthman and Ali

Levant · the geographical region comprising Syria, Lebanon, Jordan, Israel, Palestine, and parts of Iraq and Turkey.

Louis Farrakhan · a Nation of Islam member who recreated the movement, along with its original vision and beliefs

Madrasa · a school for studying the Quran

Mahdi · a Messiah figure in Shi'a Islam who will come and rule Earth for a period of time, ushering in an era of great justice prior to Judgment Day

Malcom X · Elijah Muhammad's right-hand man and fervent recruiter for the Nation of Islam; tried to steer the movement more toward orthodox Islam and was assassinated for his efforts

Masjid al-Haram · also known as the **Grand Mosque**; the mosque in Mecca in which the Kaaba is located

Mecca · Islam's holiest city, home to the Grand Mosque and the Kaaba

Medina · originally Yathrib; the city that welcomed Muhammad and first fully embraced Islam

Messengers · a unique class of the most important prophets that God has sent to Earth, such as Moses, Jesus, and Muhammad, whose words have been preserved in a written text

Mihrab · a niche in the wall indicating the direction of Mecca, the city toward which Muslims are obligated to pray

Million Man March · spearheaded by the Nation of Islam, the largest Black protest in American history

Mosques · also known as **masjids**, "places of prostration"; Islamic houses of worship

Mother Mosque of America · the oldest surviving mosque in the United States, founded in 1934 in Cedar Rapids, Iowa

Mu'awiya · the fifth caliph who established the Umayyad Caliphate

Muezzin · the man who issues the adhan from atop a minaret

Muhammad · the founder of Islam; the last and greatest Messenger of God

Muhammad Ali · a famous American boxer and convert to the Nation of Islam

Nation of Islam · the Black Muslim movement popularized by Elijah Muhammad and Malcom X that condemned White oppression and encouraged a sense of pride, purpose, and strength among African Americans

Night Journey · Muhammad's sole miracle, during which he was taken by night from Mecca to Jerusalem on a winged horse, ascended to heaven to pray with the Judeo-Christian prophets, and then returned

Nikah · Islamic marriage; a legal contract meant to protect women in case of widowhood or abandonment

Osama bin Laden · the mastermind of the September 11, 2001, attacks; killed by US Navy Seals in 2011

Paris Peace Conference · the 1919 conference at the end of World War I in which the victors—Britain, France, Italy, and the United States—split up the world into various nation-states, generally without the consent of the peoples and regions involved

People of the Book · a term in the Quran for Jews and Christians that references their shared religious heritage with Islam; sometimes mentioned favorably and other times considered unbelievers to live in a state of subjection

Qibla · the direction Muslims face during prayer; originally to Jerusalem but changed to Mecca during Muhammad's tenure in Medina

Quran · "the recitation"; the words of the angel Gabriel to Muhammad that related God's final revelation to humankind

Quraysh · the tribe into which Muhammad was born

Rashidun · also known as the **Rightly Guided Caliphs**; the first four Muslim caliphs: Abu Bakr, Umar, Uthman, and Ali

Reconquista · the Christian military endeavor to reconquer the Iberian Peninsula from Muslim rule

Ridda Wars · also known as the **Apostasy Wars**; a series of wars launched by Abu Bakr against self-proclaimed prophets who arose after Muhammad's death

Rumi · an influential thirteenth-century Sufi from Persia/Turkey who was renowned for his poetry and beloved in multiple religious traditions

Salah · ritualized prayers practiced five times per day

Sawm · required fasting during the daylight hours of the holy month of Ramadan

Seal of the Prophets · Muhammad is known as this, meaning that there will never be another divine revelation after him, nor will there ever be another earthly prophet until Judgment Day

Shah · the secular government in Iran that was overthrown in 1979, with Islamic scholar Ayatollah Khomeini elevated to leadership in its place

Shahada · a testimony of faith; the public confession that "there is no God but God, and Muhammad is the Messenger of God"

Shariah · literally "the path leading to water"; a legal code derived from the laws of God

Shayatin · devils or demons that were created from the fires of hell and are grotesque in appearance; they tempt humans by whispering into their hearts

Shi'a · the sect of Islam based largely in Iran, Azerbaijan, and Iraq that believes the caliph should be in the bloodline of Muhammad

Sixth pillar · a term sometimes used to refer to jihad to emphasize its importance in Islam

Sufism · a school of Islamic mysticism that rejects luxury and legalism in favor of following a path of loving and ecstatic unity with God

Sunnah · the traditions and practices of Muhammad

Sunni · the largest sect of Islam, representing 85 percent of the ummah, that believes the caliph need not be a direct descendant of Muhammad; they also reject the innate authority of an imam in favor of elevating the Quran and the Hadith as the ultimate sources of authority

Surah · each of the 114 chapters of the Quran, arranged from longest to shortest with the exception of the al-Fatiha

Taliban · a fundamentalist Islamic group in Afghanistan that eventually solidified control over the country in 2021

Tariqas · "paths"; communities or schools that form around influential Sufi teachers

Tawhid · the Islamic doctrine of the indivisible oneness of God

Twelvers · the largest subsect of Shi'a Islam; named after their belief on how many imams came after Husayn

Umar · also known as **Omar**; the second caliph and father of one of Muhammad's wives; an extremely successful warrior who conquered the Sassanid (Persian) Empire, as well as two-thirds of the Byzantine (Eastern Christian) Empire, before falling to a Persian assassin

Umayyads · an Islamic dynasty that ruled from Damascus, Syria, from 661 to 750

Ummah · the global Muslim community

Umrah · pilgrimages not taken during the month of Dhu al-Hijjah

Universal Islamic Declaration of Human Rights · a 1981 statement of the human rights protected by the Quran and Islamic doctrine

Uthman · the third caliph and husband of two of Muhammad's daughters who conquered more Persian territory, part of Afghanistan, and part of Armenia; one of the oldest caliphs in history

Wahhabi · a conservative, reactionary school of Islam that began in 1744 to oppose Western imperialism and revive Muslim culture; primarily found in Saudi Arabia today

Whirling dervishes · Persian Sufis who meditate while spinning in place for long periods of time, even hours

Wudu · the washing process in which Muslims engage prior to praying

Yathrib · later renamed Medina; a city 250 miles north of Mecca that invited Muhammad to become its leader and from which Muhammad eventually conquered Mecca

Zakat · a mandatory almsgiving, generally 2.5 percent of one's income, used to support widows and the poor

Zayd bin Thabit · Muhammad's secretary and scribe who committed the words of the Quran to writing, since Muhammad was illiterate

Zaynab bint Al-Harith · a Jewish woman who served Muhammad a lamb shoulder seasoned with poison in an assassination attempt; Muhammad survived and showed her mercy, but some of his companions perished, and their families sought justice by taking Zaynab's life

CHAPTER THIRTEEN

Aetherius Society · the first known UFO religion, founded by George King in the 1950s around the belief in extraterrestrial intelligences called Cosmic Masters, who can help humans with their earthly concerns

Agnosticism · the classification in religious studies for people who do not take a stance on whether or not there is a god

Ann Lee · an eighteenth-century religious leader and founder of the Shakers

Apocalyptic · religious movements which anticipate the imminent end of the world as we know it, often accompanied with promises of a new era of divine peace

Atheism · the conviction that there are no gods nor anything supernatural or metaphysical

Bab · "the Gate"; the founder of the Bahai'i Faith who was executed for blasphemy and treason in Iran, though some Shi'ite followers believed him to be the Mahdi

Baha'u'llah · "the Glory of God"; the Bab's successor, who claimed that the Bab had prophesied about him before his death; spread the message of inclusivity and the validity of all religions

Bahai'i Faith · a monotheistic NRM which branched off of Islam, teaching that all prophets were necessary during their time, and the ultimate goal of all religions is harmony and peace for all people and all nations

Christian Science · an NRM founded by Mary Baker Eddy around the idea of prayer-induced healing and a rejection of secular medical care

Church of Scientology · a controversial NRM founded by science fiction writer L. Ron Hubbard around the psychological self-help book *Dianetics*

Clear · the status in Scientology when one is free of engrams

Cults · a pejorative classification for NRMs which has fallen into disuse

Druidry · a modern NRM of harmony and connection to the natural world, based loosely on the religion of the historical Druids

E-meter · a machine in Scientology which measures one's electric currents

Ellen Gould White · a nineteenth-century visionary and mystic who founded the Seventh-day Adventists

Engrams · in Scientology, memories that cause psychological trouble because of the negativity attached to them

Entheogenic plants · naturally occurring substances that alter one's consciousness

Existentialism · a philosophy which emphasizes our current existence as opposed to some nebulous future existence in heaven or in a future life, prioritizing the will over reason, the practical over the theoretical, and the personal over the collective; important for its rejection of the possibility of objectivity

Falun Gong · a Chinese NRM established by Li Hongzhi in the 1990s; today based in Dragon Springs, New York, with millions of followers, mainly in China despite severe government opposition

Fox sisters · Leah, Margaretta and Catherine Fox; three sisters who created the NRM known as Spiritualism by purportedly channelling spirits of the dead

Haile Selassie · an Ethiopian emperor believed by Rastafarians to be the second incarnation of Jesus Christ

Hasidic · an ultra-Orthodox Jewish revivalist movement

Helena Blavatsky · a founder of the Theosophical Society

Hong Xiuquan · the self-proclaimed brother of Jesus Christ, who founded his own rebel theocracy in southern China with heterodox theology

ISKCON · the International Society for Krishna Consciousness (ISKCON), a Hindu-based NRM also known as the Hare Krishna movement; founded by Swami Prabhupada, who famously translated the Bhagavad Gita into English

Jehovah's Witnesses · a Christian-based millenarian NRM founded by C. T. Russell known for its rejection of the Trinity and its emphasis on eschatology

Mary Baker Eddy · a nineteenth-century writer and healer who founded the Church of Christ, Scientist

Mormons · known formally as the **Church of Jesus Christ of Latter-Day Saints**, an NRM based on Christianity and on a new testament which God revealed to Joseph Smith in nineteenth-century North America

Native American Spirituality · practices such as crystal healing, the channelling of deceased people's spirits, and veneration of the Earth; drawn from the religious traditions of Indigenous Peoples

New Atheism · a school of thought intolerant to religious belief, holding that religious superstition is irrational and should therefore be eradicated

New Religious Movements (NRMs) · alternative religious traditions which have arisen in recent times and have not yet achieved the longevity and the global adherence of world religions

Postmodernism · the current historical and philosophical movement, which draws heavily from existentialism in its belief that all truth is relative

Raëlian Movement · the most well-known UFO religion, founded in the 1970s in France by Claude Vorilhon, who later took the name Raël; the movement believes that humans were created by a superior extraterrestrial species known as the Elohim, who have sent 40 Elohim-human hybrids to earth as the great prophets of the world religions

Rastafarianism · an NRM from Jamaica linked to the "back to Africa" movement; believes that the Ethiopian Emperor Haile Selassie was the Second Coming of Christ, ushering in a new Zion for members of the African diaspora who return to Ethiopia

Religiously Remixed · a categorization for people who draw on various traditions from multiple religions for their own personal spirituality

Sacralization · a theory countering the secularization thesis, which posits instead that the world's civilizations are growing more religious

Secularization · the decline of religious authority and religious influence in various spheres of social life

Secularization theory · the theory that the world is becoming more secularized and less religious

Self-Realization Fellowship · an NRM started by Paramahansa Yogananda in Los Angeles, California, in 1920, which brought the practice of Yoga to North Americans

Seventh-day Adventists · an NRM founded by Ellen Gould White which observes a Sabbath on the seventh day of the week and prepares for the imminent return of Jesus Christ

Shakers · a Christian-based NRM known for its ecstatic worship (including bodily shaking), speaking in tongues, communal living, gender equality, and advocation for complete celibacy

Sokka Gakai · a Japanese NRM founded in the 1930s and based on the teachings of the 13th century monk Nichiren, along with a reverence for an important Buddhist text known as the Lotus Sutra

Søren Kierkegaard · a nineteenth-century Danish philosopher known for his existentialism

Spiritualism · an NRM started by the Fox sisters which uses seances and mediums to commune with spirits

Taiping Heavenly Kingdom · a nineteenth-century NRM which arose under the leadership of Hong Xiuquan, establishing a theocratic rebel state in China for over fifteen years before it was put down by the Chinese government

Theosophical Society · a Western interpretation of Hinduism that birthed a variety of NRMs that brought together religious ideas from both the East and the West

Transcendental Meditation · an NRM led by Maharishi Mahesh Yogi which became popular in the 1960s and 70s due to the endorsement of the Beatles

The Unification Church · an NRM founded in 1954 in South Korea by Sun Myung Moon, who borrowed several themes from Christianity and claimed that he would establish the Kingdom of God on earth

Vedanta Society · an NRM established in New York in 1894 by Swami Vivekananda with the message that all religions are essentially the same, but the Vedanta—or the Upanishads—are the supreme articulation of divine truth

Wicca · a witchcraft NRM that combines a reverence for ecology and feminism

NOTES

Chapter 1

[1] Lao Tzu, R. B. Blakney, trans., *The Way of Life*, (New York: Mentor, 1983), 102.

[2] William Woodville Rockhill, trans., *Udanavarga from The Buddhist Canon*, 1882, https://archive.org/stream/in.ernet.dli.2015.283948/2015.283948 .Udanavarga-From_djvu.txt. See section "Agreeable Things," v. 18.

[3] "Peace Prayer of Saint Francis," Loyola Press, www.loyolapress.com/catholic-resources/prayer/traditional-catholic-prayers/saints-prayers /peace-prayer-of-saint-francis/.

[4] The Shema (Deut. 6:4–5) is the holiest scripture in the Torah: "Listen, O Israel! The LORD is our God, the LORD alone. And you must love the LORD your God with all your heart, all your soul, and all your strength." Following the Shema is the command to "Tie them to your hands and wear them on your forehead as reminders" (Deut. 6:8).

[5] Abby Day, *Believing in Belonging: Belief and Social Identity in the Modern World* (Oxford: Oxford University Press, 2011).

[6] Jane Goodall, *Reason for Hope: A Spiritual Journey* (New York: Warner Books, 1999). See, for example, page 144.

[7] See https://www.pewforum.org/religious-landscape-study/.

[8] Michael Lipka, "10 Facts about Atheists," Pew Research Center, December 6, 2019, https://www.pewresearch.org/fact-tank/2019/12/06 /10-facts-about-atheists/.

[9] See Mary Eberstadt, *How the West Really Lost God* (West Conshohocken, PA: Templeton Press, 2013).

[10] M. Scott Peck, *The Road Less Traveled* (New York: Touchstone, 1978), 15.

[11] See Christopher Ellison, "Religious Involvement and Subjective Well-Being," *Journal of Health and Social Behavior* 32:1, 80–99. Ellison writes, "The positive influence of religious certainty on well-being . . . is direct and substantial." See also David Larson, Kimberly Sherrill, et al., "Associations between Dimensions of Religious Commitment and Mental Health Reported in the *American Journal of Psychiatry* and *Archives of General Psychiatry*: 1978–1989," *The American Journal of Psychiatry* 149:4, 557–59. See also Neal Krause, "Valuing the Life Experience of Old Adults and Change in Depressive Symptoms: Exploring an Overlooked Benefit of Involvement in Religion," *Journal of Aging and Health* 24:2, 227–49.

[12] Colin Baier and Bradley Wright, "'If You Love Me, Keep My Commandments': A Meta-Analysis of the Effect of Religion on Crime," *Journal of Research in Crime and Delinquency* 38:1, 3–21. See also Kenneth Ferraro and Seoyoun Kim, "Health benefits of religion among Black and White older adults? Race, religiosity, and C-reactive protein," *Social Science & Medicine* 120, 92–99.

[13] Sigmund Freud, *Civilization and Its Discontents* (Vienna: Internationaler Psychoanalytischer Verlag Wien, 1930).

[14] Daniel Pals, *Nine Theories of Religion* (Oxford: Oxford University Press, 2015). The book was preceded by previous editions *Seven Theories of Religion* and *Eight Theories of Religion*, pointing to the fact that even experts struggle to understand how many meta-approaches there are to something as complex as religion.

[15] See Pals, *Eight Theories of Religion*, 293.

[16] This helpful concept comes from William Paden in his book *Interpreting the Sacred: Ways of Viewing Religion* (Boston: Beacon Press, 2003).

Chapter 3

[1] Ayodhya is located in the north of India and is often in the news because of a Hindu–Muslim conflict that reached a head in 1992 when Hindus demolished a mosque (Babri Masjid) that had been built on the site of Rama's birth. Around two thousand people died as a result of these clashes, and the tensions continue.

Chapter 4

[1] See Census India, "Distribution of Population by Religions," https://censusindia.gov.in/Ad_Campaign/drop_in_articles/04-Distribution_by_Religion.pdf.

[2] For a further explanation of Jain worship traditions, see John E. Cort, "External Eyes on Jain Temple Icons," Object Narrative, in *Conversations: An Online Journal of the Center for the Study of Material and Visual Cultures of Religion* (2014), doi:10.223322/con.obj.2014.23.

[3] For detailed Jain statistics, see Paul Dundas, *The Jains* (New York: Routledge, 2002).

[4] For the English *Saman Suttam*, see Jain Quantum, located at jainqq.org.

Chapter 5

[1] Some Buddhists eat meat without any problems, particularly in Myanmar (Burma) and Thailand.

[2] Tibetan Buddhism is sometimes characterized as Tantric due to its emphasis on magical words and spells and its allowance of Tantric intercourse.

Chapter 7

[1] On Daoist history, see Mario Poceski, *Introducing Chinese Religions* (London: Routledge, 2009).

[2] Fenggang Yang, *Religion in China: Survival and Revival under Communist Rule* (Oxford: Oxford University Press, 2012), 152–53.

Chapter 9

[1] Gerard Russell, *Heirs to Forgotten Kingdoms: Journeys into the Disappearing Religions of the Middle East* (New York: Basic Books, 2014), 76.

[2] Jenny Rose, *Zoroastrianism: An Introduction* (London: Bloomsbury Academic, 2018), 1.

Chapter 10

[1] Jews in Israel celebrate for seven days; Jews in diaspora celebrate for eight days, based on the concept of *yom tov sheni shel galuyot*—which means that outside of Israel the holidays should add one extra day.

[2] The first ordained female rabbis in American Jewish denominations were Sally Jane Priesand (1972, Reform), Sandy Eisenberg Sasso (Reconstructionist), Amy Eilberg (1985, Conservative), and Sara Hurwitz (Open Orthodox).

[3] See Aaron J. Hahn Tapper, *Judaisms: A Twenty-First-Century Introduction to Jews and Jewish Identities* (Oakland: University of California Press, 2016), 142.

Chapter 11

[1] Todd Johnson and Gina Zurlo, *World Christianity Encyclopedia*, 3rd ed. (Edinburgh: Edinburgh University Press, 2020), 6.

[2] Rodney Stark, *The Rise of Christianity: A Sociologist Reconsiders History* (Princeton: Princeton University Press, 1996), 7.

[3] John Chrysostom, *Martyrdoms Ægyptos, Patrologia Graeca 50:693*. For further discussion, see John Wortley, "The Origins of Christian Veneration of Body-parts," Revue de l'histoire des religions 223, no. 1 (2006): 5–28.

Chapter 12

[1] Ziauddin Sardar, *What Do Muslims Believe? The Roots and Realties of Modern Islam* (New York: Walker & Company, 2007), 7.

[2] John Esposito, *What Everyone Needs to Know about Islam* (Oxford: Oxford University Press, 2002), 2.

[3] Ayman S. Ibrahim, *A Concise Guide to the Quran: Answering Thirty Critical Questions* (Grand Rapids: Baker Academic, 2020), 90.

[4] Sardar, *What Do Muslims Believe?*, 22–24.

[5] See https://islamqa.info/amp/en/answers/90071.

[6] Quran 96:1–7, located at quran.com/96.

[7] Ibrahim, *A Concise Guide to the Quran*, 31–43.

Chapter 13

[1] After the American Colonization Society (ACS) procured Sub-Saharan land from local tribe leaders in 1822, the Republic of Liberia became the world's second Black republic (after Haiti). The ACS's initial goal, financed by enslavers and abolitionists alike, was to address the "problem" of free Blacks in the United States by resettling them to Africa. In 1847, Liberia became an independent state and maintained its independence throughout the Scramble for Africa. Americo-Liberians, who can trace their ancestry to the early freeborn and formerly enslaved African Americans who immigrated to Liberia, consolidated their power and controlled the country until a military coup d'état in 1980.

[2] See Huston Smith, *Cleansing the Doors of Perception: The Religious Significance of Entheogenic Plants and Chemicals* (New York: Penguin Putnam, 2000), 20.

[3] See Karen Armstrong, *The Spiral Staircase: My Climb Out of Darkness* (New York: Alfred A. Knopf, 2004).

[4] Credit for the term "religiously remixed" goes to Tara Isabella Burton, *Strange Rites: New Religions for a Godless World* (New York: PublicAffairs, 2020).

[5] See Melinda Lundquist Denton and Richard Flory, *Back-Pocket God: Religion and Spirituality in the Lives of Emerging Adults* (Oxford: Oxford University Press, 2020).

[6] See Philip Goldberg, *American Veda: From Emerson and the Beatles to Yoga and Meditation—How Indian Spirituality Changed the West* (New York: Three Rivers Press, 2010), 329.

[7] See Jerome Sylvester, *Khristbhakta Movement* (Delhi: Indian Society for Promoting Christian Knowledge, 2013).

INDEX

ABOUT THE AUTHOR

Dyron Daughrity (PhD, University of Calgary), Professor of Religion at Pepperdine University, has taught world religions for over two decades and is the author of many books and articles in the field of comparative religion. He researches the interaction of Christianity and non-Christian religions, chiefly in India where he visits regularly. He is chief editor of the Christians in the City book series with Bloomsbury Publishing, and he also edits the Understanding World Christianity book series with Fortress Press. In recent years, Daughrity has been studying religion in far northeast India, as well as how Christianity functions in the world's great cities. He travels extensively to teach and to conduct ethnographic research in places such as India, Israel, China, Morocco, Ethiopia, and Brazil. He has written numerous books about how the Christian religion impacts, and is impacted by, global cultures, both in the Western world as well as in the Global South.